PAMELA HANSFORD JOHNSON

PAMELA HANSFORD JOHNSON

Her Life, Works and Times

WENDY POLLARD

SHEPHEARD-WALWYN (PUBLISHERS) LTD

First published in 2014 by
Shepheard-Walwyn (Publishers) Ltd
107 Parkway House, Sheen Lane,
London SW14 8LS
www.shepheard-walwyn.co.uk

British Library Cataloguing in Publication Data
A catalogue record of this book
is available from the British Library

ISBN: 978-0-85683-298-7

Typeset by Alacrity, Chesterfield, Sandford, Somerset
Printed and bound in the United Kingdom
by Short Run Press Ltd, Exeter

In 1927, *The Town Crier*, a monthly magazine published in London and aimed at professional and creative women, accepted the poem reproduced below for publication. It was the only literary offering in their March issue, which otherwise contained articles such as 'Women and the League of Nations', 'The Need for Women Police', and 'The Art and Craft of Photography'.

The Curtain

P.H.J.

Cold, blue, mysterious veils of morning mist,
What do you shield from view ? Dark factories
And reeking chimneys ? Garbage-strewn grey streets,
And shabby figures of the coarsened hawkers
Wheeling their broken barrows through the town,
Barrows whose green paint blisters in the sun,
Barrows heaped high with brown-green cabbages
And dirty purple beetroots, bruised tomatoes,
Whose scarlet lends a momentary colour
To sordid streets ? Or do you hide the forms
Of sweating workers from the factories
With cracked red hands, and hopeless, pallid faces,
Wrapped in their old brown shawls ? And do you veil
Black alleyways and soulless tenements
More cruel when touched with glinting, golden sun-
      light ?
You may.
   But when your mist clears I might see
Brown cottages, green downs and long white roads,
Bright silver streams, and purple iris smiling
Entranced at her reflection ; sombre woods
With sunlit clearings where brown rabbits play,
And, at a footfall, cock their snowy tails
And disappear in haste within a burrow ;
And clumps of ladies' smock, and meadowsweet
White, lacy, dancing ; and tall copper beeches
And silver aspens, and green, stolid oaks ;
Nut-trees, o'er which the squirrel gambols free
And impudently flourishes his tail
At the old, dusty owl that blindly blinks
Into the light.
   Draw your blue curtain, Morn,
That I may marvel at the world behind !

The editor was unlikely to have known that the remarkably self-assured poet was a fourteen-year-old Clapham schoolgirl, destined to become an acclaimed novelist and critic. This is her story.

Contents

List of Illustrations

Between pages 244 and 245

Family photographs, where not otherwise acknowledged, by kind permission of Lindsay Avebury.

Wedding photograph of Pamela's parents, Amy and Reginald (R.K.) Johnson.
2   Pierrot troupe, Clapham County Secondary School, c.1927.
3   Pamela and Amy, c.1920.
4   Pamela with Dylan Thomas, Caswell Bay, Swansea, 1934.
5   Ditto.
6   Wedding photograph of Pamela and (Gordon) Neil Stewart, Chelsea Registry Office, 1936.
7   Pamela with her children, Andrew and Lindsay, 1944.
8   Wedding photograph of Pamela and C.P. Snow, Christ's College, Cambridge, 1950.
9   Pamela with CPS and his brother Philip (in foreground), Venice, 1951. By kind permission of Stefanie Waine.
10 Portrait of Pamela, 1954, mounted by PHJ in her 'Progress Book'. By kind permission of Mark Gerson.
11 Pamela with CPS and their son Philip, Clare, Suffolk, 1954. By kind permission of Mark Gerson.
12 Russian hospitality, 1964.
13 Pamela, CPS and Sirikit, South Kensington, c.1965.
14 Launch of CPS's *Trollope*, 1975. By kind permission of Mark Gerson.
15 Pamela and CPS, Belgravia, 1976. By kind permission of Mark Gerson.

Introduction
and Acknowledgments

SOME YEARS AGO, idling while on holiday in a second-hand bookshop in Galway, I came across a Penguin edition of a novel called *Too Dear for My Possessing*. The name of the author, Pamela Hansford Johnson, immediately took me back to the time when, as a theatre-struck schoolgirl, I had loved her novel, *Catherine Carter*, centred on an actress and a player-manager on the Victorian stage. I had subsequently read and enjoyed the majority of her books, but the thought struck me that I knew nothing about her life.

On my return home to Cambridge, therefore, I searched for a biography, and discovered that none had been written. My own first book had been written for the academic market, but I was at that time looking for a subject that might also appeal to the general reader. Pamela Hansford Johnson's literary executors turned out to be the daughter and son of her first marriage, Lindsay Avebury and Andrew Stewart. Lindsay offered to meet me to discuss the possibility of a biography, and after her subsequent consultation with her brother and with her half-brother Philip Snow (the son of Pamela's marriage to C.P. Snow, and his father's literary executor), it was agreed that they would co-operate with me. Few biographers could have had as much help and encouragement than I had thereafter from all three of them; nightmare stories abound to the contrary, particularly with regard to women writers, whose families have seen fit to destroy 'clutter' after their mother's death. I was privileged to spend much time with Lindsay, the only one of Pamela's three children at present living in the U.K. and the custodian of her mother's previously unexamined diaries and letters.

I would also mention a most enjoyable interview with Philip Snow, Snr., Pamela's brother-in-law, and the chronicler of the Snow family and C.P. Snow in particular. He died in 2012 at the age of 96, but his memory was unfailing to the end; his daughter, Stefanie Waine, has also been extremely helpful. I am grateful for the interest and assistance given to me by Ishrat Lindblad, author of the monograph, *Pamela Hansford Johnson*, in the Twayne's English Authors Series, and Bill Noblett, who is currently engaged in cataloguing the material in the J.H. Plumb Archive at Cambridge University Library. The late Josephine Pullein-Thompson, together with Elizabeth Paterson, told me of their memories of the Snows' involvement with PEN; Richard Ingrams, the co-founder of *Private Eye*, provided me with insights with regard to the satire movement of the 1960s and also valuable information as the biographer of Malcolm Muggeridge.

A great deal of my time in the last few years has necessarily been spent in libraries and archives. I would first wish to thank the staff of the Cambridge University Library, particularly Neil Hudson in the Periodicals Section, and Morag Law and others in the 'West Room', who conjure up books from the Supplementary Catalogues. The latter lists works published prior to 1978 and, as the information states, 'not considered to be of academic importance at the time of receipt (for example, novels)'. As I read Pamela's novels together with her diaries, I realised how much they revealed about, and were influenced by, the social and political history of the mid-twentieth century, hence my full-subtitle.

I am also grateful to the staff of the Harry Ransom Humanities Research Center, University of Texas at Austin; Michael Basinski and the staff of The Poetry Collection of the University Libraries, University at Buffalo, State University of New York; the staff of Eton College Library, Windsor; Katharine Thomson and the staff of the Churchill Archive Centre, Churchill College, Cambridge; and the staff of the Library at Christ's College, Cambridge, together with Mary Tilmouth, the cataloguer of the C.P. Snow Archive at the latter.

For permission to quote from published and unpublished material, I am first and foremost enormously indebted to Lindsay Avebury and Andrew Stewart as executors of their mother's literary estate, to Philip Snow as executor of his father's literary estate, and to Stefanie Waine as executor of the literary estate of Philip Snow Snr. I thank Susan Hill for permission to quote from a published letter and a review by her, and from Pamela Hansford Johnson's letters to her, deposited in her archive at Eton College: David Allberry for permission to quote from his mother's privately-published memoir of her husband Charles, and the following for permission to quote from unpublished material: Andrew Dickson regarding drafts of his father's intended biography of C.P. Snow deposited in the Library at Christ's College, Cambridge, and Bill Noblett regarding relevant material in the J.H Plumb Archive, mentioned above.

For permission to quote from published material, I thank the following: David Higham Associates representing the literary estate of Constantine FitzGibbon and also the literary estate of Dylan Thomas (with the exception of the copyright of *Under Milk Wood* in the United States, for which I thank New Directions Publishing Corporation); Aitken Alexander representing the literary estate of William Cooper (Harry Hoff); Curtis Brown representing the literary estate of Bernard Levin; and Pressdram regarding excerpts from *Private Eye* magazine. I also offer my thanks to Mark Gerson for his interest and kind permission to reproduce several of the photographs taken by him of the Snow family. I have endeavoured to contact other potential copyright holders without success, but have restricted the use of material in these cases to within the guidelines of 'fair usage'.

When I began working on the biography, many of Pamela Hansford Johnson's books were out of print. Since 2012, the centenary year of her birth, however, the majority of her novels are now available as downloads or as print-on-demand through the initiative of Bello, an imprint of PanMacmillan. Encouragingly, too, several of her novels have also been brought back into print by small publishing houses.

Many friends and fellow-writers have given me encouragement and advice regarding this book. I hope that I will be forgiven any omissions, when I express my gratitude in particular to Alison Hennegan, Jane Liddell-King, Frances Spalding, Jenny Hartley, Holly Hill, Mary Joannou, Philippa Bernard, Selina Mills and Pam Hirsch. I also thank Jonathan Coe, who has kindly taken an interest in my work since he allowed me to interview him about his admiration for Rosamond Lehmann (the subject of my PhD and subsequent book), and who has been amused at the coincidence, having himself written the biography of B.S. Johnson, which won the Samuel Johnson Prize for Non-Fiction, that this biography concerns yet another writer with the same surname.

Extremely grateful thanks go to my editor and publisher, Anthony Werner, for his faith in this book, and for his constant advice and assistance during the completion process. I would also like to thank his excellent designer, Jean Desebrock, Andrew Candy who designed the jacket and Claire Peacock for proof-reading.

Finally, the 'without whom ...' acknowledgments go to my dear daughter, Beth, who has, with great grace, allowed me to spend part of what would have been her eventual inheritance on my late-in-life reincarnations as, first, a literary scholar and now a biographer, and to my partner, Iain, who was happy to travel with me on Pamela's trail around England and to Bruges, Venice, and America, who put up with countless sandwich suppers while I was absorbed in working, who gave me practical assistance with genealogical research, the scanning of documents and photographs, etc., who came up with at least one brainwave, and who has supported me throughout with loving belief.

A Clapham Childhood

PAMELA HANSFORD JOHNSON and her second husband, C.P. Snow, were to become the British and international intellectual celebrity couple of the mid-twentieth century. In 1960, the writer Ronald Blythe had emphasized the former's high literary standing, independent of her husband's, when introducing a lengthy profile of her in *Tatler and Bystander*: 'Lady Snow is Pamela Hansford Johnson, whose prolific novels [...] consistently cause critical rapture. She is also a leading authority on Proust.' Blythe later mentioned her husband as being distinguished both as a scientist and a novelist, and that together they formed 'a formidable family for literary talent, particularly as there is energy to match'.[1] In the United Kingdom, this fame was not to be without its drawbacks as it would lead to some arguably unwarranted attacks. Both Snows also, despite the Cold War, had the distinction of being acclaimed by the major literary figures in the USSR, as well as by the intelligentsia in the USA for their individual and joint achievements. In 1961, Sir Charles and Lady Snow were also deemed to have caught the public imagination sufficiently to warrant a joint photo-spread in American *Vogue*, as a couple whose titles, as the opening sentence proclaimed, 'never for a moment obscure [their] fame'.[2]

Further evidence of Pamela Hansford Johnson's popular renown in the USA may be gauged from an early Peanuts cartoon strip by Schulz, now framed and hung in her daughter's house. Lucy asks the scholarly Schroeder which authors she should read; he replies: 'You could start with Katherine Anne Porter, Joyce Carol Oates or Pamela Hansford Johnson.' Lucy's response is that she would be exhausted by the time she had read their triple names. With this in mind, I shall be referring to the subject of this biography simply as Pamela; this still distances me a little from her, since to her friends and family she was always Pam.

Pamela and Charles Snow had both come a long way from modest backgrounds. Snow's brother and chronicler Philip emphatically stated that: 'There is no doubt that we were lower middle class. We were also poor; not so badly off as some of our neighbours but poor enough to impede our progress.'[3] C.P. Snow would find that his Leicester childhood had much in common with his future wife's in South London. Biographies of women writers born in the early decades of the twentieth century commonly begin by sketching the privileged surroundings in which their subjects were born, and their aristocratic antecedents. These women might not themselves have had economic control over £500 a year, the amount famously decreed by Virginia Woolf to be the key to having 'the freedom and the courage to write',[4] but the majority were free from the necessity of working for a living in a routine occupation. They were also more likely to have been educated at home by governesses rather than at a school.

Pamela, who was born in 1912, was educated at the local grammar school, which economic circumstances forced her to leave at the age of 16; despite her evident academic promise, she had then to abandon any thoughts of university. After a short course at secretarial college, she worked unwillingly in a bank until she had established herself as a writer. As far as one can gather, her original ambitions did not stretch much beyond having poems and short stories accepted for publication in various newspapers and periodicals; she later told an interviewer that even the 'minute sums of money' she received for these had been 'extremely valuable then'.[5] But she was to become one of the most successful novelists of her period, both when measured in terms of critical acclaim, and popularity with her readers. She published 27 novels, several works of literary criticism, was a regular reviewer, lecturer and frequent broadcaster.

In a broadcast on Charles Dickens in 1949, later published in *The Listener* with the title, 'The Betrayal of Self in Fiction', Pamela maintained that:

> the writer of prose fiction, merely because he is dealing with words, may uncover a very great deal of his own interior life. [...] As he gets nearer and nearer to the springs of the character he is creating, so he

gets dangerously near to the springs of his own [...] and often he reveals infinitely more than he has intended'.[6]

She returned to the topic in her later collection of essays, *Important to Me: Personalia* (1974). In the introduction, she admitted that a writer will have 'written himself and his life into his novels, no matter how much both are disguised', although she went on to say that she was conscious of 'only two direct self-portraits in the whole of my books'.[7] Unusually, her first novels, although set in the location of her childhood, were not overtly autobiographical. Although she does not identify the self-portraits to which she refers, they are almost certainly the central characters of two novels written when she was middle-aged: Christine Jackson, the narrator of *An Impossible Marriage* (1954), and Alison Petrie, a young novelist, in Pamela's principal *roman à clef*, *Survival of the Fittest* (1968). Much of the background given to Christine Jackson, as the surname suggests, mirrors the circumstances of the author's early life, and Alison Petrie inhabits the same literary milieu as Pamela at the start of her writing career. But it is also possible to detect 'springs' from her 'own interior life' in the narrative and characterizations of several other of Pamela's novels.

Despite the near-penury of much of her childhood, Pamela's family, particularly on her mother's side, had been colourful. 53 Battersea Rise, Clapham, the substantial family house in which she was born and lived for the first 22 years of her life, had been bought by her maternal grandfather, Charles Edwin Howson, in the 1890s. Charles Howson, as an obituary in the Australian newspaper, *The Era*, related, came 'of an old and famed musical and dramatic stock', originally from England, but active in opera and musical theatre in Australia for many years. His father John, a tenor, and his uncle Frank, a baritone, had gone to Sydney from Tasmania in the 1840s, and John had at one time been manager of the chief theatre in Sydney. Other members of the family included Emma Albertazzi (*née* Howson, her husband being an Italian violinist), an operatic celebrity who took part in the first performance of Rossini's *Stabat Mater*, and, in the following generation, another Emma Howson, who regularly sang in early Gilbert and Sullivan operas, creating the role of Josephine in *H.M.S. Pinafore*. A scrapbook which has come down to present-day Australian Howson family members includes a photograph of this Emma with the actress

Mrs Patrick Campbell (Beatrice Stella Tanner) with a comment that the two were cousins. However, there is no corroborating evidence in the autobiography of 'Mrs Pat', despite her very detailed account of every branch of her family.[8]

Charles Howson came to England in the 1870s, presumably to seek his fortune. *The Era* obituary quaintly notes that: 'The deceased gentleman had essayed the dramatic art on one occasion, supplying the place of harlequin. He was a musician and instrumentalist, stringed instruments being his *forte*.' But rank and file musicians did not earn very much, his acting career evidently never got off the ground, and Charles initially supplemented what income he came by in England by copying band parts at fourpence a time. He then had a stroke of luck by attracting the attention of Henry Irving while playing in the orchestra at the Lyceum in London. As Irving's biographer, Madeleine Bingham, relates, Irving was prone to 'strange promotions'.[9] He had also found his stage manager, Henry Loveday, in the orchestra pit (in Edinburgh), and his theatre manager, Bram Stoker, working as a civil servant and part-time theatre critic in Dublin.

Charles was doubtless delighted to be offered regular employment, even though this would prove to be in the field of administration rather than performance, as he had married Helen Oborne a few years earlier, and they already had two daughters. It may well have been a shot-gun wedding (their first child, Clélia, known as Kalie, was born some six and a half months after the marriage). Helen was twenty whereas Charles was thirty-one. It is likely that neither family would have been happy with the union. Uriah Oborne, Helen's father, was a grocer, who probably viewed theatrical people as rogues and vagabonds. The Howsons, on the other hand, would have looked down at anyone in trade. Their granddaughter, Pamela, whose mother was the second daughter, Amy Clotilda, would later write of her Howson heritage, presumably in ignorance of Grandmother Helen's family background:

> I have often thought that we had no recognisable class at all. We were thought of as 'Bohemians'. I am afraid my family was afflicted with a degree of snobbery: the thought of 'marrying into trade' afflicted them as it might have afflicted a noble Victorian. But none of us ever did. (*Important*, p.65)

Charles Howson's first two posts with Irving were those of 'agent in advance' and press agent, but for the greater part of the twenty-three years he served with Irving's Royal Lyceum Company, his official and grand-sounding title was Treasurer. His duties, however, seem to have been less impressive, principally because of constant friction between himself and Bram Stoker. Howson is never mentioned by name in Stoker's two-volume *Personal Reminiscences of Henry Irving* (1906). The only reference to the position he held comes in a chapter entitled 'Finance', in which Stoker seeks to explain away Henry Irving's well-known extravagance (which, although he attempts to minimize this, came close to the point of financial incompetence). Stoker maintains that his main concern was to conceal, or 'safeguard' as he puts it, the full financial position from those he designated as 'lesser officials':

> Not one official of the theatre outside myself knew the whole of the incomings and the outgoings. Some knew part of one, some knew part of the other; not even that official who was designated 'treasurer' knew anything of the high finance of the undertaking.[10]

Stoker would doubtless have been incensed had he had access to the birth certificates of the children of this particular 'lesser official'. In the case of the elder two daughters, Charles Howson listed his occupation accurately as 'musician', but when his son Hosmer was born in 1887, when he had been working for Irving for only a few years, he described himself as 'Manager at a Theatre', and in 1889, on the birth of his fourth child Emma, 'Theatrical Manager'. As further evidence of the two men's mutual antipathy, Howson referred at home to Stoker merely as 'Irving's secretary', and, as his granddaughter related:

> One day he came home with a greyish volume in his hands, and said to his children, 'Stoker has written a beastly book. It's all about people who suck other people's blood and lunatics who eat flies.' He put it straight on the fire. It was, of course, the first edition of *Dracula*. (*Important*, pp.67-68)

Henry Irving, however, seemed content with his 'divide and rule' policy, and continued to employ both men until his sudden death on tour in 1905. They both accompanied him on his triumphant tours of the United States, and, according to Madeleine Bingham, were commended in the Boston *Journal* during the company's 1893-94 tour, as being 'entertaining men'. 'These Englishmen [*sic*]', the writer continued, 'have an unaffected manner, lacking in airs.'[11] Charles did not forget his family while away, one of his letters to the two older children, sent in December 1887, reads:

> Papa sends you a Japanese picture-book which Kalie must read. I hope you are both very good girls and love your little brother. I will send you some nice books for Christmas. Be kind to Mother, and don't forget to think of your father so far away in America.[12]

As Pamela related, 'Irving liked to deck his stage with good-looking people, whether talented or not' and this resulted in the occasional employment of Helen Howson and her three daughters in non-speaking roles in Irving's more lavish productions (*Important*, pp.64-65). At the age of 14, Kalie is mentioned as being in the company in a lively, if rarely punctuated, letter home from her mother in Dublin:

> Begorra and be jabers here we are right here! And don't I like Dublin faith and I do especially the jaunting cars and the whiskey and the Guinness stout. We were about 14 hours on the water getting here. It was very rough & they were all ill including Charlie. I was [and so] was Irving & 2 & 3 more. [...] I don't always get Charlie's company. [...] [He] is fairly well but doesn't get much time to himself. They are doing big business everywhere. [...] Manchester is their last place. They are all longing to get home. Kalie expects to be home about the 16 & she is looking forward to it so.[13]

But Irving's death virtually put an end to the family's involvement with the theatre; although Kalie and Amy continued to describe themselves as actresses and/or singers on official documents, they had few further engagements when the Lyceum Company closed. Amy did emulate her second cousin in joining the D'Oyley Carte Company, but her daughter recorded that 'she never rose higher than understudy to Yum-Yum (who did not fall ill)' (*Important*, p.65). Charles Howson died from heart failure two years after Irving at the age of 59; among those attending the funeral were many actors and musicians. Bram Stoker's attendance is not however recorded. We might know more about Charles Howson, had his diaries been preserved. Some years after his death, his daughters Amy and Kalie had found in the summer-house at the end of their garden 'half a lifetime of diaries, written in violet ink in his lovely script, in *Italian*'. And, in a rare criticism of her mother, his granddaughter Pamela continued: 'And on the grounds that nobody would be able to read them – perhaps on other grounds too – they incinerated the lot. I am intrigued to think what may have been lost by this ridiculous action' (*Important*, p.64). The family connection with Irving was an important element in Pamela's early life. The hallways in the Clapham house were hung with Irvingiana – playbills, programmes, sketches of costumes, photographs. When she was forty, all the family anecdotes were still fresh enough in her mind for her to recreate the world of Victorian theatre in her novel, *Catherine Carter* (1952), the hero of which, Sir Henry Peverel, is incontrovertibly based on Sir Henry Irving.

Clapham had originated as a mediaeval village. At the turn of the eighteenth century, an ailing Pepys moved there on his doctor's advice to have the benefit of country air. Although by the time Charles Howson established the family in Battersea Rise, Clapham was developing into a London suburb, its urbanization hastened by the coming of the railway, it still retained rural aspects. Pamela pinpointed the changes in the twenty-odd years that followed:

> We lived in a large brick terrace house bought by my grandfather some time in the eighties,[14] when it looked out on fields where sheep might safely graze. But by the time I was born, the railway had come, and the houses had been built up right over the hills between it and us. (*Important*, p.11)

Christine, the narrator of *An Impossible Marriage*, also mentions the view of grazing sheep in her description of her family home, but continues that:

> within ten years the view had been obliterated by a sudden seepage of lower middle-class houses and shops, and within another ten the seepage had streamed down through stratas of villa and potential slum to the very edges of the river.[15]

Nevertheless, in the early twentieth century, Clapham was still very different from the inner-London district it is today; the splendid eighteenth century merchants' houses around the Common were occupied by families with familiar household names, like Gorringe,

Hatchard, and Mappin, and Clapham was also the favoured neigh-
bourhood for those successful in the field of entertainment. Among
these, as local historian Gillian Clegg relates, were the prima donna,
Adelina Patti, and the music hall singer, Vesta Victoria. Clegg also
memorably defines another Clapham resident, Dan Leno, for generations who might not recognize the name, as the 'music hall singer,
dancer and clog dancing champion of the world'.[16] In 1912, the year
of Pamela's birth, the thirteen-year-old Noël Coward moved to
Clapham with his mother. In his first autobiography, he wrote of there
being 'pleasant walks in Clapham along tree-shaded roads, neatly
spaced with refined suburban houses, secure in small prosperity with
their conservatories and stained glass windows and croquet lawns'.
However, he continued that, 'from the "Plough" onwards down the
Clapham Road the atmosphere became palpably commoner'.[17] In
the crowded streets away from the Common, there were still more
modest houses with less distinguished occupants, and it was among
these that Amy Howson had found her husband.

Reginald Kenneth Johnson was born in Powerstock, Devon, the
home of his mother, Ada (née Hansford), but, contrary to family belief,
his father, Andrew, did not himself come from the West Country, but
from Huntingdon in East Anglia. Then too, family legend credited
Andrew Johnson with having 'built the Manchester Ship Canal'.
Perhaps that side of the family had felt a need to glamorize his achievements in an effort to compete with those of Charles Howson; any
connection Andrew Johnson might have had with this engineering
feat, which was constructed between 1888 and 1894, must have been
very tenuous, since Johnson, described in the 1891 census as a
'Contractors' Accountant' was based in London throughout that
period. In the same census, his son Reginald Kenneth, then 16, is
described as 'Junior Shipping Clerk'. Not exactly trade, but a family
that represented something of a come-down for a Howson to marry
into, nevertheless.

Reginald (always known in the family as 'R.K.') became a minor
colonial administrator in West Africa. His daughter accurately stated
that he was Chief Storekeeper on the Baro-Kano railway, but placed
this on the Gold Coast, rather than, as it is, in Nigeria. She was
doubtless misled by her father's frequent allusions to 'the call of the
Coast', when finding his long leaves in England tedious. Amy had

met Reginald during one of those leaves, and the Johnsons were no happier with the idea of an alliance with a theatrical family than the Obornes had been. However, their granddaughter said that they came to accept Amy as their son's wife. There seems to have been no suggestion that Amy should follow R.K. to Nigeria; indeed he was likely to have discouraged it. As Pamela later said, he enjoyed the 'long evenings on the verandahs with whisky and poker-games', and a wife and family would have been an unwelcome distraction (*Important*, pp.20-21). After their marriage, R.K. had been content to move into the Howson family home.

The couple's perception of their social status is manifest in the fact that they saw fit to announce Pamela's birth in the *Daily Telegraph*, as follows:

JOHNSON – On the 29th May, at 53 Battersea Rise, S.W., the wife (*née* Amy Howson) of R. KENNETH JOHNSON, of Lagos, late Baro-Kano Railway – a daughter.

The above form of words was standard for the time; indeed, several of the other birth announcements that day do not identify the mother other than as the wife of the father. The Johnsons' daughter was to receive the first names of Pamela Helen Hansford; there seems to have been no family connection with regard to her first name, but the two middle names were derived from her two grandmothers. It is not clear why the paternal grandmother's surname was chosen, rather than her first name, but Pamela would eventually be glad about this, since, as soon as she launched herself on a literary career, she elected to become known by the distinguished-sounding name of Pamela Hansford Johnson.

She was baptized at St Mark's Church, Battersea Rise, on 11 August 1912, then it was back to Nigeria for R.K. (it seems significant that he had given his address as Lagos in the *Daily Telegraph*), leaving his daughter with her mother's almost undivided attention. Their closeness was to become something of a burden in later life, but she certainly did not seem to resent it for the first twenty-five years. Again, this gave her a different perspective on life from more privileged writers, whose mothers were distant figures, and for whom a nurse-maid or governess might have been far more important. Grandmother Helen, sadly changed through illness from the lively girl who had followed her husband around the world with Irving's company, completed the manless family. She was to become totally blind by the time Pamela was ten. Aunt Kalie was a frequent, but at that time disruptive, visitor; she had never married, possibly because her father was said to have discouraged several suitors. Aunt Emma did marry, and moved out of London to a bungalow at Laleham in the Thames Valley. Little is known about the life of Pamela's uncle, Hosmer Charles, who died at the age of 37, when she was twelve.

Amy took at face value the title of a baby book she kept for Pamela. This was 'The Progress Book: An Illustrated Register of the Development of a Child from Birth till Coming of Age'. It was the sort that most first-time parents, even with the best of intentions, keep only for a year or two. They record the baby's first steps, first words, first illnesses, but entries soon lapse. But Amy faithfully noted the major, although somewhat pedestrian, events in Pamela's life up to the age of 18. Her first word, recorded as having been uttered at the precocious age of seven and a half months, was 'Dad-dad', and she is alleged to have mastered 'Pop Goes the Weasel' at about nine months. She had the usual childhood ailments – 'Measles (real – not German)' at two years, whooping cough at five – but was not to have mumps until the age of 16 nor chickenpox until 29 years old. Surprisingly enough, Amy did not record the constant blinding headaches (not at that time recognized as migraines) from which Pamela suffered throughout her life.

The most serious illness suffered in her childhood was nasal diphtheria when she was nine. In *Important to Me*, she described her stay in the Stockwell Fever Hospital as 'some six Dickensian weeks'; in fact, she was there from 15 January to 17 March 1922, nearly nine weeks. She did not feel particularly ill, she said, but she found the regime harsh. She was hungry and cold most of the time, and when she wrote about this to her mother (who was evidently not allowed to visit her), her letters were heavily censored. She also suffered greatly from her treatment from one of the nurses, who mocked her accent to the whole ward, thinking Pamela 'above herself' as, thanks to being brought up in a theatrical family, she spoke standard English. More than fifty years later, one particular humiliation to which that nurse had subjected her when in sole charge of the ward still rankled in her memory, and may account for her antipathy to hospitals later in life:

She would usually fetch me a bed-pan and sit me up on it (I would never demand one till the last vital moment) but then leave me there, despite my pleas, for any time up to three hours. She was the only dyed-in-the-wool sadist I have ever personally encountered in my life. (*Important*, p.37)

One important omission from the Progress Book was any mention of the birth of a sister, Beryl, when Pamela was seven. With her mother having observed the customary reticence of the period, Pamela had no awareness of the pregnancy, and suffered acute jealousy when so abruptly supplanted from her priority status. She had been brought up to be a religious little girl (her mother recorded her as being able to recite 'Gentle Jesus, meek and mild' at the age of two, and two years later, reciting the Lord's Prayer every night). Accordingly, she prayed with fervour under the hollyhocks in the garden to feel glad about the new baby. But, she later wrote: 'When she died of marasmus, a wasting disease, at the age of five or six months, I tried, under those same sacramental hollyhocks, to feel sorry. I couldn't. It was the beginning of guilt' (*Important*, p.22).

The importance of religion in her early life is further manifest from the fact that she gives the subject first place in the series of topics that comprise *Important to Me*. She had first been taken to nearby St. Mark's Church, where: 'On the whole, sermon apart, I enjoyed it: I revelled in Broad Church ritual. The Stanford *Te Deum*! There was a real male choir in those days, and I would wait breathless for the great basses to come in with "the holy company of the apostles praise thee".' When she was fifteen, however, her aunt Kalie began to attend Clapham Congregational Church 'under the ministry of the brilliant, histrionic George Stanley Russell', and insisted on her niece accompanying her there. Pamela too fell under the spell of Russell, 'a tall, rubicund, rather portly man with a magnificent voice', and took her first Communion in his church (*Important*, pp.11-13). In later life, she was torn between the Church of England and the Congregational Church, and ended up, albeit with guilty regrets, only rarely attending either church. Nevertheless, a defining feature of her writing is her strong sense of morality, doubtless inculcated in her from her religious education. As John Raymond was later to comment: '[Pamela Hansford Johnson] is a profound moralist, though of a deliberately unpretentious kind, and each of her books is at bottom concerned with a moral situation.'[18]

As befitted a theatrical family, Pamela was introduced to the
cinema and theatre at a comparatively early age; she saw her first
moving picture show at the age of two. She later annotated the
progress book to record that *A Midsummer Night's Dream* had been her
first Shakespearian experience at the age of nine; the same year, she
went to *Peter Pan* and to several Gilbert and Sullivan operettas. The
family went on holiday to the seaside regularly, and she was introduced to the delights of paddling, donkey rides and piers. Her first
holiday abroad was in 1926, when she went to Heyst-sur-Mer in
Belgium with her mother and her aunt Kalie (the sisters had attended
school in Ecloo in Belgium at the height of their father's prosperity).
She was to develop a lifelong affection for the country, which plays a
significant role in three of her novels. Under the heading 'Mental
Progress', Amy recorded her daughter's grasp of the alphabet at
'3 years 3 months', and ability to read at six years old. However, doubtless hoping, at that relatively affluent time for the family, that Pamela
might follow her into musical theatre, Amy took more interest in her
daughter being 'exceedingly forward in memorising tunes'. At the age
of two and a half, she proudly claimed that her child 'could sing over
30 songs, exclusive of nursery rhymes, tune perfect', and that she had
an 'excellent musical ear'.

Pamela went to a local primary school, and, on passing the elemen-
tary examination of the Associated Board with 119 marks out of
150, won a place at the Clapham County Secondary School, a girls'
grammar school. Within a year, however, the family's comfortable
life in the big house on Battersea Rise had been shattered by the death
of R.K. Home on leave, he had come to a sudden but unheroic end
(later twice to be fictionalized by his daughter)[19] in the lavatory in the
middle of the night. His consistent lack of success in those poker
games on tropical verandahs meant that he left nothing but debts.
He did, however, unknowingly leave Pamela with one legacy about
which she wrote towards the end of her life. In a newspaper article
dealing with xenophobia and racialism, she wrote that she had never
consciously experienced either of these prejudices:

> This was probably in reaction to my father, an old-style civil servant
> on the Gold Coast [*sic*] for 20 years or more, who believed in pater-
> nalism and, I believe, practised it; but his racial attitudes would seem
> to most of us intolerable today. I remember that if, on his rare leaves,

he got on a bus with my mother and myself, and a black man got on also, my father would speedily get my family off again. He was a good man according to his lights, and his administration was said by his juniors to be a very fair one. They had sensed the wind of change that was coming, but not he. I was only 12 when he died, but my memories of his attitudes are very sharp.[20]

For some years even before her father's death, the family had been making economies; they could no longer afford to occupy the whole of the house. Amy and Pamela had moved from their flat at the top of the house to share the semi-basement sitting-room as a bedroom, and their former accommodation was let to 'all manner of lodgers':

one was speedily removed, being suspected of sleeping sickness: one, a rubicund Welshman, got into fights on the stairways with my Uncle Charlie: one, who posed as a doctor living with his sister, sat quietly upstairs manufacturing pornographic literature, until the police caught up with him. (*Important*, p.67)

R.K.'s widow now had the burden of her husband's debts to clear, and, unable to take a full-time job because of her ailing mother, she took in typing to supplement their modest income. Pamela might therefore not have been able to continue at the grammar school, since the fees were £5 per term, not a negligible amount for them at that time. Amy was forced to plead with an acquaintance among the governors that the fees be remitted, and fortunately this was agreed.

From all accounts, Clapham County Secondary School (also known just as Clapham County School) was a model grammar school, and Pamela always acknowledged the crucial role it had played in her intellectual development. Up to the time of her first marriage, she continued to be involved with the Quondam Club (a much more interesting name, it had been decided, than CCS Old Girls), and she remained close to Ethel A. Jones, the headmistress throughout her time at the school, until the death of the latter in 1966. At her Memorial Service, Pamela (by then, Lady Snow) spoke with great affection of the woman she had known as 'Jonah'. This had been, she said,

an absurd nickname, meaningless except in relation to her surname [...]. Indeed, she seemed no more the kind of woman to have a nickname than Jane Austen. 'Miss' Austen, 'Miss' Jones. That was how it should have been. Yet the mere fact that everyone called her Jonah (her old pupils still do) indicated something of her popularity.

Her genius, she continued, had been 'for bringing girls up the way they should go, without them really being aware of the process'.

Pamela thrived in the grammar school environment. She had already begun to write poetry, and at the age of 10, the youngest in a school of 550 girls, had a poem accepted for the school magazine. Thereafter she contributed at least one poem each year, and sometimes two; she became editor of the magazine in her final year. (The poem reproduced on the fly-leaf remained the only one to be published elsewhere until she was 18.) 'English, and particularly French, literature', she reminisced, 'were thoroughly taught, and I immensely enjoyed both: but I never realised how narrow the syllabus was in both cases.' Her love of the theatre was undiminished by having to study Shakespeare as a school subject:

> From the age of eleven to about fourteen, I and a few like-minded schoolfriends saved up for our Saturday treat. This was invariably the same. We would climb to the top of the Monument, where we would eat our sandwiches, and look out on the panorama of London. Then we would go to the Old Vic – Lilian Bayliss' theatre – to sit on a hard gallery seat – price 6d – (or, I should say, 2½p) – and watch Shakespeare.

'What is there about Shakespeare', she wondered, 'that can intoxicate many children?' (*Important*, pp.87-88).

But in all the mathematical subjects, she proved unteachable: 'When it came to trigonometry, the mistress threw me over in despair: and actually gave me permission to sit at the back of the classroom and write poetry' (*Important*, p.83). This failing would in any case have frustrated Jonah's hope that Pamela would follow in her footsteps by reading English at Oxford; it was essential at that time to pass maths in order to matriculate, no matter how high a student's marks might have been in other subjects. And Pamela did achieve a Distinction in English and in Oral French, but as previously mentioned, for financial reasons, university was out of the question. 'Grants were very slender then,' she said, 'and that I could have supported myself, let alone my mother, was inconceivable' (*Important*, pp.68-69). As far as her mother was concerned, there were only two possible careers for Pamela, those with which she herself was familiar: her daughter could be an actress, or a secretary. With first-hand knowledge of how unlikely financial success on the stage would be, Amy had to abandon her first ambition for her daughter, and the latter occupation was chosen. Pamela seemed to regard this decision as inevitable, although towards the end of her life, after a visit to the National Youth Theatre, she was to wonder whether, had the latter 'excellent institution' been founded during her girlhood, it might have changed the path of her life. 'I never doubt', she wrote, 'that I <u>should</u> have had a fine acting career, if migraines hadn't stopped me during all those terrible years.'

Amy, however, was determined that her daughter should attend a 'good' secretarial college, rather than the local technical college, and despite the strain on her resources, enrolled her on a six-month course at the smart Triangle Secretarial College in South Molton Street, Mayfair. Pamela fictionalised this episode in *An Impossible Marriage*, although in this book, Christine's mother has died before she left school. Nevertheless, the account would seem consistent with Amy's aspirations for her daughter:

> It had been my mother's desire that eighty pounds of her insurance money should go to training me at a really good secretarial college, where I should meet the right kind of girl, and perhaps go straight into a really high-class post. If she had to see me as a secretary at all [...], then it was as something she called a 'Social Secretary', one who sent and accepted invitations for a duchess, and did the flowers. (*Marriage*, pp.30-31)

There is no evidence in her diaries that Pamela harboured resentment about being denied higher education. Indeed, she later said: 'I believe that, to a creative writer, a university education would have been nothing but a hindrance. A course in Eng. Lit. has rotted many a promising writer. It is only as a critic that I should have welcomed it' (*Important*, p.83).

Nonetheless, it seems extraordinary that, within thirty years of her leaving school, in the booklet compiled to commemorate the first fifty years of her *alma mater*, Pamela is listed as one of their most distinguished alumnae, as follows:

Pamela Hansford Johnson (Lady Snow) – novels and criticism, broad-caster, on regular panel of The Critics and on B.B.C. Brains Trust.

She would have many obstacles to overcome in those thirty years.

CHAPTER 2

Aut Inveniam Viam, Aut Faciam

T HE TITLE of this chapter is a Latin motto, attributed to Hannibal, the English translation of which is: 'I will either find out a way or make one'. Pamela copied this onto the flyleaf of all the diaries which she kept, with some exceptions to be explained later, throughout her life. The earliest still in existence is for 1929 and covers her final two terms of school, and the first few months of her secretarial training. Her diaries for 1930 and 1932 have not been preserved, but it is possible to piece together the missing years from the 1931 diary and the reminiscences in her memoir. In the beginning, she used the year's Boots Home Diary, which measured 8" x 5", with a week over a two page-spread. Her remarks are necessarily therefore brief and factual; the language she used is often slangy, and one can safely say that her early diaries were not written with a view to future publication. Later, when established as a novelist, she used day-to-a-page diaries, and later still, notebooks rather than diaries, and therefore could write at greater length on matters of importance to her. It will be seen that she did occasionally express ambivalent feelings with regard to the possibility of a future biographer reading her entries, but the view of her family is that she would have left instructions for her diaries to be destroyed had she not wanted her story to be told.[1]

The general picture of Pamela gleaned from the early diaries is that of a popular and talented adolescent, yet she frequently mentioned feeling depressed, or, in a contemporary slang expression, 'pipped'. This was generally occasioned by her difficult home life. Her mother, grandmother and aunt were constantly warring: typical entries record "atmosphere pea-soup', 'grannie truculentissimo [...] battle royal all day', 'simply appalling upset with Kalie before bed – hysterics &

all the rest of it'. But, in the lulls between confrontations, her mother managed to welcome her daughter's friends to their home. Pamela had inherited the good looks of the Howson branch of the family, and Amy, her daughter later wrote, 'was, in some respects, a wise woman':

> So that I should not sneak off to meet boys round street corners, as she (fearing grandfather) had done, she kept, from the day I was fifteen, open house for the boys and girls I cared to invite. These were the dancing days: we rolled back the carpet in our pleasant semi-basement sitting-room and danced for hours. We then drank tea and ate my mother's special and much appreciated treat, called for for many years after that – of bread pudding, full of currants and spice, hot from the oven. (*Important*, p.79)

In *An Impossible Marriage*, Christine's mother had similarly insisted on a weekly open house, which had proved to be a good thing 'for she had an excellent eye to the weeding-out of undesirables'. Christine's friends, like Pamela's, were 'the local ones of my childhood, girls I had known at school, boys from the grammar school' (*Marriage*, p.31). Pam's closest female friends were Babs Freeman, and Dora 'Dick' Turbin (the nickname presumably being a pun on Dick Turpin). Her first serious boyfriend was Jack Davies; at the age of fifteen, she wrote a long, romantic poem about a visit they had made together to her aunt's house on the Thames. They had found an island they could reach across stepping-stones, 'our Paradise', she called it:

> The glory of it! . . . with the long white clouds,
> The humming river, and the spiny grass!
> Then after tea, can you forget the hours
> Spent in the twilight, by the loving fire,
> You playing for my singing?

Pamela's circle also included several other boys, with whom she had more or less platonic friendships, and with whom she kept in touch for a number of years. The longest lasting of these friendships was with a young man called Teddy Lamerton. Amy had no qualms about the mixed parties at home, but became nervous when the time came for Pamela to go out to dances; in particular, her daughter fondly remembered, she worried about 'my spectacularly good-looking friend, Teddy', because he had been brought up in Malaya, 'and she had a strange fear that he would slay me with a *kris*, and leave me in some awesome hiding-place on Wimbledon Common'. 'A sillier fear could not be imagined,' Pamela commented, 'Teddy was the soul of gentleness' (*Important*, p.115).

Writing of that time, she acknowledged that the gatherings in the basement did lead to 'romantic attachments', but continued that:

> in those days, for boys and girls of our middle-class upbringing, these were only expressed in flirtation and in surreptitious kisses in the hallway. [...] No one went to bed with anyone else, nor would have thought of such a thing. (If anyone did so, he or she kept it dark.) No one suggested to us that otherwise we would be frustrated, would wither on the vine.' (*Important*, pp.79-80)

Significantly, in addition to their passion for dancing, they had been, she said, 'on the whole, a literary set'. One of them, who appears as a character in *An Impossible Marriage*, was nicknamed 'Take Plato', as he would frequently start a sentence with those two words. Her friends expanded her range of reading; they shared constant new discoveries:

> Someone had found out Dostoevsky, someone Liam Flaherty, someone Nietzsche, I think this was 'Take Plato'. And one day, Teddy burst in, full of excitement, to tell us of a novel called *Look Homeward Angel* by Thomas Wolfe. (*Important*, p.80)

Pamela wrote in that year's diary: 'A wonderful book – I don't know when I have been so deeply <u>moved</u> by any novel.' The influence of the novel on Pamela did not diminish over the years; it can be sensed in her first novel, and would lead her much later to write a critical study of the author.[2]

Her own literary discoveries were prodigious, as revealed in the lists of 'Books Read' on the flyleaves of her early diaries. In 1929, she listed only 'favourite books' read that year, with a preliminary comment: 'Shakespeare head & front first of course'. In the early part of the year, the influence of the school syllabus was still in evidence. She was reading Webster, Jonson, Kipling, Victor Hugo, and re-reading *Jane Eyre*, commenting about the latter: 'Favourite now & always'. Having left school that year, presumably her choice was then subject to the availability of books in the public library (she does not mention being a subscriber at Boots Booklovers Library, or any similar private

lending library). But the books she was able to borrow bear testimony
to that period having been a golden era for public libraries. She read
recently published novels by British authors – among them, Michael
Arlen, Clemence Dane, Philip Gibbs – and for light relief, P.G. Wodehouse, and several Father Brown detective stories by G.K. Chesterton
(the latter genre being a regular favourite, which would result in her
collaboration with her first husband in the writing of, it has to be said,
less successful whodunnits). She was also able to widen her reading
with past classics, as well as with books by American authors in
addition to Thomas Wolfe, including four novels by Theodore Dreiser,
and with works by European writers, including Stefan Zweig, Erich
Maria Remarque, and Lion Feuchtwanger.

In the 1931 diary, despite by then working full-time, she listed a
total of 90 books (nearly two a week), and included brief critical assessments, many of them shrewd, despite her self-deprecating preamble:
'These are my own personal comments & are doubtless all wrong.' She
appended asterisks to recommended books, across all genres, from
humour (*1066 And All That* was the 'Funniest book ever'); through
detective stories (an Agatha Christie omnibus had been 'Gloriously
absorbing – enjoyed every moment of it'); to novels by D.H. Lawrence,
Richard Aldington, Robert Graves, and Colette, among others, which
have entered the literary canon. She was, in general, open-minded
about sexual content, though occasionally mentioned reprovingly that
a book had been unnecessarily 'grubby'. A similar criticism was not
levelled by her at *Look Homeward Angel*, despite the novel's frequent
and explicit descriptions of the hero's developing awareness of sexuality. 'Young men and women between seventeen and twenty-three
years of age', she would later write, 'felt that in some obscure way
Wolfe was their spokesman [...]. His lyricism was the expression of
their own longing to put into words the wonder and strangeness
of coming out of childhood.'[3]

However, Radclyffe Hall's *The Well of Loneliness* provoked a violent
reaction, albeit mingled with appreciation of the book's aesthetic
qualities:

> Intolerably moving plea for a dreadful cause. Beautiful and inoffensive
> up to about two-thirds of the book, and I couldn't understand why it
> was banned, but the last part was dreadful and repulsive, almost beyond
> belief. The last paragraph superb. Should be read gravely and carefully.

While this might appear to be a standard *petit bourgeois* response, it might also have been occasioned by a suppressed memory: a note in the margin of her 1929 diary during her last term at school read: 'About this time, I was having an affair with a dame. The least said the better.' (This was almost certainly no more than a schoolgirl crush.) It is elsewhere proof of her judgment that the majority of the non-asterisked books, and those about which she is most scathing, have not survived. She dismissed *The Crucible* by an anonymous author as: 'The <u>worst</u> rubbish of the year. APPALLING nonsense', and this book cannot be traced in any library catalogue. Others she simply called 'bunk', or, in one case, 'dull, dull, dull'.

She had by now become ambivalent about her attendance at church, though she still went frequently. One Sunday in March 1929, she wrote in her diary: 'Church this morning & communion; very beautiful. I felt much "gooder".' But a few weeks later, on Easter Sunday, the entry reads: 'Went to church in morning & was very bored which makes me miserable as I hate to feel I am not blessed on a Sunday.' By 1931, her visits to church were even more sporadic. She went far more regularly to the cinema. Her mother, possibly through her former theatrical connections, was able to get free tickets for trade shows. Pamela did not list these as she did with regard to books read, but frequently mentions such visits in her diary. Even in 1929, many of the films she saw were still silent. A rare visit to a 'talkie' at one of the splendid new 'picture palaces' was an event: 'Went with Teddy to very good "Talkie" at the Regal, a very lovely, if ornate, cinema.' Pamela's two favourite actors, John Barrymore and Greta Garbo, were fortunately among the few silent film stars able to make the transition to talking pictures. Other regular pastimes included long walks around Clapham Common, baking cakes, embroidering 'fancy work', making small woodwork items, giving piano lessons, and enjoying ice-cream sundaes at Lyons Corner House. She also was evidently a proficient artist, and was commissioned to design a dust-jacket for a book, *The Sloping Garden*, by Phyllis Austin, which was published by Collins. Phyllis Austin seems to have been a friend, or possibly a client of her mother's, but Pamela was delighted to receive a fee of four guineas.

In her penultimate term at school, she was chosen to be the chief character in a one-act play, *St. Simeon Stylites*, by Francis Sladen Smith, which was to be entered for a drama competition. She had to make her own costume, with her mother's help, and they 'evolved something quite wonderful out of an old sheet!' She then tried on the dress and make-up, '& scared the cat into fits'. She thought that the first performance went really well, despite 'a good deal of prompting', and the following day heard that they had got through to the final in April, which would entail an evening performance 'thrown open to the public, so that will be jolly nice'. The day of the final was, she recorded, 'a Red Letter Day'. *St. Simeon Stylites* won the competition, and Pamela's performance was singled out by one of the judges to have been 'a splendid performance'. 'I got so worked up,' she said, 'that I was streaming tears when I came off the stage.'

The play was the highlight of her last year at school. Despite hearing that she had, as usual, been top in her English exams, she wrote that, though pleased, she had 'lost much interest in things scholastic!' She bought a bicycle from a schoolfriend for 7/6d., but the family reaction was 'so appalling that I shall have to sell it, though it was one of my dreams to have one'. As ever, she did not blame her mother for this opposition. When she mentioned her mother, it was always with affection and admiration, as on her final Sports Day at Clapham County School: 'Went to Sports with Mother & showed her off. She looked much the prettiest woman there.' Despite her later tributes to the school and its headmistress, Pamela's entry on her final day betrayed no sadness at leaving. She wrote: 'Left school for ever. HALLELUJAH! Very exciting morning: signed 150 autograph albums, etc. Lots of handshakes and goodbyes.'

Earlier that year, Pamela's relationship with Jack Davies had been the cause of several family disagreements. Her unmarried aunt Kalie was living with them at that time, and disapproved of the degree of latitude her sister allowed her niece. In May, Pamela wrote of 'A terrible horrible row – Mother & Kalie – in which Mother seems to have been temporarily vanquished – and our liberty with Jack curtailed.' Quite why Kalie was in general allowed to dictate terms with regard to the family ménage is uncertain, but it would seem that Amy could not withstand her sister's tantrums. However, a few weeks later, an ecstatic Pamela wrote: 'KALIE CONSENTED to let Jack stop 4 days with us. Jubilate.' On the Whitsun Bank Holiday, Pamela's entry was lyrical: 'Dream Day. Just wonderful. Jack & I to

Wimbledon till 5.30. It was all green & gold. One of those idylls that only occur once in a blue moon.'

The relationship with Jack became doomed when he revealed that he had theatrical ambitions. She wrote solemnly at the end of June:

> Today has been a very sad milestone in my life. Jack seemed very funny all day. I enquired why & he told me he was crazy to go on the stage & was considering a job there. I have always told him that if he did, it was goodbye to me forever. I sent him away.

Presumably, it was the knowledge of the insecurity of an actor's life, dinned into her by her mother, which swayed her; her concerns about the financial stability of her suitors were also to blight subsequent relationships. However, she bounced back quite quickly from 'utter misery'. She rarely went for more than a few weeks without a boyfriend, and soon after Jack's dismissal, went to the cinema, and, as she put it, 'clicked with an artisan bloke!' Doubtless, she realised that neither Amy nor Kalie would have approved of such a suitor, as nothing more was heard of him.

A longer lasting relationship resulted from a summer holiday with her mother in Bruges. For the first week, she was an assiduous tourist, visiting the Cathedral, museums and churches, seeing 'Memlings and some fine van Eycks'. She rowed her mother on 'a lovely journey down the canal', passing 'little cottages on one side & willows on the other, & an old château', by which they moored. This memory would inspire a significant episode in the acclaimed first novel of her 'Helena trilogy', *Too Dear for My Possessing* (1940). She rejoiced in the mediaeval buildings, the picturesque townscapes, and canal scenes, and spent much time sketching and composing poetry about them.

At the beginning of their second week, she was watching a religious procession when she realized that she was being 'tracked in most flagrant style' by 'a darling ginger-headed man'. He followed her around for the next two days, but she was always accompanied by her mother; eventually Pamela went to an evening band concert on her own, and he seized the opportunity to get into conversation with her. She had decided because of the colour of his hair that he must be Scottish, and was calling him 'Ian' in her mind. He turned out to be Swedish, although his family lived in London, and to be called Oscar John

Swanson, but throughout their relationship, Pamela called him Ian, or when she was in fond mode, Iany. 'He seems to have a violent pash – Gawd knows why!!!', she confided to her diary that evening.

The following day, Pamela introduced him to her mother, and *he* evidently found favour with her, as for the rest of their stay, he accompanied wherever they went, and Pamela was able to indulge in her favourite pastime, dancing with him at the Terrasse Tea Rooms. On the morning of the day before she and her mother were to leave, the two young people were for once left alone to walk by the canal. There are three lines heavily deleted in her diary entry, and 'very pleasant' substituted; presumably there were *some* things she wished to keep hidden from Amy. They danced that evening (chaperoned by Mother), and said farewell at midnight. But that was not to be the last that they saw of 'Ian' in Belgium: 'When Mother & I arrived at Bruges station for the sad return journey, who should we see but Ian! He had sat up ALL night so that he "shouldn't fail to be early enough to see us off."'

Pamela and Ian started to see each other regularly in London, and she met his father, who, she said, was charming to her. However, the year was 1929, and contemporary events intrude in Pamela's diary for the first time. In September, she wrote that: 'Ian's father is at a great crisis on the Stock Exchange.' But, for the time being, nothing could quench her youthful enthusiasm for her new swain: 'Phone from Ian: Would I come to Tea Dance at Wimbledon Palais? What ho! So I went & we had a topping time.' He soon told Pamela that he loved her, and she was 'divinely happy'. He proposed, and she accepted, but immediately afterward, his father was served with a bankruptcy writ, and two days later she recorded that he was now 'ruined'. Any marriage plans had to be shelved.

She was not enjoying her secretarial training at the fashionable Triangle Secretarial College. Although she was not actively unhappy, Christine Jackson's time at a similar college must have been based on Pamela's own experience:

> I made no friends there, for all the girls were richer than I and many
> of them were doing their training, not in order to earn a living, but to
> have some sort of career in their hands either to while away the time
> before they married or to maintain themselves if ever it became neces-
> sary for them to leave their future husbands. (*Marriage*, p.31)

Pamela found business practices dull, and struggled with shorthand; however, within two months, she was jubilant about having succeeded in a 50 words per minute test. Her typing proficiency would also stand her in good stead when she became a writer.

At that time, there were few, if any, secretarial employment agencies, and employers would apply to colleges for school-leavers if they had a vacancy. It was through the Triangle, therefore, that Pamela found her first, and virtually only, permanent job. Her mother recorded in the Progress Book: 'May 26 1930: First business position as shorthand-typist, secretarial work, at Central Hanover Bank and Trust Co., Regent Street, at £2 per week (3 days before 18th birthday).' The office was the West End branch of an American bank, where, as Pamela wrote later, 'very little banking was done; it was really designed for looking after the needs of travelling Americans' (*Important*, p.69).

Pamela's secretarial status at the bank was undermined by her arch-enemy, Mr Price, the under-manager, on whom the character, Mr Baynard, in *An Impossible Marriage*, was almost certainly based. Christine, the first-person narrator, dislikes Mr Baynard at once, not least 'because on my very first day [...], he robbed me of my fine title and labelled me, conclusively, "the Junior"'. Christine 'realised sensibly that I must resign myself to detesting Mr. Baynard with the same unemphatic and incurable detestation I should always have for spiders and east winds' (*Marriage*, pp.62-63). Typical entries in Pamela's diary recorded Mr. Price as being 'at his worst', 'in a real nasty mood', or 'in one of his obscene little tempers'. The office in the novel is identified as a travel agency, rather than a bank, but the business transacted, as with the real-life bank, was mainly on behalf of their American customers. This meant that they were exceedingly busy during the summer months, but Christine had little to do for the rest of the year, yet had to appear constantly occupied 'because of the faint chance that some official from the Other Side should arrive unexpectedly'. Pamela's diaries similarly frequently recorded entries like: 'Positively atrophied with inaction at office' during the winter. Christine is again clearly identified with her author, when she explains that she was selling poems regularly, and therefore she often welcomed the hiatus 'as my fury of creative energy was growing [...]. I could sit and scribble industriously hour by hour upon pink "second copy" paper' (*Marriage*, p.65).

Pamela's own creative energy was indeed mainly, like Christine's, directed at writing poetry, but not all of this was intended for publication, especially her 'Office Odes' (excerpts below) which caricature her colleagues, Price, Miss Cobban, the senior secretary, and Mr Nichols, the branch manager.

> See Mr. Price with furrowed brow
> Engaged in speculating how
> To ship the wealthy Mrs. J.[4]
> Cosily back to USA.
> Miss Cobain grimly draws the dough
> From Mr. Mauger down below,
> And gets into an awful state
> If it is fifteen minutes late,
> And tells all calls on the 'phone
> That Mr. N. is NOT at home.

Her own frustration with the trivia of office life was also recorded:

> Miss Johnson gets a little peeved
> When burdened with reports received:
> She's rather tired of putting scores
> Of dirty papers into drawers,
> But always seems distinctly better
> When she's allowed to TYPE A LETTER!

Pamela handed her wage packet over to her mother each week; in her memoir, she recorded that Amy then gave her back ten shillings 'for fares, food, and the ten cigarettes which I could not even then do without'. It was only on payday that she could afford a hot meal in a restaurant where she would have 'an omelette and chips, and a blackcurrant sponge pudding'. 'I should wish to say', she continued, 'that I have never enjoyed, in my life, any meals as much as I did those' (*Important*, p.69). She sought, therefore, ways in which to supplement her salary. Despite constantly submitting her prolific output of often excellent poems to various publications, she became inured to their rejection. She had also started to write short stories, but had not succeeded in having any of these published either. Eventually, she found a profitable, if aesthetically unsatisfying, sideline in writing doggerel verses about children for *Woman's Friend*. The first to be published, in November 1930, celebrated the birth of 'Princess Elizabeth's Baby Sister':

> A jewel in a Royal crown
> Into the world a Princess came,
> And all the fairies, smiling down
> Upon her, sought to find a name.
> But they could think of nothing meet
> For one so small – so very sweet.
> Yet, as she glowed both soft and bright,
> Cuddled within her cradle-bower,
> They all agreed to name the sprite
> After a jewel and a flower;
> So, with one voice, the fairies chose
> To call her Margaret and Rose!

(Note: the name Margaret means a pearl.)

Later, the embarrassed poet scribbled 'Awful' alongside these verses in her scrapbook. Nevertheless, from 1930 to 1932, she was a regular contributor to the magazine, whose readers presumably enjoyed following the fortunes of baby Jennifer Jayne each week, from 'Her First Smile' to her first day at school, and later the scrapes of naughty but evidently lovable schoolboy Timothy, here making New Year 'wesolushuns':

> 'WESOLVED: to be more careful and keep my jersey clean,
> An' never rob the larder, 'cos that is *very* mean,
> To go to bed when *told* to, and put away my toys,
> An' share my weekly pennies with all the other boys!'

> I read the 'wesolushuns', and smiled at Timothy.
> 'I hope you think they're good ones,' he whispered timidly.
> So I had to stoop and kiss him, and I answered (wouldn't you?):
> 'I think they're simply *Splendid*, and I know you'll keep them, too!'

Pamela would make no reference to these first published works later in life.

By the beginning of 1931, Pamela's relationship of Ian Swanson was cooling. When he visited her on New Year's Day, she 'was in rather a nasty mood', and 'let the poor little soul see it'. She had begun to go out with a more sophisticated young man, Frank Saunois, having met him and his brother, Charles, quite frequently when visiting her aunt in the Thames Valley. The brothers were part of the country club set in Laleham, and lived in Mayfair. Ned Skelton, the 'impossible' future husband of Christine Jackson, has a similar background, and in this passage, the author is almost certainly remembering her own entrancement with:

> W.I. It had a magical sound in those days for the young living far beyond in the greater numerals: S.W. 1 1, N.W. 1 2, S.E. 1 4. Perhaps it still has. It meant an excitement, a dangling of jewels in the dusk, music and wine. It meant having enough money not to get up on the cold, sour mornings and catch the crowded bus.' (*Marriage*, pp.107-08)

On 2 January, in a diary entry adorned with exclamation marks, Pamela recorded that Frank had told her that 'he was terribly in love with her'. She lost no time in telling Ian that:

> though I loved him (which I do) I wasn't in love with him. All went well & I thought he was taking it all right until he absolutely broke down as he was going. I felt dreadful. Long letter from Frank. Feel utterly wretched – realise I have been contemptible and deserve all I get. Can only pray for guidance.

Frank almost immediately asked her to marry him, and she told him that he must wait for her answer. However, only a week later, she yielded to his pressure to become engaged. She then found that the aura of luxury emanating from the W.I. address had been illusory. Frank sent her a long letter which was 'more or less a statement of financial condition', which she had found 'rather worrying'. Pamela had not initially realised that he was a hairdresser, probably not the occupation she would have envisaged for a future husband. He was then hoping to open his own salon, but he evidently did not have sufficient capital, and she was not altogether sympathetic. Christine Jackson, looking back, says that: 'We should not lightly condemn the snobberies of middle-class youth' (*Marriage*, p.106), and in February 1931, Christine's creator was exhibiting a stereotypical reaction to Frank's reluctance to seal their engagement with a ring. After several weeks of rows on the subject, alternating with days when she 'had never been so in love', Frank finally gave her a ring with 'a sapphire surrounded by small diamonds', and she duly took huge pleasure in showing this off at the office the next day.

This aspect of her engagement having been satisfactorily resolved, Pamela could turn her attention to other pastimes. The Quondam Players, the amateur dramatic offshoot of her old school's alumnae association, were ambitiously staging George Bernard Shaw's *Caesar and Cleopatra*, under her direction. 'I shall play Cleopatra,' she noted in her diary (as she probably had announced at the casting meeting), and she then spent an 'arduous evening' cutting the play to suit their requirements. After some travails, she was delighted to record that the play 'went simply MARVELLOUSLY! Raging success', and that it had won 'awfully good notices' in the local newspaper.

Pamela fretted a little about her mother's obvious dislike of Frank, which she could not understand, and also regretted that he did not get on well with her more intellectual friends. Further, while Pamela usually described him as 'precious', it would seem that he could also sometimes be sexually aggressive; her diary entries reflect her girlish alarm at Frank being 'so hard to manage' on one occasion, 'almost ungovernable' on another. Their relationship became still more volatile when he managed to open a hairdressing salon in Twickenham, since the enterprise was stressful, and would ultimately be unsuccessful. He was sometimes 'inexpressibly adorable', and sometimes intent on starting 'one of our vicious but enjoyable and innocuous rows'. On one occasion, when he had been in a 'peculiar mood', she gloomily wrote: 'Now I know why girls murder their lovers.'

That autumn, it wasn't just Frank whose business was failing. In an effort to stabilize the economy, Britain came off the Gold Standard, and the bank was besieged by clients. 'Terribly busy day at work', Pamela wrote, 'clients lined up against the counter, clamouring for money like a lot of tigers at feeding time.' Within a week, things were back to normal, and Pamela had an exciting day when: 'A very wealthy American called Santa (client) took me to lunch at the Monseigneur & made several most exotic proposals – mainly dishonourable!' (The Monseigneur was a newly opened restaurant and nightclub in Piccadilly, with a resident dance band led by the renowned bandleader Roy Fox.) When Christine Jackson is asked out to lunch by young James A. Dewey III, a millionaire client of the agency, she, with her 'heart beating', suggests the Monseigneur, and

then agonizes because her coat has a torn lining, which might attract
the derision of the waiters. She therefore resolves to keep her coat on
through lunch, despite the temperature being like 'that of a steam-
room of a Turkish bath' (*Marriage*, pp.67-77). Pamela's daughter
remembers her mother telling her a similar story, so again this episode
was based on her own experience.

It was something of a come-down to return to Clapham and Frank,
who seemed 'a bit of a pig' to Pamela that evening. The year drew to
a close with no possibility of the young couple being able to set a date
for their wedding. Pamela ended her diary for that year:

> Darling F. over in evening to see New Year in. F. adorable as usual, and
> so ends 1931 – wonderful year for me, on account of my dear & much-
> loved Frank, and rotten for poor Mother on same account & because
> of a surplus of Grannie. No one's fault, but wretched for her. May I be
> married & she be living alone in 1932!

But 1932 turned out to be very much like 1931. Pamela was still
dissatisfied at work, and frequently was sent by the Triangle for interviews, which proved unsuccessful, for other jobs. She had no further
work published, and Frank's business was still in difficulties.

1933 began inauspiciously with family sadness. Despite the constant
arguments between her mother and her grandmother (in which she
had always taken her mother's side), Pamela was extremely upset
when her grandmother became critically ill. On 5 January, she was
allowed to return home from the office at 11 a.m., to sit with her
grandmother for 'a good bit of day', and the following day, she
'worried about Grannie all day at work'. Helen Howson lingered for
a further week in the house to which her Charlie had proudly brought
her and their young family some forty years earlier, but died there on
14 January, 'very peacefully & mercifully'.

Pamela and Frank Saunois had now been engaged for two years,
and were still, she said ironically, having 'jolly' evenings, 'talking over
our miseries and our poverty'. His financial situation worsened as he
fell into arrears with the rental of his business premises. Problems at
the office continued; Mr. Price, she said, was 'a great cosmos of fidget',
even 'a common, shouting little pipsqueak'. 'How I loathe that job,'
she wailed, 'and no outlet.' All in all, it was hardly surprising that, in
language unbefitting a craftsman with words (for she was still

writing poetry), she exploded with envious rage after a visit from an old friend. The afternoon had, she said, given her, '<u>the bleedin' 'ump</u>. Gwen brought her baby to tea. Lovely little boy, but made me wretchedly jealous. Why should <u>she</u> have all the luck?'

But two months later, Pamela's luck would undergo drastic changes: she would begin to find the promised way from her motto, and this would result in her first steps on the ladder of literary fame – and she would fall in love with an *enfant terrible*.

CHAPTER 3

'My Darling Dylan'

WITH NO PRIOR notification, on a quiet Sunday afternoon at home, glancing through that day's newspapers, Pamela was startled to see her own name. She had entered a poem in a recently inaugurated competition run by a short-lived but moderately influential newspaper and she found herself named as that week's prize-winner. 'Tremendous excitement', she recorded, 'when I found I had won the 'Sunday Referee' poetry prize with "Chelsea Reach" & had been cited by a lambkin critic as "one of the most exquisite word artists of our day".' 'Cor Lumme!', the exquisite word artist giggled. It *is* occasionally hard to reconcile the writer of often banal diary entries with the sensitive girl who wrote the prize-winning poem, the first and last verses of which were:

> Soft gulls drifting on the grey river,
> Faint gulls floating on the black night,
> While the lanterns on the stream shiver,
> Keep my body and my soul white.

The 'lambkin critic' was Victor Neuburg, a man with a scandalous past, though it is unlikely that either Pamela, or her mother who was later guardedly warned about him from a barrister friend, knew the full extent of his earlier notoriety at that time. In his twenties, Neuburg, a young Jewish poet from London, had fallen under the spell of the occultist Aleister Crowley, a man famously dubbed 'The Wickedest Man in the World' in a leading article in *John Bull*, attributed to the magazine's founder and editor, Horatio Bottomley.[1] Although Neuburg was regularly abused by Crowley, both sexually, and verbally with crude anti-Semitic gibes, he agreed to travel to North Africa with him. In a location authoritatively given in various sources as having been in Algeria or the middle of the Sahara – or, and possibly the most likely, just a few miles beyond Marrakech, Crowley attempted to summon up the Devil, by means of Neuburg's ritual sodomization. A story was circulated (and evidently was believed for some time) that when the Devil failed to make an appearance, Crowley entirely blamed Neuburg and, using his alleged magical powers, turned Victor into a zebra (another version maintains that the animal was a camel), and sold him to Alexandria Zoo.[2]

Now aged 50, with his youthful indiscretions far behind him, Neuburg had set up a small publishing company, the Vine Press. As editor of the *Sunday Referee*'s 'Poet's Corner', according to Constantine FitzGibbon, he was paid an extremely small salary, probably £2 per week, and the prizes offered were commensurately modest, 'half a guinea to the winner with curiously childish consolation prizes, such as a penknife or a pencil, for the runners-up'.[3] Neuburg was assisted by his constant companion, Runia Tharp, also known as Sheila Macleod, the wife of a painter (the exact nature of the relationship between Neuburg, who was by this time married but separated from his wife, and Tharp has never been established); the pair divided their time between Steyning in Sussex, and a series of rented flats in north-west London. It was to one of the latter that Pamela was invited to meet him, having received an 'amazing letter', she recorded in her diary. 'Think he must be boopsy!!' The visit to 'the Neuburgs', as she mistakenly called Victor and Runia, was her first introduction to the literary circle they assiduously cultivated. Pamela was thrilled: 'Delightful people & had a delightful evening. [Neuburg] was charming re my work, and is the most intriguing person. Wouldn't let me go till ten to eleven. Grand time.' The next day, her thoughts were 'full of my entrancing Victor Neuburg'.

But there was another still more captivating man simultaneously in her life, thanks for once to her detested job. The secretaries were occasionally asked to work for visiting clients of the bank, and Pamela had been asked to take dictation from the charismatic conductor, Leopold Stokowski, who, though English-born, was then based in the USA. Although he was twenty years her senior, and married to his second wife, a Johnson and Johnson heiress, the naïve Pamela was overwhelmed by his glamour, and seemingly unaware of his reputation as a philanderer. She recorded:

> The most exciting day. Simply don't know <u>how</u> to tell it. Leopold Stokowski gave me handbag for all I'd done (!) & asked me to his flat to 'take a letter'. Was perfectly adorable & said he felt terribly drawn to me in 'sympathie' & that we must be great friends although he returns to States tomorrow. Quel honneur!

The following day, 'Stokowski came in to say goodbye & left for Philadelphia at 11 by the boat train. Just a look & a handclasp & goodbye.' Pamela's still regularly-kept reading list contained no works by romantic novelists, but that last sentence was worthy of the contemporary doyenne of the genre, Ruby M. Ayres.

Poor hairdresser Frank didn't stand a chance. Two days later, Pamela broke off their engagement. Her poem, 'Retrospect', written at this time, is clearly autobiographical. It begins:

> ... Two wasted years,
> Striking the match of love, blowing it out;
> Only the night air knows the whispered dreams
> Blown into dust upon the morning sun [...].

It was not, however, a clean break; for a fortnight, she agonised, as he besought her to take him back. Each diary entry was more melodramatic than the last: 'A dreadful, dreadful day. [...] Dreadful evening of misery. Tears & pleas and me fighting to do what was right, but in the end I made it goodbye.' 'A day in Hell – quite honestly I feel at the end of everything.' 'A night and half a day of most <u>ghastly</u> mental agony.' But eventually the tone lightened. Her two closest friends, Babs and Teddy (whom she had been seeing less frequently because neither of them got on with Frank), came in for an evening – 'very nice & jolly – really like the good old days' – and, the following day, she wrote of feeling:

> such a wonderful freedom & happiness – better than I've felt for months. It seems too good to last! Walk by myself – lovely evening – clouds floated in an apple green sky like the Isles of Greece. If only there had been an apple-tree – "The Singing & the Gold!" were there already.[4]

Years later, she would recreate that mood when Christine Jackson experiences an 'exaltation of freedom' after similarly ending an early relationship:

> The wet grass soaked into my stockings, the edge of my skirt; the soles of my shoes made a suck and a flap as I ran. The coolness was strange and delicious, and so was the dark. I was free at last, light as air. I might have been running barefoot in the surf of some marvellous sea, along the edge of a land where nobody knew me and I knew nobody. [...] I had known a lightness and joy that was like rising from some crippling illness to discover what limbs would obey the will, were mastered, and were whole. (*Marriage*, pp.27-28)

And Pamela proceeded to enjoy her summer. She was invited to Steyning; Victor and Runia were 'both charming' to her. Their house seemed to her to be 'a fairy-tale cottage', although the critic Arthur Calder-Marshall, who had grown up in Steyning, called the house 'tumble-down'.[5] As she was to find was the norm whether in London or Steyning, several other people came in for a discussion, led by 'the Vickybird', as the circle he dubbed the 'Creative Lifers' called him. Pamela was continuing to write poetry, at least one poem a week. She went to stay with her aunt in Laleham, but now hated the trivial chatter of the 'B.Y.P. screaming & yelling '"But my <u>dear</u> ...!"'[6] She had an occasional treat in the form of 'a letter from precious Leopold enclosing personal handwritten note. <u>So</u> sweet.' And it cannot have been entirely coincidental that she became an avid concert-goer at that time, proudly recording a visit, among several others, to the Proms: 'Gorgeous concerto by Hindemith that nearly cleared the hall save for a few enthusiasts.' She was exchanging poems with Stokowski, and may well have sent him her poem 'Philharmonic Concerto: Hindemith', with its dramatic final verse:

> This is the oldest music in the world,
> Wild as the storm that tipped the Garden through,
> Wild as the bird within the breast of Eve;
> Most beautiful, because it knows no shame;
> Most terrible, because it knows no leash;
> Age shall not slay it – for it knew no birth.

On 3 September 1933, 'Poet's Corner' awarded first prize to a little-known Welshman called Dylan Thomas, for his poem, 'That Sanity

Be Kept'. Pamela was very impressed by it, and possibly remembering how thrilled she had been to receive letters of praise from unknown
readers, she wrote to him. Within a few days, she had his reply. It was
the beginning of a remarkable correspondence, with each commonly
sending about twelve pages to the other every few days. This time-
consuming task was more feasible in his case; his first, and for many
years, only paid full-time job, as a junior reporter on the *South Wales
Daily Post*, had come to an end. He had been, according to a colleague,
'without doubt the worst newspaper man there ever was'.[7] He was
attempting to earn a living from freelance journalism, but this left
long gaps in time in which to compose, and then neatly rewrite (as he
admitted), these long letters. It began as a literary correspondence,
but later the subjects would become wide-ranging, and Dylan's style
would vary between the polemical, surreal, romantic, or just the very
funny. She, on the other hand, could only reply in fits and starts, when
work was slack at the office, or by staying up late at night. She preserved the majority of his letters, and these have now been published
in full;[8] all hers to him have regrettably been lost. But his appreciative comments about her letters and her brief diary entries tell a tale
of the relationship that differs substantially from the versions given by
Dylan Thomas's biographers.[9]

Some discrepancies can be accounted for because Pamela had sold
her 1933-35 diaries, together with Dylan's letters to her, to the
Poetry and Rare Books Collection at the State University of New York
at Buffalo in 1963. Dylan's biographers have, in the main, taken
the chronology of their relationship from her chapter on Dylan in
Important to Me, which she wrote in the 1970s, when she didn't have
the diaries available for consultation and her memory was, as she
admitted, fallible. More importantly, the perspective of Dylan's biographers does not reflect the huge impact that Dylan had on Pamela's
life, both emotionally and with regard to the trajectory of her development as a writer, and, indeed, vice versa.

Dylan Thomas was then a month away from his nineteenth
birthday, although he told Pamela in his first reply that they were the
same age. He added that: 'You say one has enough time, when one is
21, to be modest. One has enough time ahead, too, to regret one's
immodesty' (9 September 1933). She was not to discover the truth
about his age for a year and a half; certainly she could not have divined

this from his immodesty about his own poems, and the authoritative tone of his comments regarding hers. In that same letter, he commented that Neuburg's previously mentioned description of Pamela as an 'exquisite word-artist' with regard to 'Chelsea Reach' was 'a large and *almost merited* [my italics] compliment', but then added that he couldn't however agree with Neuburg's opinion that 'Prothalamium', another of her prize-winning poems, was 'The Real Thing'. Dylan said that he hadn't liked the first stanza of this poem at all: 'Too many adjectives, too much sugar. And the fifth and sixth lines are pure cliché.' The reader may wish to make up his or her own mind as to whether the criticism was just. The first stanza is as follows:

> The fir-trees lace the liquid golden sky,
>   And in their tangled web, an early star
>   Has wandered, wondering, and lost her way;
>   Across the lawn the sunset shadows lie,
>   The lake is still; and from the woods afar
>   A bird sings requiem to the dying day.

Since a prothalamium is a poem in celebration of a marriage, the lushness and romanticism seemed justified.

Victor Neuburg is credited with having 'discovered' Dylan Thomas. The blurb on Jean Overton Fuller's biography of Neuburg, describing him as Dylan's 'literary godfather', is, however, an exaggeration. Young as Dylan was, before his appearance in 'Poet's Corner', he had had several poems published in Wales, and two in England. The first of the latter was an early version of one of his most famous poems, 'And death shall have no dominion'; it had been published in May of that year in *New English Weekly*, edited by A.R. Orage. This periodical was the successor to Orage's celebrated pre-First World War *New Age*, in which he had published poetry by the major English and American modernists. The second poem had appeared in *Adelphi*, an even more respected periodical. Although he was later to admit some indebtedness to Neuburg, Dylan mocked the concept of the feature he had inaugurated:

> In the very interesting copy you sent me of the first Poet's Corner, it is explained that when, during any week, no poetry is received, the best verse would be printed. That would be perfectly all right if it did

happen. But the pretentious palming off of <u>doggerel</u> (not even verse) as 'arty' poetry is too much.

It was on the same grounds that I objected to 'Poet's Corner' as a title. There was a time when only poets were called poets. Now anyone with an insufficient knowledge of the English language, a Marie Corelli sentiment, and a couple of 'bright' images to sprinkle over the lines, is called a poet. He can't even leave his excretion in a private spot. They give him a public 'Corner' to leave it in. (9 September 1933)

Feeling he might have gone a little too far, he added: 'A vulgar metaphor! I hope you don't object.' Within a few days, he was to write to her again, and a slightly bewildered Pamela noted in her diary that she had received a 'charming & very, very modern, not to say rude, letter from Dylan Thomas'. Perhaps she decided it would be expedient to destroy this letter (in case her mother should read it?); it was not among the correspondence which she was eventually to sell.

Pamela, free from Frank, was thoroughly enjoying life, seeing old friends as well as meeting new ones. She was writing a satirical version of *Cinderella* for the Quondam Players ('I have got to play Cinderella, alas'), and Teddy Lamerton was composing music to go with her lyrics. She had evenings with her friend 'Dick' Turbin, at which they talked about 'everything from Darwin & Freud to Harry Champion' (the latter was a music hall-star who was an especial favourite of hers). She would squabble amicably about religion with Dick and Teddy: one such occasion had ended with her being 'worsted and bloodied but unbowed. The worst of my agnostic pals is that they clap me in a mental dog-collar & leave me for a crank!' (As will be seen, she evidently told Dylan about these conversations, and most of her other activities.) She went to concerts, the theatre, and the cinema, with a variety of friends.

But above all, she was meeting exciting people at Victor Neuburg's, and she wrote to Dylan about evenings with two young poets, Reuben Mednikoff, who was later to be better known as a painter, and the surrealist poet David Gascoyne. Mention of the latter aroused Dylan's ire — for Gascoyne was even younger than he was, but had had his first book of poems published when he was sixteen. He replied:

David Gascoyne and Reuben Mednikoff! You move in exalted company. I read the Russian Jew's (is he?) effort in the Referee, and agree

with you – as a poet he's a bloody good painter. But Gascoyne? And
seventeen, too? Tut, tut, what are the boys coming to? I read a thing
of his – before your letter came – in the new New Verse, and thought
he was raving mad. There are more maggots in his brain than there
are in mine. (15 October 1933)

Mednikoff was smitten by Pamela, and bombarded her with letters
and phone calls. She frequently went to his flat, ostensibly because he
was painting her portrait. Although Amy usually accompanied her
when she went to see Victor and Runia, she did rather strangely allow
Pamela to go to a man's flat alone. When David Gascoyne was also
present, he and Mednikoff talked art until Pamela's head reeled; she
was glad of the occasions when she found Reuben on his own.

Her diary entry for 29 October 1933 is marked by triple lines:

Excitements – I won the prize of having my own book of poems
published for sending into the Referee the best work in six months!!

She received congratulatory calls from all her friends and her new
literary acquaintances. Dylan had already sent her detailed critiques
of most of the works that would appear in the collection, which was
to take its title from the longest poem, *Symphony for Full Orchestra*.
He told her that he only objected to one phrase in this poem:

> '… Weave the straining clouds
> Into maddened shrouds',

has too many words – and the wrong words in it. The rhyme is a
jingle. The adjectives add nothing. Polish up or remove that phrase, &
I have no quarrel with the poem from beginning to end.

But, despite going on to praise it, he again had to add a qualification:
'*In its limits* [my italics], it is as lovely as anything I know.' (The
'straining clouds' and 'maddened shrouds' do not appear in the
published version.) Dylan continued:

What a strange, unequal selection of poems and verses you have sent
me. You have sent me the sugariest custard, the cheapest port, & the
most delicate white wine. I never remember mixing my drinks so
quickly, &, at the same time, so satisfyingly.

However, he did respond very generously to the news of the forthcoming book, saying: 'I take as much interest in the publication of

your poems as I do in the publication of my own. And if they were my own, I could not be more delighted to hear that your poems are to be published' (letter undated). (And six months later, she was to be able to congratulate him on becoming the second Referee Poet, though publication of his *18 Poems* would be delayed until December 1934.)

Pamela's status at the Neuburg gatherings was greatly enhanced. Jean Overton Fuller remembered the first time she encountered her there – 'a petite, slight girl, with dark hair and intelligent eyes. From the cheer with which she was greeted, I knew she must be someone of consequence.'[10] The first party Pamela attended after there had been a 'tremendous blurb' about her in the *Referee* was at Reuben's flat. It was, she said, 'a dreadful "crowd"', and she was 'ghastly embarrassed & nearly went mad'. She obviously wrote about the evening to Dylan in more literary style. A short extract of his lengthy as always response, headlined '<u>The Arty</u> Party', follows:

> The type of party you describe – and you describe it very well indeed – is a menace to art, much as I dislike the phrase. Wyndham Lewis has struck them hard in 'Apes of God' [...] Roy Campbell, in his 'Georgiad', has trampled them down under the feet of his eighteenth-century charger; but still they flourish. [...] With a smattering, often incorrectly memorised, of encyclopedia learning, with the names of the transient stars of their decade on the tips of their tongues, with their men's breasts shaped with the aid of wadding, the young women speak on. Sodomhipped young men, with the inevitable side-whiskers and cigarettes, the faulty livers and the stained teeth, reading Lawrence as an aphrodisiac and Marie Corelli in their infrequent baths, spew onto paper and canvas their ignorance and perversions [...]. This is the art of today; posturing, shamming, cribbing, and all the artifice of a damned generation. (Week of 11 November 1933)

Their correspondence was becoming increasingly personal. They exchanged photographs, Dylan writing that he could only send her a photograph that was two years old, evidently to maintain the pretence about his age. On receiving Pamela's photograph, he told her that he had not expected her

> to be so full and bright and strong, with such a British chin. What a dominant personality. Tut, girl, what a zest for life! And here I am, small, chinless, and like an emasculate Eton boy. [...] You are very,

very, pleasant to look at. There is meaning and strength in your face. I shall hang you in my room. [...] So now, if I look long upon your photograph, and you, looking upon mine, exercise your imagination in the details of age and cleanliness, we shan't be strangers to each other.

'I seem,' he concluded in the same letter under the heading 'A Piece of Sentiment', 'to have been writing these nonsensical letters of mine for ever, and for ever to have been receiving those of yours. But it can't have been for more than a few months. Yet I know you as well as I have ever known anybody in my life' (Early November 1933).

At this time, the occasional arrival of letters from Stokowski continued to thrill her. One in November was 'very affectionate' and enclosed a poem for her. This might well have been a response to her unpublished ode, 'The Conductor', ('verse', or worse, in Dylan's terms, although it's unlikely she had sent *him* this hero-worshipping poem to criticize). It opens with the lines:

> There you stand, silent, in a pool of light
> Your arms upraised. The humid autumn night
> Stands on tip-toe. Above you, tier on tier
> The spell-bound audience hold their breath to hear
> The first frail notes; then hearts are opened wide
> That timeless ecstasy may slip inside.

That month, a party was held in Pamela's honour by Victor and Runia. Her diary entry reads: 'This evening was a yell. [...] About 20 there. An awful swine, Dr Coplans, <u>would</u> make a speech about me, and sat at my feet, a perfect beast. Everyone else nice – everyone was decent to me.' Dylan replied to her account of that evening: 'Why didn't someone kick that perverted doctor in the bottom? Aren't <u>any</u> of the Creative Lifers men of action? Here in barbaric Wales, where men are men, he would have been stoned to death by members of Y Gobaith Cymru Wrdd.'[11] In the same letter, Dylan denounced contemporary sexual mores (again the following is only a fraction of this section of his letter); he was obviously hoping for a positive response from his correspondent:

The medieval laws of this corrupted hemisphere have dictated a more or less compulsory virginity during the period of life when virginity should be regarded as a crime against the dictates of the body. [...]

The body must be kept intact for marriage, which is rarely possible before the age of twenty; the physical expression of sex must be caged up for six or more years until, for the price of a ring, a licence, and a few hampering words, opportunity is presented with all the ceremony of a phallic religion. But so often the opportunity comes too late; the seed has soured; love has turned to lust, and lust to sadism; the mind has become covered and choked by the weeds of inhibition; and the union of two starved creatures, suddenly allowed the latitude of their sexes, is doomed from the start.

Pamela had evidently recently told him something about her previous romantic relationships. Dylan responded:

Thank you for telling me about your lost, but not forgotten lovers, and if the pages did occasionally remind me of Ella M. Ruck, that composite novelist and poet, they were none the less sincere for that.
     And that was a horribly patronising remark [...] I'm very sorry. It probably took a great deal of courage for you to tell me about the frigid reader of newspapers upon whom you wasted such a lot of your affection. [...] You paid me a compliment by telling me about him, & the G.N.L. & the British boy (your taste doesn't seem to lie in the direction of the arty & poetical young men) & the emotional part of me thanks you very much. Never mind the intellectual part: that is nothing.

He then recanted completely: 'It didn't remind me of Ella M., really. I loved it, only I'm too xxxx self-conscious to say so, damn my rabbit's eyes!' (early December 1933). She seems to have limited herself to telling him only about three of her past boyfriends (and to have omitted Reuben, who would indeed have fitted the description of an 'arty & poetical' young man). Dylan, at this time, according to his biographers, had yet to have a serious girlfriend, and the consensus among them is that he was probably still a virgin. Jonathan Fryer convincingly maintains that: 'As the letters to Pamela become increasingly intimate, they bear all the hallmarks of a young man who senses that the forbidden fruit of carnal knowledge may at long last be within reach.'[12]
Pamela did not record the outpouring of his sexual philosophy as being 'modern' and 'rude', as she had with that letter much earlier in their correspondence, but as a 'long and entirely delightful letter from

my little Dylan', and, misleadingly as he would discover, answered in similar mode. The paradox was that, although at this time *she* was certainly a virgin and timid with regard to physical sexual contact, she was knowledgeable (her naivety about Stokowski seems to have been an exception) and outspoken on the subject, both in letters to Dylan and in her writing. In his next letter, Dylan delightedly addressed her as his 'sweet, Rabelaisian Pamela', and pronounced that:

> You must, you know, be an awfully entertaining little girl. Anyone who can be intelligently artistic, artistically intelligent, and downright vulgar <u>must</u> be nice. [...] It's remarkable how few of the moreorless cultivated young women one meets can be honestly vulgar. They talk, possibly, of matters, which a 100 years ago, were not supposed to exist, but they talk in a sly, subtle, sophisticated way, and their jokes – when they tell any – depend upon innuendoes. Now <u>you</u>, to your shame and credit, have a decidedly coarse wit [...].

She had, with her mother's permission, invited him to stay with them over Christmas, but he had to refuse: 'My sister, brother-in-law and uncle will be down here for the holiday, and great fun will be had by all. Will it, hell!' But he continued: 'I'm flattered to receive a Christmas invitation from you, from you who have known me for such a little time and in such unusual ways – more flattered (and terribly pleased) than I can tell you.' Importantly, he then went on to enquire whether she had written any prose, and asked if she could send him any examples:

> I remember you told me something in a very longago [*sic*] letter about some stories you'd put on the fire. But aren't there <u>any</u> stories not used so harshly and, I'm sure, so needlessly? I think you should be able to write very good prose.

She had not recorded writing any fiction that year, so Dylan's question might well have encouraged her to take up the genre again. Dylan was now increasingly acknowledging that his interest in her went beyond the literary:

> the little, pulsating bits in your letters – when you defend your theism before a pack of negative-brained scoffers, or dwell, unhappily but unbrokenly, upon the passing of juvenile loves – are of immense

interest to [me], who am also pleased by the fact that I have your confidence. My little Welsh ear is open for all secrets. (c. 21 December 1933)

He sent her a book of poems by Robert Graves for Christmas; she
more prosaically sent him cigarettes.

Pamela's collaboration with Teddy Lamerton on the play she had
now named *Cinderella Réchauffée*, led to a sudden upsurge in the
latter's feelings for her, which seems to have amused her rather than
to have been reciprocated. 'O why, o why?' she asked herself, as each
evening they spent together ended in 'osculatory adventures' in the
hall. But she didn't totally discourage him. On Christmas Eve, she
had a party at home with a 'peculiar mixture' of friends, including
Reuben and Teddy. At the end of that year's diary, Pamela summa-
rized 1933, as 'all in all' a good year:

> I kiss it goodbye with regrets. I have had a lucky escape for which I
> can never thank God sufficiently both for Frank's sake and myself.
> I have had my good fortune with my poetry, my letters from Dylan,
> my absolute mental freedom. I am grateful for Mother, and for my
> friendship with Teddy. And so, here ends my diary for 1933. I wonder
> what on earth I shall write for 1934.

1934 started with 'a rush of work at the office and a pea-soup fog',
and with rehearsals, 'ultra-sweet' letters from Reuben, clothes buying
– 'bought charming grey swagger coat and skirt, wool, for 1 guinea,
in sales' – and films, including *Counseller-at Law*, with her favourite
actor, John Barrymore. 'J.B.,' she said, 'is, to my mind, well away the
finest actor on the screen. He gives himself completely to his audience, sparing neither himself nor them.' The teasing correspondence
with Dylan continued; on the address page of her 1934 diary, although
she listed the addresses of her closest friends, in the case of Dylan, she
wrote: 'Why write it? I know it' (although 5 Cwmdonkin Drive,
Uplands, Swansea, was not the easiest of addresses to memorize).
Evidently Pamela gave as good as she got with her criticisms of the
poems Dylan sent her for comment. He replied in a letter she received
early in the New Year:

> The last poem I sent you, the one you didn't like, is <u>not</u> very good,
> and I'm glad you attacked it [...] and thank you, too, for expressing

– in your remarks about the hiding of light and the running around
in the same weary and minor track – much that I myself have felt
and have never been able to express. [...] But [...] one day I hope to
write something [...] larger, wider, more comprehensible, and less self-
centred; one day I may even come up to your expectations. And if I
do, if ever I do, much of the credit will belong to a delightful (I will
say it) young woman I have never seen. (25 December 1933)

The next letter is further proof, should it be needed, of how much
time Dylan had on his hands. Pamela recorded receiving a 'darling
letter – in play form from Dylan who is coming up soon!' (January
1934). The 'one-act play never to be presented' is called 'Spajma and
Salnady, or Who Shot the Emu?', and the author rather unnecessarily
explains 'that the names of the two principal characters – Spajma
Oh-no-nel and Salnady Moth – are anagrams upon the respective
names of the present reader and author'. Constantine FitzGibbon
dismissed this as 'largely nonsense', which belongs, he said, 'if anywhere, in a volume of his juvenilia',[13] and indeed it was eventually
included in a collection of Dylan's early prose writings.[14] The play ran
to eight foolscap pages in Dylan's tiny neat handwriting. Nonsense it
may be, but glorious, surreal nonsense which could well have been
written by Spike Milligan, as the two protagonists visit the Spirit of
Poetry in search of 'a quick half pound of inspiration all about pimps
and gasworks'. In the guise of Salnady, however, Dylan voices his
anxiety about his forthcoming visit to Spajma (it will be seen that the
real-life pair have already identified some areas of contention):

Spajma   Don't you like Norma Shearer, Lionel Barrymore, Clark
         Gable, George Raft, Joan Crawford, & Uncle Tom Navarro
         and all?
Salmady No. I like abstruse poetry, symbolical fiction, discordant
         music, & beer. Oh, yes, I like you too, by the way.
Spajma (coyly) Wait till you know me proper, flesh and all.
Salmady Don't be pornographic. I said I like you, and I do. When I
         know you better, I shall like you better, I know. It's I'm the
         trouble. There's the great possibility, or even probability,
         that you won't like me at all.

It had been agreed that Dylan would come to London in February
to meet Pamela (and her mother) and stay for a few days at their house;

with excitement, she recorded that, to make the final arrangements: 'DYLAN phoned – such a rich, fruity old port-wine of a voice.' (This seems to have been the first time they had spoken on the telephone; neither would have been prepared to meet the cost of a trunk call.) The Friday of his arrival turned out to be a very special day in Pamela's life. She received the first copies of *Symphony for Full Orchestra*, and there were 'great celebrations' at her office. The book was well-produced, in hard-cover, and priced at 2/6d. The frontispiece was a sketch of her by Reuben Mednikoff, not, it has to be said, a particularly flattering one, as she looks middle-aged, but perhaps this was to lend her gravitas. In a foreword, Victor Neuburg, using an early feminist neutral pronoun, wrote that:

> If the reader be poet, or poet-lover, heshe will not easily let fade from memory this, [Miss Johnson's] first book, which holds poems that, unless my view of them be wholly partisan, will endure while Poetry endures.

Pamela was interviewed at the *Referee* offices (although when the result was read to her over the phone, she was not happy about it). And that evening, Dylan arrived to spend the weekend – 'charming, very young-looking, with the most enchanting voice'. In retrospect, she wrote of herself and Dylan then: 'By this time, we were, of course, fully prepared to fall in love' (*Important*, p.141).

In 1953, she began her contribution to the Dylan Thomas Memorial Number of the international review, *Adam*, with an account of that meeting:

> He arrived very late on a dull grey evening in spring, and he was nervous, as I was. 'It's nice to meet you after all those letters. Have you seen the Gauguins?' (He told me later that he had been preparing the remark about the Gauguins all the way from Swansea, and having made it, felt that his responsibility towards a cultural atmosphere was discharged.)[15]

'He looked,' she said, 'like a brilliant audacious child, and at once my family loved and fussed over him as if he were one.' (None of them, however, seems to have guessed at his real age.) The visit was a great success; Dylan was 'delightful', 'very ridiculous & funny', and 'quite the dearest thing'.

That Sunday, Pamela's photograph and a short interview with her appeared in the news pages of the *Sunday Referee*. Her misgivings about the trivialization of her achievement were justified. Under the headline, 'Girl Poet's Success', the story read:

A young woman poet whose talent first received definite recognition through the columns of the SUNDAY REFEREE has leapt into prominence this week-end by the publication of her first book of poems. [...] The author of 'Symphony for Full Orchestra' is Miss Pamela Hansford Johnson, a slim pretty girl in her early twenties, whose home is at Battersea Rise, S.W.

Miss Johnson told a SUNDAY REFEREE representative yesterday that she wrote her first poem when she was five. She appeared in print at fourteen.

From nine to five every week-day she works as a secretary at a bank, and in the evening, when she is not helping her mother or dancing – her favourite passion – she writes her poetry.

'It meant weeks of disappointment before I could get my verses published', she added. 'They were invariably to be found on the mat next morning, but when the Poet's Corner started, however, I was given a real chance.'[16]

Nevertheless Runia, Victor and Reuben visited them that evening to celebrate the book's publication, and Pamela relished the 'most glorious hokum' of Dylan's arguments with them.

Dylan had been hoping to find work in London, and although, after his 'few days' with them had extended to a week, he had managed to sell three poems and two stories, he told her that he had not had any job offers that suited him. Accordingly, she said, 'after a half-hour of supreme depression', she went with him to Paddington Station to see him off back to Wales. Three days later, she received a letter 'from darling Dylan telling me that he loved me. Oh it is so difficult to reply! I don't know how I feel or what to do.' This letter does not seem to have been preserved. Pamela 'managed some sort of an answer', which seems to have prompted a further, also unpreserved, reproachful effusion.

For the time being, Pamela returned to her love of amateur dramatics, and the Quondam production of her Cinderella spoof. Two dress rehearsals were played 'to an audience of corpses from the morgue in the afternoon, and to a slightly better one in the evening'.

The following day, the play went 'marvellously'; all her friends, including Vicky and Runia, were there. The programme announced that
words and music were by Pamela Hansford Johnson, except for the
songs for which music had been written specially for the play by
Mr E.G. Lamerton. The production was ambitious except in one
respect; a note proclaimed that: 'The Management regrets that owing
to a slight indisposition, the Transformation Scene will be unable to
appear tonight.' She wrote to Dylan telling him about the success of
the pantomime, and in his reply, he first apologized for his emotional
outburst after his visit to London:

> I still regret that now famous letter with all the conviction of my murky
> conscience. And I do regret having hurt you, as you said, in my last
> outpouring. I do regret that letter. It gives me a pain where I eat and
> where I sit down.

She described the remainder of the letter, however, as 'rather acrid',
as he had continued:

> I'm so glad your pantomime was a success; it deserved to be; I, from
> my prophetic couch, willed that it would be so. Mind, I allow you a
> little congratulation for the success; you wrote it and acted it, I admit;
> but I had an awful lot to do with it, too. But why say it didn't amuse
> me? It struck me as being very good. It's not the sort of humour that
> makes me laugh uproariously & bite my neighbour's ears, but that's
> my fault & not yours. (c. 21 March 1934)

Dylan returned to stay with them for a week at Easter. When
writing *Important to Me*, she confused this stay with a longer one later
in the year. She said that Dylan's second stay had lasted six weeks,
during which time:

> We were deliriously happy. We talked of marriage, certainly we would
> marry some day, when Dylan had a job. He talked of becoming a
> bicycle salesman, doing his rounds in yellow rubber hood, cape and
> boots. (*Important*, 142-43)

They were certainly happy for that week. He told her again he loved
her, and this time she didn't demur. A typical diary entry read:

> Met my darling Dylan for lunch – we went to Alhambra to see
> "Merchant of Venice". Vilely bad, but we enjoyed it – we'd enjoy any-
> thing together – came home, buying some chips on the way & had
> lovely evening.

She began to refer to him as 'my love Dylan', and she was desolated
when he had to return to Wales.

A few days later, she received 'a lovely, lovely letter from Dylan, my
love, that made the whole world seem different', as the following
extracts demonstrate:

> You are my only friend. I say quite seriously that I have never really
> spoken to any other human being, & that you are the clear point of
> faith with which the psalmist lifted his eyes to the hills. When I went
> away from you, it seemed you had abandoned me to myself. And when
> I was with you, after all these years of pursuit, we were face to face,
> alone. [...]
>
> The composition of my own letter and – best of all – the having of
> yours, has become the greatest event of any week, holier than the
> ritual of the bath, than the linking of sweet airs & phrases, than
> the night and its dreams. [...]
>
> Shall we live on an island, somewhere in the Mediterranean, writing
> & reading, loving & sleeping, singing our sweet, rude rhymes to the
> seals? I love you, darling.
>
> Goodbye. Dylan. X. (15 April 1934)

Two further days after receiving this, the clearly love-sick Pamela,
feeling in a 'quiet & appeased frame of mind', burbled to her diary:
'Dylan, my Dylan, my Dylan', and later acknowledged that she found
that she had to keep his name on every page of her diary.

She had been delighted with a 'very decent press notice' of *Symphony
for Full Orchestra* in the *Times Literary Supplement* (19 April 1934): the
reviewer[17] said that the spirit 'that informs her verses as a whole is not
primarily that of youthful bravado, but of delight in the world', and
that 'her verse is full of reflected radiance, of the "ever-changing light"
that plays across the face of Nature, liquid, gold, sparkling, or
subdued to a wintry grey'. A shorter critique in *Poetry Review* that
month praised 'the essentials of good poetry in Miss Johnson's work
– emotion, restraint, colour, imagery, and a happy handling of a
variety of themes'. However, she was beginning to be realistic about

her future as a poet, and, although she didn't mention reading it, an article in the same issue of that periodical would have given her little hope. Writing about the poetry of Rose Macaulay, who had already established herself as a novelist of distinction, one S.W. Powell declared that

> Great women poets are rare. So much so that, when called upon to name any, one thinks at once of Sappho and then hesitates. One wonders a little at this rarity, and cannot ascribe it to the alleged inferiority of woman's intellect, since poetry is not, primarily, of the intellect, but of the sub-conscious intelligence, or intuition, in which woman is supposed to be specially gifted. [...] Probably, however, the rarity of great women poets is due to the fact that greatness itself is rare in woman – rarer at least than in man [...].

Although this might seem ludicrous in the twenty-first century, his remarks were not untypical of contemporary attitudes. Although there was a renaissance of poetry written by both sexes in the 1930s, women poets are almost entirely omitted from literary histories of the period.

At the same time, Dylan was continuing to encourage her with regard to her prose compositions. She had sent him a story, called 'A Man Had a Monkey', and he told her that:

> With pruning & the removal of the too many & too emotional adjectives [...], the story might easily be as lovely as Anatole France's "My Lady's Juggler", a story that, in no way disparigingly [sic],[18] it at once brings to mind. [...] This is, perhaps, the first prose piece of yours that I would willingly print in any prose anthology [...]. Yes, you are going to write good stories, very good stories. You've written one now, slight as it is. But it's no slighter than "My Lady's Juggler". And that's a story that will last, as yours might last. Go on, my love, go on. The sky's the limit.

Dylan's opinion matched that of the literary editor of the periodical *Time and Tide* to which Pamela had submitted the story; it was accepted only on condition that she cut it by half, which originally horrified her, but she was nevertheless pleased when it was eventually published in January of the following year.

However, other matters about which Dylan was writing were more worrying. Although he fantasized delightfully about their future life

— 'I believe with all my heart that we'll live together one day as happily as two lobsters in a saucepan, two bugs on a muscle, one smile, though never to vanish, on the Cheshire face' — the dreary financial problems she had faced with Frank Saunois surfaced. At least, Frank had had a business of his own, albeit an unsuccessful one, but Dylan had none. He wrote, plaintively:

> I'm willing to work. I do work, but in an almost anti-mercenary direction. Which is no good at all for you or me. Something has to be done, but Christ knows what it is. And Vicky can't help. He can do little more than keep himself alive, & that not very comfortably. And the arty people I know are almost as broke as I am. (2 May 1934)

Although the bulk of his letters continued to be criticism of her poetry and short stories, and judicious advice as to which magazines she should submit her work, the letters always ended on an irresistibly romantic note, as in the following:

> I love you, Pamela, more every day, think of you more every day, and want to be with you more every day. Don't take too much notice of my rantings and rumblings [...]. I love you and love you. I only believe in you. Nice, round Pamela,[19] I love you. All the time. Always will, too. Write very soon and keep me alive. [...]
>   P.S. What do you want for your birthday? Books? Rings? Wurlitzer Organ? (13 May 1934)

But, instead of any of the above, on the day before her 22nd birthday, she received an extraordinary letter from him, a letter she found so 'appallingly distressing [that]', she wrote, 'I cried lustily all day & had to write telling him it must finish, so an end to that affair.' She ended her diary entry with a self-centred wail: 'When am I going to have some happiness?' The gist of Dylan's letter was that he had been unfaithful to her. He told her that he had been staying in Gower with a friend from his days on the *South Wales Daily Post*, and the friend's fiancée had unexpectedly arrived:

> And she was tall & thin and dark with a loose red mouth & a harsh sort of laugh. Later we all went out and got drunk. [...] I slept with her that night and for the next three nights. We were terribly drunk day and night. [...]

I'm just on the borders of D.T.s darling and I've wasted some of my tremendous love for you on a lank redmouthed girl with a reputation like a hell. [...]

Darling I love you and think of you all the time. Write by return. And don't break my heart by telling me I mustn't come up to London to you because I'm such a bloody fool.

XXXX. Darling. Darling oh. (27 May 1934)

Since Dylan verged on being a congenital liar, his biographers differ as to whether the above story was true. Constantine FitzGibbon, who, soon after this alleged episode, became a close friend of the poet, thinks that Dylan's pain is evident, and that there can be 'no question of "poetical" posing' in his letter. It is, he says, 'a desperate cry for help and sympathy to the woman who loves him'. Yet, as FitzGibbon admits, ten days after writing this letter to Pamela, Dylan had been 'as boastful as any adolescent about the same incident' in a letter to his Swansea friend, Trevor Hughes, telling him of his entanglement with 'an erotic girl with whom I indulge in unrepeatable displays of carnality'.[20] Hughes certainly believed him replying: 'How I envy you your erotic female, and – yes – that unrepeatable carnality.'[21] Paul Ferris is altogether more sceptical. He tracked down a woman of the name Dylan gave, a dancer he had known, and she firmly denied that she had been 'the scarlet woman'. 'The story,' he says, 'sounds too good to be true. It fits Thomas's stereotype of wicked behaviour. [...] If he had wanted to tell a tall story involving sex, perhaps half hoping to put an end to his relationship with Pamela, the dancer with red lips was a useful ingredient for a fantasy.'[22] A third, and to me more convincing, theory (one of five possibilities offered by Jonathan Fryer)[23] is that he was trying by this means to provoke Pamela into sleeping with him. Later that year, he did say in a letter to her: 'I've always wondered why you won't come to bed with me; it just seems silly to me' (October 1934).

Whatever the truth about the letter's content, there is no doubt that Pamela believed it. She got through the day of her birthday 'in the solid glacial way one has to get through things'. But her resolve to finish with Dylan weakened the following day, when he sent a further letter pleading for another chance. She decided to answer as before, 'but with a grain of hope', and added: 'It was such a lovely letter that it cheered me anyhow!' Her volte-face cannot be fully accounted for, as this second remorseful letter from Dylan has not been preserved, but she nevertheless agreed to let him return to stay with them the following month.

This became the stay that she remembered in retrospect as 'deliriously happy', but it lasted two weeks, not six, was not altogether blissful, and began, as it went on, with evidence of his chronic unreliability. 'My darling Dylan', as she was again calling him, was due to arrive on 4 June, but that day there was no sign of him, and she 'fretted all day about him'. The following day, she was finding 'the uncertainty v. worrying', and wrote to him to that effect. By return (the postal service, even between England and Wales, being a great deal more efficient in those days, with three deliveries a day), she received 'a letter – snooty, but letter, nevertheless, from Dylan'. Love was evidently still blinding her to his faults, as she didn't respond in similar vein, but 'wrote to the darling old fishface forgiving him & hoping for better luck next time'.

He arrived nine days later, and the first few days were indeed idyllic. It was probably during this stay that Dylan persuaded Amy to type stories from his dictation, some of which Pamela later recalled were 'of inconceivable impropriety by anybody's standards'. Her mother would stop typing to protest: '"Dylan, you *cannot* say that"', but Dylan, waving his hand, would respond: '"Put it in, Mrs. Johnson, just put it in. It's all right – I assure you, it's *perfectly* all right."'[24] Yet Amy continued at that time to be as besotted with Dylan as his daughter was. Pamela wrote in her diary that Dylan was pressing her to marry him – 'but I won't – yet'. In her memoir, she wrote how they would make trips

> across the river to Chelsea – to both of us having an aura of high romance – and sit in the garden of the Six Bells, near the little fountain that dripped its tears, while we watched the shadows of the players on the bowling-green as the sun fell. (*Important*, p.143)

Another entry in her diary records an evening 'too happy for words', when they sat in that garden 'arguing, laughing', but she was less happy about going with him to the Fitzroy Tavern in Bloomsbury (and Alison Petrie, in *The Survival of the Fittest*, would be given similar reservations about this haunt of literary intelligentsia). Pamela was also beginning to have misgivings about his drinking, and decided to talk about this with Trevor Hughes, who was now living in London. As a result, they 'came to a very definite understanding re forming a watch over Dylan'. As Constantine FitzGibbon, another Fitzroy regular, commented: 'There were to be many such watch committees in the years to come, almost always the creation of a woman who was, or thought she was, in love with Dylan.'[25]

At this point, the Leopold Stokowski episode reached its inevitable conclusion. The conductor had written a letter Pamela had found 'comic' to let her know he was returning to London. On arrival, he invited her to tea at his London flat, and evidently made an unequivocal pass at her. She found this 'very trying'; even though 'Leopold was very emotional, [...] I had to tell him I had nothing to offer him', she wrote with the injured innocence of a Victorian heroine. The next day, he came into the bank, and was 'very haughty & went out again, thank Heavens'. She heard nothing further from him.

Dylan went back to Swansea at the end of June, determined to return to London to live. The correspondence resumed, although his letters were now more sporadic than before, and she continued to fret about him. 'No letter from prize pig Dylan,' she wrote in July, 'Am afraid the little terror is in trouble again.' Throughout this turbulent time, Pamela never ceased her creative writing; Dylan envied her for her industry. 'You do work, darling, don't you?' he wrote prophetically, 'You're going to be prodigiously prolific one day.' She was following his advice and concentrating on short stories, and the literary agent J.B. Pinker had agreed to represent her. Her self-belief was evident when they returned her first submissions to them as 'unmarketable'; 'Hell to them', she wrote, 'We'll show 'em.' Dylan was now far more positive in his criticism of her work:

> Your story is as lovely as all the last stories you've sent me. You've got a style and a matter of your own. Little as they are, I can't think of anyone's stories printed today that are better. You are bloody good, you know. [...] You've got nearly everything that Katherine Mansfield possessed & a good deal more. [...] Go on, go on, my darling lady.
> (3 July 1934)

Dylan was not unaware of the fact that their relationship was becoming increasingly problematic, but optimistically wrote to her that:

> Sometime in August, I think I shall have someone to sit (again!) on
> my face so that, meeting, you won't recognise me, and we can start
> being in love again. A dirty desire. I love you. Bloody-face loves you.
> (20 July 1934)

Nevertheless, early in August, Pamela continued to be 'a trifle
worried' not to have received any news 'from love-child Thomas';
again, he then wrote to announce his imminent arrival, and again
arrived several days late. This did turn out to be a stay of several weeks,
but although there were still some happy evenings together at the
Proms, or at the Six Bells when he was 'sweeter than he has ever been
since I knew him', there were also rows about his unreliability, and
she had doubts about his excuses.

Soon after Dylan had arrived, Pamela had a short story, 'Suddenly
a Woman', accepted by a new periodical, *New Stories* (Dylan's story,
'The Enemies', had appeared in its second issue). H.E. Bates and
Arthur Calder-Marshall were on the editorial board, and the publication attracted some distinguished contributors, including Stephen
Spender, John Lehmann and T.C. Worsley. However, in their prefatory note, the editors warned that contributors would have to forego
payment for their work 'until such time as the margin of profit over
the costs of production can allow'. There is no evidence that that time
ever came. Nevertheless Pamela was delighted at the news, and the
publication of the story was a further step forward in her literary
career.

Compared with the lush romanticism of her poetry, 'Suddenly a
Woman' is a simply told story of a young girl's meeting at a fair with
a man whose 'line of hair on his upper lip' marks him as being older
and more experienced than any of the boys she had previously known.
She allows him to touch her breasts 'because she didn't want him to
think she was soft', and she realizes that she is now 'not a girl but a
woman, and that life had begun in earnest'. They kiss and fondle each
other until it grows dark, but when he tells her that she can't go home
because: '"I haven't loved you properly yet, do you understand me?"',
she resists strongly, and he releases her and walks her to her bus. As
she jumps aboard, he calls out: '"Next Tuesday, same place, seven
o'clock?"' She feels superior to the other people on the bus, with 'a
lovely aloneness in her loins'. The subdued eroticism of the final paragraph is very effective:

She touched her breasts as he had touched them and they remained
cold. She caressed her thighs as if she were feeling the shape of a vase,
and they were sweet and strange to her. [...] She was very happy in
her new flesh and her new thoughts.

The man is never named, but the girl's name is Elsie, the name that
Pamela would give to the very similar heroine of the novel she would
start to write in September.

Pamela and Dylan's relationship remained volatile. He was often
depressed about his lack of progress in establishing a literary career,
and, she felt, 'very wretched about his writing & me – I'm afraid'.
She and her mother had arranged a fortnight's visit to Wales, staying
at the Mermaid Hotel, Mumbles, near the Thomases' home. The
journey started inauspiciously with 'a blinding row with D. before
breakfast', and then with their nearly boarding a train to Devon
instead of to Swansea. Pamela later said that she thought that he had
deliberately directed them to the wrong train, being 'prepared to go
to Torbay or anywhere else, as long as it wasn't home' (*Important*,
p.144). But all went well for the first week. Pamela had already met
and liked Dylan's schoolmaster father, but both she and her mother
found Dylan's mother Florrie exhausting company. The first time
Dylan had suggested a visit to Wales, before they had met, he told
Pamela that his mother was 'a vulgar humbug', an unkind description
of a woman whose principal fault was garrulity. His criticism of her
probably shocked Pamela, the model daughter, more than any of his
deliberate attempts to be controversial. On first meeting, she found
Mrs Thomas 'kind, silly & sweet', but on a later occasion, she wrote:
'Ma [...] gabbled all day till we nearly went frantic.' But Dylan
was being 'adorable', and seeming 'so very in love'. He took her to
his favourite places on the Gower peninsula, which was, as he had
promised her, 'as beautiful as anywhere'.

But then it started to rain – and it rained incessantly for days –
'Just sopping. Not merely raining, but <u>sousing</u> down.' She was now
working steadily on her first novel, and felt content enough to have
time to do this, but eventually, as she wrote in her diary, 'my nerves,
for some extraordinary reason, went smash, and I cried & cried & then
had hysterics'. Contrary to the theories of Dylan's biographers, this
does not seem to have been caused by rows with Dylan (during her
relationship with Frank, she had positively seemed to enjoy their

frequent rows), and in fact on the day of her collapse, she wrote that Dylan had been 'perfectly sweet & darling to me'. The next day, she went to see a doctor in Swansea, who said she was suffering 'from strained heart, nervous debility, anaemia, etc., & was not to go back to work yet'. He also recommended that she should cut down on cigarettes – and on writing (presumably, on the grounds of an all-too-common pseudo-Freudian correlation of the time between women, writing and madness).[26]

Pamela wrote to her employers to tell them of the doctor's opinion with regard to the necessity to take further time off, and received a 'nasty official letter' from the bank the next day. She and her mother returned to London, and she resigned from the office. To her surprise, she received a letter of regret from her old enemy, Mr Price. Amy and Pamela had decided to move to Chelsea, and found a flat to rent without too much difficulty in Tedworth Gardens, between King's Road and the Embankment which had inspired her prize-winning poem. Despite the Welsh doctor's advice, she continued to make progress on her novel; indeed, her rate of composition was, as it would be throughout her life, astounding. Within a month, she had completed nine chapters; Dylan had offered to proof-read her manuscript, and she sent him the first 20,000 words, which he duly promptly returned with some minor corrections.

One of his suggestions was to backfire, however. Her original title for the novel had been *Nursery Rhyme*, but at Dylan's suggestion, she had changed it to *This Bed Thy Centre*. This, as she would later realize, proved to have been a bad decision, as, in the main, it would seem that the reviewers did not recognize the quotation as being the last line of John Donne's poem, 'The Sun Rising', and were predisposed to find the book salacious. Ishrat Lindblad, the author of, so far, the only full-length academic consideration of Pamela's work, convincingly argues that the original title would have been more appropriate. She points out that:

> In this book the author is essentially concerned with describing the break from the nursery that adolescence involves and in order to emphasize this theme she has woven references to several well-known nursery rhymes and fairy tales into the fabric of the novel.[27]

Other work was coming Pamela's way. Peter Davies, the publisher, asked to see further stories from her, having read 'Suddenly a Woman'. Her agents, having originally said that they would not be able to sell her poems, managed to sell one for three guineas, and were enthusiastic about the first chapters of her novel. She began to hope that she might be able to make a living out of writing; in the meantime, she was able to bring in a little money by helping her mother with her typing tasks, and by taking occasional temporary jobs, found for her by the secretarial college she had attended.

As they were preparing for the move to Chelsea, Dylan was also achieving his aim of moving to London. He was planning to share a room with Alfred Janes, an artist friend from Swansea. He wrote to Pamela, in typically nonchalant fashion:

> In reference to my prospective studio, Janes and I will be coming up definitely about the second week of November, by car fortunately, bearing with us typewriters, easels, bedclothes, brassières for lady models, & plum-cakes for Nelson's lions [...]. We want a room about fifteen shillings per week: it must be as large as possible, larger if possible, unfurnished, with good light. [...] But don't worry about looking for one: we will procure one, even if it is a little out of Chelsea. [...] Have you a mattress & a chair either to give or sell to two poor, unrecognised geniuses? [...] Don't forget, my prospectively philanthropic clother & furnisher of the artistic poor! Table, mattress, chair! I don't want to buy them from a second-hand shop, owing to the possibility of disease. (October 1934)

The unrecognised genius could not, indeed, afford Chelsea, and had to settle for a bedsitter rather than a studio in West Kensington, shared not only with Janes, but with various other transient lodgers. Pamela and her mother did sort out some furniture, surplus to their move from Clapham, to give to them, and added a dozen yellow dusters. Her chagrin, on first visiting the bedsitter, regarding the use to which Dylan and two friends had put those gifts was manifest in her account in her memoir:

> They had reached a peak of artistic romanticism. It was the setting of an up-dated *La Bohème*. The divans had been upended, so that their legs looked like tiny truncated posts of tester beds. The dusters, for decorative purposes, adorned the walls. They greeted me uproariously; and at once I knew that I was not wanted.

I was no longer of their kind. That I had written a successful book made it, for Dylan, worse: like Scott Fitzgerald, I don't think he wanted another writer in the family. I went away stunned with misery. (*Important*, p.145)

In fact, from her diaries, it is clear that she had still not completed *This Bed Thy Centre*, and it had certainly not been accepted for publication at that time. The reason for his changed attitude towards her seems much closer to her further conclusion:

I was not right for him. I did not care to wear the arty clothes he liked – I never have – and I feared and detested the Fitzroy Tavern, the denizens of which all seemed much cleverer than I could ever be. (*Important*, p.145)

In an author's note to her 1968 novel, *The Survival of the Fittest*, Pamela stated that Kit and Alison were composite characters 'each drawn from three separate sources', but in episodes which mirror these incidents, it is scarcely credible not to see Kit as Dylan and Alison as Pamela. Although Alison's successful novel had been published prior to her meeting with Kit, on her first visit with him to the Fitzroy, she tells Kit's friend Jo that all the other people there had made her feel inferior. Pamela was finally able to express her resentment at the Fitzrovians, making Jo argue that she had no reason to feel that way:

'You've done something. Don't you realize that at least three-quarters of this lot never will? They only talk. It's *better* to talk about the books you're writing than to write them. Talked about, they sound like genius, but when you see them – Ah, my little one, then comes the let-down.'[28]

There is little about Pamela in the biographies of Dylan for the remainder of 1934; they concentrate on his joyous entrée into the louche literary scene in Soho and Fitzrovia. Andrew Sinclair is among the apologists for Dylan, his attitude towards him being manifest in the American title of his biography, *Dylan Thomas: No Man More Magical*. Dylan, he says, had merely undergone

a first great love which had showed the contradictions of his nature and his society. He enjoyed the free love of an intellectual affair with a poetess, but the free love of their bodies was impossible in the suburban surroundings of the depression years.[29]

But through that autumn, in Chelsea rather than in suburban surroundings, and seemingly not overly affected by the Depression, the
said poetess suffered greatly from Dylan's virtual disappearance from
her life. Pamela's diary entries are very affecting: 'puzzled to death by
the extraordinary vagaries of Dylan'; Dylan 'called for an hour in the
morning – & could get <u>nothing</u> out of him. Am sure of one thing –
that he wants me no more'; 'No sign of Dylan today either. If <u>only</u>
he'd tell me what's really up!' But there was to be one bizarre twist.
In mid-November, her incoherent entry reads: 'Well! Well! Well!
Dylan along in evening – said he'd been keeping away because he
wanted me so much & I arranged to marry me! [*sic*] – within 3 weeks
or so!' He told her that they must go to Chelsea Register Office the
very next day to put up the notice. (Of course, she still didn't know
his real age, so didn't realize that he couldn't get married if his
parents got to know of his intention and withheld parental permission). She spent 'a dreadful night and a dreadful day', before deciding
'to do nothing of the sort'. Dylan phoned to say he would come in the
evening, '& <u>he didn't</u>'. Her mother, whose original love for Dylan had,
not surprisingly, waned as Pamela suffered, later recalled this episode
dramatically, if nevertheless erroneously; she told Philip Snow, the
brother of C.P. Snow, that her daughter and Dylan had got as far as
the steps of the Register Office, but that she had followed them there
and forbidden the marriage.[30] In fact, Pamela had heard nothing more
from Dylan for nearly two weeks. She was distraught; she entered 'no
sign of Dylan' each day, until she considered giving up keeping a diary
which had become 'a daily record of depression'. But she hadn't totally
lost her sense of humour; on one of the blank interleaving pages of
the diary, she sketched herself as a bride, with the running feet of a
disappearing man just visible in the corner.

An additional complication was that Dylan had the first draft of
the manuscript of Pamela's novel, which she desperately wanted to
complete. She could not bring herself to visit him unasked, and
eventually, her mother took charge, and went to his bedsitter in an
attempt to retrieve the novel. Dylan was out at the time, so Amy left
a message for him, and eventually Dylan sent the draft back without
a word. Despite all the distress she had been enduring, Pamela
delivered her completed manuscript to Pinkers on 3 December,
an astonishing three months after starting the novel. She made a

resolution not to whimper if the novel was rejected, and two days later was making tentative notes for a new novel. She still hadn't completely given up on Dylan, despite receiving a letter from him announcing that 'drink had won'. This 'upset me <u>plenty</u>, but surprised me little', she wrote. He still occasionally came to see her, leaving her still more confused: 'HAVE I lost Dylan or haven't I lost Dylan?', she asked herself. On one of the visits, he boasted to her about what she called 'all his rather revolting Bloomsbury fun & games'. He went back to Wales for Christmas without saying goodbye, then phoned on Christmas Eve, and Pamela sadly recorded that he 'said, oh he said, he loved, but [some indecipherably deleted words] he's lying'.

The year should have ended on a high note. On 28 December, Pamela received amazing news: 'My novel <u>accepted</u>! To be published by Chapman & Hall in March!! […] With a hey nonny nonny & a hot cha-cha!!!' There are parallels between the swift acceptance (and, as will later be seen, the reception) of *This Bed Thy Centre*, and of *Dusty Answer* (1927), the first novel by Rosamond Lehmann. I have written elsewhere about the difficulties facing an author with regard to the placing of a first novel,[31] and quoted Frank Swinnerton, a contemporary publishers' reader, and later a best-selling author, who, in his manual, *Authors and the Book Trade* (1932), maintained that: 'At the outside, the reader will find about 5 per cent of the unsolicited books worth a second opinion; not more than 1 per cent will be accepted for publication by his firm'.[32] Rosamond Lehmann, however, was asked to make substantial changes to her manuscript; Pamela's was accepted unconditionally. But Pamela's euphoria soon wore off. New Year's Eve arrived, and she was spending a 'deadly quiet evening', when the phone rang. It was Dylan, she thought, from the few words she could hear, but then the line was cut off, and she spent the rest of the evening 'longing for him, for my dear darling'. She annotated the entry the following day, after she had heard that it had not been Dylan, but 'someone with a lousy sense of humour playing a lousy trick'. Her final words on that momentous year were:

> And so goodbye to '34, with literary progress beyond all my dreams & some terribly happy moments with my precious Dylan that may never come again.

CHAPTER 4

'A Remarkable English First Novel'

DESPITE THE IMMINENT prospect of having her first novel published, 1935 opened gloomily for Pamela. She obviously did not think that publication would mean that her financial problems would be at an end, and continued to take temporary secretarial work when on offer. Dylan returned from Wales, and continued to drop in, uninvited and usually drunk, at any time of the day. On one occasion, he dramatically told her that he still loved her, but couldn't resist 'Comrade Bottle'. Pamela was still vacillating about their relationship. On 8 January, she wrote that she had 'told him I was kissing him goodbye for good', then added: 'But I dunno!' Three days later, his parents arrived for a visit, and it was then that: 'Ma [Thomas] let out shattering news that D. is 21 next October! The world completely bouleversée at the moment.' The revelation has to be put in the context of an age when to contemplate an alliance with a man almost three years one's junior was almost unheard-of, and still more so considering that the man in question was legally a boy until his next birthday. Nevertheless, she could not bring herself to break with him completely: on a typical evening, she 'wrote a bit, thought about Dylan far more than a sensible woman should'. This pining continued for months, contradicting the final mention of Pamela in Paul Ferris's biography of Dylan, which is summed up in the terse index entry relating to March 1935: 'she writes him off'.[1] She may have given that impression at around that time, as Dylan tended to ignore her when in London, but to write again to her when visiting his family in Wales. In an undated letter received early in March, he admitted that:

I should have written what's much too long a time ago, because there's so much to explain and so much that, perhaps, will, and should, never be explained – it means such a lot of belly rubbing and really tearful apologies on my blasted part.

Pamela was not, however, swayed by this seeming repentance; she recorded in her diary on 7 March: 'I wish he hadn't written. I'm going to write very cold answer.' However, as will be seen, they continued to see each other frequently all that year and, intermittently, in the subsequent one.

Pamela was not at this time without other admirers. She still regularly visited Victor Neuburg and Runia, now living in Hampstead in what she later described as 'a rambling, book-heavy flat with a rambling, overgrown garden beyond'.[2] Various Creative Lifers endeavoured unsuccessfully to take Dylan's place in her affections. The future poet and novelist Herbert Corby, described by Neuburg's biographer, Jean Overton Fuller, as 'a cheeky little Cockney sparrow with bright eyes and a neat appearance',[3] took her to the cinema, but infuriated her 'by trying to maul'. Pamela had evidently forgotten Dylan's warning about Corby the previous year:

H. Corby seems a dirty boy. But you're too old a bird to be stoned by him. I think I should like to quarrel with H. Corby about the Justification of the Phallus in Architecture, or The Influence of Sodomy on Wickerwork. What a perverted time us boys could have. (9 May 1934)

A German painter, Richard Ziegler, who later became a war artist, invited her to his flat ostensibly to paint her, but on the first occasion, he told her he was too tired to draw, but not too tired, as she tartly recorded in her diary, to try to seduce her. As with Stokowski, she 'managed to calm him down', but nevertheless found the episode upsetting.

She had made a start on a second novel, then temporarily abandoned it for one she called *Roaring Boy*. The title suggests that this book might have been inspired by Dylan, but she wrote only a few chapters, now lost, before returning to the previous novel, which would become *Blessed Among Women*. She did eventually begin to feel excited as publication day of *This Bed Thy Centre* approached. There had been a good deal of interest from the USA, and her agents eventually negotiated sale of the American rights to Harcourt Brace, a well-respected publishing house. She had received an advance of £25 (less Pinkers' commission) from Chapman & Hall, but the advance from the American publishers was £80: '$400!', she added in her diary entry, obviously feeling that this sounded a lot more impressive. It did of course represent about six months' work in terms of her previous salary from the bank (she had been earning £3 per week in her final year there).

Despite her preoccupation with her writing, in March, events in Europe did impinge on her consciousness. 'Alarmist news re war & Hitler', she wrote in her diary, although she evidently didn't fret for too long; the entry for the following day reads: 'Another miracle of a day. The sort of weather that makes you feel young, smart & a bit of a dog.' She had virtually completed *Blessed Among Women* (again, the writing had taken barely three months) before the publication of *This Bed Thy Centre* in April. On receipt of a 'very nice letter' from Dylan, she did take up his offer to proof-read this second novel.

She seems to have been quite unprepared for the furore that followed publication of her first novel on 5 April; far from delighting in her sudden notoriety, she suffered mental torment. The change of title did, indeed, seem to influence the reviewers. A typical reaction came from the Irish novelist, Seán Ó Faoláin in the *Spectator*: 'Miss Johnson [...] has circumscribed herself so much by insisting on the reality of sex that her "bed" might be thought less a centre than a circumference'. The first review to appear had been by Ralph Straus in the *Sunday Times*, and it should have given Pamela pleasure. Although Straus called the novel 'outspoken – in places, painfully so', he continued:

> But it is honest. It has something to say, and says it plainly. What is more important, it builds up a picture which, if at moments acutely unpleasant, is lifelike. Also it tells a story, terse, dramatic, unsentimental, and, fortunately, not too one-sided. There are ugly tragedies in it, but there is humour as well.

Nevertheless, Pamela felt 'beastly all day'. A few days later, attending a Foyle's Literary Luncheon at Grosvenor House as an invitee, she felt 'hysterical and terrible throughout'. Although the following day was quieter, and later reviews were still more favourable, she nevertheless felt 'very rotten mentally'.

The remarkable feature of the initial critical reception of *This Bed Thy Centre* is that a first novel by a totally unknown author, appearing under the imprint of Chapman & Hall, a middle-of-the road publisher, should receive such serious consideration by the relevant newspaper's or periodical's principal reviewer. Writing in the *Daily Mail*, Compton Mackenzie judged it to be 'an extremely promising first novel with a gallery of well-contrasted suburban portraits and a particularly sensitive appreciation of the suburban scene'. In several cases, it was reviewed alongside the latest novel by a major literary figure of the time, William Faulkner. Cyril Connolly (*New Statesman*) delivered a relatively unfavourable judgment on Faulkner's *Pylon*, but praised *This Bed Thy Centre* as being 'a remarkable English first novel', one in which the psychology of the many characters, 'their dialogue and circumstances of living are admirably grasped'. Chapman & Hall delightedly quoted Connolly in prominently-placed advertisements in the following week's Sunday newspapers, adding: 'This brilliant first novel is rapidly becoming a best-seller.'

As mentioned in the previous chapter, Pamela's reactions resembled those of Rosamond Lehmann on the publication of her first novel, *Dusty Answer*, in 1927, and for very much the same reason. Lehmann wrote to her publisher that it would be 'quite awful if it's going to be taken merely as a study in sexual relationships. I never dreamed it could be [...].'[4] After two months of constant attention, she was still finding it 'rather terrifying' that 'a thing you have made for yourself, very privately, becomes so very public'.[5] Lehmann was, however, a Cambridge graduate from a literary family, and she was 27 and married, not a girl of 22 who was essentially timid, despite her attempts at bravado. In a preface to a 1961 reprint of *This Bed Thy Centre*, Pamela emphasized that she had then been 'far and away outside of the academic world or the working literary world'. She continued, paraphrasing Hamlet:

Living in isolation from literary people, I shrank beneath the reactions of some of my kin, and some older acquaintances less than kind. I was given to understand that I had disgraced myself and the entire area of Clapham Common. It was as though a huge white finger had prodded through the clouds to point out, for ever, an indelible pool on the carpet. I was absolutely miserable. My dreams were black with fear of the Public Prosecutor. The happier my publishers, the unhappier I. I did not want another single copy sold.[6]

Pamela was saddened to receive a 'rather cruel' letter from Dylan; accordingly to James A. Davies, this was in the form of a card which read, 'God, how I hate you.' Davies comments that this might have been intended to be facetious, but probably was 'not wholly so'.[7] Yet Pamela forgave Dylan when, within days, he rang up and asked her to meet him at the Six Bells in Chelsea where they had previously been so happy. He took her home and stayed for the evening, and she told her diary: 'It was very, very lovely – perhaps transitory, but unbearably sweet all the same.'

Although, as mentioned, she had discussed the writing of *This Bed Thy Centre* with Dylan, there is no evidence that he acted in any capacity other than sounding-board and proof-reader. Nevertheless, Davies is emphatic in his contrary judgment:

> The book bulges with suburban repression, social and religious presssures, fear of marriage, tense marital relations, and powerfully written suicides. The content, even at its calmest, quivers on the edge of sensational.
> Here, doubtless, was the influence of Thomas.[8]

He does not, however, consider the reciprocal influence that Pamela's first novel may have had on Dylan, in particular with regard to his most famous work, *Under Milk Wood* (1953). In her 1961 preface, Pamela explained that she had thought of *This Bed Thy Centre* 'simply as an attempt to tell the truth about a group of people in a London suburb, whose lives were arbitrarily linked'. The opening chapter of the novel, entitled 'Locality', introduces both the setting and the characters through a series of vignettes. The first of these does not deal, as might be expected, with the main protagonist, 16-year-old Elsie Cotton, but with a sour middle-aged woman:

> The morning, drawing within itself, moved in sun and shadow over the Common and through the pond till it came to the houses. In Haig Crescent, Mrs. Godshill angrily opened her Bible in search of solace for the coming day. [...] A stream of sunlight poured through the windows into her eyes, reminding her unpleasantly of Mrs. Maginnis, who had golden hair and no God. At this very hour, Mrs. Godshill

thought, she is sleeping with a man. Closing her eyes to the light, she
added aloud, "Dirty Beast."[9]

In swift succession, the reader then encounters Patty Maginnis sliding
out of bed to comb her hair before her new lover awakens, lifting her
hands to her face, 'smoothing the lines of age away' (p.10); Elsie
Cotton dabbing a 'cold flannel in her armpits. Ten minutes to breakfast, and she was still in her knickers' (p.11); her art-teacher, the
exotically-named Leda Chavasse, thinking of Elsie, and acknowledging lightly to herself that she had 'definite abnormal tendencies
in that direction' (p.12); and various of the regulars of the local
public house, The Admiral Drake.

Paul Ferris mentions that the probable genesis of *Under Milk Wood*
was a thirty-minute radio script written by Dylan Thomas in 1946 and
in which he took part when it was broadcast on the African Service
of the BBC.[10] 'The Londoner' begins: 'It is summer night now in
Montrose Street. And the street is sleeping ...'; *Under Milk Wood*
famously begins: 'It is Spring, moonless night in the small town,
starless and bible-black [...]. And all the people of the lulled and
dumbfound town are sleeping now.' As the opening of the play
visits in turn 'the tradesmen and pensioners, cobbler, schoolteacher,
postman and publican, the undertaker and the fancy woman' of
Llareggub, it is possible also to see their genesis in Pamela's Clapham.
Dylan's Mrs Ogmore-Pritchard 'in her iceberg-white, holily laundered
crinoline nightgown under virtuous polar sheets' has much in common
with Mrs Godshill, and Pamela's Patty Maginnis would empathize
with Polly Garter, to whom Captain Cat addresses the question: 'Polly,
my love, can you hear the dumb goose-hiss of the wives as they
huddle and peck or flounce at a waddle away?'.[11]

Pamela denied that the novel sprang out of her own direct experience, but nevertheless it did mirror the confusion that she, in common with 'good' middle-class girls of her generation, felt about sex.
At the age of sixteen, Elsie Cotton still does not know about what was
then called 'the facts of life', despite sly hints from her classmate, 'fat
Joan'. When she blurts out to her art-teacher that she desperately
needs to know '"what men and women – do [...] when they're
married"', Leda tells Elsie that she must ask her mother (pp.16-17).
In the subsequent, quietly amusing scene, Mrs. Cotton, 'emboldened

to tremendous bravery by the surprise of the moment', gives Elsie a direct answer:

> After that, she could feel the silence gripping her head like a tourni-
> quet. She looked down at her lap, counting the many flowers on her
> apron. My little girl. My little girl. All the bloom brushed off.
> 'I think,' Elsie said, "that I will be a nun.'
>   Relieved at the uncomplicated normality of this remark, Mrs. Cotton
> summoned up enough courage to say: 'Eat your nice toast.'

But although Elsie's relationship with Roly Dexter, the son of the well-to-do Town Councillor, is central to the novel, Pamela also explores with great sensitivity the emotional lives of a range of men and women seemingly far beyond her own experience. Roly, it is true, does have some aspects of the now known to be only twenty-year-old Dylan about him, in this pithy description:

> Passing, by normal stages, between the ages of seven and nineteen,
> from Plasticine to Meccano, from Meccano to wireless, and from wire-
> less to love, Roly Dexter felt that, take it all in all, he excelled in the
> love. A mental rake and a temperamental virgin, his experiences had
> necessarily been limited on account of his fears. (p.73)

However, it is not only the young who have ambivalent feelings about sex. Leda Chavasse's unsuccessful poet lover, John, has tracked her down after several years' absence. She allows him back in her bed, but that night:

> John slept soundly, while Leda, sick with the horror that follows a
> manufactured love, lay long awake. Loathing the sight of his dark face
> on the pillow, of the lips, puffing and deflating with the contentment
> of satisfied slumber, she tried to think: I hate him because I'm still
> asleep. In the morning I shall love him, and be humble to him because
> I doubted. (p.51)

Patty Maginnis too has no illusions about her latest lover:

> In the night he was hotly male, with a chaining threat in his face, man
> to her woman, muscled Adam to her youthless Eve. In the morning he
> was just a thing who came to her for food and flattery, a shape with
> no shadows. (p.89)

But, despite the opinions of most of the critics, the novel is not only about sexuality, but investigates the social and economic factors governing the lives of its characters, with a light hand, and often with a good deal of humour. Maisie, the daughter of the publican of the Admiral Drake, has spent years trying to become engaged to Harry Wilkinson, in ignorance of the fact that he is an inveterate and unsuccessful gambler:

> One night, when [Wilkinson] was sombrely drunk, the idea of proposing marriage to Maisie had occurred to him with almost psychic lucidity; unfortunately he had acted on it without waiting to see how he felt when he was sober. So here he was, horribly in debt, without a hope of straightening himself out, engaged to a pink-and-white barmaid who loved him with suffocating intensity. (p.118)

Maisie immediately throws an engagement party, and tells her friends of her plans:

> "I want quite a small house somewhere [...] easy to run [...]. I'm going to have a blue drawing-room with a walnut suite, and I shall make Harry buy me one of those dressing-tables with a long glass and a stool attached, for the bedroom." [...]
> It was at this point that Wilkinson decided to commit suicide. (p.121)

However, he is comically unsuccessful even at this; he confesses his addiction to Maisie, who pays off his debts, and, abandoning her dreams of domesticity, continues to run the pub for her father.

In my discussions of Pamela's novels, I do not want to spoil the enjoyment of any reader encountering them for the first time, so I will in general be unspecific about their endings. Suffice it to say in this instance that there is finely-drawn tragedy in other episodes, and towards the end of the book, the changes in the lives of the central characters are paralleled in the transformations in the locality itself:

> The Neighbourhood fell with the fall of the year. At the end of August a whole block of houses in Lincoln Street [...] was bought and demolished, and out of this ruined Pompeii arose a large picture-palace, with one thousand seats for sevenpence, and a noble façade, moulded with stags and Greek notabilities. (p.279)

Gentrification of traditional public houses proves evidently not to have been a manifestation of the latter part of the twentieth century.

'Maisie, seeing all these changes, and realising that the march of progress was inevitable, had the outside of The Admiral repainted, and the bar and back-parlour knocked into one', and, as a finishing touch, bought 'some palms in Wedgewood pots, a few glass-topped tables, and some tub-chairs' (pp.279-80).

But Pamela was very unsure about her own 'march of progress', and was glad that she had been invited to spend Easter with the Thomases, who were very kind to her. However, Dylan had remained in London, it rained a lot again in Swansea, and she had little to tell her diary other than that she had written a lot, with 'a heart too full of my Dylan'. Many invitations awaited her when she returned to London. By mid-May, by which time her book had reached a fourth edition, she was fêted at literary cocktail parties. She had now recovered sufficiently to find these 'wildly exciting', recording on one such occasion that she had met 'Arthur Waugh, G.B. Stern, Lady Cynthia Asquith, James Hilton, S.P.B. Mais, Ralph Straus & many others', drunk 'losh & losh of champagne', and been invited to dinner afterwards with distinguished guests including the pioneering Socialist, Ellen Wilkinson.

She did not, however, neglect less well-known friends, and spent a pleasant evening with Trevor Hughes, her former collaborator in respect of 'Dylan-watching', but fortuitously, in the early hours of the following day, Dylan turned up at her house 'blind drunk'. Angrily, she told him she no longer loved him, and perhaps somewhat naively, she phoned Hughes the same day to tell him about this. Dylan and Hughes had fallen out, and perhaps Hughes saw his chance for revenge. It is also quite likely that Dylan had boasted to him of sexual exploits with Pamela as with 'the redmouthed girl' in Gower, whether or not the latter *had* existed. Whatever his motives, Hughes now laid siege to Pamela with avowals of love. Despite her attempts to discourage him, she wrote that Trevor 'seems quite happy in loving me no matter what I might think'. Dylan was evidently not unaware of Hughes's campaign; in the summer of 1935, he wrote to Bert Trick, another Swansea friend, that:

> Trevor Hughes, of the undiluted letters, is no nearer the looney bin, but the smell of the padded cells is floating about his nostrils. He has lately become a friend, counsellor, & admirer of Pamela J., who has spurned me as a small, but gifted, Welshman, of unsocial tendencies & definitely immoral habits.

With a touch of jealousy, he continued: 'Her last novel has sold well, & is now in a fifth edition. Her next honourable addition to the shelves of libraries & the welfare of widow wombs is to be called '"Blessed Above Women"'.

In pursuit of Pamela, Hughes became an occasional visitor to Victor Neuburg's circle. The 'Creative Lifers' had now renamed themselves the Zoists at Vicky's suggestion. He explained that '"*Zoos*, in Greek, means living. It could mean people putting more life into things. I only thought of it because it begins with a Z and so few things do."'[12] One day, when Victor and Runia were out, the group met in an attempt to formalize their objectives; Pamela arrived, escorted by Dylan and Geoffrey Lloyd, a young Marxist just down from Oxford. The meeting soon became chaotic, thanks to Dylan's having brought in some bottles of beer, which, with Runia absent and therefore their reluctance to search in her house for glasses, those present had willingly drunk in turn from the bottles. Runia was however furious about this when she came in, expostulating that the smell of beer was repugnant to Vicky. Geoffrey Lloyd, who died in the Spanish Civil War, was then yet another of Pamela's would-be lovers. Dylan and Lloyd (with Hughes tagging along) returned back to her home – 'G. very loving & Dylan telling me he still loved me which – God help us both – I half believe to be true.' Although she had thought the meeting 'terrific fun', she rang Runia up the next day to apologize, but she was implacable in being, as Pamela wrote, 'unnecessarily unpleasant re "orgies" and "bear-gardens". Jean Overton Fuller, who had also been present, commented that, after that meeting, Pamela did not return to the Zoists for a long time.[13]

Indeed, she would have scarcely had time for the Zoists' meetings. In addition to working hard at the final draft of *Blessed Above Women*, and writing short stories, nearly all of which were now accepted by well-respected periodicals, she was out most nights with various men of the Zoist circle, all professing their love for her despite her continuing rejection of sexual advances beyond kissing. She mocked Trevor Hughes, in terms that recall her attitude towards Teddy Lamerton, for being 'almost distressingly pah-ssionate & osculatory in [the] hall'. But gradually, she began to warm to the advances of Geoffrey Lloyd, whom she classified approvingly as '<u>highly</u> "intelligentsia" but not too dusty'. On one occasion, she went to Taplow in Buckinghamshire with him, and 'walked, lunched, necked, finding G. <u>very</u> amusing – "the bad seducer"'. Another time, she spent 'a divine afternoon with darling Geoffrey', and a few days later, after an evening at the Six Bells when Geoffrey was 'very loving', she wondered 'whether this business is serious or just another "affair"'. It is possible that she was concealing more than she was revealing to her diary. Many years later, she disclosed to her friend and frequent correspondent, the novelist Kathleen Farrell, that she had had:

> a single joyful, uncomplicated, brief and absolutely insignificant affair in the early summer of 1935. Perhaps it is because it was so joyful, in its small way that the Freudian censor has no need to go to work. In that summer three young men, including Dylan, told me they loved me at different times, on top of the same bus, on the same evening.[14]

This occasion was almost certainly the return from the aforementioned meeting of the Zoists. Since she usually attached only pitying epithets to Trevor Hughes in her diary entries, the joyful brief affair must have been with Geoffrey Lloyd. In July, when she went to Bruges for a fortnight with Amy, she had correspondence from all three men, four letters from Trevor, two from Geoffrey, and one, inevitably, 'from an unusually loving Dylan' which she found 'upsetting', and did not preserve.

But shortly after her return, in the company of her mother at their local café, the Lombard on Chelsea Embankment, she met a 'quite nice Australian lad'. The next day, she recorded a row with Geoffrey which had resulted in her walking out on him 'furious', and despite a letter of apology from him, this seems to have ended their relationship. A short holiday in Swansea with the Thomases (again in Dylan's absence) intervened before she met the Australian again, this time by chance in the Six Bells. She named him as 'one Gordon Stewart' and once again, described him as a 'nice lad'; he evidently met with Amy's approval as, after another unplanned meeting at the Lombard the following evening, they invited him back to their flat, and he stayed until nearly half-past one.

Gordon Neil Stewart had been studying art in Paris where his parents, Morven and Jane, were then living. The Stewarts, like the Howsons, could trace their family back through several notable Australian generations. Their Scottish roots went back to the High

Stewards of Scotland in the 12th century. Donald Stewart had been the first of his clan to settle in Australia, after having been exiled for treason after fighting for the Jacobites in the 1745 rebellion. In the following century, another relative, William Stewart fought with distinction in the Peninsular Wars and in North America, and was appointed as Lieutenant-Governor of New South Wales. A daughter of one of William's bastards, Charles Augustus Stewart (he took his father's name, as was common at the time – with no Fitz prefix), was Mrs Moleworth, the writer of Victorian children's books. Morven Stewart, however, had a less illustrious career; having made, as he thought, sufficient money as a motorcar agent in Melbourne in the 1920s, he had decided to give up work for ever and to live in Europe off his investments. Accordingly, in the early 1930s, with his wife and son, he had taken ship to France. His son had subsequently come to England in the hope of becoming a journalist; before long, Pamela was to find that he preferred to use his second name, although his parents continued to refer to him as Gordon.

Their burgeoning relationship was complicated by the frequent, unannounced reappearances of Dylan, usually drunk or wanting to borrow small amounts of money. He would even sometimes insist on staying the night, muddling Pamela's feelings towards him. On one such occasion, she recorded that they had spent the 'usual maddening pleasant evening', and added: 'Oh, hell!' But the adjective 'darling' in her diary was soon transferred to Neil from Dylan and Geoffrey, the latter now referred to in her diary as a 'ci-devant lover'. And Neil was not quite as importunate as her Bohemian would-be (or, in that single case, actual?) seducers; he was, Pamela wrote, 'very delighted & surprised to find I was a "good girl", as he ingenuously termed it'. A month later, barely six weeks after their second meeting, he formally made a proposal of marriage, 'followed by the most lovely yellow roses'. She told him she had to declare a moratorium, but in the ensuing weeks of 1935, references to Neil in her diary become unequivocally loving. His name is rarely mentioned without the epithets, 'sweet', 'precious' and 'my love'. It seemed clear to the young couple that any marriage could only take place with the approval and hoped-for financial backing of Neil's parents, who soon came on a visit to London. The two families' first meeting was 'passable', but Jane Stewart took Amy out on a later occasion, and upset her with regard to Neil's prospects. 'Self so dreadfully upset', Pamela wrote. There were echoes of her first relationships with Ian Swanson and Frank Saunois when Neil then came to her, 'worried re father & business & self worried in proportion'.

In the meantime, Trevor Hughes did not give up easily; he sent her 'awful, agonised letters'; he also often arrived at their flat unexpectedly, behaving 'foully & disgustingly sulky', and eventually Neil came to soft-hearted Pamela's rescue. One evening, when, she recorded, Hughes had arrived drunk and 'got drunker, beastlier & beastlier [...], Neil socked him on the jaw, threw him out, and I had hysterics.' Despite the hysterics, she was grateful: 'Neil', she continued, had been 'marvellous'.

The year ended with a 'Walpurgis Night' with 'everyone tight', and she summed up 1935 as 'the most successful year & the most worrying I have ever known':

> The first part of it was hell; I really thought I'd go mad with grief & worry. I have had some sort of success – always with a fly in the ointment. My financial position has improved; I have found the man I really want to marry, though I'm desperately afraid, by the example of my own bad luck before, that I shall be wretchedly disappointed again. The year, the latter half of which was really happy because of Neil, in whom is all my faith & trust, ended on a beastly note. I pray sincerely for my own renewed courage & strength & for my happiness with Neil.

On the first Memoranda page of Pamela's battered Timothy White & Taylors Household Diary for 1936, she wrote: 'On the day I marry I shall discontinue these diaries,' continuing:

> Even now I am tired of my own curt recording of the terrible & the beautiful days, of these morse notes on my own development, my own loves, my own fears. I have no time nor inclination to write fully. I shall look back regretfully at my ridiculous summaries of people & of events; I have no heart to deal with anything faithfully. I love and relove, sorrow & re-sorrow. Now I love, and I pray it is for the last time.

Yet although the last sentence clearly refers to her love for Neil Stewart, she evidently had not totally relinquished a tendresse for Geoffrey Lloyd, because on another of the preliminary pages, she wrote fragments of a never-completed poem, 'For July 1935', the last verse of which was:

> The cigarette burned down to amber,
> You touched me and my eyes were wet.
> And that is all I can remember
> And that is all I must forget.

Later she crossed this out, perhaps recognizing that it came danger-ously near plagiarism of Christina Rossetti's 'When I am Dead, my Dearest', and then added a savage self-judgment: 'TRIPE'.

The first event of the New Year for Pamela had been expected to be the publication of her second novel on 23 January. *Blessed Above Women* did receive two pre-publication favourable reviews in the *Daily Mail* and *News Chronicle*, but the king, George V, had become seriously ill, and died on 20 January. 'Everything beastly depressing. Nothing but "King" talk', Pamela somewhat self-centredly wrote in her diary two days later, and she further bemoaned that there had been 'No book excitement on a/c of King', the day after publication.

For the setting of *Blessed Above Women*, Pamela moves away from the Clapham of her first novel initially to a small West Country village, dominated by 'the batwinged tower of the local asylum', and later to a Bloomsbury boarding house. She also moves from a number of char-acters of equal importance to focus on one, Cecilia Hobchick, who is, at the start of the book, a middle-aged school-teacher. The novel is arguably a greater achievement for a young author than her first full-length work; she has the courage to make her protagonist unlovely, unhappy, and obsessive to the point of derangement. Yet the first emo-tion Miss Hobchick arouses in the reader is an amused sympathy:

> Miss Hobchick, dust-haired, flat-chested, leaned heavily upon her thirty-eight years. I was a pretty girl once, she would say sometimes to the mirror. And all the men were after me. Then she would add, for she was honest with herself, No, I was not, and they were not.[15]

Her favourite pupil is the six-year-old Joah Sullivan, although the little boy is terrified of her non-partisan scolding. Her mother is dead, her younger sister has also died, and she has no comfort from her father, who spends his evening dreaming of his youth: 'Then he had been [...] big, sporting and lecherous, a man's man by day, a woman's man by night. Now he was Old Hobchick, fat, money-respected and slow on the feet [...] (p.12).

One evening, after being belittled by her father, Cecilia meets the local milkman, Tom Cribb, and, despite knowing that, in village parlance, he was 'wanting' (p.3), she agrees to go for a walk with him, thinking him harmless enough. But Tom is 'soft with the beer that was in him', and Miss Hobchick seems to him to be 'wearing a moonstruck beauty'. 'What happened then nobody ever knew.' (This episode has a resemblance to the mystery of what happened to Adela Quested in the Marabar Caves in E.M. Forster's *A Passage to India* (1924), which Pamela is likely to have read.) However, the novel continues: 'It was some two months after this, with the coming of the autumn, that Miss Hobchick went funny; she went funnier even, people thought than Tom Cribb [...]' (pp.15-16).

After being taken off to the batwinged tower for two years, Cecilia is released. Her father has died, and she is now a wealthy woman. She moves to the house in London where her father had taken in paying guests, and eventually hears that Joah, now 24, is coming to London, and will be looking for lodgings. She turfs one of her tenants out in order to give Joah her best room. Joah becomes involved with a Bohemian group of would-be artists and writers, and spares very little time for Miss Hobchick, but this is enough for her. On one occasion, after rowing with his girlfriend, he slams the front door on his return, and 'out came Miss Hobchick from the kitchen. Running like a spider she was, slattern-footed, the small knob of hair askew on the crown of her head'. She holds out her hand to Joah: 'He stared at it, for it was trembling and the little violet veins were strong in the crumpled flesh.' He takes her hand, and: 'Her heart hopped with joy. [...] All the loveliness she had missed in life drew together to be concentrated in a moment. This should content me, she thought; I should die now, before the years spoil my memories for me' (pp.154-57).

Blessed Above Women is the most recognisably Modernist novel written by Pamela. The two first sentences of the final chapter contain only two words apiece: 'Time passes. Goes on.' 'Time Passes' is the title of Part II of Virginia Woolf's *To the Lighthouse* (1927). The subsequent paragraph is written as a stream of consciousness, but we do not initially know who it is who is musing about life:

> The year passes; hot and cold, hot and cold, less clothes in summer and more clothes in winter. Life hurt me last week. This week I cannot remember how or why. Anyway, I am not quite the same as I was.

That's the consolation of living – we can't change life, but life can change us. […] If everything comes to nothing and nothing comes to everything, why think at all? (p.290)

These are in fact the thoughts of Joah, not Miss Hobchick as the reader might have imagined from similar passages entering the latter's consciousness throughout the book.

This change of narrative technique was not commented on by contemporary critics. There was a sharper division of opinion than in the reviews of *This Bed Thy Centre*, with some critics describing the theme as 'unpleasant' (Howard Spring, *Evening Standard*), 'a study in abnormality' (Cyril Connolly, *Daily Telegraph*) and 'morbid and decadent' (*New York Times*). Pamela was downcast by these reviews, recording 'Rotten notice from Howard (bloody) Spring', 'lousy personal review by Cyril Connolly which <u>infuriated</u> me', and 'lousy blackguarding review' in the *New York Times*; after the latter, she commented: 'If anyone else calls me a brute & a sadist, I shall begin to think I am.' Surprisingly, she ignored that nevertheless these reviewers praised her abilities, Cyril Connolly for example describing her as 'a very accomplished writer', and she dwelt far less on the more favourable critiques, other than one by John Brophy in *Time and Tide*, which was, she said, the best that she had ever had.

It was left to her publishers to recognize that overall the reception of her second novel (usually a minefield for a new writer) had been highly satisfactory. Two weeks after publication, two-thirds of Chapman & Hall's large advertisement in a prominent position on the book pages of the *Sunday Times* was devoted to *Blessed Above Women*. An attention-grabbing quotation from John Brophy's review – '**Her career is of importance to literature**' – featured as headline, with further excerpts below from his and other reviews (underlinings are as featured in the advertisement):

Ralph Straus, *Sunday Times*: Here, I feel, is a writer with an individual outlook ... <u>she is a writer to be watched</u>.

L.A.G. Strong, *Yorkshire Post*: Miss Pamela Hansford Johnson joins the select company of novelists <u>whose second novel is better than their first</u>. One puts down her story with a lively respect for its author.

John Brophy, *Time and Tide*: *Blessed Above Women* <u>so stimulated me</u> that I immediately broke all the rules of the Unincorporated Society of

Over-worked Reviewers and got hold of a copy of her first, *This Bed
Thy Centre*. I have no doubt at all that Miss Hansford Johnson is already
<u>one of the most gifted and interesting of the younger novelists. Her
career is of importance to literature.</u>

There is even a brief quote from the review by Howard Spring which
Pamela had so disliked: 'Miss Johnson is a good novelist, and when
she takes a person in hand that person lives.' *John o' London's Weekly*
carried a photograph of Pamela at the top of the front page of its issue
of 25 January, together with perhaps the most insightful review of the
novel by Campbell Nairne. 'Not for [Miss Johnson]', he wrote,

> the nice old lady with the grey hair and the gentle, understanding
> smile. She uncovers all the emotions – jealousy, possessiveness, hatred,
> self-reproach – which beat at the thin wall of Miss Hobchick's sanity.
> She realizes that the young have no monopoly of passionate feeling. It
> is a wholly credible study.

The next month, Pamela received an invitation to become a
reviewer for the latter publication, and John Brophy's admiration led
to a recommendation from him to the Literary Editor of the *Liverpool
Post*, for which newspaper she was also to review novels for many years.
Reviews in this paper at this time carried much the same weight as
those in the two other main provincial newspapers, the *Manchester
Guardian* and *Yorkshire Post*. Pamela was justifiably excited when one
of her first reviews for the *Liverpool Post* was quoted in the *New Statesman* '<u>with my name</u>', she emphasized. This review was not for a novel,
but for C.E. Vulliamy's *Mrs Thrale of Streatham*. Jonathan Cape, the
publisher of this biography, had taken a full-page advertisement on
the front page of the periodical's Spring Literary Supplement (9 May
1936) to announce just two books. Pamela's name was indeed given
great prominence in the quotation from her perceptive review of
Vulliamy's book:

> If Mrs. Thrale of Streatham was as fascinating to Dr. Johnson as she is
> to the reader of Mr. Vulliamy's book, it is easy to understand why such
> a woman should have stamped her baroque personality so ineradicably
> on her own age and on the ages to come.
> PAMELA HANSFORD JOHNSON in the LIVERPOOL DAILY
> POST.

Pamela's gifts for swift reading and succinct opinions now came into play, as she would be sent up to five books and be expected to return her critique within a few days; in fact, she usually managed to do this in two days. Many of those books have never been republished, but her judgments of those that have stood the test of time have been proved to be sound. She found Cecil Lewis's *Sagittarius Rising*, a memoir of his service in the Royal Flying Corps from the age of 17, and which was to become a First World War classic, 'extraordinarily exciting'. She praised the excellent writing, but also the fact that the author 'gives us no romantic nonsense about war, no jingo-ideal; he writes sanely and very seriously'.[16]

She was not intimidated by having to pronounce a verdict on established authors, although when reviewing Hugh Walpole's *A Prayer for My Son*, she said that:

> It is a ticklish business, when dogmatising on the subject of a great novelist, to state emphatically the quality most contributory to his greatness, because great novelists, for the most part, carry a complete set of tools.

But as she applauded this novel's 'mesmeric power', she defined Walpole's major quality as springing 'from his perception of evil in the inner life'. 'No other living novelist', she declared, 'can come to the grotesque with such grandeur and conviction as can Mr. Walpole.[17] The review which followed, of Francis Brett Young's *The Far Forest*, showed some bravado, as well as some humour, in dealing with a novel she found 'tepid', which she considered puzzling considering that during the course of it:

> Jenny, the heroine, loses her lover David, has an illegitimate child by Charley, is slung out of doors by Aunt Thirza, marries Fred who is subsequently hanged for murdering his mistress and finally after a thoroughly bad time, returns to David.

She admitted that Brett Young's 'descriptive powers are justly famous' but, that being said, she thought that they comprised the beginning and the end of the book's virtue. 'To read it', she concluded, 'is like peering through the wrong end of a pair of opera glasses at a lot of people moving over a beautiful landscape.'[18] And the best she can say about *And Then You Wish* by John van Druten is that 'most people will like this novel enormously. It is the kind of book one reads at meal-times.'[19] On another occasion, reviewing *Summer Will Show*, and despite the care she took in writing and then painstakingly editing her own novels, she interestingly took issue with Sylvia Townsend Warner's technique:

> In Miss Warner's book, her technical brilliance protrudes between the reader and the story. [...] Her prose is cool, lovely, mannered, irreproachable. Her descriptions create a series of admirable paintings of faultless colour and design. What then is the trouble? [...] It should be credible; it is not. It should be interesting; it is not. The trouble is the fact that the book is over-subtle, so highly polished that it is impossible to look into the mirror for the shine upon the glass.[20]

In addition to Pamela's realisation of the added prestige that reviewing would bring, she was also glad to have the regular income, which she supplemented by selling the review copies as soon as read. Neil had not found a job, and their hope of getting married had accordingly stalled. On one typical evening, they had 'V. depressing talk re prospects. Mother brought in some whisky, & I got pretty tight to drown sorrows.' But she remained very much in love with him, and now became influenced by his political views. Although Dylan and the Zoists had flirted with radical views, they were essentially more interested in literary than in political affairs. Constantine FitzGibbon indeed attributes the demise of what he calls 'this little literary coterie' to their having been 'too eccentric and too old-fashioned for the age of Hitler'.[21] Neil, however, already had strong Left-Wing political beliefs which he continued to hold throughout his life. Now a night at the cinema might not mean the latest Barrymore film, but going to see, as they did, *Battleship Potemkin*, and, on another occasion, *Three Songs of Lenin*, the documentary celebrating the achievements of the Soviet Union, with an address by Harry Pollitt, the General Secretary of the British Communist Party after the showing. Pamela had fond recollections of that period of her life:

> Believe it or not, to the young the years leading up to the war, and the earlier years of the war itself, may have been days of acute anxiety and activity, but they were often *fun*. Great fun. The problems for the Left were simple: you didn't like Hitler, nor Mussolini, nor Franco. (*Important*, p.127)

Despite bouts of poor health, she was continuing to write prolifi-cally. In addition to working on her next book, *Here Today*, and her book reviews, she had five short stories published in 1936, one in *Nash's*, three in *John o' London's Weekly*, and one in the *Left Review*. These also provided a welcome addition to her finances, as she received an average of twenty guineas for each. Her short stories have never been reprinted in a collected edition, but Pamela shows great skill in this difficult genre. An example is her story, 'Judas and the Jug', published in *John o' London's Weekly* on 18 April 1936, in which an unnamed girl is waiting for the first visit to her home of Jack, her 'new young man' who is evidently of a higher social class. She is obviously ashamed of the shabbiness of their home, and is attempting to make superficial improvements. Her mother is aiding and abetting her, and the girl is pleased to see that her mother has smartened herself up 'under her overall', but her father is less compliant, refusing to put on his Sunday suit, or to change his 'straw-soled woman's slippers' for his best black ones. While her mother is looking out doyleys to put on the plates '"so the chips wouldn't show, or where the paint's rubbed off"', her father is jeering: '"I'm not going to eat no bits of paper with me tea!"'

For the first half of the story, it seems therefore that it will be no more than class-driven social comedy. But the title refers to his daugh-ter's Judas-like repudiation of her father when she sees as shameful his insistence on going down to the nearby pub just before his tea to fill his jug with ale (since he hates '"bottled"'). Later, she tries to excuse her father to her young man by saying that her mother had married '"just a little bit beneath 'er"', but then discovers that her father had been within earshot. For the rest of the afternoon, she is terrified and miserable, and comes to the poignant realisation:

> Love didn't matter any more – not love, nor Jack, nor the long twi-light walks, nor the hope of being married in white with a retinue of jealous friends in pink dresses and picture hats.
> Nothing mattered to the girl but the cold, sinking dread of the moment that must inevitably come, when she would have to speak to Dad with a steady voice and look straight into his lost eyes.

By contrast, Pamela's next published novel unfortunately shows signs of the haste in which it was written and the strain she was under.

One day in March, she wrote 4,000 words, which, she said, 'got my nerves all woolly and [I] nearly had hysterics'. She abandoned at least two partially-written novels, entitled *Dance in the Dark* and *Pilgrimage to Four Corners*, and in her anxiety to complete what she said she hoped would be her last book, she revisited the South London of her first novel. The foreword of *Here Today* engenders unfulfilled expectations of a fine novel:

> This is a story of the small life, of the shop closed down and the shop re-opened, of the blank shutter and the letting-board, of the turning of a corner and the slip of a bolt. It is a story without end, without significance, and its stem is curiosity. In the alleyway is the petty grotesque, under the stone is the placid slug, under the snail is the slime of silver. As the world cools, as the ants build palaces and sky-scrapers, as the blowflies destroy, so the little roads dissolve; but so slowly that the eye without auxiliary sees no depletion.[22]

But the characters seem to have stepped out of her first two books; indeed Patty Maginnis from *This Bed Thy Centre* makes a brief and somewhat gratuitous appearance. Otherwise the story revolves around a young couple wanting to marry against parental opposition, the girl's brother who is 'not quite right', the pub landlord who is cheating on his wife with a milliner, who in turn is being blackmailed about the affair by a lecherous florist, and a chorus of Cockney charwomen offering home-spun philosophy to justify the title:

> "That's life, that is. I work, she lah-di-dahs on the shays long. I go on living [...]. It doesn't matter. Sometimes I don't know what we're put 'ere for at all, we're so quickly forgotten with all our nine days' wonders. 'Ere today and gone tomorrow and the world not a penny the worse."[23]

In the monograph written in 1968 for the British Council in the Writers and Their Work series, Isabel Quigly commented that 'in *Here Today* Pamela Hansford Johnson frankly repeats herself for what seems to have been the only time'.[24] Nevertheless, the reviews, when the book was published early in 1937, were reasonably good, and John Brophy, who was now becoming a close friend, warmly praised the novel in the *Liverpool Post*, and went on to analyse her methodology. 'Miss Hansford Johnson,' he said, 'has her own themes and her own methods of tackling them: she is a realist, but for her realism is not an end in itself, it is a means to the understanding of human experience and the creation of imaginative art.' This judgment would prove still truer of her later works.

Throughout that year, Dylan continued to call in unannounced, and expect to be allowed to stay the night. On one occasion, Neil had just left when Dylan appeared with friends, and a 'second Walpurgis night ensued. D. stayed – of course.' Despite Neil's dislike of him, they went to a lecture Dylan gave at the City Literature Institute, which Pamela found 'very amusing' if 'pretty smutty'. In June, they all met again on the opening day of the London Surréaliste Exhibition, at which André Breton and Herbert Read spoke. 'Saw everyone in the world', recorded Pamela. Dylan's parents also continued to visit (not unannounced). In August, when they came to tea, Pamela had to go with them to redeem their son's overcoat from the pawnshop. Afterwards, Dylan walked in, and, for the first time since their break-up, Pamela experienced something other than exasperation with him. He looked so wild, that Pamela felt 'ghastly afraid for his mind – so pathetic – seems to cling to me & so fearful for him, so upset all evening.' According to Constantine FitzGibbon, Dylan had contracted gonorrhea from a prostitute around the time of the Surréaliste exhibition, and the treatment prevailing at that time meant that he had to abstain from alcohol for several months. Because of this, he had returned to Cwmdonkin Drive, to recover from 'an illness he must disguise from his mother's sympathy'. He later described those months as 'the most horrible of his life'.[25]

Clearly, he also did not confide the reason for his condition to Pamela, and he also seems to have neglected to tell her that, earlier that year, he had met his future wife Caitlin Macnamara. 'Dylan used to say,' FitzGibbon wrote, 'that they were in bed together within ten minutes of their first meeting – a characteristic exaggeration. Caitlin, however, has informed me that they did have an immediate and most passionate affair.'[26] It should be mentioned that Dylan had also lied to Caitlin about his affliction just before going back to Swansea; while telling her that he had merely been suffering from bronchitis, he felt the need to dramatise what might be seen as an unglamorous complaint by referring to its having resulted in his having to endure 'days of almost-death'.[27]

Pamela's concern for Dylan did not last long as he once more disappeared out of her life. Virtually their last meeting would take place the following year, when she and Neil met him by chance in the Six Bells, and it was then he told them that he had met 'the most glorious girl, the most beautiful girl in the world. Her name was Caitlin Macnamara. [...] He was alight with happiness' (*Important*, p.146). It seems appropriate to mention here that Pamela's contribution to the previously mentioned Dylan Thomas Memorial Issue of *Adam* (1953), ended with two short sentences: 'I only knew him as a boy. He is that to me still.'

For the remainder of 1936, Pamela and Neil were engrossed in trying to overcome parental opposition to their marriage. By November, they were considering a secret marriage, but then thought better of it in the hope particularly of placating Neil's parents, who had returned to Paris. They finally got grudging permission from Morven and Jane Stewart, and immediately announced their plans to all their friends. 'Lots of presents' arrived, but the Stewarts only sent a cheque for £15 (£5 less than Pamela's usual payment for a short story). However nothing, it seemed at that stage, could spoil Pamela's happiness, until she received a 'ghastly poison-pen letter', which gave her 'the horrors' for several days. (These letters were sent intermittently at key times in her future life, but the writer was never identified.) She gradually recovered, and gave all her time to the wedding, which would take place on 15 December 1936 at the Chelsea Register Office. (The abdication of Edward VII on 10 December was noted by just one sentence in her diary.)

The night before the wedding, she wrote a final, somewhat cryptic, entry:

> Quiet, lovely, contented evening; my mind peaceable & prepared.
>
> So now, my darling diaries, I leave you for a while, because I'm going to be married tomorrow. You have been a great comfort to me – almost a necessity. I love Neil. I'm happy.
>
> I want to be a decent wife & a good woman, to start again, living for myself & for others.
>
> Good-bye, diaries. I'll start you again perhaps someday, and look on the unwritten pages without fear.

CHAPTER 5

Married Life
amid the Clouds of War

PAMELA KEPT to her resolve not to keep a diary for the following two years, so there is less evidence for this period, compared to other phases of her life. Looking back at her early married life when writing her memoir, she focused, as might be expected, on her happiest memories:

> I remember the pre-war trips we were constantly making to France – mostly to Paris, but sometimes in rucksack hikes around the Seine Valley – Les Andelys, Caudebec-en-Caux. We were both extremely pressed for money, for my writing brought me in little, and I do not know how we managed it. But we did. For [Neil], I have little but gratitude. (*Important*, pp.80-81)

But she had admitted in the same paragraph that, at home, since perforce they had to continue to live with her mother, life was made difficult by Amy's 'irrational hostility' to her husband. Naturally enough, she did not dwell on this aspect of her marriage when replying to a letter of congratulation on her latest novel from her former suitor, Reuben Mednikoff. 'Neil and I have been married nearly ten months now, which is a long time, isn't it?' she wrote. 'We're enormously happy and placid. Or as placid as possible. Anyway, we don't row at home or in public, touch wood.' She also proudly announced that Neil's first book was about to be published by her own publishers, Chapman & Hall. Amy's dissatisfaction with her new son-in-law may have been compounded by his having devoted so much time to writing *The Fight for the Charter*, a history of the Chartist movement, a book unlikely to have contributed much to the joint family income. (It is still occasionally referred to in journal articles, but never went to a second edition.)

Due largely to Neil's influence, Pamela had become actively involved in left-wing politics, joining the local branch of the Labour Party, which produced, she recorded, 'a cyclo-styled weekly, written mainly by myself, called *The Chelsea Democrat* from the shabby party headquarters in The World's End'. This apocalyptic address is that of a pub at the then unfashionable end of King's Road, Chelsea, and would become the title of her next novel. Unfortunately, no copies of *The Chelsea Democrat* have survived the intervening years. Despite, she said, being 'rather successful', the publication folded 'because of editorial exhaustion: I had too many other things to do' (*Important*, p.127). The 'other things' included the afore-mentioned novel, *World's End*, published in 1937, and *The Monument* published the following year. Both focused on the precise moment of history in which they were written, when the nation was trying to recover from the economic slump associated with the Great Depression in the USA, Fascism was sweeping through Europe, and the immediate concern of many was the onset of the Spanish Civil War.

Arnold Brand, the protagonist of *World's End*, is the first of Pamela's male focalizers; at the beginning of the novel, he is thirty years old, out of work, and living on handouts from his father, and the earnings of his wife Doris, a draper's assistant. He is strumming a banjo for want of anything better to do, remembering boys and girls on the commons listening to the 'soft heady songs of the slump'.[1] He strikes one at the outset as the precursor of John Osborne's Jimmy Porter, playing his trumpet in the 1950s. As a boy, Brand, as he's usually referred to, had been sent by his family from his home in the West Country, in the hope of furthering his education, to stay with a rich aunt who had died before he could take the Oxford entrance examination. His ambition had been to become a writer, and in order to stay in London, he had abandoned school, and worked as a clerk when there had been plenty of jobs available. Soon after his marriage to Doris, and to her alarm, he had given up his safe job in order to concentrate, without success, on writing. Now, as the slump deepens, he has little chance of returning to work, and spends much time with a group of equally unsuccessful bohemian friends. In the last quarter of the book, the background turns from economical hardships to the uncertainties of the political situation, with events in Spain and Germany recounted alongside the account of Brand's marriage, and he finds a *raison d'être*. At this point, he diverges from the attitude of the post-war generation in the way that Osborne defined in the often-quoted diatribe from Jimmy to his friend Cliff, bemoaning the fact that: 'We had it all done for us, in the thirties and the forties, when we were still kids. There aren't any good, brave causes left.'[2]

The novel was published in February 1937, and achieved great critical success. Elizabeth Sturch, reviewing for the *Times Literary Supplement*, shrewdly commented that the characters 'live in World's End in more senses than one', being 'surrounded by a terrifying sense that all ordered life is hovering uncertainly on the brink of disaster'. Wilfrid Gibson in the *Manchester Guardian* declared: 'Miss Johnson is a born novelist, and her characters are living, breathing people who instantly engage and persistently hold our absorbed interest.' Despite its London setting, it appealed as much to the American critics, although E.H. Walton in the *New York Times* was puzzled about its effect on him: 'Due to its very simplicity, it is hard to explain why "World's End" is so exceptionally good. For one thing it is a novel unspoiled by trickery and artifice. These young people, Arnold and Doris, are presented with scrupulous honesty.' He ended with a quite startling statement for an American reviewer: 'The English critic who likened Miss Johnson's novel to Hemingway's "Farewell to Arms" is not so far astray as one might think. It gives one the same live sense of an overmastering love.'[3]

Pamela's next book, *The Monument*, published in September 1938, deserved similar critical acclaim, but the reviews were mixed. The general opinion in the British press was that she had been too ambitious in the structure of the novel, which follows the stories of three characters, Albert Whye, Annie Sellars and Mary Captor, initially unknown to each other, who happen simultaneously to be visiting the monument to the Great Fire of London at the start of the book. She was also criticized by Frank Swinnerton (*Observer*) for her emphasis on the social and political background, despite his saying that 'Miss Johnson is exceptionally able and very experienced', and that he had 'strong belief in the author's talent'. The American reviewers, however, were far more favourable when the novel was published in the USA in

September, and approved of her interweaving contemporary events
into the narrative. N.L. Rothman in the *Saturday Review of Literature*
saw this as inevitable as her characters were 'a group of Londoners
whose lives are touched at every point by contemporary history, by
fascism, communism, the struggle for democracy, Spain, China,[4]
strikes at home', and he applauded her skill in demonstrating that:
'Their lives may be colored, altered, by events, but their minds within
them are strong and sovereign.'

Albert Whye's story is one of hardships, endured because of his
unwavering love for his delinquent brother, Teddy, who was rejected
by his harsh father, because he blamed him for his wife's death in
giving birth to him. At that time, Albert had just left school and had
been about to start a job as office-boy, with the intention of going to
night school in order to 'get on quick', but he sacrifices any chances
of bettering himself in order to care for Teddy (p.87). His story does
not interlock with that of the other two.

Perhaps the best-drawn figure in *The Monument* is Annie Sellars, a
working-class activist whose characterization runs contrary to the
stereotype of left-wing political action of the period being confined to
male trade-unionists or intellectuals:

> To Mrs. Sellars London was a field of battle, a field to be sown with
> the dragons' teeth of knowledge. [...] She, at least, laboured in her
> spare hours [...] to awaken in the minds of her own people a real under-
> standing of their daily bread; where it came from, who sold it to them,
> what happened to it on the days when it didn't arrive. To her ever-
> spinning thought it was fantastic that men and women should not
> know to the full the workings of the system that ordered their lives.
> [...] they watched, moving over a plane far remote from them, the
> figures of those whom they had voted into governance; and they voted
> just as their fathers had voted, without a single question asked.
> Ignorance, souring cankerous ignorance![5]

It is not only in the field of politics that Annie sees ignorance as an
enemy to rational existence. She had, not without trepidation, yielded
to her lover on 'one sad, hysterical night' before he went to the front
in the First World War (p.49), and when he returns safely and they
marry, they cannot afford to have a family immediately. She had agreed
therefore to go to a family planning clinic,

where her fears were so neatly smoothed away and the workings of her body so coolly and practically explained to her that she began to wonder why so many other women were superstitious and scared. (p.57)

She had joined the Labour Party in response to the end of the General Strike, in anger at the way the strike had been 'abandoned as neatly upon the summit of its success as the ark on Ararat' (p.59), and continues her efforts for the party despite her husband's inability to work due to ill-health. She is not totally idealistic, being pragmatic about some of the downsides of political activity, as when she reflects after a long day:

> Tomorrow there is a Party meeting. Unconstitutional. Point of Order. Refer it back to the G.M.C. That knocks the glory out of you for the time being, but it's there all the same like the solid drum beneath the wailing of the fifes. (p.115)

The chairman of the local committee wonders at her dedication: 'She goes out charing all day, works three evenings on and off for the Party, serves on the Local Relief Committee and helps run the Left Book Club group' (p.183).

A chance meeting with a writer, Mary Captor, another of the main characters, at a Medical Aid for Spain meeting, however, resolves Annie Sellars' financial problems. Forrest Reid in the *Spectator* may have thought Mary's sections of the narrative 'more commonplace', and similarly Doreen Wallace in the *Sunday Times* criticized Mary 'and her crowd' as being 'two-dimensional', but this is to ignore Pamela's bold analysis of different forms of contemporary British anti-Semitism in this section of the book. Mary's admirer, Rafael Barrandane, is a rich Jewish exporter and art connoisseur, who takes Mary to a dinner party to celebrate his father's birthday. The other guests are a world-renowned classical pianist and his wife. They discuss a new novel which evidently reflects prevalent right-wing views, and Mary supports the pianist's 'quietly blasphemous opinion' of the book:

> 'I can't understand how any artist of any kind can give pen-service to Fascism, which professes contempt for all intellectual effort and has already muzzled some of the best brains in countries under its domination. Franco burns volumes of Dickens and murders Lorca. Hitler burns the books, puts the ban even on Heine.' (pp.74-75)

Rafael's father, Marcus, illustrates the ambivalent feelings of even a most successful Jewish immigrant when, towards the end of the evening, he begs the pianist's wife to sing for him a Yiddish folk-song, *Roshenkas und Mandelen*. As she finishes, he wipes his eyes, and then says: '"I don't know what I'm snivelling about [...] because the new days are happier for me than the old ones, by a long chalk' (p.80).

But later, Rafael encounters overt anti-Semitism when he stops at a coffee-stall where a gang of roughs tell him that all the ills of the country were due to its being run 'by aliens and dirty Yids'. Rafael (albeit trembling) tells them that he is a Jew, and one spits at his feet. '"Go back to Palestine [...] and take your sweat-shop friends with you."' But he bravely asks them why they only persecute the Jews in the East End. '"Why do you beat up only the poor Jews, throw bricks through the windows of small Jewish shopkeepers? Why don't you hold your marches up Park Lane where the Jewish rulers of England are supposed to be?"' (pp.251-52)

A still more insidious instance of anti-Semitism is later related. A copy of a Fascist periodical had been noticed in the desk of Miss Herriott, the secretary of Rafael's father, Marcus. He had always been a benign employer, and after a discussion with the equally kind-hearted Rafael, they decide not to confront her about this in case it had been accidentally left by someone else. Miss Herriott eventually voluntarily leaves the company, and they think no more of it. Mary and Rafael marry, and, despite being at an advanced stage of pregnancy, she agrees to speak at a Save China meeting. As she is about to address the gathering, she sees Miss Herriott in the audience, pointing her out to a pack of Fascists, and leading them towards the lectern, shouting: '"Get back to your dirt and your Jew!"' This time, the mild Rafael responds with a physical charge at them in defence of his wife, the mob is thrown out of the hall, the appeal goes on and collects more money than would otherwise have been expected (pp.381-82). None of the reviewers of *The Monument* noted this subtle and sympathetic portrayal of a family of rich British Jews in this fraught period of history.

The same awareness of the spread of anti-Semitism in Britain is manifest in an article by Pamela published in *The Spectator* in December 1938, recounting the bigotry to which an unnamed aunt now has recourse. The aunt, formerly 'a kindly woman', greets her one afternoon with a diatribe:

> 'I have never liked Jews,' she said, 'never. There's something about them. Of course, I can't approve of Hitler's methods, but the idea is sound. They keep us poor, they own the country.'[6]

Her niece uses the same arguments as Rafael. England was owned largely by rich Gentiles as well as rich Jews, so why should the poor Jews be beaten up?

> [Her aunt] looked first at the door as if to make sure no one was listening. Then she beckoned to me and, when I leaned forward, advanced her little lips to my ear. 'They're not poor,' she said, 'that's all show. They may live in dirty places, but they've all got money put away.'

The niece reflects: 'It was no use arguing with her; she had found a scapegoat for her own misfortunes.' Later, the aunt broadens her aversion to include other groups, warning her niece that: '"We're all going mad. The world's going mad. That's because evil spirits are working among us, trying to destroy us."' After her death, the niece finds a scrap-book in her room, with the heading 'in staggering block capitals, Good Lord deliver us':

> Inside the book was pasted the most comprehensive collection of clippings I have seen for a long time, all of them relating to the sickness of the world. There were House of Commons reports and debates on bombing in Spain and China, cuttings of German and Austrian atrocities from yellower papers and magazines, headlines from journals of the right and left, and lastly, a half-page article on the air massacres in Canton. I read them all, and for one clear moment saw my aunt sitting under the lamp murmuring each word aloud to herself.

I had initially assumed the aunt to be fictional, as I could not believe that Pamela would have written in this way about either of her mother's sisters, and although she now had little contact with her father's family, I also did not think she would have written about one of them in an identifiable way. However, in her 1942 diary, she mentions a visit to Wynnie, an elderly relative of Neil's, who is, she says, 'quite barmy, poor soul, & crazy about British Israelites', and therefore might possibly earlier have been the inspiration for this character.

When Pamela resumed her diary-writing in 1939, it was clear that, despite being in what should have been an idyllic period in her personal life, her thoughts also dwelt on current affairs a great deal and unhappily. The signing of the Munich Agreement in September 1938 was followed a few months later by the end of the Spanish Civil War. Pamela wrote of the latter event:

> The trauma of the defeat of the Spanish Republican forces in the Civil War was something beyond which the earlier trauma of Munich almost paled.
>   I remember standing in Belgrave Square, when the Republican flag was hauled down, and Franco's went up. [...] I could not stop crying: and there were many, men and women alike, in the same condition. (*Important*, pp.127-28)

Her Boots Home Diary & Ladies' Note Book now had, among the Household Hints, two pages on Air Raid Precautions, headed 'Some Useful Hints and Suggestions in the Selection and Preparation of a Refuge Room'. A typical hint was: 'Fill all cracks where gas can leak through with paper mush, and paste over with paper.' She and Neil joined the ARP (the largely voluntary Air Raid Precautions organization) in January 1939, they attended lectures on 'High Explosives', and collected boxes of gas masks 'for distribution when – if ever'. In June, they were issued with ARP boiler suits in which they looked 'irresistibly funny', providing them with the 'only laugh for a week', yet she still continued to believe that there would be no war – 'just another Munich'.

Pamela listed, in copper-plate italics, on the first memorandum page of the 1939 diary the people who were most important to her. Neil of course came first, but Buzz, their new cat, took precedence over Amy. Her old friends, Babs, Teddy and Dick were also there, as well as an actor friend called Henry, who frequently called to solicit her advice regarding what she called his *'affaires du coeur'*. It would seem that Henry was Jewish, because she was aghast when, on meeting him, her father-in-law 'dropped one frightful anti-Semitic brick'. But the diary pages also mention the names of new acquaintances in the literary world, among them, Stevie Smith, a 'toothy, pleasant girl', Graham Greene, 'looking clever & inhibited', Julien Green, Richard Church, Walter Allen, Irene Rathbone, and Storm Jameson.

The entries for this year were a mixture of the domestic, the historic and the political. A typical entry on 15 March 1939 reads: 'Went shopping with Mother. Bought a lovely coat & frock. Hitler marched into Prague. L.P. meeting at Town Hall – film show, awful flop.' For the first half of the year, her Labour Party work continued to take up a great deal of her time. She and Neil supported Stafford Cripps who advocated the creation of a Popular Front linking the Labour Party with the Communist Party and anti-appeasement factions from the other political parties, and were aghast when this led to Cripps being expelled from the Party, though they did not themselves consider resigning. At this time, she recorded events much as her creation, Annie Sellars, might have done:

> Spent morning with N. scrubbing & cleaning Party rooms. L.P. Conference at Friends Meeting House in afternoon – [Herbert] Morrison & Susan Lawrence dealt out platitudes like bags of damp oatmeal & 50-50 audience quarrelled over Cripps.

Pamela's personal obsession at this time was her failure to become pregnant. She had always marked the start of her period in her diary, and now alongside that asterisk was the comment, 'another disappointment', felt particularly keenly perhaps when, in February, she tersely recorded: 'Dylan has a son.' When in August, her period was particularly late, she said its arrival had provoked a 'sort of brainstorm, hysteric fit or something [...]. Am aching & aching for my baby.'

Neil's second book, a biography of the 19th century French revolutionary, Louis Auguste Blanqui, was published in January by Victor Gollancz, with a reprint as a Left Book Club edition; however, it received sparse attention, and evidently, like his first book, yielded little income. As usual, through economic necessity, Pamela managed to write a novel in a matter of weeks, although *Girdle of Venus* can be counted among her less successful works. She confessed later in life to an interviewer that she felt that she had, in the period immediately following the publication of her first novel, written a good many novels of which she could respect but a few.[7] Indeed, she had great doubts about this latest novel at the time of its completion, and it was initially rejected by Chapman & Hall, who were possibly antagonized by the knowledge that her agent, Ralph Pinker, had been negotiating with Collins to publish her future books. But Chapman & Hall eventually agreed to publish *Girdle of Venus*, and, to their surprise as well as to Pamela's, it became a Book Society Recommendation, although it was to receive poor reviews on publication in July 1939.

The opening scenes of this novel, like *This Bed Thy Centre* and *Here Today*, take place in a London pub, in this case in Rotherhithe. It would seem that Frank Swinnerton, reviewing in the *Observer*, was influenced by this to write condescendingly that: 'If [Miss Johnson] could be always at her best, she would produce an outstanding novel about people in pubs, in trade, in lodgings and in jobs'. However, not altogether unjustly, he found her latest offering overall 'hasty and defective'. Ralph Straus (*Sunday Times*), despite calling it 'this new and very sprightly yarn', said that: 'Once again Miss Johnson shows us that she has no particular type of story to tell, and no one manner in which to tell it.' Marjorie Grant Cook (*Times Literary Supplement*) similarly damned the book with faint praise summing it up as 'a novel full of racy little scenes and warm vitality'.

All the reviews show a considerable misreading of the novel, in which the central character, Marcia Trapper, in an attempt to recover from various tragedies in her former life sets herself up as a clair-voyant in a seaside town, then has cause to bitterly regret having misled several women. She scarcely therefore lives up to Ralph Straus's description of her as 'the cheeriest of frauds'. Early in the novel, as Marcia, now 'Madame Marjanah', reviews her recent clients, she comes to the conclusion that she is offering them a necessary service:

> Nearly all had been women; smart women with an hour to spare, seedy big-eyed women with an insatiable curiosity about themselves, pitiful women so racked by the terrors tightening over Europe that they sought escape at any price, little girls eager to find out whether they would marry [...]. Women, women, women, pouring their money away for the pleasure of being able to talk about themselves and hear about themselves for half an hour on end.[8]

As the narrative moves forward into the year in which it was written, the women's needs become still more urgent, as they seek reassurances:

> 'No war, no war, no war', Marcia repeated doggedly, as they came to her sick not for themselves alone but for their families also and for the whole structure of their lives. The voice had sounded from Nuremberg,

trumpeting the great threat. If the tortured Sudeten Germans cannot help themselves, we will help them. At home, people began to wonder whether the Sudeten Germans were not, perhaps, being tortured after all. From lip to lip the fear scurried. What was Czechoslovakia, anyway? A foreign-sounding place. [...] Dread and fear and doubt ran like spiders through the web of England. (p.288)

Nevertheless in the month of her book's publication, Pamela and Neil, equally convinced that there would only be 'another Munich', set off for their usual holiday in France, travelling around without any set plan. Her diary dwelt on various minor discomforts, 'ghastly' rough crossings, 'appalling' mosquito bites, a stay in one 'extraordinary & mysterious', yet overall 'awful', baroque hotel, where they had 'a curious lunch [...] of sheep's foot, mutton chops & peaches', and another 'smelly' hotel, journeys either on 'stinking petrol buses', or hiking between towns and villages, often in 'drenching rain'. Running out of funds, they contacted Neil's father in Paris, only finally to receive 300 francs from him, roughly the equivalent of £1. 10s. 0d. There had, however, been compensations. At Pont de l'Arche, 'a lovely little town', they sat on the river bank to watch a 'dreamlike sunset & Corot trees'. In Rouen for Bastille Day, they saw 'a grand torchlight procession', and enjoyed the 'showy but appallingly noisy fireworks'.

On their return to England, they found ARP exercises in full swing. A full blackout was ordered on 10 August, and Neil and Pamela patrolled from 12 midnight to 2 a.m. in 'fatigue suits & tin hats', the latter causing her 'a bloody headache'. On 21 August, came 'shattering news on late wireless of Soviet-German non-aggression pact', and they spent the following day 'thinking & worrying', and coming to the conclusion that the 'Russian thing must be a bargaining lever'. Two days later, 'another hell's day beginning with signed Russian pact with no escape clause. Panic very bad. [...] Everyone thinks there will be war; N & I still think not.' On 31 August:

Awful panicoso all day – evacuation ordered – fleet mobilised – & so on. Pictures in afternoon. [...] Busy comforting Kalie when mobilisation orders for ARP arrived – rushed round in my ridiculous suit – only to sign my name! Real old footle. Hitler's peace terms over 11.00 news – not satisfactory, but huge concessions.

On 1 September:

How can I write of today? Hitler invaded Poland. Mobilisation of
Britain & France. Kalie is horribly upset – couldn't soothe her this time.
N & I patrolling from 8 – midnight. So it is war; a filthy, unnecessary
bestiality loosed on ordinary people – I want to love Neil & have a
baby & write. And still one has to hope.

Like many, when war was actually declared on 3 September, Pamela
had become more or less resigned. She worked regular shifts at the
ARP post, and started writing up her experience in 'A Journal of a
Warden', completing 10,000 words within a few days, but did not
continue when Collins, her new publishers, refused to take it. In fact,
there had been, as yet, little on which to report. '<u>This is a damned
funny war</u>', she wrote. On 17 September, however, there was a further
shock when Russia invaded Poland. Neil attempted to reassure her
that this was 'an anti-Nazi move', but she was unconvinced. Many
days thereafter remained blank, with only an odd remark, e.g., 'Oh,
the bore to end war.'

Pamela was still reviewing for the *Liverpool Post*, and occasionally for
Time & Tide and the *Spectator*, but was not writing or planning another
novel. One day in November, she was feeling 'horribly depressed when
Pinkers rang up to say they'd sold – of all things – "<u>TIDY DEATH</u>"!!!
to Cassells for £35 advance'. This was a detective story that she and
Neil had written together, more or less for fun, but she evidently felt
it had so little chance of being published that she had not previously
mentioned it in her diary. It was, she said, an 'extraordinary & awful
book, but who cares?' They had used the pseudonym Nap Lombard,
for reasons that had mystified her children until recently, when I
pointed out to them that the Nap presumably stood for 'Neil and
Pamela', and Lombard was the name of the café in which they had
first met (it had been thought that they had met elsewhere).

In November, with the 'Phoney War' still giving the ARP volunteers little to do, she and Neil were moved to a different post, at the
'Third Feather', presumably then a pub, now a youth club in Earl's
Court. She had got on well with the other volunteers in the previous
post, but the tone of her entries reflects the still warmer camaraderie
that she now experienced. It was, she wrote in her memoir, where she
encountered 'the Classless Society [...], genuinely classless: I have
never met with it since':

We waited for yellow messages (preliminary warnings) and drank cup after cup of revolting stewed tea, which left an orange film on the tongue. [...] With us were Ron, ex-printer, ex-everything, one of the cleverest self-educated men I have ever met; 'One-Arm Harvey', an ex-sailor, [...] an ex-chef from the Savoy, and four extremely pretty women. (*Important*, pp.129-30).

In her diary, she described the warden at the new post as 'a tasty lad' called Freeman. In her memoir, she merely identified him as John Freeman, 'later Ambassador to the United States' (*Important*, p.129). It might therefore be thought from this that Freeman was a career diplomat, and it seems somewhat strange that Pamela did not mention that Freeman had become a Labour M.P. for ten years after the war, then, among other journalistic achievements, editor of the *New Statesman*, nor, perhaps even more surprisingly, given her own later career in broadcasting, the inquisitor on the renowned BBC Television interview programme, 'Face to Face' between 1959 and 1962. But in 1939, he was only 24 and awaiting his call-up, and he and his wife Elizabeth became firm friends with the Stewarts. On quiet nights, Pamela enjoyed literary conversations with Freeman, and this may have provided the stimulus she needed to start a new book which took no account of Frank Swinnerton's advice to concentrate on the proletariat. It would prove to be one of her most successful novels.

On 1 December 1939, Pamela wrote in her diary that she had 'made a start on [an] odd novel [...] which may come to something but probably won't'. Much of this novel had to be written while on duty in the Warden's Post, and it seems more impossible than ever that she could have been able to write such an intricately-plotted and exquisitely-worded work within so short a time-span. As time went on, she began to feel that the book 'isn't at all bad', and felt an 'absurd fear of some damned blitzkreig' before she can finish it. But on 13 January 1940, she merrily crowed: 'All right, Hitler, blitz away: I'm through!!!' Pamela had toyed with various titles for the novel, including *The Fiery Bushel*, and *The Glory and the Dream* (the latter from Wordsworth's 'Intimations of Immortality'). It was not, however, until just before submitting the manuscript to her agent that her mother suggested, and she was delighted with, the novel's actual title, *Too Dear for My Possessing*, which comes from the first line of Shakespeare's Sonnet 87.

Several studies of British literature written during the Second World War agree with Robert Hewison that, at that time: 'Instead of confronting the present, many writers turned to the related themes of autobiography and childhood'.[9] This may well have been Pamela's unconscious reason for setting Parts One and Four of this novel in Bruges. In her Author's Note to the Penguin edition of *Too Dear for My Possessing* (1976), Pamela explained that 'the novel was suggested to me by *place*', continuing:

> Belgium was the first foreign country I ever visited (I was fifteen) and Bruges the first foreign city. It caught hold of my imagination in a way that has never been loosened, and indeed, I go back to Bruges for the peace, the pictures and the bells, whenever I possibly can.[10]

In Part One, the narrator, Claud Pickering, is thirteen years old and had been living for two years in Bruges in semi-exile with his father, who had been unable to obtain a divorce in order to marry his flamboyant mistress, Helena, and live with her respectably in England. Parts Two and Three move between Paris and London, and in these, the novel is an excellent example of Hewison's further contention:

> There is a reason for this outpouring of memory, and it is not simply that writers found it difficult to deal with the immediate present. The probing back into the past was in search of some explanation for the crisis of the times.[11]

By the end of Part Two, it is 1929, Claud is 20 years old, working in London for the English branch of an American bank, and writing art critiques for little magazines. He feels he is having the time of his life, but Pamela, in the persona of the older Claud reviewing his life, provides a nightmarish summary of the period:

> These were the Twenties that crashed with Wall Street. Stockbrokers came flying out of sky-scraper windows like damned souls from a Bosch heaven; the Comus masque of bulls and bears grew ugly in the pity and the storm began to travel the Atlantic. The Thirties came, bringing a milestone between wars. Till 1930 people talked about the last war; after 1930 they talked about the next. As the world plunged, the unemployment figures soared upwards. America knew the breadline, England a sharpening of social conflict, Germany a degradation that was to father a remedy worse than the sickness. (pp.163-64)

When Hitler comes to power in Germany, Claud still denies any interest in politics, and again his older self breaks into the narrative to comment: 'Not interested! I did not realize that politics were becoming interested in me, in us all, that every man's nose would, before a year had passed, be ground into their dust' (p.210).

The heart of the story, however, is not the historical background, but a doomed love affair. When they are both thirteen, Claud has a friendship in Belgium with a girl called Cecil Archer; at their first meeting, he describes her as 'an under-sized child with the reddest hair I have ever seen, so violent in colour that it made almost invisible the features in the peaked, triangular face beneath it' (p.36). After the deaths of both his parents, he moves to London with Helena, and discovers that Cecil has become a successful singer, currently appearing in a musical comedy. The now seventeen-year-old orphan boy weaves fantasies

> in which I would meet Cecil at the stage door, be recognized by her and by her be taken into a world in which, miraculously, I should find myself accepted and loved. [...] I had held [Cecil] in my heart all this long time, waiting for her to come like a rich inheritance into my possession. (p.132)

They do in fact meet by chance at a party, at which all the men 'came all about her like filings to a magnet' (p.152), she does recognize him, and they talk briefly in a room alone together. As she tells him they must return to the gathering:

> We stood in the dark-blue twilight, neither of us stirring. Her white, peaked face was below mine and her eyes were terrible in beauty, old, demanding eyes amused and unafraid. The electricity of love moved along my spine, to the roots of my hair, to the tips of my fingers. (pp.155-56)

Nevertheless, believing Cecil to be out of his reach, Claud later makes an ill-advised marriage to Meg Ettrick, a typist in his office, of whom he reflects:

> I was fond of her because she was pretty and capable and kindly, but of desire I had not so much as would fill a second. She loved me without fire and was content that there should be none, wishing that love

should be temperate in season and out, and that it should look on no tempests. (p.205)

Some years later, when Claud has been transferred to the bank's French headquarters and they are living in Paris, and Meg seems much smitten with a visiting South African cousin, Claud cannot resist attempting to see Cecil, who is appearing in cabaret at a club off the Champs Elysées. The events of that evening are described in some of Pamela's most sustained lyrical passages, recalling her initial recognition as a poet.

Claud goes to wait outside the club, and, as he says, 'as I stepped out into the warm twilight, the dream came to meet me, and with a full heart I accepted it':

> I walked the Paris streets under the rainbow glory of the lamps, walked on night-green grass and over pavements shining like diamonds. [...] I was looking down a great arcade cut through the building in which she was. The stonework was of reddish marble with gold in it, the pavement tessellated in a design of suns and stars.

When she emerges, she is unsurprised to see Claud, saying: '"I wondered when you'd come."' The impossible dream continues for him as they enter the waiting taxi, and, in the vivid description:

> at once we were swept into the great avenue of jet and diamond, moved off pursued by the driving rain, the following thunder and the wind bearing down upon us like a regiment singing on the march. (pp.233-35)

There is no explicit description of that night, the only one they are destined to spend together. Pamela was later to defend her romantization of Cecil Archer, since:

> She was little more than a tenacious dream to Claud, in any case, and I do not mind thinking of her in Paris in the early morning, in evening dress, her face streaked with tears, even as the carnations she held were streaked and streaming with colour.[12]

By placing this unattainable, in some ways mystical, relationship within the framework of the tempests shaking Europe, Pamela made a significant move forward from the straightforward narratives of her earlier novels. At the end of the novel, Claud returns briefly to Bruges to relive his childhood memories on the brink of war. It is the second day of September 1939, and he reflects that he will no longer be able to withdraw from political involvement:

> Well, tomorrow we shall know; and then there will be no peace, for there dies tonight, I think, the last epoch in which men can set their home and heart affairs foremost, can find their personal troubles of primary importance. (p.303)

Family finances being in their usual parlous condition, Pamela was delighted to hear from her agent (invariably referred to by her only by his surname, Sagar) at Pinkers, that he had negotiated an excellent deal with Collins, who were prepared to pay half the advance payment on delivery of the manuscript. She hastened to send it to him, and within a few days, Sagar rang to say he thought the novel 'magnificent', and shortly afterward that Carrick & Evans, at that time her American publishers, were 'very enthusiastic'. She had some differences on opinion with her new editor at Collins who suggested alterations which she dismissed as being 'just plain fantastic', but with Carrick & Evans now being 'crazy' about the book, the changes she had to make were minimal. She also recorded a visit to Sagar when Ralph Pinker, the head of the agency, 'rushed out to make more of a fuss re TDP than since This Bed'. (There would, however, be reason to worry about Pinker later that year.)

While she was awaiting publication of that novel, the detective story by 'Nap Lombard' was published by Cassell in April. She and Neil were pleasurably surprised by two good notices in the Sunday papers. The notices were also proof of the popularity of new books, including crime fiction, at that time. With wartime shortages of paper, both the *Sunday Times* and *Observer* were reduced to 18 pages (from 32 in the former case, 28 in the latter), but both still found room for four pages of book reviews among the war reports. Milward Kennedy in the *Sunday Times* praised *Tidy Death* for being 'a spirited and fast-moving story', and Maurice Richardson in the *Observer* on the same day 'strongly recommend[ed] it to all connoisseurs'.

Neither critic mentions the strong resemblances in the plot and characterizations in Nap Lombard's first published work to those found in the early detective stories written by one of Pamela's adolescent favourites, Agatha Christie. Lombard's happy-go-lucky amateur detectives, Andrew and Agnes, have much in common with Christie's Tommy and Tuppence, rather than with either Miss Marple or Hercule Poirot. However the plot, which revolves around a disparate collection of people sent mysterious invitations to a garden party, there to receive further instructions, after which, one by one, the most unlikeable come to various forms of grisly end, does resemble Christie's similarly plotted *Ten Little Niggers* (1939).[13] Sinister foreigners abound in *Tidy Death*, and Agnes and Andrew, with little help from the police, uncover motives relating to black magic and drugs. Andrew's aristocratic cousin, a Commissioner at Scotland Yard, berates the couple at the end for their derring-do, just before they are going off to get married, saying: 'Never in all my experience, never in all my years of dealing with criminals and lunatics, have I come across such a damn case of criminal lunacy as your behaviour throughout this affair.'[14] Agnes, unchastened, says: '"We might just fall into adventures time after time, like Bulldog Drummond and Phyllis, like ..."' (p.275). The ellipsis might have been intended to refer either to Tommy and Tuppence, or to another prototype of a wacky crime-solving married couple, mentioned favourably in Pamela's diaries, Nick and Nora Charles from Dashiell Hamnett's *The Thin Man* (1934). There was, however, only to be one further novel by Nap Lombard rather than the hoped-for series or film adaptations.

For two months, Neil became a paid Post Warden. His small salary was undoubtedly useful, but the long shifts he now had to work played havoc with their relationship. On an average day after a night shift, he 'slept & slept & swore when anyone awoke him'. Pamela was not altogether sorry when he lost the job when their post was amalgamated with another. Despite having Australian nationality, Neil had had to register for military service at the start of the year, and had various abortive interviews with the Tank Corps and Field Intelligence. Their friends were gradually being called up. Henry, 'all splendid in his uniform', left to join an Anti-Aircraft Battery. John Freeman's last night at the post came around, and Pamela commented that it was 'all rather pathetic. He is a b. good P.W.', although she did cryptically add 'whatever his other shortcomings'.

Dylan Thomas, however, was not among those going off to the war. As Constantine FitzGibbon remembered, Dylan 'regarded the war as a personal affront' since it interfered with his writing and 'dried up such slender sources of income as he possessed'. FitzGibbon also mentioned that on 3 September 1939, Dylan had sent Pamela a copy of his just published collection of poetry and prose, *The Map of Love*, and had inscribed beneath the date: 'Dylan-shooting begins.'[15] Pamela did not think this important enough to record in her diary, but in April 1940, she did mention that 'Dylan, fat & blotto' had come to tea, and the following day that: 'Blasted Dylan called when we were out to borrow money.' In fact, according to FitzGibbon, with a wife and child to keep, Dylan was then trying to borrow money from all his acquaintances, and considering all the alternatives to avoid active service, including registering as a conscientious objector (although he was not keen on the idea of a tribunal). He did sneer to his friends about 'all the shysters in London [who] are grovelling about the Ministry of Information',[16] but had himself applied to the Ministry unsuccessfully. In the end, his machinations were unnecessary; in a medical for what he hoped would be a cushy army assignment, he was deemed to be in the C3 category, sufficient to disqualify him from active service if not from non-combatant units.[17]

Shortly after Dylan's visits, Pamela and Neil were able to take a week's holiday together, and went to Stratford-on-Avon in time for the Shakespeare birthday celebrations, the season continuing as usual despite the war. Despite her delight in being in Stratford, Pamela's critical faculties were unblunted: the first play they saw, was a production of *Measure for Measure*, which she said was 'inaudible & poorly acted', and altogether an 'absolute disgrace to commemorate our national hero so', and the next, *The Merchant of Venice*, was 'poorish'. 'What a set of Venetian skunks', she commented, 'enough to make one sick. Last scene thrown away.' Her judgments may have been a little harsh. The cast lists for the Shakespeare Memorial Theatre's last pre-war season had included many young actors whose careers were suspended the following year by service in the armed forces. In 1939, John Laurie had played Othello and Richard III, Alec Clunes had played several other leading roles, and Michael Goodliffe, Geoffrey Keen and Trevor Howard, comparatively minor roles. All of these had played several seasons in Stratford, and would have successful post-war careers, but in 1940, there were almost no familiar names either among the men or, indeed, the women. But it was not necessarily the

'Venetian skunks' which were making her feel queasy. While they were away, she was expecting a period, and on the third day late, she was 'wondering – I hope not too pathetically – whether I might not be pregnant'. Despite being 'steeled to disappointment', she began to believe that her longed-for baby was on the way, although her doctor would only say when she was fourteen days late that 'he definitely suspected pregnancy'.

War news filled her diary for the intervening days before she would have the results of 'a biological test'. She recorded the German invasion of Holland, Belgium and Luxembourg, though omitted to mention that Winston Churchill had taken over the reins of government the same day. Her first entries regarding Churchill are quite disparaging, despite his dogged anti-appeasement stance in the late 1930s. After quoting Churchill's famous first speech as Prime Minister in the House of Commons, saying he could offer nothing but 'blood, toil, tears & sweat', she merely added: 'What a stinking legacy this world has!' And she dismissed his first broadcast to the nation as 'very panicky', without quoting from it at all. Presumably this hostility emanated from her left-wing standpoint, but in that broadcast, Churchill proclaimed that:

> I have formed an Administration of men and women of every Party and of almost every point of view. We have differed and quarrelled in the past; but now one bond unites us all – to wage war until victory is won, and never to surrender ourselves to servitude and shame, whatever the cost and the agony may be.

Politics then became sidelined as her pregnancy was confirmed. 'Am so happy about it, despite everything!' she wrote. In her euphoria, the Dunkirk evacuation from May 26 to June 3 passed virtually unrecorded in her diary. She mentioned on 28 May that the British Expeditionary Force appeared to be on the point of withdrawal, but continued: 'Everyone horribly upset. Still, it's no time to whine. Anything may happen.' On 14 June, she recorded that the German army had entered Paris, and remarked: 'Couldn't they have armed the workers to defend the city?', and on 17 June, a terse entry read: 'France surrendered – NOT surprising.' At this point, they were anxious about Neil's parents from whom they had not heard since the onset of the war, but they would find out quite some time later that Morven and

Jane had managed to leave Paris for Bordeaux, make their way from there to Casablanca, and eventually reach the Dominican Republic, where they saw out the war.

As often happens, an individual sadness seemed to impinge itself more on Pamela's consciousness than the mass fate of the troops in France. She was 'very shocked & upset by news that poor little Vicky Neuburg died last night. Felt so dreadful about it. Wrote to as many "poets" as I could rake out.' She attended his cremation at Golders Green, perhaps feeling guilty that she had not seen him for some years. Much later, she later told Jean Overton Fuller that she had gone less often to Vicky's after she married Neil, because he 'was not in sympathy with the ambiance and was rude to the Lady [Runia] about "yogis and bogeys"'.[18] Dylan was among the poets to whom she wrote; he was then living in Laugharne, and did not attend the funeral, but he later wrote to both Runia and Jean Overton Fuller. To the latter, he said that he was 'very grieved' to hear the news, and that Vicky had been 'a sweet, wise man'.[19]

With some reluctance, she and Amy decided to move out of London. She realized that 'no-one would want a pregnant warden', and that Neil's call-up was imminent (*Important*, p.130). They rented 'Cotswold', a bungalow with a delightful garden, between Laleham and Staines, and close to 'Sideways', the home of her Aunt Emma. (Her 1936 diary had recorded that she agreed with Neil that Laleham was 'a stinking pesthole', but this was evidently forgotten in the present circumstances.) Just prior to the move, she wrote: 'Now feel I can hardly bear to wait before I shake dust of Chelsea off my feet.' On moving day, her main concern was for Buzz, but the cat settled down 'miraculously'. Pamela, however, didn't. For days, she recorded feeling depressed, even though she tried to reassure herself that she supposed 'it's only ole baby!'. 'Feel in rotten state', she moaned, 'and am so disappointed. Can't adjust myself to this place.' The Thames Valley was scarcely a war-free zone; night after night, there were 'huge air-fights' overhead, and 'bombs, guns, biffs, thuds'.

Too Dear for My Possessing was first published in July in the United States, and her delighted publisher sent her a 'raving enthusiastic notice' by Jane Spence Southron in the *New York Times*. Headlined 'New Work by a Brilliant Writer', the review began: 'This is a book of queer enchantment; of strange, astringent realism; a book stripped utterly of sentimentality but deep with feeling that is both psychic and sensuous.' Southron expressed her wonder at 'how far Pamela Hansford Johnson has come in the few but pregnant years that separate this beautiful pain-dogged book from her promising first novel', and ended:

> The tough, clear-eyed decision that gives the finale its strength and special significance is the writer's answer to the challenge of contemporary events. Pamela Johnson, looking back at her own generation's less than thirty years, has taken stock of them, given them their meed of due, nostalgic longing and swept them into the discard. With quiet confidence, she speaks here for the young intellectuals of her day and country.

The British edition ('quite inoffensive and quite without charm', she had commented on receiving it from Collins) was published the following month, and also received good reviews: Ralph Straus, in the *Sunday Times*, applauding the 'real feeling in her writing', and singling out 'one sign of fine work – her people linger on in your memory'. In the *New Statesman and Nation*, despite a patronising headline, 'The Ladies', in his review of books by four writers he describes as 'lady-novelists', Desmond Hawkins congratulated Pamela for having written 'in the first person, as a boy and later as man: a difficult feat of male impersonation which is strikingly successful and which must inevitably be labelled a *tour de force*', and continued: 'This is a full-fathoms-five novel to drown in, ample in dimension, packed with carefully elaborated characterisation and incident.'

Pamela was eagerly awaiting her royalty cheques early in September, when the afore-mentioned problem with her agent, Ralph Pinker, became manifest. As Selina Hastings categorically states in her biography of Rosamond Lehmann, another client of Pinkers at that time: 'J.B. Pinker, the firm's founder, had been a distinguished figure in the book world, but his son, who took over the business, was a crook [...].'[20] Pamela had rows on the telephone with him, and eventually received a cheque when her solicitor threatened him with a writ. Her American publisher opted to bypass Pinker by directly sending her a cheque for $250, and her solicitor continued to harass Pinker for the balance of the British royalties until they were fully paid. In November, John Brophy rang to tell Pamela that Pinker was 'v. much in queer street; might be bankruptcy & even prosecution'. It was in fact to be the latter in 1943, when Pinker received a jail sentence for fraud, and his company was forced to close down. Pamela's persistence had ensured that she did not lose by his malpractices, as did others among his notable clients. Pamela then appointed Spencer Curtis Brown as her literary agent.

Throughout the remainder of the year, London was suffering heavy bombing. Pamela certainly had cause to regret her flippant remark mentioned at the beginning of this chapter about it being all right for Hitler to start a *blitzkrieg* once she had finished her book. 'Poor, poor London,' she wrote. Aunt Kalie left her job in London, 'horribly shaken and depressed', and her sister Emma eventually agreed to let her stay with her. Friends phoned most days to tell of the high death toll and number of casualties. While a couple called George and Doreen 'Don' Musgrove, visiting from London, were telling them 'all the stories from the bombed areas', a heavier than usual raid began which, despite themselves, they all found fascinating to be watching from the distance. This may have been the occasion about which she wrote in *Important to Me*: 'One night we watched, from our garden, the City burning. It was a beautiful and terrible sight, the sky a vivid rose-colour behind our apple-trees' (p.132). (More will be heard about Don Musgrove later.) Elizabeth Freeman came down to Laleham with news that their old warden's post at Milman Street had been blown up with deaths and casualties among their former colleagues. Pamela's old friend, Teddy, arrived looking 'quite appallingly strained & worn out', and when the evening brought the usual cacophony of sirens, anti-aircraft gunfire and steady procession of planes, he told her that this was, comparatively, 'a picnic'.

Neil's call-up papers finally arrived, and he left for a training camp on the Norfolk coast. Despite the success of her latest book, she still had money problems, and needed the Army allowance to supplement her writing income from book royalties and from reviewing. On the first day of December, Neil was appointed Battery Commander's Assistant in Great Yarmouth. On the last day of the year, she went into labour, and their son was born the following morning. (Neil had been unable to persuade the army to grant him compassionate leave and so was not present.) But a seemingly routine event between these two landmarks would eventually change the course of her life.

She had been continuing to review for the *Liverpool Post* despite her advanced pregnancy, and at the beginning of the month, her consignment of books included one called *Strangers and Brothers*[21] by a relatively little-known author called C.P. Snow. Snow was then a Civil Servant in the Ministry of Labour, but had always hoped to become fully accepted as a writer, having published one successful detective story, *Death Under Sail*, and two other moderately well-received novels in the early 1930s. He had now conceived the idea of a sequence of novels, roughly following the trajectory of his own life, and reflecting contemporary shifts in society, education and politics; later he would fully admit to interviewers that there were many autobiographical elements in his depiction of the one character common to all these novels, 'Lewis Eliot', and that many of his other characters were either single or multiple portraits of people he had known. When during a series of taped interviews, later published as *C.P. Snow: An Oral History* (1983), the questioner, John Halperin, remarked: 'I'm trying to disentangle Lewis Eliot from C.P. Snow. It's not always so easy', Snow's reply was merely: 'No, it isn't.'[22] 'George Passant', the central character in *Strangers and Brothers*, was based on Bert Howard, a schoolmaster at Alderman Newton's School in Leicester, the grammar school which Snow had attended, and who gathered a group of young men, including Snow and the future distinguished historian, J.H. (Jack) Plumb, around him. The friendship of the latter two was to continue for many years, both becoming fellows of Christ's College, Cambridge. They also continued to keep in touch with Howard despite a later scandal, which Snow anticipated in this novel but fictionalized as concerning financial irregularities, concealing his supposition that any disgrace would in fact originate from Howard's then allegedly platonic relationships with boys.

Pamela would then have known nothing about Howard's misdemeanours. Perhaps with memories of the small literary coterie of her girlhood, led by the young man they had nicknamed 'Take Plato', Pamela's review began:

> In the twenty years that followed the last war, influences small yet powerful were nibbling away at the English scene. Little cults, too swiftly-withering to seem the harbingers of vast change, sprouted all over the intellectual soil. Men like George Passant, the young solicitor's clerk, were gathering about them in the provincial towns, their

cliques and 'circles' of young people, dedicated to a fuller cultural life and a wider personal freedom. Dr. Snow's first novel of a series of four books[23] dedicated to the world between wars is rich with understanding of such prophets and their followers.

She concluded: 'I recommend "Strangers and Brothers" as one of the most striking and vital literary products of five years or more. [George Passant's] excitement lingers in the mind like a reflected fire.'[24]

C.P. Snow, who had been cast down by early reviews (as will be seen, he was everlastingly prone to deep despair when receiving adverse criticism) was naturally delighted with this review; he wrote to his brother Philip, then working as an administrator in the Colonial Service in Fiji, that there had later been 'a few sturdy voices proclaiming that I was a good writer,' particularly Pamela Hansford Johnson, whom he described as 'herself a good novelist', and who had said '"the portrait of George was as good as anything in modern fiction"'.[25] Snow duly wrote to Pamela on 30 November, thanking her:

> I have just seen your review of my book, with excessive pleasure. It is nice to be flattered by anyone, of course, but particularly so by a writer as good as yourself. I think I have read all your books ... your first I thought a work of astonishing promise, and the last, <u>Too Dear for My Possessing</u>, much your best. I've admired and envied and talked about your gifts: and sometimes been angry with you for not being more ambitious in the use of them. [...] If you want, you can become quite easily the best *woman writer* {my italics} in the world [...].
>
> I've nearly taken the trouble to tell you this before, but now your review gives me a good excuse. [...][26]

He ended his letter by suggesting that they should meet in London so that he might expand upon his views, but the meeting necessarily had to wait. On 30 December, her doctor decided to 'doom' Pamela to 'a jorum of caster oil tomorrow, which he said <u>might</u> precipitate labour'. Her mother got into 'a grand flap', her two aunts arrived the next morning to make the bungalow 'smell like a hospital', and this, she wrote, was how 'this terrible, awful, wonderful year ended', with a 'grand orgie d'huile'. She went into labour at 12.30 p.m., and her son, Andrew Morven Stewart, was born at 10.15 a.m. on New Year's Day.

CHAPTER 6

Surviving on the
Home Front

I N SOME WAYS, Pamela's life was a good deal easier than that of
other young mothers whose husbands were in the armed forces,
because she had her mother with her, and her two aunts nearby,
to help look after her young son, Andrew, usually referred to as 'sweet'
and 'adorable'. She was thus able to continue with her writing and
reviewing. She went to the cinema once or twice each week, shopped
regularly in Staines, cycled short distances as necessary (usually, however, 'with trepidation') and took part in events in the Village Hall.
Nevertheless, she evidently found life away from London stultifying.
Neil sympathized with her in an undated letter, probably sent towards
the end of 1941, from his Officer Cadet Training Unit in Shropshire:

> The discussion group seems to be the only bright spot in Laleham's
> mental landscape. It is very good for you to get up & speak, & develops
> self-confidence, mental agility, etc. After being in the army my mind
> is about as agile as a young elephant.[1]

With nothing else to do one day, she reread her 1934 diary, and
thought 'how interesting & wild & sad' it was, 'compared with the
dull record of these days!' The lack of local intellectual stimulation
must have made her continuing contact with C.P. Snow all the more
of consequence to her. They had first met briefly during 1941, according to Donald Dickson, a would-be biographer of Snow.[2] Snow is
mentioned only fleetingly, and only by surname, in her 1942 diary.[3] He
came to visit her in Laleham on one occasion, having evidently proved
unreliable on at least one previous occasion. So, while she prepared for

his visit by cooking as best as wartime restrictions would permit – a 'prune flan & a vanilla mould' – she added that it was 'for Snow, if he <u>does</u> arrive tomorrow'. And indeed that 'tomorrow' came and went, but he did arrive by train at 4.30 p.m. the following day. They 'talked, went for walk, all about', and she added: 'That's all.' He stayed overnight, but there can be no doubt that this was entirely a matter of exigency, and after he left before lunch the following day, she commented to her diary that he was a 'curious sort of man & in an unexplicable way, unnerving'.

Snow's early correspondence with Pamela resembles that between herself and Dylan (minus the jokes and the many sexual asides for which Dylan usually later apologized). Very soon after his first contact with Pamela, Snow sought, as Dylan had done, to give her guidance as to her future literary direction:

> You write well of trends in the political world, and you make these trends sharp in your characters: and I agree with your political attitude by the way. Nevertheless, I don't believe it's your proper theme: i.e., I don't believe you've yet set yourself your deepest theme. It would be easier for me to tell you than to write it. [...] I don't think politics, in the deepest sense, is in your blood; I think you have got interested in the doom of our world through your intellect, and that it has not just passed into your unconscious experience. This world in any case can be harder for a woman than a man, I suppose, and particularly hard for a woman of your age: I am 35 and have had a pretty lively consciousness of doom since 1930: yours can't have begun till about 1934 or 5?[4]

One can only speculate as to whether these and subsequent words of advice influenced Pamela's choice of genre for her next novel. *The Family Pattern* (1942) is a domestic chronicle following three generations of a family through a complex sequence of cross-class marital alliances from the early 1890s to the first year of the First World War. As Ishrat Lindblad points out, the primary theme of the novel reveals 'the way in which class-distinction is deeply rooted in England'.[5] She tellingly quotes a passage halfway through the book:

> The nineteenth century outlived its own lifetime [...]. It should have died with the bell of the last midnight, or at least, with the death of the Queen; but it was the great century of the middle-class, and the middle-class was reluctant to face the ugly speeding of time, time that

must inevitably blur the class outline, paint out the clear-cut edges and smooth them into the great, dangerous, unknown classes on either flank.[6]

Perhaps the mood of the nation halfway through another world war, with a conviction that a victory, should it come about, would lead to a utopian classless society, was not receptive to a more pessimistic analysis. Pamela had been even more dubious than usual about the novel prior to publication, and was therefore unsurprised to receive 'a bunch of lousy reviews of F.P. which is most certainly a flop!'

Pamela's own political views were fluctuating at this time. Her initial suspicion regarding the Coalition government was beginning to wane, although in January 1942, she had suspected 'grubby Tory work going on', when a motion of No Confidence was defeated in the House of Commons with only one dissenting vote. But, after the fall of Singapore, which Churchill described as 'the greatest military defeat in the history of the British Empire', Pamela wrote in her diary: 'We should keep him at all costs, but I hope he does do something about Cabinet reconstruction.' Throughout the year, her entries inevitably interspersed reports of the progress of the war in the Far East, North Africa, and, perhaps with most anxiety, on the Eastern Front, with domestic matters, and her work.

During Neil's leaves the year before, they had collaborated on a second Nap Lombard book, *Murder's A Swine*, featuring the now-married Agnes and Andrew, and were annoyed when it was rejected by Cassells on the ground that it was 'callous', a criticism they felt could be levelled at most thrillers. It was however published in 1942 by Hutchinsons to 'Book Production War Economy Standards', on flimsy paper with a greatly reduced print size. Despite being approximately the same length as its predecessor *Tidy Death*, it was crammed into 160 pages as against the bulky 280 pages of the latter, and was thus ideal for an army kitbag. Whereas the style and substance of the pair's first adventure was firmly rooted in prewar England, *Murder's A Swine* (retitled *The Grinning Pig* in the USA) was contemporary, and the tone was less frivolous. A corpse is found by an off-duty air-raid warden, in the block of flats in which Agnes and Andrew live and thereafter there is a convoluted plot, involving a number of mysterious porcine incidents, the resolution of which, again Christie-like, relates to a past grudge about which the reader could have no knowledge. Nevertheless the book was reasonably well received and brought in some modest but welcome royalties.

At the beginning of 1942, Neil was stationed in an officers' training camp in Shropshire, and Pamela was able to visit him there, although this involved long and very cold train journeys; before such visits, she recorded always feeling 'half-happy, half-apprehensive'. He was fretting a great deal about the possibility of being 'R.T.U.'-ed, the acronym standing for 'Returned to Unit', that is, being rejected from officer training, and their meetings were clouded by his anxiety. Things improved when he was moved to a camp on Salisbury Plain; he was much more optimistic about his prospects during his next leave. However, Neil's service career, and indeed his life, might have ended with this new posting. On 14 April 1942, Pamela was alarmed to read a newspaper report to the effect that, two days earlier, fourteen men & a Brigadier had been 'killed on manoeuvres in Tidworth'. Shortly after this, she was relieved to receive a telegram informing her that Neil was in the military hospital with only a minor injury. *The Times* carried the official statement issued jointly by the War Office and Air Ministry that an accident had occurred during combined exercises, as a result of which 'a number of soldiers' had been killed and injured'. The *Daily Telegraph*, however, was more enterprising in sending a reporter to investigate; his account of the tragedy, headlined: 'Tried To Warn Diving Pilot: Death Roll of 23 in Army Accident' was seemingly uncensored, and the facts he uncovered were later admitted to be true. The deaths could hardly be classified as having occurred during 'manoeuvres', as described in the earliest report. The men killed, including high-ranking army and air force officers, had been watching a demonstration of power-diving to strafe specific targets when one of the Hurricane pilots mistook their grandstand for the objective. As Neil was at that stage non-commissioned, he had been outside the officers' enclosure, but he had nevertheless been shot through the heel by a stray bullet of the live ammunition, which, the *Daily Telegraph* reporter said, had been used to add 'realism to the demonstration'. Naturally enough, Pamela wrote in her diary: 'Thank God [the injury] was no more.' And two months later, she proudly attended her husband's passing-out ceremony in Larkhill Barracks, Wiltshire.

The following month, Neil was transferred yet again to an artillery unit in Lamberhurst, near Cranbook, Kent, which should have made life easier for them. At other camps, the accommodation she had been able to find ranged from pubs, bed-and-breakfasts, and in Amesbury, 'an awful little shop-café, all full of texts and restrictions'. On her arrival in Cranbrook, she was delighted to find 'the George Hotel, extremely good & the food prewar!' But disillusion lay ahead: she recorded 'such a disappointment, as I shall hardly have any time with him!' The reason for this was that the Battery Commander there, who had earned the nickname 'Twitty', 'doesn't approve of wives', and Neil therefore had to leave her early each evening 'quite stranded and lonely, & fed up to teeth'. On her following visit, she did her best to be an obedient army wife, staying nearer the camp albeit in 'a bleak pub with awful food', watching a 'chilly football match', and attending a 'sergeants' dance in evening'. At the latter, she met 'Twitty' for the first time, and evidently charmed him, as he permitted Neil to spend the night with her.

The Lamberhurst experiences were to give her the basis of her next novel, *Winter Quarters*, the setting of which is the scarcely-disguised 'Christenhurst' village and army camp. The lengthy cast of characters in this book warranted, probably at the suggestion of her editor, a list giving the rank of each soldier and the occupation or family connection of the civilians, and indeed this reader certainly needed frequently to refer back to this. The Battery Commander, Major Cameron-Leckie, nicknamed 'Sadness', is clearly based on 'Twitty', since the opening conversation between two lieutenants establishes that Sadness is 'not keen on wives'.[7]

One of the characters is one that we have met before – Claud Pickering from *Too Dear for My Possessing* – but here in a minor role, together with his stepmother Helena and stepsister Charmian who make still briefer appearances, particularly superfluously in Helena's case. There is no first-person narration in this novel, as in the former. In an Author's Note on the flyleaf of *Winter Quarters*, Pamela explains that her aim had not been to generalize by representing 'a "typical" cross-section of army life', since there could be no such thing, but 'to explore the reactions of "ordinary" men to an "extra-ordinary" way of living'. The difficulty is that her army characters are in a state of stasis, awaiting active service; it is the sections about the civilians, and especially the women of the village, whose lives are substantially altered by the arrival of the temporary camp, and the quandaries of the soldiers' wives, which are the more compelling. One can hear the author's own voice speaking through the character of Stacey, at the end of a short visit to her officer husband:

> How many ghosts we must leave behind us, we visiting wives to the war-time inns; but ghosts that do not haunt our successors, nor are heard by human ears. When the bus has carried us away the chamber-maids go upstairs to exorcise our spirits with swab and broom and duster; not even the scent of our powder is left upon the air. You would think that something of the love, the hunger, the loneliness for a moment assuaged, would remain behind, that the voice of the girl who had slept last week in the maple bed would say to this week's girl, 'Yes, I, too, was glad to see him; I, too, dare not think about war without end; I, too, always try to disbelieve it when the old men prophesy (as if our lives were worth nothing at all) that it will last five years, seven years, ten; for if I did believe I should be sick with grief.' (pp.166-67)

Although Pamela wrote this novel at her usual swift rate (often a chapter per day) throughout the autumn of 1942, it was unusually not to be published for more than a year. She ended 1942 on an optimistic note, following Allied victories in North Africa: 'The tide of war appears to have turned. I hope, humbly, next year to see Europe freed of Fascism, my Neil home, & my Andy promised a decent life without fear & the abnormal dangers.' These hopes were of course premature, as the war continued for a further two and a half years.

It is not clear whether or not Pamela kept a diary in either 1943 or 1944. The first eight months of 1943 brought little change to Pamela's wartime way of life, other than that she now occasionally broadcast. Neil remained in England, although expecting at any time to be posted abroad. Meanwhile, Pamela's intermittent literary correspondence with C.P. Snow had continued, but their relationship moved onto a different level in August 1943, when in responding to an invitation to dine with Pamela and Neil during one of the latter's leaves, Snow touched on personal matters:

> I should have written long before, but I've been going through a painful time. My closest friend was killed over Essen in April, and the circumstances are more tragic than that kind of loss need be. He was one of the most gifted men in Europe (the best Coptic scholar in the world at the age of 32); he went into the RAF because of a self-destructive streak that dominated his life; at the time of his death, he

was just beginning to feel that he might be happy, through an unexpectedly successful marriage; a son has been born since.

Also I've been a good deal hurt by a love affair which began in great happiness and turned into misery.

But I'm just beginning to recover from these blows and it is high time I saw people I like. I want to hear about your books; I have reproached myself for not finding out before, because it is very important that you should get settled in a literary sense. [...] [8]

The 'closest friend' was Charles Robert Allberry, another Fellow of Christ's College. Snow would later fictionalize Allberry as 'Roy Calvert' in several of the novels in the *Strangers and Brothers* series, notably, and controversially, as the central character in *The Light and the Dark* (1947). The love affair to which he referred was with a Wren officer, Sheila Palfreyman, often identified as another of Snow's future characters, 'Sheila', in several of the novels, but, as Snow explained to John Halperin, 'Sheila' was also partly based on a girl called Stella Eames with whom he had been in love while an undergraduate student at Leicester University.[9] Stella's father owned a coalmine, and Snow had been bitter when she rejected his proposal of marriage, believing her decision to have been class-driven.

Some explanation of Snow's early relationships with women seems appropriate here, since, in self-defence, he established a pattern of wilful non-commitment and some reliance on safety in numbers which would continue for the rest of his life. Snow did not have great success with girls in his youth; as his brother candidly put it: 'Charles was singularly unprepossessing in appearance, making him not one for the girls.'[10] During his early years at Cambridge, he made a virtue out of his enforced near-celibacy. In 1931, he wrote to a friend, Harry Hoff, with regard to the proposed marriage of one of their acquaintances: 'In my austere code, the best people oughtn't to lose control of their conscious minds, even when they're persuading themselves that they are in love.'[11] (After the death of Charles Allberry, Hoff was to become Snow's closest friend; although a few years younger than Snow, he had attended the same Leicester grammar school, followed his mentor to Cambridge, and later into the same department in the Civil Service. In due course, Hoff decided that he, too, would prefer to be known as a novelist; he wrote, for reasons which will later be explained, under the pseudonym of William Cooper.)

Snow told John Halperin that, as he became a tutor and later a Fellow of Christ's College, he avoided any long-term entanglements by, as he put it, having 'one or two girls for purely carnal entertainment'.[12] He failed, however, to mention to Halperin, and, it would seem, also to Donald Dickson, a relationship, recently unearthed by Lesley Chamberlain, with a Russian refugee, born Katerina Speransky, whom Snow met in Cambridge in the early 1930s. (After her second marriage to an English man, she anglicized her name and became known as Kathryn Barber.) The dedication of Snow's first novel, *Death Under Sail*, read: 'To Kathryna, who was Generous', but this tribute, as Chamberlain points out, was omitted from a revised edition published in 1959, despite Barber's contention in the 1934 *Authors and Writers Who's Who* that the novel had been 'a collaborative effort'.[13]

In 1938, Snow met another refugee, Rachel, a Jewish scientist, 'who', he wrote to his brother Philip, 'attracted me enough to make me wonder whether I ought to pursue her' although he had doubts on the grounds that she was 'coolly self-centred like most of the women that I fall for.' Soon afterward, he told his brother: 'I deliberately didn't see Rachel again: I daren't get entangled with a woman just now.' His consolation, he explained, was a reversion to his previous modus operandi: 'I sent for Rosie from Nottingham and had a distinctly satisfactory champagnerous Edwardian sort of night,' and his conclusion was that: 'I've decided that I prefer women that I don't have to respect.'[14]

In answer to a further enquiry from John Halperin about his later relationships with women, he averred: 'I'm a good deal like a machine [...]. I can pursue an active life almost irrespective of emotion.'[15] There seems to have been some retrospective self-deception in this answer, as he had admitted in a long letter to his brother, written in the same month as his previously mentioned letter to Pamela, that his utter despair with regard to the relationship with Sheila Palfreyman had affected his work. Snow had begun by apologizing to his brother for a long hiatus in their correspondence despite his concern about the possibility of a Japanese invasion of Fiji, the country in which Philip Snow had been working as an administrator for the Colonial Service since 1938. His excuse was that he had been going through 'perhaps the most acute experience I've ever known. [...] it's ended in disaster, and I'm desperately miserable.' 'I was harassed,' he continued 'to the roots of my nature, actively unhappy and ashamed, unable to see any solution.' He had now been seconded to the Ministry of Labour as Director of Personnel, but as he went 'from committee to committee, going through all the motions', he could only hear himself making speeches 'with a kind of hopeless distrust'.

Snow had known Sheila for two years, but, it would seem, had never mentioned her to his favourite brother and confidant. 'I knew from the beginning she was eccentric', he said, 'but I was extraordinarily exhilarated; life took on a brightness & intensity that I'd never known before, not even with Stella.' After a long panegyric detailing Sheila's appearance, her virtues, her 'wit, originality and great distinction', Philip must have wondered why his brother should have felt: '(a) this could only end in catastrophe, and (b) I should never meet a girl of this quality again.' Yet the 'catastrophe' seems to have self-initiated by Snow's 'coming across another young woman' with whom he thought he could 'conceivably enjoy' himself enough to forget Sheila, since 'in all theoretical respects', this other girl 'would be a most suitable wife'. So, for nearly eight months, he confessed, 'an absurd Box-and-Cox act proceeded', with neither girl knowing of the other. Nevertheless, he claimed: 'During all those 8 months I was miserable. [...] I was harassed to the roots of my nature, actively unhappy and ashamed [...]'. Matters came to a head when Sheila told him she was in love with someone else, but nevertheless was willing to go on seeing him. This seems to have made his mind up for him, and he told both women he would no longer see them; he did nevertheless continue to correspond with Sheila. 'I am left with an intolerable sense of loss', he wrote, as he ended this section of his letter to his brother:

> There are a fair number of women of deep personality & lofty spirit,
> but usually they don't capture one's imagination and drug one's senses.
> This one did, and I'm sure I shan't find anyone like her again.

It was only after this outpouring of grief with regard to Sheila that he went on to mention to his brother how much the death of Charles Allberry had also affected him.[16]

In 1988, Donald Dickson interviewed Sheila Palfreyman while compiling material for his uncompleted biography, and she presented him with over fifty letters that she had received from Snow between 1941 and 1945. Most of them, addressed to 'My dear Sheila' and signed

'Cps', are cool in tone, and concern arrangements to meet. The longest by far, and the most revealing, was written on 12 September 1943, after Sheila's rejection, and in it, Snow dropped any pretence of indifference. Addressing her as 'Darling', although still signing himself with his initials, he detailed the course of his attachment to her. From the first, he said, he had found that her 'intelligence, wit, and creative spark were a complete delight'. But caution prevailed, as he explained in a much-rewritten self-analysis:

> I like emotional relationships, but [...] some flaw in my temperament makes me choose them when I can be to some extent detached, free from the demands of my own egotism, not pre-occupied by the pettier claims of self. It is a deep flaw, & I don't know exactly why it exists in me; but it makes me extravagantly distrustful when I feel drawn to someone who might strip my detachment right away. I felt this acutely about you; you threatened the security I had built up, painfully cunningly, self-prohibitingly.

Only now, when their relationship seemed irrevocably ended, did he feel free to tell her how much he had loved, and still loved, her. He told her that he had intended to ask her to marry him in March 1942, but just as he was preparing to do this, Sheila had been 'swept with a wave of ill-temper or tiresomeness or irritation, almost as though a current had been switched on', which had made his blood run cold. It had been, he said, 'the most dreadfully strangulated scene I've ever taken part in in my life', and one from which, despite trying to interject some humour, he still hadn't fully recovered. He continued:

> I must admit that there is something strangely ludicrous about it all; it is rather as though a Victorian young man was just about to get on his knees to propose & the girl has playfully tugged the hearthrug away from under him. But somehow, after my struggle with myself about falling in love, after my deliberate passiveness for so long, it seemed like death. It had caught hold of my imagination, & it's still fresh and unsoftened after eighteen months.
>
> After that I retired into as near an approximation to the passive attitude as I could manage, but now, of course, it was a sheer pretence as I was tormented by love.

If Snow hoped that Sheila would be moved by his anguished account to reconsider her decision, the final section might have been unwise, as he went on to tell her about the other woman with whom he had been involved at that time, and whom he now realized that he had wronged, by acting 'like a fool and a cad':

> I've done her great harm, I've taken away her confidence, which was never strong enough, I've made it hard for her to make the sort of marriage which will satisfy her. I couldn't have done much worse if I'd tried, and there is nothing I can do now or say.

He ended by reverting to his feelings for Sheila: 'It isn't easy to write the truth after concealing it for so long. I love you. Cps.'[17]

Unaware as she was of Snow's complicated attitude to women, Pamela doubtless felt great sympathy for Snow with regard to the deep hurt he had sustained with regard to Sheila, and also his grief at the death of Charles Allberry. However, her mind was then occupied with her own personal family and literary concerns as, by the autumn of 1943, she had become pregnant with her second child, Neil was on the verge of embarking for military service in India, and she was working on a new novel. *Winter Quarters* was published in December, and received only moderately good reviews.[18] R.D. Charques in the *Times Literary Supplement*, while commenting that the book was not in 'an exacting or particularly original vein of fiction', ended with acknowledgment of '[Miss Johnson's] interested and alert eye'. Pamela had to wait until February of the following year for a more enthusiastic review from John Hampson in the *Spectator*, praising the book as being 'both ambitious and entertaining', and one which, as such, 'can be warmly recommended to the bulk of the novel reading public and should gain the author many new admirers'.

Pamela's next novel, *The Trojan Brothers*, has a music-hall background (the comedian Billy Bennett had been a family friend during her childhood, and his death the previous year may have given her the impetus to write about a rapidly disappearing world), and features Sid Nichols and Benny Castelli, two variety artistes who appear as a pantomime horse. Sid, the back end of the horse, falls obsessionally and ill-fatedly in love with Betty Todd, a cousin who has married into money. It may not be too fanciful to consider that Snow's confidences about his equally unreciprocated passion for Sheila may have planted a seed in Pamela's imagination. Indeed, when Snow read the early chapters of the manuscript of this novel in advance, he himself saw a parallel between Sid and himself. 'I wouldn't have believed,' he wrote to Pamela in December 1943, 'that I could be so deranged by any human relations; I feel great kinship for poor old Sid in your horse, and the circumstances are not dissimilar.'[19]

Although the sexual relationship between Sid and Betty is the main focus of the book, there are several other, more tender, relationships revealed: Sid's unselfish love for his mother; the wistful, undemanding love for Sid of Anna, a Russian Jewish refugee he has befriended; and, as a constant framework, the rapport between the back end of the horse with the front end. Sid and Benny could supply another example of the literary pattern of male homosocial desire identified by Eve Kosofsky Sedgwick in her brilliantly-argued study, *Between Men: English Literature and Male Homosocial Desire* (1985). The description of their music-hall act which opens the book makes the centrality of this relationship palpable. After various antics at which 'the house roared', the horse falls 'neatly apart', and then:

> The halves of the horse moved blindly, vermicularly, in search of each other [...]. The halves met, adhered; it was like a miracle, some enactment of the impossible at the wrong time, some awful seriousness intruding upon a moment without depth.[20]

Their act similarly ruptures because of Sid's increasingly irrational behaviour with regard to Betty, re-forms, then breaks again irrevocably. But their seemingly asexual love for each other survives, and at their last meeting, in response to a magnanimous gesture from Benny, Sid finds himself crossing a taboo boundary:

> It seemed to Sid that he must somehow express the emotion Benny's offer had called forth, whether or not it damned him. Damnation was a small price to pay for such a splendour of friendship. The inhibitions of his sex rose in him, making him cold as ice; but he fought them and he won. He went to the little man and kissed him on the cheek.
> 'Sid!" Benny cried in a thin sad voice, and put out his hand.' (p.225)

Neil, in one of the few surviving aerogrammes sent by him to Pamela soon after his arrival in India, commented on another theme of the novel: 'Your new plot has tremendous possibilities as an attack on the "arties". I wish I was there to talk it over. In some ways it could be the best plot you've had so far.'[21] Betty's circle of friends comprises would-be patrons of the arts, flitting between whichever branch seems currently in fashion. After amusing herself for a while with Sid, Betty leaves him for Arnold Dench, a novelist 'who had succeeded in writing, in a brilliantly intellectual manner, a novel that could be enjoyed, gushed over and sniggered over by the silliest wife of the silliest husband' (p.157).

Another episode also offers insights into contemporary social history. Sid briefly becomes a film actor just before the advent of the talkies. The director, who hopes to employ Sid in the future, warns him:

> 'Then you'll see some people making a pile, some people losing money, and hundreds of musicians thrown out of work, poor devils. [...] you'd better start learning elocution, Sidney. Papa, potatoes, poultry, prunes and prisms.' (p.143)

The plight of vocally-challenged actors is still remembered, the effect on musicians following the change-over to soundtracks, less so. Sid's beautiful co-star Gwenda kills herself, not however for fear of the talkies, but because she finds out that her husband had been unfaithful to her throughout their marriage, which she had believed to be idyllic. Pamela's description of the press coverage of this fictional event still has resonance in the twenty-first century:

> [Gwenda's] death came at the harvest time of the sensational news-paper. Perhaps because she was distraught, perhaps because she desired at the last to punish the man she had loved so dearly, so unquestion-ably, she had left a suicide note; and the public learned the circumstances from it. Her photographs, serious, misted, appeared on the front pages under headlines calculated to force out the easy tear and render the subconscious sadist a little more conscious of his potentialities. Her secretary, a quiet girl who had always seemed harmless and discreet, accepted a large sum of money for her signature to a series of articles on the dead woman's life; they were inaccurate, colourful and bathetic, oozing a kind of domestic purulence. (p.145)

Sid's descent into mania is figured by a solipsistic cloud in which he moves, albeit with some awareness. At one point with Anna, he recalls the moment when, for him, his rival, the writer Dench, had meta-morphosed 'from an idea into a man', but realizes that despite his deep, fatherly fondness for Anna, to him, 'Anna was still an idea'. The omniscient narrator continues: 'Vaguely [Sid] wondered, though he was unable to form the question coherently, whether she had an existence at all when he was not there to give her one.' The subtle characterization of Sid Nicholls lingers long in the memory of the reader.

At this time, the background to Pamela's novels was generally familiar territory to her, but the characters and situations were predominantly fictional. As previously mentioned, this was not the case with Snow. Early in 1944, he had told her that he was already contemplating incorporating his recent emotional experiences into Lewis Eliot's story. 'I've learned more of the sadic life in the last two years (mainly through Sheila, and in part through its effect on me),' he wrote, 'and I shall want to write about it when I've calmed down, if ever I do.' He went on to draw a slightly more plausible comparison than between himself and the back end of a pantomime horse: 'Most people's insight seems to go all askew on it. Even Dostoevski's did sometimes, although he knew more about it than any great novelist.'[22]

Neil, in India, was not yet involved in any combat, and, happy as Pamela must have been about this, she must have felt some envy reading, in the freezing conditions of a wartime winter, his description of a typical day:

> Today I was due to go for a long walk & a picnic with a couple of officers. This morning they cried off: they felt they couldn't stand the heat of the day! Some people here feel the heat dreadfully – it is winter, too; they will be quite useless in the summer when it is really hot. As for me, I thrive on the heat; even in the hottest part of the day I feel as lively as a cricket.[23]

Also around this time, Pamela received a letter from Neil's father in the Dominican Republic, showing a typical lack of concern for his daughter-in-law, grandson and the grandchild about to be born. He said that he was 'well content' that Neil had not been sent to Europe, since he felt that his health was not suited to 'war in the snow and ice'. But the Caribbean weather did not suit Neil's mother Jane, and Morven continued:

> I have a sort of feeling that I will have to get her out of this climate though I dread the idea of London in war time for her, one has the impression that you are fairly short of heat and then we might be separated by being put in war work, and I couldn't look after her.

He was already anticipating the end of the war, and trying to decide where to live. Returning to Australia did not seem to have occurred to him as an option, as he pondered:

> We will all be fairly broke and I have to keep well in mind that our families have the habit of living to 96 in spots and one must find a country and dig in and start a bit of work that pays for the drinks, in case everyone lives on unreasonably.[24]

If Pamela *was* then keeping a diary which has since been lost, she would doubtless have made some acerbic comments about her in-laws' self-centredness. Pamela and Neil's second child, Lindsay Jane, her 'D-Day baby' (*Important, p.*132), was born in May, and, like so many children born at that time, would not meet her father for nearly two years. With all the anxieties of wartime, exacerbated later that month by the first V.1 bombing raids, Pamela must have felt that the Stewart side of the family was in general having an easier time.

The Trojan Brothers was published in November of that year by Michael Joseph, with whom Curtis Brown had negotiated an advantageous contract for Pamela. With one exception, Pamela would have been happy with the reviews, but the virulence of James Pope-Hennessy's review in the *New Statesman* must have dismayed her. With no mitigation, he condemned the novel as being:

> nothing but the luscious Edwardian novelette in a new and hideously protracted form. What makes the best-sellers of forty years ago seem unreadable today is not their euphemisms nor their reticences. It is their real bad writing. And judged by this standard such a novel as *The Trojan Brothers*, for all its showy psychology and frankness, is intolerable.

Alan Pryce-Jones in the *Observer*, however, judged it 'a really excellent novel, which is also more ambitious in theme and structure than anything [Miss Hansford Johnson] has written so far'. Maurice Willson Disher in the *Times Literary Supplement* was much of the same mind:

> Clowns in love are commonplace. Now it is the turn of the hind legs of a pantomime horse. Perhaps the idea will seem preposterous before "The Trojan Brothers" is opened. After a very few pages imagination is prepared to follow the author anywhere. She has taken the music-hall for place and the nineteen-twenties for period, but in any setting

her ability to give dignity to human life, [...] would ensure respectful attention.

British National Films evidently did not share Pope-Hennessy's verdict on the novel, as *The Trojan Brothers* was, the following year, to be the only one of Pamela's novels to be adapted for the screen. Pamela was originally told that Sid would be played by John Mills, and was delighted about this. In addition to being physically suitable for the part, Mills was already recognized as a fine film actor, having starred in David Lean's *In Which We Serve* (1942). However, to her dismay, the role was eventually played by David Farrar, a handsome matinée idol.

The friendship with Snow continued. Pamela had been introduced by him to two of his female friends, generally known as 'the two Ks' – the novelists Kay Dick and Kathleen Farrell. They had a turbulent relationship in which Pamela now often had to act as mediator, and she had been drawn into their Hampstead circle. Kay Dick was then editing *Windmill*, a literary magazine, to which Pamela occasionally contributed. In a flippant note on a postcard, Pamela had mentioned to Kay that she was trying 'to date old Snow up'.[25] Kay's response evidently did not find favour with her, as by then, Pamela was not seeing Snow's comparison of himself with Dostoeveski in his letter to her of 11 February 1944 as being unduly hubristic. She tartly responded to Kay: 'Snow is a <u>Great Man</u>. Not that I expect his work to be fully recognised for about 20 years.'[26]

CHAPTER 7

'Waving Flags on Top of a Huge Rubble-Heap'

I N THE FINAL MONTHS of the Second World War, Pamela's pessimistic streak was well to the fore. On 1 January 1945, she wrote:

> In these days of waiting I find myself looking forward to very small events with disproportionate pleasure, almost inventing incentives for waking up next morning. During the whole of today, for instance, I have been looking forward to writing in this neat new book, because it is always so pleasant to write on clean, unmarked paper. But diaries are very frightening; I should hate to know now what I shall be writing in mine before the end of the year.

The 'neat new book' was a blank notebook, enabling her to vary the length of her entries, and to include longer accounts of the latest news of the progress of the war. 'One clings to the radio', she wrote, 'for every fresh news bulletin.' When, later that month, German troops led by General von Rundstedt were reported as advancing towards Alsace, she commented that:

> Even to the most pessimistic about the war (& I have always been conservative in my hopes) this setback to hopes of an early end has proved a blow. One grows less resilient as this agony drags on – & God knows we have little to complain about, compared with the occupied countries.

She acknowledged that pessimism might be considered a sensible British trait in another lengthy entry:

It is very interesting, at this juncture of the war, to see the British exercising their hard-won caution. Once they absurdly underrated Hitler. Now it's the reverse. It isn't <u>probable</u> that a German collapse will come about with a month, nor that Zhukov will be in Berlin within that period: but <u>both</u> these things are now possibilities. The British don't, however, admit of them. They really take Hitler, to a degree, at his word, & the witch-doctor stuff is sufficiently potent to make them believe that Germany might stage a miraculous recovery & let the war go on for another ten years. [...] We have been "had" too often, & no one is going to catch us again. This is an excellent thing: God knows what might have been saved if we'd been cautious from the first. We may, however, be caught quite unpreparedly by The End, when we might have conceivably expected it, but resolutely refused to permit ourselves any such expectations.

All this commonsense did not prevent Pamela from suffering fits of depression. She was finding it hard to settle down to creative work; several novels were started, then abandoned. In the meantime, however, she was broadcasting more frequently, mainly about books. The back pages of a diary contained her jotted-down comments on radio technique. There may be one million listeners, she scribbled, but one should address two of them in a room, and since those two might not be actively listening, one had to 'dramatise the book: make it provocative: try to make appeal personal'. But a major drawback for a woman, she continued, was 'the distortion of the female voice'. (Her mother had not spared her by concealing her 'horror' of hearing her daughter on the airwaves for the first time, and Pamela similarly disliked her transmitted voice intensely.) 'So,' she concluded, 'do not condemn any woman broadcaster who sounds like an elderly female SS guard – she is probably young, pretty, & of charming personality. The microphone is her worst enemy.' Other work producing a further modest income at this time included the production of film treatments for the Ministry of Information, although she disliked being thought of as 'a literary odd-job woman'.

She was also re-establishing her literary circle of friends, since, with the easing-off of the V2 rocket attacks on London, she travelled more frequently to the city. She became a regular attendee at the meetings of PEN, the organization established in 1921 to promote literature and human rights, enjoyed lunches with friends, and went again to the publishers' parties which had now resumed. On a typical example of the latter, she recorded lunching at the Dorchester in Heinemann's party at which the fellow-guests at her table included Snow, Kay Dick and Robert Henriques, but she regretted that the occasion had been killed 'stone dead' when Clemence Dane 'gave an exceedingly tedious & dramaticoso monologue about Kipling'. She and Kay stayed on for a while afterwards, talking 'of how fine it would be when <u>we</u> could hog all the conversation'. New acquaintances at this time included writers Lettice Cooper, Storm Jameson, Georges Simenon, Norah Lofts, and Vera Brittain, and the film actress Phyllis Calvert.

Snow was continually in the background, at PEN meetings, and advising her on her broadcast material. Despite all her family and work commitments, she still found time to help Snow when he decided to move from his cramped bachelor flat, and involve her (and both Ks) in his search for what he might consider to be suitable accommodation for his anticipated enhanced status. (He was expecting to publish further novels in the Lewis Eliot sequence as soon as the war was over.) Notwithstanding her admiration for him, Pamela felt he might be over-reaching himself when he put his name down for a set of rooms in Albany (the prestigious, originally bachelor, apartments in Piccadilly), and asked her if she approved. She told Kay Dick that she had answered as follows:

> (a) Yes. Because I don't know anyone to visit there and shall be able to put on immense side. (b) No. Because the [*sic*] Albany is artistically wrong for him. If anything happens to Snow <u>it will be too much money</u>. He'll be buying a house in Carlton House Terrace next. Perhaps I feel Snow shouldn't start behaving like a Great Man until he is generally acknowledged to <u>be</u> one. And Proust was born to the French equivalent of the Albany – Snow was not. The whole thing is, as Chesterton would say, the wrong shape.[1]

She was not to know that the service flat in Hyde Park Place, Bayswater, into which Snow eventually moved, was found and furnished for him by another woman in his life, Anne Seagrim, then his secretary at the English Electric Company, where Snow was now working as Director of Technical Personnel. In the 1960s, Snow sold his manuscripts and material relating to his work both as a scientist and as a writer to the Harry Ransom Humanities Resource Center in Austin,

Texas. He would also later deposit from time to time in his archive there much correspondence of a purely personal nature, some with an embargo precluding access until a certain time after the deaths of the people concerned. His letters from Anne Seagrim are in the latter category; his to her, now deposited in the Churchill Archives, Churchill College, Cambridge, are even more stringently embargoed, together with the typescript of her unpublished memoir, revealingly entitled *Partners and Lovers*.

Pamela believed herself then to be greatly missing Neil (whose unit had moved on to Burma), intellectually, emotionally and physically. On a warm February day, she wrote: 'I felt all day (the spring weather!) that I wanted to see a man – any man – so that I could feel female again. I am beginning to feel vaguely asexual, like a tree or a cabbage.' The following month, she felt 'restless and goatish', and a few days later, admitted: 'I am much troubled by the flesh – knowing it's no good, I find myself craving for excitement – any sort – as a substitute.' She tried to remind herself of her resolve during the worst times of the blitz – 'I shall never again complain about being <u>bored</u>. What Heaven to be bored instead of frightened!'

In March, there was a resumption of bombing raids, and again Pamela derived some comfort from her pessimism:

> I felt dog-tired & strained, & worried about leaving Mother & the babies when I go to town – yet damn it, I <u>anticipated</u> this, & never allowed myself the 'let's-tear-down-our-shelters-the-war's-nearly-over' optimism. Pessimism has served me well. If I've never had the fun & relief of sharing the exaltation of victories, I've never suffered quite so bad a let-down over setbacks as the optimists.

Her parents-in-law, however, evidently erred on the optimistic side, as, without any warning, towards the end of that month, she received a telegram informing her that they had just arrived in Glasgow from the West Indies, and peremptorily demanded that she meet them in London to help them find accommodation. She was then visited by two men from the Ministry of Health, explaining to her that there had been a smallpox case on the ship on which the Stewarts had travelled, and that there was a possibility therefore that they might be carriers of the disease. Father-in-law Morven, in search of a temporary home, was inclined to disregard medical advice, and assumed they could stay for the time being in Laleham; Pamela had to tell him that she absolutely forbade him to come near her children. She was to find later that her ban did not in any way trouble Morven or Jane. When they were out of quarantine, and settled back in London, they were still in no hurry to visit their son's family. 'I thought I'd ceased to expect common humanity from those two,' she recorded, 'but it still seems to me quite fantastic that they make <u>no</u> efforts to see their grandchildren.' (It would be more than two months before the world travellers did manage to negotiate the 20-odd miles from London to Laleham.)

Gradually as the Allies advanced through Germany, even Pamela began to believe that the war was in fact coming to an end. It was a wonderful spring; she wrote that she had never seen the lane in which she lived looking as lovely. But there were horrific revelations acting as a counterpoint. One warm evening, she walked with her mother along the riverside, enjoying the peacefulness, the crescent moon and 'the green and gold twilight in the water', but on her return home, they listened in to 'Ed Murrow's ghastly story of the overrunning of Buchenwald'. 'The <u>children</u>,' she expostulated, 'Christ! I would take parties of German citizens every day through Buchenwald, men <u>&</u> women, over 18. <u>Every day</u>.' Three days later, the radio and news-papers were full of 'more atrocious reports from the Belsen concen-tration camp'. This led her to recall her personal involvement with anti-Fascist organizations in the 1930s:

> What makes me sick is the way that, during the first six years of Hitler's government, gentlemen here would go & shoot, or hobnob in various ways, with the swine, <u>despite the constant exposure of condi-tions in the camps by the labour organisations here</u>. It makes me vomit to see how many people are regarding the exposure of Buchenwald & Belsen in the light of a <u>surprise</u>.

There were small landmarks, like the end of blackout on 23 April. 'We used to imagine, somehow,' she mused, 'that the lights would first go up on Peace Night. I suppose a little of the thrill has gone for the event, for most people. Not for me. I pray it will mean that my beau-tiful babies are safe from terror in the air.' At this time, she was approached to stand as Labour candidate for the Chelsea constituency in the postwar election which now at last seemed to becoming a reality. Reluctantly, she could not see how she could combine this with all her other commitments. When she wrote to Snow about her decision, he replied:

> I'm glad you're not standing for Chelsea. You wouldn't get in: & politics is no fun unless one does it professionally. And a writer of your gifts oughtn't to do it professionally. If you were offered a safe Labour seat, I admit that I should be torn.

And then came the hugely longed-for event, which Pamela dated in full at the top of the page:

> 1st May – 1945 – Tuesday
> **HITLER DEAD (?)**
> Last hours of Battle of Berlin. Russians take <u>Brandenburg</u>. Churchill preparing country for the finish.
> Missed first announcement of Hitler's death, for which Home Service was interrupted. Hitler said to have died of a stroke in the Chancellery at Berlin. The news was almost a shock. Twelve years of worry & misery caused by that swine, most of a continent in ruins through the triumph of an anachronism. I want to write about it but can't; not now. God help us to a quick end of the war <u>everywhere</u>, & God help us to make a proper future.

The following day, she went to London to see the documentary about the liberation of Buchenwald. Her diary entry, painful as it is to read, is important evidence of her deep humanity. 'The audience', she began, was 'dead silent with horror':

> I shall remember this film above all the events of this day. It wasn't the dead bodies, piles of bones, that made one sick. It was the living. Tottering, trotting skeletons in absurd striped clothes over their deformed & fleshless bodies. That's the ghastly crime – not to make a man into a beast, but to make him into a circus freak. It was unspeakable. Unspeakable.

Six days later, on the day of the German surrender, with the next day designed as 'VE Day', she was bewildered that she could not wholeheartedly join in the rejoicing. She was not alone in this; she quoted the leader-writer in the *Evening Standard* saying: 'One doesn't shout for joy when one has just escaped being murdered.' 'But not only that', she wrote, 'I feel we are all waving flags on top of a huge rubble-heap. The symbol of the war, to me, is that poor tottering mindless thing going through the compound at Buchenwald.'

Soon Pamela was experiencing a new and acute worry. Churchill made a speech shortly after VE-Day in which he stressed the need for continued friendship between the United Kingdom and the United States, 'but nothing of the sort', she noted, 'for Russia.' Churchill had continued with 'a warning that we must be prepared that the sort of democracy we had in mind was established in Europe, & that Fascism should not give way to another sort of totalitarianism.' Pamela's reaction was that:

> This is obviously directed against Russia, & makes me shudder with horror. How, after what we have been through, can anyone even contemplate the manufacturing of a rupture with USSR? I think I am praying for a miracle even harder than I prayed for it at the blackest moment of the war. After all we have been through, I cannot endure the thought that this peace may be momentary. We are, I think, a damned generation. [...]
>   The whole world is in hideous peril. Nor can I despise Virginia Woolf as I did, for making her own end because she couldn't face the future. I still think this is wrong, because no solution is right. That isn't the solution of ALL. But I can't be smug about it.

Her spirits were briefly raised on a visit to the National Gallery, where paintings, removed from London during the course of the war, had been rehung within a fortnight of VE-Day:

> [I] went to National Gallery where about 100 pictures have been replaced including the Piero Nativity, & the Arnolfini, the latter so beautiful[ly] cleaned it was like a handful of jewels. This was the event of peace I'd most longed for, & it lifted my heart.

Despite naturally, given her party allegiance, hoping for a Labour victory in the post-war election, she still retained sympathy for Winston Churchill. After he had made what she described as a 'pathetic election speech', she acknowledged that he had been 'a great war leader', but that, 'now he is tired, & has nothing to say. Wish they'd give him a dukedom & let him rest.' Although polling day was on 5 July, the results were not announced for three weeks, in order to include votes from servicemen abroad. On 26 July, she 'spent whole day listening hourly to election results, my knees giving under me with excitement', and she then implored: 'Now, for God's sake, I hope Labour does the job it promised, & does it toughly.'

No sooner had the jubilant post-election parties come to an end than, in this see-saw summer, there was further cause for distress. On 6 August, following a broadcast, she went as usual to the BBC Club for drinks, and there met the newsreader Frank Phillips, who told her that the Allies had a 'new atomic bomb, no bigger than a biscuit can, force 1000 times that of 10-ton bomb'. The 'thought of it', she wrote, 'makes me vomit.' When confirmation came through that an atom bomb had been dropped on Hiroshima, and a second on Nagasaki, signalling the end of the war in the Far East, her personal concerns for her husband warred with her abhorrence. Nevertheless, when reading of the aftermath of the bomb, her final judgment was that it had been 'damnable to use it, & there can be no moral justification. I am sure of that, and ashamed.'

Despite her deep concern about the international and domestic political situations, Pamela's conversations and correspondence with Snow at this time mainly centred on their work. When writing, she still began 'Dear Snow', as he had directed her to do when they first exchanged letters, but he now addressed her as 'Dear Pam' and signed 'With love, CPS'. Although she had not started another novel, he was in the course of writing *The Masters*, which dealt with the election of a new Master of the deliberately unnamed Cambridge college of which Lewis Eliot is a Fellow (but which is universally agreed to be based on Christ's), and Pamela was flattered that he sought her advice on the draft chapters he sent her. She singled out his response to one of her letters in August as being particularly 'charming'. Snow had written:

> I was delighted with your letter. I don't think I've ever told you – I'm excessively articulate in some ways and dumb in a few – how much your support has carried me through one of the darkest patches in my life. If you hadn't been scheming to keep me going as a writer, I shouldn't have had anything to give me hope at all. I shan't forget. When the time is appropriate, I shall say so in a public place. [...]
>
> I wish I could help you in return, my dear. Don't hesitate to ask. I don't often show you unselfish inspiration – perhaps no man is likely to – but I'm willing to learn. And I think I am no more self-centred than you are.[2]

Pamela was unaware that he was also continuing to use Anne Seagrim as a sounding-post, as he had done in the past, and that there was yet another woman with whom Snow had an on-off emotional relationship to whom he was sending his manuscripts for comment at this time. The aristocratic Anne Whyte had been a colleague in the Ministry of Labour, and, at the end of the war, was awaiting a transfer to the Political Division of the Control Commission for Germany. Before she left for Lubbecke, he had asked her to read a novel then entitled *Charles March*, which he had written before the war but then had decided to postpone its publication. Whyte's criticisms tended to be forthright: she boldly took 'Percy', as she invariably called him, to task about his usage of words she saw as pretentious, an example being her admonition that: 'You simply cannot talk of "fundament". In normal usage it means the human behind or arse [...].'[3] Her overall opinion of the novel was not quite as totally admiring as Snow doubtless would have wished: 'It is still not a moving book [...]. But it is absolutely absorbing. The great mind is there, but the great heart not quite.' Her reaction to *The Masters* was more personal: she protested that his characterization of Lady Muriel, wife of the dying Master, Vernon Royce, had clearly been based on her mother, and thus the Royces' daughter Joan on herself:

> Lady Muriel is pure <u>stealing</u> – I thought I had made it clear that she was copyright. Even some of my best verbal gems are shamelessly incorporated. [...] I look forward to the day when Mama reads this book – to see if the portrait strikes home.[4]

CPS did later confirm that the character of Joan Royce had been based on Anne Whyte, whom he described as 'a young woman of the time [...] clever, strong-willed'.[5]

Meanwhile at this time, Pamela might have been able to make rational judgments as far as Snow's work was concerned, but her own emotions were confused. She constantly wrote in her diary about her longing for Neil's return, and her anguish when, despite the end of the war with Japan, he had not been able to obtain his discharge. Neil had written to her in October that he was 'a bit scared of being sent to Indonesia & [felt] his duty is to his family rather than to Dutch oil interests', an argument which evidently did not carry any weight with the military authorities. Yet she was increasingly drawn to Snow; after one of their frequent meetings, she recorded finding him 'fascinating as ever, in that "voice under the moss" manner'.

An extract from Pamela's lengthy diary entry for the Heinemann party early in November gives evidence of how rapidly the publishing world was recovering from the difficulties of the war years, and of how she and Snow were now becoming a focus of attention:

> Bizarre affair – packed like the cabin in the Marx Bros. film. Met Gerald Kersh – a wild, rather pathetic type, half-seas over, his noisily-glamorous wife, Brophy, Clemence Dane, Barbara Noble, Lord Huntingdon (Red Viscount Hastings that was), Georgette Heyer, etc. Kay got dreadfully tight, & when Snow arrived, overwhelmed us both with loving & embarrassing idiocies. So drunk Snow had to get her on the tube – 'in the general direction of Hampstead'.

Afterwards Pamela dined 'at Veglio's[6] with Snow & Harry Hoff – all delightful, witty & very slightly phantasmagoric'. She arrived back home 'with the elation that covers a *cafard*', the latter perhaps resulting from her guiltily recalling the plight of her husband. 'Hope & pray', she ended this entry, 'my dear Neil won't have to go to Indonesia.' But the following month, she received a 'letter from my darling Neil to say he is in Sourabaya – went into action immediately on landing.' 'It is a bloody disgrace', she wailed, 'a Labour govt. sending British troops – assisted by Jap – to quell a National Independence movement.'

Snow's grand plan for publishing his sequence of semi-autobiographical novels chronologically had now received a setback. The above-mentioned *Charles March* should have been the second of the series; it was the story of Lewis Eliot's years as a trainee barrister in London, and his friendship with the scion of a wealthy Jewish banking family. The eponymous central character was based on Snow's friend, Richard (Dick) Cohen. March/Cohen falls out with his autocratic father when he decides to give up a promising career at the Bar in order to become a doctor, a profession he believes to be of greater use to society. On the brink of publication, the blow had fallen; Snow was often insensitive about family relationships, and he evidently had not comprehended the enduring bond between Cohen and his father despite their differences of opinion. Pamela recorded receiving a letter from a 'deadly worried' Snow, telling her about the problem:

The March family are objecting to my publishing "Charles March"
while the old gentleman is still alive (he is in the eighties, but pretty
hearty). [...] I must try to persuade them, but as you can imagine from
the story, there are a good many deep psychological currents flowing.
If the worst happens, I shall have to hold "Charles March" back &
produce another No. 2. "The Masters" is excellent as No. 3, but
wouldn't do for No. 2. It's hard: but better men have had to fare worse.[7]

It seems significant that he refers to the 'March family' as though they
were more real to him than the Cohen family (admittedly this might
have been a slip of the pen), but this would not be the only time when
his lack of perception with regard to the effect of his work on the originals of the characters portrayed would manifest itself. As will be seen,
his substitute 'No. 2' – *The Light and the Dark* – was to prove even
more distressing for the protagonist's family. Snow did in fact have to
promise not to publish the 'Charles March' novel until after the death
of Dick Cohen's father, and Pamela sympathized with him about this.

Yet again, Pamela's main concerns at this time were domestic; she
had been trying to arrange a move back to London. Her father-in-law
had dragged her to see grandiose and quite unaffordable houses with
the idea that they might share the accommodation, an idea that she
could only envisage agreeing to as a last resort. However, on 'a fantastic day' in December, she had a letter from the 'Chelsea Housing
people' offering her a house in what twenty-first century estate agents
would call, 'the highly desirable Cheyne Row'. Lapsing, unusually into
an American expression, she said that the house was 'swell, but a bit
small: but as we can have it for £2. 16s. p.w., can only accept'. Her
finances were, as it happened, in a reasonably healthy state, thanks to
the popularity of *The Trojan Brothers*; in addition to the advance already
received from Michael Joseph, she had been delighted in August to
receive royalties of £400 for this novel (compared with a cheque for
£20 from Macmillan the same month for the American edition of
Winter Quarters). Further, disappointed as she had been with the film
version when David Farrar invited her to the Trade Show, she did
console herself with the thought that she could regard the £1000 she
had received for the film rights as 'Heartbalm'.

So 1946 dawned with a return to the Chelsea so beloved of Pamela
and her mother. But the first month there was 'a perfect misery of
cold', with the boiler constantly breaking down, and the children

ill and fretful. Her father-in-law came twice, ostensibly to help with the move, but chose to spend the time telling her at great length that he was contemplating suicide, a threat she dismissed as self-dramatisation, while she 'worked and <u>worked</u>!' Fortunately, she was able to call on extensive help from her former ARP colleague, Ron, but even *his* practical skills were unequal to the vagaries of the boiler. Over and over again, he believed that he had fixed it, only for it to go out again as soon as he had left. For the first month in 6 Cheyne Row, Pamela wailed that the boiler was driving her frantic: 'I eat, sleep and dream Boiler.' But one evening, after a day spent 'washing, cooking, fighting with boiler, etc.', it came into her head that she wanted to write another book about Helena, her creation as Claud Pickering's stepmother in *Too Dear for My Possessing*, and within a day or so, she had found a title, *An Avenue of Stone*, and started to write it. There would be a fourth novel, entitled *A Summer to Decide*, in which Helena and Claud Pickering would feature. Helena is central only to *An Avenue of Stone*, and she dies in an early chapter of the final novel, but the force of Pamela's portrayal of her led to *Too Dear for My Possessing*, *An Avenue of Stone* and *A Summer to Decide* to have become known as 'the Helena trilogy', rather than, with *Winter Quarters*, 'the Claud Pickering quartet'.

Pamela's response to the end of the war is mirrored in the early chapters of *An Avenue of Stone*. Claud Pickering, reinstated as narrator, has returned from active service to a posting in the War Office. He is therefore in England on VE-Day, and walks with his step-sister Charmian 'slowly along the streets where flags hung limply beneath a thunderous sky'. Claud reflects that:

> It was quiet where we were, all the celebrations, I supposed, being effected in the West End [...]. I felt unaccountably depressed, my spirits at rock-bottom [...]. There was a quietude in the world, or so it seemed to me, more ominous than the noise of war.[8]

An Avenue of Stone would not be finished for nearly six months, mainly because Neil was at last on his way home. In the interim, Pamela was continuing to spend time with Snow. Being based back in town, she could return some of his dinner invitations; after he had come to dinner at her house one evening, she recorded that 'a talk with Snow is always like a current of some magical energy'. Dining together soon afterward at the Connaught Hotel, he mapped out her new 'Helena book', and it had been, she wrote, a 'delightful evening'. However the following day, she reflected that: 'Every evening with Snow leaves a curious hangover-feeling of talk cut too soon, a hundred ideas unexchanged, jokes unmade, thoughts unexpressed.' Possibly again feeling a sense of guilt after she re-read this entry, a note was added (clearly at a later date): 'It has been such an intellectual starvation since N. went away.'

Pamela was to spend very little time with Snow for the rest of the year; unknown to her, his relationship with Anne Whyte had reached a crucial phase. Whyte had been in attendance at the Nuremberg Trials (she sent Snow a copy of her discerning observations on the appearance and demeanour of the main defendants)[9], but had endeavoured to see him on her short leaves home. In a letter to Snow in March 1946, she dropped her usual bantering tone, writing:

> Dearest, it meant so much to me to see you again for longer than a few hours. It was valuable beyond words because it proved to me how much you mean to me. Over the last year, I have tried quite hard to get away from you, & I believed I could do this. I did succeed for a while, but I now know it was false, & I know also that I did not really want to. I love you now as I have loved you for sometime. I don't think anything can change that. [...] All I know now is that, as far as it is humanly possible to know anything, I love you forever.[10]

The same month, Neil had come home to Pamela, to the son he had left as a baby and to the daughter he had never seen, but, after the first euphoria, like so many forces' personnel now demobilized, he found it difficult to adjust to civilian life, and sought work in vain. He was low-spirited most of the time, and as Pamela continued to write her new novel, passages convey his state of mind as well as her own. A Stewart family outing, a tram-ride around South London, was cut short by Neil's despair. Pamela wrote in her diary:

> N. felt sick, said everyone was dwarfed & deformed & mad, & refused to accept my own lively vision of the bombed, dusty & decayed streets. N. is in poor health, I think: his nervous tic is pronounced, he seems to see everything through a veil of dust.

This experience echoes Claud Pickering's feelings as he contemplates his future when his army service comes to an end:

All in all, the interest of life seemed suddenly to have run dry, and I could not imagine from what new source it might spring again. It was not, indeed, a good world for renewals, was like a patient awakening sickly from a major operation, still leaden with the anaesthetic. Outside the slow-waking world of England (here a finger moves, here a leg twitches, an eye slews round in a paralysed face) was the universe of chaos, of hunger, of displaced persons, of the great crocodile of the dispossessed moving from nowhere in particular to nowhere that bore a name, but always moving, moving. (*Avenue*, p.133)

Back in 6 Cheyne Row, the hostility between Pamela's mother and husband resurfaced, and Pamela as usual was piggy-in-the-middle. During what she described in her diary as a 'run-in with Mother [...] re misery in this house', she told Amy that she wasn't 'going to be dragged about as by wild horses between her & N.' Nevertheless, the next day Pamela suffered 'an intense *cafard* – feeling that I was locked inside my own mind & couldn't look outwards on other people – all things external to myself no longer real.' In June, she and Neil were in no mood to join in the Victory Parade celebrations, despite going to see the crowds the night before. She wrote that it had seemed:

> [...] like a nightmare – people milling along glassy-eyed, squatting on the kerbs for a night-long wait, sailors rigging hammocks to trees and lamp-posts, Bobby-Soxers wearing red, white & blue clowns' hats, or cellophane bonnets inscribed "Squeeze Me". It is a purely worked-up hysteria. What we want in this, still sick & rocking world is another National Day of Prayer, rather than a wild junketing in the middle of starvation. Long bread queues in the King's Rd this morning didn't add to the charm. The whole thing, without Russia, is a great cynical farce.

Perhaps it was a yearning to portray an insouciant character who could contend with the post-war era that had led Pamela back to Helena, the arch-chameleon. The young Claud's memories of his tyrannical stepmother which open *Too Dear for My Possessing* are of her as a force of nature, a former Irish music-hall singer, 'queer and handsome in her black way', who, in dying her hair 'yellow as broom [...] had made herself not hideous, but barbaric and magnificent' (*Too Dear*, p.14). By the end of that novel, Claud's father has died, and Helena has undergone a transformation after her marriage to the wealthy Daniel Archer, the father of Claud's lost love, Cecil:

Imitative as a monkey, she caught the manners and bearing of his friends, had smoothed the superfluous richness from her speech and had, in fact, almost perfectly disguised herself as something she was not. (*Too Dear*, p.264)

When Archer later receives a knighthood, Claud's reaction is that:

So Helena, Heaven help us, is Lady Archer. [...] Termagant Helena, tamed to dark colours and matrons' hats! Magnificent Helena who had run out in red slippers on to the Dyver shouting and screaming after a boat-load of boys and who was now wife, hostess and Lady with a capital L. (*Too Dear*, p.291)

Class consciousness is an important theme throughout the Helena trilogy, but it comes to the forefront in *An Avenue of Stone*, which opens with Claud observing Helena grandly presiding at a formal dinner-party, and declaring '"As a class, [...] we are doomed"'. She indicates 'consciousness of her absurdity only by a bright flash in [her stepson's] direction' (p.7). Claud muses on his way home that:

When I first knew Helena she was outside class, something apart from any social category; not a Juno at the Palace, or a Minerva at the High Table, or a Diana in the hunting field, but perhaps an Iris, a professional entertainer, in demand at all the best masques. (p.22)

Helena would, of course, have been thought thoroughly *déclassée* in the milieu in which she now moved, had it not been for 'the freakish and magnificent match' (p.22), she had made with her second husband. She is now surrounded by sycophants, who sponge off her, despite their feelings of class superiority. However, they turn on her after Daniel Archer's death, when she acquires as a protégé a young man called John Field, formerly a subaltern in Claud's battery. Their spokeswoman, Charmian's atrocious mother-in-law Mrs Sholto, archly describes him in Helena's hearing as a '*sigisbee*, a *cavaliere servente*', presumably in the hope that Helena would be unfamiliar with either term (p.122). Helena delightedly afterwards tells Claud that she would indeed not have known what Mrs Sholto was talking about, had the former word, meaning a young admirer or lover, not been the answer to a clue in a crossword puzzle she had recently completed (p.125). Pamela manages to wring further dry humour out of the class that

Mrs Sholto represents with regard to her reaction to Labour's victory in the post-war election. Charmian tells Claud her mother-in-law '"was really upset; I believe she expected the mob to break in at any moment and hang her on a lamp-post. She took me aside and said, in a trembly voice, *This is worse than losing the war.*"' In response to Claud's reply in the form of an abusive comment, Charmian laughs in agreement, but continues:

> 'Oh yes, yes [...] but from her point of view it's logical. If Hitler had ever got here she'd have collaborated like fun. You know, my hairdresser told me that during the worst of the invasion scares one of his customers came in for a perm. She said, "If the Germans do come, I think it's up to us all to look our best."' (pp.151-52)

In the course of writing the final part of the novel, she and Neil had had to arrange for Amy to convalesce after treatment for various ailments in a residential hotel (they dubbed such establishments as 'Sausage Castles'). When eventually they decided on 'a fairly hopeful one', the Imperial in South Kensington, Pamela commented that she felt 'that the British Empire is beginning to look like S. Kensington – respectably shabby grandeur falling into dust & rubble'. (Amy's 'rest cure' was to prove to be no respite for Pamela, as her mother insisted on returning home most afternoons.) In the final book of the trilogy, the fate of being consigned permanently to a similar residence is suggested to Charmian by Claud to solve the problem of Mrs Sholto's finances now being reduced to the point when she can no longer keep up appearances in a flat in Kensington with a living-in maid:

> 'The private hotels are full of Mrs Sholtos, all living angrily on the memory of grandeur. The lounges are full of Jew-haters, Negro-haters, Indian-haters, trade-union haters and daughter-in-law haters. She'd be happy enough.'"

It is possible that Pamela partly based Mrs Sholto on her own mother-in-law in revenge for Jane Stewart's self-centredness and her continuing disparaging attitude towards her and her mother.

It is also likely that Pamela's current emotional turmoil regarding Snow spilled over to her description of the key relationship between Claud and Helena in *An Avenue of Stone*. In a fine, lengthy Jamesian passage (the full paragraph, part of which I quote below, almost occupies a whole page), attempting to analyse his feelings for his mother-in-law, Claud recognizes 'a tormenting emotion that lies between friendship and love':

> It may exist between man and man, or between woman and woman, but, as it has some undefined sexual element, it exists more frequently between man and woman. It is a torment of understanding that can have no physical expression. For a lifetime it may remain unexpressed; if it seeks the normal expression of love it is ruined. It is, if one must give a name to it, the highest form of friendship, and is mysterious in origin. [...] Each may be partnered in complete happiness by another person; but were he to lose the friend with whom he shares this third emotion his life would lose, irretrievably, a shade of colour, a degree of light.

Further, some time after this book had been completed and sent to the publishers, in a rare diary entry regarding her self-identification with any of her characters, Pamela admitted to an empathy with her chief protagonist:

> Obsession with my <u>looks</u> continues – have the wildest regrets for my twenties – keep feeling – don't know what – a loss – something missed. At 34 I feel as Helena felt at 67. So much of that book I actually felt with every nerve. Find myself now a mass of violent emotions, all utterly false in basis, as they can go as suddenly as they came, between one sentence & another.

What Helena wants at 67 is to feel that her life is not over. She knows her attachment to John Field is unequally reciprocated, but she tells Claud: 'This is the last important thing that will ever happen to me' (p.131). Field is weak, but nevertheless representative of the many thousands of ex-servicemen experiencing problems of post-war adjustment, and Helena throws him a lifeline in the way of accommodation and some financial support. She tolerates his acquaintance with one of her former husband's mistresses, and even encourages his friendship with Naomi, a young woman of his own age, on the basis that they are too poor to marry and anyway unsuited (she even considers that Naomi might be a more appropriate wife for Claud). But eventually an aunt of John Field provides the means for him to marry Naomi, and in his typically cowardly fashion, he does not tell Helena about his marriage until it has taken place, and then only by letter,

ending: 'Do be pleased, Helena. God bless. Gratefully and affectionately, Johnny' (p.267).

Claud sums up Helena's reaction in the final chapter, and again one
wonders if he is articulating the author's thoughts about herself:

> The sense of being 'left behind' may never again arise from any one
> specific thing; but I believe it comes inevitably with the understand-
> ing that one has grown old. For years we cling to the belief that we
> are young for our age, that young men and women appreciate us far
> more than our contemporaries do. Our minds are strong, and our legs
> also. We are still learning, we can still change. And then, suddenly, we
> realize that the marchers are passing us by, and we are taken by pure
> panic. Soon we shall be alone upon the interminable road, seeing in the
> distance only the jolting, merging backs of those that continue on.
> (p.275)

Pamela had her usual doubts about the novel when she was typing up
the manuscript and making final adjustments, but was later reassured
when she received a 'most heartening' letter from Robert Lusty, then
the Managing Director of Michael Joseph. He told her that their most
highly regarded reader with 'a considerable name as a critic' had highly
praised the subtlety of the novel, which he had found 'admirably
written', and further that 'its psychological analysis is most perceptive
and expressed with frequent brilliance of phrase'. Lusty ended his
letter by congratulating her 'upon what is quite clearly a notable piece
of work'.[12]

In August 1946, Pamela and Neil were able to take a fortnight's
holiday together in Belgium with their son, leaving their daughter
with Amy and Kalie. They stayed with friends in Bruges, and despite
feeling 'still raw in my nerves', she was able to revisit her favourite
places. One day, she recorded:

> I went off alone to N. Dame & St. Sauveur. Sat on Dyver, & time just
> passed. After supper, Guigui [their friends' daughter] sang for a while,
> & then [we] went to café near Port d'Ostende & ate wonderful cream
> cakes & ices with thick cream. All rather like a fairytale.

However, the following day, her demons returned; she and Neil went
for a 'long and rather nightmarish walk in the dark, discussing our
problems'.

While Pamela and Neil may have had the common difficulties of many other couples attempting to remake their lives after the disruption of war, those problems undoubtedly included their domestic ménage. Years later, when she included a loving tribute to her mother in *Important to Me*, stressing Amy's beauty and great sense of fun, she admitted nevertheless that, on Neil's return, Amy's continual presence had played a significant part in the deterioration of their marriage. 'She had had me (and the children) too long to herself', she wrote, 'and I think she became jealous' (*Important*, p.121). One evening, after going with Neil to see *Claudia and David*, a then very popular film about the travails but ultimate triumph over adversity of a young married couple, Pamela evidently derived no satisfaction from what she described as its whimsy and mawkishness. 'What stuff!!', she continued, 'What an artificial slant on life.' Additionally, since Neil had not been able to find work, she was now struggling to maintain a family of five; she couldn't help being envious during a visit to Kathleen Farrell's parents' home, later recording the impression there of 'money, money everywhere, pots of it'.

Among her correspondence when they returned from Belgium had been a 'disagreeable surprise [...] in shape of filthy, poison-pen card [...], pretty intimate in detail', the first for ten years, but evidently sent from the same but still unknown source responsible for the missives she had received before her marriage. Pamela and Neil put the card in the hands of the local police, to no avail, and she continued to brood about it. Dining with Snow soon afterward again at Veglio's, she recorded that she had felt 'sad and puddingy & probably bored him'. It was typical of her to take the blame for an unsatisfactory meeting; the fault might well have been with her dinner companion, since yet another of Snow's relationships had come to an abrupt end, and he was likely to have taken this badly. Anne Whyte had just written to him to say that she had decided to marry a cousin, despite adding: 'Percy dearest, I shall love you always in some way.'[13]

Pamela's main solace continued to be her work, this time an ambitious foray into the genre of extended literary criticism. She had decided to write an essay on Thomas Wolfe, the author she had so admired in her youth, and relished what time she could allow herself for research. After a rewarding afternoon in the Reading Room of the British Museum, she wrote that: 'Wolfe's character is beginning to obsess me – I dream about him.' As she neared the finish of the first draft of the essay, she reflected: 'Work, when I get down to it, is so satisfying & invigorating, like a great reviving drink. Wish I could get drunk on it more often. Tom Wolfe still obsesses me.' The publisher, A.S. Frere, who had recently become the managing director of Heinemann's, was very encouraging and persuaded her to expand the essay into a monograph to be published by his company. Although Wolfe had died in 1938, there had been no similar study then published, even in the United States, and, to Pamela's delight, Frere sent her manuscript to Maxwell Perkins, Wolfe's renowned editor at Scribners for comment, and it received his approval.

1946 ended unhappily. Throughout December, Pamela was dreading Christmas, with Amy hysterical, and Neil either monosyllabic or subject to outbursts of rage, and her own worries about the cost of it all. Christmas Eve was, she wrote, the worst for years:

I was in an agony of misery all day [...]. Shops this year laden with fruit and luxuries for millionaires only. Christmas seems for the majority not a religious festival, but just an orgy of eating, drinking, & spending, spending, spending.

When she summed up the events of 'rather a bad, frustrating year', with 'too many nightmares by day & by night' and 'domestic affairs in a foul mess', she cryptically added: 'I feel I have drawn away from the thing that sustained me during the war.' It is almost certainly not a 'thing' to which she was referring, but a person, Charles Percy Snow.

CHAPTER 8

Chill Outside and Within

THE FIRST THREE months of 1947 are still remembered for the severity of the weather throughout Great Britain, and the extreme cold compounded Pamela's state of misery, as a typical diary entry in mid-January attests:

> A thoroughly beastly day. I froze out in incredible cold, & came home chilled to find N. in process of some imbecile row with Mother. All <u>entirely</u> unnecessary. I was furious with him, as Mother got dispropor-tionately upset, & I had my work mucked up for rest of day. Managed to get a chapter [of *Thomas Wolfe*] typed, but was thoroughly worried & depressed. It is <u>damnable</u>. Sometimes there seems to be no con-sideration for me, & my plea that a pleasant atmosphere shall be main-tained if only that I may earn money in peace goes for nothing.

Urban areas suffered as much as the countryside under several inches of snow for long periods; in Cheyne Row, the pipes constantly froze, and Pamela could only work with the greatest difficulty by candle-light because the hours of electricity were drastically cut.

However, she did manage to finish her *Thomas Wolfe* treatise, while sorrowing: 'Dear Tom, I shall miss him. But I haven't done him justice. I shall be as nervous till I hear from Frere as a young writer submitting her first novel.' Her anxiety stemmed from her occasional fretting about her lack of tertiary education; on re-reading Cyril Connolly's *Enemies of Promise* at this time, she revealed:

> I felt, as I always do with stuff of this type, first humiliated because I am so relatively illiterate & haven't been to a university, then stimu-lated – 'Damn your eyes, I'll still write you off your fat feet!' Tom Wolfe & I have many emotions in common.

Her *Thomas Wolfe: A Critical Study* was published in October and received reasonably good reviews in the *Times Literary Supplement* and the *Spectator*. She was to be particularly delighted when, following its publication in the United States (under the title, *Hungry Gulliver*) in January of the following year, the reviewer in the *New Yorker* described the book as 'an extremely acute appraisal of Thomas Wolfe by an English critic'.

In the meantime, Pamela was being offered increasingly prestigious work as a literary critic, although one of these assignments began inauspiciously. The British Council had commissioned her to write the booklet on Ivy Compton-Burnett in their *Writers and Their Work* series. Having received an invitation from the author which Pamela assumed was for a preliminary discussion, she recorded that first encounter in her diary with some dismay:

> Went to dinner with Ivy Compton-Burnett in evening. Started off badly by arriving 30 minutes late, due to a misreading of her card. She lives in a flat in one of those Kensington Baronial horrors with Margaret Jourdain, who is like a Mervyn Peake drawing. [...] a bizarre, nightmarish evening. God knows how I went down – probably with a thud.

She amplified the description of this and other meetings in a chapter of her memoir. There had been little or no opportunity to talk about the proposed work on the first occasion. The eccentric 'Miss Compton-Burnett' (as Pamela always referred to her, until she became a Dame of the British Empire), Margaret Jourdain and an unnamed female friend scarcely addressed a word to her, although 'there was a good deal of gossip about displeasing creatures the three of them met, in some place or other' (*Important*, p.190). The next meeting, a formal tea, was equally frustrating as Compton-Burnett attempted to steer Pamela toward her own chosen direction to dictate which works she wanted included in the survey. A third meeting, however, yielded 'a source of excitement': in answer to a question from Pamela about how contemporary critics had viewed her work, Compton-Burnett brought her a large cardboard box full of reviews, but then disconcertingly began to talk – to herself. Pamela recalled: 'As I leafed roughly through [the reviews], I heard her talking busily above my head, but not to me. It was an uncanny experience'. She did not let these more or less hostile encounters alter her opinion of the writer's abilities. 'Whatever Dame Ivy's personal relations with myself (and I think she would have disdained admitting to have had any whatsoever)', she wrote, 'I admired her as an artist inordinately. She was a great original' (*Important*, p.191). Perhaps not surprisingly, due to the combative nature of her subject, her esteem was not reciprocated. Compton-Burnett wrote to a friend with regard to the finished product that Pamela Hansford Johnson 'works in such haste that her words cease to have a meaning and a mind seems to be going to waste'.[1] Ivy's biographer, Hilary Spurling, considers this judgment harsh, more sympathetically describing the essay as 'a dashing affair, full of enthusiasm if at times inaccurate and understandably nervous in tone'.[2]

At the other end of the literary spectrum, an initial approach was made to Pamela by Metro-Goldwyn-Mayer to write an unspecified 'film story'. When she was invited to Claridge's to discuss the project with the MGM executive, Kenneth McKenna, she discovered that they were planning a sequel to their Academy Award-winning wartime film, *Mrs Miniver*. They could scarcely have found a less willing writer; in 1942, Pamela's opinion of the original film had been that it was 'a glossy, fake bit of slop', which, she suggested, should have been subtitled: '"War in S. Kensington"'. Furthermore, as she recorded on this occasion, McKenna 'didn't mention money – said he was looking for someone who would be "immediately fired by" the idea. How he hopes to fire any English writer on a beastly job like that <u>without</u> mentioning dollars, God knows. I came home cross & bothered.' She heard nothing further from the film company, although the sequel did go ahead some years later, with Ronald Millar as one of the co-writers.[3] However, a writing credit on this film would have scarcely enhanced her literary standing. Halliwell's Film Guide considers *The Miniver Story* (1950) to be: 'A glum sequel […] with the dauntless heroine finally succumbing to a glossy but fatal disease.'[4]

What may have seemed a more routine assignment, reviewing books for the *Sunday Chronicle*, was also to prove fraught. Pamela had been delighted and disbelieving when she was contacted by the editor, Reginald Simpson, and offered twenty guineas for each column, four times the fee she received from *John o' London's Weekly*, and, according the Retail Price Index, the equivalent of roughly £695 in 2014.[5] The introduction of a new book critic was given considerable prominence in the edition of 6 April 1947. Pamela was announced as being 'herself a top-rank author of 11 novels', who would be 'well-known to readers from the film version of her recent best-seller "The Trojan Brothers"'. Broadcasts which gained her 'wide popularity' were also mentioned, but Pamela was unhappy with the whole heading of her first column, which she thought 'nasty & vulgar'. Below the introduction, the first headline stated (one feels, with some condescension): 'A Woman Reviews Three Women's Novels', and the subheading was *This Is Not Written For The Squeamish*. 'Damned if I'd do it', she confided to her diary, 'if I didn't want the money so much.'

She was, however, pleased when she was invited to extend the range of her reviews to genres other than the novel. Her entire column of 20 April was dedicated to a review of the diaries of Count Ciano, Mussolini's son-in-law, edited by Malcolm Muggeridge. Ciano, as Pamela explained to the readers of the *Sunday Chronicle*, had been the Foreign Minister of Italy until the tide of the war had turned away from the Axis powers in 1943, whereupon he made overtures towards the Allies. Some nine months after his dismissal from the Italian government, Ciano was executed for treason by the Germans on his father-in-law's orders. 'The book,' Pamela wrote, 'is an invaluable contribution to history and most fascinating reading':

> The thing that emerges most strongly is the mediocrity of the Fascist leaders. Against a background of intrigue, palace-skulduggery, bedroom farce and place-seeking, the "tattered lackey" Mussolini struts and shouts and claims to follow in the tradition of the Borgias.

The headline on this occasion was more arresting; it was 'A Muzzled Hardy and a Foaming Laurel', a reference to Ciano's account of an interview between Hitler and Mussolini, with 'the Fuehrer talking, talking, talking, and [el Duce] silently fuming, looking constantly at his wrist-watch, and unable to get a word in edgeways.'

Later, Pamela's column varied in size at the whim of the editor; she was used to having as much space as she wished in the *Liverpool Post* and uncut full-page spreads in *John o' London's Weekly*, and she found this interference irksome. Initially she was also displeased with the quality of the novels she was sent, but later it would seem that she was able to make her own suggestions as to the books she wished to review. Within the then relatively small community of literary

London, it was inevitable that sometimes, whether deliberately or coincidentally, an author might be personally known to the reviewer, who might then let friendship or animosity colour the critique. In 1945, Pamela had articulated her dilemma in the former case while preparing a review of *The Human Face*, by her mentor and now close friend, John Brophy:

> Reviewed Brophy's book in evening – a thoroughly trying job. It is so difficult for me. He's so kind & good I hate to hurt him in any way – but what sort of violence should I do (a) my reputation (b) my conscience, if I gave it a straightforward boost?

I have not been able to trace this review, so possibly she made some excuse so as not to file it.

A contrary instance concerns the work of P.H. Newby, then a young man on the threshold of his career as a novelist. Before meeting him, Pamela had reviewed his first novel, *A Journey Into the Interior*, in *John o' London's Weekly* (28 December 1945), and had been very impressed:

> P.H. Newby is a writer interesting enough to cause me to be careful of my adjectives; this is a new and most striking talent, and I have a feeling that it will not be long before Mr. Newby's books are discussed whenever the modern novel is a topic of conversation.

By 1947, they had met several times, since Newby was now included in the literary circle of the two Ks; Pamela recorded her impression of him in one of her succinct character portraits in her diary:

> I like Newby – he has a fine brow & dark eyes. Though his face goes to nothing below the nose. He is v. nervous & jumpy, & tends to conceal nerves by a sort of tutorial dogmatism, but he is really very sympathetic & his eyes are full of kindness.

But Snow was hostile to what he considered to be Newby's rapturous reception by some critics (his first novel had won the Society of Authors' Somerset Maugham Prize), and Pamela may have been influenced by Snow's bias to make her approval of Newby's second novel, *Agents and Witnesses*, more ambiguous. While still retaining the same adjective to describe him, she wrote in her column of 11 May that the new novel by 'that extremely striking young writer, Mr. P.H. Newby, appears to me full of things concealed between the lines. What they

are I don't really know. If there's a message, I didn't discover it.'
Damning with faint praise, she ended: 'It is, however, a good enough
story without one.'[6]

An Avenue of Stone was published in May, to a mixed reception, which
seemed to depend on whether the reviewer was enchanted or exasperated by Helena. Ralph Straus, in the *Sunday Times*, commented
that: 'Old ladies (in fiction) can be at once pathetic figures and the
greatest fun,' and that in the 'rich portrait' of Helena that Pamela had
painted, the reader 'cannot help watching her antics with an amused
affection'. Marie Hannah's review in the *Times Literary Supplement*
started similarly with general remarks about 'the elderly beauty who
cannot quench her desire for love' being 'a stock figure of fiction', but
came to the opposite conclusion to Straus, when she judged that, in
this novel:

> Sympathy with the heroine could have been won only by an extraor-
> dinarily vivid and vital presentation of someone who was an exception
> to all the rules. This Miss Hansford Johnson does not achieve. Judged
> by her conversation and behaviour, Helena is a tiresome, egocentric and
> devouring personality from whom it would be a duty to flee at any price.

Pamela did not, however, seem particularly downcast by the moderate reviews, perhaps because she had much to distract her.

Her feeling of estrangement from Snow had continued. He had left
in February for two months in America, on behalf of English Electric,
and Pamela seems only to have received one letter from him during
that time. On his return, he gave her a present of '3 pairs of American nylons!!!' for which she was indeed most grateful, but their meetings for several months were few, and usually either in the company
of other friends or at home with her family. On one occasion when she
and Neil were expecting him to come to dinner, she wrote in her diary
that at 5.45 p.m., Snow 'rang up & said he was in bed with lumbago.
N. answered the phone. I rang up to condole, but couldn't get a reply.
Odd. Can only think he "stood us up" which is a poor show!' When
Snow did come home to tea with her after a PEN meeting, she mentioned that she had been finding him 'quietly infuriating politically
since he went to America'.

The frosty atmosphere at home was also continuing throughout the
year. Pamela recorded persistent *cafards*, some of which threatened to

overwhelm her. 'I am worried', she wrote in July, 'morning & night, seeing the last of my youth rusted out like this.' A short holiday in Paris with Neil in May had proved disappointing, as she was so tense that she had been unable to sleep, and a fortnight in Birchington in July, with Neil and the children, but *sans mère*, was equally unsatisfactory. She was bored for the first few days, then described having a 'deadly fit of accidie', which she ascribed to the strain of the past eighteen months. They returned home to face again 'A's pathological hatred of N & exaggeration of every small thing concerning him'.

Despite all her domestic problems, in August, Pamela began the third book of the 'Helena' trilogy, *A Summer to Decide*. On the penultimate day of the year, she wrote in her diary that 'it is dreadfully hard to finish this book. God knows what it is like – I wobble between hope & fear.' Nevertheless, she worked on the final chapter on New Year's Eve, sandwiching it between baking and icing the birthday cake for her son's seventh birthday, and before the day was out, recorded that she had written 'The End, with usual dash & doubtfulness'. With, as mentioned, Helena's death shortly after the beginning of this novel, Claud Pickering now takes centre stage again. He is working part-time in the gallery owned by a friend, and writing little-read books on art history. He sees himself as 'one of the legion and the uselessly and futurelessly employed, sitting on a sun-warmed but very small rock in the middle of quicksands' (p.23). Pamela wrote modestly in a preface to a 1975 reprint of *A Summer to Decide*: 'I think the background of the immediate post-war years may be of some interest – I hope so. They are very sharp in my memory.'[7] Her contribution to communal memory of the years of austerity is indeed valuable and constitutes one of the great strengths of this novel as in the preceding one. Nearly twenty years later, reviewing another of her novels, A.S. Byatt commended this aspect of her work: 'In her wartime trilogy, Pamela Hansford Johnson created in precise detail a whole world of black market, shell shock, rationing, requisitioning, button-polishing.'[8]

In real life, Pamela had always been uneasy about visiting people who, because of their wealth, were clearly flouting wartime regulations. Her character Helena had typified those who saw no harm in people willing to provide her with the luxuries she misses; when her rich second husband was alive, there was always black market whisky and plenty of food in the house, although she professed not to know the source of these. In the previous novel of the trilogy, she had insisted that '"Everyone gets a bit on the side, anyway."' Claud's response is:

'I made a promise to myself at the beginning of this war that I wouldn't touch the black market with a barge pole – wouldn't wangle petrol, whisky, butter, or clothes coupons – and I haven't. And do my pastors and masters admire me? Not a bit of it. I simply get regarded as a harmless lunatic. My faith in common morality has gone to pot.'
(*Avenue*, pp.45-46)

In *A Summer to Decide*, Pamela examined two further forms of transgression against the many controls imposed by the post-war government. In an introduction to a collection of essays, entitled *The Age of Austerity*, editors Michael Sissons and Philip French compare the fiddling of the small-time racketeers with 'whiffs of spivvery on the grand scale and in high places'.[9] How the first form may have influenced the second is examined by T.E.B. Howarth in *Prospect and Reality: Great Britain 1945-55*:

One element of the post-war underworld which flourished with relative impunity in the face of benevolent legislators and overworked policemen was the black market. [...] This sort of exercise was the standard activity of the so-called "spiv", beloved of the cartoonists with his flashing rings and cuff-links, his striped shirt, curly-brimmed hat and pointed "co-respondent" shoes. A similar disregard for both the letter and the spirit of the law soon became prevalent at much more exalted levels of society.[10]

Even the lower levels of racketeering could, however, culminate in more serious crime, as in the case of the notorious murder of a successful spiv, Stanley Setty, by his underling, Donald Hume, in 1949, as it happened, the same year as the Lynskey tribunal investigated alleged bribery of high-ranking government officials at the Board of Trade.

Pamela's fictional creation, Helena's protégé, the seemingly helpless John Field, becomes involved in both these forms of corrupt behaviour in *A Summer to Decide*. An aunt who is a high-ranking official in the Ministry of Labour has exercised some nepotism in finding him a job as secretary to an M.P. Claud Pickering, told of an impending political scandal regarding an improper leakage of information, immediately wonders if Field could be involved:

It would not be out of character for him to obtain information from a
venal or foolish young Labour man having some business or other concerned with the House, and to convey this knowledge [...]. The more
I thought of this the more likely it seemed, and then the more wild
and coincidental. (*Summer*, p.65)

Claud finds that he is indeed right in his suspicions; he confronts Field,
who tries to bluster his way out by minimizing his actions: '"[...] it
wasn't quite so – so dirty as you think. I only collated one or two
things of common knowledge – nothing really secret, and certainly
not disgraceful."' '"It was worth paying for, though"', Claud
comments, and Field gives 'a little gasp like a man beset by injustice'
(p.119). Field promises to end his shady activities in the field of
politics, saying that Claud had brought him to his senses.

However, before long, Claud is surprised to hear from his sister
Charmian, that Field has joined forces with her unsatisfactory husband
Evan Sholto in a new enterprise, ostensibly in the belief that they
could, by some honest means, cash in on post-war shortages by opening a second-hand car showroom. Claud Pickering, prompted by his
sister's misgivings, goes with her to inspect their place of business, the
resultant passage being a testament to Pamela's descriptive power:

There are no roads more sad, more hopeless, than some of the by-roads
of South-East London. [...] The houses are tall and mournful,
skulking back from the dank front gardens like pockmarked invalids
shirking the public street. Before the war the paint hung in tatters, and
the sodden letting-boards were split and ragged with damp. It is just
the same now, except that there is nothing to let and that here and
there are no houses, only heaps of rubble over which the weeds crawl
and tangle and riot. [...] We passed the great cinema, tawdry in the
heavy rain, [...] an amusement arcade that gave forth a fitful blare of
music from a horrible jungle of meat-red and gold, [...] countless pubs
and dress shops, [...] a hoarding half concealing an enormous bomb
crater. Behind it death was still fresh; sixty lives were lost there, and
the twilight of fear and agony clung still to the pit where the fireweed
clambered out of the crumbled stone.

Claud and Charmian then see an advertising hoarding on which posters
hung in shreds, and notice, as a final irony, that: 'A new one, intact,
announced an Atomic Dance to be held at the Town Hall' (p.161).

Shortly after this visit, with the mystery of the nature of Field's and Sholto's motor enterprise still unsolved, Claud leaves for a lengthy business tour of the United States. On his return, he finds the two still prospering, to the extent that they have now been able to open a restaurant, clearly dependent on their ability to obtain black market food; 'Sholto and Field', Claud thinks, 'are the bluebottles growing fat on the decay of a society. This is their golden age; there is more filth than their stomachs can cram' (p.184). Eventually, retribution does catch up with the hapless pair, both unskilled at covering their tracks, and they receive prison sentences. Their garage scam is revealed to have been the precise modus operandi of that of the real-life Setty and Hume; new cars being impossible to come by, and second-hand cars almost as scarce, they acquired the log-books of derelict cars, then stole vehicles that roughly corresponded with them, resprayed them, and sold them to customers prepared to ask no questions with regard to provenance. The more serious matters of Government leaks and corruption of ministers do not warrant prosecution in the novel, as indeed was the case following the Lynskey tribunal; some minor officials lost their jobs through their indis-cretion, but were not otherwise punished. According to Howarth, however, the legal process had satisfied the British public, who 'felt that a corner had been lifted of the hitherto impenetrable curtain, behind which everybody but themselves seemed to have access to whisky and nylons and bananas and steaks and petrol and foreign travel'.[11]

The parallels between fictional and actual events might seem coincidental, taking into account the fact that the revelations following the Stanley Setty murder and the findings of the Lynskey tribunal were not made public until 1948. However, throughout the latter part of 1947, while Pamela was writing *A Summer to Decide*, she had resumed her frequent correspondence and occasional meetings with Snow to discuss their current works in progress. Snow had remained a part-time adviser in the Civil Service since the end of the war, in addition to his job at English Electric. As David Shusterman says, in connection with Snow's own political novels, this experience had enabled him 'to know well the inner manoeuvrings of government'.[12] It is therefore possible that Pamela gleaned some information from Snow at this time; on one occasion, after lunch with him and one of his colleagues, she recorded that the latter had given her 'some invaluable stuff' for her book, and the following year, before Pamela delivered the manuscript to the publishers, she sent it to Snow to read, and he returned it to her 'with 30 or 40 magnificent pages of notes', for which she said she was 'deeply grateful'.

Around the middle of 1947, Harry Hoff had started to play an ambiguous, probably deliberately mischievous, role in Pamela's relationship with Snow. She had met him, usually in Snow's company, on various occasions, but not recorded much about him until one evening the previous year when Neil had been out with a friend and Harry had invited her out to drinks on her own. She found him: 'V. queer – like a Michael Arlen character who had died, been prettified by an American mortician, & then reanimated. But all v. amusing.' Throughout 1947, Harry would occasionally drop in to Cheyne Row unannounced to confide in Pamela about 'his sorrows' about a married woman with whom he was in love; he also regularly invited Pamela to the theatre. Before long, he would seem to have been playing the part of another character, actually called 'Harry', in one of his future novels, whom the narrator sees as 'a sort of non-sexual voyeur, whose ferreting out of details about everybody's lives somehow fed his sense of power', but whose curiosity leads him sometimes to acts of 'motiveless malice'.[13]

In one specific instance, Hoff phoned Pamela one day in August, to make arrangements for one of their theatre visits, and then casually mentioned that 'by pure coincidence, Snow would be coming that night with "an old flame", & that we could meet for supper afterwards'. Pamela's suspicions were aroused; she commented that it was a 'damned odd coincidence'. It turned out to be a most awkward evening; the play was J.B. Priestley's elsewhere well-received *The Linden Tree*, which Pamela dismissed in two words: 'It stank.' Her frame of mind was probably not conducive to a dispassionate verdict on a play featuring an unhappy family, nor evidently did she enjoy being sidelined by another woman. The four did go on to dine together, but Pamela made little comment about this, other than to say that they had had champagne with the meal and that Harry had taken her home by taxi. She thought Snow's guest was called Ann Siegman, but she put a question mark by this, as she was obviously unsure if she had got the name right. At some later date, she added a footnote identifying the woman as Anne Seagrim, and commenting, with some, as it will turn out misplaced, relief: 'Turns out to be "P.A.", – not "old flame".'

Pamela seemed at this time to be realising how little she really knew about Snow; an American met at a cocktail party bemused her by telling her that 'he remembered going to tea with Snow & his wife', after which she added 'as I rather suspected'. And when, at another party, novelist Alec Waugh insisted to her that Snow was homosexual, she wrote: 'Never thought I would be baffled on such a score, but I am.' She then inserted an indecipherable shorthand note punctuated by exclamation marks, and continued: 'So much evidence in favour of theory – & so much against.'

As the year went on, despite their literary communications, personal relations between Pamela and Snow continued to be strained; she described them as being 'on quietly bad terms' on one of the few occasions when they dined alone. But, following the postponement of his 'Charles March' novel, his replacement 'No. 2' – *The Light and the Dark* – was to be published in November, and Pamela was determined to do it justice in the *Sunday Chronicle*, despite feeling, she said, 'like the chameleon on plaid' in trying to please both the author and the newspaper's editor. On the day of publication, she wrote in her diary:

> I know this to be a literary event, whether or not it is immediately recognised. In a way, I feel melancholy; for seven years I've kept his name going in utter belief. Now he's handed over to the other critics – let them do what they will. My job, such as it is, is at an end.

But she evidently had overcome Simpson's objections to giving her the space she believed the novel warranted, as the review ran at far greater length than was usual. She began (without identifying herself as Snow's first advocate):

> I suppose every reviewer lives in the hope that one day he will be able to say of a new book, "Here is a masterpiece".
> Since 1940, the literary bush-telegraph has been putting around the name of C.P. Snow. Seven years later, here is "The Light and the Dark", to test the rumours, and to contest the theory that the English novel is dying, like an india-rubber pig, on a long whistle and a wail.

She continued with an admiring resumé of the plot (which, as mentioned

earlier, told the story of Snow's friend, Charles Allberry, thinly disguised as 'Roy Calvert'), and concluded:

> For Mr. Snow there is no "good" or "bad"; only very rarely does he pass
> judgment. What he does do is to probe into the minds of men and
> women with an almost frightening skill. As I was reading his book
> I felt that he knew, not only the innermost secrets of his characters,
> but my secrets as well. [...]
>   Is it an easy book to read? No. Not very. Not at first. But I believe
> that Mr. Snow is engaged upon the making of an English masterpiece;
> and though, for the ordinary run of novel, we have only a week or so
> to spare, to our masterpieces we can bring a lifetime of enjoyment.

'The other critics', into whose hands she had said she was now
willing to commit Snow were, however, far less laudatory. Pamela had
now been made aware of Snow's angst before the publication of a
novel, and experienced for the first time his extreme reactions with
regard to what he considered to be unfavourable reviews. Harry Hoff
told Pamela that Snow was 'in the depths of despair over a slating
in Times Lit. Supp.'. The review, by Anthony Powell, would seem,
however, relatively benign: '*The Light and the Dark*', he said, 'is a
painstaking and readable account of university life seen from high
table. It would give a foreigner a fair idea of the types he might meet
and the opinions he might hear expressed in such circles.' Pamela
thought Snow's anguish 'quite absurd,' but acknowledged that 'no
sort of logic will help him.' She nevertheless telephoned him in an
attempt at consolation the following day, but the line was bad and
he spoke to her 'in a sort of remote Lazarus-voice'. He did, however,
manage to write a letter to her shortly afterward, explaining his
despair:

> The TLS review twinged itself on one nerve, but now I can begin to
> emerge. I'd better confess that I am as vulnerable as Tom Wolfe to
> certain kinds of criticism. The TLS went right through the cracks. It
> seemed to me incredible & upsetting that any literate person could get
> so little from one of the profoundest experiences of my life.

He told her that he was even considering abandoning writing altogether, but this was not because he was assailed by self-doubt. Indeed
he went on:

I'm not modest about what I think its worth is; it's not in the class of War & Peace or Karamazov, but I think it can hold its own with Fathers & Children or Bovary, i.e., the rank of novels just below supreme masterpieces. [...] I find it bitter, bitter almost beyond bearing that the chances of time (& some personal chances) will not allow it more than some genteel applause from an odd selection of people [...].[14]

Pamela evidently did not take her presumable inclusion in the above 'odd selection' personally, nor question Snow's judgment on his own work; she felt, however, that the letter revealed to her his 'surprising temperament, so hideously & absurdly vulnerable'. Another letter shortly afterward written by Snow to his brother in Fiji is further evidence of his near-paranoia with regard to critics in certain publications. He said that, while 'the *private* critical reception' of The Light and the Dark had been 'very warm', and he had had twenty-eight good reviews, the only two bad reviews to date, 'though contemptible', were indicative of the treatment he expected from those and other 'coterie' journals. While he did not expect these to affect sales, he continued that:

I had hoped to conquer this kind of hostility as I must before I get a really solid reputation. I am writing in the teeth of a strong, though ridiculous, literary movement; at present I'm too "human" for them. I'd hoped they would be outfaced by this book, but that has not yet happened. It may take several books and some years. But with good fortune I shall win through.[15]

Eventually, Snow wrote to Pamela saying he was 'climbing out of the abyss', only to be appallingly downcast yet again three days later by what she had to agree had been a 'perfectly foul attack' in a publication he would have presumably defined as a coterie journal, the *New Statesman & Nation*. The reviewer, distinguished literary critic Walter Allen, was a regular acquaintance of theirs, but obviously did not feel the same scruples that had troubled Pamela with regard to John Brophy and P.H. Newby. Allen had started his 'New Fiction' column with a review of Malcolm Lowry's *Under the Volcano*, which he praised highly, although mentioning some minor quibbles. He ended: 'All the same, it makes most contemporary novels appear slack and unconsidered. It certainly shows up *The Light and the Dark* for what it is.' After a description of the plot of Snow's novel, he ended with the overwhelmingly damning verdict:

The Light and the Dark is, quite simply, not the masterpiece of the year, as has been claimed, but the most pretentious novel of the year. It is pretentious because it tackles the most serious subject a novelist can tackle without the necessary sensibility or adequate technique.

With Christmas not far off, Pamela was as almost always dreading the festival, but she revealed this year a further reason for dismay. Snow invariably left London for a protracted stay with friends for the holiday, and Pamela wailed, 'Now, S. won't see me for about another three weeks!' Her wedding anniversary that month reminded her, by way of contrast, of her husband's good qualities. 'Dear Neil', she wrote in her diary, 'I do think I made a satisfactory marriage. He is so unfailingly good to me.'

CHAPTER 9

The Dark and the Light

T
HE EARLY PART of 1948 followed a similar pattern to the
previous year. Pamela's contract with the *Sunday Chronicle* was
renewed with a slight increase in remuneration. She continued
to broadcast regularly, and she made her first television appearance
in an afternoon magazine programme. While she was still receiving
substantial royalties from *The Trojan Brothers* in addition to those from
An Avenue of Stone, Neil was continuing to search for regular employment while gaining a small income from freelance journalism.

Snow was now sending Pamela drafts of the next instalment of
Lewis Eliot's narrative, *Time of Hope*. On receiving Part II of this novel,
which she found 'very fine', she commented: 'I have had a recent
"recovery of affection" & a lessening of the resentment caused by his
peculiar performances during the autumn – sulking, misery, avoidance,
etc.' She and Neil visited Cambridge in February, and were entertained
at Christ's College by Snow's friend, Jack Plumb, whom Pamela had
evidently already met in London. Pamela fell in love with the city,
adding it to Stratford and Bruges as the places she constantly yearned
to revisit. She was thrilled on this first visit to encounter E.M. Forster
in the college rooms of a mutual friend, to walk along the Backs
and to visit King's College Chapel and the Fitzwilliam Museum. But
her depressions resumed on her return home, and she worried that:
'I simply can't bring myself to do any work – it hardly gives me
pleasure to feel the pen upon the paper, which is unusual, as the mere
mechanical act of writing is usually pleasurable.'

Telephoning Snow one day, she found *him* once again in the depths
of despair, accountable, as I have suggested with regard to the characters identifiably portrayed in *Charles March*, to his lack of forethought

with regard to his *modus operandi* throughout the Lewis Eliot series.
This time, it was the parents of Charles Allberry, who had been grief-
stricken by the 'fictional' portrait of their son as 'Roy Calvert' in *The
Light and the Dark*. They had written a deeply reproachful letter to
Snow, emphasizing their hostility by returning to him the letters of
condolence Snow had written to them at the time of their son's death.
Pamela's sympathies were all with Snow. 'I never knew', she wrote, 'a
man who has such luck, or is offered so many blows just at the time
he feels on the verge of recovery.'

It does seem almost unbelievable that an intelligent and sensitive
woman should not have found it possible to sympathize with parents
for a portrayal of their dead son, in the words of Hester W. Chapman,
reviewing *The Light and the Dark* in the *Spectator*, as one who was
'spiritually tormented' and 'morally maladjusted'. While 'Roy Calvert'
is portrayed as the embodiment of erudition, grace and wit, he is
nevertheless shown as suffering from what 'Lewis Eliot' identifies as
'the black night of melancholy: [Roy] had already felt the weight of
inexplicable misery, the burden of self.' The narrator goes on further
to say: 'He was born with this melancholy; it was a curse of fate, like
a hereditary disease. It shadowed all his life.'[1] Eliot believes that
Calvert seeks to escape this curse by means of promiscuity and, at one
point, most controversially, by means of finding possible personal
salvation in Nazism. Finally, he sees Calvert's choice to become a pilot
in Bomber Command as a final surrender knowing it will lead almost
certainly to death. And when the inevitable happens, the final pages
are dedicated to an account of Eliot's grief alone.

It is also difficult to comprehend that neither Snow nor his publishers had foreseen, and in some way tried to assuage, not only the
reactions of Allberry's parents, but also those of his young wife,
Patricia, who had been carrying their unborn child at the time of his
death. Nearly forty years later, after rereading Snow's novel, that son,
David Allberry, asked his mother whether his father had 'really been
like that', and in response, Patricia Lewis, as she then was, published
privately her own recollections of her first husband.[2] She also wrote
to his remaining friends and contemporaries, including those from
Cambridge, and Christ's College in particular, in order to quote from
their responses. Mrs Lewis recorded meeting Snow on only two occasions. 'He seemed,' she wrote, 'a big, genial man, but I cannot recall

much about him.' Snow had perhaps never recovered from his initial baffled reaction on hearing about Allberry's engagement in 1941; he had written to Harry Hoff that his then best friend's fiancée was 'a nice simple pretty girl of 20', whom Allberry had met when working temporarily at Bletchley, prior to enlisting in the R.A.F. 'I am puzzled', Snow continued, adhering to his previously mentioned austere code, 'as to whether he believes in it himself, or whether it is a Dostoevski trick; and I have no idea what will become of it.'[3] Mrs Lewis made it clear that neither she nor her parents-in-law had any advance knowledge of the subject of the novel before publication; Snow 'didn't tell me at any time', she said, 'that he was writing a novel partly based on Charles. Hearing about it in 1947, I bought it at W.H. Smith's and, like his parents, was distressed by what I read.'

Among those who replied to Mrs Lewis in 1984 was Jack Plumb, who had fulfilled his ambition to become Master of Christ's, having recently completed a four-year term. He somewhat disingenuously said that Snow 'never intended Roy Calvert to be a totally life-like portrait of Charles'. However, it should be said that Snow made little attempt in his novel to make any variation between Calvert's highly specialized field of Orientalist scholarship and that of Allberry in real life. In personal matters, the majority of those who replied to Mrs Lewis agreed that Snow's portrayal was 'greatly exaggerated'. Mrs Lewis introduced their various responses with her own testimony, addressed to those who did not know her husband, and would have 'difficulty in differentiating between the true and fictional qualities portrayed in the book':

> I can vouch for the facts: that Charles was never sexually immoral, the reverse was true – he was a man of high moral and religious principles; [...] he was not pro-Nazi (as events later proved). [...] He detested their treatment of the Jews and other dissidents and the disservice [the Nazis] were rendering to universal scholarship. He did admire the German people, especially their industry and enthusiasm, the cleanliness of their towns, their music and poetry.

Back in 1947, the letter from Allberry's parents had not swayed Snow's determination to continue to offer portraits of his close friends as well as acquaintances in all the subsequent Lewis Eliot novels (indeed, he identified them himself to interviewers, and assisted in compiling the list which is an Appendix to Philip Snow's *Stranger and Brother*). He was amazed and hurt by any adverse reactions from the people he depicted, and Pamela would continue to offer him solace and support.

In the case of *The Light and the Dark*, Pamela's aid went beyond her praise in the *Sunday Chronicle* review. She regularly contributed a book column to *Windmill*, and in March 1948, five full pages of that periodical were given over to Pamela's further discussion of Snow's novel. She opened with a justification:

> Because a considerable time has passed since the publication of *The Light and the Dark* […], it may not now seem too gross an impropriety to comment upon a certain remarkable element noticeable in much of the immediate critical comment. This was a positive resentment, not against the novel itself nor against the author, but against the hero.
> Roy Calvert was attacked as if he were a living man.

At no time in this essay, did she acknowledge that this might have been because the novel had been recognized, within the milieu in which they lived, as being, for the greater part, a *roman à clef*. Since she and Snow had so frequently discussed his work, she had to be fully aware of the autobiographical nature of the project and of the real-life origins of the main characters, but she chose to disregard this here. Perhaps it was still in her mind that, coincidentally, she had recently defended Thomas Wolfe from somewhat similar accusations of defamation of his own background. In her monograph on Wolfe, she had answered his home-town critics, who saw "Altamount" in his novels as being a condemnation of his real birth-place, Asheville, North Carolina, and for Wolfe, one might say, also read Snow, even if the latter had only distressed individuals rather than an entire community:

> 'Altamount' believed itself pilloried, disgraced, and above all things, found out; and despite the powerful autobiographical character of *Look Homeward Angel*, a character the author always, by a complex reasoning, violently disclaimed, Wolfe was stunned by the reaction. The fact that he did feel this sense of terror and amazement is comprehensible enough to any writer. The novelist is always far more innocent of malice than the neighbours think. He may use them as framework for his people; but once the new characters are elaborated, thickened in,

they do become to him things of his own creation, emancipated from the originals. (*Thomas Wolfe*, p.6.)

By extension, therefore, Pamela would have believed 'Roy Calvert' to have been 'emancipated' from Charles Allberry. '*The Light and the Dark*', she proclaimed, 'is a Novel with a Hero, a tragedy upon the classic scale. Roy Calvert is as richly gifted as a T.E. Lawrence or a Saint-Loup,[4] and like them, harbours in his nature the seed of his own destruction.' She praised Snow's 'delicately and meticulously observed' portrayals of other senior members of the college, while admitting that 'every character functions as a support for Roy Calvert, the Hero conceived upon the most audacious scale'. She ended her lengthy panegyric by placing the novel within the context of Snow's grand scheme:

> Mr. Snow writes of men and of Man. He plans, in his projected series of novels, to make a vast portrait of his own times, studying them from all social levels. There has been no English work planned on so vast a scale for twenty years past. [...]
> *The Light and the Dark* is part of an English masterpiece, a novel not of a "school" but of an historic tradition. That is why recognition of its quality is unlikely to be immediate. [...]

At this time, Pamela was herself feeling in need of support. A series of depressive days led to what she described as a '<u>cafard</u> out of <u>hell</u>', precipitated in this case, she thought, by worries about the crisis in Czechoslovakia where, under pressure, the President, Edvard Beneš, had appointed a Communist-dominated government, thereby giving legal sanction to a Communist *coup d'état*. She knew that Neil would welcome this, but felt herself to be 'terribly uncertain politically'. In a long, impassioned outburst in her diary (abridged here), she wrote:

> Don't know what to think, & dread to thrash it out with N. [...] In my deep heart I feel as despairing as any of the young writers who are in such terror & doubt. It is as though God gives no help now & it is absolutely silent above & around the abandoned earth. I want to see Snow, who helps me & lets me talk things out, but he seems locked in his own silences & doubts. I hate to write like this, to feel this sick failure of faith. [...] All this is dreadful & I must stop, though it helps me to write even so much.

She wrote to Snow, suggesting a meeting, but received no reply, so contacted Anne Seagrim as his secretary; Seagrim told her that Snow was away and had absolutely forbidden her to forward any mail. 'How kind he can be in large things', Pamela mused, '& how hurtful in small ones.' At the foot of that page in her notebook, she added: 'All his virtues are the great ones, & all his faults extraordinarily petty.'

Neil's solution to her despair about the state of the world (and presumably, his own despair at the state of their own small world) was that they should leave England for Australia. Pamela understood the logic of this, but her reaction was that:

> the thought fills me with such awful desolation & I can't take decisions. Won't something happen to help? To reassure me & the world? I don't know how much of my mind is actual & how much neurotic. My handwriting is still calm. I wish I could see Snow – get help – get affection – I must pull myself together & see straight. This is absolutely essential.

Her doctor's response was to prescribe Benzedrine, a potentially addictive amphetamine, widely recommended by the medical profession at that time for a wide range of disorders. (When later that year, Neil had a bout of undiagnosed ill-health, the same doctor prescribed for him 'benzedrine, cod liver oil & malt, & an iron tonic'.) Pamela was to become reliant on the drug for many years.

An illogical lack of faith in her own work had been another reason why Pamela wanted to contact Snow at this time. In 1945, she had written a play called *Corinth House*; it had taken her a fortnight, and she put it on one side, imagining that there was little chance of a stage production. When the text was published in 1954 together with an essay, 'On the Future of Prose-Drama', she wrote that she had written the play merely 'as a laboratory experiment' in order to extend her critical range, by gaining 'some idea, certainly more than before I chanced my own arm, of the problems with which the prose-dramatist today has to contend'.[5] She was, however, approached in 1947 by Frederick Piffard, a minor impresario, with a view to staging *Corinth House* for a short run at one of the little theatre clubs which proliferated in London at that time. 'Personally', she had written in her diary, 'I hate the damn play, & don't want it done at all.' Her feelings remained the same early in 1948, when Piffard began to press her further, and she felt Snow was the only person who could give her 'real guidance'. However, with his still being incommunicado, she went ahead and, with some trepidation, agreed terms for the play to be produced at the New Lindsey Theatre Club in Notting Hill, at the end of May.

Pamela's misgivings about the play were temporarily shelved as she started work on an ambitious project. The novelist Rayner Heppenstall, whom she had met years previously when he had been one of Dylan Thomas's first friends in London, was now working as a producer for BBC Radio, and invited her to contribute to a series called 'Imaginary Conversations' on the Third Programme. She saw the offer as a chance to compose a programme about the work of an author who, like Thomas Wolfe, had become for her a *grande passion*. During the period of her wartime literary exile in Laleham, she had a visit from Royston Morley, coincidentally another BBC producer, whose family was living nearby. As she remembered:

> That day, he spoke of something which was to be of great importance in my life. He spoke of Marcel Proust. Had I ever read him? I said no, and he lent me Part I of *Swann's Way*. From the beginning, I was enthralled. Having earned rather more than usual from one of my books, I bought the entire set. [...] I have read it ever since, yearly, for the rest of my life, both in English and in French. (*Important*, p.201)

Her bold concept for the programme was to move Proust's characters forward in time to Paris in 1941, the first year of the German occupation. She knew she was running the risk of enraging Proust purists, but was willing to take the risk.

In the meantime, rehearsals for *Corinth House* were going ahead. Pamela was still uneasy about the exposure of her play to an audience, although she could not precisely understand why. The action of the play does rely on an initial coincidence, but once disbelief in this is suspended as being the *donnée* of the play, it becomes a tense drama. The setting is a South Kensington residential hotel. In the essay which accompanied the published text, Pamela explained that her startingpoint had been the wish to portray 'the classical idea of the Hunter and the Hunted, and the ancient theme of the relation between the two', and the eponymous name of the hotel was therefore intended 'however faintly' to make a classical implication (p.22). The Hunted is Miss Malleson, a retired headmistress; the Hunter, Madge Donnythorpe, a former pupil of hers, who had been forced to leave the school 'voluntarily', rather than being expelled, after some never-named transgression, which Miss Malleson remembers as being 'unspeakably ugly', but Madge insists that: 'It was only ugly because you made it so. I was truly innocent then ... there was no good or bad ...' (p.85).

The text of the play offers lengthy stage directions, which, if included in the working script would have left the actors no need to ask the producer/director, Gordon Crier, about the background or motivation of a character.[6] For instance, Miss Malleson's character is established by the description of her bedroom:

> Silver-framed photographs are everywhere, mainly of schoolgirls and young women; all are signed. [...] This is the room of a woman who loves to live in a clutter of small evocative possessions, yet somehow contrives to keep everything perfectly tidy. [...] There is not an article in it, however trivial, that has not a meaning for her, that is not a part of her past. (p.57)

The audience is therefore disposed to feel sympathy for her even before her appearance. She is described as being 'little and plump, with a round, contented face'; a long psychological analysis of her character follows, including the following extract: 'It would be unfair to describe Miss Malleson as self-satisfied, for she thinks too little of self to be either satisfied or dissatisfied with what she finds' (p.60). Madge Donnythorpe, however, while superficially 'a handsome, dark girl', has sharp, thin features: hers is 'an ectomorphic face stamped with the restlessness of one who gnaws through her life, past, present and future, as if she were worrying a bone' (p.74). But first impressions can deceive, and swings in the audience's sympathy between the two adversaries provide much of the tension of the play. There is also a well-drawn cast of minor characters, and one wonders whether Terence Rattigan might have seen the play, and drawn some inspiration from it when writing *Separate Tables* six years later.

Pamela had to admit that her play was being well produced and had been satisfactorily cast, with the established character actress Nora Nicholson playing Miss Malleson, and a somewhat excitable film starlet Patricia Laffan playing Madge. (The peak of Laffan's career was to be playing Nero's wife, Poppaea, in *Quo Vadis* in 1951). An early set-back for the producer was the discovery that there would be a clash on the proposed opening night in June between their little theatre production of *Corinth House* and the much-heralded first London performance of Tennessee Williams's *The Glass Menagerie*, directed by John Gielgud, and starring the award-winning American actress Helen Hayes. Assuming, as he told Pamela, that the only review of her play would therefore be written by 'the office boy at the *Daily Worker*', he shifted their opening to 31st March, only to find a further clash with a very different American star, Sophie Tucker, the 'Last of the Red-Hot Mamas', making a rare London appearance. No further adjournment was possible, and indeed the first review which Pamela read did appear in the *Daily Worker*; whether or not the reviewer was the office boy, Pamela was pleased with the critique which said that the play showed 'a fine sense of drama and a feeling for personality'. The subsequent reviews in the *Times* and the *Daily Telegraph* were more moderate in their praise, but not unsatisfactory. Patricia Laffan, who had now become a friend of Pamela's, rang her however in a state of 'mild hysteria', as only the *Daily Worker* had commended her performance, while the other two papers had singled out Nora Nichol-son, and Una Venning, who played Mrs. Beauclerc, the unfeeling hotel manageress.

Pamela had other concerns; at the final rehearsals, as she later wrote in the published edition, she had felt that the play was falling flat 'as it deserved to do: and still I could not see the way'. 'I doubt', she continued, 'if I should ever have seen it had I not watched the play on a stage before an audience [...]' (p.24). She would have thoroughly appreciated a comment made by Bertolt Brecht regarding his difficulty in coming to a decision on a turning-point in *The Good Woman of Szechuan* at a time when, for political reasons, his plays could not be performed before an audience. 'It is impossible,' he wrote in his *Arbeitsjournal*, 'to finish a play without a stage; [...] only the stage can decide about the possible variants.'[7] Pamela persuaded Gordon Crier to let her rewrite the final act in time for the last few perform-ances. Most of the cast co-operated, but Patricia Laffan, to Pamela's mind, ruined the effect of the last act. Friend or no, Pamela got tough, and the next day recorded her triumph:

Rang up poor Pat in morning & chewed her up thoroughly re last night's performance. Awful screams & protests, but she said she'd play it 'hard' in the evening. [...] Pat telephoned to say she'd done last act as I insisted, had got a round of applause on her exit, & 5 curtains!

The revised play was later to have successful radio and television productions, as well as a revival at the Q Theatre in 1951, and numerous amateur performances. Reviewing the published text with its preliminary essay in the *Times Literary Supplement*, Anthony Cookman wrote that, while appreciating that 'the evolution of a good play from the earliest draft to the final text may be exasperatingly slow', he thought that Pamela had identified a problem common to many playwrights who suffer from the consequences of a premature production. His judgment was that:

If *Corinth House* had been in its definitive form in 1948 [...] it might well have reached the West End and made an even bigger name for itself. [...] In its final form, it is an admirably tense study in feminine psychology on a higher level than much that the London stage has offered its audience in the present season.

Although many of Pamela's friends had attended the opening and subsequent nights of the play's run, Snow was absent until the final performance. When he had returned from his voluntary isolation in the early months of that year, he had recovered his spirits; he was more active in PEN, and this had led to one of the more bizarre entanglements of his emotional life. Maureen Gebbie was one of the administrative staff at PEN, and that year was involved in the organization of their annual conference to be held in Copenhagen at which Snow was to be one of the main speakers. In May, just before the delegates left, she held a party to which Pamela and Neil were invited. Pamela tartly recorded that Maureen 'was wearing a frock that exposed her bust almost to the nipples & went for N. with the persistence of Potiphar's wife, occasionally sneaking a glance at me to see how I was taking it'. She was thus outraged when Snow phoned her on his return from the conference and highly tactlessly told her that Maureen had insisted to him in Copenhagen that it was Pamela who had '"wanted all the men at her party"'. Pamela continued: 'When I expressed mild indignation, Snow went very Father Zossima[8] & urged me to charity. All I can say is that if she spreads this kind of thing abroad, I'll threaten her with a slander action.'

Before long, Pamela realized the reason for Snow's partisanship. At the next PEN meeting, she witnessed 'Maureen G. all over Snow in wreaths'. 'I simply cannot bear that woman', she wrote, 'it takes all my moral & social control to be even polite. What has happened so v. obvious.' Quite what right she felt she had in condemning the relationship between two single people may only be surmised; nevertheless, the day after that meeting, she recorded feeling 'rather sad [...] – as if a long friendship will never be quite the same'. There are three further sources of information regarding *l'affaire Gebbie*: the first is another bosom-beating letter from Snow to his brother Philip; the second is a fictionalized version by Harry Hoff; the third is the cache of personal letters in Snow's archive in Texas. The letter to Philip Snow in Fiji was not written until August, but told of Snow's having been distracted by:

> a violent love affair which began in May and from which I have just extracted myself. I wasn't in love, but the circumstances were melodramatic – a wild, upper-class girl of 24 suddenly conceived an infatuation for me, mainly because she felt I could bring some stability into her life. Not that stability wasn't necessary, since she was (a) drunken (b) liable to sleep with any man at sight (c) fantastically extravagant (she cost me hundreds of pounds in three months). In fairness, I ought to add that she's also intelligent, has formidable character and is voluptuously attractive to a degree. [...] All of which is a singular mélange for a middle-aged gentleman of quiet tastes. [...] Someone ought to produce a nice girl for me to marry: otherwise I'm still liable to get into these predicaments. [...][9]

When Harry Hoff decided to follow his friend into the realms of semi-autobiographical fiction, he initially disregarded his knowledge of the problems Snow had encountered from the Cohen and Allberry families. The first book in his new genre, *Scenes from Provincial Life*, was set in a provincial town, easily identifiable as Leicester from the description of the 'wondrously ugly' clock-tower,[10] and the characters, though portrayed with a more humorous touch than Snow's, are based on the ex-Alderman Newton's School's circle of friends depicted in Snow's *Strangers and Brothers* (later, as mentioned, retitled *George Passant*). However, when the manuscript was ready to go to press, as will be seen in the next chapter, one of those friends objected vehemently. Hoff was more than willing to adopt a pseudonym so that publication could go ahead, thus becoming better known in the literary world as 'William Cooper'. According to Pamela's diary, it was Snow who had suggested this compromise; he may sometimes have had some regrets that he had not chosen a similar course himself, but it is likely that he would not have wanted to forgo recognition of his name as a scientist as well as a novelist.

Hoff is 'Joe Lunn', the hero, or anti-hero, in his *Scenes from ...* series, and Snow is a barely-disguised 'Robert', Joe Lunn's friend in the first novel, and superior in the Ministry in which the two men work in later novels. Snow would have had no reason to object to Hoff's portrayal of him, as introduced in the first novel:

> Robert [...] was a few years older than us. He was clever, gifted and wise; and he had a great personal influence on us. We had appointed him arbiter on all our actions, and anything he cared to say we really accepted as the word of God.[II]

Harry Hoff may therefore have been confident that 'Robert' would never wish to sue 'William Cooper', but when he included a version of the Gebbie imbroglio in another *Scenes from ...* novel, several years after the event, it was Pamela who forbade publication because the distress the episode had caused her continued to be keenly felt. *Scenes from Metropolitan Life* was therefore not published until 1982, after the deaths of both Snow & Pamela.

In this book, Robert is 'triumphant' to Joe when the young and beautiful 'Julia' (clearly identifiable as Maureen) telephones to invite him away for the weekend. Robert boasts to Joe in a rather adolescent fashion: '"Of course we shall be going to bed together."' Julia then decides she wants to marry him, and he frets that this would mean indulging 'her very expensive tastes'. Still more clinchingly, like Maureen, she has a wayward lover who had previously been paying the rent on her flat (a Pole in the book, an Italian in real life) and now expects Robert to take over this responsibility. This is the final straw for Robert:

> '"It feels," said Robert, "like taking on a responsibility that ought to be reserved for very rich men only."
> '"But you are very rich," I said. [...]

"'If I did marry her, it would mean I should never know when I was going to come home and find her drunk or in bed with another man."
'I thought: "He isn't going to marry her." '[12]

Snow telephoned Pamela in a 'voice of doom' early in July, barely two months after the start of his relationship with Maureen, and told her that he wanted to make her 'a confidence', following a lunch they were both due to attend. He then confessed about his liaison with Maureen Gebbie, which had indeed begun in Copenhagen, but assured her that it had come to an end. She duly sympathized with him, recording that:

> It has been a fantastic affair, quite crazy & dangerous, he dreads repercussions & I'm sure he'll get them. However, we went back to his flat & talked all afternoon, on a more sure & confidential basis than we have been before. I am so glad it's over – sorry for her, glad for him. It would have been disastrous. And selfishly, I dreaded the wreck she would have made of our friendship – and of the "Group" solidarity, come to that.

The 'more sure & confidential basis' was something of a myth; a fortnight after telling Pamela that the affair was at an end, he told her that he had agreed to write a 'testimonial' to Maureen's mother, Mrs Kilroe. It seems even more surprising that he should have later sent copies of their correspondence to the archive in Texas, thus providing the third strand of evidence mentioned above. He told Mrs Kilroe that he loved Maureen very much and longs to make her happy. He continued:

> I am quite sure of my own heart; but before I can take care of her I must be sure that she herself is making the right choice. I am a good deal older than she is and have known much unhappiness, and I haven't much confidence when someone is as precious to me as Maureen is.
> So I have suggested to her that she should go away and rest and think things over. [...] It is a risk for me, since she may decide against me. [...] If I am the man to provide [enduring happiness for her] I shall count it the greatest good fortune of my life. [...]

Maureen was duly sent off to Menton and, to Snow's great relief, he gradually managed to disentangle himself from her, although not as immediately as he had told Pamela. One of his last letters to

Maureen that year was couched in language far more passionate than he allowed any of the characters in his novels, as the following extract demonstrates:

> I am profoundly grateful to you, my love – you know that, don't you? Until Copenhagen, I had felt nothing deep about a human being for two years. I was coming to think that I had exhausted all I could feel. You brought me alive – and, much more, gave me a period of almost undiluted happiness. It was short, but one doesn't measure these things by the ordinary clock. Throughout that time, I knew the joy of being with you in perfect harmony, and for the first time in my life never wishing to be elsewhere, free from angst and claustrophobia, lit up by your presence and longing that such days would never end. I had not believed that such bliss was possible for me; and I shall find life empty unless and until I have the luck to stumble across it again.
> For that revelation I am grateful to you now and shall always be.[13]

Pamela, who felt that Snow had been 'inconceivably silly', and who had been much relieved on his behalf once she believed that Maureen was out of the way, had no idea, however, of not only another ongoing relationship but the advent of a new woman in his life. She did of course know of Anne Seagrim's existence, but had accepted Snow's assurance that she was no more to him than a fellow-employee at English Electric. His brother, however, was aware that this explanation of Anne Seagrim's role in Snow's life fell short of the truth. He had been unsurprised to receive a letter from CPS that October, regarding the making of a new will, and asking that, as executor, he ensure that: 'Anne Seagrim receives either the copyright of *Charles March* or *The Masters* or a sum of £2,000 – whichever she prefers', adding somewhat arrogantly, 'the copyright is the better bet'.[14]

The existence of the final woman in Snow's life that eventful year, the year in which he had described himself to his brother as 'a middle-aged gentleman of quiet tastes',[15] might never have been discovered but for his lack of reticence when talking to Donald Dickson, combined with the evidence of particularly personal letters deposited in his archive. In his never-completed manuscript, Dickson has a chapter entitled 'Snow and Women', which began by saying that:

> Although CPS was coming to the conclusion that his literary prospects would best be advanced were he to enter into marriage with Pamela

Hansford Johnson, predictably he could not resist pursuing favours elsewhere.

Anne Seagrim, of course, had been in the wings from 1945, and privately had hopes of marrying him. From 1948 Maureen Kilroe [Gebbie] had come on the scene, while Pamela Hansford Johnson couldn't escape the conclusion that marriage to Snow would solve her own marital difficulties. Not content with the intricacies of keeping this formidable triangle on the qui vive, [...] Snow broke new ground.

The 'new ground' was in the person of Holly Southwell, a mathematics teacher, daughter of Sir Richard Southwell, former Rector of Imperial College, London, who had introduced her to Snow in Oxford. It would seem that their friendship did not become a love affair until after Snow's involvement with Maureen Gebbie, but Holly then wrote over one hundred love letters to Snow from August 1948 to the end of 1949. She seems to have been exceedingly understanding, writing to him at the beginning of their relationship: 'You would have preferred slightly, wouldn't you, if no-one close to me, knew we were in love. Why, sweet? No-one's going to hold you to anything.'[16] And the next day, she continued with a perceptive comment, in a letter beginning: 'My very, very darling love':

> I love you so [...]. Sometimes, I almost wish that I didn't yet know you loved me, and that I was still just thinking you're a darling and hoping to know you more and more, and minding very much about your books. Being in love with an autobiographical novelist, particularly during production, is a queer feeling, I have decided. Among other things it involves a curious feeling of slightly seeing double all the time [...].[17]

In William Cooper's *Scenes from Married Life* (1961), Joe muses as to why Robert has reached the age of forty-four without getting married. (Snow was 46 in 1948). Joe concludes that:

> In fact, there was more to it than common reluctance, in Robert's case. [...] In the past he had fallen so deeply in love as to overcome common reluctance. But on each occasion the girl had been so odd, so eccentric, or even so crazy, that somehow the upshot, partly through her own actions and partly through a final move for self-preservation on Robert's part, had been no marriage. (*Married*, p.43)

This explanation is valid for Snow's decisions not to marry Sheila Palfreyman or Maureen Gebbie, but either Anne Seagrim or Holly Southwell would have fitted the desire he expressed to his brother that someone should find him 'a nice girl' to marry. It is hard not to come to the same conclusion as Donald Dickson, that Snow's priority now became the consolidation of his literary partnership with Pamela, and that he was considering combining this with marriage if there were no other way. And there were still obstacles in Snow's path; in Pamela's case, of course, a husband, in Snow's case, chronic indecisiveness.

There is no evidence that Snow had yet communicated this decision to Pamela; she was baffled for the remainder of the year by their seesawing relationship. She received a 'v. affectionate letter' from him, while holidaying in France with Neil and Andy, which nevertheless contained a rebuke 'for lack of Christian charity in the matter of Mrs. G.', which incensed her sufficiently to write 'rather a snorter in reply'. The two of them had a fierce political row when they dined on her return, and she was doubtful as to whether the breach would heal, since she felt that the underlying cause of their estrangement was lingering bitterness on her part regarding Maureen Gebbie. But a few days later, Snow rang to apologize for his 'fouler remarks', and she had hopes that 'relations were re-established at their happiest'. She also showed some glee in recording that he had then told her that Maureen had, 'in an excess of frustration', bitten him in the hand.

In the meantime Pamela was busier than ever with a variety of literary activities: she had started a new novel, *The Philistines*; *An Avenue of Stone* was to be published that autumn; and her Proust pastiche, 'The Duchess at Sunset' was broadcast in September. The latter, to her great delight, was very well received, both by critics and by friends and acquaintances, including Ivy Compton-Burnett, all of whose opinions she valued. If she had any ignoble thoughts, she might have been particularly pleased when Kay Dick told her that 'a superlative review of my <u>Duchess</u>' which appeared in the *New Statesman* under the name of William Salter had in fact been written by Snow's recently fierce critic, Walter Allen. Salter/Allen had acknowledged that Pamela's concept had been a daring one, with obvious difficulties and dangers. Nevertheless his judgment was that:

The Duchess at Sunset seems to me a most successful and exciting programme, and that this should be so I take as an index not only of the reality of Proust's characters but also of Miss Johnson's literary skills and tact. [...] If, as I think, Miss Johnson has not written for broadcasting before, then, on the evidence of *The Duchess at Sunset*, she is the most exciting newcomer to the art for a long time.

The reviewers of *A Summer to Decide* were equally laudatory when taking the opportunity to re-evaluate the trilogy as a whole; Ralph Straus in the *Sunday Times* described it as 'a remarkable piece of work', and Lionel Hale in the *Observer* went much further:

The last novel of her trilogy [...] finally and brilliantly confirms Miss Hansford Johnson as in the first flight of contemporary women novelists. All her virtues, in this study of the scene of today, are somehow clarified: a prose which is close without being stingy, an eye which is straight without the deflection of malice, an instinct for story-telling which is leisured without being lazy. [...] this is post-war England most penetratingly observed.

Despite this triumph, Pamela was still too often subject to bouts of depression. 'Life,' she wrote, after one routine day, 'seems v. full of cinders.' She had been at loggerheads for most of the year with the features editor of the *Sunday Chronicle*, and had finally been informed that her contract would not be renewed in December. At the beginning of that month, however, she recorded an evening spent with Snow, which she highlighted with two lines in the margin of her diary; Snow had been 'very kind to me', she wrote, '& I felt the President of the Immortals had let Tess off his sport for a while.' Snow spent Christmas in Devon with Jack Plumb and Bert Howard, but returned to take Pamela to a New Year's Eve party at which Hattie Jacques had sung. However, Pamela did not enjoy the party at all, dismissing the other guests as being 'a dim lot of high earning professional people', and she left early, having been visited once again by 'le cafard – horrible – complete'. She ended that year's diary with two fraught lines: 'That's all. Can't say more. This has been a tormented year. Success – loss – le cafard – no. Can't say more.'

Matters seemed to worsen in the first week of January 1949. Neil, who had felt ill throughout December, was depressed and morose; Pamela was worried about money, and concerned about both her children, as usual wondering if she was at fault, as a neglectful mother, engrossed in her work. A typical diary entry read: 'A hellish day in this thoroughly black patch.' She only had short telephone conversations with Snow that week; the reason for this was likely to have been that, according to information given to Donald Dickson by Snow, his affair with Holly Southwell had then been at its peak. (Holly was working in Lincoln as a mathematics teacher, and before her term started that January, she stayed at the deluxe Connaught Hotel in London at Snow's expense.) In total ignorance, as she would remain, of Holly's existence, that same month, Pamela's relationship with Snow became again a source of comfort and hope to her. Dining with him to discuss the eleven pages of textual criticism he had compiled on *The Philistines* had made for a 'very happy & peaceful' evening, and the following day, her diary entry read: 'Felt serene today, & as if it would come out all right. Always nervous of these feelings, but one needs courage about them.' Another day, after Snow had shown interest in the background to her first novel, they went together on a tour of Battersea Rise. 'He was very amused by it all', she wrote '& felt that despite my own "Arabian Nights" atmosphere, I had got rather more reality into the book than he had thought.' Holly, on the other hand, was aware of his friendship with Pamela, but believed that she was just one of the 'sad friends' Snow felt obliged to help. 'Poor Pam', she wrote to him in January 1949, 'You're a good man and a good friend. I adore you.'[18]

Snow had told Pamela that he had decided to follow her example by writing a play, and that, to do this, he would need to take himself off to the Dudley Hotel in Hove for three weeks in isolation. The resultant play, *The Ends of the Earth*, was not in the manner of a French farce, but had it been, he would not have been short of his favoured source of inspiration, namely autobiographical material. His isolation was not unbroken; Holly visited him there one weekend, even though she afterwards wrote to him apologizing for having behaved 'abominably',[19] and Pamela was surprised to hear casually from the equally volatile Maureen Gebbie that, one Saturday, *she* had been to visit him. Pamela evidently immediately telephoned Snow in some perturbation, and, by the 4 p.m. post the same day, he 'explained' that Maureen had descended on him 'out of the blue [...] thereby wasting a valuable afternoon before I rushed her off after dinner'. Further to allay any suspicions Pamela might still have about Maureen, he added: 'I don't need to tell you that she is a wild and dangerous creature, though to be pitied', and as balm to an older rival's ears: 'By the way, I've never seen anyone of her age wear physically before one's eyes.' Add to these incursions, the possibility that the life-changing correspondence between Snow and Pamela that month might have prompted *her* to make a spontaneous, unheralded, visit, at the same time as one of his other female visitors, and the peace of his supposedly monastic retreat might have been irrevocably shattered.

CHAPTER 10

'I Have Been Infinitely, Infinitely Enriched'

P AMELA AND SNOW exchanged an enormous volume of correspondence throughout 1949, which is revelatory, not only with
regard to the consolidation of their emotional relationship, but
also in its testimony to their joint literary ambitions.[1] The first letter
sent by Snow from Hove on the first of February 1949, makes clear
that, before leaving London, they had finally made some form of declaration of love, however equivocal, to one another. (There is an indecipherable shorthand note in her diary following a mundane account of
their last meeting in January.) Snow's handwriting on small sheets
of hotel notepaper, always difficult to decipher, is noticeably more
cramped, possibly caused by awareness of the major step forward he
was taking. He began by evidently continuing a recent conversation:

> My dearest Pam,
> I say again: I would not have it otherwise. Do not think of that as
> arrogant – I often am, as with all else you accuse me of, but not with
> you. I mean that you have enriched my life in more ways than any
> other person:[2] and I believe that, not quite to the same extent, I have
> made a difference to you. That no one can take away from us. It will
> always be so. Fate has played an ironic trick, and sometimes I find it
> very hard to take, and shall for a long time. But it is a comfort to say,
> just for once, that I shall never admit any woman to the place you hold,
> never till I die.

He continued more mundanely by discussing the difficulties he was
experiencing regarding his play, adding some comments about her

work in progress, but signing for the first time 'My love, Charles'. Almost always to the other women in his life, he had signed himself 'CPS', as I will henceforward refer to him.

In her diary, Pamela warily merely recorded: 'V. beautiful letter from Snow.' Her reply the same day initially addressed him as usual by his surname:

> Snow, my dear, No one has ever written to me anything more beautiful. If I answer you at all dully, it is because I am at the moment too moved to get my thoughts in order. They are still swimming about me in a haze [...]
>
> I too wouldn't have it otherwise; I have been infinitely, infinitely enriched. I am glad that we can talk a little – it's better that way. I was beginning to wonder [...] how much I had invented – how many overtones I'd caught that did not exist, whether it simply wasn't true. I don't know when I have been in a state of such utter bewilderment.

She continued, this time allowing herself the pleasure of using his first name:

> Dear Charles (I shan't use your first name generally, only upon occasion) – you know the worst trouble of my heart & the nagging fear of <u>hurting</u>. Not only you, but – oh, you know. And it's a heavy thing, to make up one's mind never to hurt. But I must not do this, because I couldn't bear it.
>
> Meanwhile, part of me is preposterously happy & the world so rich. (2 February 1949)

CPS evidently took 'the worst trouble of her heart' as meaning that she could not bring herself to leave Neil, and told her:

> Do you think that I don't know how important it is for you to act in the way that seems to you good? Do you think that I don't know that, if you acted violently out of accord with what you feel is good, you would carry a weight that would darken life? (6 February 1949)

In a long reply, Pamela began by hastily denying that she had meant her first reply to be understood as 'a valediction': 'Last night, while I was struggling to sleep, I suddenly saw the whole of my letter to you, & I knew for certain that you would misread it. It isn't your fault – it is mine. What an ass I am!' (8 February 1949). CPS happily seized

the chance allowed by the non-existent 'valediction' misunderstand-
ing to prevaricate a little:

> I did misread your letter slightly. Not quite so much as you thought,
> but still enough. Dear, let me say one thing in return for yours. Just
> now we ought to try not to worry about each other. You are in the
> same world, to use your lovely phrase. So am I. Let's bask there for
> a bit. You've had more than enough to cope with – without new
> dramas, ordeals, or what you will. (9 February 1949)

In her letter of 8 February, Pamela had in turn interspersed further
emotional outpourings with discussions of their current literary work
and their long-term aim to defend the novel of realism against the
current vogue for experimentation. Hearing that CPS's publisher had
expressed admiration for *Time of Hope*, she said: 'So he should! My dear,
things will go <u>for</u> us, & soon. We have to touch the young people.'
She continued with an account of a lecture she had given the previous
day at the Student Movement House: 'My students were mostly girls
& boys in their twenties from London University, all very indoctri-
nated by <u>Horizon</u>, muddled, leftish, & shocked by my denigration of
fashionable gods.' And she finished that section of her letter with a
presumably rhetorical question: 'There couldn't be something wrong
with <u>us</u>, could there?' (8 February 1949).
  In another letter, she was highly indignant about the reaction of her
agent to the first parts of *The Philistines*:

> Spencer had read my chapters, & was tepid about them. It was very
> <u>precise</u> writing, he though. He doubted if it would go in America. He
> wanted to know if anything was likely to happen. Suggested it would
> be drab, & finally said with a beady, tender & false look, "Pamela,
> darling, why don't you write me a best-seller?" He was, in fact, at his
> most trying, & in the mood that makes unperceptive artistic persons
> fail to love him.

A favourable review of P.H. Newby's *The Snow Pastures* by George D.
Painter in *The Listener* caused her to expostulate: 'I am so tired of these
<u>childish</u> intellectuals, with their shallow undergraduate tastes. [...]
"Ungrownupness" is one of the things we must attack. We must get
it into the heads of the public that we are Bigger & Better intellectually – which is true! Is it not, my love?' (10 February 1949).

Little definite action regarding their way forward had been agreed between them before CPS's return to London after some three weeks, after which they continued for some time, in Snow's word, 'basking'. They dined alone together occasionally, and took advantage of random free time after PEN meetings. As will later be established, at this stage, neither of them appears to have suggested consummating their declared love for each other. Nevertheless, onlookers were aware that their relationship was undergoing some form of change; the novelist Irene Rathbone later told Josephine Pullein-Thompson, a fellow committee member of PEN, that she remembered the atmosphere of the meetings of the House Committee and the Programme Committee of which both Pamela and Snow were members at that time as being 'sultry'.[3]

Pamela had included a reference to her recently completed novel in that joyous letter of 2 February: 'I owe you so much. If <u>The Philistines</u> turns out as we hope, I shall owe it to you utterly, and it will be yours as nothing else could be.' Despite the fact that CPS had read and discussed with her each part of the book as it was written, there seem to be only marginal traces of his influence, either in content or style, in contrast with more noticeable features in some of her later novels. *The Philistines* is not overtly autobiographical, compared with CPS's Lewis Eliot sequence of novels, yet the theme of a young woman marrying unwisely just before the onset of the Second World War, and entering into a close but unfulfilled relationship with a colleague while her husband is serving abroad, does have echoes of Pamela's own experience.

The setting of *The Philistines* is an outer London suburb, which is the antithesis of the sympathetically-described inner London suburbs of Pamela's early novels. She possibly had the years of her exile in Laleham in mind, as she portrayed the parochialism of 'Branley'. The novel opens, however, with a lyrical description of the central character, Gwen Burgand, awakening the morning after her wedding, in the country cottage lent to her and her new husband Clifford for their honeymoon:

> The sun had risen behind the fringe of tall, dry grasses, the headless stems of the opium poppies. Streaming across the field beyond the house, it filled web and stem with scarlet light. She shivered a little in the chilly young air of the day, enjoyed the pull of the nightdress across

her moist body. All sensation was beautiful, even to the movement of a finger, the flutter of a lash. All sensation was heightened by the joy of utter relief. Having doubted so long, she found herself a proper woman; she had known already the small, sure promise of pleasure. She was satisfied with the discovery of love.[4]

Gwen's father, a country solicitor, had died when Gwen was ten years old, leaving very little money, so her mother had had to move to London to find work, and scrimp and save to send her daughter to university. At seventeen, Gwen had 'dreamed of becoming a painter' and had 'bright and detailed pictures of success to come', but found herself, by her mother's choice, reading sociology, and then working in East End settlement housing (p.11). She goes reluctantly with a friend to a tennis-club dance in Branley, and is immediately courted by Clifford Burgand, to her amazement as her friend has made clear that he was 'regarded as the local Prince Charming'. Clifford is handsome, has a steady job as head cashier in a local bank, and she is flattered by his attentions, and feels 'loved and mastered' (p.15). Before their engagement had been announced, Gwen has become more clear-sighted about him, her feelings being elucidated in Pamela's elegant and insightful prose:

> She was more sure than ever before in her life that she was truly in love; and then, for certain moments that were like falls into a cold and tremendous space, infinitely less sure. She watched him closely, trying to separate her thoughts from the excitement of her body. In the daytime he seemed not so glorious – this she could admit; but she succeeded in finding in him a boyish quality, something a little pathetic, which filled her with a tenderness great enough to engulf the faint nag of disappointment. (p.16)

After their marriage, they move in with Clifford's mother and spinster sister on what is planned to be a temporary basis, but which drifts on indefinitely. Gwen finds the pettiness of suburban society hard to bear. With her background in social work, Gwen becomes assistant almoner at the local hospital during the war after Clifford has been called up, and is posted abroad. She is befriended by Paul Smith, one of the specialists, who gives her a lift home some evenings, and they later occasionally have dinner together, and talk about literature. The physical characterization of Paul Smith bears little resemblance to CPS, yet his effect on Gwen may well reflect Pamela's see-sawing feelings towards Snow during Neil's absence. One evening, when he has invited Gwen out for a drive: 'He said good night in his usual solemn, warm, casual fashion, and left her standing beneath the corner lamp-post, trembling, half-angry, bewildered by the chaos of her thoughts.' (p.43)

Two years of these platonic meetings pass by, and the war comes to an end, and Gwen, like the dutiful wife she wishes to be, gives up her work to be at home full-time when Clifford returns. Soon afterward, Paul tells her that he will be working for some months in Austria, and Gwen believes that her attachment to him had been no more than 'a fancy dragged out of romantic childhood to add a little gilding to the present'. In what was presumably an unwitting plagiarism from the final scene of Noël Coward's *Brief Encounter* (1945), she now looks at Clifford and thinks: 'My darling, I've come back to you; and you never knew I'd gone away, did you?' (p.74). But very soon afterward, when Paul comes to say goodbye until the following year, she admits to her recent self-delusion:

> 'I love Paul, of course', she said quietly to herself, 'but I shan't let this love do me or anyone harm. It will not lessen and it will not grow. I shall keep it as the illumination of my life. To make me better, not worse. To make me more kind. More strong.' All this she said aloud, but so softly that in her ears it was like the voice of another person a little way removed, trying to reach her through a dream. (p.76)

Gwen is however equally deluded in this resolve, for life in Branley now seems to her to be 'more than usually stale and restricted, conversation more stupid'. Whereas she had previously deliberately not reacted to reactionary remarks, 'now she was finding it less easy to be silent, the itch of her own loss, her own frustration, like a demon standing inside her body, already ready to thrust some word of bitterness or contempt through her lips' (pp.145-46). After a particularly fraught evening with local people, the spokeswoman for whom is one Doris Hedley, Gwen realises that she has pointlessly gone too far:

> It was impossible to change these people, who would be as they were till the day they died. Why had she arrogated to herself the right to chasten them? In many ways they were better than she. They might be thoughtlessly cruel in speech, but in action they were usually kind.

They were ordinary, unthinking, unharmful people who would never tear to pieces the structure of the life about them. (p.196)

For the remainder of the novel, she attempts to resign herself to her marriage and to a prosaic life.

Pamela was exhausted when the novel was finished, and hoped to spend the rest of the year merely writing 'profitable oddments'. In March, she spent a week in Cambridge without Neil. With some defiance, she had mentioned to CPS in Hove that: 'If I disappear just as you come home, I shall only have the melancholy satisfaction of feeling it serves you right. You disappear for long enough, God knows.' She was indeed on her own for the first two days, and wandered around the city, first 'in a sort of nervous half-delightful dream', and the following day being 'attacked by nerves, melancholy, a sense of unreality'. CPS arrived later to attend a Feast at Christ's (to which she was not invited), but they spent little time alone together, indeed she saw more of Jack Plumb that week. Back in Chelsea, she and her husband were increasingly leading separate lives; she recorded Neil being out most of the evenings that she was at home, but seemingly without too much curiosity as to where he went or with whom.

Later in March, Pamela was delighted with an approach from the *Daily Telegraph* with regard to her becoming a regular reviewer for them. She had a tussle with her conscience regarding one of their conditions, which was that she should no longer review for *John o' London's Weekly*. She knew that this would inevitably upset her long-standing colleagues at the former journal, for which she had been working for many years, but eventually accepted the offer, particularly because she felt that it would give her greater opportunities to broadcast her views. Since the end of the war, Malcolm Muggeridge had reviewed a mixture of non-fiction & fiction in the one column allocated to book reviews. More space now being available as newsprint restrictions eased, Muggeridge continued with non-fiction, and Pamela took over reviews of new novels.

The 'Peterborough' column in the *Telegraph* welcomed Miss Pamela Hansford Johnson to their literary staff on 29 April 1949, adding to a short biographical sketch, the opinion that she was 'one of those rare people who have made their name as a critic as well as an author'. In that same issue, Pamela laid out her stall emphatically. The three novels under review were *Elephant & Castle* by R.C. Hutchinson, *The Best Days* by Hugh Massingham, and *Doctor Faustus* by Thomas Mann. Before coming to her judgment of the first two books, she began:

> Some of the most admired of English novelists today have turned aside from the rich and lively humanism of the national tradition to work almost exclusively along the extreme edges of human sensibility. They work out and away from the heart, almost as though they fear it; the major experiences of human life give way to the suggestion of a distaste, the hint of an affection.
>
> Their books – narrower & narrower, increasingly subtle, almost private – are directed to persons of similar specialised sensitivities, and never to the vast mass of readers seeking more and more for what Dickens gave them, and Trollope, and Tolstoy, and other great writers of the 19th century.

Although she had some criticisms to make about the novels by Hutchinson and Massingham, she applauded both authors for 'trying to write in the English tradition, on a large scale, of people in their full stature'. She then went on in her review of *Doctor Faustus* to tackle the European tradition as exemplified by Thomas Mann, evidently not intimidated by his stature (Mann had received the Nobel Prize in Literature in 1929). 'The Enormous, Stately and Ponderous has a way of disarming criticism', she began. 'One does not carp at an elephant.' Nevertheless, her overall judgment was that: 'Mr. Thomas Mann's vast work, built up in layers, philosophical, political, theological, musical, is very impressive and almost unreadable.'

Meanwhile, *Corinth House* had been successfully adapted for the radio, with the distinguished actress Gladys Young playing Miss Malleson. Pamela also extended the range of her radio programmes from talks for the Third Programme to participation in a long-forgotten programme, 'Stump the Story-Tellers', with Richard Dimbleby, Denis Norden and Frank Muir, which she found 'great fun'. Her mother, her aunt Kalie and CPS were among the studio audience. When she listened to the recording, she wrote: 'I did sound a snooty bitch! – But was astounded by my own presence of mind!' Sadly, virtually all her programmes are among the many whose tapes were wiped by the BBC. Despite these achievements, Pamela nevertheless continued to worry about the future; on April 1, she wrote of feeling 'unspeakably depressed all day, trying to greet the unseen – not with a cheer, but at least with some of honourable fortitude. God knows what it will bring.' (On this occasion, as on many others, she found comfort from her small daughter; taking her out that afternoon cheered her a little, as Lindsay had been 'very gay & sweet, & my heart's comfort'.) When a few days later, CPS's work took him to Preston to inspect a new aeroplane, and she didn't hear from him while he was away, she reflected that so few people knew of their relationship that no-one would think to tell her if he were to be run over.

In the Easter holidays that year, Kay Dick and Kathleen Farrell suggested that Pamela and her now eight-year-old son, Andrew, should spend a week away together in Buckinghamshire, close to the homes of the parents of both Ks, so that they could be entertained by them all. CPS came to dinner on the second evening and stayed the night with the Dicks; Pamela only recorded that she had had to hurry off to be back at her lodgings by midnight. However, meetings as brief as this seemed to suffice for CPS; he wrote to her as soon as he had returned to London:

> Darling Pam,
> On Tuesday night I found myself wishing that this particular moment could go on for ever. Cowardly, if you like: but I don't know. I think we've both got some excuse for cowardice. To be engaged, day in, day out, in a war on three fronts is pretty hard, even for us. Against ourselves; and others: and all we have set out to do. No wonder we are tired.
>
> I wish our public battle was at a stage when we could sit back and relax [...]. We must strengthen each other again, my darling. I suppose it would be better if I began another book. I am glad the cricket season is coming: it sounds silly, but for an odd afternoon it takes the edge off one's thoughts. I wish you had a sedative like that. Anyway, you must come with me, and I shall wish that afternoon prolonged to all eternity ... (14 April 1949)

It is significant that he specified 'all we have set out to do' as one aspect of the 'war' in which they were allies; Pamela only recorded having received his letter without adjectival comment. Since, as she later testified, she could not pretend that any form of games really absorbed her (*Important*, p.199), it was unlikely that she would have empathized with his looking forward to the panacea of afternoons at Lord's.

The remainder of the week scarcely offered the respite for which Pamela had hoped. The relationship between Kay and Kathleen was, as so often, in one of its more explosive phases. However, she reflected that: 'It served (so selfish is human nature) to remove my mood most blessedly from my own troubles.' She sent a long account of the situation to CPS, in which it is clear with whom her sympathies then lay: 'Kay', she wrote, 'is nice-natured but hopelessly weak. Kathleen can be very cruel, & doesn't hesitate to remind her of her dependency.' She did not speculate as to whether their rows that week might have been caused by Kay's notorious infidelities. (Earlier that year, in fact on that fateful second of February, she had recorded in her diary that: 'Kay Dick rang up fantastically to ask, with much circumlocution, whether I knew a doctor who would do an abortion!!' Pamela had told her that she did not have that kind of doctor.) Her son, oblivious of the atmosphere, had enjoyed the visit, particularly the riding lessons which had been arranged for him, and his explorations in the woods around their lodgings with his mother, and when Neil came for the last two days of their stay, Pamela was pleased to have his company.

As the year progressed, Pamela's wish to work only on 'profitable oddments' was only semi-fulfilled. She was indeed busy with 'oddments', reviewing, broadcasting, lecturing and writing short articles, but they were not sufficiently profitable to keep the household afloat. Her usage of Benzedrine increased, but she justified this to herself by describing it as a necessity for 'keeping in trim'. Eventually, Neil found a job with the Hungarian News Agency, which did mean she was no longer the sole breadwinner. They still participated in the round of literary parties and dinners, which occasionally led to uneasy confrontations, as when she met Elizabeth Taylor for the first time, having recently, as she put it in her diary, struggled to be fair to the novelist, 'whose work is a prototype of everything I hate'. Pamela depicted her as 'pretty & mousy, & obviously ready to attack me with an axe', but added: 'Can't blame her for this, naturally.' She and Neil gave their own evening party at the end of May (taking CPS to a local pub beforehand to dine); it was, she thought, 'a great & crowded success', with the guest list almost entirely composed of Pamela's literary, broadcasting, and publishing acquaintances.

Time of Hope was now at the proof stage, and CPS sent it to her for her further comments; this novel, a *bildungsroman*, is chronologically the first of the *Strangers and Brothers* series. Lewis Eliot therefore is the central figure, recording the events of his life, from the genteel poverty of his childhood, to his success as a barrister, and to the torture of his marriage to the unstable Sheila Knight, a thinly disguised portrait of Sheila Palfreyman. Because of the hopeless love Eliot has for Sheila, Pamela had found discussing the novel with CPS as presenting 'peculiar difficulties', although she had tried not to let this affect her critical faculties. Indeed, she told him in a letter, that she believed that 'this is a great novel, & no one with any taste or human feeling at all could fail to see it'. However, she confessed that 'Paragraphs 3 & 4 on p.414 touch a raw nerve'. In the final chapter of the book, Lewis Eliot realises he is incapable of sending his wife away, despite the knowledge that: 'I was about to sentence myself for life.' In one of the paragraphs to which Pamela referred, Eliot then further explains that his bondage to Sheila was 'no chance':

> Somehow I was so made that I had to reject my mother's love and all its successors. Some secret caution born of a kind of vanity made me bar my heart to any who forced their way within. I could only lose caution and vanity, bar and heart, the whole of everything I was, in the torment of loving someone like Sheila, who invaded me not at all […].[5]

Pamela clearly felt that CPS was here revealing as much about himself as about his fictional alter ego, and told him that, while she felt Eliot's analysis of himself held good, it had made her worry about her own role in the author's life, because: 'There are times when I feel I would rather not be an oasis – ever.'

CPS had written to her that he had meant to dedicate the book to her, but had changed his mind: 'I think it would be a mistake until the battle is won, and that our self-denying ordinance still applies.' However, he then announced his intention eventually to dedicate the whole series to her as 'the only possible step which can express all I feel' (20 June 1949). This would give him some breathing space as he proposed to do this 'probably in three or four books' time'. Pamela was however thrilled by this promise, writing in her diary: 'I feel it to be an almost impossible honour, & which touches me beyond words.'

Time of Hope became dedicated to 'Dick', his friend Richard Cohen, with whom, despite the Charles March affair, he had remained on good terms.

In June, CPS's circle was shaken by another acrimonious dispute regarding identifiable characters, this time, as previously mentioned, involving Harry Hoff, who had finally found a publisher (Jonathan Cape) for *Scenes from Provincial Life*, the satirical novel which was to prove the springboard for his literary career. It would seem that it was to the surprise of both Hoff and CPS that it was J.H. Plumb who was threatening legal action with regard to Hoff's character, 'Tom' — he is never given a surname 'for reasons of delicacy' (*Provincial*, p.15). Bert Howard, with rather more cause, had not objected to CPS's portrait of him in *Strangers and Brothers*, and might indeed, with anyone's knowledge of his Alderman Newton's School circle, believed himself to have again been portrayed in fictional form as Tom in Hoff's novel, yet it was their historian friend Plumb who maintained that Tom could be thought to have been based on him, despite the character's early description as being red-haired, Jewish and an accountant (pp.15-16). Nevertheless, when CPS phoned Pamela to tell her about this, her reaction was: 'God knows how we [*sic*] shall think our way out of <u>this</u>. Jack has an excellent case & is, in fact, being poorly treated, but it will drive H. to suicide if he can't publish this.' Her sympathy was however reserved not for either of the two main adversaries, but as usual for CPS, because he was, she wrote, 'in desperation'. Although CPS had changed the cause of the downfall of 'George Passant', Hoff had no qualms about revealing Tom's predilection for young, generally male, uneducated partners. But Tom, unlike George Passant, does not suffer ignominy, but ends up married and living in America, where he found 'a limitless field for his bustling bombinations, spiritual, emotional and geographical' (p.215).

Plumb decided that he could let publication go ahead once Harry Hoff had metamorphosed into William Cooper. Speculation about the sexual orientation of all three Leicester-born friends never, however, quite faded away; the novelist Francis King, a waspish member of the two Ks' Hampstead and Brighton clique, included the following innuendo in his obituary of 'William Cooper' in the *Independent* (6 September 2002):

Although Cooper seemed always to open himself out to company like a flower to the sun, one none the less suspected, as with C.P. Snow and another close friend, Jack Plumb, a secret life of which there was no hint in even the most autobiographical of his novels. Whether that secret life existed, and, if it did, what was its precise nature, some future biographer will no doubt eventually tell us.

CPS attempted to convince Pamela that the matter had so exhausted him that only three weeks away in Devon would revive him. She meanwhile could have no such release from constant anxieties and felt injured by his lack of support for her. Harry, in one of his almost daily phone calls, 'joked about how a certain person always found slaves', which, she wryly remarked to herself, was 'only too true'. Hoff, CPS's confidant with regard to all his liaisons, might well have teasingly had Holly Southwell in mind rather than Pamela. CPS had not severed his relationship with Holly, who was not financially independent, and indeed, according to her letter to him in May, he had offered to part-finance her purchase of a 'hypothetical flat' to enable her to move to London. 'Sweet', she wrote to him, 'from the pride point of view, I don't care <u>what</u> I take from you provided I'm sure always I didn't make it hard for you.' She had evidently been kept informed about the state of affairs regarding Pamela as she continued: 'I hope I don't ever make it harder for Pam by taking any of you further away.' Somewhat ambiguously, she continued: 'I couldn't, could I, you being what you are!'[6] The following month, Holly visited CPS again, and subsequently told him that: 'Times with you get nicer and nicer, and this time was <u>specially</u> close, somehow.'[7] Snow did go to Devon in July; Holly was not able to join him there, although they did discuss this, as his weeks there clashed with her school commitments.

That month, Pamela was preparing to give a talk, entitled 'The Limitation of the Novel', to be broadcast on the Third Programme.[8] Things started inauspiciously when she left her only copy of the draft in a taxi, and found herself 'absolutely staggered' by what she called 'this relatively small misfortune', even though, disproportionately, she then maintained that she felt like Carlyle.[9] She found the rewriting onerous, and her difficulties continued. She had already found the BBC producer, Anna Kallin, 'too bossy for a person in my exacerbated state', when meeting her in February in connection with the Dickens broadcast mentioned in my first chapter; in fact, Pamela had continued then: 'I could have brained her with a blunt instrument if one had lain to my hand.' Now Kallin was again her producer and attempting to interfere with the content of the talk, in which Pamela hoped to reach beyond the readers of her *Daily Telegraph* column to proclaim her beliefs about the current literary climate. She began by 'outlining the problem of the ordinary cultivated reader and his unconscious enemy, the esoteric critic'. The latter, she went on to say 'has thrown his entire influence into the support of experiment as a be-all and end-all.' She continued, still more forcefully:

> If the English novel goes to its death, it will have been driven there by the most deliberate campaign to narrow and restrict its scope in the history of English criticism. It is being diverted from its mainstream, deprived of its force and richness, and reduced to the mere expression of a certain type of nervous sensibility.
>
> The great novels of the world have been stories about human beings, deeply and fully realised, living the major experiences of their lives in the surroundings of their time.
>
> Mr. T.S. Eliot has declared that the novel is no longer of any serious value. I do not believe this is true. [...] There are already signs of hope, signs of a renaissance, signs of a new vitality and strength.

Finally, in support of that argument, she quoted the concluding passages from two contemporary novels, which, she said, sounded 'the note of the English tradition at its most robust, stoical, humane and forward-looking, the note of affirmation: it affirms the indestructibility of the spirit of man'. One of these is from Joyce Cary's *The Horse's Mouth* – the other is from CPS's *Strangers and Brothers*. She recorded in her diary that she had had a 'tense argument with Anna Kallin re including the Snow extract in my talk. I will <u>not</u> tolerate dictation on matters of taste from these people & made it clear'.

With all this going on, and feeling generally 'drab & tired' in CPS's absence, Pamela wrote directly to an unknown future biographer, who might be the first to read her diaries:

> When I read these diaries I think how tiresome I shall one day seem to anyone who reads them, & how they will think themselves clever to realise that I must have been infinitely trying to everyone about me. Let me tell them that <u>I</u> realise it. This kind of nervous unhappiness is

horribly selfish at core – we touch bottom when we realise the pleasur-able element – that we do <u>not want</u> to be quite cured again. Yet I do try not to make life too bad for everyone at home – indeed, I think N. is unharmed by me.

(To insert a personal note, when I noticed that the entry was dated 17 July, which happens to be my birthday, this biographer felt all the more keenly, as other biographers must, should they come as close to their subject's inner thoughts, a voyeuristic guilt as well as great sympathy.)

It didn't help then that Pamela was feeling insecure about her relationship with CPS and wondering whether she had yet another rival, the splendidly-named Lady Germaine Elizabeth Olive Eliot, divorcée daughter of the eighth Earl St Germans. CPS had told Pamela that he was contemplating visiting an old acquaintance, 'Liz', as she was generally known, while in the West Country, as she had now returned to living in the family seat, Port Eliot, in Cornwall. His first letter from Devon, however, was full of vexation at the news that his aristocratic friend's first novel, *Alice*, had become the October Book Society Choice, and he wrote to Pamela that it was more imperative than ever for one or other of them to get 'a resounding success'. 'It's hateful', he continued, 'being the prey to this kind of petty envy':

But Alice is about 1/10 as good as [*Time of Hope*] or [*The Philistines*]. Fancy beginning with that kind of luck! When we need it to get hold of our steady 30000 public – which is what we must have.

It might have been understandable for Pamela, with all her financial problems, to have yearned for that number of sales, but although CPS had a more than adequate income from his dual salaries, his ambition was to take early retirement and live on his earnings as a writer. Nevertheless, it is arguable that a conflict might have arisen between their aim for higher sales figures and their joint desire to be acknowledged as major intellectual writers. As his brother recorded, CPS's sales in the 1950s averaged around 12,000,[10] a respectable amount for the latter aim, but higher sales, and Book Society nominations, would have left him on the brink of the popularity which might have had a deleterious effect on his literary standing.

CPS had ended his letter unwisely by fuelling Pamela's suspicions about Liz Eliot, as he continued in mock self-effacing mode:

> God knows, we oughtn't to begrudge Liz her luck. She is 38 and has had a most unhappy life [...]. She has never found love where she wanted it. I ought to confess more things to you, and hide less: so I now confess, with my usual sense of outrage, that she has thought once or twice that I was a man whom she could respect. I wish she'd find some decent and intelligent man." (19 July 1949)

Pamela responded that he should indeed hide less, telling him that: 'I spend such a lot of time guessing, and usually guess right. [...] I reveal things by the notes of my voice, you by your silences and changes of subject. I should be more at ease with you if you told me more' (21 July 1949). In a follow-up letter, she apologized having possibly made him feel 'dark & guilty', but explained that: 'I did feel bad & deserted & overweighed, & couldn't keep it out of my letter.' She then hastily changed the subject to let him know about her current work. One item illustrates her generosity to writers she admired whose abilities had not as yet been recognised. She was still occasionally acting as a publisher's reader, and she told CPS delightedly:

> I have discovered a novelist!! Her name is Doris Lessing. She is in her early twenties. I had her first MSS from Joseph's, the story of a South African Madame Bovary, called <u>In Black & White</u>. If Michael doesn't publish this he is quite mad. [...] The depth of this work is surprising, & the faults only those of youth – & very few at that. I am really badgering Joseph's about this work. (25 July 1949)

The future Nobel laureate's novel was indeed to be published by Michael Joseph the following year, as *The Grass is Singing*.

CPS was at that time fretting over losing his American publisher, and was seeking sympathy and reassurance about his own literary career. Pamela told him in her following letter that 'half the writers of repute' in Great Britain had similar problems as regards publication in the United States, including Newby 'with all his absurdly inflated reputation here'. Nevertheless, she was currently feeling emboldened about the worth of her own writing as well as his. She was due to record her talk on the state of the English novel that day, having evidently won her battle with Anna Kallin. She told CPS before she left for Broadcasting House: 'I am quite sure there is a strong feeling <u>against</u> me at the BBC – which I shall deepen triumphantly today, when I record my arrogant talk and declaim the end of S & B.' And, still in defiant mode, she concluded:

> Who so beset us round, my heart, with dismal stories, Do but themselves confound – our strength the more is.[12] I am afraid of none of these people, & I am certain they cannot frustrate us for ever. Have you the slightest doubt of the value of your own work? – No. Nor have I of mine. (Except in a few bad moments.) (26 July 1949)

In his final letter from Devon that summer, CPS eventually answered her unspoken question as to his present relationship with Liz Eliot, with a denial which, perhaps in this case, might have been justified:

> You blame me for things when I'm to blame – and just occasionally when I'm not. I could no more 'spring' a name of importance on you, casual-like, than I could fly. I am secretive, I try to hide a depression and guilt of which I am ashamed and which links with flaws in my character. But that state is purely internal and has no real relation to a situation or person or persons, and no such person or person has a claim or hold upon me. I don't like you thinking ill of me for good reason: and I don't like it much better when the reasons aren't so good. You couldn't think that I should 'spring' a situation, in the vulgar sense, upon you? My dear girl. (1 August 1949)

When CPS returned to London, Pamela was able to meet him on several occasions. The evening on which they listened together to the transmission of her recent talk was, she wrote, 'the happiest I've ever spent in his company'. Later, evidently without any objection from Neil, they were both weekend guests at Spencer Curtis Brown's house in Suffolk. Soon afterward, Pamela was herself away from London, having arranged a holiday in Rottingdean with her mother, aunt and the two children. To her surprise, Harry Hoff telephoned shortly after their arrival to tell her he had decided to spend a week of that time in Brighton, and was thereafter in constant attendance. Whether Harry was, as in a Shakespearian plot, trying to test the fidelity of his best friend's inamorata, cannot be established, but he certainly gave Pamela the impression that he might be 'secretly too fond' of her.

'This may be pure vanity & <u>obtuseness</u> on my part,' she wrote in her diary, '[but I] am far too attached to him to contemplate this with equanimity.' CPS only came down for one afternoon during the twelve days that she was away, but they corresponded fondly throughout. Pamela's first letter from Rottingdean to her now 'darling Charles' was a mixture of poetic description, praise for his latest work, and playfulness:

> The downs were splendid. There was a lavender sky below & a grey & lemon one above the horizon: the hillsides were covered with lights, & a violin was playing somewhere in the valley. I stood all by myself & looked at it, & thought about you with joy.
>
> You and I are secretly dominated – really – by <u>hubris,</u> but I wasn't worrying about it just then. [...] I'll write about the play tomorrow. It is splendid! (When you come down I shall give you a "look of devotion". I tried it today, but can't get quite the right sort of look yet. Perhaps it is the look I call Assessment. My love! You are such fun!) (20 August 1949)

CPS replied: 'Your letter was enchanting and gave me nothing but delight from the first word to the last. When you are in high spirits you're not earth-bound at all.' He went on however to discuss whether they should necessarily fear hubris:

> I was happier, more than that, more joyful last Friday night than for years past. As though the years were abolished and there was no weight at all. I felt free and innocent. I felt we were even living alone in the world. Hubris, God knows. Of course, we are both upset by it. Perhaps it's natural. After all, we have each sacrificed much (not through an act of will, but because we were made that way) for the triumphs to come. We can't help the dread that, when we are exultantly happy, we shall pay somewhere else. I think hubris is a deep component of all people such as we are. (22 August 1949)

(Pamela had recorded in her diary, but without censure, an example of his hubristic tendency only the previous month, when he had told her that *Time of Hope* had been selected as a Book Society 'Recommend', rather than the monthly Choice, and that this had made him feel 'like Aeschylus receiving 4th Prize in the Greek Drama Festival!')

The play to which Pamela had referred was CPS's *The Ends of the Earth*, which had been televised earlier that year, but, in a revised version, was now in production for a short run at the Lyric, Hammersmith. Pamela had found it difficult to be objective about the play, as she felt that the central character was a self-portrait, while her Aunt Kalie, on reading the manuscript, had insisted that CPS had based the love interest, somewhat bizarrely called Anne, on Pamela herself. Kalie's judgment had, she told CPS 'initially flabbergasted' her, although she admitted that there could be said to be a 'poignant resemblance'. Nevertheless, she told CPS that she approved of the revised version:

> The big love scene doesn't come too suddenly now. This play will always wring my withers, even when I am eighty & the withers are almost too dry to be wrung. It is odd, when you do make a self-portrait, how harsh you are with yourself. You always hint that you are nastier than I think. I maintain that you are nicer than you think. Anyway, you are the way I like you to be.

The play ran at Hammersmith for the allotted week with moderate success, and then CPS became wildly excited when the impresario, C.B. Cochrane, began negotiations for a West End transfer.

Family holidays over, Pamela was now able to fulfil her dream of some uninterrupted days with CPS in arguably the most romantic city in the world. She had been invited to address the PEN Congress in Venice in September, and although CPS had not planned to attend, she persuaded him to go with her a few days in advance of the start of the official proceedings. Yet, despite their passionate correspondence throughout the year, their acknowledged 'self-denying ordinance' was even to survive their visit to 'La Serenissima'. Pamela (unlike the uninhibited Maureen Gebbie during the course of a similar event in Copenhagen, the previous year) still did not wish their relationship to be consummated sexually, and it would seem that CPS did not press her. After a ferry crossing, they travelled to Venice by train; Pamela found the whole journey 'wildly exciting', but she found a difficulty on arrival. She had asked PEN to arrange some modest accommodation for her, but no booking had been made. CPS had arranged to meet some old friends, the best-selling novelist Francis Brett Young and his wife Jessica, at the expensive Hotel Cavalletto, close to the Piazza San Marco, and so they booked them both into their hotel, in separate rooms, for the first evening. Presumably Brett

Young did not read all his reviews, or at any rate, did not remember a mocking review of his novel, *The Far Forest*, by a tyro reviewer in the *Liverpool Post* in 1936, as Pamela did not record any froideur between them.

The next day, with the help of the hotel management, Pamela was able to move to the Taverno Fenice, a hotel more within her budget. CPS, who would be remaining at the Cavalletto, accompanied her there. She recorded that: 'They first thought S & I were together & gave us a huge preposterous double room. Then moved me into a tiny squalid one!' The next two days were not particularly blissful; her glands were troubling her, it was cold with heavy rainstorms, and they had to spend much of the time with the Brett Youngs. But on the third day, the BYs (as she called them) were too tired to dine with them, and Pamela and CPS were able to spend the evening on their own. After dinner, they went for a long walk, and had a long talk; an indecipherable shorthand note (and evidence from a letter written by Pamela to CPS shortly after he left) points to this having been a watershed in their relationship. But, to use Pamela's analogy from *Tess of the d'Urbevilles* in her diary at the end of 1948, 'the Immortals' were still attempting to have sport with her, because the following morning, awakening in her own hotel, she discovered herself to be 'mutilated and half blind with mosquito bites'. She had to telephone CPS to ask him to escort her to the 'dreary inaugural meeting' of the congress, where she felt 'ugly and awful & an object of pity'. (The painful experience would prove to have been not totally without value for her, as she would later fictionalize it in an entertaining episode of her novel, *Catherine Carter*.) The Brett Youngs again came to her aid, and insisted on moving her back to the mosquito-free luxury of the Cavalletto (presumably at their expense). And even the weather changed for the better; she and CPS spent a quiet, happy afternoon in a little park by the Grand Canal 'which was superb with sun & jade green water'.

The next day was CPS's last full day in Venice; they dined 'magically at the Gritti Palace', and the next morning she watched him riding off 'statelily in a gondola'. Pamela could not articulate her feelings in her diary: 'Can't write of Venice at all – it is <u>too</u> glorious. It has all been <u>so</u> much!' But in an ecstatic letter to 'my own Charles', she found herself able to express herself freely:

I shall never forget this week: I think neither of us will. Let me thank
you again, darling & kiss your nose – what <u>can</u> I say? It has been
perfect, <u>trenta-tre</u>,[13] mosquitos & everything – everything! [...]
Dear love, I shall never forget anything you have said to me this week,
never, until I die. It has been pure magic – but more than that, a
magic that has become a part of life itself, a heat, & a light, something
in the very essence of my whole being. Does that sound pompous? I
am more articulate than usual today – on paper, at least – & can talk
to you.

She went on to tell him that she had had an intriguing letter from
her mother, who evidently favoured CPS as a replacement son-in-law.
Amy had written, 'maddeningly', to say that she had made an
'exciting discovery that may be of use', although it was 'one which she
wouldn't put on paper'; it seemed that she had been more suspicious
than Pamela about the many evenings on which Neil had been out
late, ostensibly at committee meetings. While Pamela had had no
reason to believe that he had not been telling the truth about these,
she nevertheless ended her letter to CPS by saying:

> Sweetheart, we must break free somehow. I am so happy with you that
> it is like an entirely new form of living – something unsuspected &
> world-transforming. I hated you to leave me, yet the glow of joy was
> so much there that my spirits kept high.
>   My love – ! Pam. (18 September, 1949)

The PEN Congress lasted three more days; the 'considerable
ovation' that Pamela had received after her speech on criticism, might,
she wrote self-deprecatingly in her diary, have been influenced by the
fact that she was '(a) female and (b) brief', but she was nevertheless
delighted. Storm Jameson, she added, had been particularly nice to
her. Various rows concerning the wording of resolutions did not burst
her bubble of happiness, and, on a post-Congress outing, she enjoyed
fending off an amorous Polish delegate who insisted that she was 'the
Byzantine beauty he had been looking for all his life'. She went to bed
that evening 'v. tired, amused & pleased with my brilliance at staving
off Gentlemen'.
    Deflation followed soon after her return to the tensions at home,
compounded by her anxiety about a decision she and Neil had come
to, which was that their son Andrew was to go that week to a

preparatory school in Eastbourne. Was this the way, she wondered, in which 'we "bourgeois" torture our children?' With Andy safely settled (according to the Matron), she determined to have a showdown with Neil. However, the following day, there was no opportunity, as he was out all day, and she could not resist an early evening invitation to Princess Marthe Bibesco's party at the Ritz, particularly because the famed Romanian writer of the *Belle Epoque* had been a close friend of Proust. She then went to see CPS, and was regaled with the details of what she called 'a <u>new</u> complex' of his, about which she had to comfort him. He told her he had been sick at intervals for the last three days, although whether this was caused by emotional turmoil, or his usual pre-publication nerves (*Time of Hope* was to be published the following day) cannot be established. She went to bed as soon as she got home, and so had no idea when Neil came home. '<u>Must</u> speak tomorrow', she resolved. And that day, she recorded the following evening, was a turning point in her life.

CHAPTER 11

'Divorce-Nausea',
'Wounded Pride',
finally 'Wondrous Joy'

T HE CONFRONTATION with her husband, over which Pamela
had been agonizing, went more smoothly than she could have
dared to hope. She had scarcely begun to broach the subject of
the apparent breakdown of their marriage before Neil freely confessed
to her that his mother-in-law's suspicions had been well-founded. His
late nights had, for the most part, not been caused by attendance at
political meetings, but had been the result of the affair he was having
with their friend, Don Musgrove (last heard of in 1940, sitting with
her husband in Pamela's garden at Laleham). Neil was, Pamela wrote
in her diary with some surprise and much relief, 'as willing as I that
we should get a divorce', and they had agreed to do this 'amicably and
without recriminations'. Even by the end of that day, however, Pamela
was worrying about how this might come about. Neil wanted to marry
Don, but was doubtful about whether she would wish to be cited as
co-respondent. CPS had been 'semi-hysterical' on hearing the news,
and she felt tired and muddled, and 'in a general state of mind utterly
beyond description'.

The next evening, however, CPS had rallied, taking her to dine at
96 Piccadilly, one of their favourite restaurants. 'He was so wonderful', Pamela wrote, and emphasized her surprise that he wanted them
to be married in church, by underlining the sentence. She was also
overwhelmed that when she had tentatively suggested that her mother
might now make her home with her sister Kalie, CPS had responded

that 'happiness cannot be built on the unhappiness of others'. In her memoir, written years later, she wrote that this had been 'splendidly unselfish, but I am not sure that it turned out to be wise' (*Important*, p.115). Perhaps it was not entirely unselfish; CPS could probably see the benefits of live-in help with his soon-to-be stepchildren.

CPS returned to becoming more distant when poor reviews of *Time of Hope* led to his usual post-publication dejection. There had been, however, one exception to the unsatisfactory reception: in her review in the *Daily Telegraph*, Pamela devoted more space to the novel than to any she had previously reviewed. 'I believe', she wrote, 'this is an English novel of the highest order, a classic of our time [...]', and continued:

> Mr. Snow has extraordinary insight into the motives of the heart [...].
> "Time of Hope" is a wonderful book. I think it can hardly fail to move any reader of human tastes and appetites who believes that the greatest art is the art most closely related to the fundamentals of human life.[1]

This praise notwithstanding, a few days later Pamela recorded that CPS 'was still v. low about his book, & I am low with "divorce-nausea"', and asked: 'How long will this awfulness continue?' At the beginning of October, Neil came to collect his belongings, and this led to a 'really dreadful and distressing' scene in which all the theatrically-inclined Howson women participated:

> I cried, & so did he, & it was horrible. Said this mightn't have happened if we'd talked a year ago. I said it was inevitable & tried to comfort him – but the whole weight of thirteen years was an <u>agony</u> of spirit. I broke down hopelessly, & so did Amy & Kalie. [...] I phoned Charles & managed to distress <u>him</u>.

CPS responded with a 'rather fierce talk', reproaching her for 'being all too frank about misery'. He subsequently wrote about his predicament to the ever-understanding but clear-headed Holly at this time, as her reply testifies. 'My poor sweet', she replied:

> I think I had better come up and see you. At least I think it would be better for me, and unless you would very much rather I did not, and can say so, I think it would be unkind of you to put me off. We needn't talk of this – of Pam, of our perhaps parting – unless we want to, which I don't. [...]

I have been feeling blank and resentful and self-pitying about you, having had no word for so many weeks [...]. But all that's wiped away at a stroke by your letter, my darling [...].

As to this happening at the worst possible time for you – I think I've said before that you are past-master at maintaining a steady run of worst possible times. I refuse to stop laughing at you. [...][2]

The reviews of Pamela's *The Philistines* had also been generally unfavourable. Julian Symons, the writer of the unsigned review in the *Times Literary Supplement*, said cuttingly that:

the novel fails particularly because Miss Johnson never convinces us that Gwen is sufficiently imaginative or sensitive to be a misfit in Philistia. [...] At the end, the reader is less inclined to congratulate Gwen on her escape from Philistia than to condole with her hosts for their long endurance of her company.[3]

Pamela was normally less inclined than CPS to brood for long about adverse critical reaction, and certainly not at this time, when she was 'dreadfully anxious to get the divorce under way'. Neil had still not made any arrangements to provide evidence of unfaithfulness, and in the course of a probably boozy lunch at the Café Royal with the temporarily reconciled Ks, Pamela was warmed by Kathleen Farrell's 'cheerful offer' to act as his co-respondent. 'Absurd,' she wrote in her diary, 'but could friendship go further?'

Pamela, of course, should have had no hand in arranging her husband's counterfeit infidelity, as if collusion between the parties were proved, her petition for divorce would have been dismissed. However, she lost patience with his procrastination and enlisted the assistance of her old friend Teddy Lamerton, now a solicitor, to act as go-between, and eventually Neil agreed to go, with an unnamed woman, to a hotel ('in Dorking!', Pamela expostulated, as though the location particularly offended her). She wrote afterwards to Kay Dick:

Neil has committed whatnot this weekend and I am waiting for the evidence. Then I shall go to my lawyer and I suppose all sorts of sordidness will set in again. Snow doesn't have to suffer from all this and I don't think he realises just how edgy I am – quietly, most of the time. [...] But this business of being neither maid nor wife, widow or thing of naught, even, is dreadfully unnerving.[4]

And indeed, all was still not plain sailing, as when she subsequently had a meeting with her divorce lawyer, 'he didn't like N's evidence at all, & made me thoroughly hopeless & miserable'. (Later the lawyer relented and did allow the evidence to be submitted.) CPS was over his disappointment about the reviews of his last novel, but was now absorbed in Cochrane's renewed interest in his play and overwhelmed by the possibility that the recently knighted Laurence Olivier might take the lead (as previously mentioned, the character identified with CPS himself, therefore not, one must say, exactly type-casting). Accordingly, he frequently brushed Pamela's problems aside in phone calls, as she complained to her diary. I 'was bleak with [Charles]', she wrote on the day of her visit to the divorce lawyer,

> because I felt bleak, but also because I feel somehow that he lets me down
> – 'When I've finished the play we'll have fun,' he says, not realising
> that in the middle of all this strain, 'fun' might be helpful to me now.

Pamela endeavoured to keep going with her work commitments, but she had no impetus to start another novel. Her usual round of literary cocktail parties became something of an ordeal as some of her friends knew about the pending divorce, while both she and CPS were reluctant to give ammunition to those they both thought of as their enemies by making the news of their proposed marriage fully public. Nevertheless, some of the other guests at those parties feature in further vignettes in her diaries: Georgette Heyer, was characterized, in an image hardly likely to have been surmised by the readers of her frothy Regency romances, as 'that great noisy pirate', and Rex Warner as 'a dry, antiseptic man, rather like a brand-new kitchen unit'. Meanwhile, Olivia Manning had been 'v. bitter as usual'.

Eventually, the divorce hearing was set for the end of January, but Pamela was further galled before that date by discovering that Neil was to be cited as co-respondent by Don's husband. She wrote in her diary: 'If only this had been done in the beginning!' She was also fretting about breaking the news to her eight-year-old son, and despite visits to him at his boarding-school, decided to leave that unhappy task until the Christmas holidays. CPS made a mild effort to get to know her five-year-old daughter, accompanying Lindsay and Pamela on a walk in Battersea Park, which Pamela found 'v. sweet', and showed that he was 'v. determined to get used to the "Children" business'. But he frequently pleaded exhaustion; he did still have a 'day job' with English Electric in addition to his writing and reviewing.

CPS arranged as usual to go to Devon for Christmas, and Pamela docilely agreed that he needed 'a <u>really</u> good rest'. However, after dining with him and Harry Hoff at the Connaught the week before he was due to go away, she felt that the evening had gone badly wrong, and, as usual took the blame, albeit with a touch of bitter humour. 'Am suffering from worry re Andy', she wrote, 'sexual frustration, & an unkind conviction that if C. says he wants to go to bed early once more, I shall SCREAM.' An unwelcome reunion with a figure from the past was avoided one evening during all this turmoil: she had, she wrote, been preparing to go to bed 'when DYLAN rang up – not sober – saying he wanted to come around. Hung around till midnight, but no sign of him. I was exasperated but heartily relieved.'[5]

As soon as Andrew was home for the holidays, Pamela told him about the pending divorce, and his initial reaction was that of a phlegmatic British schoolboy. 'He said', she recorded, '"Hard cheese" and then "It isn't nice for you"', so, in her relief, she went no further, deciding, somewhat to Neil's annoyance, not to mention her proposed marriage to CPS for the time being. The Christmas period passed quite peacefully, and she felt that both children enjoyed the extra attention they received from both parents. On New Year's Eve, she took them to the pantomime, followed by a children's party, then 'raced off' to see CPS just returned from Devon. Her 'darling Charles' ended the old year, she wrote, 'with a rather solemn scene, admonishing me for causing him <u>angst</u> with my bouts of manic-depression. But we were happy all through the 'scene', & greeted the New Year in love & hope.' This did not include spending the night together, but when she belatedly found that she could get no transport home, CPS, she gratefully recorded, 'walked with me right the way back, all through the revellers, under a lovely starry sky. Home about 2, hardly able to move my feet, but v. happy, & grateful to God for helping me to a chance of a new life.' The epilogue to her 1949 diary read:

<u>The End</u>

of one of the most remarkable years in my life – first being in love, & frustrated & miserable – then Venice – then sudden release. I want good things not only for the children, Amy & myself, but for Neil too – one must look out in hope.

The 'good things' were, however, slow in coming, as she chronicled copiously in the notebooks that had replaced the diaries she had previously used. Early in January, on the day of the first, although abortive, house-hunting expedition with CPS, Pamela felt uneasy: 'I want to keep the "even emotional flow" C. demands of me', she wrote, 'but am troubled by two fears':

> One: does he want to marry me to make himself happy, or to make me happy? If it were the latter I couldn't bear it. Two: how far is his memory of 'Sheila' a rival to me? Because it would be hard for me to play second fiddle to a man's memories. Wish I were certain of these things one way or another. Wish I understood C. better – & myself better, come to that. I could always go on alone.

Shortly after this, CPS told her a little about his 'worries' with Anne Seagrim, and this, Pamela said, 'was a comfort to me, because this kind of confidence is the most open sign of love that he can show'. She became mildly irritated when CPS continued to fret about Anne who was on the verge of leaving English Electric, but she didn't consider her to be a threat in the same way evidently as his memories of Sheila Palfreyman, nor was she in any way as jealous of Anne as she had been of Maureen Gebbie. Perhaps she was given reason to believe that CPS was still just taking a kindly interest in the problems of a colleague.

Pamela and CPS had one or two happy evenings together, but then suddenly a volte-face on the part of C.B. Cochrane precipitated a period which she headlined in her diary: 'Start of the misery and disappointment.' Cochrane had decided not to take up his option on CPS's play, *The Ends of the Earth*, leaving 'C. in dreadful state', she wrote. Later the same day, she added: 'C. rang up, dark as the grave, to tell me shortly that he was going "away for the night". No explanation.' When he returned, he still would give her no further information. 'I do not know if he loves me. I simply do not know,' she wrote, 'But I think he doesn't love me enough for life to be happy for us both.' However, she concluded with, for the first time, some asperity: 'Things may be different when Charles recovers from his shock & misery & wounded pride.'

Some of her feelings of wretchedness may have spilled over into her *Telegraph* reviews that week, and would later provide ammunition for

the literary feud between the Snows-to-be, and the more experimental younger writers. Pamela's review of P.H. Newby's latest novel
was scathing. 'It is not a happy thing to have to admit', she began,
'that "The Young May Moon" is an uninspiring work. Since his
striking first novel, "Journey to the Interior", Mr. Newby's work has
not been improving; he seems to have had less and less to say [...].'[6]
CPS also now had a platform for their joint campaign; as the
American academic Rubin Rabinovitz points out in a thorough study
of CPS the critic: 'Snow had always opposed the experimental
novelists, but it was not until [1950] when he became a regular book
reviewer for the London *Sunday Times*, that he had the opportunity to
put his critical views forward.'[7] As it happens, this appointment would
provide him with another, perhaps spurious, reason to temporise about
making his relationship with Pamela public; in April, Pamela wrote
to the two Ks:

> We want to keep our proposed marriage between our intimate friends
> at the moment [...] for the very practical [reason] that C. will lose his
> job on <u>The Sunday Times</u> the moment it's official. This has been
> intimated to him in no uncertain terms.[8]

In fact, CPS continued to review fiction for the *Sunday Times* every
fortnight until the end of 1952.

Pamela and CPS only had agonizing telephone conversations as the
allotted day of her divorce hearing approached. She began to recover
some of her *amour propre*, and to become still further critical of CPS:

> C., when hurt, hurts everyone around him, using a sort of mental
> knout, & then says no one must reproach him. I <u>cannot</u> go on behaving
> like a saint, & possessing myself in entire patience, & self-abnegation.
> Why the devil should I? Tonight I have at least the comfort of being
> angry.

She wrote to Kathleen Farrell, the same day, explaining the current
situation with some bravado:

> Poor dear, he [CPS] can't really help his behaviour-patterns; but it is
> plain hell for me. He tells me in nice round terms that he doesn't need
> me while he's suffering and expects me to go away and play shove-
> ha'penny until he can bear the sight of me again [...].

I don't know that I shall marry him. I suppose I will [...]. I should like to make NOBLE GESTURES, but the thought of life without him is so indescribably bleak [...].

Don't take my distracted frame of mind too seriously. Charles and I are both absurd people, only he's worse.[9]

Pamela was nevertheless ill-prepared for the reaction to the lonely ordeal before her in the Divorce Court, which proved to be, she said, 'one of the most anguished – quite the most anguished – day of my life'. She had never, she continued, 'realised the nightmarish, hallucinatory horror of it, & the exposure. Was in box about 5 minutes, & it seemed like an hour.' The decree nisi was granted promptly, but she nevertheless returned home 'desperately upset', and then:

Charles didn't ring. I was so frantic with misery I didn't know what to do, with past & future both shut alike so far as I can see. Then found my divorce was in both News & Standard & that upset me worse. Finally phoned C & found him laid low with his 'neurotic sickness'. But his tone sounded as if there was love, & he says we must meet & talk things over. He is writing me a letter. We must work out our 'clash of wills' somehow: I have so much to give him, & he to give me.

The letter she received the next day was apologetic in tone, but, as she said, 'still giving no answer'. He did not mention her divorce, but tried to explain his reactions to any setback:

Ever since I remember, I've reacted to disappointment or humiliation in the same fashion. It is intolerable to me in such conditions not to be alone. I curse myself for it; it exposes some of the pathological things about me. [...]

No-one that I've known is as magnanimous as you. But, as you said the other day, that isn't the whole of you; in both of us it is in part the selfish force that gives us our effectiveness. Oh my dearest, it is there that we clash, there only, on the plane of will. You think that I don't treat you as an equal: I believe that in every issue between us, major or minor, you have always got your way. You say I want a lesser woman: sometimes I have felt overburdened – but that wasn't what we meant.

Let us get a bit restored. It wouldn't be wise to talk just yet.

My love, Charles.[10]

Pamela's remark about his wanting 'a lesser woman' would seem, in the light of his past and future relationships, to have been discerning, but, in the longer term, she would suppress such suppositions.

Throughout February, they suffered physical reactions from their individual mental torments, Pamela feeling 'utterly exhausted and rotten', but CPS, she feared, was still worse than she was, scarcely eating, and looking 'so queer & so thin'. She tried to be understanding – 'He must have his unhappiness his own way, & I must leave him to it, but it's hard.' Occasionally her resentment flared up as when she was expecting to see him after visiting her son at his boarding-school on a freezing day:

> When I got home, C. had telephoned. Told Amy he was 'low' again & was going straight to bed. This really is getting past endurance. How long am I to tolerate this uncertainty, this lack of real contact – anything? I will never reproach him for these awful weeks, but I cannot think of Jan 26 [the date of the divorce hearing] without the tears coming to my eyes. I do not know what we are going to do, or what life has for me. Even now I don't know.

They had dinner together the following evening, but it had been 'an appalling strain', and she felt that 'C. is now throwing up every obstacle of worry he can in order to escape planning our own future.'

Pamela had a minor success that month: *Corinth House* was televised with Gladys Young again in the principal role, and received good notices. When C.B. Cochrane once again came into their lives by expressing an interest in staging the play, CPS was, perhaps surprisingly, delighted. Pamela attributed this reaction to his belief that this could lead to theatrical success for both of them, but more realistically, considered that possibility as being no more than a chimera, 'the damned crock of gold at the end of a rainbow'.[11] Pamela's diary entries for two further months continued to reflect the precarious nature of her relationship with CPS: 'We swing', she wrote, 'from joy & hope to awful gloom and suffering.' She felt herself to be beset by enemies; she was distressed to be told that the novelist Norah Hoult, to whom, she wrote, she had given 'the most appreciative critical attention', was among those spreading tales of 'virulent scandal' against her. She turned again for comfort to Kathleen Farrell:

> I have the self-pitying impression at the moment that I am surrounded by persons who wish me ill and delight at my misfortunes, and I have

to think of you and Kay to get back into balance again. Sometimes I find myself counting up the people who actually like me and don't want to claw me to death [...].[12]

In optimistic spells, she and CPS continued to view various London properties, and after much soul-searching on his part, in April CPS bought 1 Hyde Park Crescent, an elegant and spacious house in Bayswater, to be their first marital home. The decree absolute now having been granted, Pamela continued to suffer from sexual frustration and bewilderment, occasioned by CPS's apparent reluctance to consummate their love. But in May, they had a short holiday in Shrewsbury, and on the third day, she recorded: 'Glorious happy day. [...] Spent afternoon indoors – happiest of my whole life', and the following evening was 'wondrously joyous', because 'Charles formally asked me to marry him'. 'Sounds foolish', she added, 'to write this after all this time, but it was of profound significance to us both.' Before their wedding later in the year, illustrating her awareness of a moral dilemma (a theme that would emerge in several of her later novels), she felt compelled to justify their anticipation of the marriage vows. She wrote that she had realised how important it had been 'for C & I to become lovers for the first time at Shrewsbury & that there would have been no happiness for us at all if we had not had reassurance in this. Nor does it make our marriage less, but only the desired confirmation & new beginning.'

At last, Pamela was beginning to feel the anguish of the first five months of the year was over. A slight disappointment was that, as she was a divorcée, they were unable to have a full church wedding as they had originally envisaged, but they compromised by arranging a civil wedding, followed by a religious ceremony in the chapel at Christ's College. On the day she went to the Paddington Register Office to make the necessary arrangements, she received her engagement ring from CPS; it was, she wrote, 'the most exquisite sapphire set in a beautifully designed diamond mount. Have never had anything so glorious in my whole life – never. [...] I love Charles so much & am assured now that he deeply loves me.' Her faith in him was not even shaken when he departed the following day for three weeks in Cornwall, leaving her to cope with all the wedding arrangements, with the necessary repairs and redecorations in their new house, with her move from Chelsea (with mother and daughter), and with his move from Hyde Park Place. The latter involved, among other things, her taking on the task of boxing up all his library, one day recording having 'dusted, stacked & covered 250 cricket books', and not surprisingly, arriving back home '<u>sick</u> with weariness'. She did nevertheless that evening manage to write a brief letter to Kathleen Farrell, mock-seriously complaining that: 'C. will return from Cornwall bronzed and rested to find a tottering wreck. Me ...'.[13]

CPS was feeling optimistic again at the news that his new play, *View from the Park*, was to be staged at the Lyric, Hammersmith, with the Australian actor John McCallum, then becoming established in English films, in the leading role. He was working in Cornwall on the final corrections to *The Masters*, the latest (and the most enduring) novel in the 'Strangers and Brothers' sequence, and light-heartedly wrote that he hoped it would be a financial success since this would enable him to shower her with 'rings and dresses, as befits the only literary popsy ever manufactured'.[14] Pamela responded gleefully to this suggestion, fantasizing that when he was rich, 'I shall riot in jewels and frocks, like a true popsy. It has often occurred to me to wonder whether my brains spoil my looks or my looks my brains.' In the same letter, she told him that fortunately Ron, her old ARP friend, had happened by chance to get in touch with her, and he had volunteered to help her again, as he had done when she had moved back to Chelsea after the war. He had become 'a quiet comfort', as well as giving her much practical assistance, and Pamela gave CPS, who was about to return, the firm instruction: 'Darling, you must spend every ounce of niceness you have on my Ron, without whom I should be in an asylum.'[15]

CPS continued to keep in touch with Holly Southwell that summer, although they may not have met. Holly had been kept fully informed by the man she still called her 'funny and most curious love', and she generously told him to 'have a good time with Pam, sweet. Goodness knows you deserve it.'[16] Following his instructions, from then on, she addressed her letters to him c/o his club, the Savile. He returned to London just three weeks before his wedding to Pamela, for whom the happiness of their restored relationship overrode all the last-minute problems at the new house.

The day before their Paddington Register Office wedding, Pamela was 'terribly happy', even though she said: 'Cannot <u>believe</u> I am marrying Charles tomorrow. It is just like an agreeable but not too convincing pretence.' But the following day, they were indeed married 'in a pink room, by a comic registrar', and she thought that: 'perhaps we were the only couple who have ever <u>looked at</u> each other while making our responses, or kissed each other for so long when it was done.' They went to Cambridge immediately after the civil ceremony, CPS departed for his stag night, and Pamela spent the evening with her mother and aunt at the University Arms. 'I am Charles' wife', she wrote, 'I simply cannot believe it yet. I love him so much.' She wrote that 'everything went most beautifully' at the chapel service the next day; Bert Howard was CPS's best man, and Jack Plumb, then Steward of the college, arranged a wedding breakfast for about 130 people in the Hall at Christ's. Some twenty years later, the latter provided a typically sardonic alternative account of the blessing in the course of an interview with Carl Bode, an American professor, who was another to contemplate, but not complete, a biography of CPS. 'It was really', Plumb began, 'a comic occasion':

> Pam had got into a dress that was perhaps a trifle too tight – a grey silk – so when they had to go forward and kneel at the altar (it was pretty comic seeing Snow kneel at an altar anyway), there was a tremendous sort of move forward because Pam might split.

Then, he continued, the officiant, Ian Ramsey (later Bishop of Durham), gave 'the most extraordinary sermon about Charles and Pam Snow', representing their marriage as 'a spiritual Kon-Tiki expedition'.[17] Nothing, however, could blight Pamela's happiness; she and CPS then left for two days in Huntingdon (they had agreed to postpone a proper honeymoon until the autumn) and, for once, she was unable to put words to her emotions: 'Impossible to write much more about today because these things cannot be written.'

Pamela, Amy and the children did not move into their new house until a week afterwards, and CPS kept prevaricating about leaving his bachelor flat until all the building works had been completed. She had bought a beautiful four-poster bed, and began to despair about when she would actually share it with her new husband, who seemed content to take her out to dinner, after which they would return to their separate homes. Eventually Pamela got angry 'feeling he had nothing but concern for his own adjustment problems & little for mine', and insisted he stay that night at least, although she slept badly and they quarrelled in the morning. On another night, 'he stayed till midnight in the Wonderful Bed', and this time she let him go back afterwards to his flat, since she was 'never so deeply in love in him', and felt reassured that: 'We shall often have our difficulties & strains, but, I think, more often touch Heaven like this.'

Pamela had constantly been fretting about how much the house renovations were costing, despite now having a husband who at least was in regular employment, but CPS now reassured her that she should go ahead and employ staff, preferably a husband and wife, to run their big house. She had no idea what problems would lie ahead of her in this respect. An employment agency sent them two Latvians called Zanderson, whom they interviewed and liked 'immensely'. They moved in the next day, and although Arvid, the husband, seemed nervous serving at table, his wife served them an excellent dinner, and Pamela thought: 'All looks hopeful & a foretaste of luxury & peace.' But her diary entry for the following day sadly recorded:

> Alas!! Exit Zandersons! Arvid threw violent temperament in morning & went off to pace the street. Mrs. Z in tears. Arvid finally returned, green-faced & frenzied, saying he could not do the job, he was a builder!! Atmosphere so awful I suggested they went at once, & they were off by 3, to total loss of about £4 to us! Diabolical!

'Luxury and peace' was now postponed both domestically and professionally. *View from the Park* had a pre-London première in Brighton; on the first night, 'C. was in an awful state, and self as bad.' They returned to London where the situation was that: 'Children had been hell, no staff, & C. so wretched he retired to bed. But in evening I sat down to help with his play & between us we slogged out a new Act III better than ever before.' The now identifiably middle-class Pamela then had an 'exhausting crazy day with the servant problem'. She first of all engaged an 'Italian cook with no English & very temperamental parlourmaid', then decided she preferred an Irish couple, albeit still with misgivings. She was terrified that the four of them would arrive the following day, but fortunately the first couple didn't show up. The following week, she went with CPS to see the second try-out of his play at Malvern; Pamela thought the final act was a 'vast improvement', but was unconvinced by McCallum's performance. She thought he had charm, but was 'a pretty poor actor'.

Pamela had booked the usual August seaside holiday with Amy, Kalie and the children, but decided that she couldn't miss CPS's London opening night, so sent her family off to Bognor in advance, causing her to receive letters of 'woe' and 'worse woe' from her mother. Throughout the first performance, she and CPS were 'in a state of pure misery', not being able to gauge the audience's reactions. The next morning, CPS went to buy all the newspapers, and came back announcing: 'It is an utter failure'. The early reviews in the dailies were indeed poor, leading in the Snow household to 'a day of sick misery & faint, courageous revivals'. W.A. Darlington, the long-standing theatre critic of the *Daily Telegraph*, obviously unaware of the staging the previous year of *The Ends of the Earth* at the same theatre, presumably meant to be encouraging when he wrote:

> C.P. Snow's first [*sic*] play, tried out at the Lyric, Hammersmith, last night, has in it so much that is good that one is left wondering why the whole is so ineffective. The answer simply is that it is his first play; he has not yet got the hang of the theatre.
>
> His dialogue has the ring of real talk, yet it ends by defeating itself and confusing the mind. [...] A clever cast [...] makes what it can of the material.[18]

The reviewers in the Sunday papers were moderately more favourable. Harold Hobson (*Sunday Times*, 3 September 1950) described the play as 'an exceedingly intelligent study of ambition in a high Government official'. He continued, however, with comments that mirrored Pamela's verdict:

> It is a theme which calls for great talent in the author (which Mr. Snow has), and also in the actor. Mr. John McCallum does not quite match the stature of the part. [...] He rarely suggests greatness, and he smiles too much.

With CPS 'determined to feel better', Pamela felt that she could not now delay joining her family in Bognor. She was also excited because her head was 'burning' with a new idea for a novel about the theatre, which, as usual, she had already named; it was to be called *Catherine Carter*. She may well have been inspired by CPS's recent experiences with difficult theatrical managements, temperamental actors and backstage machinations, but, as mentioned in Chapter 1, she set the novel in the latter part of the nineteenth century, incorporating some of her mother's and aunt's reminiscences about Henry Irving's company, in addition to her own considerable further research. On arrival at the Beaulieu Downs Hotel, she found her mother had not exaggerated its failings. It was, she said, 'a gone-to-seed nightmare' and Bognor itself 'a sort of slum dormitory under the grey sky'. However she asterisked these comments to admonish herself for being 'very snobbish & wicked & self-indulgent', and did her best to entertain the children for the remainder of the holiday, buoyed up by the prospect of her impending honeymoon.

This started idyllically as they re-enacted together their journey of the previous year, the channel crossing, the overnight train to Venice, and the 'magical gondola ride' to the Hotel Cavalletto. 'I could hardly realise,' she wrote, 'that we had ever left there'. But they *were* back in an altered state following their marriage, and her ecstatic entry continued:

> This must be the most entrancing place under the sun. It is incredible to be back here with my darling husband. It is possible to reconstruct or repeat experience & important that this should be realised.

Her lyrical descriptions of the city and the lagoon would later indeed be reconstructed in the novel she was planning, and they recall the quality of the poetry she had written as a girl, a time she recollected after dining on the roof terrace of the Hotel Danieli overlooking the Grand Canal. That evening, she wrote, had been 'the most intense realisation of all the romantic dreams of my youth'. Returning to their hotel another evening, she witnessed 'the most wonderful sunset I have ever seen, with all the cineraria blues, lemons, oranges & magentas in the world'. 'At one moment', she continued, 'the blues & pinks fused, & the whole sea turned to glittering violet. Only lasted two minutes, but I shall never forget it.' The month did not pass, however, without a few days on which they had 'misunderstandings' to cloud her joy, but she attributed this to all the tensions they had suffered throughout the year.

While they were away, Pamela also received what she saw as a major blow in the shape of a letter from George Bishop, the Literary Editor of the *Daily Telegraph*, informing her that they were terminating her reviewing contract. 'Really', she wrote, 'what caddishness of the most

indefensible order to deal it on a honeymoon!' The tone of the letter
was, she thought, 'half-embarrassed, half-enraged [...] explaining the
enormities of my reviewing system, especially in regard to the Hemingway article'. The background to this dismissal was that the *Telegraph*
had sent her between three and five novels to review each week, daunt-
ing enough in itself, and also frustrating when she had wanted to
dedicate most of the space to just one novel, as she had boldly done not
only with her panegyrical review of *Time of Hope* the previous year, but
also, earlier in the present year, when reviewing another novel which
conformed to her credo, *Winter Song* by James Hanley. 'If Mr. James
Hanley had written in the 19th century', she had begun, 'he would
have been recognised instantly as a great novelist', and continued:

> The technical experiments of this century however in streamlining of
> narrative, economy of words and increase of pace, tend to make us
> impatient of the novel which is slow and diffuse, and Mr. Hanley's
> books are both. Nevertheless, I believe he is among the three or four
> living English novelists with sufficient power and stature to approach,
> or to achieve, greatness.[19]

In the article which she considered her nemesis as weekly reviewer,
she had deviated from her appointed task by again devoting her
column to one novel, not this time to praise, but to muse on what she
saw as a reviewer's dilemma, in the context of discussing a recently
published novel by Ernest Hemingway. She began:

> It is very important that the critic should not deny his own pleasure,
> or fall into the error of believing that enjoyment is necessarily conso-
> nant with admiration. The critic who has never in his life had pleasure
> from the second or third rate can be a dull dog, removed by his own
> sensitivity from the joys of his fellow-creatures. A writer may be a poor
> stylist and a romantic dodger of the realities, yet still work from so
> humane, vigorous and delighted an impulse that something humane,
> vigorous and delightful comes through. Let us, by all means, disap-
> prove of him: but let us not pretend that we didn't enjoy his book.

She then discussed at some further length what she dubbed 'the question of the Bogus':

> We see that a certain novel, in terms of human truth, is in fact bogus:
> and we know perfectly well on what grounds to condemn it. Yet we

cannot, if we have any honesty of spirit, deny that this contemptible work has moved us. Why should we be moved by the *Bogus*?

For the final third of the column, she did turn 'from this imaginary work to Mr. Hemingway's new novel, *Across the River and into the Trees*'. 'The title', she said, 'is an incantation. So is the book. Accept it as such, and the magic works. Read it in cold blood and all you will see is the nonsense.'[20]

It is unlikely to have been Pamela's judgment on this novel that provoked the letter from George Bishop, as the book, which had been published simultaneously in London and in New York, received outstandingly adverse reviews on both sides of the Atlantic. A typical review by the renowned critic Maxwell Geismar judged it to be:

> [...] an unfortunate novel and unpleasant to review for anyone who respects Hemingway's talent and achievement. It is not only Hemingway's worst novel; it is a synthesis of everything that is bad in his previous work and it throws a doubtful light on the future. It is so dreadful, in fact, that it begins to have its own morbid fascination [...].[21]

One can only therefore speculate that Bishop had been seeking an excuse to fire Pamela, possibly because of a perceived lack of impartiality in her critiques, or a tendency, as in the case of the Hemingway article, to deliver a disquisition rather than a straightforward review.

For the next few days of their honeymoon, Pamela and CPS opened their forwarded letters 'with awful gingerliness', but there was no further bad news. Nevertheless, they both continued to feel 'absolutely overstrung', until Venice started to weave a spell of happiness around them again. They settled down in the mornings to write plays together or separately in Quadri's, their favourite café in Piazza San Marco, visited churches or galleries in the afternoons, and, as she put it on several occasions, 'drank rather more than usual' with their evening meals. On the last day of what she summed up as a 'magical honeymoon', they were 'both terribly sad at leaving our darling Venice, where we have been so happy'.

Three days in Paris on the return journey proved anti-climactic; Pamela found the city 'garish and sad'. She had also reason to worry, from Amy's letters, that she would be returning to staff problems at home, as indeed this proved to be, reflecting post-war attitudes to domestic service. Pamela had had no complaints about the capabilities of the wife of the Irish couple, who had followed the Latvians, nor with the wife of the English couple, nor with the wife of the Hungarian couple, all following in quick succession, but in each case, the husbands were reluctant to perform the menial tasks that would have been expected of pre-war male staff. Each of these couples started well, but then subjected Pamela to several months of sulks before abruptly leaving for another position, seemingly without any need for a reference from her.

Aware as she was that she now had no income from reviewing, and had not published a novel for over two years, Pamela attempted to disregard these distractions, as she was now engrossed in writing *Catherine Carter*. It would prove to be by far the longest of her novels (469 pages in the original edition), but she completed it within three and a half months. She had worked in Venice on the characterizations and structure of the book, in a notebook which has been preserved and which gives evidence of her meticulous preparations.[22] Within five weeks, she was able to record: 'I worked blazingly hard on CC today – best day I've had – & at 9.30, all in, finished Part II (about 80,000 words).' 'Cannot believe', she continued, 'work that so carries me with it can have no merit.'

Marriage to CPS had not quite lived up to all her expectations, as they both had to cope with busy working schedules and the usual round of literary parties. There are already hints in her diary that her sexual frustration continued on occasion: CPS would prove to be a more ardent lover in his extra-marital liaisons than in the marriage bed. In one of several similar diary entries, she wrote: 'C. home earlyish: both fell into state of love & excitement, & then old trouble intervened. C. dreadfully upset & self shaky.' Many years later, she told her daughter that she believed that scientists had a lower sex drive than other men; perhaps CPS had persuaded her that that was the case. Nevertheless, her round-up of the seesawing events of 1950 stressed that it had been:

> the most wonderful & _teaching_ year of my life. I have been more unhappy than ever before, & infinitely more joyful. Profoundly grateful

to God for his goodness. As someone said, "God can be terrible, but never cruel", & that is so. But I have much of bad behaviour – even wicked – to regret – & guilt towards many. I can't however regret the passing of a year which has brought me such enormous joy.

CHAPTER 12

A Fragile Start to a
Second Marriage until the
Arrival of 'Borox'

D
UE TO HER pressing domestic concerns towards the end of the
previous year, Pamela had to some extent shrugged off the
loss of her regular fiction review column in the *Daily Telegraph*.
Now she had time to reflect, and to register her frustration at feeling
'gagged'. CPS was still reviewing for the *Sunday Times*, but, perhaps
surprisingly, she brushed aside his potential contribution to their
common aim when writing in her diary:

> I began this certain school of criticism, & feel that neither C nor
> anyone else will carry it through to its logical conclusion. I was the
> most trenchant voice in English reviewing, & am now very effectively
> muzzled. Now it is as though I don't exist. I never get asked to do
> critical stuff, & I feel as if I had been deprived of the exercise of a gift
> – as if I were a singer whose vocal chords had been deliberately cut.

Once the euphoria of their honeymoon had worn off, Pamela was
distressed at feeling constantly 'weary & nerve-racked'. CPS had
adjusted reasonably well to married life, since she allowed him to continue in many of his set bachelor ways. He often dined with friends
without her or at his club, returning in a state which she euphemis-
tically described as 'popular'. His most regular companion remained
Harry Hoff who (despite Pamela's previous suspicions that he was
'sweet' on *her*) had followed his mentor to the altar only a few months
after him. His bride was called Joyce Harris, and became lovingly

portrayed by 'William Cooper' as Joe Lunn's wife, Elspeth, in *Scenes from Married Life* and *Scenes from Later Life*. Pamela had previously seemed hardly aware of her existence, but, Joyce being seemingly as accommodating as Pamela, the two marriages did not affect the lasting close friendship between the two men.

A further strain on Pamela in the early months of their marriage was her failure to become pregnant. As each menstrual period relentlessly led to 'disappointment', she became increasingly worried that she would not be able to give CPS the child she was sure he wanted. Although she was not yet 40, late pregnancies were the exception at that time, and she did in fact feel that her menopause could not be that far away. She began to mark in the margins of her diary the occasions on which they were, as she usually put it, 'very happy at night', which, with the 'old trouble' never far away, were never too frequent. After one unsuccessful episode, she wrote that: 'I am in a really poor nervous state, exhausted & drained, & am in constant danger of the daemon that drives me to quarrel with C. over matters best left alone.'

Nevertheless, and particularly as she was aware that rumours about the state of their marriage were already circulating in some literary circles,[1] Pamela issued a warning in my, or another writer's, direction:

> It does occur to me now & then how any biographer of the future – if I am ever worth one – will get hold of my diaries & try to prove from them that C & I are not happily married. Which we are.

She cited her disbelief of the portrait of the marriage of Robert Louis Stevenson, as presented in a recent biography by Malcolm Elwin. (In this, Elwin alleges that, contrary to previous accounts, 'Stevenson's married life was undoubtedly shadowed by his wife's querulous temper and morbid habit of mind', and that 'her insistent interference with his work caused acerbity in argument'.)[2] As Pamela wrote the above admonishment, she was completing the last chapters of *Catherine Carter*, and it does not seem mere coincidence that Ishrat Lindblad sees this section of the novel as portraying 'the only kind of marriage that is possible' between two 'ambitious and strong people determined not to be subdued by each other', and that Lindblad also praises the author for her descriptions in this novel (as well as in others), not only of 'sexual happiness, but [...] sexual longing and frustration in women as well'.[3]

Catherine Carter, however, is primarily, as previously mentioned, a brilliant evocation of the London theatrical world in the late Victorian era, a time when the standard fare consisted of often butchered Shakespearian revivals, turgid verse dramas, and barnstorming epics like Henry Irving's famous vehicle, *The Bells*.[4] The eponymous heroine is engaged by Henry Peverel, the most celebrated actor-manager of his day, and she progresses from being a walk-on to being a leading lady. In her 'Author's Note' to the first edition, Pamela admitted that: 'Students of the stage will not fail to observe that I have given to Henry Peverel the physical appearance, many of the mannerisms, and an approximation to the speech-rhythm, of Sir Henry Irving.' She continued, however: 'Here the identification ceases. The story is not Irving's story. The dates do not coincide. In Irving's Lyceum there was never, as in Peverel's Belvedere, a Catherine Carter.' She then went on to claim that none of the other characters had their origins in real life.[5]

Her preliminary notes do, however, contain an outline of Irving's life, and her deliberate choice to alter dates to make Peverel younger than Irving, so that he might be a suitable husband for Catherine. One further character who definitely can be identified is Lord Norroway, a poet-laureate, (indeed, Pamela wrote 'Tennyson' after this name in the list of characters in her notebook). Peverel is determined to stage Norroway's narrative poem, *Harold Hardrada*, despite all advice to the contrary and a complete lack of grasp as to practicalities by the author. Not surprisingly the play proves to be Peverel's first major theatrical disaster; Irving had similar difficulties in staging Tennyson's *Becket*, but it did remain in his repertoire. Catherine Carter is not, as Pamela makes clear, Ellen Terry, but, despite her disclaimer, it would seem that she did at least partly base her heroine on a living person, namely herself. The physical description of Catherine in her notes began: 'Small. Looks like P.H.J., only much prettier.' Many of the character traits she went on to list for her protagonist emerge in her own diaries, among them the following:

> Strongly sexed, but v. single-minded.
> All ups & downs: wildly happy or wildly miserable.
> Sensuous, romantic, but attracted by colour rather than form.
> Sense of sin considerable (but not so much in sexual matters: is easily oppressed by this sense over some minor bad behaviour –

remembers small unkindnesses out of her own past, i.e., to her mother
– impatience, or roughness).

The episode in the novel which can be most closely traced to
Pamela's own experience concerns Catherine's bold move to escape
from her unhappy first marriage by going to Venice on her own, in
the expectation that Peverel will follow her. His eventual arrival is
much delayed by his failure to be informed of her whereabouts by his
secretary, Willy Palliser.[6] Both Henry and Catherine have visualized a
scene of high romance when they eventually meet there, but as Henry
attempts to stroll nonchalantly into the lobby of the Danieli, 'racing
down the handsome red staircase was a small, distraught, weeping girl
with the face of a goblin, swollen, bruised and disfigured, a girl with
hair roughly pinned up and dress awry [...]', whose opening words to
him are: ' "Oh, Henry, Henry, I'm so glad you've come! Can you give
me some money?" ' Catherine, like Pamela, had forgotten to shutter
her window one night from the marauding mosquitoes, and the delay
in Henry's appearance had meant that she had misjudged her finances
and, terrified of eviction from the hotel, she is on her way to throw
herself at the mercy of the manager. Henry has to restrain his
laughter: 'This was his true Catherine, his preposterous Catherine,
destroying all the grandiose inventions of his imagination in half a
dozen words' (p.277).

Once Catherine's face has healed, they spend idyllic days together
which live up to their previous separate imaginations. On their final
day, one of Pamela's honeymoon diary entries (quoted in the previous
chapter) was clearly the inspiration for her description of the splendour of a Venetian sunset, which unites her lovers in profound delight.
As their gondola drifts down the Grand Canal with the sun sinking,
Henry feels 'a spur of jealousy' that Catherine seems to '*see* more
passionately than any human being had ever seen before', but then:

he gave an exclamation of wonder, for something happened which was
so marvellous that it enabled him to *see* no less than she. For the past
few minutes the giant rage of colour had been melting away, scarlet
and gold dying into rose, and purple into periwinkle blue. Suddenly
rose and blue fused together, and the sea became a shrine of parma
violets, stretching as far as the eye could reach into a great mass of
petals, packed and glistening with dew. There was violet above and

below: they were floating upon violets, the oars hewing their way through the massed miraculous flowers. (p.285)

Perhaps influenced by the period in which this novel is set, Pamela made a significant change as regards its narrative structure. Her previous novels had either been written in the first person, or from the point of view of a neutral omniscient narrator. *Catherine Carter* has two main focalizers, Catherine and Henry, but the narrator occasionally also intervenes, in the manner of one of Pamela's favourite Victorian authors, George Eliot. Catherine's lonely vigil in Venice before Henry's arrival recalls Eliot's description of the recently wed Dorothea Casaubon in the galleries of Rome in *Middlemarch*. For both, the master-pieces of Italian art can make no coherent impression but reflect their inner state of mind. In the case of Dorothea who is fighting against bitter frustration and disappointment with her new husband, the withered scholar:

> [...] all this vast wreck of ambitious ideals, sensuous and spiritual, mixed confusedly with the signs of breathing forgetfulness and degra-dation, at first jarred her as with an electric shock, and then urged themselves to her with that ache belonging to a glut of confused ideas which check the flow of emotion.[7]

Catherine, in the grip of pre-mosquito-attack romantic love attempts to be 'like a proper sightseer', studying Venetian art through the medium of her guidebook, yet is 'so ravished by a shimmer of blue light falling through the stained glass windows upon one of the great pillars, that she lost interest in everything else' (p.265), and the narrator extrapolates the following interpretation:

> The blue light upon the gothic pillar is for ever out of reach: it cannot be touched, cannot be captured, cannot be bolted into the heart of the man who stares at it until his eyes begin to ache, and he is forced to turn away. In human love man sees, desires, pursues and may possess. And it is all very well to say that the possession is the end and the destruction. There are more renewals in love than man has ever believed possible, and they will continue to astonish him [...]. (p.266).

This and other similar authorial comments add depth to a well-researched story with characterizations which may be compared to another of Pamela's favourite Victorian novelists, Charles Dickens, and various episodes are similarly related with a great deal of Dickensian humour.

There would, however, be a longer than usual delay before *Catherine Carter* would be published, due to a problem, which was to prove persistent, namely, anxiety over the newly-married couple's financial affairs. CPS generally brushed aside any of her concerns, but Pamela began to realise that: 'To be honest, we are both <u>very</u> incompetent with money, bad on details, & generally uncomprehending.' It happened that, on a day when her bank manager had rang up to warn her about her over-spending, and she felt that she simply didn't know where to turn, their evening was to be spent at 'a hugely rich' party given by a visiting American. She felt, she wrote, 'gay & hopeless among so much wealth', and seemed to have moved away from the principles that had informed her creation, Claud Pickering, as she mused that: 'These people are, of course, the villains of the DW [*Daily Worker*], & I still feel that's true in a sense, but the villains are so much more <u>agreeable</u> than the non-villains.' In the circumstances, when her agent approached her shortly afterward with a generous offer of £400 for the serialization of *Catherine Carter* in the popular weekly magazine, *Woman*, she could hardly refuse, although she did have misgivings, both because of the necessary aforesaid delay in publication, and because of her fears that abridgement of her novel in a decidedly non-intellectual periodical might have an adverse effect on her literary reputation,

Meanwhile, CPS, despite similar concerns about his status as a novelist, was nevertheless anxiously awaiting the decision of the Book Society with regard to his much-postponed novel, *The Masters*. The previous year, at the urging of Spencer Curtis Brown, they had both had signed publishing contracts with Macmillan. In CPS's case, he had the more difficult choice in deciding to leave the more prestigious imprint of Faber and Faber, but he had been dissatisfied with their low expectations of sales when they had printed only 6,000 copies of *The Light and the Dark*, and their subsequent low-key marketing of that novel. Pamela had been vigorously courted by A.S. Frere of Heinemann, as well as by Macmillan. She went to discuss the situation with her current publishers, Michael Joseph, and the meeting turned into 'a fearful row, conducted on a level of remorseless <u>politesse</u>'. With some amusement, she continued:

M.J. refuses to let me go, just to spite Frere, & claims that Frere only
wants me to spite him. Meanwhile Spencer, that combination of a were-
wolf & Groucho Marx, has been writing M.J. the most frightful letters.
I gave Spencer a rocket on the phone, & he merely shrieked with mad
laughter.

In the end, she could not resist the offer that Curtis Brown had
conjured up from Macmillan of £1,500 per book, and Michael Joseph
reluctantly conceded defeat.

There was no news about *The Masters* on the day of the Book
Society committee meeting, and CPS was 'in the depths'. In the early
hours of the following day, he attempted to explain to Pamela that
success was, for him, 'an organic need', and, as usual, she felt frustrated at her inability to get him to see things in proportion. Fortunately,
finding an excuse soon after daybreak to phone Daniel George, a
member of the Book Society panel and a supposed friend (but, as
mentioned earlier, occasional mischief-maker, if not downright enemy,
of them both), she discovered that CPS had indeed been given the
Fiction Choice, and she wrote: 'Really felt the top of my head was
coming off with relief.'

With that matter resolved, and *Catherine Carter* with the publishers, they were able to put their literary worries aside temporarily, and
enjoyed a few days in Stratford-upon-Avon, where the Memorial
Theatre was that year staging Shakespeare's history plays. The company consisted of distinguished established actors including Michael
Redgrave and Anthony Quayle, with the addition of the 26-year-old
Richard Burton, playing Prince Hal and Henry V in his first and
what was to be his only season there. Kenneth Tynan wrote that: 'His
playing of Prince Hal turned interested speculation to awe almost as
soon as he started to speak; in the first intermission local critics stood
agape in the lobbies.'[8] Pamela, however, thought that Burton had only
offered 'a new reading of the Prince – cogent up to a point, but
basically unsound'. She had similar ambivalent reactions to seeing him
off-stage, when he came into the Dirty Duck public house where she
and CPS were drinking. She registered 'young Burton' as being 'a
marked personality with a stubby, alive face, the brow overhanging v.
bright eyes, & a transforming smile', yet considered his 'figure bad,
stocky, short, slouching & not enough leg'. (They returned to Stratford later in the season, to see his Henry V, about which she conceded

that his reading was 'peculiar rather than inferior: a sort of insecure, schizoid Henry', but felt that 'his two levels of voice' were 'not good for poetry'. It would be three years before Burton's voice would prove unsurpassable in the iconic radio production of her former swain's *Under Milk Wood*.)[9] Another outing in this hiatus in their lives, a visit to the Festival of Britain, received still more withering criticism, and here CPS's opinion was likely to have carried weight with her, particularly as, unusually, she used the first person plural for her comments:

> We think it quite <u>awful</u> – the worst modern type of 'chichi', 'smart', 'amusing'. Thin, & second-rate. Scientific section plain idiotic. The whole thing a curious gloomy half-lit incoherence. V. few people there. We were both nightmarishly depressed by it.

The two months' wait until publication of *The Masters* seemed interminable as Pamela had to deal with CPS's customary apprehensions. During this time, when she wrote that her own nerves were in a particularly 'frightful' state, CPS was telephoned in some excitement by J.H. Plumb, inviting him to Christ's the following day to dine with the renowned cricketer Bill Edrich. Forgetting all his anxieties, CPS dropped all his appointments in order to meet his hero; a disgruntled Pamela wrote that she realised that this would be to her 'the equivalent of being asked to dine with Proust', but, to her shame, she could not refrain from reproaching him for leaving her. Her faith about his literary abilities never, however, diminished, and she continued to believe that everyone must share her opinion. Recording the events at a 'grand party' held by the publisher Victor Gollancz, she expressed her delight at seeing that her husband 'really <u>is</u> greeted very much as a great man now'.

Publication day finally arrived, and started well enough with good early reviews and a lunch with the publishers who were predicting sales of around 20,000 (although that figure was not to be immediately achieved). In the evening, the Brett Youngs hosted a celebration party for CPS at the Connaught, but, however, made the 'fatal error' in Pamela's opinion, of not providing enough drink, hence: 'Charles became sober & miserable, & by bedtime was back in the grip of an appalling anxiety state.' He then became reasonably satisfied overall with the novel's reception, especially with the reviewers who emphasized, as J.D. Scott did in the *New Statesman and Nation* that *The*

Masters was not only 'in itself beautifully done' but also 'a harmonious part of a larger whole'.

But yet again, CPS's use of real people as a basis for his characters was to threaten his equilibrium. In this novel, the choice of a new Master lies between two men, Paul Jago, the popular Senior Tutor with, however, a wife who might be thought to be a hindrance, and Crawford, a scientist, with 'a quiet, comely wife', but a man whose popularity may be gauged from the fact that we do not learn his first name until the penultimate chapter, describing the day of the election, and then it comes as a surprise to most of the Fellows that he may be voted for either as plain Thomas Crawford or Redvers Thomas Arbuthnot Crawford.[10] When writing *Stranger and Brother*, CPS's brother Philip asked him to identify the originals of the two contenders, and he was informed that Jago was based on Charles Raven, Master of Christ's from 1939-1950, and Crawford on Sir Robert Watson-Watt. Neither man appeared to have been unhappy about the novel; perhaps Mrs Raven did not read the book, otherwise she might well have felt traduced by possible association with Mrs Jago. Nevertheless, CPS was in some trepidation when rumours came to him that Sidney Roberts, the current Vice-Chancellor of the University of Cambridge, 'had been uttering violent abuse against him'. He became increasingly convinced that a libel suit might be looming, and Pamela suffered a further long week of 'dreadful strain' on his behalf. However, eventually CPS received a letter of praise from Sydney Grose, Senior Tutor at Christ's, and the following day 'the kindest & most enthusiastic' letter from Brian Downs, who had succeeded Raven as Master. From these two communications, he was reassured that he was not *persona non grata* at his college, and would continue to be invited to Feasts.

The summer passed with the usual arduous family holiday *sans* CPS, this year in a grey, cold Bournemouth. Left behind in London, CPS continued to fret about the reception of *The Masters*, and to sense a wider conspiracy against them both. He wrote to Pamela: 'We seem to live surrounded by madmen.' He singled out 'dirty Daniel' [Daniel George] as a ringleader of 'this foggy hostility', writing somewhat cryptically:

> we are, for purely careeristic reasons, unlucky in our friends (the real careerists don't carry their friends with them, but make friends among those already arrived). But it is time that a few open words were said.[11]

These concerns were temporarily shelved as Pamela and CPS left for a month in Italy and France, initially also cold and rainy. They visited Florence en route to Venice, and a diary entry betrays the casual homophobia of the times. In a restaurant, they observed 'three fascinating inverts at next table; one elderly & arch & gay, one young, & one old & distinguished', who were engaged in the 'most frank public conversation I have ever heard'. An asterisk in the margin led to a possible identification: 'Bernard Berenson, we think', although it is not clear whether Pamela was referring to the first or third diner. Their first week in Venice was not the idyll she had hoped for, being blighted by illness; both had heavy colds, and Pamela also had a stomach infection. Shortly after recovering, they were joined by CPS's brother Philip, now returned from his colonial service in Fiji, who had volunteered his services as a driver, since they wanted to vary their usual schedule by returning home by car, via the French Riviera (neither Pamela nor CPS had ever held a driving licence). The journey wasn't altogether successful; while she loved Verona and the subsequent drive to Genoa ('glorious scenery, strange huddled villages like a child's toy houses flung on a hillside, sunsets of radiant peach & deep lavender'), she was disappointed in the 'tatty' Italian Riviera, didn't care for Antibes, and found Nice still 'horribly battered by war'.

On her return, she found that the Book Society had made *Catherine Carter* their Fiction Choice for January. She mentioned, with a shade of satisfaction, that this was 'exactly the same thing as C. had', and that, although her agent was disappointed that it had not been the main choice, it had restored her *amour-propre*. She did, however, later record meeting at a party two members of the Book Society panel, the historian C.V. Wedgwood and the publisher Alan Bott, both of whom offered further balm to her soul by telling her that they had been furious that it hadn't been the overall choice. I would surmise, however, that she would have been reluctant to outdo CPS in this early, somewhat fragile, stage of their marriage. Indeed, CPS was yet again downcast about the progress of his literary standing, this time blaming the American reviewers, while forever maintaining faith in himself; in the course of a business trip to the north of England, he wrote to Pamela:

> The most unpleasant fact, which we've got to face, is that my reputation hasn't crystallised enough to force attention in the slick New

York papers. This is a defeat, and mustn't be minimised: all wise and humane writers have an occupational risk of being passed over as good but not journalistically interesting. That is the greatest danger in front of me [...].[12]

Pamela was now occupied with a small-theatre production of a dramatization by her friend, John Ireland Wood, of parts of the Helena trilogy, principally *An Avenue of Stone*, although, despite her lifelong interest in the theatre, and unlike CPS, she was always less than happy about her own work being staged. The play, which was to star the well-known film actress Olga Lindo, was to focus on Helena, and was originally entitled *Here is Helena*; however a more anodyne title, *Sunset in Knightsbridge*, was later substituted.

Towards the end of the year, Pamela would have reason to feel still more relieved that *Catherine Carter* had not been in direct competition with *The Masters*, when, to CPS's chagrin, the latter was omitted from the *Sunday Times* Books of the Year list, and he became even more 'dreadfully miserable <u>au fond</u>' when the novel was similarly missing from the *Observer*'s list. 'Why is it <u>always</u> like this at the year's end?', Pamela asked, and then reminded herself for the future that 'the final week of December is always going to be hell'. Unusually, she did not even try to summarize 1951, only writing in her diary on New Year's Eve, that the year was ending 'in a state of affectionate gloom'. 'My poor C.', she continued sympathetically, 'feels his career has suddenly wrecked itself & that he will never recover. He will, of course; but it is bad for a man of his temperament to endure so many blows (both real & imagined).'

CPS's despair about his career as an author continued throughout January of the next year; he was 'so down', she wrote, 'that it is like living within a great cold pudding'. On the evenings when they were at home together, he could only take comfort from what she always described as 'looking in'; he would sit in front of the television (which she had never previously had in her house), 'for hours, watching the most banal rubbish with an air of detachment'. She felt a personal failure in being unable to make him happier, although she now had reason to hope that they would shortly have something to celebrate. She did not even confide to her diary that she had missed a period until she missed a second, although even then she wondered if this just meant an early menopause. Despite tests, it would take several

more weeks before her doctors were prepared to confirm unequivocally that she was indeed pregnant.

In the meantime, the first night of *Sunset in Knightsbridge* and
publication day for *Catherine Carter* were both approaching. Pamela's
misgivings about John Ireland Wood's play proved well-founded,
although the play's reception was not in fact injurious to her literary
standing. The critics in both influential Sunday papers stated their
preference for the original source. Harold Hobson in the *Sunday Times*
declared that the play lacked 'the richness of the novel by Pamela
Hansford Johnson from which it is adapted', and the unnamed
reviewer in the *Observer* said that *Avenue of Stone* had introduced him
'very readably to plausible people with their failings not over-stressed,
whereas *Sunset in Knightsbridge* [...] seemed to put them on a lower
level of sanity and credibility'.

On the same day, the *Observer* fiction column on the opposite page
to the review of the play featured Pamela again, as the author of
Catherine Carter. (One of her friends rang to say that her name seemed
to be 'everywhere in the Sunday papers with the exception of the
Stocks and Shares column!'). Giving her novel pride of place,
Marghanita Laski was extremely enthusiastic:

> "Catherine Carter" will be and deserves to be a greatly enjoyed and
> very successful novel. [...] Miss Hansford Johnson has written with a
> spacious sweep admirably suited to her period and theme. She has
> stinted neither words nor invention, with the result that we are able to
> feel, as we were with the real Victorian novels, that we have been
> deprived of nothing that could make a large, long story interesting and
> intelligible.

However, Pamela had been downcast by a review, slightly ahead of
publication, by Seán Ó Faoláin in *The Listener*, particularly as this was
a periodical for which she was occasionally commissioned to write
articles. Ó Faoláin, who, it may be remembered, had been harsh in his
critique of her first novel, had made use of her present novel to side-
swipe the Book Society. Their current choice, *Catherine Carter*, was, he
wrote:

> the sort of novel that the average bookseller calls a good novel: a long,
> easy story, with uncomplicated characters and sufficient incident, suit-
> able for the rapid reader. [...] Miss Pamela Hansford Johnson employs

sentiment rather than wit, and very rarely cuts the greasepaint. This indulgent method is certainly not in the topical mood. [...] Evidently the Book Society knows whom it is catering for. It is not primarily catering for connoisseurs of The Novel.

Pamela's long-time champion, John Brophy, was so incensed that he insisted in responding to this, although she implored him either not to send a letter at all or to make it very brief. He did not yield to either of her requests, but the brief excerpts below not only give the flavour of his letter, but also illustrate the battleground of the literary wars of the period:

> You change your reviewers of fiction often enough, but the more they change, the more uniformly they adopt a now familiar attitude of superciliousness towards most of the novels they are paid to report on. Today I find Mr. Seán Ó Faoláin discussing *Catherine Carter* by Pamela Hansford Johnson [...] with an air of condescension that would be infuriating in a nonagenarian patriarch.

Brophy particularly took issue with 'the shameless principle' with which Ó Faoláin made use of 'the old reviewing device of calling technical skill "competence" in the hope of disparaging it'.

Meanwhile, Pamela was more concerned that her London doctor was still refusing to commit himself regarding her possible pregnancy; she quaintly recorded that he only felt it 'likely' that she might be 'with child'. She decided to consult John Sanctuary, the doctor in Laleham who had supervised the births of her first two children, and to her delight, after examining her, he confirmed that she was indeed pregnant. 'I can't believe it', she wrote, 'Somehow I <u>can't</u>. I dare not. But Sanctuary should know – !!' She and Charles celebrated with champagne that evening (medical wisdom of the time did not advise mothers-to-be to abjure either alcohol or nicotine). A few days earlier, Pamela had had a jealous tantrum after they had dined with a banker and his wife. She expostulated to her diary: 'I have rarely met such a thoroughly dislikeable, strident, ill-bred woman as Betty K[...]. For the first fifteen minutes she behaved as though C. & she were in some secret from which I was utterly excluded, reminiscing about 'old times' [...].' Pamela had found the whole evening 'strained & beastly', and had 'blown up like a volcano' on their return home. She now had a useful excuse for such reactions, writing: 'I think my condition is affecting me rather poorly this time, & I think I must try to remember the fact whenever I want to misbehave.'

As it happened, King George VI had died the day after that dinner party. Pamela had been sorry to hear of 'the quite unexpected death of poor old King at Sandringham', but soon afterward felt optimistic about the reign of Queen Elizabeth II, her love of Shakespeare prompting her to rejoice: 'Now we are Elizabethans again!' The event seems to have prompted CPS to mention casually to Pamela that Anne Seagrim had landed the prestigious position of secretary to the Duke of Windsor, primarily concerned with assisting in his writing of his memoirs, and had duly moved to Paris to take up her duties. (This had in fact happened, as CPS was well aware, some eighteen months earlier.) With this reassurance that at least one of her former rivals was safely out of the way, Pamela now felt able to tolerate another erstwhile adversary, when their paths crossed at the next PEN meeting, at which, she observed with some amusement, all the women, other than herself, were dressed 'in <u>dead</u> black, like crows, as if they were claiming personal relationship with King'. Even more satisfyingly, she noticed that Maureen Gebbie was putting on weight, and continued: 'Found I was able – thanks to my condition, I think – to contemplate her not merely with equanimity but with an utter lack of interest.'

It is not clear who initiated the idea that the Snow ménage should now leave London. Pamela was initially enthusiastic about the scheme to bring the family up in a house with a big garden, especially when they were sent the particulars of Nethergate House, a fine half-timbered building, dating from the sixteenth century, in Clare, Suffolk. CPS made it clear to his brother Philip that another attraction for him would be the opportunity to commute regularly to London and resume his bachelor existence there.[13] Before long, Pamela started to have qualms about the move; after a visit to Clare, despite the delighted reactions of her two children to the lovely house with its garden leading down to the river, she felt 'horribly upset, as though I'd rather cling howling to Nelson's column than be torn away from London. [...] Nethergate looking beautiful – but O, my Paddington, my Bethnal Green!'

Nevertheless, the sale of their London home and the purchase of Nethergate House went ahead. In an effort to feel less isolated when 'torn away' from London, Pamela determined to take driving lessons.

After a fortnight of 'bloody tuition', she admitted defeat: 'I really <u>have</u> met my Waterloo – I am <u>not</u> getting on, & I am so frightened. Shall have to give up, though I hate it.' Her mother, who had receded somewhat into the domestic background as she had fewer household or child-minding duties and still preferred CPS to her previous son-in-law, now moved to a more central position, further undermining Pamela's equilibrium: 'Amy having fits of violent <u>angst</u> about the mere journey to Clare, which couldn't be easier; & myself in a corresponding state of <u>angst</u> as this is infectious.'

The last day at 1 Hyde Park Crescent inexorably arrived. The removal vans left them in 'a shell of desolation'; CPS looked in after his day at the office, and promptly departed for his club. Pamela howled to her diary that she had had an intense wave of grief after he had gone,

> knowing it is the last time I shall see him <u>here</u>, hear his key in the lock as he comes back after work, & puts his briefcase down in the hall, the last time I shall bathe in <u>that</u> room & watch him shaving – I love him perhaps more than I ought & the memories of two <u>wonderful</u> – despite all minor worries & sadnesses – years, contrasted with this emptiness, grime & echo, were too much. [...] Goodbye to my darling house, & I must greet the new life with hope.

The first weeks in Clare were chaotic; CPS arrived for two days at the end of the first week, spent nearly all the time sorting his books, and returned to London, leaving her in despair. 'Oh God', she wrote, 'I saw living in the country as somewhere to be <u>with him</u> & not this abomination of desolation.' The only good news received at that time concerned the sales of *Catherine Carter* on both sides of the Atlantic; she received an interim cheque from her agent in respect of UK sales for £500, which paid off all her personal debts, about which she had been fretting, and she learned that the novel had had excellent reviews in the USA and was high on their best-seller lists.

The following week, Kalie, who, over the years, had very much calmed down, and become transformed into a much-loved maiden aunt, joined them to help with the domestic chaos, but promptly fell over and broke her leg. Pamela, now in the third trimester of her pregnancy, had to arrange for Kalie to be operated on at Addenbrooke's Hospital in Cambridge, and was extremely anxious about her. She continued to have little support from CPS, and was already 'trying to repress a real repugnance to this sequestered life'. Predictably, just over three weeks after the move to Clare, Pamela woke in the night with a show of blood and some irregular pains. Somewhat apologetically, she aroused CPS to call the doctor, who promptly sent her off to the maternity hospital in Cambridge in an ambulance. CPS did not accompany her, but she did not seem to expect this as she drove 'through such a blazing dawn, after leaving darling Charles & poor, harassed Amy'. She was, she said, 'not in the least fearful for myself, but only for too premature a baby. I <u>want</u> this baby so desperately for Charles.' The following day, the labour pains had ceased, but her doctor advised against her returning home. She 'smoked till I ran out of my few remaining cigarettes', and having not, in her haste, brought in anything to read, was reduced to reading the women's magazines that were all that was on offer. The following day, to her relief, a neighbour brought her in some cigarettes, together with Joyce Cary's latest novel, *Prisoner of Grace*; as an admirer of the author, she was delighted and also amused at the coincidence that she had been reading his novel, *The Horse's Mouth*, while awaiting the birth of her daughter in 1944.

It is entirely possible that CPS would not have been in the vicinity while his wife was giving birth, had it not been for the fact that he was due to attend a dinner at Christ's the same evening, and looked in on her for the first time since she had left in the ambulance. As she remembered many years later: 'I shall never forget that night [...], hearing C. go off to a College dinner [...], and as I heard his footsteps retreating, my waters broke!'[14] She did not consider calling him back, although the labour pains were now strong. Just before midnight, after a 'very short & sharp' accouchement, their son, to be named Philip Charles Hansford Snow, was born.

The baby weighed just under 4½ lbs. at birth, and Pamela was not initially allowed to leave her bed to see him in the premature baby ward. CPS came in to see his son at 10 the following morning, and pronounced him to have 'a large wise brow' and a 'very solemn' look. She was relieved when he also added: '"He looks such a dear!"' He had instantly nicknamed Philip 'Borox', derived from an obscure Snow family joke.[15] Despite bad after-pains, she declared herself to be 'so wonderfully happy to have given C. his longed-for son'. It would be two days before the baby would be transferred to the main nursery, and she would be able to hold him in her arms. There were many more anxious days before he was fully out of danger, and when Pamela recorded some time later that sales of *Catherine Carter* were rising in the US best-seller list, she added: 'I'd swap the lot for 1lb. gain in Philip's weight'. She was briefly able to breast-feed, during which time she had, she wrote:

> three wonderful hours with Charles, who was able to hold him & see me feed him: felt I must at least dare to be free of <u>angst</u> for that time, & try to enjoy our happiness without fear. Charles is a real father, with the kind of love for the baby which is beautiful to see – rich & unembarrassed [...].

'On the comic side', she added, 'I learn that C's first practical action was to put Philip down for the MCC!!' But then she was disappointed when, with little tact, the obstetrician told her that Philip was not receiving enough nourishment from her, with the judgment that: "Some are good cows & some aren't, & you <u>are</u> forty – [...]".

CHAPTER 13

Second Exile from the City

I T WAS ALMOST four weeks before Pamela could take their baby
home to Clare, and in that time, she attempted to come to terms
with the changes in her life. It may seem strange that she had
initially embraced the idea of living in a small country town, considering how, blitz or no blitz, she had pined for London during the Laleham years, but perhaps CPS's enthusiasm carried her away. She had
certainly believed that he would be spending the majority of the time
with her in Suffolk, and the last few months had proved her wrong
about this. She admitted to her diary:

> I now dread returning to Clare, & making <u>the act of fresh vision</u> needed
> to begin a new life there. It is so shadowed by the events leading up
> to Philip's birth that I can only see it through a sort of Gothic haze. It
> is wrong & foolish, & it must be conquered. The country is right for
> the children & right for Charles, & they <u>must</u> come first.

CPS did take a month's leave soon after Philip's discharge from
hospital, but spent a great deal of it working on his next novel, *The
New Men*. Fortunately, the baby was now thriving and allowing them
undisturbed nights. Once the month was over, CPS reverted to
spending the week in London, generally staying at the Savile. Holly
Southwell, now living in Kensington, had written to him shortly after
Philip's premature birth, offering to end their relationship without any
recriminations:

> [...] if [the baby] lives, he'll need more than concern for his survival,
> and if you truly feel absorbed in him, I think I should find that a last-
> ingly good reason for our parting. I have always thought that might
> turn out to be so. [...]

> I doubt a little whether, by now, you love me, except as a waif and flukily as flesh. If that's so, you most emphatically ought to quit, or you'll wear yourself out on me for nothing lasting.

CPS temporised for a relatively brief time. Throughout November, the month after his return to work, a nanny having been found for Philip, Pamela was herself in London quite often as she had now joined the prestigious panel on BBC radio's 'The Critics'. This involved seeing beforehand a current London play, film and exhibition, and Pamela expected CPS to accompany her to these. At this time, they both generally stayed in London overnight with CPS's friend, the English scholar, [Samuel] Gorley Putt.

By early December, however, CPS did resume his relationship with Holly. It would obviously not have been possible to have a rendezvous with her either at Gorley Putt's flat or at his club, but his compliant lover readily agreed to another solution, writing:

> How lovely. I am so glad. Yes of course it will be <u>lovely</u> to have you come to my flat. I have <u>no</u> tremors and at the moment I have no iota of strain either. I feel completely that we are right, from my side of it. But my dearest, I want you to cry off even without notice at the last minute, either if as may well happen, it becomes practically awkward or chancy, or if you suddenly don't feel right about it. [...][1]

Pamela sensed a difference in CPS's behaviour towards her, but had no cause for jealousy as all his previously-known girl-friends were accounted for. She was just delighted that he had been 'very dear to me lately', and she felt 'so much in love', thinking of him as she returned to Clare after one particular evening in London in December 'in a kind of renascence of all my earlier feeling'. She endeavoured to involve herself in local activities, but an 'interminable Coronation Committee meeting' resulted in her crying through the night. 'I can no longer pretend', she wrote, 'I like rural life [...]'. She reiterated that she had not realised that she would lose so much of CPS by living in Suffolk: 'Life without him is nothing – a sum of days wasted.'

Her 1953 diary reflects her comparative social inactivity during the time spent in Clare. She had reverted to a standard day-to-a-page desk diary, but very few pages are completely filled. Many of them simply but proudly record the baby's gains of weight and hours of sleep. It

may also be significant that, having written her name on the inside
front cover of her 1951 diary as Pamela Hansford Snow, and simply
Pamela Snow in 1952, she now reverted to proclaiming the diary to be
that of Pamela Hansford Johnson, perhaps an unconscious attempt
to reclaim her individual identity. She continued to voice despair
about her isolation, about CPS's continuing moodiness, often related
to money worries (the house in London being still unsold), about
domestic crises (they had taken Friedel, their current German housekeeper with them from London, but the move had resulted in Friedel
on occasion being 'intolerably moody'), and, last but not least, about
the regular invasions of bats and spiders into Nethergate. Pamela
also had to fit in regular visits to her aunt Kalie, who had never fully
recovered from the accident just before Philip's birth, and was now
permanently living in a nursing home in Clare. Within a few months,
however, staff matters at least improved. Friedl decamped back to
London, and Pamela had been able to employ a married couple, the
Bowdens, who lived in a cottage which formed part of the Nethergate property, the wife to cook, and the husband to act as gardener,
handyman, and part-time chauffeur. She was also continuing to
employ Nannie Page, as she invariably referred to the nurse who had
originally come to her for the fortnight after she had been able to bring
Philip home, but who stayed for eight years (quite the longest period
served by any of their staff until much later).

    In addition to CPS's usual week-day working in London, he
also occasionally had to make journeys around England for English
Electric. Pamela sometimes accompanied him, and they tried to fit in
lecturing engagements at the same time. A visit to engineering works
in Yorkshire with CPS was the first time she had visited the north of
England, and it fulfilled her typical southerner's expectations: 'Sun
came out, pale yellow & blazing, just before Wakefield & gave me the
apocalyptic impression I had been wanting. Impression of vast
grandeur & squalor & a sort of blackened nobility.' They gave a joint
lecture at Wakefield with Phyllis Bentley in the chair, and then at
Batley and Huddersfield. Despite her constantly reiterated belief that
CPS was the greater writer of the two of them, Pamela was quite glee-
ful at her own reception. 'C. finds no-one seems to know him here,
while I am pretty well La Reine du Nord! But he has it all the time
in London!'

It is also likely that her success at these events could be accounted for because she was the better lecturer. When, later that year, CPS had to spend nearly two weeks in Germany on English Electric business, and Pamela was fulfilling engagements in London, Gorley Putt took her to dinner at the Athenaeum, and she recorded 'one lovely thing':

> G. told me in secret how Charles, lecturing to the students of E. Acton in 1949, had said, on putting my name on the blackboard, 'who, by the way, is an extraordinarily beautiful woman'. If I <u>were</u>, only for him! Touched to pure delight by this.

Many years later, by which time both CPS and Pamela had died, Putt published a memoir in the course of which he recounted a different version of this incident, which he said had taken place at a Summer School for foreign students at Exeter University. He also gave a less than complimentary account of CPS's communication skills and general effect on his audience. Being familiar with his guest speaker's normal speech, Putt had advised him to attempt to address his audience clearly and slowly; however, as he remembered:

> His opening words, in true Snovian burbling mumble, were: 'I'm given to believe that I'm not specially audible.' Nor was he specially stable, for ambling to and fro across the platform in his customary totter, he caused his listeners to open their eyes as wide as his own peering pop-eyes, when several times he seemed about to pitch forward and land among them.

Putt had asked him to write the names of the eighteenth- and nineteenth-century novelists he had been discussing on a blackboard, and then add the names of recommended contemporary novelists in what space was left. There was in fact only space for one name because CPS, 'starting in huge capitals and scrawling the rest in the last few inches',

> mesmerised them all by incanting, while writing, PAMELA HANSFORD JOHNSON ('Pommela Hahnsford Jawnson'), and then wheeling to face them with the unexpected critical commentary: 'Who, incidentally, is an ex-straw-dinarily beautiful wooman'.[2]

Putt's recollection of the location of this lecture may later have been faulty, but the manner of its delivery (almost certainly impaired to some extent by alcohol) is likely to have been accurately described.

Despite having feared throughout 1952 that she would never again be possessed by a creative urge, by the end of January 1953, Pamela had decided on a subject for her next novel, to be called *An Impossible Marriage*, and she derived some comfort from being again engrossed in the process of writing. As previously mentioned, this is the first book in which, possibly influenced by CPS's use of autobiographical material, many of the incidents in the opening chapters can be seen to be derived from her own youthful experiences, and not just set in the South London background of her early novels. The epigraph Pamela chose for the novel was an acknowledgment of those sources; it is an untranslated quotation from the penultimate paragraph of Marcel Proust's *Le temps retrouvé*, the final volume of *À la recherche du temps perdu*, in which the author records feeling

> un sentiment de fatigue profonde à sentir que tout ce temps si long non seulement avait sans une interruption été vécu, pensé, sécreté par moi, qu'il étais moi-même, mais encore que j'avais à toute minute à le maintenir attaché à moi, qu'il me supportait, que j'étais juché à son sommet vertigineux, que je ne pouvais me mouvoir sans le déplacer avec moi. [...][3]

More specifically, Pamela confided to her diary that: 'It is so difficult to tell the truth so that it is literary truth as well as actual.'

An Impossible Marriage begins with the former Christine Jackson reluctantly standing on the doorstep of Iris, a friend she has not seen for many years, and echoing Proust in her thoughts:

> I do not like looking back down the chasm of the past and seeing, in a moment of vertigo, some terror that looks like a joy, some joy crouched like a terror. It is better to keep one's eyes on the rock-face of the present, for that is real; what is under your nose is actual, but the past is full of lies [...]. (p.1)

Iris had been her self-obsessed, glamorous 'best friend', who had insouciantly blighted her life by always capturing the attractive boys initially interested in Christine, and it was fear and jealousy of her that precipitated Christine into marrying the older and sophisticated Ned Skelton. She had instantly fallen in love with Ned at their first meeting, a phenomenon which the older Christine examines (and here a parallel with the nature of Pamela's burgeoning love for CPS is recognisable):

I know through this experience that love at first sight is possible – I have proved it empirically. What I see no reason for claiming is that love of this kind is the best, for the most enduring love in my life, which is no part of this story, did not at all begin in such a fashion. It was upon me suddenly in joy, bewilderment and something like fear, when, after years of knowing, and of complex but unanalysed friendship, I had looked upon the object of it with new eyes. (p.47)

Pamela was always adamant that Ned was not a portrait of Neil Stewart, and indeed it would seem that Frank Saunois might have been the inspiration for this character. The Skeltons, like the Saunois family, live within the magic postal district of W.1, and after his marriage to Christine, Ned starts up a business which proves disastrous.

The pattern of Christine's life does not thereafter follow Pamela's, but some further insight into her state of mind when writing the book is offered by a passage in which, shortly after the birth of her son, Christine is consumed by self-pity but refuses to condemn herself for this. 'I never know why self-pity is considered especially disgraceful', she muses, and continues:

It seems to me neither a virtue nor a vice, but simply an inevitable emotion. The sympathy of others is an uncertain thing at best. A friend may be genuinely sorry for us for an hour, but forget his sorrow the moment affairs of his own divert him – which is perfectly natural and right, but no consolation to us, in whom unhappiness may endure day in and day out. We have to be sorry for ourselves: nobody else can sympathise with us as steadily, as loyally as we, and it is from such sympathy that we draw strength to put a decent public face upon our misfortunes. (pp.290-91).

Once Pamela had got over her self-criticism as regards the transmission of her voice on the wireless, particularly during unscripted discussions on 'The Critics' in which she felt she sounded 'like a peculiarly brutal wardress in a woman's prison', she enjoyed her visits to London for that purpose. She was, however, forthright in her judgments, and often recorded there having been lively debates and considerable differences of opinion with others on the panel. For one edition of 'The Critics', for example, she had attended an elsewhere well-received revival of the Restoration tragedy, *Venice Preserv'd* by Thomas Otway, with a stellar cast which included John Gielgud, Paul Scofield and

Eileen Herlie and remarked to her diary: 'It is a lousy play & I don't know why about 75% of the total talent of the English stage has been poured out upon it.' The exhibition under discussion for the same programme was the major Graham Sutherland retrospective at the Tate Gallery, and again her criticism was unflinching. 'What is he', she asked her diary, 'but a magnificent decorator with the horrors? The Hugh Casson of the Crucifixion Route. No, no, no, this is not great art. All manner: no profound feeling.' Almost certainly, these were the views she expressed on air.

By contrast, on another occasion, she had enormous pleasure from a 'really exciting and interesting day', far removed from the realms of high art. To share in CPS's lifelong passion for cricket, she went with him and several other members of his family to see that year's Tourists, Australia, play Leicestershire. In the evening, they all went on a 'fantastic pub-crawl' with the legendary commentator John Arlott, the Australian captain Lindsay Hassett in his last tour in England, and 'the large fascinating Bill ["Tiger"] O'Reilley', the recently retired Australian bowler, now working with Arlott as a commentator. Hassett was, she recorded, recalling her childhood visits to the theatre and cinema, 'just like a great musical comedy star of the Nelson Keys/ Leslie Henson era'. It was to be the year in which England retained the Ashes, and, to her own amazement, Pamela took an interest in all the matches, and rejoiced in the eight-wicket victory in the final Test.

Pamela had made another new acquaintance at this time. She had written earlier in the year to Rosamond Lehmann, sympathizing with her for 'the N.S. scurrility', by which she meant a very hostile review in the New Statesman (11 April 1953) by Honor Tracy of Lehmann's The Echoing Grove (Kay Dick had been among those who had defended the novel in subsequent editions of the periodical). In due course, Pamela was invited to visit Lehmann, whom she summed up as 'a huge, affectionate, wounded creature', and whose interrogation, she amusedly described as being 'in the manner of High Bloomsbury lost to my generation' (Lehmann was in fact only eleven years older than Pamela): '[She] asked me all manner of personal questions dead on the mark. Didn't mind – I never do: though I remembered Dylan saying [T.S.] Eliot behaved as though he (Dylan) were "from Pit Boy to Poet".'

Diary entries reflect the workings of the literary partnership between Pamela and CPS. The latter was completing The New Men,

I *Wedding photograph of Pamela's parents, Amy and Reginald (R.K.) Johnson.*

2 *Pierrot troupe,*
Clapham County
Secondary School,
c.1927 (Pamela,
centre front row).

3 *Pamela and Amy,*
c.1920.

4 & 5 *Pamela with
Dylan Thomas,
Caswell Bay, Swansea, 1934.*

6 *Wedding photograph of Pamela and (Gordon) Neil Stewart, Chelsea, 1936.*
Left to right: Emma Oram (née Howson), Pamela, Neil, Katie Howson, Amy Johnson (née Howson).

7 *Pamela with her children, Andrew and Lindsay, 1944.*

8 *Wedding photograph of Pamela and C.P. Snow, Christ's College, Cambridge, 1950.*

9 *Pamela with CPS
and his brother
Philip (in
foreground),
Venice, 1951.*

63

42ⁿᵈ

Photograph at ~~21st~~ Year.

10 *Portrait of
Pamela, 1954,
mounted by PHJ in
her 'Progress Book'.*

11 *Pamela with CPS and their son Philip, Clare, Suffolk, 1954.*

12 *Russian hospitality, 1964. Clockwise from bottom left: Oksana Krugerskaya, the Snows' regular interpreter; unknown bandaged man, the host, Viktor Bokhov, CPS, Pamela, Lindsay (partially hidden), Betty Linn Smith; unidentifiable heads in foreground include that of Philip Snow.*

13 *Pamela, CPS and Sirikit, South Kensington, c.1965.*

14 *Launch of CPS's Trollope, 1975. Front row: CPS, Harold Macmillan, Pamela; second row includes, far left, their editor, Alan Maclean, and Maurice Macmillan behind his father.*

15 *Pamela and CPS, Belgravia, 1976.*

and, as usual, asking Pamela for her opinion. (She had completed the first reading on a train journey with, she wrote, 'C. lowering at me as if expecting me to damn it. He always does this.') The following day was 'ghastly' as, despite thinking that the book was 'so fine', she attempted to argue minor changes with CPS, which left him 'down in the depths. I had to go out for a walk to get free of his spiritual pressure so that my own judgment remained free.' This led to CPS's conviction 'as usual' that the book was a total failure, and it took a further day's cajoling before she calmed him down. On the other hand, shortly afterwards, when, after reading the almost completed *An Impossible Marriage*, and, while telling her that it was 'splendid', CPS suggested that she should attempt to 'deepen' a central section, her reaction was one of agreement and gratitude: 'It is an inordinate comfort to us both to have a professional & affectionate opinion on the spot – it is hard for the writer who works alone, having no Flaubert he can trust.'

In July, she and CPS managed to have 'Our first holiday – real holiday – in years!' in Stratford-upon-Avon, the Company that year including Peggy Ashcroft and Michael Redgrave. She was censorious about Ashcroft's Cleopatra – 'a cut between Electra and a high female civil servant', although Redgrave's Antony received her approval, and she also disliked the production of Richard III, 'marred by a Richard [Marius Goring] without sexual charm'. Nevertheless, an ecstatic diary entry recorded:

> How happy & serene we've been, this short holiday! Feel I loved C. more with every day that passes – & tomorrow we shall have been married three years. How impossible to make any despairing young man or woman realise that it is possible, on the edge of middle age, to know the supreme felicity of life.

The previous month, less than a year after their move to Clare, Pamela had persuaded CPS to put Nethergate House up for sale, although it would be another three years before a buyer was found, and throughout that time, Pamela became ever more desperate to return to London. Her feeling of being 'landlocked in [a] mood of despondency' continued through the autumn. Her visits to London (now augmented by having been recruited onto the Book Society panel of judges) were not always compensatory. The two Ks were fighting yet again, and Pamela was torn between them. On one day in London, she lunched with Kathleen, went on to see 'a grey-faced, raging Kay', and ended up in a 'great hot crush' at 'Goose [Stephen] Spender's party for his tedious new magazine [*Encounter*]'. Kathleen came to spend a few days with Pamela at Clare, but this was scarcely restful for either of them, as Kathleen's parents had locked Kay out of the house she had been sharing with their daughter, and Kay bombarded Clare with phone calls, express letters and telegrams, the latter being so frequent that Pamela had to tell the Post Office to stop delivering them as it was wearing the aged local postman out.

Then a deeper sadness intervened in the shape of Dylan Thomas's death in New York in November of that year. Her diary entry was more touching and revealing than her contributions to various obituary compilations would be, but posterity has disagreed with her judgment as to his lasting reputation:

> There seems so little to say about Dylan. I loved him for a year, & we thought of marrying, & all turned cold & ugly. There was a very brief spell of intense misery & afterwards no feeling at all; & never has been since. He was an odd minor genius & I think will have his place among the literary oddities of English literature – with Peacock, Beddoes, Firbank, I.C.B. – at best, with Hopkins. He was a fascinating, self-absorbed, highly-self-conscious & not, ultimately, a likeable man: everyone else was a 'feed' to him, as to a leading comedian. Once he was a beautiful boy, full of high, ridiculous humour & I did love him: but he tended then to <u>use</u> people. He may have changed. I haven't seen him for 15 yrs. Drink was not only an obsession with him but a <u>romance</u>. I have often known him pretend to be drunk when he was not. Yet how I loved him once!

Throughout 1954, Pamela continued to spend time in London in connection with 'Critics' broadcasts and Book Society meetings. On these visits, she now usually stayed in a single-bedded service flat, owned by English Electric, in Dolphin Square, but she was frustrated that CPS would only rarely stay there with her. He was continuing to be 'desperately wretched' at each perceived reverse in his literary career, but a new possibility was opening up for him. After giving a talk on the Third Programme, the producer Freddie Grisewood suggested that CPS might become 'officially a sort of adviser on contemporary thought – allying Science & Art [...].' 'This seems to me', Pamela wrote, 'full of pleasant potentialities.' It would be several years before this proposition bore any fruit.

An Impossible Marriage was published in March, and received mixed reviews. Pamela was now beginning to react like CPS to any critiques which were not unequivocally laudatory, and was not prepared to balance a relatively good review in *The Times*, praise in the *Manchester Guardian* for 'the author's integrity as an emotional reporter', and a 'lovely notice by Betjeman' in the *Daily Telegraph,* against others less favourable. A typical entry in her diary is that of 2nd April: 'I had a pretty condescending review in <u>Statesman</u> from Giles Romilly & a filthy one – this a blow – from some little cretin in the *TLS*, and a messy one in <u>Spectator</u> – how <u>out</u> my luck is!' That last comment seems especially significant since she had always previously had belief in her own abilities rather than relying on 'luck'. The 'little cretin' responsible for the unsigned review in the *Times Literary Supplement*, was in fact Julian Symons, who was exactly the same age as Pamela, and then well established as a critic; her reaction reveals her unwilling-ness to consider whether she might take some encouragement from this review and indeed learn from it. Symons's judgment was in fact far from being, as Pamela said, 'filthy', beginning as it did:

> *An Impossible Marriage* is written with sincerity and no little skill, yet it is not the distinguished novel which Miss Hansford Johnson has always promised to write. [...] between the honourably realistic intention and the act has fallen a shadow, the shadow of sentiment.

The book became successful financially when bought by Odhams for their Companion Book Club reprint offshoot, which meant royalties of around £1,800 and guaranteed a sale of 170,000. Pamela neverthe-less brooded in doggerel:

> Wealth & fame, they fill my cup
> But I'd <u>rather</u> have a Middle in the Times Lit Supp!

The 'Middle' for which both Pamela and CPS were pining was not the literary equivalent of a Playboy centrefold, but a lengthy article variously situated within the *TLS*, usually spanning between one and a half and two pages, devoted to a contemporary author's most recent work, together with an overview of their oeuvre to date. Pamela had acknowledged, the year before, that she had had to make 'an effort of generous spirit' to attempt to feel glad when Olivia Manning, one of the Hampstead set, was the subject of what she termed 'a preposterous "middle"' (*Times Literary Supplement*, 4 September 1953). Pamela surmised correctly that this had been written by their mutual friend William Gerhardi, and metaphorically raised her eyebrows at the writer's frequent use of the word 'genius', as in the judgment: 'Miss Manning is handicapped by her genius [because] genius eschews predigested conclusions.'

CPS was continuing to work hard on the next novel in the Lewis Eliot sequence, to be called *Homecomings*, but this time would tell Pamela nothing about it, leaving her feeling 'left out, unneeded, discouraged'. Several American publishers turned down *The New Men*, making him 'immoderately depressed & down again (if he was ever up)'. But even when their agent managed to place the novel with the well-regarded firm of Scribners, his depression continued, making Pamela desperate. She triple-lined an entry: 'It has been so dreadful for months.' *The New Men* was published on 30 April, and the early reviews in the daily newspapers were also a mixed bag. The weekend broadsheets were more encouraging: 'Thank God,' Pamela wrote, 'Lambert's review decent, & Stevie [Smith], in Observer, doing her mad-Ophelia-like best. So C. far more cheered than he would really show.' Her entry a few days later reverted to despair: CPS was 'all mouth-tucked-in again'. The 'Lambert' to whom she had referred was Jack Lambert, then the Assistant Literary Editor of the *Sunday Times*, and he had taken it upon himself to acquaint CPS of 'the opposition existing against him in certain circles, mostly centred around The Observer'. 'As if we didn't know!' she sighed, continuing:

> But it does C. no use to put all this nonsense into words, & it merely left my darling miserable again. When I think how generous he has been to his own friends, to young writers, how much he has always been willing to give, it saddens me to think of the malice he has to endure.

A week later, however, CPS did have the consolation of the desired '*TLS* Middle' (7 May 1954), which, although unsigned, it seems that they knew had been written by Julian Symons (whereas his identity as the author of the 'filthy' review of Pamela's book fortunately seems to have remained unknown by them). Their first reaction was that the essay was 'awful, but a second view comforted us: it is pretty silly in many ways, by a man who is not too bright [...]', but nevertheless Pamela was delighted that CPS had at last achieved this recognition. The accolade might, however, be thought to be double-edged. Symons praised *The New Men* for its subject-matter, but his final paragraph concentrated on CPS's limitations as a writer:

> At last, however, critical consideration of Mr. Snow comes back to his style, that style which in its alkaline flatness blandly ignores half a century of experimental writing. The style is not the man. Mr. Snow is not imperceptive of the revolution in the novel's technique connected with the names of James Joyce, Mr. Wyndham Lewis, Mr. Joyce Cary and many others; he ignores them deliberately in pursuit of an aesthetic which has never been openly formulated, but is perhaps his own version of realism – a realism that looks back to Trollope rather than to the symbolic naturalism of Zola [...]. The style is that of a lucid and uncommonly honest record, rather than of an artist.

It would be nearly five years before Pamela received her own unequivocally laudatory *TLS* 'Middle', following the publication of her novel *The Unspeakable Skipton*.

Pamela's feelings of isolation from London literary life and dislike of Clare continued, yet when her mother complained about their exile, Pamela did not feel gladdened by her corroboration of her own secret thoughts, but considered that Amy should try to make the best of things. Pamela had further reason to bemoan her own lot; she was, she wrote, 'much troubled by an excess of sexual feeling', which CPS did not appear to share. Evenings in London, if spent together, now usually ended with a game of Scrabble and an early night. One evening, when CPS had pleaded a bout of depression, for which she could find no reason, she wrote:

> WHY? Really felt rather fed up. I had hoped for a gay evening, but no. [...] Went to the pub, & I still hoped for cheerful evening, but after a sober, friendly, muffled pint, we came [back] & went to bed. HELL! I am brimming with energy tonight. I'd like a PARTY!!!!

In the autumn, despite all the complications of her family life, Pamela managed to get away from Clare for five weeks, although not for the peaceful holiday she might have chosen in her beloved Venice. CPS was asked to go to Canada on English Electric business, and they decided to combine this with a visit to literary friends and acquaintances in New York. They had a very rough crossing on Canada Pacific's elderly liner, Empress of Scotland. As Pamela later recalled:

> The ship creaked horribly, and the gales roared. We were not being helped by the fact that, at intervals, our Irish steward would come in, cross himself, and say, 'By the grace of God, we shall come through.' (*Important*, pp.40-41)

Safely on dry land, she fell in love with Quebec, 'an enchanting city of green copper roofs & rose-red brick. Very French', but detested Montreal, 'a brash, noisy, vulgar, bastard place'. Niagara Falls exceeded her expectations 'by miles – apple green water tumbling down on to great brown rocks & then spraying upwards in a cloud a hundred feet high: & over it all today, just a strip of cobalt sky'. In Toronto, they were feted at the University Women's Club, and interviewed for television. Pamela also had a surprising, but disappointing, encounter there with one of the heroes of her girlhood, the formerly charismatic George Stanley Russell, no longer in Clapham, but now the highly-paid minister of the large Deer Park United Church. He was still preaching, she recorded, 'with prodigious drama', but, after being invited back to tea with him and his wife, she sadly had to acknowledge that 'he is really megalomaniac these days, & very tired, & ill'.

She was eagerly looking forward to her first visit to New York, as she wrote in her memoir: 'New York! Who has not hallucinated a first visit? Those glorious skyscrapers, by night all silver and gold, splitting the indigo skin of the sky? The overriding exhilaration?' But on arrival by train 'into a murky, smelly station', she asked herself: 'Where was the glory and the dream?' Her perception of the city the following morning was little better; the overall impression, she said, 'was of a magnificent engineering feat which had achieved only pomposity and discomfort' (*Important*, pp.44-45). Nevertheless, she found intellectual stimulation there, meeting, at grand publishers' parties, writers whom she had never previously met, but with whose work she had been familiar since her first indoctrination into American literature by Teddy Lamerton and 'Take Plato'.

They returned home on the Queen Mary. The sea was rough the first day out, but thereafter they were able to enjoy shipboard activities that had been impossible on the outward sailing. The highpoint was CPS's progress into the last round of the table tennis competition, his final opponent being Professor Werner Heisenberg (of the 'Uncertainty Principle'). Pamela admiringly reported on the event as being 'surely the most intellectual game of Pingpong ever played? A wildly exciting match, as the Professor had all the ghastly solidity you would expect from a Nobel Prize winner.' Since she did not identify the winner, presumably it was Heisenberg.

In the final six weeks of the year, she had to make up for the time lost during their extended visit to North America. She took part in three 'Critics' programmes with their concomitant visits to events, and was involved in the rehearsals for 'Mme de Charlus', another of her Proust reconstructions. She was delighted with the principals, a very young Prunella Scales playing the eponymous role, and Max Adrian the Baron. She also wrote an article about 'Contre Sainte-Beuve', Proust's rebuttal of some of the ideas of the French literary scholar, two short stories, 15,000 words for a television feature, and somehow managed to slot in reading about fifty Book Society proofs. Over Christmas and the New Year, her elder son was confined to bed with a high fever and chest infection, and she had to cope with three extra house-guests, CPS's brother Philip, with his wife Anne and daughter Stefanie. Scarcely surprisingly, on the penultimate day of the year, she recorded being 'rather drunk, dead-tired, utterly despondent', and concluded: 'I HAVE TOO MUCH TO COPE WITH.'

Little changed the following year, which started with more than three months of unbearably cold weather, leading to all members of the family being ill in turn. A typical diary entry described Nethergate House as being 'a sink of gloom'. She now fully realised the folly of their having decided to buy the house in midsummer, only to be made aware much later that the draughts rushing down 'the huge stone entrance hall', with its two fine curving staircases, made that 'interesting architectural feature [...] uninhabitable for the greater part of the year' (*Important*, pp.121-22). That winter, CPS's back pains were almost continuous and the analgesics prescribed by their local doctor did little to allay them. A consultation with a London specialist was scarcely more help: he diagnosed posture problems, and told CPS to stop the bending exercises he had previously been advised to do, and to endeavour 'to keep erect'; otherwise, his opinion was that CPS was 'sound in every other respect' and should be able to enjoy 'a first-class life'. The following day, Pamela recorded CPS's attempt to follow the specialist's advice: 'C. sitting in bolt-upright position all day looking (I tell him) like a cross between Queen Victoria & a stuffed parrot. Had dreadful attack in evening, after a better day.' There would in the future be reason to believe that his presumed 'lumbago' was always a misdiagnosis.

Pamela had no broadcasting commitments until May when she began a seven-week stretch of 'The Critics', in which the first topic under discussion was the work of an Australian painter then relatively unknown outside the country of his birth. Sidney Nolan had moved to London a few years earlier, and the privately-owned Redfern Gallery off Bond Street was now giving him a one-man show. Pamela was 'much struck' by his paintings and his use of the outlaw Ned Kelly as a constant symbol, and, as she put it, 'did my best, though ramblingly' for the artist on the subsequent radio programme. A few days, later, she and CPS spent an evening in a London pub with the Nolans. His wife, Cynthia, she said, 'looks like Queen Elizabeth (I), but dark and ill'; she found Sidney to be 'a dear, but a very shrewd go-getter. C & I call him "Simple Sid."' For some years, the two couples remained friends; the Snows bought several of Nolan's paintings, and, on their return to London, the painter was to agree to loan others to them, on the assumption that thereby their flat in London could act as an unofficial gallery.

Other experiences which Pamela and CPS might not have had but for the selection of items for 'The Critics' included seeing Danny Kaye at the London Palladium (they both agreed that his performance was 'most lovely and joyful', and one in which 'one feels not only the physical grace, but a kind of spiritual grace'); the Academy Award-winning *Marty* ('a charming, highly naturalistic American film – quite unique in its truth-telling'); and a tour of the recently completed Queen's Building complex at what was then called London Airport, now Heathrow ('v. struck by its lightness & gaiety: rarely have I liked contemp. architecture so much').

By the beginning of the summer, Pamela felt that *she* must spend some time away from home distractions to enable her to write without interruption.

It is almost a physical pain to be jerked out of the kind of concentration I <u>have</u> to achieve, if I am to write well at all. Think I shall have, somehow, to do a good bit of my creative writing away from home. I'm not young any more & not so resilient as I was: & when I lose an idea, it <u>doesn't</u> come back again.

Accordingly, she chose to stay at CPS's former retreat, the Dudley Hotel in Hove, and this clearly inspired her to start a new novel, *The Last Resort*, in which the greater part of the action takes place in a very similar hotel, which she calls the 'Moray', on the south coast. Although she initially thought that the break had greatly benefited her (at a Book Society meeting fitted in on her way home, she had felt 'well & even witty', and that 'starting work again had been miraculous'), back in Clare, she soon relapsed into a state of frustration at the conflict between her writing and her domestic commitments. Nevertheless, within three weeks, she recognized that she was nearing fifty thousand words, and while she admitted this was 'preposterous', she continued: 'But I cannot stop. I must get this book driven through at the highest possible pressure.'

Even when returning to the Sussex coast in August for a fortnight's holiday with her two older children (Philip presumably having been left in the care of Nannie Page), she continued writing her novel in any time which seemed spare; on one occasion, this forced her to begin a chapter at 1 a.m., and she was 'dizzy with sleep' for the remainder of the day. A visit to the Edinburgh Festival with her fellow-Critics made a further inroad into her attempts to complete the book, but the intellectual stimulus of all the conversations with her companions made up for this. Returning to London on the overnight sleeper, the panel headed straight to the customary lunch before the recording took place, and the resultant programme, she said, was very lively, especially as, unusually, there was no use of preliminary scripts. She hoped that this would set a precedent for the future. A week later, she completed *The Last Resort* 'on a final great jag'.

In late October, Pamela and CPS left for almost a month in Italy, combining an initial short holiday in Venice with visits to English Electric contacts in various cities which she had not previously visited, and in which they both lectured for the British Council. Beforehand, she indulged in her ritual self-flagellation about leaving the now three-year-old Philip, as well as Lindsay and Amy, being torn between her longing to travel with CPS and her superstitious dread of what might happen in her absence. Venice, as ever, did not disappoint her, despite constant rain (duckboards out in the Piazza San Marco) and an increasing degree of Americanization. She found Turin to be a 'huge, heavy, uninteresting, grandiose city', but Bologna 'entrancing'. She was delighted with her reception at a packed lecture in Milan, and at the subsequent party, at which 'an enormous fuss' was made of them both, but particularly herself, although, as she self-deprecatingly put it, she thought that they were 'deluded into thinking me more important than I am'.

They were in Rome for four days, entering under a huge double rainbow, and immediately going for an 'exciting walk under fantastic sky, almost pitch-black with thundercloud [...]'. In the dark, they more or less stumbled by chance on Trajan's forum, although they didn't really know what they were seeing 'except that it was romantic & overpowering'. She was 'wildly excited by my walk! & by Rome!' They lectured again successfully to a crowded audience, then left for what she had hoped would be an idyllic short and work-free stay in Sorrento. But it was 'grey, wet and cold', and although staying at the five-star Albergo Vittoria in a magnificent room overlooking Vesuvius and the Bay of Naples, judged the only appeal of the town to be its 'situation of unique splendour'. Otherwise, she dismissed it as 'an Italian Brighton', with 'shops full of appalling rubbish', with the peace and quiet she had hoped for constantly disturbed by 'the constant rip & bang of those awful little Vespas'.

Back at home, Pamela was informed by Kay Dick that the Hampstead set were atwitter with speculation as to whether 'My Books are my Children', a short story she had recently written for inclusion in a collection called *Winter Tales*, was a reflection on her present marriage. The story begins with the emphatic statement, '"Mrs. Bell, [...] how proud you must be of your husband!"', said by an American student, one of a group of enthusiasts visiting George Bell, a novelist only very recently enjoying a cult following, despite, or because of, having only published two semi-autobiographical novels, with a thirteen-year gap between them. His wife Lois, herself a novelist, considerably more successful than her husband in terms of sales, reacts with 'the familiar, uncontrollable sting of irritation that George's addict should have called her by her married name', albeit with the knowledge that:

> the sting was a wretched one, a silly one, for was it not she who had insisted, at the beginning of their marriage, that she should be first of

all his wife and addressed as Miss Audley only upon her own professional occasions? She had done this out of love and respect. She knew
he was a better writer than she. All the same, despite her financial
success, she was by no means a bad one. [...] it was impossible that
even George's addicts should simply not have heard of her.[4]

The Bells' marriage is childless but happy, except that George does
regret his lack of universal acclaim. Like CPS's desire to make Pamela
a literary popsy, showered with his gifts, George lives for the time
when his sales will equal or overtake those of his wife, and then, he
promises Lois, '"we will ride in our carriage and eat pâté de foie gras
every night" (p.175). The visiting student has begged George to write
another novel in the autobiographical sequence he has begun, not
knowing of the existence of a chest in which 'the false starts lay, six
of them. Three, though false, were complete. Each of the other three
wanted from between ten to twenty thousand words more' (p.169).
When the acolytes leave, George and Lois resume 'the pattern of their
shared life', by working on one of his more promising drafts (p.174).
Lois has yet another success shortly afterward with her latest novel;
George meanwhile works away but refuses to believe Lois when she
tells him that his manuscript is now 'wonderful'. '"It will be all right"',
he says, '"when I've tinkered with it."' '"You mustn't tinker"', she
responds, '"Leave it as it is."'

> But she knew he would not leave it. Tinkering was, for him, the breath
> of literary life: it had been his undoing. He had spoiled all his ships, in
> the last seven years, by bestowing upon them far too many ha'pences
> of tar. (pp.178-79)

George is then diagnosed as having a weakened heart, but he continues tinkering with his book, eating and sleeping well, and making
love to Lois, although she has qualms in the latter respect: 'She was
afraid he might die in her arms – not calmly, peaceably, as she had
hoped to die in his, but in a sudden agony, making her not only his
widow but his murderer.'
But George in fact dies in a traffic accident, and Lois, to her
surprise, goes on living. George's literary reputation does not initially
suffer; Lois begins to realize that 'his death had made him something
like a great man, not now to a few addicts, but to several thousands
of them' (pp.182-83). She is pestered with requests for any unpublished

work, and types up his last manuscript, now 'free from the tinkerings', with the intention of offering 'this treasure' to those who loved him. But after another visit from the American student and an English undergraduate both still working on George's writing, and completely ignoring her attempts to introduce her own work into the conversation, she has a *volte-face*. She goes through the contents of the chest, other than the manuscripts:

> Methodically she read, tidied, preserved, destroyed. She destroyed three love-letters from somebody he had known before they were married. She destroyed a young photograph of herself that he had loved, but which she disliked because it made her look fat.

After going to sleep for two hours, she found herself worrying about whether the kitchen boiler might have gone out, goes downstairs, and without any apparent conscious thought, pushes all the drafts and the new typescript into the boiler. Far from feeling any guilt, from then on, she sensed George's 'presence steadily, his comradeship, his approval' (pp.186-87).

As time goes on, Lois begins to acquire addicts of her own, including a Miss Breitman, 'a bright, dumpy, rich little girl from Connecticut who was majoring in contemporary literature and proposed to write her thesis upon Lois's work'. Faced with Miss Breitman's sympathy for her now solitary state, Lois tells her that she has compensations. She comes near to voicing the words of the title of the story, but embarrassment at uttering 'a cliché so pretentious, so preposterous, that George would think she had gone mad' prevents her, and she continues by signifying her present situation by merely stroking the green and gold spines of the collected editions of her own novels (pp.187-89).

Pamela's indignation at the reaction to this story of those in London literary circles that she already saw as her enemies, hovering like vultures to detect flaws in the Snow marriage, seems, in the least, naïve. '[I] begin to wonder', she wrote, 'if any of them can imagine the idea of fiction at all', especially when she heard that 'idiotic' Olivia Manning was among those making wild conjectures as to CPS's feelings. Pamela clearly had not consciously meant the story to be self-revelatory, but for a while, it continued to add fuel to the flames of petty jealousies.

At the end of the year, CPS completed *Homecomings*, the novel from which Pamela had felt excluded, and gave it to her to read in its entirety. She realised that the reason behind his reluctance to discuss the novel as had been usual throughout the course of writing was that it covered the period in which Lewis Eliot remarries, and, the second wife, 'Margaret Davidson', was acknowledged by both of them to be at least partly a portrait of herself. Eliot and Margaret do not share a common profession, but the description of their early relationship, brought to an end by Eliot's reluctance to commit himself fully to her, certainly would have resonated with Pamela. Margaret tells Eliot that she is unable any longer to bear the situation:

> 'With those who don't want much of you, you're unselfish, I grant you that,' she was saying. 'With anyone who wants you altogether, you're cruel. Because one never knows when you're going to be secretive, when you're going to withdraw.'[5]

Margaret marries someone else, and they have a child, but five years later, she and Eliot resume their affair, and her husband agrees to a divorce. It is only in the last short chapter that the narrator admits to how marriage to Margaret and the birth of their son has brought to him 'a homecoming such as I had imagined when I was lonely, but as one happening to others, not to me' (p.320).

On finishing the first part, Pamela wrote that she had been reading 'a great book, agonisingly painful but enthralling'. She finished the novel within two days, and, with great relief, recorded that:

> All sense of being 'shut out', the anxieties of its inception, were swept away by its grandeur. I hope he gets his due <u>now</u>. I have no doubt – I never had any, since I first read <u>S. & B.</u>, not knowing him from Adam by the fire at Cotswold in 1940, that posterity will give it him. It is deep & true & heartrending: & for once – for him – joyful. [I] needed to be alone with C., & close to him, just to let him know how I feel about him as a husband – whom I could not love more profoundly – or as a writer – whom I could not honour more profoundly. I am proud to be Margaret or the part of her that is me.

CPS was 'happy to feel' that she not only thought his book was 'magnificent', but also that she was 'in no way hurt by it'; Pamela added somewhat wryly, 'I don't think he ever knows what I <u>am</u> hurt by!'

Snow's brother Philip's memoir, *Stranger and Brother*, was published the year after Pamela's death, so she was never to read an anecdote therein, which would indeed have bewildered and hurt her. According to this, CPS had been asked some years later by the evangelist Billy Graham for a gift of some value to be auctioned in aid of research on multiple sclerosis. CPS had declined on the basis that he had nothing suitable to offer, but had expressed his particular regret because: 'A very dear friend of mine was afflicted with the disease, and I have never been able to forget it.' Philip Snow identified this 'very dear friend' as being the original of Margaret Davidson, although he did not name her then, or in his Appendix naming 'Some Characters Identified in C.P. Snow's Novels'.[6] He did, however, unequivocally identify Margaret Davidson with Holly Southwell in a further book of memoirs, *A Time of Renewal* (1998).[7]

At the time of publication of *Homecomings*, Holly Southwell's health was beginning to fail, and the following year she was diagnosed as suffering from multiple sclerosis. CPS's continuing deep feeling for her is manifest in a letter sent by him in 1961 in response to a question from a German student as to the meaning of the overall title of the Lewis Eliot sequence. He explained that there are times when each person is alone, and thus a stranger to all around him, and times when 'we can and should feel for each other like brothers'. He continued:

> [...] the brothers side of the overall theme contains a completely
> definite hope. But some aspects of the individual life do not carry the
> same feeling. Have you ever seen anyone you love die of disseminated
> sclerosis? That is the strangers part of the thing.[8]

By this time, Holly had been hospitalized, and CPS was visiting her regularly there until her death in 1964; letters in his archive from a close friend of hers attest to the importance of these visits to Holly.

1956 began, however, with what Pamela perceived to be a period of exceptional closeness in her marriage (although Anne Seagrim had returned from France in the autumn of 1954, her relationship with CPS was not resumed until 1957).[9] However, an event of great sadness lay in wait for Pamela. She had got used to her mother's many reports of ailments, and put most of them down to 'Howson' hypochondria. Early one morning, a few days before the first Book Society meeting of that year, Amy complained of 'frightful pain between her shoulders'.

Pamela put her back in bed, and called their local doctor who said that there was 'nothing much wrong'. As the day progressed and Amy's pain increased, a second doctor examined her and came to the same conclusion as the first, but Amy became delirious and frequently sick. Pamela stayed up with her all night, attempting at the same time to take care of Philip because his nanny was temporarily away. After two more days of 'fright and pain', Amy seemed a little better. CPS returned from London since they were both supposed to attend an anniversary dinner at Christ's, but although he went to this, and the doctor said that there was no reason for Pamela not to go, she did not, feeling that Amy would have felt 'let down and miserable'. Nannie Page came back a day early from her break, and became a tower of strength. Nonetheless Pamela thought it would be better for Amy to go overnight to the nursing-home in which her sister Kalie was living and to stay there for the day she had to be in London; she promised to be back that evening. At 8.30 the next morning before leaving for the train, she phoned the nursing-home to be told that, after her mother seemingly having had a good night and having ordered break-fast, she had found dead when the tray was taken into her room. Pamela's account in *Important to Me*, written nearly twenty years later, revealed how painful the memory still was to her, yet how, in retro-spect, she realised what an influence Amy had been:

> I passed through a period of intense grief and guilt. I can write nothing about that. Amy. I had greatly loved her.
>
> Possessive, I suppose, she always was, though in my earlier years I was not aware of it. [...]
>
> But what fun she had been! How much I owed her! The songs she had sung in her small, pretty voice! The anecdotes, always enthralling, about her schooldays, her memories of Ellen Terry, her theatrical experiences! I now try to think of her only like that.
>
> (*Important*, pp.125-26)

Amy was buried in the graveyard at St. Mark's in Clapham; although Pamela took some comfort in leaving 'my dear in the neigh-bourhood that had mostly been her home', she continued to feel 'very low and desperate' for months, while attempting to fulfil her engage-ments. Another of her Proust reconstructions, 'A Window at Mont-jouvain', was broadcast, but, although this time she had thought that

Rayner Heppenstall's production was superb, the aftermath did nothing to lift her spirits. She wrote:

> Well, I am the mute inglorious Milton, & my name is writ on water.
> I can never hope for any creative work of mine to be so flawlessly
> matched by interpretation: & there is not a damned word in the press
> & nobody cares.

She gradually returned to enjoying her Critics sessions, and the battles at the Book Society, but had to resign from the latter due to a conflict of interests regarding whether *Homecomings* should be a Choice (which eventually it was not).

June brought at last an exchange of contracts for the sale of Nethergate House, heralding the family's return to London. They had visited a flat, owned by the brother of a friend, in Cromwell Road, South Kensington, which seemed ideal, except for the minor difficulty that the owners did not want to move out until the following February. Nevertheless, the Snows went ahead with the purchase despite having to make complicated arrangements for the interim period. World events were about to dominate Pamela's diary entries, although her first remark about the political scene in that momentous year was fairly flippant – 'Nasser has pinched Suez Canal' – and she seemed more concerned in rejoicing at Jim Laker's achievement in taking nine Australian wickets for 37 runs in the Old Trafford Test Match on the same day in July.[10] Subsequently, she became fearful at the prospect of an escalating war, and condemned Eden for his handling of the crisis.

Pamela had a welcome boost with regard to her literary standing when she was twice mentioned in a *Times Literary Supplement* special edition, 'Frontiers of Literature' (17 August 1956). In an essay entitled 'New Patterns of Society', she was included in a list of 'best novelists with substantial sales' in the company of Joyce Cary, Anthony Powell, L.P. Hartley and Ivy Compton-Burnett. Even more gratifyingly, the author of another essay, 'The Illusion of Involvement', quoted at length from *The Philistines* to illustrate 'the curiously direct force of realism, felt when a novelist is confident enough to speak *ex cathedra*', and concluded from that passage that Miss Hansford Johnson was shown to be 'an energetic, truthful and sympathetic writer'.[11] She had been 'really enthralled' by this, writing: 'I had not expected a line at all. Felt so gay I danced around the hall.'

The following month, the publication of *Homecomings* sent CPS into his usual 'abject misery'. Again, there were some good reviews, and indeed a second Middle in the *TLS*, although Pamela thought this 'idiotic & rather caddish in tone'. She attributed the critique to 'that bum Maclaren Ross'; fortunately, the anonymity still granted to *TLS* reviewers prevented her from discovering that the author had in fact been her radio producer, Rayner Heppenstall. The latter's mild criticism, however, was admixed with praise, as he wrote, by way of apology, that: 'One carps, it may be, because Mr. Snow has sometimes written so wonderfully and one is furious when he falls short of his best. [...] It is not too late to hope for a perfect recovery.' However, there was no anonymity granted to Daniel George, whose review in the *Spectator* was judged by Pamela to be 'a piece of rancour [...] that exceeds anything I could have expected [...]. I never saw such naked hatred. He really is a detestable man.' George did start by acknowledging that *Homecomings* deserved 'nearly all the praise it has elsewhere been awarded', but continued by suggesting that CPS should have a word in Lewis Eliot's ear:

> 'Eliot', he might say, 'this is going to hurt you more than it hurts me, but the fact is that readers are complaining that you are becoming just the teeniest bit of a bore [...] too fond of the opaque, curious, obfusc, subfusc. I must give you credit for bringing in some unfamiliar words: sadic, pantocrator, labile, snurge and so on: they keep the reader from dropping off.
> 'Just one other thing: I do wish that when you tell us about making love to your wife you wouldn't say you 'had her' or 'took her' – it makes you sound like a gangster and you were far from that, old chap. [...] But watch it: you can't expect new readers to guess, when you are being so pompous and omniscient and humourless and such an old busybody, what a splendid fellow you actually are.'

'Pots and kettles', the Snows might have thought, in view of the fact that this mockery came from the author of various pedantic compilations, such as *Alphabetical Order* (1949), described in the subtitle as being 'a gallimaufry composed [...] for the diversion and solace of the ruminant reader'.

No sooner, however, had CPS recovered from George's sneers than he heard that the review by Richard Mayne in the *New Statesman* amounted to another attack, and before the periodical went to press, he put pressure on Janet Adam Smith, then the Literary Editor, to delete at least 'one offensive sentence'. Pamela, as ever, suffered as much as her husband, feeling 'sick with anger' on his behalf. The subsequent glorious autumn day was ruined for them both by CPS's 'abject misery':

> (a) on account of that skulduggery on the *NS&N*, (b) because sales aren't so good. Now saying he will never get what he wants – never attain even the position of Cary – etc. It is pitiable to watch, & hard to hold him up. His temperament is such a difficult & delicate one, his kindness & sensibility so acute that I hate his enemies more than I could ever hate my own.

The following day, however, CPS managed to locate a copy of the *New Statesman* in nearby Sudbury and found that the review was 'not as bad as all that'. And indeed it was not; the episode is evidence of CPS's constant and sometimes ill-founded fretting and its effect on Pamela. Mayne gave the novel first place in his Fiction Review which was headlined: 'Major Read Ahead'. He explained that he had never previously read one of C.P. Snow's 'roman-fleuves', but that *Homecomings* could be read on its own, and be judged on its own terms. 'What terms are these?', he continued. 'The words, "solid, workmanlike, skilful", spring to mind, perhaps to mask a sharper word: "old-fashioned".' The latter adjective was the only slightly negative comment. Mayne continued by praising CPS's 'masterly' exposure of 'intrigues and power politics' in his Whitehall scenes, and ended by saying that the novel overall had 'obsessive readability', leading him to look forward 'with relish to devouring the rest of the saga'. Pamela's relief was only short-lived; their subsequent successful joint lecture tour in Scandinavia was almost wrecked by CPS's reaction to what she described as 'very silly savagery' in an unsigned review in *Time* magazine, which also reflected on her own long-term championship of CPS's work. The reviewer described the author of *Homecomings* as being 'a latter-day Galsworthy', and continued:

> Critics who for more than a decade have touted him as a new Stendhal are simply chasing the wrong literary genealogy. In the Snow-Galsworthy vision, the middle class can have no Stendhalian tragedies, only troubles. The scent of *Homecomings* is well-bred but unmistakable: it's Yardley Soap Opera.

There has been much evidence of CPS's sustained belief in himself, and his assumption that those against him were either merely ignorant or deliberately malignant, but the extract below from a letter written to Pamela just before the family move from Clare also demonstrates how far he attempted to influence her as to how she should regard herself and their literary partnership.

> There is just one thing which I think you ought to be clear about. Your position in literary circles is considerably higher than when you left London: partly through The Critics, Proust, etc., Book Society, partly through not being in contact with the literary world at too low a level for your real status. Owing to our origins and independence, we have never made the high literary world: we have, in fact, not made it to an extent unparalleled by any people of our serious reputation. This will be an advantage sometime: but it's very important that we should neither <u>be</u>, nor <u>seem to be</u>, in a literary outer world. I like seeing Kathleen Farrell for her own sake: I don't like seeing K[ay]: in any case you're committed to them for life. But this kind of literary sub-world is the worst possible for people of our present standing and future hopes. Apart from old friends, one ought to keep right out of that kind of literary society – and, in my view, as much out of all literary society as we reasonably can. I know you like it, and I don't: and I know you want some, and the pleasure is real, and we ought not to sacrifice pleasure too easily: but strategically I have no doubt I'm right. When we're much grander we can do anything we like.[12]

On 22 October 1956, there could be no doubt about where Pamela's 'real pleasure' currently lay. She headlined her diary entry for that day in large black capitals:

LEFT CLARE for good.

CHAPTER 14

'"And have You Ever Written, Lady Snow?"'

THERE NECESSARILY had to be an enforced hiatus before the Snows could move into their new London home. Pamela's son Andrew was continuing to be away at boarding-school, and her daughter Lindsay became a temporary boarder at her school in Clare for the remainder of the autumn term. Aunt Kalie had to be left behind in the Clare nursing home, where her niece feared that her morale was sinking. Pamela, with CPS, their son Philip and his nanny, went to their Hove refuge, the Dudley Hotel. Her euphoria at leaving Clare swiftly evaporated; she began to brood about the ageing process, and to have doubts about her literary ability:

> I have looked so much younger than my years for so long: & now I find it hard to confront the race of those years into my face. Pride in 'youthfulness' has contented me for a lack of beauty. Seven years ago, when I was wildly in love, I think I looked beautiful, more than ever in my life. Now (& I am still in love) I seem to be paying for that halt in time. It is ignoble. I think of Proust, & how he found the defeat of time in art. But, oh God, I think, why couldn't I have been a better artist?

Before long, however, anxiety about the critical world events of that autumn added to her personal worries. In late October, in the Middle East, Israel's invasion of Egypt, with the support of Great Britain and France, began two days before the publication of *The Last Resort*. Even when an overwhelming vote of censure was passed at the United Nations, Pamela still was under the illusion that the British Prime

Minister Anthony Eden had 'a rabbit to pull out of his hat', but almost immediately realised that 'the "rabbit" was the rapid victory that didn't come off'. Two days later, her left-wing sympathies left her shocked at the Soviet invasion to quell the Hungarian uprising, with 'a rush of cowardice as frightful as any I've known'. When the Suez crisis seemed resolved by a ceasefire, she remained 'in the most appalling state of fear', even though CPS felt she was exaggerating possible dangers ahead. She tried to put her own concerns into perspective, writing: 'As for my wretched book, it appears to have sunk without trace. I was proud of it. But one can hardly care.'

Pamela had originally intended to call this novel *The Well Beloved*, until Kathleen Farrell had reminded her that this was the title of one of Thomas Hardy's lesser-known novels. At CPS's suggestion, she changed the title to *The Last Resort*, a rather unfortunate punning title which would seem to relate to the setting rather than to the predicament of Celia Baird, her protagonist.[1] Although some of Pamela's earlier novels had featured characters (Claud Pickering, for instance) facing a moral dilemma, *The Last Resort* is the first of her novels to make that theme central. Celia cannot be classified as the heroine of the novel, because Pamela had moved on from the romantic world, for instance, of Catherine Carter, to the later phase of her writing, which, as Isabel Quigly perceptively analysed, while offering 'minutely exact observation, pinpointing exactly this or that class, time or age group', nevertheless 'within that class, time or age group, [deals] with people who are intensely individual, quite outside the run of fictional characters that can be labelled hero, heroine, young, old.'[2]

The narrator of the novel is Christine Jackson, Pamela's alter ego from *An Impossible Marriage*, now an established novelist, but there are no grounds for believing that Celia is not a purely fictional creation, although other characters may be amalgams of the Farrells' literary and artistic circles in Rottingdean, near Brighton and Hove. (Having read the novel pre-publication, Kay Dick sent Pamela a 'maddening wild, upsetting letter' insisting that Kathleen <u>was</u> Celia, which Pamela ridiculed.) A chance meeting in the 'Moray Hotel' leads to a renewal of the previous slight acquaintance of Christine and Celia, which now deepens into a close friendship. Celia's parents are permanent residents at the hotel; she divides her time between weekends with them and weekdays in London. Her father is gruff and opinionated; her mother is interfering, and professes to be protective of her only child while in fact attempting to safeguard herself from a lonely old age. Celia loses no time in making Christine her confidante with regard to the affair she has been conducting with the architect Eric Aveling, an old family friend whose wife, Lois, is incurably ill and in a local hospital. Celia is a complex character, a dutiful daughter, a moderately successful business woman, and a frequenter of cheap bars and dubious night-clubs.

Neither she nor Aveling have moral qualms about their relationship as long as Lois remains in ignorance about it. However, Lois reveals to her husband her knowledge of the affair just before her death; it will transpire that she can only have been informed by Celia's mother who will do anything to ensure that her daughter remains with her. Aveling is stricken with remorse and feels that the memory of Lois will always come between him and Celia, should they continue their relationship. He cannot bring himself to explain his coldness to Celia for many unhappy months; when he does, she too agrees that, while they will remain friends, they must never again be lovers. She explains to Christine: '"I can't live with guilt, and I have felt guilty enough to die."[3] There is an unexpected twist in the dénouement of the novel.

Some of the reviewers were unhappy with the form of the novel: Tom Hopkinson in the *Observer* felt it suffered from being narrated in the first person by a writer 'who takes great pains to dissociate herself from the unhappiness and muddle in which her characters are involved', while the *New Yorker* reviewer also criticized the narrative mode, but for an opposite reason, alleging the story to be 'dimmed by the constant presence of a nondescript, morbidly sympathetic narrator'. It might, however, be recognized that Pamela had found an excellent compromise between the story being told in the first person by Celia with inevitable melodrama, or by an omniscient narrator; Christine's views can, by this device, be separated from those of the author's. Her thoughts about Celia's selflessness after Aveling's confession are conveyed in a passage of the fine writing which characterizes this novel, and would almost certainly have resonated with many readers. Christine compares herself to Celia, and concludes that, while her friend is 'of the company of those who can make and keep resolutions which must change a whole life; a member of that most incomprehensible of companies in which are the martyrs and the saints', she herself is among those incapable of such resolve:

> For most of us can conceive the noble idea, suggest it to ourselves, even go so far as to begin to put it into practice: but the secret planner of the mind knots the invisible safeguards, weaves the safety-net beneath us. We are in no danger of falling too far. We do not quite speak the irrevocable word: we only suggest we are about to speak it. [...] The majority of us are expert recanters; we can do it with infinite grace and the minimum of blameworthiness when the time is ripe. (p.189)

Unlike Celia, Christine is aware that she would always optimistically await 'the galloping horse, the shout from the edge of the crowd, the white paper flashing like lightning in the air, the reprieve' (p.190).

The novel is also a document of its time in the way that Pamela portrays a subsidiary but important character, Eric Aveling's homosexual junior partner, Junius Evans. The Wolfenden Report was a year away, and the language she uses to describe the quixotic and meddling Junius is initially guarded. He lives in a 'very chichi' house at Black Rock (located on the eastern side of Brighton, traditionally a gay enclave). When Celia first mentions him to Christine, she tells her: '"I'm afraid he isn't to everyone's taste, but he can be fun"' (p.37). Pamela seems to have had no problems about gay women, being, despite CPS's admonitions, always loyal to, if somewhat exasperated from time to time with, the two Ks, but, in the privacy of her diary, she does make disparaging remarks about homosexual men, especially if their sexual orientation might impinge on her work. She had initially been suspicious about what she saw as flamboyant tendencies in John Ireland Wood when he was adapting the Helena trilogy for the stage, although she later came to the conclusion that he was 'not a bad old "queer"'. Adverse reviews from critics known within literary circles to be homosexual were not so easily forgiven. When the scripts for her Proust reconstructions were published in book form, Simon Raven (*Spectator*, 27 March 1958) dismissed her concept as being 'literary romancing of the utmost falsity'. He focused on her treatment of Marcel's overtly bisexual friend, Saint-Loup, declaring that: 'Saint-Loup is the child of the living, creative intelligence of Proust and Proust alone, and Miss Hansford Johnson's Saint-Loup is just a clever tricked-up zombie and as such plainly obscene.' Pamela dismissed

Raven as being a 'typical pansy with rabies'. There does therefore seem to be something autobiographical in her rendition of Christine's attitude to Junius. When he accuses her of being among those who '"don't really like people of my persuasion. All tolerance outside, all Pilgrim Fathers within"', she replies 'that he was trying to have it both ways': '"It was unreasonable for 'people of his persuasion' to expect women to admire them, at least until the latter were past the stage of hoping for physical joy"' (pp.261-62).

There is another fault in the novel which might have somewhat alienated Pamela's regular readers; unusually the reader may occasionally need to reach for a dictionary to check words like 'mithridated', 'monergism', 'camarillo', 'ichor', and 'steatopygous', despite the narrator being known to have had minimal formal education. To Pamela's annoyance, this tendency was also mentioned in Tom Hopkinson's review. Worse still in her eyes, possibly because there was some basis of truth, it seemed to be CPS whom he was targeting when, echoing Daniel George's review of *Homecomings*, Hopkinson attributed this 'cause for uneasiness' to 'a curious streak of common-room pedantry'. Whether or not, CPS had suggested these words in the course of their regular mutual consultations, it is noticeable that Pamela reverted to using words in everyday usage in the remainder of her novels.

Despite Pamela's despair at the first adverse reviews followed by the possibility of the novel being subsequently ignored by other publications, once the newspapers were no longer full of the political crises, *The Last Resort* received the usual amount of notice, with the majority of the remaining reviews being favourable. Michael Swan in the *Sunday Times* praised her departure from being 'a detached analyst of London suburban life' to a concern 'with the new interplay of classes produced in post-war England', and thereby making 'the tragedy of her central character, Celia, one peculiar to the social revolution of our time'. Norman Shrapnel, in the *Manchester Guardian*, applauded her ability to 'embroider everything she touches; but always with point (if sometimes petit-point) and a fine accuracy'. *The Last Resort* was also to be among her novels cited some years later by Walter Allen as examples of 'the pure novel [...] concentrating on human beings and their mutual reactions'. Bracketing it with her following novel, *The Humbler Creation*, Allen wrote that both rendered 'beautifully the complexities, the discontinuities, the contradictions of human behaviour and the necessary recognition of the frustrations attendant upon it'. 'They seem to me,' he added, 'to have the sad, honest, lucid acceptance of life we find in George Eliot [...].'[4]

In November, the Snows left the Dudley to stay in a boarding-house in South Kensington, a more convenient base for Pamela's radio commitments and for making the necessary arrangements for their move. Her diary entry for December 3rd is marked by several thick vertical lines in the margin: 'C. offered a knighthood. He isn't sure he will take it, because of his writing. We shall have a heavy week's thinking.' It only in fact took him two days to decide to accept the honour; he did ask for an undertaking that 'services to literature' would not appear in the citation. (The honours list, as posted in *The Times* on New Year's Day, 1957, would describe him merely as 'Commissioner & Scientific Adviser, Civil Service Commission'; whether there had been any intention to do otherwise is questionable.) CPS wrote to his brother Philip, prior to the official announcement, to say that he was pleased that he was only being rewarded for his official career, because:

> These things are of course nothing but a nuisance to a writer; it will do me a slight but perceptible amount of harm. However there are inducements on the other side. People who compare me with Trollope ought to realise that I've gone much further in the Public Service than he ever did.[5]

Their move into the ground floor flat at 199 Cromwell Road began three days later. CPS's contribution was to absent himself by taking Philip to the Zoo, while Pamela and Nannie Page coped with unco-operative moving men, who left behind them 'a ghastly mess', and most seriously in Pamela's eyes, resulting in their book collection being 'to hell'. So she spent the following two days putting everything in order before they finally left the boarding-house. Her son Andrew remembers how dark the mansion flat seemed to him after the house in Clare, but it was large and very suitable for the entertaining which the Snows envisaged. There were five bedrooms and several reception rooms, including a large open hallway used as a dining room, and a spacious sitting room, facing onto the main road – but also directly opposite a bus-stop. This became something of a problem when both Snows became familiar to the general public through their television appearances, and they would become aware of faces peering down on them from upper decks of buses. Among their new neighbours was the charismatic Moura Budberg, a Russian Baroness rumoured to have been a Soviet spy; CPS's acquaintance with her dated from the 1930s, when she had been one of H.G. Wells's many lovers.[6] She kept weekly open house for a wide range of guests, and she and the Snows frequently exchanged visits.

Another new influence entered their lives at this point. Pamela had to find a family doctor and was recommended to Dr. David Sofaer; her first reactions were not favourable; she thought him 'perky & rather horrid', although probably clever. Any time that young Philip was ill, both parents worried inordinately about him, and they found Sofaer initially to be 'a pretty intolerable man'. Gradually however they began to rely heavily on their new doctor, and this would have repercussions on the health of both.

Pamela and CPS's brother Philip accompanied CPS to Buckingham Palace for the Investiture Ceremony in February. The night before, Pamela reflected that everyone else in the family seemed to be in a state of excitement which neither she nor CPS fully shared:

> […] for C., the fuss is about something that is not the most important thing to <u>him</u> – & as for me, 'Mrs. C.P. Snow' was the proudest of titles. As 'Lady Snow', I might be any battleaxe in the provision department of Harrods.

She enjoyed the splendour of the Palace, but was less appreciative of what she described 'the tea shop music' which accompanied the proceedings. CPS was dubbed Sir Charles as the Household Band played 'The Surrey with the Fringe on Top' from *Oklahoma*; his brother commented that it would have been more fun if the bandleader had chosen 'When I Marry Mr Snow' from *Carousel*.[7]

The yearned-for move from rural isolation had not solved Pamela's worries about her literary standing. In diary entries a month apart, evidently without any awareness of the repetition, she commented: 'If I wrote <u>War & Peace</u> <u>now</u>, nobody would take the slightest notice.' On the second occasion, she continued:

> <u>The Last Resort</u> is, I know, a good book. It simply died, through Suez, & through the sheer lack of attention that I see no way of circumventing. I have been writing novels for about 23 years, some good, some

bad, some indifferent. That's the trouble. And now I write a really good one …. Well, I suppose I shall have to plod on. I am comforted by the knowledge that my dearest C. is being recognised by all those slow sunkets who couldn't see what he was in the first place. Still, I'd like a small degree of recognition myself – i.e., that I can, on occasion, write a novel of quality.

The following day, she voiced other problems. Despite CPS's financial stability compared to that of her first husband, she still felt her own earnings to be essential:

I am considering retiring from active writing, if only I can make enough to finish educating the children. I'd rather back out on a good book than a bad. I shall have to consider this really seriously. […] I am too worried to write – or to think: anyway, it is bloody hard being a woman, simply because one's life is so fragmented.

Shortly afterward, when Sidney Nolan brought them one of his Ned Kelly paintings to hang in their new flat on loan, she consoled herself with the thought that: 'I do claim to have discovered Charles & Dylan & set things going for Nolan. If I am to have nothing for myself, I at least have that. I should have set up as a cultural talent scout perhaps.'

An opportunity to gain further recognition for herself *had* recently come her way. The long-standing radio discussion programme, 'The Brains Trust', was now being televised, and she was invited to join the panel, initially for one episode. She found herself in 'a thunderous atmosphere', because, in an early example of potential dumbing down, the lightweight Canadian presenter, Bernard Braden, had taken over the chair, and Jacob Bronowski among others was threatening to resign. Nevertheless Pamela felt 'cockahoop' after the recording; she was told by the producer that her contribution had been a great success and that she would be asked to appear regularly. (Later in the year, CPS also occasionally joined the panel.) She was much less happy about her participation in:

a perfectly <u>dreadful</u> I.T.V. programme called "Crosstalk", chairmanned by that false man [Edgar] Lustgarten, with Ruby Miller (an old & abominably garrulous gaiety girl), Spike Milligan (quietly & sinisterly mad, hopelessly dissociated in fact, as well as his own brand of humour) & poor old Hugh Casson.

In June, the Snows were invited to Malta for another joint English Electric and British Council-sponsored visit. They dined soon after arrival at the Governor General's residence; she felt the evening had been 'exceedingly glamorous – lights in trees, beautiful garden – starry night – oh, a <u>long</u> way from Clapham Junction'. The following day she was seated next to the Prime Minister, Dom Mintoff, at a dinner party for members of the Government. She enjoyed the experience, finding him 'very much the type of Bonaparte (peppery – determined – impatient – roughly sardonic)', and was even more impressed by him when they were invited to lunch alone with the Mintoffs in their home. Pamela's lectures were successful, and she was generally delighted with all she saw in the island nation.

The late summer of 1957 saw a change in the previous Snow/Stewart family holiday arrangements. With their son Philip now being nearly five years old, both parents wanted to enjoy holidays abroad with him and the older children, rather than Pamela taking the children to British resorts without her husband. For the next few years, they chose to stay in a small village, Le Coq sur Mer, in Pamela's beloved Belgium. They took Nannie Page with them, and this arrangement facilitated side-trips, as when Pamela took CPS and her elder son to Bruges for the day. She was 'charmed', she wrote, 'to show C. the town that had meant so much to me since I was 15. The quays, the paintings, the paddock of Notre Dame, the Béguinage [...]'. The sixteen-year-old Andrew, tensely awaiting his GCE results, was generally appreciative, but, as mothers of teenage children might recognize, nevertheless shied away from Pamela 'like a frightened horse <u>in case I should give him information</u>'. Philip's enjoyment of the holiday was less equivocal; the fond mother recorded him saying: '"I adore <u>here</u>!" – and "I am the owner of the sea!"' A fictional Belgian coastal resort would be the setting for Pamela's novel, *The Holiday Friend* (1972), but she returned from this first holiday *en famille* with an idea for another book, already given the title, *The Humbler Creation*, and which would be published in 1959. She credited CPS for having suggested the theme of this novel; this is possibly the only occasion when the initial idea had not generated with her, but it helped her to overcome the despair about her writing that she had experienced earlier that year.

In addition to working hard on the new book throughout the autumn, Pamela also had a brief but welcome return to reviewing when she occasionally stood in for Walter Allen and Maurice Richardson, the regular reviewers of novels in the *New Statesman*. Her first column on 21 September displayed her powers of criticism at their best; she was prepared, where she felt it necessary, to praise and damn equally unequivocally, justifying her shrewd judgments in fluent prose. The first novel she discussed received her highest commendation: this was *Pnin* by Vladimir Nabokov. The author was then relatively little-known in England; although the writing of *Lolita* had predated *Pnin*, and had been published by the Olympia Press in France the previous year, outrage at the theme prevented its publication in the USA until 1958, after which the English publishers Weidenfeld and Nicolson followed suit in 1959. 'Nabokov', Pamela began, 'writes in the tradition of Chekhov, Svevo, William Gerhardi. [...] [He is] a highly "literary" writer, whose style though oddly eclectic is excellent for his purpose. [His] comic style is catching, and is flattering to the reader's detective sense – here is Kafka, here Proust, here [...] is Joyce.' But she particularly pointed to what she described as a 'sweetness' in the novel, without which 'this book would be not much more than a first-class Third Programme comic strip. As it is, a hero who is at one level absurd is simultaneously endowed with dignity and moral grace. This is a remarkable feat.' After moderately good reviews of Colin MacInnes' *City of Spades*, and Compton Mackenzie's *Rockets Galore*, however, she ended with a harsh critique of John O'Hara's novella-length, *A Family Party*. She began sorrowfully, explaining that O'Hara's first novel, *Appointment in Samarra* (1934), still seemed to her to have been 'a serious book', but concluded tartly:

> If you decide to write a book that shall be extremely short, simple and profound, you'd better be sure that it is profound: because being short and simple alone won't save it. There have been many short, simple and profound frauds in literary history. Mr. O'Hara's story is a commonplace piece of simple rah-rah bunkum by a very clever man who ought to know better.

O'Hara does not seem to have reacted to her condemnation, but Pamela was later in the year distressed at a 'ferocious' letter she received from an author she had considered one of her discoveries. She had, as mentioned, much admired Doris Lessing's first novel, and in reviewing her new collection of short stories, *The Habit of Loving*, she began: 'Mrs. Lessing [...] has never written better, nor shown so fully the range of her literary capabilities.' However, Pamela continued:

> I was worried about Doris Lessing's Martha Quest series, partly because the heroine was treated with so conscientious a heartlessness, so honourable a lack of self-indulgence that she gave the impression of being a repellent person; and partly because the discipline of an overtly political framework destroyed a great deal of the writer's intuitive flexibility.

Evidently, Doris Lessing was not placated by having been given pole position in the column, and not even by Pamela's sweeping final judgment: 'With these short stories [...] I am no longer in any doubt that Mrs. Lessing is one of the best writers in England, male or female.' It has to be said that Pamela's surprise at Lessing's reaction showed her as a reviewer to be seemingly oblivious of her own displeasure at critiques that sandwiched a modicum of censure within praise of *her* creative works, and perhaps even more so with regard to similar judgments of those of CPS.

Early in December, Pamela accompanied CPS to Exeter for a speaking engagement; she wrote that he lectured 'really admirably on "The Two Cultures"'. This is the first reference in her diaries to this title, which was of course to lead to considerable controversy a few years later. As the year ended, Pamela had a number of worries. She was again taking Benzedrine on a regular basis, although reassuring herself that the amount she used to spur her when she flagged seriously did not amount to 'a drug-taker's addiction'; her youngest child had been ill over Christmas, and she felt that she could not leave him behind to join CPS on a tour of the USA, nor, as was suggested, take Philip with them; all in all, she felt that her 'nervous exhaustion' was coming to a crisis. Yet she managed to finish *The Humbler Creation* in January of the following year, by which time she already had an idea for her next book, which, as a satire, would mark her entry into a different genre of writing: it would be based, she wrote, 'on a Corvo-like paranoiac'.

The Unspeakable Skipton would become one of her most successful novels, the composition of which brought her nothing but delight, which she shared with CPS, who, she said, read each completed chapter as a serial, roaring with laughter. She recorded a typical working day: 'Succeeded, between bouts of cooking, in writing about 3000 words of my comedy. I have never been on such a creative jag, nor so oblivious of the feelings of others in its execution.'

Pamela's dilemma about the American tour was resolved by a compromise. They would sail to New York together, leaving their son at home with his nanny, but she would return after a month, leaving CPS to stay in the USA to complete his commitments. Their first engagement was at Columbia University, where they both lectured; she rejoiced then in how well CPS was known there. But gradually, a sour note crept into her accounts of their reception. His American publishers, Scribners, gave a party for CPS, which was 'a tremendous success for him', but her publishers, then Harcourt Brace, did not do the same for her. For some reason, she switched to French to write: 'Je n'aime pas cette ville, mon dieu, je ne l'aime pas!' A typical entry recorded:

> what was, to me, a nightmarish party with the Harvey Breits[8]. She is a very rich girl, like a beautiful witch-doll, & they live in an almost repulsively luxurious apartment on Park Avenue. I was tired & very irritated. Most people v. drunk by time we left. Detested James Jones, a wretched writer [of, most famously, *From Here to Eternity*] & horrid man, with whom C. mysteriously insisted on becoming chummy.

Things nearly came to a head at a party given by the literary agent Edith Haggard:

> All useless except for meeting John Cheever (though he is v. awkward in conversation). [...] I was pretty enraged at outset of party by Edith's failure to explain to her guests that I wrote too. (After all, she is also my agent). I dislike – "And have you ever written, Lady Snow?" – petty beast that I am. But I was good, & did not hurl the Rockingham.

Even shopping, which at that time she normally enjoyed, did not reconcile her to the city. At the Captain's table on the Atlantic crossing, she had met the wife of a director of the luxury Bergdorf Goodman store on Fifth Avenue, who had insisted on taking her there for a visit. Pamela was all too aware that there was almost nothing that she could afford to buy, and felt intimidated by the clientele, wryly commenting that it had been 'hard to keep my genet from slipping off my shoulders & genuflecting to the mink'.

They travelled to other cities where the pattern remained the same. CPS was fêted, although principally as a scientist, rather than a novelist; her engagements were generally confined to lunch or dinner with 'absurd women's club groups'. 'A very dim day for me', she commented after one of these dinners. At a party after CPS's lecture at the University of Chicago, however, Pamela enjoyed talking to the novelist Saul Bellow, whom she described as 'a nervy ectomorph, but OK when he gets going', and at Cornell University, she met Vladimir Nabokov, whom she found 'v. good value – a sort of "inspired ass" in the Russian tradition, as C. says'. But these meetings did little to compensate her for the fears she endured on the internal flights, nor for some of the drives they had to take, which proved nightmarish because the East Coast was experiencing heavy snowfalls. It was with considerable relief therefore that Pamela embarked for the return journey on H.M.S. *Queen Elizabeth*, despite the prospect of being parted from CPS for more than a month. Her feelings about the subsidiary role she had been playing are manifest in this extract from a letter she sent from the ship to her brother-in-law Philip:

> Charles in on his way to becoming a Great Man in certain circles in US. He had made a tremendous impression, and is so good at it that I feel only a cross between Cleopatra and Boadicea could be a fit help-mate for him.[9]

Dick Cohen's father, the model for the patriarch of the March family, had recently died, allowing the novel which CPS had originally intended to be the second in the Lewis Eliot sequence to be published. Pamela had suggested the final title, *The Conscience of the Rich*, and CPS dedicated the book to her. It was published just after Pamela's return from America on her own, so she had the task of relaying information about the reviews to her ever-apprehensive husband. He would have been pleased to receive the news that the novel had received lengthy reviews in all the Sunday papers, but less happy if Pamela had expressed her views on them as she did in her diary:

> Long, thoughtful, uncomprehending one from {Cyril} Connolly, strange Jemmy Twitcher[10] act in *Observer* from {John} Davenport, J.H. Priestley throwing in sponge & predicting Nobel Prizes & OM. Feel this is a bit premature and something of a mistake.
> It is odd how C's work, especially his deliberate & peculiar style, precisely matched to subject, is misunderstood. Nobody has written sensibly since I had to stop doing it.

CPS did not seem to have taken Priestley's prediction lightly, but his paranoia about those he saw as enemies among English critics bubbled over in his letter to Pamela sent from Stamford University:

> I am feeling much better, occasionally a little strained by the thought of the sheer hatred that must be simmering about us in England. Of course, they know what we set out to do; and now we're somewhere near it, they don't love us any the more. I didn't think Connolly's review was inspired by hate, by the way, just puzzlement. But John D's was. And I expect like you to meet some in the Spectator and the Listener. I <u>think</u> my English enemies will just do me out of the Nobel – unless the Jewish sociological critics over here redress the balance.

Priestley was at that time reviewing for *Reynolds News*, a popular Sunday paper, probably unlikely to have been read by the Nobel selection committee. (The Nobel Prize in Literature that year was awarded to Boris Pasternak.) The *Spectator* reviewer was Frank Kermode, and his judgment was, as CPS predicted, luke-warm at best; he asked 'why this deeply serious undertaking, for all its magnanimity and justice, for all its humane and devoted craftsmanship, is so clearly hindered by some serious loss of power?' Both CPS and Pamela usually feared the *New Statesman* critics; there was an unpromising opening to the review of *The Conscience of the Rich* in that periodical by the scholar Helen Gardner (later to be the Merton Professor of English Literature at Oxford). She declared that 'C.P. Snow has no talent for rendering scenes, nor does he create strikingly alive characters', and that she had formerly written off the Lewis Eliot novels as being 'no more than intelligent entertainment'. However, she continued that she had now realised that she was judging his aims from the wrong standpoint, and her final judgment was that: 'The whole enterprise seems to me the most impressive attempt in our generation to explore through fiction the moral nature of man.' CPS commented to Pamela: 'I thought Helen Gardener [*sic*] had seen the major point of the game, which is important, but was (a) too unflattering to me as a novelist pure and simple, (b) too flattering to me as a moral seer.'

Pamela was now to have a scare of her own about a possible libel action concerning her depiction of a character in her next novel awaiting publication. Originally Macmillan had been so enthusiastic about *The Unspeakable Skipton* that they decided to publish it before *The*

Humbler Creation. The central character in this satire was indeed based on a real-life writer, who had, however, died in 1913 and therefore was unable to be litigious, much as it would have suited his confrontational and avaricious nature. In the note on the flyleaf of the novel, Pamela acknowledges that: 'Anyone familiar with the life of Frederick Rolfe will detect some of my sources [...].'[11] Rolfe, under his own name, or as 'Baron Corvo', a title which he might or might not have been entitled to use, became re-introduced to the literary generation of the 1930s through the publication of an idiosyncratic life of the author by A.J.A. Symons (coincidentally, the brother of Julian Symons, whose reviews of their books rarely pleased the Snows). In *The Quest for Corvo*, A.J.A. Symons explained how his interest in Rolfe/Corvo came about, and all the difficulties he had encountered in writing what he called 'An Experiment in Biography'. In the course of idle conversation with a friend, Christopher Millard, about 'books that miss their just reward of praise and influence', Symons was persuaded to read a book of which he had never previously heard, Rolfe's *Hadrian the Seventh*.[12] He was to find it:

> a feat of writing difficult to parallel; original, witty, obviously the work of a born man of letters, full of masterly phrases and scenes, almost flabbergasting in its revelation of a vivid and profoundly unusual personality. (p.4)

Symons demanded more information about Rolfe from Millard, who was in possession of some letters from the mysterious writer, written towards the end of his life when he was living a hand-to-mouth existence in virtual exile in Venice, and having to resort to offering his services as a guide to the 'perverse sexual indulgencies [available in] the dark byways of that Italian city' (p.12). Symons determined to write a 'Life of Frederick Rolfe', although, as his brother pointed out in a preface, the resultant book became 'an unusual example of the biographer's art, because its revelations of the compound nature of biography are conducted with such engaging frankness' (p.vii).

Pamela's satire moves the Corvo character in his declining years from Venice to Bruges, possibly because of her greater familiarity with that city. Symons describes his subject as passing through life 'in a state of opposition and exasperation, giving and taking offence without cause or scruple' (p.15). The reader meets Pamela's Daniel Skipton as he is composing a letter to his patient publisher who has had 'the impertinence' to offer him 'a small loan of money', which nonetheless he will accept since, 'if you think that I am going to starve for your benefit, so that you may pirate my work after my death, you are a sillier man even that your pug-dog's eyes and slopping lips would indicate'. (p.4) After posting the letter with some satisfaction, Skipton makes his way to the Grand Place where he proposes listening to a band concert on a free seat in one of the cafés, while spinning out his consumption all evening of a single coffee (not having sufficient money for the beer or wine he would have preferred). His fortunes seem to be on an upward turn when he is able to make the acquaintance of a party of English visitors, chief among them being a woman he thinks he recognizes. From the recesses of his memory, he triumphantly produces her identity:

> She was Dorothy Merlin, Australian-born playwright, whose verse-dramas had given her a vogue in esoteric circles in London and were inevitably produced in reading editions with long, admiring prefaces by herself. He had not read any [...] but he had gathered with repulsion that her plays were all about motherhood on some spiritual plane where the carnal and the mystical came clammily together.

On giving birth to her seventh child, Merlin had written her most famous poem, 'Should seven in the womb be made', as a prologue to her play, *Joyful Matrix*. Later in the novel, she insists on reading this poem, twice, in a British Council lecture she gives in Bruges; it ends to Skipton's intense embarrassment:

> In mirth
> the afterbirth,
> And in the prayer, and in the pregnant sheaf
> My groan,
> My grief.

To Pamela's surprise and considerable annoyance, her editors at Macmillan had come to the conclusion that this character was 'a wild libel on E. Sitwell'. They insisted on her making some changes – for example, Dorothy had not in the original version been Australian – but they were still not placated. They then sent her a copy of the *Collected Poems of Edith Sitwell*, which Pamela read 'with stupefaction'.

These contained, she wrote, 'only 3 references to maternity, & only a maniac could think <u>Should Seven</u> resembled them in the least.' With the matter still unresolved a month later, CPS wrote directly to Edith Sitwell, explaining the situation, and a few days later (on Pamela's birthday, as it happened), he received a 'most cordial phone call' from the poet, telling him that 'his letter had amused her more than anything for weeks'. Two days later, Pamela received the following letter from her:

> Dear Lady Snow,
> How much I laughed when I received Sir Charles's letter! I am, at the same time, alarmed, for I am, at the moment, finishing a book called 'The Queens and the Hive', which is about Queen Elizabeth I and Mary Queen of Scots, and contains a rousing account of Catherine de Medici planning the massacre of St. Bartholomew's Eve. I am now terrified that this may be supposed, by any readers I may have, to be a malicious portrait of you. After all, you are not Italian, do not persecute Protestants, and are not the mother-in-law of Mary Queen of Scots, so the likeness springs to the eyes!
>   What do you suppose I have done with my seven offspring? Eaten them?
>   Nonsense apart, it is an ill wind that blows nobody any good. I am a very great admirer both of you and of Sir Charles, and have longed, for ages, to know you both.
>   And now I shall![13]

Dame Edith soon followed this letter up with an invitation to both the Snows to join her and a group Pamela described as her 'court' for lunch, at the Sesame Club, or to give the establishment its full title, the Sesame Imperial and Pioneer Club, in Mayfair, which was Sitwell's permanent London base. Pamela described her hostess on that first occasion as 'a hilarious monster', but they were to become firm friends, especially when Sitwell discovered that they had both been close to the man she called 'our dear, ever-missed, tragic Dylan'.[14] They were also to find common ground in their opposition to the views of F.R. Leavis; Pamela had initially found some sympathy for Leavis when Sitwell recounted tales of her persecution of the critic, but it would not be long before she had her own reasons to agree with her new friend's judgment that 'Leavis is a tiresome whining pettifogging little pipsqueak'.[15]

Since her return to London, Pamela had been faced with attempting to follow CPS's advice to break with the set which, apart from the two Ks, included Olivia Manning and her husband Reggie, Francis King and the Snows' particular bête noire, Daniel George. Since CPS's acquisition of a title, bitchy gossip from 'Hampstead' frequently reached Pamela to the effect that the Snows were now considered by them to be social climbers. Nevertheless she had attempted to stay loyal at least to Kay and Kathleen, inviting them generally when CPS was (ostensibly) at his club. One of these occasions, however, was so painful to her that she twice described the evening as having been 'beastly':

> Kay very drunk, & with a quietly insulting undertone. Learned that Daniel had somehow got from MacM. the impression that my book was "obscene", & was broadcasting the fact. That supreme louse in the locks of literature[16] is an absolute curse to us all. [...] C. in <u>more</u> than popular — in fact, I had to put him to bed, & those women wouldn't go — Kay rowdy & silly, Kathleen tightlipped.

The following day, she wrote: 'What I'd give now to cut clean away from Hampstead! The crowd up there is hostile, even K & K are at heart, & I have been a damned fool to trust them so much.' Nevertheless she was never to break completely with either of the latter.

There *is* evidence in Pamela's diary during 1958, however, to fuel Hampstead sniping, and it has to be remembered that some of that set, in particular Daniel George, now the chairman of the Book Society panel, were in positions from which they could influence literary opinion. The Snows' circle of acquaintances had now widened to include eminent but non-literary figures; after a lunch at the Dorchester Hotel, for example, she described Nancy Astor as 'looking like pastel-painted steel', remarked that Clement Attlee was 'very, very small when he sits down', and that she had been seated next to Viscount de L'Isle, whom she had found 'vivacious, chatty, witty & a bit simple'. At an evening event, she had been introduced to the Queen Mother — 'a dainty little body. Very pleasant: white net crinoline with sprays of green fern, emeralds & diamonds. Has a superlative air of enjoyment.' And heaven knows what Daniel George would have made of Pamela's entry later that year: 'C and I to ATV "Bookman" party, where we were treated with quite preposterous deference, & followed about by photographers [...]'. She did, however, add: 'God alone knows why.' Soon after this, a new friend entered their lives:

C & I to lunch with Bill Astor at Cliveden – my first private visit to a great house, & very fascinating. 22 at lunch. Bob Laycock, that nasty Lennox-Boyd (it gave me a Thirtyish frisson of self-betrayal to be talking to the Friend of Franco at <u>Cliveden</u>, of all places), the Jellicoes, Lady Tennant, Duchess of Roxburgh (a nice, rather simple woman), George Weidenfeld, Freya Stark, etc. [...] But I liked Astor, who seems somehow desolate in all that grandeur.

The Unspeakable Skipton was published on 8 January 1959; the following day, in Pamela's words, became 'the great day of my writing life, the greatest for twenty-three years'. If it seemed to her curious that this significant boost to her literary standing had not been occasioned by a work about which she had felt more deeply, she nevertheless rejoiced in the 'superb' *TLS* 'Middle' which she knew to have been written by John Raymond, and the 'fine review' by Walter Allen in the *New Statesman*. The latter echoed the judgment of several later reviewers both in England and the USA, when he concluded:

The Unspeakable Skipton is a brilliant piece of sustained writing, which, as an original and successful comic work, challenges and compels us to revise our former notions of the nature and scope of Miss Hansford Johnson's talents.

John Raymond's lengthy retrospective of Pamela's work to date began:

Miss Hansford Johnson belongs to that group of writers – they are perhaps most to be envied – whose fame has climbed slowly on the wings of each new achievement. In the past ten years she has become well known to the reading public as a novelist of great craftsmanship and distinction and to readers of the weeklies as one of the best contemporary reviewers of novels in the language.

In the course of reviewing her previous non-fiction writings, he particularly praised her essay, 'On the Future of Prose-Drama' (which was, as mentioned, the preface to the published script of *Corinth House*), judging it to have been 'the best thing that has been written on the aesthetics of the modern theatre'. He discussed some of her previous novels very favourably, including *The Last Resort*, which

Pamela had felt had been unfairly ignored, and she would have been delighted to read his approval of that novel's 'superb characterization with its accompanying and unique gloss on the fruits of human action'. *The Unspeakable Skipton* was 'all the more of a surprise, since it is so unlike anything that she has written before'. However, he did then acknowledge similarities between *Skipton* and her other works: 'The same qualities are there, the same crisp, business-like style shot through with flashes of poetry, the same wit, the same pointed observation [...].'

Raymond then focused his attention on an episode in which, like Rolfe pandering to his clients in Venice, the ostensibly reluctant Skipton agrees to arrange a dubious 'spectacle' for Dorothy Merlin and her friends for, of course, remuneration both from them and from a kickback from Mimi, the impresario of a ludicrous enactment of the seduction of Leda by the Swan. The latter was played by 'a coke-washer' by day, who wore, for this performance, 'large wings made of wire and cotton wool, and nothing else except a corn-plaster' (*Skipton*, p.49). Raymond found this to be 'one of the funniest and most perfectly managed scenes of sexual comedy that has been written since Isherwood chronicled the escapades of Mr. Norris and his friends in the Thirties', but also pointed to 'how brilliantly yet soundly Miss Hansford Johnson has always handled the sexual side of the human comedy through its whole gamut'.[17]

Pamela's reaction to this deluge of praise is instructive; there is no reason to doubt the sincerity in the diary entries in which she feels that she can only be content with her own achievements with relation to those of CPS. She appears to have forgotten her many successes prior to his, as she recorded that the reception of *Skipton* had been 'what I dared not hope for, when I used to pray that I wouldn't let my dear Charles down by seeming hopelessly inferior to him. Inferior I am: but not hopelessly.' Lionised for her own sake 'as a new fashionable idol' at a party given by the publisher George Weidenfeld, she found all the 'Küss die hand' bewildering and 'rather disgusting', and she worried specifically that her success might be used 'to kick Charles'. 'If so', she continued, 'I would rather not have had any. Charles is Alpha +. I am, perhaps, at best Alpha − : but no more.'

Soon after this, Pamela became, yet again, embroiled in the intricate relationships of the Hampstead set. The two Ks were, it would seem, finally parting, and each took it in turn to attempt to involve her. She had previously believed that it had been Kay who was bisexual, while Kathleen had been her faithful lover throughout their relationship. The final straw between them had come when Kay had broken open a cache of Kathleen's letters, and found evidence that the latter had been conducting an affair with none other than the man frequently described by Pamela as 'execrable' – Daniel George. 'Now the cat is among the pigeons', Pamela commented. For a month, she was besieged with visits, letters, and phone calls from them both, finally telling them bluntly that she was putting a stop to 'all this Kay/Kathleen/Daniel bosh' since it was 'futile and time-wasting'.

While the Snows were now extending their own circle to high society, they still retained their left-wing sympathies. CPS's novels were selling well in the USSR, and they were frequently invited to the Russian Embassy. The cultural attaché then asked them if they would be willing to host gatherings of British writers to meet distinguished Russian authors visiting London. The first of these events, which would lead to several exchanges of visits, was in honour of Mikhail Aleksandrovich Sholokhov, the author of *Quiet Flows the Don*. Pamela recorded that, while she had found the author 'harsh & ungenerous, especially to his fellows', the party had been a great success with Jacob Malik, the Russian Ambassador, who had been 'in fine form'. Their own guests had included Isaiah Berlin, Anthony Powell, L.P. Hartley, Doris Lessing, John Lehmann and Walter Allen. Before Sholokhov left, the Snows attended a luncheon party for him at the Embassy, where they met Paul Robeson – 'a nice man but not clever' – in Pamela's view.

At the beginning of May, a sketch of the Snows occupied the main part of the cover of the *Times Literary Supplement*, the first in a series entitled *Writers of Our Time*.[18] Pamela was very pleased with this recognition of their status, and was probably somewhat put out by a letter of commiseration from her now regular correspondent, Edith Sitwell, and wondering what gossip might have reached her. Sitwell wrote:

> I can imagine the condolences you must both have received on figuring in that painfully prominent position in the T.L.S. You must both have repined on the utterly indelicate publicity! Are not people incredibly envious and spiteful? When, some years ago, the Sunday Times published a very kind People, or whatever they call it, of me, John

Hayward said to me that "the whole of London is saying <u>Osbert</u> must have written it, because no-one else would"!!! Yet I had never been anything but nice to J.H.[19]

On 7 May, CPS delivered the prestigious Rede Lecture at the Senate House in Cambridge. Pamela had been delighted when he had received the invitation to give this lecture, snorting partisanly to her diary that it was 'the first time that ungrateful University has done a thing for him'. His title was 'The Two Cultures and the Scientific Revolution', a topic which, as mentioned, had passed without disputation when CPS had previously lectured on it, both in England and in the United States. There was also little suggestion of a future contretemps in the lengthy report in *The Times* the following day. The headline of the respectful article, the lead story on the Home Page, focused on the second part of his argument; it read:

West Must Give Money, Men and Good Will
Sir Charles Snow on Way to Avert Three Menaces Facing Mankind.

The problem which CPS defined was that the industrialized countries were getting richer, while those in non-industrialized countries were at best standing still. The three menaces mentioned in the headline were 'H-bomb war, over-population, the gap between the rich and the poor'.[20] The latter, he maintained, could be addressed, but: 'If we are short-sighted, inept, incapable either of good-will or enlightened self-interest, then [the gap] may be removed to the accompaniment of war and starvation: but removed it will be' (pp.43-44). Standing in the way was the paucity of sufficient 'trained scientists and engineers adaptable enough to devote themselves to a foreign country's industrialization for at least ten years out of their lives' (pp.44-45). It is therefore obligatory, he ended, 'for us and the Americans and the whole West to look at our education with fresh eyes' (p.48). The *Times* report only briefly touched upon the starting point of his lecture, his belief that this state of affairs had arisen because:

the intellectual life of the whole of western society was increasingly being split into two polar groups – literary intellectuals at one pole, at the other, scientists – with between the two a gulf of mutual incomprehension.

There was comparatively little adverse reaction when his lecture was published shortly afterwards in *Encounter*. As Stefan Collini commented in the introduction to a 1993 edition of the lecture, now simply known as 'The Two Cultures', contributors to a small symposium of immediate responses in that periodical were 'overwhelmingly favourable', with CPS being 'praised for his "brilliant delineation of the divide between the cultures"'.[21] For the time being, the occasion seemed a great success. Shortly afterward, Pamela had a further boost to her own career. *The Humbler Creation* was chosen to be the Book Society Choice on publication in September. 'My very first', she crowed, 'and to hell with Daniel George'. (Soon afterward, another member of the Book Society committee told CPS that George had twice 'bitched' Pamela's book, but he had finally been outvoted.)

The Snows' flirtations with the aristocracy continued with an extended stay at Cliveden. On this occasion, Pamela forsook all her left-wing qualms, and relished in recording the highlights:

> I have never seen quite such fantastic luxury (indeed, why should I?) – lily-surrounded swimming bath heated to 80? – I <u>swam</u>! – & entrancing park. Party rather too large for my real taste – that is, about ten extra people get added for lunch & dinner. Staying in the house, Mrs Vincent [Brooke] Astor (charming little cat's face, & a very nice kind woman) with an emerald like a field in heaven; Mary Roxburgh who is a dear, Lord Banbury, who is fat, sad & diffident, Joan Aly Khan ('the mother of God', as Bill Astor said), Jimmie Smith (of W.H. Smith) & Nancy Astor – who is a diabolic old lady, & must have been more diabolic in earlier years. I now believe every <u>word</u> about the 'Cliveden Set'! Nancy tried to bully Charles playfully after dinner & got the worst of it.

The occasion was Nancy Astor's 80th birthday, and they witnessed a ceremony at which commemorative kitchen garden gates were unveiled; this was followed by the formidable doyenne giving, in Pamela's opinion, 'a really <u>atrocious</u> speech to the tenantry!' The only cloud on Pamela's horizon during this stay was experiencing one of her 'ferocious' migraines; she mentioned that 'a pet osteopath called Shaw*, who came to lunch, massaged it & gave it a jerk', but continued that this had done '<u>no</u> good'. (The asterisk by his name marked an amendment dated 22/9/64: 'No, Stephen Ward!'). Some three weeks later, she recorded that her neck was still stiff, and wondered if 'that wretched man at Cliveden had anything to do with it'.

On 27 August 1959, Pamela recorded being 'pretty astonished to find a biting attack on us' in the *Times*. This was to be the first of several wounding spoofs regarding the Snows' public profile and their literary aims. Pamela had no doubt that they were being targeted as 'Sir James' and 'Olivia' in a supposed discussion in the book pages by 'George Cloyne', whom Pamela knew to be Alan Pryce-Jones, the editor of the *Times Literary Supplement* from 1948 to that year. The starting point for this, the fictitious interviewer 'Henry' says, had been an article in an undergraduate paper, *Cambridge Opinion*, criticizing 'social awareness' as being 'the obsession of writers of England over the last ten years', and continuing with 'something about the importance of people rather than society'. 'Olivia' addresses her husband:

> Surely they can't be disloyal to *us*. I remember lecturing in Cambridge on your books the same term you lectured on mine. We both made it perfectly clear that if anything had happened in English literature during the last ten years it was ourselves. [...]
>
> I greatly admire James's books very much. Otherwise I should not have married him. We married because we were both socially aware [...]

'Sir James' responds: 'And genuinely think that society is more interesting than the individual.' He continues:

> I think I can say that we have a unique position. I am asked to recommend a lecturer for Paraguay, and I immediately think of Olivia. She is asked to help choose the Crump Lecturer for 1960, and she at once thinks of me. That is what I call society: congenial people pulling together and rejecting insecure elements.

Olivia explains further: 'You see, James and I think the aim of writing is to gain power. Oh, for the good of others, of course. Readers have to be protected from themselves.' Pamela did admit that while generally the article was 'absurdly unfair', she did laugh at some of it, probably acknowledging some truth in the picture Olivia presents of their activities:

> The writer's task today is to keep society up to the mark. We throw off a play here, a pamphlet there, we join every committee, we plug a

hole with a novel, we stop a breach with a course of lectures, we shore up a ruin on the radio and whack our enemies over the head by volleying back at them on television. James, so to speak, stands up to the net; I, as a woman, do better on the back line. That's modern literature.

There was no acknowledgment in the article of the Snows' frequent support for aspiring writers, an outstanding example of which had been Pamela's response two years earlier to a letter received from a fourteen year old Scarborough schoolgirl asking for advice. Pamela began: 'I read your letter with great interest and attention. I can't see any reason why you should not become a writer. You write easily and you love doing it; these things are important and basic. [...] When you are ready, write a book.'[22] She followed this with detailed recommendations as to preliminary reading, and wished 'Miss Hill' well.

Susan Hill had now felt ready, and had sent her mentor her first novel. Pamela quickly read the book of the girl she was now calling her 'protégée', and immediately replied: 'There is no doubt in my mind that you are going to be a novelist. [...] For a girl of your age (what, now, precisely?) to handle a theme like this is very daring, and it is done with great skill.'[23] Two days later, she followed this up with three typewritten quarto pages of analysis, ending: 'I will do what I can for you with it, that is, if you want me to and would like me to try. Hutchinsons New Authors Series is the thing for you, at this stage.' Pamela also introduced her to her own agent, and eventually Hutchinsons did indeed publish the novel, *The Enclosure*, in 1961, but on their main list, not in their New Authors Series. Soon after the 'George Cloyne' affair, Susan had written to thank Pamela for all her advice and support, saying that she intended to dedicate her first novel to her. Pamela's reply encompasses an analysis of the forces she believed to be currently against her:

> I am most grateful and touched by your offer of a dedication. But I am going to accept it, if I may, for your SECOND PUBLISHED NOVEL. This is not because I have doubts of the one I've read [...]. Firstly, it would preclude me reviewing it, if my chance arises, or doing anything to help you when you most need it. Secondly, a young writer doesn't want to acknowledge sponsorship of any kind. You have no idea how easily reviewers are prejudiced. If your book fell into the hands of someone who disliked <u>me</u> (there are some), he would be a Robespierre

of incorruptibility not to let some reflection of that fall upon your work. And at lowest, some asses might think that I had something to do with it.[24]

After several visits to the Snows' home, being around the same age as the Stewart children, Susan became a family friend.

In September, *The Humbler Creation* was published; it is the story of Maurice Fisher, a vicar of an unfashionable West London church. Maurice is trapped in an increasingly unhappy marriage, and faces a religious and moral dilemma when he falls deeply in love with a former acquaintance, Alice Imber. Alice, now widowed, has returned to the neighbourhood where she once lived to care for her ailing father; she admits to being a non-believer, but agrees to help with various church-related duties. It is possible to see a benign influence from CPS in the background of brilliantly-realised episodes of parochial politics akin to his accounts of the politics of university colleges, the civil service and Parliament. J.D. Scott, one of the contemporary reviewers of Pamela's novel, mused in his *Sunday Times* column about the neglect of clergymen as central characters in fiction since the turn of the century, when in his opinion, 'a clergyman today makes as interesting a hero as he did a hundred years ago'. He then continued: 'Miss Pamela Hansford Johnson has understood all this, and in *The Humbler Creation*, like someone discovering uranium in an abandoned coal mine, she has made masterly use of what others have passed by.'

The novel is particularly rich in the characterizations of those who surround Maurice Fisher, recalling Pamela's multi-populated earlier novels. The members of the Church Council, who will sit in judgment on the vicar as the plot unfolds, are introduced at a meeting early on. The Treasurer, in the Chair, is described as:

> Broad-shouldered, short-necked, his skin lined and muddied by almost forgotten suns, [...] his ginger moustache squeezed into a short upper lip, Kitson looked like a retired Colonial administrator: which he was.

Johnson-Black, 'sinking lower and lower in his chair' as the meeting progresses, is the Vicar's Warden, and that title defines him: he is, as Maurice recognizes, 'my man'. The considerably younger Jeremy Fawcett, the People's Warden, on the other hand, is 'a highly-active

churchman of impenetrable conceit' (p.26), who constantly badgers
Maurice. Also present is Plymmer, the organist whose recent innova-
tions have not found general favour. The Council is, apparently as
before, divided in this respect, Hannaway, the Secretary, insisting that
the music is 'tremendously stimulating', others dissenting. The Chairman sums up that item for the Minutes 'with his odd, dry humour':
'"Question of organist raised and not dealt with as usual. Excellent.
I move we pass on to the next business"' (p.30).

Another matter on the Agenda of that meeting establishes Maurice's
conventionality at the beginning of the book: a homosexual couple,
Peter and Lou, who are enthusiastic members of his congregation, have
volunteered to fill between them a vacancy for a sidesman. As the
narrator admits, Maurice is uncharitable in this respect, saying:
'"Neither Peter nor Lou is going to prance round with the plate in
any church of mine.' The majority of the Council agree with him, if
less openly. It is left to the organist, putting on 'his heaviest North
Country accent', to growl: '"I don't know why we can't all say what
we mean. If those two cissies want to come to God in some demon-
strative and official manner, who are we to stop them?"' Maurice
mildly responds: '"You're jarring us, Plym. Don't do it"' (pp.27-28).
He has, at this stage, no notion that his own possible transgression
from the rules he has so long accepted is near at hand.

In an excellent discussion, Ishrat Lindblad links *The Humbler
Creation* with *The Last Resort* in her chapter entitled 'Love and Renun-
ciation'. She points to their both dealing with 'one of the central
conflicts in the "great tradition" of the English novel – the conflict
between love and duty,' while treating an '"old-fashioned" theme in
a modern context'. 'Her protagonists', she continues, 'know that their
society claims to have jettisoned the moral values that continue to
govern their own conduct.'[25] The title of the novel is taken from a
hymn, based on Psalm 104, 'O Worship the King all glorious above!',
which also contains the lines:

> Frail children of dust, and feeble as frail,
> In thee do we trust, nor find thee to fail.

Edith Sitwell wrote immediately after publication to Pamela, congratulating her on her choice of title, and praising this novel in the
most extravagant terms:

Thank you. <u>Thank you</u>. If this is not a great book, then I don't know
what greatness is. What anguish! [...] And what flawless and impeccable shape and wording. I am not given to being a cry-baby, but the
end really did break me down. There has been nothing like the anguish
in the English novel since Wuthering Heights [...]

I am convinced that you and Emily Bronte are the two great woman
novelists. As a rule I dislike the sexes being segregated in literary matters – just as I fall into a frenzy if I am called a poetess. But with women
novelists there is a peculiar insight and sensibility (added to passion)
which differentiates them from the male insight and sensibility and
passion. [...]

I really don't know how you <u>can</u> know so much about human nature![26]

The contemporary critics were more measured in their judgment, but
the reviews were generally favourable; it was fortunate that Daniel
George was not among the reviewers, as he might have delighted in
chastising Pamela, as he had CPS with regard to *Homecomings*, for
referring to the act of love as the man 'taking the woman' in this novel
(pp.33 & 116).

While being reasonably satisfied with the reviews, Pamela was
nevertheless somewhat baffled that the novel seemed not likely to
be, as she put it, 'a Skip success'. However, as proof of her current
standing, in the cases where *The Humbler Creation* was reviewed with
others, it almost always took first place, with writers of the calibre of
Jack Kerouac and Alan Sillitoe second. An exception was the review
by Graham Hough in *The Listener*; he chose to discuss Ivy Compton-
Burnett's latest novel, *A Heritage and its History*, before Pamela's, but in
this instance, this could not be construed as a demotion. The relationship between the two writers had never mellowed into friendship, and
this review would doubtless have galled Compton-Burnett. Hough
ended his less than admiring discussion of the latter's novel with:

So there we are; the addicts will have one more item to feed their
passion; the allergic will know what to avoid; and newcomers to Miss
Compton-Burnett's world could as well begin here as anywhere, for it
is all of a piece.'

Hough then praised Pamela's 'distinguished' novel as being 'as good
an example as we could find of the opposite way of going to work',
with her characters 'giving a compelling sense of being a part of the

great continuum of contemporary London life'. Continuing the direct comparison, he wrote:

> I cannot help feeling that this, the central traditional methods of the novel, is a more exacting way of working than Miss Compton-Burnett's. She has only to be consistent with her own spare and highly stylized conception; Miss Hansford Johnson has to be consistent with all the multiplicity of our daily experience [...]. In this she never strikes a false note; indeed a resolute refusal to stray from actuality into novel-land is the mark of her writing.

After a thorough discussion of the plot, Hough ended:

> There are no heroics and no romanticisms; we are held firmly to the terms on which life is actually lived. The impression of reality so thoroughly overcomes the awareness of fiction that we are almost in danger of overlooking how finely the book is written – and how finely felt.

When the book was published in America early the following year, it received similar praise. Notably, a lengthy review by Gerald Sykes in the *New York Times Book Review* compared Pamela's writing favourably with that of Virginia Woolf. While acknowledging that Miss Johnson did not possess 'anything like Mrs. Woolf's verbal magic [...] although she writes with masterly precision', he continued that 'she goes deeper [than Woolf], knows her people better and faces up more squarely to their problems'. Sykes saw the book as 'a symbolic portrait of Britain today', and 'a kind of "Pilgrim's Progress" for our times, except that this pilgrim makes no progress, but simply tries to carry on'. He concluded:

> The novel is not grandly conceived; it is content to make its tough, neo-Puritan point, to tell its single story and be done. But it makes that story indirectly so pertinent, and tells it with such an effortless flow of flawless detail, that unless I am mistaken it is going to enter the small pantheon of the significant books of our day.

The Humbler Creation has proved to be, however, yet another example of a neglected novel by Pamela that should still be in the canon of twentieth-century literature.

The Snow family holiday in Belgium in August that year had been spoilt by bad weather and illness, and on her return, Pamela wrote: 'I don't know when (since America) I have been so hopelessly tired. [...] Absurdly rundown, after what is called a "Holiday".' She was continuing to suffer from a number of ailments, among them, persistent attacks of migraine and conjunctivitis Only two months after that summer holiday, however, she was committed to accompanying CPS again to the USA for a lecture tour, and wailed to her diary: 'I feel sick with worry. How can I go? How can I be sure? This is really tearing me to bits, after a year of awful work & no leisure.' She then used a description that often appears in her diaries when under stress: 'Hat far too tight.'

Their schedule on this trip was, however, not as taxing as the previous one. After a few days in New York, with Pamela now beginning to feel more at home in that city, they spent a week as guest lecturers at Haverford College, outside Philadelphia. They lunched with Ralph Sargent, the Professor of English, on arrival. Pamela found him and his wife 'very high thinking & pretty plain living'. The college had been founded in 1833 'to ensure an education grounded in Quaker values for young Quaker men'; at the time of the Snows' visit, it was still an all-male institution, although it did have a close connection with the nearby women's college, Bryn Mawr. The main problem for the Snows was that those values meant that most gatherings were alcohol-free, and the food relatively sparse. Pamela felt that a joint lecture they gave at the college had been very successful, but yet again, thereafter, CPS was the more lionised. She enjoyed a big party following his lecture to a large gathering in Philadelphia, 'apart from being introduced (a) as Sir Charles and Mrs. Snow, and (b) as Miss Pamela Jones'. She also ruefully recorded that her solo lecture on Proust at Haverford had 'an audience of 2 French dons here (one who hadn't read Proust), 1 from Bryn Mawr (who had), & about eleven students (who hadn't, & whose eyes slowly closed)'.

Back in New York, they had no lecturing commitments, and now, in addition to seeing literary and scientific friends, they renewed their acquaintance with the recently widowed Brooke Astor, who, as a blessed relief for the Snows after the Spartan regime in Pennsylvania, entertained them lavishly at the St. Regis Hotel, and escorted them on a tour of Hyde Park on the Hudson. Pamela very much enjoyed this, despite finding Franklin D. Roosevelt's home to be 'the nadir of the Awful Unpretentious', and the Vanderbilt Mansion, 'the zenith of

ostentation'. On a visit to the United Nations, they were both introduced to the then Secretary-General, Dag Hammarsjøld, whom
Pamela pithily summed up as 'a blue-eyed bore of the first order',
while nevertheless adding: 'Thank God for such bores. He should be
sent to every field of battle to talk them into a better frame of mind.'

Soon after their return home, Pamela was informed of the death
of her aunt Kalie, whom she had continued to visit regularly at the
nursing home in Clare since moving back to London. Her mother's
once lively and beautiful elder sister had been declining in health and
spirits for many years, but Pamela was still very distressed. She went
to Clare the following day to adorn Kalie with a necklace which had
been a present to her from her brother Hosmer. Pamela said sorrowfully that her aunt had looked 'so yellow and so <u>small</u>', and she
reflected: 'It is a lie that people look beautiful in death. We are
terrible when the spirit has left us.' Kalie was buried in the Clapham
cemetery close to Amy.

CHAPTER 15

East and West

A T THE END OF 1959, CPS had resigned from the Civil Service Commission, and had come to an arrangement with English Electric whereby he could take extended leaves. Much of 1960 for the Snows, therefore, was taken up by two visits, the first a cultural exchange arranged by the Soviet Embassy, the second an even longer than usual stay in America encompassing an invitation to CPS to become the Regent's Professor of English at the University of California at Berkeley for three months. Both visits would lead to controversy, and provide fuel for their increasing number of detractors.

In the first few months of the year, they had many social and literary engagements in London, and Pamela's diary entries continue to include pithy comments about their acquaintances. She portrayed 'detestable Bernard Levin' as being 'quiet, like a snake, & you might think him modest if you hadn't seen him sting'. The American novelist Nelson Algren, invited for a drink before dinner, prolonged his visit so that she was forced to ask him if he would eat with them (although this meant that she had to ask her daughter to sacrifice her own meal). She couldn't fathom out why Algren had come, and found him 'markedly schizoid'. 'If I found myself in an American city where he was', she wrote, 'I would take wings to another one.' They had several meetings with Stephen Spender in connection with their forthcoming visit to Moscow, as he had just returned from a similar stay. 'Spender', she wrote after she and CPS dined with him, 'in his cunning pseudo-masochist way, manages to shred reputations away quite a bit during the course of an evening.'

Proof that her own judgment could be affected by partisanship is offered by her reaction to criticism of CPS in 'an idiotic essay in

Twentieth C. by a pinhead'. The writer, so castigated, was Bernard Bergonzi, then a young academic, but later to be acclaimed as a literary scholar and critic. The article, which was twelve pages long, took as its starting point the pamphlet on CPS published the previous year in the British Council 'Writers and their Work' series. The ostensible author of this appraisal was scarcely impartial; it was Harry Hoff, writing as usual as 'William Cooper', but Pamela had also been involved. In her 1958 diary, she had mentioned a falling-out between herself and Harry, who had told her off 'with incredible rancour for rewriting some of his pamphlet'. She was bewildered 'as he had asked me to do anything I thought fit'. Whether or not this fracas had reached the ears of 'Hampstead' and subsequently Bergonzi cannot be ascertained, but the latter certainly seems to be hinting at a close connection between writer and subject when he wrote that Cooper was 'rather more concerned with Snow's intentions, on which he writes *with some authority* [my italics], than with his actual achievement'. Bergonzi conceded that the *Strangers and Brothers* sequence appealed to contemporary readers for 'the extent and variety of its social observation', and would probably prove of interest to future social historians, but continued with a crushing judgment about Snow's prose, 'at worst so arid as to be almost unreadable [...] and at best efficacious but banal'.[1] After a further ten pages of somewhat less scathing criticism devoted to the individual novels, he returned to the British Council pamphlet to refute 'Mr Cooper's confident prediction' that the sequence 'must inevitably be regarded as a key-work of the decades in which it was written'.[2] At a party in Manchester shortly afterward, Pamela met Bergonzi, and memorably described him to her diary as 'the Cliff Richard of the Redbrick World'. She might have decided to dismiss Bergonzi as an unimportant lightweight, but *Twentieth Century* was an influential monthly periodical, and attacks on CPS like this lengthy article were becoming more frequent.

CPS had, however, been notified in February that his latest 'Lewis Eliot' novel, *The Affair*, would be the Book Society's main choice for April. Nevertheless, immediately before publication, she recorded CPS being in his usual 'dreadful pre-publication state [...]. Fears the knives are all out for him this time. May be.' Nevertheless, she continued: 'We shall survive.' The early reviews after publication were in fact reasonably good, only for them both to be downcast with regard to 'an absolutely abominable notice in TLS, spiteful, full of personal animus: more than probably from that embittered little swine, Rayner'. The author was indeed Rayner Heppenstall; he assumed that the novel's title was intended to draw a comparison with the Dreyfus affair, and pointed out that the fate of the central character, a brilliant scientist, Donald Howard, who is being reduced to having to teach 'at a grammar school in Cambridge [...] hardly seems an equivalent to Devil's Island'. Considering that Pamela and Heppenstall had collaborated on her Proust reconstructions, she would have been particularly incensed by his further mockery, which she took to be also aimed at her, that the novel was clearly influenced by Proust, leading to the inclusion in CPS's lexicon of 'a new sprinkling of French words [...], some not in Larousse'.

Then, after what Pamela described as 'tolerable notices in the weekend papers', she again despaired after reading 'the most virulent attack' in the *Guardian*. W.L. Webb declared that: 'The trade-marks which show Snow's achievement to be a high-grade synthetic substitute for art are less prominently displayed than they have been in the past [...] but one does not have to look far for them.' It was evidently of little comfort to them that the review ended: 'If Snow could wipe the steam of nostalgia from his spectacles [...] and apply his genuine powers of psychological insight and strong narrative skill to the donnish scene as it actually is today, the next instalment [...] might be a really valuable bit of chronicling.' The American reviews were, however, favourable in general, and as further proof of CPS's standing as a novelist in the USA, the University of Texas had just bought his manuscripts for the then considerable sum of £4,000. The Snows were therefore looking forward to their next visit to the United States, after their other eagerly anticipated first visit to Russia.

On May 1, two weeks before a scheduled Summit meeting in Paris between Dwight Eisenhower and Nikita Khrushchev, however, an international crisis erupted with the shooting down of an American U-2 reconnaissance plane over Russian airspace. The timing, Pamela felt, could not have been worse: 'Both of us deeply disturbed about Russian/US trouble on eve of Summit – & of our visit, I may say.' It took nine days before the Americans admitted that the plane had been on a spying mission, and the Summit went ahead, albeit in an atmosphere of mutual suspicion. Pamela thought that Khrushchev had sounded 'demented' at his final press conference in Paris, commenting: 'One can only imagine internal pressures in Russia are driving him crazy as the rest of us.' Fortunately for all concerned, in a speech in East Berlin two days later, Khrushchev was more conciliatory, and said that he did not propose to intensify the Cold War. 'C & I', Pamela wrote, 'felt rather eased.' Her view of the Soviet leader and of the political situation at the time of their visit had become still more benign by the time she wrote her memoir: 'We went first to Moscow in June 1960. That was in the springlike, early days of the "thaw", under that wayward, Dostoevskian but essentially progressive figure [...] Khrushchev' (*Important*, p.159).

They were met at Moscow airport with flowers and a warm welcome from a delegation from the Russian Writers' Union. It was also their first meeting with Oksana Krugerskaya, who was to act as interpreter for them on this and future visits. Oksana, Pamela wrote 'was the most wonderful oral interpreter' and 'also a bit of an actress', able to appreciate and transmit any jokes they might make. 'She was a dedicated Soviet citizen, though', Pamela added, 'always ready to argue a case' (*Important*, pp.159-60). Their days were fully programmed with organized sightseeing and cultural events. They were taken to the Bolshoi Theatre to see Prokoviev's <u>War & Peace</u> ('a stupendous production, very <u>long</u>'), and to the Moscow Arts Theatre, to see some rather elderly actors in a Russian version of *The Winter's Tale*. They gave joint talks, the first at the Foreign Literature publishing house, after which they were entertained with the 'usual Georgian wine, chocolates, tea, oranges'; Pamela remarked: 'Russians turn everything into a party.' They addressed a course at the Writers' Institute to an audience of 'Red Army men, sailors, etc., all studying to be writers. Cheerful young men, battering us with questions.' They travelled by train to St Petersburg, then still known as Leningrad, where Pamela was overwhelmed by its beauty – 'the sweet pea colours – green winter palace – glories of peacock blue & white of Smolny Convent'. Description of the Hermitage defeated her: 'No words for this that others haven't used.'

They were also invited to informal meals in the dachas of Soviet writers; on one of these occasions, however, after lunching in the country beneath the trees with Aleksei Surkov and his wife, Pamela almost re-enacted her (and Catherine Carter's) nightmare – 'got appallingly bitten by mosquitoes & quite blinded in one eye'. Nevertheless, Pamela enjoyed the day with them. Surkov was then the Secretary of the Writers' Union, and they found him 'most frank'; she recorded that 'he and C. had a bibulous & honest evening. Impressed by S. You may not always like what he means, but he does <u>mean</u> it. And he has an extremely attractive personality.' Back in Moscow, they had a packed final day, which included a World Literature meeting, lunch with a group of writers, a 'rather glum visit' to the British Embassy, a visit to 'battle-axe Evashova', a professor at Moscow University, who, despite that description, Pamela believed to be 'one of the most liberal forces in literature', and participation in a television broadcast with Surkov. The following morning, before driving them to the airport, their hosts insisted on their joining them in 'a farewell breakfast with vodka, wine & huge meal'.

On their return to England, Pamela was disappointed with the reaction to their Russian visit from her new aristocratic friends. Dining at the home of the newspaper editor David Astor (the brother of their friend William, Viscount Astor), she wrote:

> They all want to know our impressions of Russia, & then receive the most moderate account (of a favourable one on the whole) with smiling disbelief & hostility. I feel v. depressed about this <u>kind</u> of establishment. I like our system & not the Russian, but to imagine they are all panting for Czarist Restoration or a foreign liberation is plain crass.

She and CPS were nevertheless ill-prepared for the outright attack in Astor's newspaper, the *Observer* (7 August 1960), launched by the novelist John Wain, with whom their paths had briefly recently crossed. Wain had been in Russia having received a Somerset Maugham Travel Award, and evidently believed that this had enabled him to be more open-minded, more able to resist what he described as the 'terrific, all-pervading, crushing propaganda'. In an open letter to the Russian establishment, Wain declared that: 'There will always be the Western visitor who is impressed by the sight of so much endeavour. While I was in Moscow, I met Sir Charles Snow. As an official visitor, he was being given the full treatment, particularly on the theme of education. He had been to all the university buildings and seen all the classrooms and the laboratories.' This seems a gross exaggeration, as there was scarcely a mention of even one such visit

in Pamela's diary. However, Wain alleged that CPS had played into
the hand of the Russian propaganda machine; he sarcastically ended:

> When the homeward boat put into Stockholm and we were able to
> buy Western newspapers for the first time, I went ashore and got the
> *Guardian*. Headline: British behind Russia in Education: C.P. Snow's
> Impression. At it already! That must have pleased you, comrades. To
> get a statement like that out of an acute and informed man like Snow
> is worth a thousand volumes from half-baked fellow-travellers. I salute
> you.

Evidently still smarting from these and future memories, Pamela later
wrote:

> If I write of [the Soviet Union] too warmly, fanatic Russophobes in this
> country will say I have been 'conned'. If I write too critically, I may
> cause pain and anxiety to many of my Russian friends. [...] I may say
> that Charles and I, having made many trips to the U.S.S.R., found no
> attempt by anyone to 'con' us at all. They did not think we were fools.
> For one thing, we refused to play 'politics', which is a trap into which
> western visitors often fall: so they learn nothing whatsoever. We made
> acquaintances both on the left and the right (I use these terms for
> convenience) and it was rare for either side to refuse to talk to us freely
> and argue late into the night. (*Important*, pp.158-59)

Chief among CPS's speaking engagements in the USA that autumn
was the invitation to give the Godkin Lectures at Harvard University.
Following what was then perceived to have been the success of his
Rede Lecture, his topic was to be a related one, entitled 'Science and
Government'. In August, Pamela read CPS's draft which she found
'magnificent', and made her feel 'so proud of him!!'. But CPS anticipated that any forthcoming public pronouncement by him might
become fraught when *Encounter* published an article by Rayner
Heppenstall, entitled: 'Divided We Stand: On "The English Tradition"'.[3] The first two paragraphs took the form of gratuitous insults
with regard to CPS's Rede Lecture. As Heppenstall made clear, he had
written the remainder of his article before the latter event, but before
submitting it for publication, he considered whether it should be
rewritten to be 'explicitly collated with what Sir Charles had to say'.
'Unfortunately,' he continued, 'I did not find his argument of much
interest.' He then mockingly differentiated between Sir Charles, the

scientific civil servant, and C.P. Snow, the novelist, implying that the public might be misled into thinking that CPS was speaking for both camps, when, to his mind, the Rede Lecture had been purely 'a Civil Servant's lecture [...] part of a recruiting drive for more scientists'.

The remaining three pages of the article have little relevance to the subject matter of CPS's Rede Lecture, so those opening remarks do seem superfluous, and it is not surprising that Pamela saw the matter as 'a new Heppenstall outrage'. CPS was so affected by Heppenstall's hostility that he immediately wrote to Melvin J. Lasky,[4] the Editor-in-Chief of *Encounter*, informing him that he would not now give permission for extracts of his Godkin Lectures to be published in that journal, as his Rede Lecture had been. 'And about time, too', Pamela commented about her former friend and colleague: 'Heppenstall's spite has been going on for years now, & though one can stand most things, this is ceasing to be funny.'

Pamela's usual misgivings about their next extended absence from home were allayed to some extent by having been able to make arrangements for her two younger children to accompany them to America. Moreover, again much to her relief, their initial travel did not including flying: they crossed the Atlantic on the Queen Elizabeth. She declared herself to be 'a proud Mamma' when her daughter Lindsay was much sought after as a dancing partner, although there was a whiff of regret that her own dancing days seemed to be over. After ten days in New York, the family continued to California by train. Pamela's published memories of that trip, including their first experience of 'sitting on campus' at Berkeley, emphasize the positive aspects – the intellectual stimulation of friends in New York, and their charming accommodation with splendid views of the Golden Gate Bridge in San Francisco (*Important*, pp.45-48). Her diary, however, reveals great, but suppressed, unhappiness, of which she was ashamed. 'It is odd', she wrote, 'but this country does something <u>bad</u> for me, & makes me feel hateful inside.' She felt 'demoniac possession by a kind of <u>Mrs Jago</u> figure':

> I am envious, miserable, angry. And all this is contemptible. It is won-
> derful to watch C's success – he is <u>really</u> famous here. Sometimes I am
> afraid I resent my own lack of it: but I don't think it's that. I believe
> I am afraid that in America I <u>lose</u> Charles – & God knows if I go on
> being such a bitch I shall deserve it. Not that I don't repress most of

it. But I cry here, by myself, I always have, & I am not sure why. If
I were C., I should detest me.

Eventually, Pamela found herself a role at Berkeley: she and CPS kept
open house in the afternoons twice a week for any students who wished
to talk to them on any subject, and she found this moderately rewarding. After the first month, she even began to plan a new novel, which
would become *An Error of Judgement*.

The whole family got caught up in the excitement of the forthcoming Presidential election in which Vice-President Richard Nixon
was being challenged by Senator John F. Kennedy. Here again, her
written account conflicts, at least initially, with her diary entries. 'We
were all passionately pro-Kennedy', she unequivocally declared in her
memoir (*Important*, p.50). Yet her first view of him after watching a
television documentary was that he was 'a 3rd rate man'. Her opinion
of Nixon was however even more despairing (and it has to be remembered that his resignation as President after the Watergate scandal was
fourteen years in the future); after watching the first Nixon-Kennedy
television debate, she wrote:

> I suppose one can only prefer a third-rate man with a glimmering of
> decency to a second-rate scoundrel. V., v. dreary, & all curiously unreal-
> istic. To think of either of those two as leader of "The Free World!"
> O, for Stevenson, at least.

Pamela did, however, indeed become pro-Kennedy by Election Day,
by the end of which she thanked heaven that his opponent was not
elected. She nevertheless found the television coverage of the defeated
candidate's wife 'heartrending', as she noted that, while 'looking
absolutely ravaged & desperate, near to tears', Pat Nixon continued
'mechanically flashing great smiles on & off'. It may not be too fanciful to consider that she felt fellow-feeling for Mrs Nixon because of
her own continuing struggle in America to perform the expected
subservient wifely role. She remained deeply in love with CPS and
genuinely delighted in his reception there, but she could not come to
terms with her self-labelled 'Mrs Jago status'.

Towards the end of their stay at Berkeley, the Snows flew back to
the East Coast, primarily for CPS to deliver the Godkin Lectures. His
main contention was that 'cardinal choices' in any contemporary
advanced industrial society were invariably made by politicians, 'men

who cannot have a first-hand knowledge of what those choices depend on or what their results may be'.[5] As he later wrote in the Preface to the published edition: 'Giving three lectures on three successive nights is pretty rough on the lecturer, not to speak of his audience' (p.vi). He surmounted this problem by illustrating his argument with a gripping account of 'two men and two choices' (p.4). As Pamela wrote in her memoir, 'Charles has his own brand of cunning', ending, as he had, the first two lectures with cliff-hangers in the manner of a detective serial. 'After the first', she continued, 'one professor was heard to whisper to another – "And *did* the butler do it?"' (*Important*, p.104).

The two men were Sir Henry Tizard, in CPS's view, 'the best scientific mind that in England has ever applied itself to war', who became an advisor to the Air Ministry, and the man Tizard always referred to Lindemann, who became better known as Lord Cherwell, Winston Churchill's principal scientific advisor before and during the Second World War (pp.4 & 10). The two men had been friends in their youth, but became bitter enemies during the 1930s when they advocated different priorities for defence preparations, and their enmity continued during the war over the issue of strategic bombing. The point that CPS wanted to emphasize was that the final decision on both vital matters was inevitably determined by neither eminent scientist but by the politicians. The reception of CPS's Godkin Lectures differed considerably between the USA and the UK. In the former, they were a great success; Pamela reported the attendances as being 'sensational', and the published version was an American Book of the Month choice. In the UK, however, as CPS's brother remembered: 'Controversy erupted among scientists, administrators and specialists in telecommunications.' 'Eminent wartime figures took sides', Philip Snow continued, with the pro-Lindemann factions believing that CPS was challenging 'Churchill's own sagacity and judgement'.[6] There would be a further twist in the tale the following year when CPS received an angry phone call about his lecture from Tizard's son Peter. 'Considering his Pa is the hero', Pamela commented, 'this seemed extraordinary.' Nevertheless, CPS agreed to 'give both sides' more evenly in a postscript when the talks were reprinted that year.

Pamela was glad that their stay in Berkeley was coming to an end. Her daughter Lindsay had begged to be allowed to stay in America to study, since she had continued to be in touch with Alfred Harrison,

a student at Harvard who had been her principal suitor from their
outward transatlantic crossing, and Pamela had spent much time
making the necessary arrangements. Before the return home for which
Pamela was longing, however, they spent the Christmas holiday period
in New York. CPS was continuing to be fêted (she had written earlier
to her brother-in-law that 'Charles is as famous as Napoleon in the
U.S.')[7] and she was nearing the end of her tether. For once, her diary
is critical of him; on the penultimate day of the year, she grumbled:

> C. had appointments all afternoon, & I never got to shops after all.
> I never get to do anything I want to do here, & am never helped to do
> it. [...] Dined with Scribners. C., who claims to be exhausted, stayed
> far too late, 1.15 when we got home, & I just burst into what C. calls
> a "scream of tears" [a phrase he had used in *Time of Hope*]. But of course
> he was virtually asleep by then.

Their return to London in the New Year, however, brought further
problems. Indeed throughout 1961, Pamela's diary recorded a litany
of ailments, constant migraines, conjunctivitis, mystery rashes, and
evermore persistent bouts of depression. (She would write frankly
about the latter in *Important to Me*, Chapter 29). Now in her late 40s,
she attributed most of these symptoms to the menopause, despite her
periods remaining regular. Her general unhappiness in January was
heightened by guilt as she prepared for the departure of the eight-
year-old Philip, to a boarding preparatory school in Sussex. After seeing her 'v. brave', but 'a little pale' younger son off at Victoria Station,
she returned with CPS to 'a silent house' for the first time in 20 years
for her – no Amy, Lindsay in America, and her elder son Andrew now
studying engineering at CPS's old college, Christ's, Cambridge. While
she sensed that this state of affairs as being something of a relief for
CPS, she wrote, echoing, in the final sentence, a plaintive cry of her
son Andrew when a similar age to Philip: 'Darling, darling Philip!
Darling Charles! But – I want, I want, I want.'

One of the things that she wanted was to have 'a real holiday' with
CPS, but on one occasion when she tried to discuss this with him, she
was met 'with such blank opposition' that she admitted to sulking for
the rest of the day. It was some comfort to her at this time that she
made contact with some of her old friends, although with mixed
results. She attended an Old Girls' Reunion at the home of her

former headmistress, whom she was delighted to find 'straight as a dart & wonderful'. 'But,' she wrote, 'all those <u>very</u> old girls are <u>very</u> dull. I am a <u>very</u> old girl too.' She was pleased on another occasion to find the former Babs Freeman 'still lively, witty, & [with] a touch of her old glamour', but downcast by a visit from Teddy Lamerton, evidently unhappily married and 'looking so grey & stooped'. 'What a frittered life!', she commented. Age was clearly becoming a major preoccupation for her: on her 49th birthday that year, she recorded being 'In my 50th ... year ... SO OLD!'

A minor difficulty that had awaited them on their return from America was the announcement of their live-in housekeeper that, after nearly five years with them, she was leaving to be married. Pamela hated the process of interviewing applicants. She was on the verge of employing 'a glossy, talkative Miss A', who had declared herself to be 'a dévotée' of Pamela's novels, when she received a letter from Miss A's former employer, exposing her as a nymphomaniac – 'a letter with deadly ring of truth!' So they settled for a Mrs Owens – 'Heaven grant she is good! Red hair, rather ectomorphic, pleasing Scottish accent: may be bossy. Hard to tell.' As things would prove within a few months, they might have been better off with the alleged nymphomaniac.

Neither Pamela nor CPS had a book published in 1961. Pamela had put *An Error of Judgement* aside, and did not resume writing it until June. In the meantime, they were both involved in theatre productions: Pamela had been collaborating on a translation of Jean Anouilh's *The Rehearsal* with Kitty Black, and CPS was working with Ronald Millar on a stage version of his novel *The Affair*. (The latter would be produced in September and be the first of several adaptations of the 'Strangers and Brothers' sequence for stage and later television.) *The Rehearsal* was now to open at the Bristol Old Vic and it came to the London West End shortly afterward with a stellar cast, including Robert Hardy, Alan Badel and Phyllis Calvert (better known as a film actress). The early rehearsals seemed to Pamela 'hopelessly chaotic [...] with everyone but the producer full of ideas for the production'. She thought, nevertheless, that the principal male actors were likely to be extremely good, but had reservations about Calvert ('indifferent') and thought the girl playing the ingénue role was 'naturally wrong'. The latter was Maggie Smith at the start of her illustrious career.

Compared with the way that Pamela always agonized about the reception of CPS's works, she was relatively laconic about the reviews when *The Rehearsal* reached London. The press, she merely recorded, had been fine, and the play 'should run', as it did indeed for over a year. All the cast were praised, and, despite Pamela's qualms, Maggie Smith was singled out by Harold Hobson in the *Sunday Times*, as being 'touching, sincere, and sometimes devastating'. Surprisingly, and surely gratifyingly for Pamela, the hard-to-please Kenneth Tynan begged his readers to go to see this 'striking production' with 'an even more striking translation by Pamela Hansford Johnson and Kitty Black'.

The Snows undertook two American tours in 1961; the first, in the spring, started, as it continued to be, nightmarish for Pamela. Her diary entries for the first week in Washington recorded: 'Feeling quite hysterical'; 'One of the most exhausting days I have ever spent'; 'Another demented day'; and 'Really hideous session at ICA, with Charles Eames [the furniture designer] talking so appallingly that it was like our comedian, Stanley Unwin'. They then had a week's stay in St. Paul's, New Hampshire, which Pamela described as 'the nearest American equivalent to Eton' but what should have been a restful break was spoiled by the necessity to join the boys at dinner: 'the food was revolting. On Friday, they had, God help us, a day of "self-denial". Nothing could have made the diet worse than it normally was.' However, in retrospect, she was able to find one memory amusing: 'It was pointed out to us, though, and rather pathetically, by one of the boys, that they did eat it off very good china' (*Important*, pp.107-08). After two more long journeys to other campuses, she complained still further:

> This is a terrible trip, & Charles was mad to arrange it as he has done. As a result, he is worn out, & on the defensive, & I am so exhausted I could cry for hours. He must let me arrange these schedules in future – it is too awful. We are losing our lives.

She could not even look forward to tranquillity on her return home. They had had some doubts about the religiosity of their new house-keeper when Mrs Owen had greeted them on Easter Sunday with: 'Christ is Risen. Peace be on this house.' Pamela's son, Andrew, had been staying in their flat during their absence, and some incidents between them culminated in Mrs Owen's having sent him a letter 'of such vituperation' that Pamela had to write from America to sack her. CPS, if not Pamela, was so amused by the housekeeper's letter by return that he kept it among the papers to be deposited in his archive. Addressed to 'My dear Lady Snow', it continued:

> You have forestalled me only by about the inside of a fortnight. Being far from obtuse, I am sure you realised some time ago that I found the ambiance inimical. The view of life (& your reactions to others) held by yourself and Sir Charles are, almost, diametrically opposed to mine and although I have tried conscientiously not only to do the work well, but to fit in to (forgive me) what is to me an uncivilised mode of life, I have felt for some time that it could not be done [...].
>
> It is extremely doubtful that I shall take another post as housekeeper, & if I did it would be in a presbytery.

Pamela was, however, able to enjoy the final part of this American visit. In Cambridge, MS, she was reunited with her daughter, who was to return with them on the Queen Mary; Lindsay, Pamela wrote, had grown 'so protective and sweet'. Then, in contrast to the privations of their hospitality on campus, she felt again rewarded by Brooke Astor, who on this occasion invited them for a weekend stay at her country estate at Rhinebeck, NY. After the solemnities of (inedible) academic meals, she delighted in an 'uproarious dinner, all being silly with a new party game', followed by sitting out late on the terrace – 'such magnificence – inevitably strange'.

To the relief of all the family, Mrs Owen had moved out by the time they arrived home, although not without having tried to induce Mrs Scarlett, their daily cleaner, to go with her to work for 'a Christian family', who might pay her another 1s. 6d. an hour. Mrs Scarlett revealed this to Pamela, who was amused by her 'dreadful revelations of how Mrs O prayed and prayed for Sir C. & Lady Snow but could see no improvement'. One can only think that Mrs Owen's main objection to the Snows' ménage would have been the absence of religious observance, but while CPS declared himself to be 'a pious agnostic',[8] Pamela frequently revealed in her diaries that she was not without guilt in this regard. However, a new housekeeper was soon found, proved to be an excellent cook, and they were able to resume their usual pattern of hosting dinner parties and literary gatherings.

Pamela was at this time attributing her continuing sense of unhappiness to worries about international crises, in this case, the building of the Berlin Wall and the Russian decision to resume nuclear testing. On the 11th anniversary of her marriage to CPS, her diary makes for sad reading: 'I broke down, cried uncontrollably for 4 hours. No point in going into it. Nobody's fault. Tiredness – frustrations – .' She had now resumed writing *An Error of Judgement*, arguably her blackest novel, and had incorporated into it at least one painful episode from her own life. The central character of this novel is William Setter, a Harley Street doctor, who abandons his lucrative practice because he has come to recognize that he derives both 'pleasure and disgust' at giving pain, and needs to remove himself from any temptation.[9] Later, he comes into contact with Sammy Underwood, a young man who may or may not have been involved in a motiveless group attack on an old woman in a south London side street, which had culminated in her graphically described horrible death. Setter hears that, since 'hunting for louts in that part of the world is no easy matter [...] there wasn't the smell of an arrest' (p.55). Having become convinced that Sammy had in fact been the primary mover in the murder, but that no adequate proof of this could be offered to the police, Setter feels bound to exact retribution himself.

Ishrat Lindblad, who discusses this novel in her chapter entitled 'Human Relationships and Moral Values', points out perceptively that:

> Setter [...] can be thought of as either a saint or a sinner depending upon the moral premises of the person who judges him. The novel shows how difficult it is to judge such a man and implies that either judgement would be erroneous.[10]

In her introduction to the 1987 reprint of *Error of Judgement* in the Oxford University Press 20th Century Classics series, A.S. Byatt writes of Pamela's belief in realism, associated with moral truthfulness, as her chosen literary form, and she asserts that:

> [...] the peculiar force of *An Error of Judgement* (and also of those other excellent novels, *The Humbler Creation* and *The Last Resort*) derives from the fact that the truths she wants to tell are not only psychological but in some sense religious. [...] *An Error of Judgement* is partly a wry social comedy and partly a study in good and evil, creation and destruction, paradise and the pit.[11]

In reinforcement of these dichotomies, Victor Henrey, the first-person narrator of the novel, is depicted as a semi-comic character. He is a hypochondriacal former patient of Setter's, whose wife, Jenny, experiences intense self-condemnation when her mother dies during one of her rare brief absences. Jenny's 'nightly dreams of the pit', Byatt appreciates, 'are brilliantly imagined and written'. Victor is initially sympathetic, but soon begins to find the situation intolerable:

> I had always thought of Jenny as a pretty lightweight character, and shouldn't have married her, I think, if my impressions had been different. I don't like the Siddons touch around the house. But there was nothing light about the awful, howling grief with which I had to contend. [...] She was entirely sunken in guilt [...]. (p.91)

Pamela's son Andrew believes that, in this novel, for the first time, his mother was following CPS in basing several characters on people she knew, other than herself, for example, Setter partly on their present family doctor, David Sofaer, and Malpass, a worldly priest, on Father Gerald Irvine.[12] Pamela had by now revised her initial distrust of Sofaer, and had become reliant on him for regular prescriptions of tranquillisers; they exchanged social visits, and she had become aware of, and sympathetic to Sofaer's evidently difficult private life, writing of him after an evening spent with CPS at his house: 'Poor chap, he is so difficult, & so lonely.' Irvine was a regular and popular attendee at their parties. But whereas Andrew believes the narrator to be a thinly disguised portrait of Harry Hoff, Victor's reaction at Jenny's state of mind following her mother's death, quoted above, would also seem to reflect the attitude taken by CPS with regard to Pamela's own feelings of guilt after Amy's death, and her confused thoughts about her own ailments at this time. Later that year, after struggling through a dinner party for her husband's sake, she chronicled:

> C. is not very patient about me – I don't think he likes ill women much. I do try to keep up, & have been so much better that this little set-back was bitterly disappointing. Menopause or not, I am feeling so very lonely. Think I understand how my poor Mother felt: am prepared to accept my own state as a punishment, if it is acceptable.

Her loneliness during school and university terms was exacerbated by CPS's regular evening absences.

A change of venue for their summer family holiday from her beloved Belgium to the south of France had done little to raise Pamela's spirits. They rented an apartment in Cavalaire, a small seaside village described by her as 'newly developed, bright, gimcrack, petty-bourgeois [*sic*]', with even the 'pretty beach' blighted by there being 'lots of hideous burning flesh on it'. The mistral blew for several days on their arrival, to be followed by intense heat. Pamela continued to be obsessed with the current world crises, and complained about the hopelessness of getting news; she was reduced to 'prowling around trying to get a look at other people's newspapers'. On the day that those papers carried confirmation that the USSR's nuclear tests were imminent, her near-incoherent diary entry revealed her at her most tortured:

> Felt pretty nightmarish all the hot day. On beach in afternoon, preposterous breaking out of a smooth sea & one huge wave: began dementedly to wonder whether the Russians had caused it with a really epic explosion. I even felt the colour of the <u>sky</u> was wrong.

Despite the relative proximity of the museums and sites relating to the great Impressionist and Modernist painters in that area, she and CPS did not, as they usually did in Belgium, leave the children behind so as to enjoy time alone together, visiting the local places of interest. On the day they flew home, she wrote: '<u>Was</u> I glad to get out of the claustrophobia of Cavalaire!' Unsurprisingly, the resort never became the setting for one of her novels. Her only consolation was that her children had enjoyed the holiday. Lindsay's American boyfriend Alfred had come to Europe during his summer vacation, and had accompanied her to Cavalaire; Pamela had become very fond of him, and when he left for home, she recorded a 'depressing & emotionée day' as Alfred's 'lavender eyes misted over' and he 'kissed the cat with passion'. Quite tartly for once, she added: 'C., that emotional coward, crept out to the Athenaeum.'

Pamela had, however, managed to complete *An Error of Judgement* during the holiday, although she could not bring herself to rejoice even about this, writing:

> I don't know what it is like. It worries me. It is powerful, but not, I think, really neo-realistic – just a bit dotty. Perhaps I have been too much disturbed this last year, what with one thing & another.

Unusually, she does not seem to have conferred with CPS during the writing of this book, and he did not read it until some months later. His verdict then was that, while he did not know how it would be received, 'he thinks it is (like <u>Skip</u> & <u>Corinth House</u>) among my "Insane" works, but thinks it has something of genius.' This briefly relieved her anxiety, but she soon reverted to having nightmares about the book with publication still over half a year away.

In the autumn, the dramatization of *The Affair* received exceedingly good notices. Pamela summed up the reviews in the daily papers as being: 'Wonderful press for dear C., which makes me happy, despite my own complaints.' The Sunday reviews were in general equally good, Harold Hobson writing that:

> *The Affair* is one of the few contemporary plays which satisfy at every level. It is civilised, witty, packed with picturesque characters, full of conflict, passing through situations of mounting intensity to an admirable climax.

However, despite Kenneth Tynan's praise earlier in the year for her translation of *The Rehearsal*, Pamela evidently had not warmed to him, describing him as 'a bogus left-winger', when, in his *Observer* review, Tynan criticized the slow-motion tension of the play, in which he commented that: 'Sir Lewis Eliot investigates with the sententious thoroughness relieved by flashes of acuity, that we associate with the novels of C.P. Snow.' CPS's alter ego was played, as he would be in future dramatizations, by John Clements. Pamela could scarcely have argued with Tynan's verdict that this actor had only just managed to stay 'this side of smugness', considering she had described him as 'a posturing ass, as usual' on the first night. As it happens, because Clements had other commitments, his part was later taken by Alec Clunes whose portrayal of Eliot was praised for its subtlety. The play ran for a very creditable 379 performances, to be almost immediately followed by Millar's adaptation of *The New Men*.

In October, they were invited for the weekend to the home near Stratford-upon-Avon of J.B. Priestley and his archaeologist wife Jacquetta Hawkes. Pamela commented that Priestley had 'so many chips on shoulder that he must look, to a psychic person, like a dragon', whereas 'Jacquetta, despite fierce appearance, is gentle, shy, & naïve'. Peggy Ashcroft, an actress whom Pamela very much

admired, came to lunch on the Saturday, and Pamela was delighted
to find her 'a charming, unaffected woman who looks incredibly like
Ellen Terry'. She found Iris Murdoch, who came with her husband,
John Bayley, to spend one night, far less congenial:

> Iris is heavy, low-hung, grotesque in appearance: he is little & stutter-
> ing, with a fluting voice. I rather liked him. But she is nervy, socially
> ill at ease, & not my thing at all. She is profoundly & deeply <u>feminine</u>,
> despite appearances: all those frilly heroines are compensation figures.
> I hate to seem a bitch towards her – I think her life hasn't been easy.
> This doesn't mean I can stand the incoherence of her novels.

In years gone by, Pamela might well have found intellectual stimulation in such a gathering, but in her present state, she was not at all
sorry to return home, reflecting that: 'Weekends take hunks out of
one's life, & when spent with a quartet none of whom are in the least
what they seem, psychologically exhausting.'

Despite her previous hopes that she could influence CPS not to
undertake another lengthy American tour, they left shortly afterward
for six weeks of engagements, which included almost a week at a
Science Symposium in Columbus, Ohio, and then three weeks 'sitting
on campus' at the Wesleyan University in Middletown, Connecticut.
Whereas the former was entirely for CPS's benefit, Pamela did appreciate the fact that both of them were given the status of Fellows of
the Centre for Advanced Studies at the Wesleyan, and that, as she
wrote in *Important to Me*: 'We were presented with a house – daunt-
ingly large – to live in, and beautifully appointed offices in which to
work. At what? *At our own books'* (p.III). She did admit in her memoir
that they had had some problems on arrival, but watered down her
actual diary entry for the first day, which read:

> Given a Charles Adams house, trailed around for hours before we got
> our mail – & <u>no</u> help in house, & food in club horrible. C & I exhausted:
> keeping going on odd snacks of a hasty nature & too much Scotch. Oh
> dear!
>   As Captain Scott said, on his view of the South Pole, "God, this is an
> awful place!"

She felt 'edgy being <u>alone</u> in this detestable house – it is architecture
which produces ghosts'. However, the experience was not without

reward; with *An Error of Judgement* delivered to her publishers, and
with the promise to the university that she would write during their
stay, she revived her spirits a little by transporting the sophisticated
Matthew Pryar, one of Dorothy Merlin's entourage in *The Unspeakable
Skipton*, to Cobb, described as being a 'rich American liberal arts
college', ostensibly in New Hampshire (this being a state with no
university the Snows had visited).[13]

The resultant book, *Night and Silence Who is Here?*, subtitled 'An
American Comedy', Pamela insisted, was not intended specifically to
satirise Wesleyan, as was generally thought on publication; she intended
the location to be 'an amalgam of many campuses' (*Important*, p.111).
This consolation apart, Pamela complained throughout her stay about
the lack of facilities: 'The laundry doesn't call, the kitchen equipment
is baffling, there is no help of <u>any kind</u> whatsoever.' Her fictional alter
ego appreciates that he will have to accustom himself to some changes
of lifestyle: he would not be able to rely on 'his man' bringing his early
morning tea to him, but in the morning after his arrival, he nevertheless has a 'frightening thought',

> which was, that perhaps nobody would come to make his bed for him,
> and wash up the plate and saucer he had used the night before.
> Oh, but surely, he said to himself, surely someone will. Of course,
> someone will. (p.25)

But nobody does. Similarly, even after a week *in situ*, it would seem
that having become accustomed to live-in domestic help since her
marriage to CPS had rendered Pamela incapable of improving their
present living conditions: she wrote: '[...] one prays here for a dinner
date, otherwise one has to eat biscuits or a rather stale egg from the
fridge.' She had found that the inability of either herself or CPS to
drive a car rendered the purchase of groceries, not to mention the
alcohol and cigarettes on which they both relied, near-unachievable,
and in due course, would make the automobile-phobic Matthew
suffer similarly when he finds that the only comestible available in the
college store is peanut butter (p.46).

The Snows spent a few days in Philadelphia towards the end of their
stay in Wesleyan; Pamela contemplated with some amazement how
'life was so odd in its changes' when CPS gave a lecture to a huge
audience in the Academy of Music, where Leopold Stokowski had been

principal conductor to the Philadelphia Orchestra at the time of her encounters with him, and her mind went back to the days of her servitude with the Central Hanover Bank. She also gave some lectures in Philadelphia, although not in such surroundings, after which she 'staggered back to Middletown more dead than alive', to be 'led off to a foul Ladies Dinner', after which her hosts abandoned her, leaving her: 'exhausted, liquorless. MAD!!' She had no regrets whatsoever in bidding farewell the next day to 'ghastly Middletown'.

Back at home, she admitted to having 'long-term generalised depression', which she hoped she was able to conceal from her family, but CPS was full of anxieties too. New Year's Eve, 1961, represented for her:

> The end of this black year. C. feels it is black because of the anxieties to himself. I feel it is black because nothing has happened to me, & all my literary hopes are broken. Yet what we both feel is the horror of the year in terms of politics & war. We dread the future. Charles may see the hope logically. I, so wretched a Christian, hope through God. Yet I cannot make up my mind to enter a church formally – return to Noncomformity (as I would like, but what does it matter?).

She became more positive in expressing 'gratitude to God for 21 years of life of my dear Andy. Nearly 18 years of my beautiful & kind daughter, 9 years of my beloved & brilliant Philip. All these years of my wonderful & dear Charles'; yet finally she sought absolution for her past wrongdoings 'towards Neil, my mother, towards myself'.

I admit to qualms about including diary entries clearly written by Pamela under conditions of stress, and felt duly admonished in another broadside directed at any aspiring biographer of herself the following day, written after she had been re-reading Betty Miller's biography of Robert Browning, which she considered: 'ALL wrong':

> Wish I could have a kind of Shakespearian epitaph on my tomb, cursing dogfaces[14] who might like to disinter my private life & make everything complicated and ugly. (Much has been simple & beautiful.)

CHAPTER 16

Attacks, Scandals and Distresses

P AMELA'S HOPES that 1962 might prove to be a less stressful year were immediately dashed by two major attacks, the first of which questioned her intellectual impartiality as well as that of her husband. The Snows had been invited to be joint guest editors of *Winter's Tales 7*, the annual collection of short stories published by Macmillan, to which Pamela had contributed in the past. In their hope of bridging the gap between East and West at least in the field of literature, they had chosen only works by modern Soviet writers. The first review of this book had been moderately good; the anonymous *Times* critic had indeed praised the Snows for 'their enterprise and their open-mindedness', and for contributing 'an introduction which tactfully avoids the banalities of the cold war and gets down to the serious stuff of literary criticism', but then found the stories themselves 'somewhat disappointing'. But then the historian Robert Conquest reviewed the collection and its introduction so intemperately that his critique was nominated as "Invective of the Year" by the *Guardian*. Pamela wrote despairingly: 'I hope I am not getting too cowardly, but this incessant assault is hard to bear.'

It might seem strange that, in the middle of the Cold War, and with America only just emerging from the McCarthy era, CPS was always welcome there, whereas, in the UK, some suspicion and much antagonism was levelled at the Snows for their championship of writers from Communist countries, and this despite the fact that the hospitality they offered to visiting Russian and other East European writers was as often at the behest of the Foreign Office as a request from the Russian Embassy. Conquest was scarcely an impartial judge; although he had joined the Communist Party as a student in Oxford, he later became disillusioned with Soviet policies. After the Second World War, he was recruited into the Foreign Office's Information Research Department, established to counter Soviet propaganda. He began by criticizing the Snows' choices far more harshly than the reviewer in *The Times*: the stories were, he claimed, 'poor, unrepresentative, and in the main, dull', and continued: 'The introduction is worse than the selection.' He then went on to attack the introduction, claiming that the editors had frequently used the phrase, 'the cold war', in the context of which:

> It is wicked, they assure us, to look at Soviet literature with any political considerations in mind, since we would not do so with literature of other cultures. This really is fantastic impudence! Soviet literature, as we are told day in and day out by Russian politicians, cultural bureaucrats, and orthodox writers, is (or should be) 'a weapon for Communism'.[1]

In fact, the Snows only mentioned the contemporary international standoff twice in their fourteen-page long introduction when stressing the importance for English readers not to read Soviet stories as though they were documents in the Cold War. They had maintained that:

> For forty-four years, [...] the West has been doing precisely that, reading Soviet literature in quite a different spirit from that in which it reads any other literature, scrutinizing it, in suspicion and wishful thinking, for any sign of the collapse of the régime. The process has led us nowhere: or rather, it has led us to ludicrous misjudgments of Russian art and Russian living.'[2]

Conquest was later to become renowned for his exposé of the atrocities carried out by Stalin in the 1930s,[3] and it is the omission in this collection of stories published on that theme at the time of Khrushchev's 'Thaw' in 1956-57 that is the primary focus of his belligerence. Perhaps the Snows were naïve when they wrote that, under a 'general umbrella' of acceptance by writers of 'the Communist system as the only imaginable and desirable one [...], there is room for criticism, disputation, argument, varieties of opinion [...] with remarkable and sometimes disconcerting vigour',[4] but Conquest openly accused them of ignoring accounts of the purges and the continuing discrimination against certain writers, because: 'Burintern solidarity forbids.'

Distressing and unfair, as they believed the attack to have been, the Snows were aware that the *London Magazine* had a limited circulation, and since they were determined not to respond to the article, they felt that it was unlikely to have repercussions. But the following month brought an unpredictable onslaught which remains in the public consciousness to this day. On 21 February, she wrote that CPS had heard from Cambridge friends that F.R. Leavis 'is apparently going to attack C. like mad in the Richmond Lecture at Downing College, Cambridge. We are so <u>tired</u> of it – the constant driving attack from all sides. Why <u>us</u>?'

F.R. Leavis was retiring from Downing at the end of the academic year, and it was also his final year as a full member of the English Faculty; his reputation and influence in the field of English literature was great within academic circles, but not perhaps at that time far beyond. His biographer, Ian MacKillop, attributes his decision to make the topic for his valedictory lecture 'The Significance of C.P. Snow' to a recent review in *Delta*, a Cambridge literary magazine, of a book of essays by Frank Kermode. Despite his mediocre review of *The Conscience of the Rich*, Kermode had mentioned CPS in one of the essays 'as a contemporary representative of Leavisian art, a 1960s member of the "great tradition"', a judgment which had piqued Leavis to the extent of feeling 'that Snow was a figure from whom he had to dissociate himself'.[5] Stefan Collini believes that the antagonism between the two men went back much further, to the Cambridge of the 1930s when the two men publicly disagreed about the merit of H.G. Wells, Leavis being 'more than hostile' to his work, whereas CPS 'admired Wells as "a great writer" and "a remarkable man"', and they had similarly disagreed about the worth of T.S. Eliot and Gerard Manley Hopkins.[6] As time went on, and CPS became acclaimed both as a novelist and a technocrat, Collini pithily reflects that:

> In retrospect, one can only feel that a malevolent deity setting out to design a single figure in whom the largest number of Leavis's deepest antipathies would find themselves embodied could not have done better than to create Charles Percy Snow.[7]

The opening passage of the Richmond lecture, delivered on 28 February, left no-one in doubt of Leavis's attitude toward CPS in general and to the latter's 1959 Rede Lecture in particular:

If confidence in oneself as a master-mind, qualified by capacity, insight
and knowledge to pronounce authoritatively on the frightening
problems of our civilization, is genius, then there can be no doubt about
Sir Charles Snow's. He has no hesitations. [...] Yet Snow is, in fact,
portentously ignorant.[8]

He continued with further *ad hominem* insults, justifying these on the
grounds that: 'Snow is a portent. He is a portent in that, being in
himself negligible, he has become for a vast public on both sides of
the Atlantic a master-mind and a sage' (p.10). He then turned still
more derisively to CPS's literary output:

> Snow is, of course, a – no, I can't say that; he isn't: Snow thinks of
> himself as a novelist. [...] The seriousness with which he takes himself
> as a novelist is complete – if seriousness can be so ineffably blank, so
> unaware. [...] as a novelist he doesn't exist; he doesn't begin to exist.'
> (pp.12-13)

The Times, the following day, carried a brief report from its 'University Correspondent' on its news pages. While admitting that while
'the first two-thirds of Dr. Leavis's lecture were devoted to abuse, the
burden [of which] was that Snow was of significance only because he
had been erected into a sage on both sides of the Atlantic' and
'consisted mainly of criticism by dogmatic and unqualified assertion',
the writer did consider that 'the last twenty minutes were much more
specific and constructive'.

There was little about the lecture in the remainder of the daily press,
as 'Ass Leavis', as Pamela now called him, had refused to release the
text to the newspapers, while simultaneously denouncing them en
masse. Pamela was delighted to feel that he would thereby be 'reap-
ing the whirlwind', but then Leavis agreed that his lecture should be
published in full in the *Spectator*. The assistant editor Cyril Ray, who
was a friend of CPS, was sent to show the text to the Snows in order
to establish whether he was intending to take legal action against
Leavis. Pamela's attitude, which paralleled that of CPS, was 'Publish
and be Damned', although at this stage, she actually showed some
sympathy for 'poor old L.', possibly after reading the sections of the
lecture in which he boasted of his own achievements. He was, she
thought, 'like Corvo & Skipton, & I sometimes feel a twinge of pity
– which I suppose is falling over backwards'. This contradicts the

impression that Cyril Ray went away with. He alleged in a letter quoted by Ian MacKillop that: 'Lady Snow showed more anger at Leavis than Snow.'[9] Publication in the *Spectator* went ahead in the issue of 9 March.

Any lenity Pamela might have felt towards Leavis evaporated during the following week, when they were besieged by reporters, and pressed to sue for slander by friends and legal advisers. At the end of that week and the following week, the correspondence columns of the *Spectator* overflowed with reactions, virtually all, however, being favourable to CPS. 'We feel,' she wrote, 'like poor old creatures besieged by Indians in a stockade, who have suddenly seen U.S. cavalry coming to their relief!' The leader of the 'cavalry' was William Gerhardi, whose letter in support of CPS was allowed to span two and a half pages. This was followed by contributions from equally well-known, if predictable, friends and regular guests at the Snows' parties, including Edith Sitwell, the psychiatrist Anthony Storr, the eminent scientist J.D. Bernal, Robert Boothby, and Ronald Millar.

J.H. Plumb turned the tables on Leavis in his reaction to what he described as 'a senseless diatribe'. 'Dr. Leavis,' the historian declared, 'accuses Sir Charles Snow of ignorance of history. But his own is so abysmal that it would require a new Dunciad to do justice either to his folly or to his arrogance.' Pamela would have been particularly gratified that the *Spectator* also chose to include a letter from her (far less renowned at that time) young protégée, Susan Hill, then in her first year reading English at King's College, London. Susan wrote of her personal knowledge of CPS as 'a generous, modest man, concerned with the intellectual and social state of the world and trying to put forward an analysis of, and remedy for, it'. 'Leavis,' she bravely continued, 'has not given me one single, valid reason for altering my opinion of Snow. He has given me, on the contrary, every reason for drastically reconsidering my former opinion of himself as a great critic.'

Leavis's own 'cavalry' did not arrive until the third week after publication, and the principal spokesman for his faction was no more impartial than CPS's supporters. His publisher, Ian Parsons of Chatto and Windus, wrote to contradict those who had questioned his author's reputation, citing the continuing demand for *The Common Pursuit* and other of Leavis's books. 'So,' he asked, 'what is all this about envying another writer's success?' In general, there were no major figures in the pro-Leavis faction, but finally, pots and kettles again come to mind when Robert Conquest joined the debate, asking: 'Cannot these matters be argued decently?' He continued:

> The sharpness – even rudeness – of Dr. Leavis was only about Sir Charles Snow's talents and tastes. That Sir Charles has many good personal qualities is evident from his friends' comments; but I do not see why criticism of his literary or intellectual pretensions should be taken as reflecting on these. Some of the counter-attacks against Dr. Leavis in your issue of March 16 were a cesspool of disgraceful attributions of motive and low-grade psychoanalysis-at-a-distance.

And there, for a time, the matter rested.

Despite all these distractions, Pamela had managed to finish *Night And Silence Who is Here* within four months of having begun writing the novel in America. She did not, however, begin another novel for nearly two years, principally due to anxieties about her own health and that of CPS. For Lent that year, she made a resolve 'to drink only with other people & never alone', but she now became more concerned about her smoking. In March, the Royal College of Surgeons published their report, 'Smoking and Health', which gained much publicity from a special programme on the BBC's much-respected current affairs programme, *Panorama*. Pamela forwent her usual television diet of light entertainment: 'I sat & looked at dreary Panorama, with horrors of the smoking. I can't stop. But I have held to my Lent drink resolution – oh how I would like a night-cap now.' A week later, the programme was still on her mind: 'Smoking rumpus upsets me whether I like it or not – since 16 I have been smoking heavily, now 40 a day. Can't stop – don't know how I'd work if I did.'

At the end of the previous year, CPS had been elected Rector of St. Andrews University. Pamela had not been happy about his undertaking this commitment; in fact, she wrote that she felt 'rather angry, as he had promised to withdraw his candidature. He will clutter life.' The investiture was due to take place early in April, but just beforehand, CPS virtually lost the sight of his left eye. Pamela initially feared that this might have been caused by a brain tumour, but it proved to be a detached retina. To her dismay, he insisted on postponing the necessary operation so that he could fulfil what he saw as an obligation to attend the ceremony in St. Andrews. As she later remembered, she 'concocted a black bandage that covered the eye afflicted, this going right round his head, and slanting over one side' (*Important*, p.217). CPS being at that time so newsworthy, photographs of him adorned with this contrivance appeared in several newspapers.

As it happened, CPS had chosen 'Magnanimity' as the theme for his Rectorial Address in advance of that year's Richmond Lecture, and he made no direct reference to his recent adversary. Nevertheless, as Nicolas Tredell has remarked, the address, whether intended or not, 'inevitably took on the aspect of a "hidden polemic" against Leavis'. Tredell goes on to summarize the gist of the lecture favourably:

> As well as providing a general definition of magnanimity and drawing examples from scientists and literary men, Snow also offers a diagnosis of Britain in the early 1960s as a culture from which magnanimity is disappearing: 'in certain ways we seem to be behaving less amiably to one another' [...].

He ends by pointing out that CPS's contentions may now have 'greater relevance than ever', with 'the development of faster and more widely accessible means of communication, especially the Internet', making it 'much easier for people from all walks of life to be publicly nasty about one another'.[10]

In the early 1960s, the burgeoning satire movement was however providing its own opportunities for being 'publicly nasty'. *Private Eye* had been launched in 1961, and Richard Ingrams remembers a cabal of ex-Cambridge English pro-Leavisite writers for the magazine being advocates for CPS to become one of their regular targets.[11] On the first occasion, he was unnamed, but clearly identifiable: Pamela was deeply wounded on her husband's behalf when his (fortunately temporary) blindness was lampooned in their pages. She wrote in her memoir about the publication of a 'malicious cartoon',

> depicting Charles, cavorting naked, wearing the black bandage I had made for him to wear during his quixotic journey to St. Andrews. Underneath was the caption: 'In the country of the blind, the one-eyed man is King.'

Pamela judged this to have been 'not just insensitivity' but 'staggering cruelty', and she shielded CPS from finding out about the cartoon for as long as she could. 'We are told,' she continued, 'to forgive our enemies. I can usually forgive mine [...] because I tend to forget even who they are: but I cannot forgive Charles's' (*Important*, pp.218-19).

On their return to London, CPS went straight to Moorfields Hospital for the operation on his eye, following which he had to lie in darkness for days. Pamela spent hours at the hospital by his bedside, reading newspapers and books to him. To their huge disappointment, the specialist then told them of his deep regret that the operation had not been successful, and that he had therefore lost sight in that eye. But at home, a few days later, Pamela believed that 'something miraculous' had happened; citing one of her favourite novels, she wrote in her memoir:

> It was straight out of *Jane Eyre*, where the blinded Mr Rochester *sees* that Jane has on a blue dress [...]. Charles said suddenly, and I saw that he was covering his good eye, 'I can see your shape against the window'. (*Important*, p.219)

For a while, it did seem as though the retina had reattached itself.

Pamela had been in the throes of organizing a party for the distinguished but later controversial Russian poet, Yevgeny Yevtushenko. The previous year, during the Khrushchev Thaw, Yevtushenko had taken the opportunity to write his most celebrated work, 'Babi Yar', about the massacre by the Nazis of 34,000 Jews in a ravine outside Kiev, and the subsequent distortion of historical fact by the Soviet government which pursued policies of discrimination against, if not downright persecution of, Jews, and had preferred to represent the victims of Babi Yar as having been unidentified Soviet citizens. Pamela kept coming up against difficulties with regard to the guest list, and recorded her worries about 'getting a paranoid feeling that everyone hates Charles & me – & if I go on like that, I shall end up like old Publicity Leavis'.

The Snows had not previously met Jenya, as they learned to call him, but he had heard about CPS's operation, and insisted on visiting him in hospital to wish him well, in a manner that Pamela later wrote, 'was full of kindness and imaginative sympathy' (*Important*, p.161). She was therefore delighted that her party for Yevtushenko proved to be very successful; she had found him 'impressive in the way that makes one suspect real genius', and memorably described him as 'reciting magnificently with his parchment head outlined on Sid's [Sidney

Nolan's] <u>Gallipoli</u>'. The following week, she attended the Russian poet's evening of readings at the Royal Court Theatre, but was shocked at the hostility shown toward him at the end:

> [...] the question-time (every cold-war warrior in London) conducted by Spender like a helpless sheep, was revolting. Came home sick & tired of it all. He is, I am sure, a great poet: & all they can do is heckle as if he were a third-rate politician.

The Snows decided to go ahead with a planned visit to America, which did not include any 'sitting on campuses' but mainly social engagements and yet more honorary degree ceremonies for CPS, but to Pamela's relief, he agreed that they should go both ways by ship in case flying caused further eye problems for him. Before leaving, he thought it necessary to send a letter to his brother. As Philip Snow was to put it, 'Charles's physical setback had naturally caused him to think profoundly',[12] and had come to the conclusion that the time had come to acquaint his habitual confidant with the following:

> You may remember Anne Seagrim. I was always very fond of her and after she left the Windsors' ménage we took up again – in, of course, the most concealed kind of way. No one – except now you – knows anything at all about it. It has been a great support and joy for me and has made a big difference to my life.

CPS went on to say that 'the thing she is finding increasingly a horror is to be cut off from news when I happen to be ill', and therefore asked his brother (who duly agreed) to act as 'a channel of information' between them if needed.[13]

Despite Pamela's having no intimation of the above, the visit was an unhappy one; she was fretting about her own health throughout, and CPS was drinking even more heavily than usual. When one of their acquaintances showed him what even Pamela described as only 'a mild attack' by Edmund Wilson in the *New Yorker*, this upset CPS dreadfully, and quite quixotically, she thought, he blamed <u>her</u> for their being in the USA at that time. After this led to them both having a sleepless night, Pamela still felt wretched the following day, writing: 'I have got through this day & done everything <u>I said I would</u> on this nightmare trip. But when my darling C. gets upset, he <u>is</u> unkind to me. He can't help it, & he is worth it. But I am sometimes so alone. At night, terrible crying.'

On their return home, there was fortunately one improvement in their domestic life which was to prove long-lasting. Emilia, her house-keeper since the departure of the judgmental Mrs Owen, had had to leave due to poor health, and her replacement, Conchita Roca, became Pamela's 'greatest comfort & blessing'. The latter comment, dated some two years later, was added alongside her entry for the day in July 1962 on which Conchita arrived. A further ten years later, in the chapter in her memoir dealing with her bouts of depression, Pamela included Conchita in her reasons to be happy, although she did then mention her housekeeper's 'Latin temperament', which led her to enjoy 'a good "scene"' (*Important*, p.209). Otherwise, that summer and autumn brought little respite. The Leavis affair was by no means a thing of the past since, as Pamela put it: 'That damned Leavis wants to publish his vomit in book form.' They had been informed about this in a 'soapy letter' from his publisher, telling them that: '"Frank" had <u>no</u> personal animus.' This hardly consoled either of them; 'Talk about envy, hatred & malice, combined with a little extra money-grubbing & a further boost on another man's shoulders!', she wailed.

The publication day of *An Error of Judgement* arrived in July, and was for the most part very well received; Pamela was particularly delighted with a lengthy review solely devoted to the novel by her fellow-novelist Elizabeth Jennings in the *Sunday Times*, which showed her understanding and appreciation of Pamela's favoured literary mode:

> Miss Hansford Johnson is a realist; there is no symbolism in her work except in the odd metaphor or comparison. One is never left wonder-ing precisely what a given novel meant, or what was its significance. Yet Miss Hansford Johnson is an extremely subtle writer, a sharp prober of moods, motives and relationships. [...]
> In this book, Miss Hansford Johnson shows us that the realistic novel can be as profound and as searching as those novels which often attract more attention simply because they are introverted and enigmatic.

Pamela's pleasure that the book was a success was soon tarnished, however, because two reviewers took the opportunity to incorporate sneers about CPS into their praise for her. Richard Mayne (*New States-man*) was the less offensive when he judged her novel to have 'a depth and an emotional reality somewhat lacking in the bulk of her husband's series', but John Coleman (*Queen*) began with what Pamela called 'the most insulting & gratuitous reference to Charles'. 'Can we all forget for a minute,' he wrote, 'that she is married to the most drearily incompetent "famous" novelist of our time?' That he then continued by saying that Pamela was overall 'quite clearly, one of our most interesting contemporary novelists', and admiring the 'vivid, intelligent courage' of the perceptions in this novel, did not placate her; she thought both reviewers had been 'simply beyond all bounds of decency'. A subsequent libel case against *Queen* was settled out of court, with agreement that they would print an apology and pay the legal costs.

There was again little consolation to be had from that year's family holiday, despite their having reverted to their favourite small hotel in Le Coq on the Belgian coast, this year taking Susan Hill with them. However, they only had one day of sunshine during the three weeks they were away; on a typical day, their plans to spend the afternoon on the beach were frustrated by 'waves [...] rolling in diagonally like liquid clay' and by being 'chilled to the bone'. Pamela generally felt very low: 'If I cannot write something less <u>nevrosé</u> in my diary before long', she wrote, 'I am going to STOP IT. I have been going through this bad, edgy time too long.' She and CPS did leave the family behind for two days to stay in The Hague, and a brief interlude became the high point of the visit for Pamela as she sat among the paintings in the Mauritshuis, engrossed in Vermeer's 'View of Delft', a painting she deemed 'irreproducible', and Rembrandt's 'The Anatomy Lesson', which she could only describe as 'a miracle'. But, back in Le Coq, with worries that her anxieties about her health irritated CPS, and with the younger family members squabbling, she could only look forward to the end of 'this dreadful holiday'.

Pamela rightly anticipated that the next onslaughts on CPS would come with the opening of the stage version of *The New Men*. At the first night on 6 September, she 'sat and sweated, & was in a worse state of nervous tension than I had ever felt at a play of C's or mine!' The press the following day was indeed mixed, and included, according to Pamela, a 'piece of pure defamation' from Bernard Levin in the *Daily Mail*, which led CPS again to consider, and this time to pursue, legal action. When the case came to court the following year, counsel for the plaintiff alleged that the review had taken 'the form of a vigorous attack on Sir Charles in terms which had been read as carrying the plain implication that he was a fellow-traveller', and that 'the play amounted to a shockingly unscrupulous piece of political sleight of hand'. Counsel for the defendant responded that this had not been his client's intention, and that he 'greatly regretted that this implication had been drawn'. Nevertheless, Levin 'unreservedly withdrew what he had said', and tendered 'his sincere apology to Sir Charles for what he recognized to have been a serious libel'.[14] (CPS was awarded damages of £1,000, which, to Pamela's pleasure, he donated to the British Migraine Association, a forerunner of the Migraine Trust, of which Pamela was to be a founder-member.)

Herbert Kretzmer, Levin's opposite number at the *Daily Express*, had contented himself with faint praise that *The New Men* could be categorized as 'a play of ideas', although it was one in which 'some of the issues have been over-simplified to the point of caricature'. Fortunately, however, the Sunday papers were, according to Pamela, 'far better than expected', an excellent notice from Harold Hobson in the *Sunday Times*, and even a review by Kenneth Tynan in the *Observer* from which the theatre management could (and did) extrapolate the phrase 'not to be missed' for future advertisements.[15]

Private Eye that week continued with their campaign against CPS, now renamed C.P. Snurd for their readers, publishing a letter purporting to have been sent by F.R. Leavis to *The Times*, and spoofing the plans already being made for the 400th Anniversary of the birth of William Shakespeare in 1963:

> Next year will see the 400th Anniversary of the birth of C.P. Snurd. We suggest that this would be an opportune moment to reopen the tomb of the Grand Old Man of British letters. Hitherto, public opinion has been restrained by the famous inscription on his tombstone:
>   'Here Lye Ye Bones of Charlie Snurd Who All His Lyfe was Quite Abfurd. Refrain from Digging It You Must For He is Onlye a Pile of Duft.'[16]

The letter then continued with the suggestion that opening the tomb might resolve the matter 'of the true authorship' of Snurd's works, which may indeed have been written 'by an obscure ghost-writer of the time named Ronald Millar, otherwise only known as the author of a few second-rate drawing-room comedies'. With CPS worrying that similar attacks could do him 'real harm in the US', as well as his continuing suspicions about a concerted campaign to deny him a Nobel Prize, it was hardly surprising that Pamela recorded at this point: 'What a ghastly year it is!' 'My various neuroses', she reflected, 'are becoming almost beautiful in their variety & ingenuity. Yet I am sure that if C & I could get a lone, calm, happy period, they would all go away.' But there would be no such relief; soon afterward because *The Affair* had received poor notices on its transfer to Broadway, CPS went to New York on his own for a fortnight, ostensibly at the urging of Ronald Millar, in a vain attempt to save the play.

During his absence, Pamela was Roy Plomley's guest on 'Desert Island Discs'. Her choices ranged from classical music (three pieces by J.S. Bach, one by Debussy and an extract from one lesser-known work, Vincent d'Indy's Symphony No. 1) to a ballad sung by Yves Montand, a Shakespearean song from Cleo Laine, and a Thomas Hardy poem read by Richard Burton (rather than one of the many poems by Dylan Thomas he recorded). Her chosen book was, predictably, *A la recherche du temps perdu*, and her luxury item, which might have suffered from being cast away with her, was Van Eyck's 'Adoration of the Immaculate Lamb'.

The next blow came when Henry Sherek, who was the impresario behind the British Snow/Millar productions, decided to take *The New Men* off after barely three months, most gallingly not because attendance figures were below the profit margin, but because he wanted to bring in a musical version of Anita Loos's *Gentlemen Prefer Blondes*. Pamela suffered from this setback along with CPS; it was, she wrote, 'awful to hear him using that frightful <u>hollow</u> voice nearly all the time'. He then decided to go into 'solitary hiding' (back in fact to the Dudley Hotel, Hove) to finish his latest book, which would be entitled *Corridors of Power*, and give its name to the future television series based on his Lewis Eliot sequence. 'Here I am,' Pamela wrote, 'alone with Conchita & the cat in ten rooms. [...] There is a sort of brief pleasure in loneliness that is wonderful, but after a little of it a quiet little madness seeps in, from one's wrists along all the veins.'

More than a little madness was now happening in the Caribbean in the form of the Cuban missile crisis. Pamela found herself in the position of having to comfort others terrified of the possible escalation into a nuclear war; these included her remaining aunt, Emma, her new housekeeper, Conchita, and Susan Hill, now an undergraduate at King's College, London, who told her that all her fellow-students had stopped work as they felt '"this was it"'. Telephoning from Hove, CPS was hardly reassuring, since he told her he was sure that there would be an American invasion of Cuba 'no matter what conciliatory moves are made'. Not surprisingly, Pamela spent, she wrote, 'a depressed, lonely evening, & no wonder. This is a poor time to be alone.' She was nevertheless dreading having to fulfil an arrangement to spend the weekend at Cliveden, doubtless thinking that her hosts and their guests were likely to be hawks rather than doves.

Her mind momentarily reverted to her own concerns when she composed 'a more than vigorous reply' to an article by Stephen Spender in *The Listener* (25 October 1962), which she felt had quoted her 'badly out of context', and had added what she now felt was becoming habitual, 'a statutory sneer at Charles'. 'I thoroughly enjoyed the exercise', she wrote, 'I feel far happier when I am allowed to fight.' Spender had included a lengthy quotation from Pamela's chapter on literature in the inter-war years in a collection of essays, edited by John Raymond, *The Baldwin Age* (1950). The concept of this book had been to offer a mixture of essays on the political and social background of that period, together with surveys of the influence, if any, of the former on the contemporary arts. It is generally accepted that modernism became the dominant mode in literature during the first part of the period under discussion, and that this, as Pamela put it, meant an emphasis on experimentation 'in verbal and oral techniques', while: 'What shrivelled away in their work was any contact between man and society.' However, Spender made her seem reactionary by omitting to quote an intervening paragraph in which she had said:

> No-one in their senses is going to decry what Virginia Woolf and James Joyce did for the novel, and the enrichments they brought to it. Virginia Woolf made it *obligatory* to see, and James Joyce *obligatory* to hear.[17]

Pamela's letter, duly published the following week, pointed out that her essay had been 'tightly reasoned, and to mutilate it as Mr Spender had done verges, to say the least of it, upon irresponsibility'. She also could not resist countering the impression that Spender might have given that, in her essay, Pamela's assessments of James Joyce's *Ulysses* and *Finnegans Wake* had been that they had been 'mere "experiments", whose discoveries have been usefully absorbed into the novels of C.P. Snow', whereas she had not mentioned CPS at all in her survey. She characterized Spender's misleading and gratuitous 'tilt' at her husband as being 'simply mob-fashion, like the Oxford bags of one generation or the beehive hairdos of another', and ended with some, one feels, less than sincere sentiments: 'I would deprive no one of his civilian uniform, if it makes him feel cosier among his friends, but I must say I am surprised to see Mr Spender wearing it.' As was to be expected, Spender responded (about which, further later), but, in the intervening week, a far more serious crisis had arisen in the life of the Snows.

CPS's eyesight had been continuing to deteriorate, causing him to return earlier than planned from Hove, which had, at least, given Pamela a reason to cancel her weekend at Cliveden, but she took little comfort from this. He was told that a further immediate operation was the only option if sight in his left eye was to be saved, and the night before the operation, she bitterly reflected on:

> the layabout spite which has chased him this year – the purely fashionable sniping, from people who have never done a thing to help their country out of its growing slumminess [...], the 'Establishment' crowd, the 'Private Eye' mob, as destructive as weevils & as useful.

CPS had urged her not to cancel her commitment to broadcast for 'The Critics' the next day, so she went to Broadcasting House as usual. At the pre-programme lunch, she received a potentially devastating phone call from his specialist, telling her that CPS's heart had stopped for several minutes towards the end of the operation, that external massage had been unsuccessful, but that he had been able to restart the heart by 'opening it up'. By the time she arrived at Moorfields, CPS was only just conscious, but sufficiently to be suspicious about her early arrival, since he had not been told that an emergency procedure had been necessary. The surgeon wanted Pamela to make the decision as to whether CPS should be told the full story, and she responded that her husband was no fool, and would soon notice that his chest was covered in bandages. When back in his room and fully conscious, CPS, the non-believer, gleefully told his ever-religion-questioning wife: '"I'll tell you what happens on the other side.

Nothing"'. In her state of enormous relief, she was happy to have merely responded that 'this was no time to discuss theology' (*Important*, p.220).

CPS regained peripheral vision in his left eye which restored his sense of balance and was soon, as Pamela recorded, 'in high old form', while she, irrationally, she felt, found herself frequently crying uncontrollably, and trying to conceal this from him. She was grateful that, on this occasion, the press had been 'decent' in reporting the trauma. Stephen Spender did not withhold a reply to her letter in the *Listener*, but clearly moderated his tone. While attempting to justify his criticism of her essay, he denied having 'joined some mob in tilting at C.P. Snow', and concluded:

> May I, at the risk of seeming impertinent, add that personally I feel sympathy and admiration for Miss Johnson and C.P. Snow, and that I am really sorry that my disagreement with Miss Johnson in a matter of literary reputations should have appeared at a moment which must be most trying to her [...].

There would be one further published letter from each beginning with almost flirtatious civilities and ending without yielding from their fixed positions. Pamela: 'I dislike quarrelling with Mr Spender, either in public or in private, but I do not propose to be tripped up by the brand-new banana-skins he has now laid down for me [...]'; Spender: 'Terrifying as it is to break another lance with Miss Pamela Hansford Johnson and not only be routed, but, to boot, unmasked for want of chivalry, may I, with the utmost gentility, question her flat assertion [...]'. The Editor of the *Listener* did not, after this exchange, have to print the standard declaration: 'This correspondence is now closed.'

Soon afterward, Pamela was determined to fulfil a long-standing engagement to speak, not to a literary audience, but to a group of scientists, the X-Ray Analysis Group of Institute of Physics, on a subject of her choice. Bravely, she resolved to discuss the Snow-Leavis affair from the perspective of a writer with only vestigial scientific knowledge. She called her lecture '1½ Cultures', and, according to her diary, 'by dint of benzedrine', she had prepared by getting herself to the hairdresser that morning and sketching some notes for the talk there, which she had typed up in the afternoon. The typescript has fortunately been preserved, and is evidence of her fluency in speaking on an unfamiliar subject with brief notes. She analysed the responses of rage to CPS's Rede Lecture, from both the literary and scientific sides, incorporating a not-too-subtle reference to Leavisites as representatives of the former: 'A certain section who really hated science and technology, harking back wistfully to a cloud cuckoo land that never was, full of jolly peasants and chortling craftsmen.'[18] Having declared that, as much as she longed to know more about 'the wonder that is going on about me', she admitted that 'perhaps to set $1\frac{1}{8}$ cultures as my own ambition might be more modest and more just'. She concluded with an appeal to the scientists in the audience to bear 'with the literary stumblers, blunderers, bunglers, even the hopelessly inept, and try to help them on', and to make a reciprocal effort, 'of course, to read their books.' She was delighted with the reception of her talk, which she deemed to have been 'really a great success'.

Life began to take an even keel. For the time being, CPS was far more frequently at home, and joined Pamela in evenings of Scrabble or 'looking in', at the wide range of programmes she classified as 'unintellectual, but soothing', from show-jumping to 'Z-Cars'; they also had a penchant for Benny Hill whom she had described on first seeing as being 'repulsive, but [with] <u>what</u> an ear, & what insights!', but later as 'a minor genius of the ineffably soppy'. CPS accompanied her on a shopping trip to Harrods where she was 'much tempted by a Siamese kitten', and, to her delight, he encouraged her to go back the following day to buy it. It was some time since they had had two cats in the house, but the new arrival, Sirikit, soon won over the incumbent feline, Skippy. Fortunately, Conchita was also a cat-lover and was happy to look after them in the Snows' frequent absences. From her childhood, cats as family pets had always been so essential to Pamela that one wonders why they do not feature in her novels, or in a chapter about them in *Important to Me*. Before long, however, Pamela's health concerns turned back toward herself; she was aware that 'this year's miseries & anxieties have played hell with me', and accounted for her greatly increased usage of cigarettes. On the first day of her resolve to cut down, she recorded smoking 'only 21 (with a great effort) as against a ghastly total, some days, of as much as <u>60</u>'. For a while, she aimed to maintain her total per day at around twenty, although she found it far harder when she went to social gatherings, when the total crept back up towards thirty.

As the year came to an end, a serious problem surfaced within CPS's long-standing group of friends, but this was one matter which he deliberately withheld from Pamela, who had decided to put all the problems of 1962 behind them by throwing a grand New Year's Eve party. Despite freezing temperatures, this was attended by fifty-one people, not including the family. Andrew Stewart remembers that around this time, one of the society magazines, possibly, he says, *The Tatler*, listed his mother as one of London's leading hostesses. The list of notable guests includes evidence of her forgiving nature as Rayner Heppenstall and his wife were among those present (although her magnanimity on this occasion did not extend to past guest Daniel George nor to John Wain, Robert Conquest or Bernard Levin). Pamela delightedly recorded that the party had been 'most gay & successful'.

The scandal CPS had decided to conceal from Pamela was the not altogether unexpected nemesis awaiting his good friend and the best man at their wedding, Bert Howard. The Snows had continued to see him throughout the intervening years; he was still living in Leicester, and teaching at Alderman Newton's, although he had not, as he and his coterie had hoped, become headmaster of the school when the post had become vacant. Howard often visited them in London, was invited to their large parties, and occasionally joined the family for a few days of their European holidays. CPS had often sent news about Howard in his letters to his brother Philip in Fiji, who had also known him well, despite being ten years younger than the original group. Philip Snow Snr. told me of his firm belief that the relationship between Bert and the young CPS had been 'nothing other than an intellectual friendship [...], the great stimulus that Charles needed, and utterly innocent'. However he admitted that eventually Bert had had 'non-platonic friendships with boys at the school, and unwisely one of these boys was the son of a warder at Leicester Prison'.[19]

It would seem that, of Howard's friends beyond Leicester, it was J.H. Plumb who was first informed of an impending arrest. He immediately contacted CPS, whose response was made clear in the following telegram, sent on 28 December 1962:

[...] DONT WISH TO INVOLVE PAM STOP [...] WILL SUPPORT ANY STEPS YOU THINK NECESSARY = CHARLES.[20]

Fortunately Pamela was never to become aware that CPS's first thought had been one of concealment from his wife, or this matter might have led to another crisis of confidence about their relationship, although another instance of distress caused to her by the secretive side of his nature was not far away. CPS's motive here cannot be ascertained, but he achieved his objective by ensuring that all correspondence between himself and Plumb regarding Bert Howard's predicament was henceforward sent from and to English Electric. On the day of the Snows' big end-of-year party, CPS took time to go to his office to reply more fully to Plumb, describing the situation as 'heartbreaking', but agreeing with him that 'recrimination is useless, and the only help is practical'. They considered some form of medical intervention, but CPS said that whereas he was sure that their friend, the psychiatrist Anthony Storr,[21] would be willing to offer some assistance, he doubted that the opinion of any 'respectable doctor' would be of any use, continuing: 'It isn't the kind of sexual truth that attracts sympathy, even from worldly & tolerant people.' The solution he advocated was that they should get Howard 'abroad at once'.[22] For some time, the friends dithered about the right course of action, but with the police about to bring charges against Howard, it was agreed that exile was the only possible solution. Even then, CPS did not tell Pamela about the part he had played in arranging this, nor to Howard's actual offences; it was left to his brother to come to see her in April with the 'horrifying' (if deliberately inaccurate?) news 'that poor old Bert was taken up for importuning', although he believed, he told her, that 'no charges would be preferred'. An asterisk to that day's diary entry noted: 'All the same, he has had to leave the country. Poor George Passant!!' She fretted about the prospect of Bert wandering around the continent, 'ageing & ill & quite unable to take care of himself, till he dies'.

Pamela's sympathies frequently extended also to people whom she scarcely knew, and had been aroused early in the New Year when Hugh Gaitskell, then leader of the Labour Party, had become seriously ill. She had been outraged by a 'revolting item' about him in the television programme, *That Was the Week That Was*, which had reinforced her opinion of this form of humour. She commented: 'There is something so sick, & so brutal, & so insanely callous in much of this "satire" that it reminds one of the last days of the Weimar Republic.' When

Gaitskell subsequently died 'after a terrible 15 days' struggle for life', she strongly identified herself with his wife, Dora, who, she said, had endured for that length of time, what she herself had suffered, during CPS's eye operation, for merely an hour before his miraculous recovery. Gaitskell had been, she wrote, 'a decent and honourable man: & everything that life would almost certainly have brought has been snatched from him.' She had no idea at that time that the consequent election of Harold Wilson to the leadership would impact significantly on her family's life.

Much of 1963 for the Snows was again taken up by protracted over-seas tours, two to the USA and one to the USSR. The first American visit passed with little incident; Pamela's usual lack of enjoyment was tempered on this occasion by the fact that it enabled her to spend time with her daughter who was now attending college in Williamsburg, Virginia. (Pamela was disappointed that Lindsay's romance with Alfred Harrison had come to an end, as she thought of him as her 'darling boy'.) Back at home, in March, she was initially mildly intrigued by the newspaper reports about a 'missing model, Miss Christine Keeler, the disappearing witness in a knifing case against a Jamaican', who, it was said in one tabloid, 'had been giving a 'spec-tacle' at Cliveden, attended by Bill Astor & John Profumo, <u>dressed up as policemen</u> & blowing whistles'. 'This probably explains (if true)', she wrote in her diary, 'the mysterious claim of Bill that he feels himself like George Passant', adding: 'I must say <u>our</u> bleak weekends at Cliveden aren't like that – C. says "Thank God they aren't [...]"'. When Profumo made his notorious speech of denial in the House of Commons, Pamela thought far too much was being made of the matter: 'It is hard to be hounded as that poor chap is being for – if true – something basically <u>absurd</u>.' It was, of course, the osteopath Stephen Ward, with whom she had had that brief acquaintance, who was to be the more 'hounded'.

Presumably in an attempt to compensate for the Leavis affair, CPS had been invited that spring to give the annual Richmond Lecture at Downing College; he had accepted, and to Pamela's relief, his talk entitled 'Education and Sacrifice' passed by without controversy, and had an excellent reception. 'Now it is over', she wrote, 'I think there must be some lighter hearts & soothed consciences around here. Many people <u>must</u> have felt ashamed.' She herself showed little charity

towards their erstwhile adversary when she spotted F.R. Leavis in a
Cambridge street, 'looking more derelict than I could possibly have
imagined'. 'When he realised we were behind him,' she gleefully
continued, 'he literally took to his heels & RAN. What could he have
thought we were going to do to him, silly little man?'

With no prior knowledge, the Snows had been surprised to read
newspaper reports that CPS was to be offered an honorary doctorate
(in Philological Sciences) at Rostov-on-Don, evidently at the insti-
gation of Mikhail Sholokhov. Pleased as they were at this, they were
also aware of an increasing literary clamp-down in Russia which
threatened Yevtushenko and others. 'One hopes for them', Pamela
wrote, 'to make a society in which there is so much to be admired that
the idea of a really "peaceful coexistence" is possible, & back they seem
to go again.'

Nevertheless, she looked forward to their visit to Russia with greater
anticipation than to their impending second visit to the USA, in
respect of which CPS had presented her with a 'grotesque schedule',
about which they had a furious row; the only compensatory feature of
this timetable, as she then saw it, was that it included her receiving
her first honorary degree, from Temple University, Pennsylvania. She
had been smarting for some time about being overlooked while CPS
had so frequently been honoured in this way. It was not to be until
nearly twenty years after his brother's death, that Philip Snow revealed
that their gruelling US schedules throughout the 1960s and 1970s had
indeed been primarily motivated by CPS's delight in accumulating
honorary degrees from each university he visited. 'Their fascination for
him,' he said, 'cannot be understood if it is not accepted that he hoped
to set a record in the number collected and variety of places in which
he had been given them, 30 in all and one posthumously.'[23]

One of the drawbacks of the schedule was that they would be away
on the opening night of *The Masters*, the latest of Ronald Millar's
adaptations of CPS's novels. Accordingly before they left, they went
to the play's first night of its pre-West End try-out at the Hippodrome,
Golders Green. Pamela, on this occasion, praised John Clements in
the role of Lewis Eliot, was generally thrilled with the play's reception, and was particularly touched by the audience clapping CPS as
they returned to their seats after the first interval. 'If this doesn't go
in London', she declared, 'the London Theatre is sick & silly.' Two

weeks later in New York, as they perceived what seemed to them to be silence from the London critics, who were likely inevitably to be less partisan than Pamela, CPS became sure that the play had flopped, and was 'as low' as she had seen him for years. But fortunately the delay had only been caused by their miscalculation of the day on which first reviews would appear; the play was generally deemed to be the most successful of the series, and would run for more than two hundred performances. Typically, however, on their return, CPS singled out a less favourable review in *Queen* as a target for his fury; loyal Pamela commented that Jocelyn Stevens, the proprietor of the magazine, was 'really like a small time gangster with a peevish delinquent past'. The unsigned review was not quite, however, the 'vicious attack' that CPS made out. Although it did contain phrases like 'cliché-capsule contrivance of the middle-brow stage', the reviewer did admit that 'having begun by thinking in the first act "who cares who wins this boring waxwork election?", you are willy-nilly caring and enjoying John Clements' brilliant performance as a waxwork'.[24]

Pamela had not similarly attempted to find out how her latest novel, *Night and Silence Who is Here*, had fared on publication but waited until she returned home. The reviews of the second book in what became the Dorothy Merlin trilogy had in fact been relatively good. The poetess herself barely makes an appearance in this novel; she is just the raison d'être for Matthew Pryar's sojourn in the fictional Cobb College since he has managed to be invited to be a Visiting Fellow there on the basis of being a world authority on her *oeuvre*, which, as he reflects, consisting as it does 'of twenty shortish poems and four slim verse-dramas' was not a demanding task (p.13). The permanent staff and students at Cobb are all well-meaning whereas eccentricity and some ineffectual plotting are left to the other Visiting Fellows. Since Matthew is such an agreeable protagonist compared with Daniel Skipton, the narrative has none of the dark tones of the first Merlin novel. Far from leaving the central character near-death and in a state of total ignominy, the dénouement of this sequel involves a reverse-gender Cinderella transformation to ensure a happy ending. The character of Jane Merle, the multi-millionairess Princess Charming was, as Pamela readily admitted, based on her friend Brooke Astor, and Matthew on Alan Pryce-Jones, whom she had soon forgiven for his mock interview of 'Sir James and Olivia' under the name of 'George

Cloyne'. (She had had frequent pleasurable encounters with him at literary parties but he had now moved to New York. At a dull dinner-party, shortly after his departure, Pamela had found herself longing 'for AP-J or needlewits of that class'.)

The novel tended to get recommended as by Anthony Cronin in the *Times Literary Supplement* as being so 'light-hearted' that 'if it some-times seems like holiday writing, [it] would at least make good holiday reading'. Karl Miller in the *New Statesman*, discussing the novel, in conjunction with other American campus novels, as being 'an efficient airy burlesque', did pay it a little more respect by praising it for being 'pleasantly eclectic as between the neighbourly traditions of the British and American academic novel', and adding that: 'It also adds a bit to the stock of pertinent criticism of the humanities. Research is made richly and revealingly comic.' In his *Punch* review, Malcolm Bradbury, obviously having suffered from the same difficulties in the USA as the Snows, explained reasons for his enjoyment:

> The plot really turns on the absence in this rich American campus of food and service, and the stratagems the English must get up to to secure them. Clearly this is deeply felt, and this, certainly, is a true observation about American academic life.

Scribners, Pamela's American publishers, took out a half-page advertisement in the *New York Times* Book Review to announce that:

> One of the most gifted of literary Englishwomen offers a wonderfully inventive comedy about a British bachelor who enters an academic community in New Hampshire as a visiting fellow. With Wodehouse-like skill, she leads him through a tangle of domestic problems and complications with eccentric colleagues to create a sharply satiric, yet affectionate, sketch of the American scene.

'It is greatly to the credit of the Americans' sporting-spirit – never lacking – ', Pamela later wrote, 'that *Night and Silence Who is Here?* had the best critical reception, in some places, rapturous, that I have ever had on that continent' (*Important*, p.112).

Her portrayal of American academic life might however have been less benign if written after their second visit to the USA in 1963. For once, there had been no lack of alcohol on the campuses visited, although Pamela did complain about the 'barbarous US habit of sousing rather hard before dinner & then nothing for the rest of the evening, which consequently gets a dying fall to it'. As it happens, she then quixotically criticized her hosts in Philadelphia because 'they give one drinks far too sizable'. CPS had been insistent that they must stay, as invited, with Violet and Arthur Ketels, and she had agreed 'unwillingly'. The Ketels had been adapting CPS's *Time of Hope* for the stage, and it was about to be tried out in Philadelphia, prior to a Broadway production. Pamela had seen an early draft of the script, which she had deemed 'execrable', and quite evidently did not share CPS's enthusiasm in particular for their hostess. Pamela's distrust of Violet, whom she described as 'a very beautiful oppressive woman', would seem to have been well-founded. CPS later boasted to Donald Dickson that, as his literary reputation flourished, women were more attracted to him, particularly in America, and that his fame over there rested in the hands of intelligent well-to-do women. He then specifically mentioned Violet Ketels, as an example of the latter, saying that she had remained 'an admirer over the years'.[25]

On the day on which Pamela received her Hon. D.Litt, at Temple University, she wrote in her diary that 'there have been distresses over this which have spoiled my pleasure in my degree. Very odd thing. Life is, & often seems to be, directed by a sadistic lunatic.' She confided later to Kathleen Farrell:

> I duly got my degree from Philadelphia and stood there all robed, with mortar board, [...] feeling like a tart who had gone to her wedding in white. It gave me huge pleasure at the time, but very fleeting.[26]

It seems likely that she had at some point been given reason to believe that her first honorary degree had been negotiated between CPS and Violet, in the latter's capacity as Professor in the English Department at Temple, to ensure that they visited them. If there had been any such plotting between the two to have clandestine meetings, the rehearsals for the play, which neither Pamela nor Arthur Ketels attended, would have proved a useful alibi (CPS and Violet absented themselves on this pretext immediately after the degree ceremony). Pamela certainly continued to be distraught, writing the following day:

> I haven't, for years, felt so much that I would be glad to die. It is as though years & years of closeness & comradeship have been swept away.

<u>Cannot</u> imagine why he misled me over this business. Yet, yet, yet – life has to go on. And love isn't love that alters – etc. But wept in the night.

The Snows left Philadelphia shortly afterward for a brief stay with Brooke Astor on her Rhinebeck estate before returning home. Rhinebeck, with its magnificent views of the Hudson River, was the retreat that Pamela had come to think of as 'an angst-reducing house', but nevertheless on this occasion, she felt that she had 'too much angst to reduce'. The one ray of happiness in her life at the time came with a communication about her elder son, who had just taken his finals: 'Found Andy had a FIRST!!! Truly delighted by this.'

No sooner was her eldest child evidently firmly on a career path than Pamela became worried about her daughter's education; she wasn't certain if she could afford the fees for the remainder of Lindsay's college course (she was always determined to give any necessary financial support to the children of her first marriage without recourse to CPS). As it happened, Ralph Maud, from the State University of New York at Buffalo, had visited her the previous year to talk about Dylan Thomas in connection with a book he was proposing to write, and she had shown him their correspondence in the 1930s. He had then excitedly contacted Oscar Silverman, the Director of Libraries at SUNY to suggest that they should try to acquire these, plus her diaries of the years of their friendship. He valued the collection in that letter at a minimum of $20,000 (approximately £6,000) since:

They are long, long revealing letters. Many of them from Swansea when Dylan was doing the Notebooks we have – talking about the poems in the Notebooks; then some after he and Pamela had fallen in love.

Without discussing any specific figure for a possible sale, Pamela had then said that she might consider selling the letters at some future time. While he could not have known about her current financial problem, Maud timed a renewed approach to her very advantageously. There was a letter from him that month, pointing out that: 'Buffalo certainly has the most substantial Dylan Thomas MSS collection in the world, most of the stuff sold by Dylan personally at a time when others were not interested in taking such risks!' He then however mentioned 'the round figure of £3,000 for the whole – or let's say a slightly more favourable round figure of $10,000'.[27] This letter was swiftly followed by a formal offer of this amount from Oscar Silverman.[28] Unfortunately, Pamela didn't haggle or the Library might well have increased the offer to nearer Maud's original valuation. As it was, she had some misgivings, later, it will be seen, to be justified, about selling the letters at all, but at the time, she came to the conclusion that: 'Think I shall have to sell, to pay L's fees. Don't <u>think</u> Dylan would mind.'

On their return from America, Pamela had been disgusted to see that the trial of Stephen Ward, on charges of procuring in connection with the Profumo affair, appeared to be taking precedence in the news-papers over the nuclear test ban talks in Moscow, the latter being, in her opinion, 'the great hope of our years'. When the talks resulted in what she described as 'a wonderful breakthrough, however limited', they both rejoiced: 'C & I feel we have played some tiny part, at some cost to ourselves, in helping to get the right atmosphere for this.' She found the press coverage of the Ward case abysmal as it utilized 'the full panoply of squalid sensation [...] with pictures of Mandy & Christine looking like bad little cats', but she was nevertheless saddened a few days later to read of the suicide of Stephen Ward following his conviction on two out of five counts:

> He had been stretched too far upon the 'rack of this rough world', & death is too high a price to pay for goatishness in the service of the rich. [...] Now, of course, we shall have lynching articles in the lower press on all the wretched girls, & howls of moral indignation from the unloved. But one is sorry for the unloved, too. V. hard to be compassionate all the time – wish I were.

Yet another of their August summer family holidays proved unsatisfactory; the party was reduced to Pamela, CPS, and their son Philip (now usually referred to in her diaries as 'Pops', 'Borox' having been dropped in favour of an abbreviation of another early childhood nickname, Philipopsky). It might be ungenerous to suggest that their decision not to go to Belgium or elsewhere in Europe that year could have been prompted by the desire to avoid a meeting, either by chance or by invitation, with Bert Howard, now living in exile in Holland, not all that far away from Le Coq, but, for whatever reason, they had chosen instead, for the first time, to visit Ireland. They stayed in what turned out to be 'a gloomy hotel on a loch' in Mulranny, County Mayo, and the weather that blighted so many of their holidays followed them there. The first week was bad enough; CPS spent the time writing around a thousand words per day, leaving Pamela feeling 'desperately lonely', despite appreciating the comfort that 'Pops' tried to give her. In the second week in Mulranny, the weather passed 'from the horrible to the unspeakable. Dashing gales, pouring rain, cold, white horses on the bay.' Evenings in the bar were 'funereal', but, in any case, Pamela was suffering so badly from migraine that she had to limit alcohol to a minimum. Her migraine attacks were becoming so frequent that she listed them at the end of that year's diary.

There would be some compensation to be had from the weather experienced by the three of them on a comparatively short visit to Stratford the following month; the day they arrived was 'a most wonderful blue, sparkling, warm day, smelling of autumn flowers, & with all the colours blazing', although Pamela was critical of the acting again that season. Despite experiencing 'another golden, blue, glossy day' and a 'magical walk by the river with P. after dinner, with swans floating home to bed, gleaming phosphorescent gold in lights from theatre', she continued: 'I am in one of my lonely fits – "and your Indian summer's done" – to paraphrase.[29] But if only I could come to terms with the fact that it is!!'

Within a fortnight, Pamela and CPS left to fulfil their engagements in the USSR. On their first visit, they had not travelled much beyond Moscow and St. Petersburg; their itinerary this time could, like that of their recent US visit, have been labelled 'grotesque', but in this case Pamela had no personal cause for such recrimination. It involved visits to many university cities at which they both gave talks, plus television, radio and press interviews. She was glad, however, that time was allowed for a visit to Yasnaya Polyana, Leo Tolstoy's family home, which she found 'deeply impressive & touching'. In the grounds, albeit followed by intrusive television cameras, she and CPS walked to the 'tiny little mound' which was the author's grave, and laid flowers there.

They arrived in Rostov at the end of the first week, to be greeted by the mayor, the rector of the university and a delegation of writers, but Mikhail Sholokhov was not among the latter, nor was he present the following day when CPS received the honorary degree which had been the main purpose of their visit. Pamela was amused with the gift he then received; it was 'a complete Cossack uniform: cap, boots, *burka* – an immense sheepskin cape, designed to cover not only oneself but one's girl-friend, when eloping with her on horseback across the Steppes' (*Important*, p.164). Sholokhov's absence had not surprised the other dignitaries in Rostov; they had explained that he preferred to keep open house 'among his Cossacks' in 'his extraordinarily palatial house in Veshenskaya', the small village in which he had been born into a peasant family (*Important*, p.162). The day after the ceremony, the whole party duly travelled the 200-odd miles to stay at Sholokhov's home on the Don, where Pamela revised her original critical opinion of Zhenya, as she learned to call their host. The Snows, fond of entertaining guests as they themselves were, became overwhelmed by the hospitality offered. The party ate, and drank after proposing toast after toast, all afternoon and evening; Pamela had to admit defeat and go to bed at least an hour before the men.

Breakfast the next day, with similar amounts of alcohol to accompany further speeches and toasts, lasted for three hours. CPS was then asked to don his Cossack uniform and pose for a photograph with a horse. The animal proved to be terrified of the burka, so would have been useless in its traditional role; Pamela had to hold the reins to calm it. Her brief notes on the last day of their stay convey the general frenetic atmosphere of life at the dacha: 'Constant comings and goings. Views of Don as necessary as views of Hudson! Earth road. Cars drive over fields. Planes land on grassy sand.' After more days of literary events in Moscow, they left Russia for Hungary. Pamela found Budapest enchanting: 'After Moscow, it is a glory to the eyes.'

While they were away, Harold Macmillan had left 10 Downing Street. (It is generally believed that his resignation was the result of poor health, brought on by the stress of the Profumo affair, having been misdiagnosed as a terminal illness.) Politics aside, the Snows had always been great admirers of his; their books had, by then, been published by the family publishing house of Macmillan for many years, and they had met on many occasions, even though Harold Macmillan had not played an active role in the company since achieving ministerial status. With a general election due the following year, there was much speculation as to the outcome. Alec Douglas-Home had succeeded Macmillan as Prime Minister, but Pamela thought 'that

Home's brand of fla-fla is not what the country needs'. After dining with Harold Wilson, CPS told her that the opinion of the leader of the Labour Party was even more dismissive; Wilson had declared that Home was 'suffering from wild conceit & euphoria'.

But then the event occurred that marked 1963 in the memory of all alive at the time, resulting, as Pamela wrote, in a realization that: 'None of the trivia of our own day seems to matter.' Watching with CPS 'an idiotic "Quiz" programme', the broadcast was interrupted to announce the shooting of John Fitzgerald Kennedy. Pamela continued: 'We both felt stunned in an almost literal sense. The awful tragedy for his wife – the uncertainty for the world. He might have been a great President. [...] Can't feel that a more bitter blow could have hit any of us, any of the nations. Now where?' She also grieved, the following day, at the news of the deaths of two authors she had much admired, Aldous Huxley and C.S. Lewis. Even after the funeral of JFK ('a great, heartbreaking mess'), she felt discussion of the assassination was becoming for her, as well as for others, 'a drug addiction. I get so tired of it these days & can't stop.'

The year had begun for the Snows with a concealed scandal (which remained so, with the death at this time of Bert Howard in Hilversum) and towards the end of the year, they joined a large Christmas house-party in the location of the notorious public scandal. Pamela's son, Andrew, was invited with them for a weekend in Cliveden, where he remembers Lord Astor seeming 'not unreasonably, to be much demoralised', while Pamela described her host as being 'as much like a nervous lizard as ever', but his wife, the former model Bronwyn Pugh, had been calm, cheerful and welcoming. Pamela was nevertheless always less than impressed by their visits to the sumptuous Italianate mansion, complaining on this occasion that it had been the 'usual tedium', made worse by the guests having to eat according to the Astors' latest dietary fad, which involved 'no bread & masses of <u>fat</u>', although there had been 'a bit more to drink – slightly'. She couldn't resist recording an awkward moment when the local carol singers, invited to perform in the great hall, launched into 'Good King Wencelas'; she commented that the 'line about "On the Feast of Stephen" sounded slightly embarrassing, all things said – and done.'

With no reviewing commitments and no work of her own in hand, Pamela spent much of December re-reading her husband's books.

Despite her mid-year unhappiness about their relationship, her belief in him as a writer did not waver. Re-reading *The Masters* again, she proclaimed:

> It is superb, & I have no doubt about C's work. This is a great series, & The Masters is among the finest novels in the English language of this century. Most of C's foes, of course, haven't read him.

CHAPTER 17

Pamela the Crusader,
Part One

B Y THE MID-1960s, Dylan Thomas's erstwhile 'sweet, Rabelaisian Pamela' had become more and more critical of the dawn-
ing era of liberalism in the arts, often dated from the verdict in
favour of the publishers in the *Lady Chatterley* trial of 1960. She
expostulated both privately and publicly about what she saw as the
new obligation to include explicit discussions of sexual matters in
novels. Her (unpublished) verdict on Mary McCarthy's *The Group*
(1963), much-praised elsewhere, was that the 'vulgar' style of this
'most unfortunate novel' consisted of 'strained sexual giggling of a
peculiarly <u>female</u> sort (pessaries, breast-feeding, potty-training & the
rest)'.

Pamela was, of course, by no means alone in these feelings; an
instance regarding the work of a male novelist led to a debate, lasting
from November 1963 to January 1964, in the correspondence columns
of the *Times Literary Supplement*. The starting-point had been the publication of *Dead Fingers Talk*, the first novel by William Burroughs to
have been published other than by the Olympia Press in Paris. John
Willetts took the opportunity to include a retrospective assessment of
Burroughs's oeuvre to date, including his best-known work, *Naked
Lunch* (1959). Willetts's full-page article was detailed and well-argued,
but his overall opinion was conveyed by the briefest of headlines,
namely 'Ugh ...'. Edith Sitwell was the first to praise this 'very right-
minded review', followed by Victor Gollancz agreeing that Burroughs's
work was 'bogus-highbrow filth', the publication of which had
'proliferated horribly' ever since. Other correspondents defended

Burroughs, including, finally, Anthony Burgess, who apologized for his late contribution, occasioned by his having been unaware of any controversy, since he had not been in England, but spending some time in Tangier with the 'courteous, hospitable, erudite, gifted and dedicated writer' being vilified. Pamela scoffed to her diary at what she called an 'immortal line, symptomatic of our times' in Burgess's letter: 'The world of the country parsonage is not necessarily more wholesome than that of pederastic Morocco.'

When Samuel Beckett's *Endgame* and Joe Orton's *Entertaining Mr Sloane* were, in consecutive weeks, the plays under discussion when she was a panellist on 'The Critics', Pamela turned her attention to the trend towards overt portrayals of ugliness and obscenity in the theatre. She had found the former play 'ridiculous', and commented: 'When all critics fall for this kind of thing, they add another nail to the theatre's coffin. Dialogue either flat or flowery, & ideas footling.' When voicing a similar verdict on air, she had no support from the distinguished panel of her fellow-critics (Philip Hope-Wallace, John Gross, Roger Manvell, David Sylvester and Jack Lambert), whom she therefore dismissed as: 'Chorus-singers all'. Nevertheless when she heard the transmission of the programme, she thought her 'blast-off at Beckett' had sounded good. She saw *Entertaining Mr Sloane* with CPS and her daughter, and deemed it to be 'coarse, badly written, & beastly'. She also felt it 'beastly to hear a largely middle-aged audience tittering', and recorded that Lindsay had left after the second act. She stood by her judgment in the following week's 'terrible, if hilarious, "Critics" session':

> I went for <u>Mr Sloane</u>, all stops out, supported by [Roger] Manvell only
> – & v. slightly: at one point, when I asked whether they'd all enjoy a
> nice black comedy about Buchenwald, I literally reduced David
> Sylvester (drunk anyway) to a terrible, gobbling silence & the pro-
> gramme had to be stopped while he recovered. Am sure when I left
> them afterwards they all sat down to a hymn of hate. Oh, for the <u>desire</u>
> to sing chorus!

At the end of the final week of her 'Critics' stint (a far more amicable session), the producer's assistant gave her six letters of support from listeners unknown to her, and Pamela commented that it was: 'Nice not to feel alone.'

That year, Mary Whitehouse founded a 'Clean-Up TV' pressure group (to be renamed the Viewers' and Listeners' Association the following year), specifically campaigning against excessive portrayals of sex and violence on BBC television; however, she and Pamela never joined forces. Pamela was, however, heartened by a talk by Laurence Kitchin on violence in the arts, broadcast on the BBC's Third Programme (reprinted in the *Listener* on 16 July 1964). While giving examples of writing about violence in the past which could be deemed to have had literary merit, Kitchin lambasted the current 'tendency of all the arts [...] towards the short cut, violence for the kicks, towards immersion in the subject-matter rather than control of it'. Offering his credentials, he declared: 'After prolonged exposure to it as a theatre critic, a film critic, a reader, a television viewer and a devotee of painting, I find this kind of souped-up, subjective, amateur's violence a massive bore.'

Pamela wrote to the periodical in support of Kitchin's 'courageous' talk, and was delighted when her response headed the 'Letters to the Editor' page. Not only was 'the "amateur violence" of stage, cinema, books' a bore, she maintained, but it was also dangerous 'because familiarity breeds, not contempt, but *affectlessness* (the total incapacity to feel for another person). Far more of the horrors of our age have been caused by affectless persons than by sadists.' This was by no means a recent conclusion she had come to (her character, Sammy Underwood, in *An Error of Judgement*, could well be included in this category). She continued:

> It is no good comforting ourselves with the thought that no adult-minded person takes the more drivelling examples of violence in art seriously, audiences are not pre-selected, and the line between art and drivel is a finer one than most people care to think.

Later in the year, re-reading for pleasure the plays of George Bernard Shaw, which were rarely staged at that time, she reflected: 'What it must have been to go to the theatre & have an evening of sharp intellectual argument, instead of finding plays of the Absurd or the Moronic.' Eventually these concerns would lead her to the theme of her next novel.

Her younger son was in his penultimate year at his prep school, Cumnor House, where he had regularly been awarded the major prizes, and with some soul-searching because of their socialist principles, the Snows had made up their minds to send Philip to Eton, subject to the entrance examination which they had little doubt that he would pass. This would prove to be a controversial decision, but one that they believed was in the boy's best interests. (The three of them had made an exploratory visit to the college the year before, and the admissions tutor had been so impressed with Philip that he had then said: 'I'll make room for him if I have to vacate my own drawing-room.')

Throughout 1964, Pamela had health scares, although she did not know whether to ascribe these to 'Howson hypochondria'. She continued to have menopausal symptoms; her doctor prescribed tranquillisers. Her New Year resolution, yet again, to cut down smoking, didn't last through January; despite the 'dreadful strain' of reducing her consumption by ten cigarettes a day, she admitted: 'This leaves me, unhappily, still smoking 35!' Their month-long tour of the United States in May, flying between seven universities, was as arduous as ever, and further blighted for Pamela by a prolonged attack of conjunctivitis. As usual, her own engagements were at a lower level than those of CPS, but she did exhibit a wry sense of humour about these. Her lecture on Proust at Brandeis University, outside Boston, had been, she wrote, 'a Wesleyan experience' (she was, of course, referring to the university rather than to the Methodist theologian):

> No food, no drink. 25 people, 5 Proust scholars of infinite inadequacy, & one clever but horrid Italian boy. At conclusion of my lecture, an old lady got up, & asked what book I had been talking about.

The problem of lack of alcohol on campus got steadily worse as the Snows visited several universities in the South until, in a case of life imitating art, they had the good fortune to meet a Miss Hutchinson, a Chaucer scholar at Georgia State University in Atlanta, who had managed to accumulate a stash of Scotch and was generous in sharing it. This real-life visiting scholar bore a considerable resemblance to Pamela's fictional creation of the previous year, Dr Maud Groby, the Slavonic Languages scholar at 'Cobb University', who similarly comes to the rescue of Matthew Pryar. CPS's penultimate engagement was to give a lecture on world affairs at the Maxwell Air Force Base in Montgomery, Alabama, which was, to their surprise and delight, 'far from dry'; they even found Scotch and Bourbon awaiting them in their room. Pamela forgot her various ailments as she enjoyed 'a very cheerful day [...]. What a change after that particular bit of Bible Belt!' In New York at the end of their visit, as it happened, she met the originals of Jane Merle and Matthew Pryar together at a party. 'Brooke had been', she said, 'spectacular in puce & emerald, with all her emeralds on at once, plus a huge diamond bracelet. She is v. pleased with my book, & I think rather proud to be Jane Merle.' Pamela mused further: 'It is a little ungrateful of her not to marry Alan Pryce-Jones, in the interests of art.'

A three-week visit to the USSR in the summer presented a different set of problems, although Pamela's version as recounted in *Important to Me* once again glossed over adverse experiences. They travelled on this occasion with Philip, Lindsay, and Betty Linn Smith, an American college friend of the latter. It proved difficult to find activities which they could all enjoy, and Pamela suffered through taking the 'responsibility for lugging round this kind of party' on her own shoulders. One consolation was that there had been, of course, no problem for the grown-ups with regard to the hospitality offered on this trip being 'dry'; the reverse started as soon as their plane had touched down in Moscow in the form, she wrote, of a 'great drink-up at the airport that got me – me – distinctly stoned'. A dacha on the Don had been booked for them, but before they could get there, they were met by Sholokhov 'half-seas over already', who insisted on transporting them to his house for a 'wild, Dostoievskian evening'. 'Shan't forget termination', she told her diary, but not the readers of her memoir, 'when C., incapable, fell in the bath, Oksana & L. had to get him out, & L & I undressed him.' The next morning, however, she reported with some amazement, he woke 'as fresh & sweet as a daisy'. The dacha, an agreeable wooden cottage, was attached to a rest home for miners; unlike the services-free American campus accommodation, a cook and 'nice Edwardian maids' were in attendance on them. The main drawback there for Pamela, whose digestive system usually went haywire on these trips, was finding that there was only an outside lavatory which she instantly dubbed 'The Place of Horror'. She couldn't find her way to it at night, and rejected the offer of a pail in her bedroom, so had to resort to crouching outside, despite frogs jumping over her feet. She told CPS that she really now knew what 'penis envy' was, since it was so much easier for him in the 'damned bushes'. Their visit ended with an exhausting week of sightseeing, talks and meetings in Moscow. Her following day's diary entry simply read: 'HOME. Ah, home! Home! HOME!!!'.

But, for a while, there was little peace to be had at home, as *Corridors of Power* initially received very disappointing reviews. One of their young American friends visited them and announced with the 'air of one who brings delight', that he had heard that Arthur Schlesinger Jnr was going to review the novel on the whole front page of the *New York Times Book Review* (unusually, the US publication preceded the UK one). Schlesinger was an eminent historian who had been an advisor to President Kennedy, but Pamela was horrified by this news as she knew that CPS counted him among his bitterest enemies. 'C. was,' she wrote, 'as shocked & down as in the bad old days.' Schlesinger's review in fact occupied more than a page in the Saturday issue of the *NYT*; Orville Prescott's review in the *NYT Book Review* the following day did not appear on the front page and was rather more favourable. Schlesinger made some stinging observations about CPS's 'dogged and sententious' style, his 'poverty of charac-terization', and, most hurtfully, his 'faltering grasp' of the politics of the situation around which the plot of *Corridors of Power* revolves. Pamela's loyal reaction was:

> I never knew any man of such creative originality & range, who devoted years of his life (& mine) to the simple task of trying to get US & USSR not to drop ridiculous bombs on each other (for it is <u>horrible &</u> ridiculous) – who was so insensately persecuted by envious or stupid or paranoid men. There is no question in my mind that the S & B scenes will be a huge landmark in 20th C. lit. I love him more every day for his courage, & his kindness. So does everyone near to him.

In the belief that CPS was in such despair that he was in no mood to accede to her wish to have the 'precious, real holiday' in Venice on which they had agreed, Pamela offered to forgo this, but in the end, they went ahead. She took pleasure as always in visits to churches and art galleries in 'this adorable city', but on the visit to the Biennale to which Pamela had particularly been looking forward, her unhappiness about the state of the contemporary arts extended to the visual sphere. She described the British Pavilion as being 'a formaldehyde disgrace' (this in the year before Damien Hirst was born). Although Roger Hilton won that year's UNESCO Prize for his exhibit, she found his work and that of Gwythr Irwin 'boring & sterile beyond belief', and dismissed out of hand the 'gimmicky & vulgar' Pop Art of Joe Tilson.

The day of the 1964 General Election was headlined in Pamela's diary as 'A PREPOSTEROUS & WORLD SHAKING DAY'. She was initially most concerned with the 'sudden shocking disappearance of Krushchev', and his replacement by Brezhnev & Kosygin, which even took the Russian press by surprise (Izvestia, accordingly, failed to appear). Pamela's opinion of Krushchev was that he was 'a wonderful old man', and she was concerned that the change of government might have adverse consequences for their writer friends. Later, she became caught up in the drama of the British election results; it became clear that, if the Labour Party was to win, it would only be by a very small margin. The following day was one of 'unmitigated cephology', as they looked in at 'comments, results, predictions, for over eight exciting hours'. Harold Wilson's Labour government *was* to have an overall majority, but of four votes only.

There had been some speculation among CPS's friends as to whether he might be asked to join a Wilson administration; the English scholar and critic George Steiner had even told them of a transatlantic rumour that CPS might be offered the Embassy in Washington. Three days later, he was summoned to 10 Downing Street in the early evening, leaving Pamela, Lindsay and Conchita 'in a state of demented excitement'. *The Times* of the following day carried the following short report, headlined 'Mr Wilson picks new men for his team':

> Sir Charles Snow, the author and scientist, called on Mr Wilson last night. This visit, and the emphasis which Mr Wilson has always put on the need to promote more scientific research, suggests that one new Ministry may be concerned with the development of science and science-based industries.

Elsewhere in that edition of *The Times*, however, there is a report that Frank Cousins, the former General Secretary of the militant Transport and General Workers' Union, had been appointed Minister of Technology, and would have to fight an early by-election in order to enter the Commons. CPS, it emerged, had been asked, and had agreed, to become Cousins's Parliamentary Secretary; Pamela considered that Harold Wilson had been 'extremely considerate about not taking too much out of him'. CPS would not be required to stand for Parliament, as he would receive a life peerage. Pamela, who would of course remain 'Lady Snow', was not particularly thrilled by his elevation, although she did think that it would be fun for their son to be able to style himself the Hon. Philip Snow. Her pleasure lay in the fact that 'C. is irradiated by the pure <u>idea</u> of doing something that might be important for us all', although she did pessimistically add: '<u>Who will believe that?</u>'

Pamela's misgivings about the peerage were somewhat assuaged by the private jokes they incorporated in CPS's coat of arms. She wrote to her sister-in-law:

> We had a great afternoon's mummery at the College of Heralds. We were choosing our Coat of Arms (for which, by the bye, one pays through the nose). Shield: symbols of 2 Cultures, telescope crossed with pen. Supporters: 2 Siamese cats, because we love them, and because they pun on Colleges of Advanced Technology. [...] Motto: Aut Inveniam Viam Aut Faciam, [...] a motto I chose for myself when I was eighteen and have hung on to with adolescent romanticism.[1]

Nevertheless on the day that the peerage was gazetted, she was still ruminating about her husband's new name seeming 'commonplace' to her, on the grounds that '"C.P. Snow" is really something. "Sir Charles Snow" had an evocative, chivalric ring. But "Lord Snow"! How dull. It hardly seems like a name at all now.'

For a short time, the satirists were kept at bay; Pamela and CPS were both happy with a cartoon by 'Vicky' in the *Evening Standard*, which depicted Wilson, Cousins and CPS on the barricades, brandishing a banner with the slogan: 'Liberty, Equality, Technology'. There were, however, two attacks in the following week's *Private Eye*, and both mentioned Pamela in passing. (One slight concession was that she was always to be given her own name rather than an *Eye* sobriquet.) The first item was the more hurtful; it alleged that CPS had insisted on being in the Chair at a luncheon in honour of J.B. Priestley, in order to keep his name before the Nobel Prize allocators, and continued:

> The hosts, with misgiving, and in fear of ugly boredom, agreed. But things turned out well. By the time he got around to delivering the

big speech, the genial Snurd was inaudible. While the guests chattered among themselves, Snurd was heard trying to read out what he said was a letter from his wife, Pamela Hansford Johnson.[2]

The second item purported to be the first scene of a new play by C.P. Snurd, adapted by Ronald Millar, called *We Are the Masters Now*, in which Wilson's inner Cabinet welcomed their new recruit. It was spread over two full pages; the short extract below gives the flavour of the skit:

Enter C.P. Snurd, wearing a ridiculous academic gown and carrying 7,000 review copies of "Corridors of Power", the latest in his Strangers & Brothers saga.

BROWN: Welcome, brother!

SNURD: Hallo, Stranger! (He emits a cautious academic laugh.)

WILSON: Come in, Sir Charles, you're just the man we're looking for. As a corpulent old bore, you represent a symbol of the dynamic new Britain we are all going to build. [...] By some mischance we've been landed with Frank Cousins as Minister of Technology, and I was wondering if you, with your infinite knowledge of the popular view of science, would be willing to lend a hand.

SNURD: I suppose this'll mean a peerage?

WILSON: Of course, my dear fellow, of course.

SNURD: Lord Snurd of the Corridor is what Pamela suggested. [...][3]

The unfortunate (for Cousins & CPS) timing of the launch of another long-running satire programme, *Not So Much a Programme, More a Way of Life*, provided a platform for further attacks on the new Minister and his Parliamentary Secretary.

In these circumstances, on the British publication day of *Corridors of Power*, Pamela was greatly relieved to find that the novel seemed to be having a far better reception at home than it had had in America. The Sunday press, she wrote, had been 'absolutely <u>admirable</u>', and her 'dear love' was 'VERY happy'. Her continuing devotion to CPS, combined nevertheless with doubts about his reciprocation, is touchingly evident in her continuation:

Listened in to Lena Horne, a beautiful singer, & perhaps because of the joys & strains of the day, began to cry. Dear C. wrote me beautiful inscription in C. of P. Think he <u>must</u> love me – perhaps he always has. It is absurd to be so deeply in love at my age.

Subsequent press notices were not so favourable, and Pamela was particularly distressed by an 'unbelievably malignant and ugly' review in the *New Republic* by Malcolm Muggeridge, previously her fellow-reviewer on the *Daily Telegraph* and a man she had thought of as a friend. In his biography of Muggeridge, Richard Ingrams quotes the description of CPS, 'that so substantial figure, that huge moon face, unsmiling, portentous', in that review, as being 'the first of many pot-shots' at the same target by him, 'one of which memorably described Snow as "a kind of tragic clown of our times, stumbling Grock-like down his own phantom corridors of power"'. Yet Ingrams (echoing Ian Parsons on F.R. Leavis) maintains that 'Malcolm [...] felt no personal animus towards Snow [...]'.[4]

A few days after Muggeridge's review had appeared, watching *On the Braden Beat*, one of Pamela's favourite undemanding television programmes, remembered now principally for its consumer investigations, she was further grieved by the inclusion of 'a vicious "comedy" attack on C.', featuring Peter Cook, 'from the old P.E. & Establishment crowd'.[5] This seemed to Pamela to be another personal betrayal; she remembered their support of Bernard Braden, 'a man whom I've always liked & admired', when his controversial appointment as chairman of *The Brains Trust* had coincided with their first appearances on that programme. 'This is becoming a nightmare', she wrote, 'I could wish I lived in any age but this one of triviality & spite. These people are like body lice – one can feel them creeping over one.'

She turned to the comfort of writing another novel, one which, as mentioned above, would encompass her current concerns, but which would utilize the weapon of satire for her own ends. The book, *Cork Street, Next to the Hatter's*, became the third novel in the Dorothy Merlin trilogy; her speed of writing was as phenomenal as ever, amounting between 1,500 and 2,000 words per day in the first week. Nevertheless, she reflected:

> I haven't the insensate drive of <u>Skip</u> yet, or the delicate, even progress of <u>N & S</u>. It may, of course, be a different kind of book. It is a <u>roman à thèse</u>, which the others certainly were not. (Anyway, not <u>N & S</u>, which was meant purely to give pleasure.)

Sadly, Pamela's return to writing about Dorothy Merlin, the character who had initiated the Snows' warm relationship with Edith Sitwell,
coincided with the death of the latter. Pamela had continued to visit
her regularly, aware that her friend's health was failing. On the day
of Sitwell's death, Pamela remembered her on the last of those occasions, 'lying under an emerald bedcover [...] looking like a small green
mound in a graveyard'. She reflected that: 'She was a wonderful friend.
They say a terrible enemy: but here there was a touch of the paper
tiger. [...] C & I will miss her very much. She had some nonsense in
her make-up, but some real splendour.'

Despite Pamela's regular resolve not to throw huge parties, 1964
ended with 'the most enormous New Year's Eve party we've ever had'.
The guest list of 130 was a mixture of their friends and acquaintances
from the world of the arts with now a moderate sprinkling of
political figures. Thus, Anthony Wedgwood Benn might have found
himself in conversation with Sidney Nolan, Robert Boothby with
Marghanita Laski, or Lord Longford with Olivia Manning. The latter
with her husband, Reggie Smith, almost always accepted their regular
invitations to the Snows' parties, although she would afterwards relay
gossipy titbits to her Hampstead cronies, such as that the Snows were
becoming pretentious in employing a butler[6] (in fact, all the helpers
were students under the wing of both of them). Pamela's magnanimity was again displayed by the inclusion of Bernard Braden and
his wife Barbara Kelly as guests.

Throughout January of the following year, Pamela recorded with
sadness the progress of the final illness of Winston Churchill. After his
death, she wrote that: 'All England is Churchill, at present, rehearsals,
lying-in-state – enormous queues of people for Westminster Hall,
miles long, in the bitter cold.' Thanks to CPS's elevation to the peerage, the Snows were allotted seats for the funeral in Westminster
Abbey, positioned in an 'excellent position under the Dome, four paces
from everyone we wanted to see'. As mentioned earlier, Pamela had
had no political animosity towards the country's wartime Prime
Minister, and thus was not averse to attending the service but she
summed it up as being: 'A beautiful piece of drill, impressive, but to
me, not specially moving, except for "The Battle Hymn of the Republic".' The organization was less impressive at the end of the service,
when, as Pamela recorded, the major political figures, including a very

frail Clement Attlee, were left outside the Abbey, awaiting their official transport, and 'shivering in the dreadful wind'. She and CPS abandoned all hope of their own hired car finding them, and went home, frozen, on the Tube.

Christmas, a New Year party and a state funeral notwithstanding, Pamela completed *Cork Street, Next to the Hatter's* within two months. The 'thèse', to which she had referred, was an attack on the contemporary Theatre of Cruelty. Tom Hariot, a young lecturer in structural linguistics, who lives opposite the bookshop in Cork Street, owned by Dorothy Merlin's husband, is drawn somewhat unwillingly into the poetess's circle. In return for a favour, he asks her if she would like to accompany him to a play of her choice. Dorothy opts to see a play which 'critics had hailed as a comedy', the latter perhaps being misled by its title, *Good for a Giggle*. This had not been the reason for Dorothy's decision; she had read a review by a critic who had actually seen the play, and who had written: '"The dialogue hisses gloriously with spite, like a drop of water spilled on a red-hot stove."'[7] During the course of the play, Tom comes to the realisation that he and Dorothy are 'by no means thinking as one' about its merits or total lack of them (p.26).

As described by Tom, *Good for a Giggle* 'concerned three psychopathic siblings who lived with their old mother, who was deaf and dumb, in a suburb of Basildon New Town'. In the hope of regular sex, they take as lodger a psychopathic prostitute, but since she is a lesbian, whose specific mental disorder is gerontophilia, she makes advances to their mother rather to them. By the end of Act II, having made no headway with the mother, the prostitute has beaten her to death. In Act III, in Tom's resumé: 'Since all three siblings had always wanted to be hanged, each took a ritual jab at the corpse with a bread-knife to ensure this pleasurable outcome.' Tom has found the play appalling in every way, while Dorothy has been captivated by it, because she has found it '"so inconceivably *true*"'. Pamela obviously based the reaction of the majority of the remainder of those present on the tittering spectators observed when she had seen *Entertaining Mr Sloane*: 'The audience, which had a large admixture of clergymen and elderly ladies, was laughing obediently away with a puzzled expression on its collective face' (pp.26-27). Tom is so incensed by the experience that he decides to write a play himself, with such repellent

content that it would be impossible to stage. He consults his friend
Harold as to what might constitute the fulcrum of such a play, but
several of Tom's suggestions are dismissed on the grounds that 'something like that has been done before'. Eventually, Harold says:

> 'Ah – wait a minute. Do you remember my brother?'
> 'He was in the Far East somewhere, wasn't he?'
> 'He was a District Commissioner in Fiji. He used to try cases, as part
> of the job. There was a man and a goose.' (pp.43-44)

(This might have been another Snow family in-joke, as a reference to
a story possibly told by CPS's brother Philip about his days of
jurisdiction in the South Seas.) Anyway, Tom agrees that the central
character in his play should rape, and then ritually kill, a goose on
stage.

Nearing completion of the play, which is now, according to him,
'almost inconceivably nasty' (p.66), Tom reveals his plan to Dorothy
Merlin's circle, and, speaking clearly with Pamela's voice, explains his
motives to them: '"I am not reactionary. I do not wish to tighten
the censorship, or to do anything about it at all. It is not merely a
necessity, it does and must exist in some shape or form [...]. No, I
only want people to think about where the line that must be drawn
is to be drawn' (pp.72-73). Predictably, when Dorothy reads the
finished product, she declares that, whatever his intention might have
been, Tom had created 'a great, *true* work of art' (p.123), and insists
on showing it to theatre managements. To Tom's horror, a young
director rhapsodizes over the play and insists on staging it. Tom has
somewhat reluctantly to agree to use a property goose, rather than a
real one, the only change he will allow.

While in satiric mode, Pamela took the opportunity to turn the
tables on other targets, the first being gossiping 'friends'. Throughout the novel, Dorothy is suffering from an unidentified illness, and
at one point she goes to a publisher's party and blacks out after
drinking no more than two half-glasses of sherry:

> This had given rise to the rumour, which proliferated through the
> literary world like convolvulus in an untended garden, that she had
> become an alcoholic. The London literary world is no kinder and no
> crueller than other literary worlds in other capital cities, but it is
> remarkably homogeneous, and any good piece of gossip, however

implausible, can make the rounds completely in a matter of forty-eight hours.

Pamela was well aware that 'friends' commented among themselves about her own intake of alcohol, and may well have experienced Dorothy's subsequent fate of having the rumour relayed back to her 'by way of another woman poet who hated the sight of her and who telephoned in tones of sisterly compassion to assure her that she, personally, never believed a word of it' (p.81). If so, Olivia Manning would be prime suspect.

There is a brief dig at literary agents in the shape of 'Mr. Cropper' (Spencer Curtis Brown?), who reduces a young female novelist to tears:

> The trouble with Cropper was that he liked his writers to be neither too big for their boots nor too small for them: if he thought they were either, he made them pay for it. He had once driven an intellectually austere woman writer to take a swing at him, simply by saying, in comment upon her latest novel, 'It's a smashing good yarn for the female market, dear' – and this at a time when she could be sure of one middle article in *The Times Literary Supplement* to every three of her books. (p.178)

But Pamela's main target was the group of critics that, in real life, she had dubbed 'the chorus'. On the opening night of Tom's play, now called *A Potted Shrimp*, he sees critics from every major newspaper in the expectant audience:

> He surmised that at least two of them had composed their views mentally before coming to the theatre. [...] He noticed the handsome Miss D. with her long black hair bouncing on her shoulders. She, he knew, was feverishly composing verbal squibs of high originality that she would somehow contrive to get into her article; he had little hope of her, since she clung to the petticoats of fashion with the frenzy of an infant terrified to be parted from its mother. (p.227)

Tom attempts to come to terms with the success of the play due to the refusal of the audience to be shocked, and 'the successful endeavour of the Sunday press to praise the play without mentioning its essential characteristics at all', but one review comes near to tossing him irrevocably into the depths of despair. It had read:

This play helps to remove from our shoulders the boring burden of monosexuality. Homosexuality, heterosexuality, how stale it all seems, how trivial! Mr. Grutch [Tom's pseudonym] would seem to offer the stage, at last, new horizons for the human condition. (p.245)

At times in the novel, Pamela leaves satire behind to go deeper into what she sees as reasons for the contemporary malaise, as in the following shrewd analysis:

Blackguarded, blackmailed by the cult of youth, the cult, that is, of early school-leavers in dead-end jobs with more purchasing power than any consonant generation in history, the English were beginning to lose their nerve. Cultivated but weakly parents were pretending to be beguiled by a smeary sub-culture because it was a craze with the children. [...] Men and women, who found self-conscious absurdity boring after the first startling ten minutes, were learning to sit through the stuff patiently, resisting the temptation to leave at the end of the first interval. Kindly people had learned to titter, though with some queasiness in their souls, at little magazines devoted entirely to a callow variety of cruelty and smut. (p.129)

Back in the Snow household, CPS had still not made up his mind whether or not to pursue a libel action against just such a publication with regard to the previously mentioned skit, *We are the Masters Now*. (There is an exchange of letters between CPS and the Prime Minister in the Government Archives with regard to this ridicule. Wilson said that he quite agreed with him that the sketch was libellous, but that he would not recommend court action.) CPS had been surprised to receive a telephone call from Robert Boothby, interceding on behalf of *Private Eye*, with a request not to demand damages as this would result in the financial ruin and the subsequent closure of the magazine. Pamela's reaction was more extreme than that of CPS: 'My temper really broke, remembering this campaign of hatred & malice for <u>years</u> towards C.' Nevertheless, they came to a final decision to drop the case.

Only two days later, however, an attack on both of them was made in a totally unexpected location, the House of Lords. In a debate, CPS had been speaking for the government in favour of comprehensive schools when he had been interrupted by Lord Eccles,[8] challenging him about their decision to send their son to Eton. This intervention became the lead story in the 'Yesterday in Parliament' report in the *Daily Telegraph* (11 February 1965). This quoted Eccles as saying:

'I am told that Lord Snow is sending his young son – to a comprehensive school? No.
A secondary modern? No.
To a grammar school, where he went himself? No, to Eton.'

Caught completely unaware as he was, CPS's justification was somewhat unwise. He snapped back at Eccles: '"In reply to your somewhat personal remarks, it is quite simple. It seems to me that if you are living in a fairly prosperous home it is a mistake to educate your child differently from the mass of people you know socially."' In what the Parliamentary Correspondent described as 'another brush', Eccles then spoke of 'the doctrine of uniformity' being put forward 'by men whose educational arguments are unsound and whose private conduct labels them as humbugs'. Lord Longford then 'sprang to his feet' and invited the Speaker of the House of Lords '"to repudiate the contemptible slur on Lord Snow and other peers. It is quite unlike anything I have ever heard in this House before."' The Speaker, the report concluded, 'remained mute'.

The Snows were in a difficult position as further attacks in the House of Commons and newspapers continued. Pamela had always given priority to her children's education, even in difficult financial circumstances. Philip had not yet sat for Election (the Eton entrance examination), but there seemed every chance that he would gain a scholarship. If he should do so, the fees would be halved, and be less, if anything, than the preparatory boarding-school fees they were currently paying. Pamela considered that it was still more important that, as a Scholar, he would enter College, the house for the most academically accomplished boys. But they had to remain silent about this situation to avoid putting undue pressure on Philip.

After what had been a pleasant lunch for critics who wrote for the *Sunday Telegraph*, the film and theatre reviewer Alan Brien, described by Pamela as 'that purple-tied bounder', began to bait her about Eton in front of a crowd of people. Referring to the name of a famous animal in the bear-baiting arena close to the Globe Theatre in Shakespeare's time, she wailed: 'People seem to think that C & I are Sackersons, for the amusement of the mob. They forget that I am not on a

chain.' And further 'steady, brutal & idiotic persecution' continued.
Fred Bellenger, a Labour M.P., wrote to *The Times*, calling for CPS's
resignation, a question was tabled in the House of Commons, and then
the newspapers turned their attention to pillorying the cost of their
coat of arms, which the Snows had assumed had been a standard
charge. Poor Pamela continued to record her acute unhappiness:

> What have we done to deserve this hell? I don't suppose these diaries
> will ever be read by anyone but myself. But if ever a stranger sees them,
> let me say this: Do not join the pack & don't persecute. You don't know
> what you're doing.

She attended Question Time in the Commons when the matter of
CPS, Philip and Eton was raised, and to her relief, this represented the
end of the affair, with Anthony Crosland for the Government divert-
ing attention by producing telling statistics, showing the generally low
percentages of Members of Parliament from all parties whose sons
attended state schools. Shortly afterward, Pamela was delighted with
an academic success in her family that could not attract adverse
comment; her son Andrew was awarded a scholarship to Harvard
University to take up postgraduate studies.

In April, Pamela's Aunt Emma made one of her infrequent visits
to London to have lunch and tea with her; Pamela remarked that
Emma was 'wonderful for 76', she added, 'but poor dear, she drains
one very thoroughly'. Pamela had never been as close to her as she
had been to her Aunt Kalie in later years. She had always tried to
support her two aunts, and had divided her legacy from her mother
between the two sisters. Having had many expenses to meet at the
time of Kalie's death, she had not similarly passed on the full amount
of that inheritance to Emma, and had obviously been reproached
about this. 'I am tired,' Pamela had written, 'of being treated as
a milch cow, & then rebuked for meanness.' It nevertheless came as a
shock when Emma's son rang her only a few days after his mother's
visit to tell her that the last of the three daughters of Charles
Howson had been found dead in her chair that morning. Pamela did
feel saddened, but when the reading of the will after the cremation
revealed that Emma had had a very adequate income, she felt assuaged
of any lingering guilt about perhaps not having helped her aunt
enough financially.

This was just as well as the next family event was an extravagant celebration of her daughter's 21st birthday. Lindsay looked 'magnificent in white satin' at a large reception at 55 Park Lane, followed by a dinner and dance for a smaller group of friends in the Terrace Room of the Dorchester Hotel. Fortunately, there seemed to have been no gossip columnists around to spoil the occasion with malicious comments about champagne Socialists the following day. Four days later, the family rejoiced in the news that Philip had indeed won an Eton scholarship. When visiting the college again to make final arrangements, Pamela did admit to being somewhat 'in awe of Eton – O, a long way from Clapham Junction!'

Pamela had recently attended a publisher's party to launch Jean Overton Fuller's biography of Victor Neuburg. This must have brought back memories of her early life when she was still living in Clapham; perhaps this was why she described the occasion as 'Beckett-like'. Nevertheless, she enjoyed meeting some old friends from Vicky's circle, the former 'cockney sparrow' Herbert Corby, 'who is now fat & has a <u>nice</u> accent', the Marxist historian A.L. Morton, 'distinguished as ever', and the Irish poet Ewart Milne. The downside for her was that 'Jean read, or mooed, one of Vicky's very <u>worse</u> poems which she is to recite tomorrow on <u>Chanctonbury Ring</u> for sound radio!!!' Pamela later reviewed the book favourably in *The Listener*, while declaring at the outset that it was impossible for her to write impersonally about it. 'I should say', she wrote, 'that [Victor] was one of the best, gentlest, and – when he put his half-histrionic nonsense aside – one of the wisest men I have ever known.' The majority of her review detailed that 'nonsense', Neuburg's involvement with Aleister Crowley, which had led to the 'magical dilemma' of the book's title. She ended:

> Miss Fuller has done a cleansing job; if the final results seem more absurd than tragic, it is no fault of hers. Had I never known Victor Neuburg's circle I think I should have laughed a good deal. As it is, I can only think: 'Poor everyone. Poor Victor. Yes, and even poor Crowley.'

That last sentence shows surprising sympathy for the occultist in view of her current preoccupation with apologists for evil-doers.

Despite the easing off of attacks for the time being, Pamela was baffled as to why states of depression continued to threaten her sense of well-being. One of her diary entries during the summer of 1965 is headed by a quotation from *The Merchant of Venice*, summing up her fear that her state of mind affected all about her:

> 'In sooth, I know not why I am so sad.
> It wearies me – you say it wearies you.' (Antonio, Act I, Sc. i)

Nevertheless, she was still capable, on occasion, of rejoicing: not long after her distress about CPS's hostile cross-examination about Eton in the House of Lords, she felt privileged to be present, with her daughter, in the Visitors' Gallery of that House on the 'wildly exciting' final day of the Lords' Debate on the abolition of capital punishment. This ended, as she had long desired, in a vote in favour, by a margin of one hundred votes. Celebrations in the Peers' Guests' Bar, followed by dinner in a fashionable Chelsea restaurant as guests of Lord and Lady Longford, completed 'a stirring day'.

She was still being pestered by the protagonists to be involved in the regular dramas of the two Ks, at this time in fact three Ks, since Kay Dick and Kathleen Farrell had now, it would seem, finally split up, and the latter was now involved with a woman called Kay Collier, with whom Pamela and CPS were now acquainted. Out of the blue, Pamela received an 'absolutely <u>preposterous</u> call' from Kay Dick, saying that she was in a 'paranoid state', because she felt that CPS was working against her in support of Kathleen. (Kay had attempted to see their mutual friend the psychiatrist Anthony Storr about this, only to be thrown out by him.) Pamela continued in her diary entry:

> When I exploded into wrath & asked why the hell he [CPS] <u>should</u>, she said she thought he had been encouraged by Kay Collier. Told her she must realise that other people had lives besides herself, & that to be brutal, Charles hasn't time to give her or Kathleen a thought. This [was] to me too much, even from Kay, & I was really angry.

Nevertheless Kay Dick would continue to telephone her regularly, mostly to say, (despite the fact that she was then enjoying considerable success as a novelist), that she was near destitution. Later that year, when Kathleen had been admitting in a letter to worrying about KD, Pamela replied:

> I even feel faintly guilty about K myself, though why I should do so after that awful tirade about Charles, I can't imagine. Some people are

guilt givers and everyone is infected by a sort of mad responsibility towards them.[9]

And the following year, she expanded further:

> I was thinking that I get on so much better these days with you than with Kay because you and I have both grown up. I did love her, and despite the breach, do: but she has simply stuck in adolescence and I cannot get on adult terms with her.[10]

That year's family holiday consisted again of just Pamela, CPS and their son. They went first to Venice, originally staying on the Lido, principally for Philip's benefit, but their usual Belgian and (1963) Irish August weather dogged them, restricted Philip's swimming, and prevented his parents from spending much time in their 'repellently expensive cabana'. Thunderstorms and low temperatures continued when they moved to a hotel in the city, and for three days in a row, the greater part of their day was taken up by chess and Scrabble. The saving grace was that the day before they were due to leave was beautiful, and enabled them to enjoy a gala lunch on the hotel terrace, watching the annual regatta – 'lovely in colour, faultless in taste – nothing shoddy'. They had two days in Brussels where CPS visited a machine tools exhibition for the benefit of the Ministry of Technology, and Pamela enjoyed introducing her son to the delights of the Musée des Beaux Arts, and then two days at the Belgian seaside, where Philip's hopes of swimming and playing clock golf were wiped out by what Pamela described as 'a monsoon'. She said that it would hardly have been appropriate if the holiday hadn't ended as it had begun with 'atrocious weather'.

Irritatingly enough, Pamela's next trip away from home with CPS started on 'a perfect autumn day', but their destination was Blackpool for the Labour Party Conference, and her aesthetic sensibilities overrode her dutiful judgment of the town as would befit a loyal politician's wife. She ranted in the privacy of her diary:

> Blackpool is the most appallingly ugly place I have ever seen in my life: it appals because it looks as though the entire wit of man had been devoted to producing something so coarse, crude, lurid & witless, that it had to be seen to be believed. Better when the lights are on, because the neo-Disney monstrosities can't be seen so clearly. How one must

despise the capacity of man to enjoy beautiful things if he is offered this degradation!

The hotel at which they were staying was 'monstrously ugly like all of them'; dinner consisted of 'boiler fowl & cold bread sauce', and 'a faint smell of stale pastry' was pervasive over the whole town. The following day, however, she did admit that the experience of attending the first session of the conference had been 'oddly vivid & exhilarating', and that 'the Winter Gardens ballroom, being in pale colours, isn't so hideous as the rest of this place, & the chandeliers & TV lights help'. She thought Harold Wilson's speech had been 'magnificent (if dodgy)'; unfortunately she didn't expand on her reason for the parenthetic adjective. He had spoken for seventy minutes, and it had seemed to her that the speech could not have lasted more than half that time. 'He is a dazzling performer', she concluded.

September ended with publication day for *Cork Street*; in anticipation of being 'in for a horrible kicking season', Pamela had decided to adopt a new motto: 'If you put the cat among the chickens, you must expect a squawk from the coop.' Some of the reviewers did 'sing in [hostile] chorus' as she had expected, but others were complimentary, not just about the novel under discussion but about Pamela's writing in general. Jocelyn Brooke in the *Listener* gave the novel pride of place in his New Fiction column, beginning:

> There must be many reviewers of fiction who, on unpacking their current batch, heave a sigh of relief at finding that it includes a new novel by Pamela Hansford Johnson. It will be sandwiched, as like as not, between huge splurging American epics, or militantly illiterate books by 'beats' [...]; and one pounces on Miss Hansford Johnson, knowing that she is invariably competent, often very funny, and always entertaining.

And he ended: 'As a satire on the contemporary "cultural" scene, this novel seemed to me first-rate.' Anne Duchêne in the *Guardian* accorded the book a separate review flanked by a photograph of the author. While she acknowledged that *Cork Street* represented 'an enjoyable and elegant capitulation to the current taste for comedy', she expressed some regret that Pamela, 'such an intelligent writer, commanding so solidly place [...] and people and their spoken and unspoken relationships' had lingered in the 'beguiling' company of

Dorothy Merlin and her circle, 'to the exclusion of others'. Referring
to the book's subtitle, 'A Novel in Bad Taste', Duchêne continued:

> Perhaps Miss Hansford Johnson may yet write another novel in truly
> dubious contemporary taste – serious and passionate, that is to say, as
> in those early books where she scoured moral relationships as remorse-
> lessly as some angry young George Eliot.

Given the mixed nature of the reviews, Pamela still felt beleaguered:
'Don't know whether I pray nobody will ever mention my name again
<u>or</u> go the whole hog & abuse me all the time.' She felt that the
timing of the serialization of excerpts from Constantine Fitzgibbon's
biography of Dylan Thomas might lead to the latter. (The previous
year, while Fitzgibbon was writing the book, she had been happy to
discuss with him her relationship with Dylan, commenting afterwards
that she thought he would do 'a splendid job', and that he had been
'grateful to find (I think) any friend of D's capable of telling the
truth'.) On October 10, Fitzgibbon's version of Dylan's 'first love'
occupied a full broadsheet page of the *Sunday Telegraph*, headed by a
photograph of Pamela as a young girl. It began with a lengthy excerpt
from an early letter sent by Dylan, describing, as Fitzgibbon put it,
'what it was like to be a boy of just 19, who has tasted briefly the
freedom and excitement of the city'. He did not mention that Dylan
had added two years to his age in his first letter to her, but perhaps
Pamela too had embroidered a little in her conversation, as she did
not comment in her diary on Fitzgibbon's version of her break with
Frank Saunois. 'Pamela had recently escaped from a youthful love-
affair', he had written, 'which had collapsed because the man had
shown insufficient comprehension of her emotional requirements that
were finding expression in her poems.'[11] For the time being, to Pamela's
relief, there was no reaction in the form of a satiric attack.

CPS celebrated his 60th birthday in October; the house was
'festooned', Pamela wrote, 'with cables from all over the place, USSR
predominating'. Among the letters received was a humorous one from
Mikhail Sholokhov, sent from Stockholm where he had travelled to
collect that year's Nobel Prize in Literature. (The Snows had evinced
some traces of hubris by considering that a long letter that they had
sent to the Swedish Academy in his support could have been a
deciding factor for the awards committee.) The Nobel laureate sent

birthday congratulations to 'our dear young man Charles', explaining that CPS was 'young, due to his character, optimism, ability to laugh and enjoy life'. He ended, signing on behalf of himself and his wife:

Respectfully, as Charles is not a common person any longer but a Lord,
M. Sholokhov Esquire

His personal keeper of the seal, treasurer and keeper of the keys to all the drawers and wine cellars,
M. Sholokhova.[12]

The Snows' travels to Iron Curtain countries continued in the autumn with a short visit to Bulgaria, where their engagements, which could have provided further ammunition for their detractors, included attending a 'fantastic celebration of Revolution at Soviet Embassy [...] sitting with Bulgarian Politburo'.

Pamela's recent novelistic stand against the Theatre of Cruelty might not have come to the notice of a wider audience, had it not been for a bizarre coincidence. Just over one month after the publication of her latest novel, Pamela crowed to her diary that 'all the prophecies of Cork Street had come true' with the production of 'the most repellent play at that sink of a place, the Royal Court, by someone called Bond, in which teenage louts smear a baby in a perambulator with excrement & stone it to death'. The deprived setting of Edward Bond's notorious play, *Saved*, resembles that of both Pamela's imaginary plays described in *Cork Street, Next to the Hatter's*. The catalyst for all three plots is the introduction of a stranger into an emotionally-subnormal family, with murder as a result. Pamela's imagination had not stretched as far as the killing of a baby, rather than the deaf and dumb mother in *Good for a Giggle* or the goose in *A Potted Shrimp*, but she was delighted to find that, when the line that she was campaigning to retain had been overstepped by Edward Bond, the press reaction had been: 'Pretty well every critic outraged! – & they do seem surprised!!'

The Times critique was typical; the reviewer said that, in addition to containing the ugliest scene ever seen by him on any stage, the play was 'full of dead domestic longueurs and slavishly literal bawdry'. It was, he concluded, 'a work which will supply valuable ammunition to those who attack modern drama as half-baked, gratuitously violent, and squalid'. In his review of *Saved* in the *Sunday Times*, J.W. Lambert made handsome amends for his previous 'chorus-singing' by acknowledging that the play was a 'concocted opportunity for vicarious beastliness', and adding:

> Miss Pamela Hansford Johnson must be laughing, if ruefully. In September, she published a witty novel "Cork Street, Next to the Hatter's" in which one of her characters deliberately set out to write a play so offensive that it could not be performed (though of course it was). She thought up some pretty nasty notions, but life has overtaken her. "Saved" has been written, and produced, and will no doubt find its champions.

Pamela was therefore interviewed about the play, which she did compare to her fictional creations, while admitting that she had not seen *Saved* nor wished to. Edward Bond then attacked her for this omission in a letter in the *Evening Standard*, quoting the opinion of 'an illustrious man of the theatre', who had indeed come forward as a champion of the play. Laurence Olivier, Bond said, <u>did</u> see it before passing judgment, claiming that most critics had been blind to 'the rare qualities shown in the play, which [...] achieves astonishing heights of dramatic prowess and contains a last scene of which Chekhov himself would have purred his approval'. Pamela wrote 'a vigorous response' to Bond's letter, but this was not published.

Before the year was out, Pamela briefly mentioned reading about an 'appalling Moors murder case'. Almost certainly, her stance on the pornography of violence had by then become general knowledge in Fleet Street and would lead to a surprising assignment.

CHAPTER 18

Pamela the Crusader
Part Two

SOON AFTER CPS had joined the Wilson administration, Pamela
had written in a letter to her brother-in-law: 'I must say C thrives
on politics. He is out far earlier and back far later, but always
comes in looking chuffed as hell.'[1] But, as Philip Snow later remembered, 'it was not long before the novelty wore thin. Not the Lords,
which he found absolutely ideal as his club and retreat into select
company, but the Ministry where he found that he had no power for
channelling his ideas [...].'[2] He was, therefore, not surprised to hear from
Pamela, almost exactly a year later, that his brother was now always
coming in 'fagged out', and that he was considering offering his resignation.[3] (As a life peer, withdrawal from political office would not, of
course, preclude CPS from continuing to attend, and to contribute to,
parliamentary debates, and from socializing in the various Lords' bars.)

Before any decision in this respect had been taken, however, there
was yet another American tour for them both at the beginning of
1966, with CPS's fifteenth and sixteenth honorary degrees to collect
(amid blizzards), and speeches for him to deliver in Washington to the
House of Representatives Committee on Science, Technology & Astro-
nautics. Pamela was proud to record that he had been given 'a really
splendid citation' at the latter event, but this scarcely compensated
for the usual extreme exhaustion from which she suffered during these
travels. CPS, on the other hand, she commented, had 'enormous
powers of resilience while these horrible trips are on, then collapses
completely at home', where she was 'semi-collapsed the whole time,
& recover more quickly at home'.

A few days after their return, CPS did send in a letter of resignation to the Prime Minister, which, to his displeasure, remained unacknowledged for some time. Eventually, the news filtered back to CPS that Wilson had been too occupied with a threatened rail strike (called off at the last moment), and had assumed that the Parliamentary Secretary to the Minister of Technology would be prepared to wait for a few weeks for a reply. As Pamela briefly recorded: 'C. said he wasn't.' However, it was to be nearly three months before he officially left political office, at the time, more convenient to Wilson, of an extensive ministerial reshuffle. Pamela did not show any animosity towards the Prime Minister for having delayed her husband's departure; she described Wilson's eventual response as being 'v. amiable & considerate'. Addressing CPS as 'My dear Charles', he thanked him for staying on at his request for the last few months, and continued:

> I am grateful for the work that you have done at this crucial phase of our policy of modernising British industry. I know how much you enjoyed it, but I fully understand that you want to take up your literary work again. I hope you will contribute from time to time to debates in the House of Lords and that, in this way, the Government and the country will continue to benefit from your wisdom and experience.[4]

CPS gave a short interview to a *Times* journalist two days later. He took the opportunity to explain that he had told the Prime Minister from the start that he would only agree to join the Ministry for a year or so. When his interviewer asked whether he had become disenchanted with politics, having been quoted as saying '"Chucking bricks at Frank Cousins and myself has become a kind of national sport"', CPS replied 'firmly': 'Not a bit, it is part of the game. If you can't take it, you ought not to be there at all.'[5]

Pamela's reactions to current events at home and abroad that year prove that her views were not entrenched. When, in a notorious trial in Russia, the verdicts of maximum sentences of imprisonment in labour camps were passed against Andrei Sinyavsky and Yuli Daniel for publishing, under pseudonyms, anti-Soviet satirical stories in foreign publications, she commented: 'I wish the Russians would temper justice with mercy: their lack of the latter makes one discouraged and sick.' She did not therefore, as the Snows' critics often assumed, support unquestioningly whichever regime was in power in the USSR, and her remarks illustrate that she also saw nothing wrong with satire, put to what she saw as worthwhile ends. She would, however, have difficulties in reconciling her views with those of their recent host, Mikhail Sholokhov, whom they had so recently supported as a worthy Nobel laureate, yet who was alleged to have described Sinyavsky and Daniel as 'werewolves' and 'thugs with a black conscience'. With regard to this trial too, as will be seen, the ambiguous attitude of Yevgeny Yevtushenko would lead to controversy in Oxford some two years later.

Then, despite her husband's recent political career, Pamela began to feel despair about the way the Labour Party was going. In the last few years, they had both been very concerned at the escalation of the war in Vietnam during the Presidency of Lyndon B. Johnson. (CPS, on one occasion, said that, if matters got worse, he would have to go there himself, although it might be asked: 'to what end?'). Now Pamela was distraught that Britain's policy to the war continued to be 'American-sucking', despite the extensive British newspaper reports that the US troops' use of napalm bombs and Agent Orange often led to civilian deaths in addition to their alleged military aims. With regard to home affairs, she condemned what she saw as 'the idiotic pandering to envy in the conception of an education in which merit is discounted', and the socialist stance with regard to the arts. In conversation with Paul Johnson, then editor of the *New Statesman*, she felt she must express her feeling about the latter, telling him of her conviction 'that the left was going all wrong on the cultural front', and had been surprised to find him a sympathetic listener.

It was in this mood of general discontent that she received what she called 'an astonishing suggestion' from the editor of the *Sunday Telegraph*. He asked if she would attend the Moors Murder Trial in Chester, and write an article about her impressions of it. From the early reports of the case, she realised that this would enable her to examine social malaise at its nadir, even though the experience was likely to be 'as disgusting as sitting through <u>Saved</u> about 90 times'. She agreed therefore to take the commission, while acknowledging that: 'This murder case is going to be the horror of all time', and worrying that 'it will be corrupting to the public to have these atrocious details day after day'. Wrestling with her conscience, having so fervently welcomed the end of capital punishment, she continued:

'God help me for wrong thinking – & thinking <u>sub judice</u> – but it would have been better if those two could have been shot out of hand.'

Coincidentally shortly before the trial, CPS had received a letter from Colin Wilson, the author of *The Outsider*, who was now principally concerned with the psychology of murderers. Wilson, who had been born and brought up in Leicester, was asking if CPS could provide any information about a trial for attempted murder in their mutual home city. The memories that Wilson's letter awoke gave CPS, Pamela recorded, 'an idea' for the penultimate novel in his 'Strangers and Brothers' sequence. It was afterwards frequently assumed that the account of the trial which is the crux of CPS's novel was entirely derived from Pamela's experience of attending the Moors Murder trial, but he had in fact discussed his outline with Pamela, before she had even left for Chester, and she was proud to record:

> I provided the title, which comprehends the failure of liberal humanism – <u>The Sleep of Reason</u>. So I have given him 3 titles – <u>The Affair</u>, <u>The Conscience of the Rich</u> & this one.

The reference is to one of Goya's most famous etchings, *El sueño de la razón produce monstruos* (The Sleep of Reason Brings Forth Monsters).

The *Sunday Telegraph* agreed that Pamela need only attend the final two days of the trial, when Myra Hindley was to be examined, because another writer, Elwyn Jones,[6] would concentrate on the evidence of Ian Brady. The day before she left, she admitted to ambivalent feelings: 'Am half-attracted by my next two days' assignment, half-sickened.' 'The press', she continued. 'has, on the whole, been excellent, & tried not to plunge the country into a sewage bath, <u>but</u> ...' It was early May, and travelling by train to Chester, it seemed bizarre to her 'that the fields, all buttercups, ladysmock, cowslips, were stringing out towards a place of horror'. She was in court to hear the end of Ian Brady's evidence and the whole of Myra Hindley's. Elwyn Jones had told her that his impression of Brady had been one of 'absolute violence, plus arrogance', but she was surprised to find him quite ordinary in appearance and relatively subdued at this stage of the trial. Hindley, on the other hand, brought to her mind the Clytemnestra of one of Lord Leighton's most famous paintings. On the second day, Pamela's seat in the press box was directly facing Hindley. At one point, their eyes met and Pamela found it hard to keep up her own gaze. '<u>I have never been in the presence of such total depravity & evil</u>', she wrote. 'Today the same impassive lying, the look of impassive hate.' After the hearing, a policeman on the case told Pamela that he had found Hindley so terrifying that she haunted his dreams, and also that the prison officers dreaded to go into her cell. She returned home 'tired & very shaken', aware that it had been 'an experience of a life-time', but wishing never to have another like it again.

Her long article (*Sunday Telegraph*, 8 May 1966) was headlined 'Creatures from Another World'. She expanded upon many of the entries in her diary, ending, still with bewilderment:

> The difficult thing was to believe that any of this was true. We knew what was done: yet to see the whole proceedings as more than a court-room play was almost impossible. It was a sensational drama, played unsensationally – for a while, that was all. And then perhaps a phrase, a look, the slightest gesture, the wound of our world broke open, and we looked into and we smelled its sepsis.

Afterwards, she felt compelled to go beyond the limitations of that essay to write an extended study which might offer some explanation. (She might perhaps have been further convinced of this necessity after dining, shortly after her return, with the Longfords. She commented then that she had found 'Frank L. peculiarly silly on subjects of women & criminals'. He was, of course, later to campaign persistently for the release of Myra Hindley from prison.) Pamela felt unnerved by her decision, and admitted to feeling 'cowardly about facing the row when the book appears'. 'But', she continued, 'I do feel I have to write it: somebody must.' She completed the first draft of *On Iniquity*, her 143-page analysis of the climate which had bred the two people generally referred to as 'monsters', within three weeks.

The prosecution had laid much stress at the trial on Ian Brady's collection of books, listed as 'sado-masochistic, titillatory and sado-Fascist'. In her opening chapter, Pamela cogently pointed out a link between the two latter categories in recent history:

> When the Nazis took on the government of Poland, they flooded the Polish bookstalls with pornography. [...] They did so on the theory that to make the individual conscious only of the need for personal sensation would make the social combination of forces more difficult.

[...] The Nazi scheme was the deliberate use of pornography to the ends of social castration. The theory was – and it is worth considering – that if you permit all things for self-gratification, you are likely to encourage withdrawal from any sort of corporate responsibility.[7]

She anticipated that the critical fracas, which she believed would follow publication of *On Iniquity*, was likely to focus on her continuing emphasis on the effect of the present easy availability of books in all three of the categories in Brady's book collection.[8] Accordingly, she wished to establish her own position about the *Lady Chatterley* case, which had taken place at the Old Bailey during the period of their long stay on campus at the University of California. While acknowledging that the verdict that the novel was not obscene had, in popular parlance, 'opened the floodgates to total permissiveness on the bookstalls', she said that she had recognized that a distinction needed to be made between those publications with, and those without, any literary merit or interest. For this reason, she declared:

> If I had been in England at that time, I should unquestionably have slouched into the witness-box in its defence [...]. It is one of Lawrence's poorest books, exemplifying his lack of any sense of the ridiculous. But if Penguin Books wished to publish the entire works of a writer of his standing, then they were entitled to include this book. (p.39)

With regard to the general responsibility of practitioners in the field of the arts, she later discussed the codification of laws of imitation by the French criminologist Gabriel Tarde (1843-1904), which she said 'in essence are still found of value by such modern experts as Hermann Mannheim' (pp.120-21). Tarde called the first of his laws 'Fashion', and Pamela asked, and answered, her own question:

> What were the fashions which attracted Brady and Hindley? They were not set by the lower strata of society, but by the upper ones. It was those upper intellectual strata, novelists, playwrights, stage and film directors who, fascinated by the violence of their imagined picture of the *lumpen* proletariat, turned that violence into a vogue, who made chic the whole paraphernalia of petty perversion, who made easily available and socially acceptable such writers as [le Marquis de] Sade, whose work had previously been more or less confined to specialist readership. (p.122)

Nevertheless, she denied simply seeking an easy solution, such as a drastic reversal to former levels of censorship. 'I am,' she said, 'only suggesting, as straightforwardly as I can, that we have a lot of rethinking to do' (p.136). She opened her final chapter with a personal statement and closed it with another question. She admitted that: 'It might have been better for me, as an individual, if I had had nothing to do with this case at all. It has left a mark which I think will never quite be eradicated' (p.137), and she ended with a moderate appeal to the reader: 'How can we live our lives so as to make the behaviour of Hindley and of Brady just a shade less likely?' (p.143).

With the book completed, Pamela's activities became more routine. She returned to listing her ailments in her diary, and paying frequent visits to Dr. Sofaer, who seemed to have limitless patience; she was, however, always shocked at the amount of his regular accounts. Unlike the fictional doctor whom Dorothy Merlin visits in the opening chapter of *Cork Street, Next to the Hatters*, Sofaer provided her with whatever pills she demanded, including Dexedrine, which she described as 'the only help' during her increasingly frequent periods of depression. These visits did lead to a moment of comedy on one occasion, as evidenced by the following dialogue between doctor and patient:

S: "You must lie down on the couch at once & let me see your legs…"
Me: "Why?"
S: "One is quite white, & the other is purplish."
Me: "Well, I've got on odd stockings."

Their son was continuing to thrive at Eton, collecting several prizes. They had previously often combined attendance at events at his preparatory school in Sussex with visits to Harold Macmillan at his nearby family home, Birch Grove; now, on Eton half-holidays, they occasionally took Philip with them to visit the Astors at Cliveden. William Astor had died prematurely from a heart attack in March that year, but Pamela and CPS, together with Philip and a schoolfriend, were nevertheless invited to Cliveden in May, and found that his widow Bronwen was continuing to offer hospitality to a large number of friends at every meal. She was persisting, however, with her food fads, and Pamela was amused by the displeasure of Wellington, the Cliveden butler, in this respect: on offering her a choice between fruit cup or wine cup at dinner, he had whispered to her:

'"I do apologise, Madam!"' Another death which saddened her at this time was that of her former headmistress, but she was somewhat comforted to record that the Memorial Service, to which CPS had accompanied her, had been in Jonah's 'own impeccable taste'.

On 30 July 1966, a significant day in British sporting history, Pamela's diary merely read: 'World Cup Final watched by Charles, Philip, & a strange old gentleman from Cairo whom Moura sent to us because her set had broken down. England won. I read about silly Queen Christina & felt I would scream if the noise didn't stop.'

She had been looking forward to a fortnight's cruise in the Eastern Mediterranean with CPS and Philip in August, but, at least as far she was concerned, it had a disastrous beginning. The first supposedly 'soothing' day at sea had been ruined, she admitted, by her 'humiliating neuroses raging'; the next day she was 'so depressed & nerve-ridden in morning, with every conceivable psychosomatic symptom, that I began seriously to worry whether I wasn't going off my head'. For the sake of her son, she went through the motions of attempting to enjoy excursions in Greece, and hoped to conceal her continuing anguish. She found that she 'loathed Turkish cuisine', which was all the more unfortunate since they were on a Turkish ship. Dreading the second week, she was, however, relieved by her enjoyment of the Turkish ports of call: she loved Ephesus; Troy charmed her more than she had antici-pated; she rhapsodized about swimming with Philip in the Darda-nelles; and in Istanbul, in addition to the obligatory visits to the Blue Mosque and Santa Sophia, she was overwhelmed by 'the wonderful mosaics & wonderful frescoes' in the lesser-known, but to her, 'superla-tive' St. Saviour in Chora. She was so revived by these visits that, at dinner aboard one night that week, she became bored with CPS's lengthy conversations with the elderly captain at whose table they sat, and 'preposterous', as she thought it was, 'to feel a young wife (aetat 54)', she realised that: 'Occasionally I do. I'd like to dance ...'

In November, she attended a publication party for Constantine FitzGibbon's *Selected Letters of Dylan Thomas*. Although other guests included Rayner Heppenstall, Arthur Calder-Marshall and Jack Lambert, she had been disappointed otherwise to meet 'very few – indeed, from my point of view – no – old friends'. She was afterwards irked that 'the press for [the] Dylan Book is plastering me all over the place'. She could in fact have blamed FitzGibbon's publishers,

J.M. Dent, for this new notoriety; she was the only named recipient of Dylan's letters in the large advertisements they took out on the literary review pages of most newspapers. Additionally some reviews, for example the one in *The Times*, which focused on Dylan's letters to Pamela as being 'the most ebullient' of the collection, might have given readers the impression that she had colluded with his portrayal in those letters of 'a comic, bawdy, and in the end, sordid, world, where every hint of the magical or beautiful has to be jokily qualified'. Julian Holland, in the *Daily Mail*, gave a more accurate account of:

> one of the most unlikely love affairs of our time [...] between the 19-year-old chain-smoking, beer-swilling, naively provincial Dylan Thomas and the "nice" 21-year-old London girl Pamela Hansford Johnson (later to become Lady Snow). [...] It was always platonic.

A few days after the party, with the past evidently still in mind, Pamela recorded having an idea for a novel, 'broadly', she wrote, 'based on the Trevor Hughes story'. She had immediately decided on a title, *The Survival of the Fittest,* and might have thought her chosen title prophetic when she soon had to withstand another calumny. Her head being inadvertently again above the parapet, this time her connection with Dylan Thomas did not escape the attention of satirists. She now rarely watched any satirical programme so her first intimation that there had been a skit about her in yet another short-lived BBC programme, *The Late Show*, came the morning after transmission, thanks to a series of phone calls from family and friends. They related in their various ways that not only did the item, featuring John Bird and Eleanor Bron, mock her relationship with Dylan, but, as Pamela put it, it also related 'repellently to my marriage with Charles. All details entirely wrong, & sexual references appear nauseating.' When she heard further that 'apparently my professional conduct was smeared, as well as everything else', she felt that she had no alternative but to put the matter in legal hands. Her solicitor advised suing for libel, and introduced her to the distinguished Q.C., David Hirst, who thought the sketch 'perhaps the most beastly libel he has ever seen, outside hard-core pornography', and thus she wrote:

> I am to sue Sir H. Carleton Greene, the scriptwriters, producer, & the BBC. [...] Hirst's idea is that C & I should sue jointly, but on reflection

we think it better that I should 'go it alone' as if it <u>should</u> go to Court, some of the filthier references to C. might only add to the gaiety of nations.[9]

Feeling, to her own surprise, 'the prospect of a fight therapeutic', Pamela returned with some zest to writing her new novel. As mentioned earlier, despite the statement in her prefatory author's note that two of the three central figures, Kit Mallings and Alison Petrie were 'composite characters', they bear very strong resemblances respectively to Dylan and to herself. She continued with an outright disclaimer about the origin of the third, and perhaps the most central, character, Kit's close friend, 'Jo'. Pamela asserts this character to be a 'pure invention', contradicting her diary entry about her memory of Trevor Hughes' infatuation with her having been the novel's starting-point. Yet, in addition to attempting to take over his friend's first serious girl-friend, 'Jo' has an invalid mother who restricts his life, and is eventually diagnosed with T.B., in all cases as in Hughes' life.[10] Without naming names, Pamela stated that only two minor characters might be recognizable as real people: 'Belphoebe [...] a poet now dead', is in fact the portrait of Edith Sitwell that Dorothy Merlin was not; 'Mamònov [...] a writer now living' is certainly Mikhail Sholokhov, but both these portraits are affectionately rendered. The remaining minor characters, many of them from the Bohemian London of the 1930s, and all alleged to be in the category of 'pure invention', include two frequenters of the Fitzroy Tavern, Clement Maclaren, a successful journalist, and Georgina, his persistently unfaithful wife; these might well be thought to have been portrayals of Constantine FitzGibbon and his first wife, Theodora. In composing the Author's Note, Pamela was probably more mindful than ever at that time of the laws of libel, although she had not deemed it necessary to rename either the Fitzroy Tavern or the Six Bells in Chelsea, both of which feature in the novel.

Pamela did not often record a great deal about the process of writing her novels, other than to list how many chapters had been completed and the total time taken, but there is more evidence than usual in her diaries about the composition of *Survival*. She began in this case by writing a crucial scene set in Russia, a banquet on the Don, which would take place towards the end of the book, while acknowledging that this was not her usual method. 'Still', she said:

it is begun, & I felt the rare exhilaration of writing with full heart & absorption, as if I were only describing what was going on around me. Hope to God I can make the rest half as good. Writing is a marvel of the spirit when it goes well, a dreariness when it doesn't.

The opening three parts of the novel are each narrated from different points of view, although always written in the third person. Part I principally reflects Jo's thoughts, Part II, Kit's and Part III, Alison's. The remainder of the book switches irregularly between the perspective of these three, and, occasionally, the more important subsidiary characters. Pamela felt she was coping with her chosen narrative method, but that the process was 'never easy & worse when the eyes of Kit Mallings are operating'. Early on, CPS read Part II, and suggested that she should not write this from Kit's standpoint, claiming that the character was not 'internally interesting'. Pamela originally wondered whether he might be right, but since she did not eventually recast it, evidently preferred her own concept. As she continued writing, she acknowledged that:

> The awful problem of the multiple-viewpoint novel is the way some characters do seem to get out of hand, & others to become so shadowy that they have to be hauled back into the limelight. It is like driving a team of about sixteen horses! I am having trouble with Alison, who will recede, & Georgina who will push herself forward.

Further, her recent campaign against gratuitous sexual explicitness inevitably led to landing herself with the difficulty 'of writing a sexual scene germane to the story, as sparely as possibly'. This was likely to have been the incident in which Jo suffers the embarrassment of an involuntary ejaculation. Pamela managed to solve her problem by injecting some stream of consciousness with a touch of humour into the account. Jo has become 'terribly excited' comforting Alison for Kit's abandonment, but hastily moves away from her. When Alison, unaware of any problem, tells him to sit back down again with her, the narrative continues:

> Bloody fool of a girl! Hadn't she the slightest idea that he was frightened of what she would see? He felt the heat, the dampness, in his clothes. [...] Keeping as far beyond the lamps as he could, he edged towards the door. (pp.47-48)

Pamela did also movingly portray adult female sexuality in the novel, bravely choosing Jo's ailing mother Bessie to be her mouthpiece. On the wedding day of her daughter Mildred, Bessie smiles to herself 'in succulent memory of her own honeymoon':

> For, though Jo and Mildred had never suspected such a thing, she had once been as highly-sexed as they. Nobody would ever know how she had suffered from bodily deprivation after her husband's death. It had taken a good deal of conquering. All that was long past. It was quite ten years since those urges had tormented her in the night, when she had lain wakeful, her teeth clenched, longing for sleep. (p.226)

It is a moot point as to whether Pamela's admiration for the semi-autobiographical novels of her husband influenced her choice of subject, which would eventually leave her open to criticism. Within *Survival*, she did articulate the problems of such fiction, when Jo attempts to write 'a delicate and sensitive' novel about characters based, he realises, despite himself, on his close family:

> His only trouble lay in his struggles to disguise Bessie and Mildred as far as possible, so he might give offence to neither: but he was apprehensive lest they might see through such simple devices as giving the former big black eyes and the latter long yellow hair. However much he tried to invent a new structure upon the basis of reality, they persisted in coming through it as the outline of an old painting will slowly but certainly make its ghostly appearance through a new painting superimposed upon it. (p.291)

Survival is one of Pamela's finest books; the characterizations go deeper than the surface likenesses to their originals, the account of the pre-war London literary scene is compelling, and, as in her Helena trilogy, the historical and political background of the war years and their aftermath is fully explored. She did not finish the novel until the middle of 1967, and it was not published until the following year.

Pamela had resolved not to have a large New Year's Eve gathering in 1966, but was persuaded by the Snow family instead to host a 'Leicestershire Supper' on the eve of Twelfth Night in 1967 (in line with the Shakespearian reference, the dress code on the invitations to 'Lord and Lady Snow at home' read simply: 'What You Will'). Philip Snow Snr devoted several pages of *A Time of Renewal* to a lively description of the party, for which he and his brother Eric transported to London by train 'two huge cheeses, a whole Red Leicester and a whole blue-veined Stilton, plus Leicestershire pork pies'.[11] Unfortunately, Pamela was 'too bewildered & anxious for people to be happy' to enjoy the occasion, but she was told that it had been a great success, and she noted to her relief that 'an enormous amount was eaten'. She afterwards wrote to her brother-in-law: 'I have scads of letters almost hysterical about the originality, gaiety and the glories of Pork Pie.'[12]

Around sixty guests were present, and, from Philip Snow's account, it would seem that the majority were literary, journalistic and theatrical friends. Pamela was all the more taken aback to receive a 'most malicious & unpleasant' phone call from Olivia Manning a few days afterward (ostensibly to canvass with regard to a protest against the export of laboratory animals). Pamela's account of the subsequent conversation was as follows:

> Olivia: "I hear you & Charles never see <u>anyone</u> but Lords these days."
> Me: "From whom?"
> Olivia (who ought to get back on her broomstick): "Oh, everyone says so."
> Me: "Then don't you think you ought to contradict them?"

Whether or not Olivia and her husband had been invited to the supper is uncertain, but they had not been present.

Pamela did mention, with an accompanying '<u>Oh</u> dear!!!' that another married couple with whom she and CPS now had a fraught relationship had only looked in that evening '<u>v.</u> briefly'. These were Sidney and Cynthia Nolan, although it was the latter who had become more and more unfriendly over the past year. Sidney Nolan's loaned paintings were still on the walls of their flat, together with two that he had created for the Ministry of Technology, and, with a retrospective exhibition in Australia scheduled, the painter had written to CPS to ask for the return of these, as well as the loan of one of the paintings that they had bought from him. Both Pamela and CPS agreed that they had no alternative but to agree, but in CPS's reply, he did ask whether there was any chance these paintings could be replaced (also on a loan basis) by any large canvasses that would not be required for the exhibition. The result (just before the party) had been, Pamela recorded,

an extraordinary phone call from Cynthia, wailing that she had to do
S's dirty work for him – & telling me they had decided not to <u>lend</u> any
more paintings, because they could trust nobody – <u>not even us</u>. Not
unnaturally, I was angry at this extraordinary statement & I told her
so, pointing out that not only had S. lent us pictures <u>he would not let
us buy</u>, but that Cynthia had lent us two that I hadn't even asked for,
just for wall-space! But it was all the more mad, & more offensive, than
I can write here.

The problem of the empty wall-space in Cromwell Road was soon
solved by Bronwen Astor, who, much to Pamela's surprise and delight,
offered her, on loan, a choice of paintings from Cliveden, since she had
moved out of the great house into a cottage in the grounds. Despite
rarely having enjoyed her visits to the mansion, Pamela found it
poignant when she went there for the last time to collect the paintings, to see the house which had, in its heyday, been so splendid, and
later, so notorious, 'now derelict, all in dust covers, v. sad'.

In February, Alexei Kosygin came to London for talks with Harold
Wilson principally about Vietnam. The Snows were invited to a reception at the Russian Embassy; Pamela described the USSR Premier as
having 'the face of a sorrowful dog, & a smile that dazzles, less because
it is dazzling but because it is so rare'. Both she and CPS had great
hopes about the outcome of the talks, all the more so because of the
cordial nature of Kosygin's departure, '<u>all</u> smiles and satisfaction &
H. Wilson bizarrely calling him "old fruit"'. But the same day,

> as a flash in the news, announcement that the Americans had resumed
> bombing – this, of course, a studied slap in the face, & brought the
> Kosygin visit to nothing. [...] Really felt for a while as I had done in
> the treacherous thirties.

The Prime Minister's televised attempt at an explanation the following day made her feel 'sicker & more furious', and again she
recalled the years in which she had been an active protester: 'I
suppose I should feel grateful that the rage of the thirties hasn't quite
fallen from me!'

The fall-out from the renewed public interest in her youthful love
affair in that decade had not quite subsided. In March, Geoffrey Grig-
son (the poet's one-time friend and supporter) took the opportunity
in his review of a number of Dylan-related books in the *Times Literary*

Supplement to categorize her as Dylan's 'submissive whetstone'. This was hardly the image that she would have wanted to project with the publication date of *On Iniquity* fast approaching. Pamela was, in any case, beginning to regret her self-imposed burden, writing:

> I sometimes wish my talents had taken me along really happy lines such as writing elegantly about Braque [...] or if I had become an art historian, & had written nothing but huge illustrated works on the Flemish Primitives!
>
> The times may be out of joint, but it's a pity that ever I felt called to set them right! (Perhaps I'm not, & this is overweening vanity. But I do feel we are making such a very ugly & violent society, & one in which the young particularly are going to get seriously damaged.)

It certainly did not help the reception of *On Iniquity* that one of the first reviews was by their old enemy Bernard Levin. He wrote a column each weekday in the *Daily Mail*, but, on this occasion, took over the newspaper's Book Page to ensure that his opinion, with the headlines below occupying one-third of the page, could not be missed by any reader:

> NO DOUBT SHE MEANS WELL ...
> Miss
> Johnson's
> useless
> road from Hell

'*On Iniquity*, by Pamela Hansford Johnson, is a foolish, useless book', Levin began, albeit, as he patronisingly continued, being 'unquestionably well-meaning and written (very readably) out of a deep and honourable sense of horror and moral outrage'. He explained that 'Lady Snow' had been 'one of that band of literary ladies and gentlemen, who, commissioned by publishers of newspapers, trotted up to Chester, sat in on all or part of the trial, were duly horrified, and then trotted back to get it into print'. He continued:

> Miss Hansford Johnson, being human, is appalled by the story she heard in that court-room; being decent, she wants to help ensure that such things will not happen again; being emotional, she believe she can; being silly, she thinks she knows how; being wrong, she has written this book.

Elsewhere, the huge amount of media attention given to her short book is proof of Pamela's public standing at that time. John Rowan Wilson, in a very favourable review in the *Spectator* described her as 'a leader of opinion', and praised *On Iniquity* as being 'like all Miss Hansford Johnson's work [...] humane, intelligent and perceptive'. And support came from unexpected sources: she was 'startled' to read a 'laudatory' review by Goronwy Rees in the *Listener*. Referring to her as 'a distinguished novelist', he applauded her for appreciating that 'any serious writer or artist has the right, and indeed the duty to scrutinize' the questions she poses. Even adverse critics like Alexander Cockburn in the *New Statesman* granted, with a slight sneer, that 'Pamela Hansford Johnson's sermon [...] has been greeted with a surprising amount of respect'. Overall, critical opinions were evenly divided, and certainly did not represent that 'barrage of abuse' against which she had steeled herself.

Pamela was interviewed for various radio discussion programmes on the subject of her book. She thought the first two had gone well, so was unprepared for the depth of hostility she encountered during the last of these. She was particularly infuriated because she was expecting, according to her contract, to discuss censorship on 'World of Books' with a single interviewer, only to find that the format of the programme had been changed to interrogation by a panel of critics. This was, she wrote, 'a really disgusting trick, which maddened me so much that adrenalin was pouring through me for hours afterwards (the more so because I had to keep even-tempered throughout this deliberate bear-baiting)'. She was shocked that the chairman of the discussion, the regular broadcaster Kenneth Allsop, who should, according to BBC policy at that time, have attempted to maintain balance between the speakers, attacked her himself 'with such violence' that C.V. Wedgwood, who was also present, felt compelled 'to put a gentle oar in'. Allsop was to continue his intemperate criticism of the book with a long article in Stephen Spender's *Encounter*, in which he criticized 'the untruths, the absurdities, the exaggerations, and the rabble-rousing hysteria' of Pamela's writing. His final shot came in a contribution to the debate in *The Listener* which had followed upon Goronwy Rees's review; Allsop boasted about his technique in the programme that had so distressed Pamela:

On *World of Books* Frederick Raphael and I, in a discussion with Miss Johnson did, I think, very forcibly comment on the muddle of non sequiturs, half-baked fallacies, and inflamed emotional haranguing that comprise her 'argument'.

In June, the Snows made a short but exhausting visit to Moscow in order to attend the Writers' Congress. They met many old friends, and had no more than a brief encounter with Sholokhov in the hall outside the congress chamber. Their presence at the event led, however, to yet another attack on CPS, this time by Mervyn Jones, a writer whom they had not only thought of as a friend, but one whom Pamela believed that she had 'damned well started [...] as a novelist'. Jones's article, 'Writers' Benefit' in the *New Statesman*, began by saying that Louis Aragon and Jean-Paul Sartre had been among the writers who declined invitations to the Congress, on the grounds that it 'followed indecently fast upon the trial of Sinyavski and Daniel'. 'Lord Snow, however,' it continued:

> was present to listen to a tirade by Sholokhov, with whom the British social realist has spent many happy hours on his Kuban farm, and who now adjured Soviet authors once more to forget all that nonsense about freedom.

This was an exaggeration of the truth, but what followed was, according to the Snows, 'inconceivable meanness'. Jones ended:

> What Sholokhov said at Moscow's Speech Day was simply that team spirit is best inculcated by a hundred lines and the odd caning, supplemented by gating if necessary. If young Snow had gone along with pater, he'd have found it quite like Eton.

It is really hard to comprehend why the Snows attracted so much vituperation, mostly from people known to them, who, as above, worked irrelevant *ad hominem* gibes into articles about their professional lives. Not surprisingly, after this period of stress, Pamela's health took another downward path, the main physical symptom being episodes of heavy bleeding, which, despite her doctor's reassurances, made her fearful and wretched. Her former fighting spirit was nevertheless still capable of resurrecting itself occasionally, as her account of a lunch at art historian John Pope-Hennessey's shows. Brooke Astor was the guest of honour, looking 'magnificent & with enough jewels

to adorn the Queen of Sheba', and Ian Fleming was also present.
'I like John & I love Brooke', she wrote, 'but talk after lunch did
degenerate into a sort of rich man's crap that made me feel I wanted
to rush round to King St. & enrol in the C.P.'[13]

Her case against the BBC was heard in the High Court in July.
As the *Evening Standard* reported: 'Lady Snow – Pamela Hansford
Johnson, novelist, poet and literary critic – received an apology and
"a substantial sum of money" in the High Court today for a sketch
which the BBC admitted "ought never to have been written or broadcast in this form".' The judgment stated that:

> this sketch went far beyond the bounds of fair comment by sug-
> gesting that the association between the plaintiff and the late Dylan
> Thomas had been improper and that this association had continued
> until shortly before her marriage to Lord Snow, and also by suggesting
> that the plaintiff had deliberately broken faith with Dylan Thomas by
> causing his letters to be published immediately after his death.

Sadly for those who might have enjoyed the salacious detail, there were
no direct quotations from the script in any of the newspaper reports,
and thus the 'nauseating sexual' innuendoes regarding Pamela and the
'filthier references to C.' remain lost.

Undeterred by Mervyn Jones's spiteful comments in May, only two
months later, the Snows went ahead with another visit to the Communist bloc, although probably wisely Sholokhov- and Yevtushenko-
free this time. They travelled with Philip (who would be celebrating
his fifteenth birthday during the holiday) and Martin Taylor, one of
his schoolfriends. The boys were provided with their own Intourist
guide in Moscow, so that they might sightsee during the two days in
which Pamela and CPS met friends and attended writers' discussion
groups. They then all moved on to Latvia for a similar visit to members
of the Writers' Union in Riga, punctuated with the usual refreshments
in the form of a 'riotous "tea" with much vodka'. When they left to
return to Russia on the night train to Leningrad (as St. Petersburg was
still then known), almost all the writers came to the station to see
them off. They were, unusually, then all free to enjoy sightseeing for
three days (Pamela chose the Smolny Convent as her favourite building).

Their next destination was Tblisi: Pamela described her reactions to
this 'ravishing city' and their rewarding meetings with the poet Joseph

Noneshvili at some length in *Important to Me* (pp.164-65). But although, in her memoir, she also described the overwhelming Georgian hospitality, which comprised enormous meals, followed by visits to each table in turn to drink toasts (in champagne instead of vodka), she did not recount that this had proved, not surprisingly, almost too much for the teenage boys. Whereas, in her diary, she said that she had thought it 'all v. wild & dotty, & good for the boys', they did in fact have to return to Moscow earlier than planned because, to Pamela's guilty dismay, Martin became ill. The last few days in Moscow were hardly more restful, as a group of mainly female Russian writers, whom Pamela nicknamed 'the Maenads', attempted to adopt them, bursting into their hotel room late at night one night, 'stoned, to épater les bourgeois'. Pamela was 'determined not to be épatée', and duly started a party. All in all, it was fortunate that it was an era before social media, and therefore no selfies of seeming excesses, some involving adolescent children, travelled back to their enemies in England.

Their Eastern European journey ended sombrely. Their final destination was Poland, first to Warsaw for the usual round of meetings with writers and publishers, and then to Cracow, from where, despite nearing total exhaustion, Pamela was determined to go to Auschwitz. In the year in which she had faced, and tried to make sense of, individual evil, she did not want to shirk encountering evidence of the greatest mass murders in history with which so many had colluded. She had given the boys the opportunity not to go there, but they both chose to go to accompany her and CPS. Pamela could only then write in her diary: 'There are no words for the horror – the gigantesque horror of it all'. Six years later, however, she emphasized the significance of their experience by devoting the second chapter of *Important to Me* to their visit. Her reflections focused on the difference in attitude between those of her generation who had lived through the Second World War and the two intelligent boys. As far as the latter were concerned, while agreeing that the Holocaust should neither be forgotten nor forgiven, they emphasized that *'it was the past*, and it was their business to remake the future'. But Pamela's thoughts had turned also to the war crimes of the Allied forces, and in particular to the use of the atom bomb to terminate the war against Japan. 'I do not', she wrote, 'subscribe to the fashionable shibboleth that "we are

all guilty". It is an escapist's excuse for not feeling guilty about anything at all. [...] But the feeling of shame persists.' She remembered
her thoughts as she watched the boys laying flowers on the Auschwitz
memorial, and here again her experience at the murder trial in Chester
must still have been fresh in her mind:

> At least – and this I took for my comfort – we had not so much col-
> lective guilt for the cruelty of individual man to individual man. This
> seems to me the worst of all, that gleeful (or indifferent) eyes must have
> met eyes in terror. (*Important*, pp.18-19)

CHAPTER 19

'This World is in a Frightful State'

C PS WAS CONTINUING to work on *The Sleep of Reason*: Pamela found the first part of his new novel 'absolutely magnificent, work at the very top of his form', and attempted to draw comfort from his example. She wrote: 'C's book revives <u>me</u>. If, at nearly 62, he can be writing at his peak, <u>so can I go on</u>, & not continue to envisage the retirement (after the S of F) that I have had in mind for quite five years past?' There is an element of self-delusion in that last statement. She seems never to have been more happy than when writing her novels, and had only rarely considered giving up during fits of depression.

In October 1967, they left on yet another trail around American campuses, which Pamela as usual endured rather than enjoyed. On a typically nightmarish day, she had yet another bout of profuse bleeding, all her clothes and jewellery went temporarily astray during an internal flight, she felt giddy, had a tension headache and acute anorexia. The latter was at its worst that evening when they had to attend a big dinner at Cornell University, where, to cap it all, Leopold Stokowski was present – 'who <u>did not</u> recognise me after 36 years!' She had fortunately recovered a little when, the day before their return, they attended 'Brooke's grand party' in New York. Other guests were 'the Nelson Rockefellers (she is quite charming)', Louis Auchincloss [lawyer, author and socialite], etc.' Brooke Astor, 'in rose pink with <u>all</u> emeralds & huge diamond belt', told her that she had thought of asking the Scribners (the Snows' publishers and major figures in New York literary salons) but she had decided that they

389

'weren't senior enough!' Those responsible for the 'malice' that Pamela believed to pursue her and CPS might have enjoyed disseminating these remarks, particularly as she ended her diary entry: 'C. & Nelson R. got on splendidly & spent most of the evening together.'

They were at home for less than a month before returning across the Atlantic, this time to Canada, where Pamela received her second Honorary Degree at York University, Toronto, this time without the suspicion and unhappiness which had surrounded the award of her first at Temple. The convocation ceremony was 'most attractive', the only drawback being her difficulties with 'a "square" far too large & too shallow, which tried to fall off every time I moved my head'. But this problem was more than compensated by 'a really staggering citation, in which I could scarcely recognise myself'.

At home again, CPS settled back into his pattern of being out most evenings, leaving Pamela disconsolately to watch television on her own or with Conchita. He almost always returned 'popular', but sometimes he exceeded even Pamela's patience. On one such occasion, she recorded the arrival of an agitated taxi-driver

> to say he couldn't get Lord Snow out of his cab! L & I & Conchita to rescue. C. quite fuddled, & it was a business getting him indoors & on to bed. Managed to undress him (rather like the night on the Don!), & he became infectiously giggly. [...] However, he had a placid night. Tomorrow, he will start being holier-than-thou for about a fortnight! I tipped driver 3/6 on a 4/- fare, & shall collect from C. tomorrow. Firmly!

They both had periods of vowing to reduce their alcohol intake, not only at social events and also at home, but, in the latter respect, they nevertheless maintained their regular order with a wine merchant. Aghast one month at the size of the account rendered, Pamela resolved to limit the amount of whisky ordered to (not too abstemiously, it would seem) '1 doz. Haig on first day of every month', though she did add that should they have need for excess at any time, they could always buy it locally.

In the New Year of 1968, Pamela yet again became embroiled in the life of one of her Hampstead 'friends'. A quadruple-underlined entry in her diary read: 'Kay Dick wants me to lend her £500. Good grief.' (The equivalent amount in 2014 was around £7,500.) She spoke to Kay's accountant, offering to lend £100 if four others would do the same: 'He sounded rather shaken – she had obviously represented me to him as a rich woman who had merely to sign a cheque.' Kay continued to phone regularly, making Pamela feel 'maddened and badgered, as if by a lunatic'. Eventually, however, Pamela weakened to the extent of agreeing to guarantee Kay's bank loan for the amount for which she had been asking. Having earlier loaned her £175, she had little hope that Kay would not renege on repayment to the bank, and gloomily wrote: 'I shall never see £675 again (plus sixpence on form, plus solicitors' fees).'

Throughout the early part of the year, she and CPS were considering a move to Belgravia, and looking at a number of properties. Their final choice was 'a v. elegant & delightful house at 85 Eaton Terrace [...]. Paved garden, central heating, all decorations & curtains charming.' Pamela wondered whether, with her two older children likely to move away from home permanently before long, it might not be too big and too extravagant, but they started negotiations with the owners. Philip was continuing to justify their decision to send him to Eton; he won the college's most prestigious award, the Newcastle Scholarship, awarded on the strength of an examination in theology and ethics. He was becoming increasingly independent of mind, and when courted by colleges at both Oxford and Cambridge, insisted on visiting them on his own, and made up his mind to try for Balliol College, Oxford. CPS was naturally a little sad that his son did not want to follow him to Christ's, Cambridge, but Pamela was content to let Philip make up his own mind.

Pamela was very much affected by the tumultuous events at home and abroad throughout 1968. Her former palliative of undemanding evening television was now constantly invaded by distressing news items. 'The horrors of the Vietnam fighting prey on me – night after night, these tormented children,' she wrote, and saw this as symptomatic of 'the general anarchy of the world', which in England currently led to 'football riots, trains, telephone booths, etc., smashed, waiting room seats ripped up with knives'. 'What', she vainly asked, 'are we all doing?' Although she did not disapprove of her daughter's attendance at the great anti-war demonstration outside the US Embassy in Grosvenor Square, she still felt that the total of 117 policemen wounded on that day proved that the demonstration had been 'far more violent – often for the mere sake of violence – than ours in the 30s' and had included many participants with 'a strong element of the non-genuine'. Before long, the assassinations of Martin Luther King and Robert Kennedy made her despair further that:

> Blake's <u>Second Coming</u> is beginning to sound like real prophecy. This world is in a frightful state – wars, rising civil violence, obsession with sex & cruelty – 'The ceremony of innocence is drowned.' In my more depressed moments I do begin to think, '<u>What</u> rough beast? And when? Soon?'[1]

She was less troubled about the student riots in Paris. She thought the ringleaders 'very dull, because their ideas are so jejeune & chaotic', and found it hard to take their spokesman 'Danny the Red' seriously, since he looked '<u>just</u> like Benny Hill'. But soon there was a further international development which caused her great concern. In January that year, Alexander Dubček, had been elected First Secretary of the Czechoslovakian Communist Party and had begun a series of social and political reforms which became known as 'The Prague Spring'. His country had been part of the Soviet bloc since the end of the Second World War, and the USSR was becoming increasingly dismayed about what they saw as Dubček's challenge to their influence. When, in May, there were newspaper reports about Soviet troop movements on the Czech border, Pamela wrote: 'Oh God, NOT another Hungary! If that happened, C & I would never go to the USSR again, nor see those friends who would be as horrified as we should be.'

Meanwhile her health problems continued, and eventually Sofaer came to the conclusion that she had a grumbling appendix. However, he thought no action need be taken for the time being, and she was happy to delay any surgery if not thought to be essential until after the publication of *The Survival of the Fittest* in May. Her pain worsened but Sofaer had gone away on holiday, and his locum merely asked her what helped. After her reply, 'aspirin and alcohol', he responded: '"Take both"', and departed. The operation was eventually arranged for one month later.

Pamela had heard in advance that Julian Symons would be dedicating his fiction column in the *Sunday Times* to a review of *The Survival of the Fittest*. As the founder of *Twentieth Century Verse* in the 1930s, Symons had published several of Dylan's poems and had been a Fitzroy Tavern regular. Pamela therefore expected a favourable judgment from him, since 'those days were precisely <u>his</u> days, & those pub-rounds more or less his'. However, to her annoyance, she thought his review 'so <u>dim</u>, as though he felt he could have done it so much better'. Despite admitting to 'an experience closely parallel to Miss Johnson's', Symons questioned whether life had really been as portrayed in her novel, and answered himself: 'I should say, not quite. [...] the colours were surely brighter, the conversations livelier, the sense of defeated hope much more acute.' The review by Stephen Wall in the *Observer* on the same day was, Pamela thought, 'long and foolish'; her opinion was almost certainly coloured by another instance of a comparison of her work with that of her husband. Although he admitted that any biographical material in Pamela's latest novel had been 'thoroughly made over into fictional terms', he did continue:

> Technically, 'The Survival of the Fittest' adopts many of the procedures of the novels of C. P. Snow's, though it is formally less complacent than they are. Miss Hansford Johnson's view of human nature is perhaps wider than C. P. Snow's, but that is not to say much.

In contrast to these reviews, Pamela was delighted with a 'long and exceptionally interesting' full-page discussion by A.S. Byatt in the *New Statesman* of *Survival* together with Isabel Quigly's recently published monograph about her in the British Council 'Writers and Their Work' series. Pamela's reaction to this demonstrates that, if she respected the reviewer, she did not wish only for unadulterated praise, but was willing to have some measured well-argued criticism of her work included. Byatt, for example, said that:

> Reading the book is a curious experience; vague and casual from moment to moment, it is nevertheless compulsive and cumulatively gripping. Its mood is elegiac: characters, places, periods, history, are evoked, suggested, rather than solidly dramatic.

In the context of Quigly's overview of Pamela's previous novels, Byatt said that Pamela's invention often flagged in the comic novels:

> But in the [Helena] trilogy, and the patient serious novels of the Fifties [...], she seemed able to create solid dramatic life, independent of her own circumstances. She seemed to write out of an emotion which appeared then one of her own primary responses to life – a greedy curiosity, detached yet sympathetic, about other people's passions.

The daily London newspapers having, in general, carried positive critiques of the novel, Pamela was unprepared for a review 'of almost unspeakable malignity' from a provincial paper. Perhaps it will not surprise the reader to find out that this emanated from a Welsh newspaper, the *Western Mail*. The reviewer, Christina Hobhouse, at no time identified 'Kit' as Dylan, but merely asked, after a resumé of the early part of the plot: 'Does Pamela Hansford Johnson's new story somehow strike a chord?' She ended:

> And what, one wonders, would Kit, the drunken and ungentlemanly writer, have made of this memorial? Would he shrug it off as "sweet, girlish drivel"? Or did Kit, did the towering dead, guess that Alison's renunciation and forgivingness concealed an acid revenge, the revenge of belittling him, of making him dull?

Pamela seemed genuinely amazed and hurt that the reviewer thought it had been 'written in <u>revenge</u> (on Dylan)!!!' Had Hobhouse, she wondered, 'no understanding of the creative process? To wait 30 years & then write 400 pages odd for such a purpose!'

The delayed appendectomy proved to be a 'bitter experience', but Pamela did not immediately attribute the blame to her doctor's poor advice, but to the incompetence of the surgeon (Mr. K...): 'I can <u>never forget</u> what he has done to me,' she wrote. 'I am weakened far more than I need have been.' She was quite happy that Dr. Sofaer came to see her regularly in hospital, even insisting, the day after the operation, on her drinking a small whisky, and he took her home, albeit feeling groggy nine days afterwards. CPS was at home to greet her, but then, to her chagrin, 'tore off to the House for Prices & Income Bill'. She often mentioned that he could not stand her being ill, but on this occasion, was not prepared to make any excuses for him. However, her daughter and her elder son were 'v. kind'. A week later, she decided to tackle Sofaer about his part in the severity of the experience she had undergone; he responded that he had never known her to be unreasonable before. A sign that she was beginning to lose faith in him was rendered by the single-word sentence, 'Maybe', following her recording of this conversation. The doctor had, unusually, refused a drink on that occasion, but said he would accept a drink on his visit two days later. However CPS was at home on that occasion, and Pamela knew that he would exhibit his suspicion of all doctors which dated from a serious illness in his student days from which he came close to dying:² 'C. behaves in [Sofaer's] presence in the most <u>loopy</u> way, retreating into a corner & almost snarling.' A further reason for CPS's hostility was that, at the time, he was convinced that he was in financial difficulties, and indeed Pamela herself was worrying about the huge bill she would be receiving from the doctor.

CPS's money worries, leaving him 'depressed to <u>absolute</u> nadir', had two origins. The first, a long-term one, was that he thought he had overstretched his resources by setting up a trust fund for the three children; the second was that, in the short term, he had relied on the increased sales that would result if *The Sleep of Reason* was a Book Society Choice, and he was now despairing about that possibility to the extent of telling Pamela that they would almost certainly have to give up any thought of buying the house, on which, she said, 'we'd all set our hearts'. Their accountant, however, persuaded CPS that he had sufficient funds to finance the purchase (although future events would prove that their faith in him was as much a misjudgement as Pamela's trust in her doctor).

They went back to Le Coq in Belgium for a family holiday in July, which started well enough. Both the resort and the hotel were very much improved, the little café on the beach which they had frequented still had the same owner who welcomed them, and it was, she said soon after their arrival, 'all very nostalgic & unexpectedly charming'. But, it would seem, inevitably, the weather deteriorated, putting an end to their games of mini-golf, and leading Pamela to comment: 'It must be the worst summer on record – verging on a sort of cosmic joke.' There was some cheer when her son Andrew wired from home: 'BOOK SOCIETY CHOSE SLEEP JANUARY', so that both short- and long-term difficulties regarding their house move seemed over, but then much distress for them all with the news from Czechoslovakia. In the hotel lounge, they watched the television newsreels showing Russian tanks rumbling through the streets, and Pamela reflected that she could understand the 'Russian terror of satellites freeing themselves one by one, but even such a risk should be borne in the name of humanity.' 'As for C & me,' she continued, '– perhaps a petty consideration – years of hope wasted.'

Pamela's next worries concerned family matters, the first of which stemmed from their now sixteen-year-old son's announcement that he intended to leave school after he had taken the entrance examinations for Oxford. He planned, at a time when gap years were not the norm, to travel the following year. Her anxiety deepened when he later announced that his plan was 'to help the Zulus in January & wander around Africa for about 6 months'. Their move to Belgravia took place in October, and, as usual, the onus fell upon Pamela, with the help of her older children. She was so exhausted that she lost track as to where CPS had retreated; in between accounts of placing the furniture, placating their housekeeper and soothing their cats, she wrote: 'C. to Club for 2 nights, & Leicester for a third (so far as I can remember).' After four days, he deemed the new house sufficiently in order to take up residence, but did so suffering from 'aching teeth (new), angst re his book (S of R) & a general grouch'.

Pamela had little time to recover from her exhaustion before their second visit to America that year, and, as a result, struggled even more than usual with their packed itinerary of events in New York, Philadelphia, Kansas City, and Fulton, Missouri. For the first few days, the main topic of conversation at both private and public functions was the imminent Presidential Election. The principal candidates were Richard Nixon and Hubert Humphrey; Pamela agreed with the general consensus that Humphrey, the incumbent Vice-President, would scrape in, if only because his running mate, Edmund Muskie, was more acceptable than Nixon's. As she put it: 'After all, if they elect Nixon & then shoot him, look what they're left with! Spiro Agnew.' The consensus was, of course, to be proved wrong.

The high point of this visit, arguably the apogee of CPS's career as a public speaker, was his lecture (given, in fact, in two parts) at Fulton, Missouri. Entitled 'The State of Siege', the lecture sought further solutions to the problems of under-developed countries on which he had concentrated in the second half of his Rede Lecture. The 'Fulton Lecture' series, which generally took place annually, had achieved international fame in 1946 when Winston Churchill delivered his 'Iron Curtain' speech there. Its proper name is The John Findley Green Foundation Lecture, and the stipulations as set out by the foundation are that the speaker should be 'a person of international reputation', and that the lectures should 'promote understanding of economic and social problems of international concern'. The lectures continue to have a roll-call of eminent speakers; among the non-

Americans later in the century were Edward Heath, Mikhail Gorbachev, Margaret Thatcher and Lech Walesa. Pamela had been in two minds about CPS's invitation; on the one hand, she was proud that he had been asked to deliver this prestigious lecture, on the other, she dreaded that the aftermath might be 'another sort of industry, like Two Cultures, involving endless work and correspondence'. She was very relieved by the enthusiastic reception of his first lecture by the large audience, and even more the following day when 'C. gave 2nd half Fulton Speech magnificently & now all wires are buzzing'. The *New York Times* reported extensively and favourably on both halves of the lecture, but there was in fact no further aftermath. Pamela should have been pleased that her forebodings were not realised, but that relief was adulterated when, on their return home, CPS was 'dreadfully down' at the 'complete neglect of Fulton Speech' in the British press. (Similarly, although the lecture was published by Scribners the following year in America, and was highly recommended by R.W. Haseltine in the *Library Journal* as a book which 'should be on the purchase list of every library', it was not published in Britain.)

The Sleep of Reason had been published in the UK while they were away. His brother quoted in *Stranger and Brother* from a letter he believed CPS had sent 'to an American Rabbi friend', but it seems more likely to have been the eminent scientist Isidore Rabi. Whichever the recipient might have been, the letter illustrates CPS's openness regarding his despondency about the British reviews:

> I cannot comprehend what some reviewers are thinking of, but they have reduced me to a state of depression which I don't think I shall easily shake off. This has been a temperamental difficulty all my life although I think I conceal it from the outside world. But now I am finding it hard to drag my feet around.[3]

Philip Snow explained in various references during his memoir that in *The Sleep of Reason*, CPS 'had "cannibalised" much of *The Devoted*', an unpublished novel which he had begun in the late 1930s, but which had long been lying in reserve, less some parts which had been transferred to *Strangers and Brothers* [*George Passant*] and *Homecomings*.[4] This might account for a certain incoherence in the first half of the book, in addition to bewilderment on the part of any reader unfamiliar with the earlier novels in the sequence. Two hundred pages elapse before the key episode of the trial of two girls in a lesbian relationship who are accused of the murder of a young boy. During the first two parts of the novel, many characters from previous novels wander in and out without noticeably being relevant to the later development of the plot; among the clearly more recent additions, there are five chapters devoted to Lewis Eliot's temporary loss of vision due to a detached retina (no experience wasted).

Eliot becomes involved in the murder trial since one of the accused is the niece of George Passant, and the narrative then gathers pace and intensity. In a collection of essays by Albert Borowicz on notorious crimes in fact and fiction, published in 1977, the first chapter is entitled 'The Snows on the Moors', and begins:

> Husbands and wives have been known to hold strong views about many things, and marriage provides no guarantee that those views will be congruent. [...] When the husband and wife in question are novelists as distinguished as C.P. Snow and Pamela Hansford Johnson, however, and the object of their views is one of the most disturbing murder trials of our day, the Moors Murder Trial, a comparison of their individual attitudes may illustrate the possibility of highly personal intellectual and emotional responses by two thinkers bound by marriage, and at the same time assist the continuing assessment and development of public views on a matter of human and social concern.[5]

While admitting that 'it can, of course, be misleading to take [*The Sleep of Reason*] to be a literal retelling of the Moors trial', Borowitz does discuss the novel at considerable length, and ends by declaring that CPS's fictional account and Pamela's treatise, *On Iniquity*, lead to the same conclusion, which is 'that intelligent people must live with and respond to the crimes and human disasters of their time'.[6]

The frequent association of the two works would seem to carry a suggestion that they were both attempting to profit from a horrific occurrence. While no commentator went so far as to insinuate that the motive was financial gain, the implication was that they might both have wanted to use the trial to promulgate what could be seen as a narrow point of view. However, the circumstances of the murder of the boy in CPS's novel differ fundamentally from the crimes of Brady and Hindley, the only possible connection being the theory of *folie à deux* which was raised at the Chester trial and in the fictional trial of George Passant's niece. Nevertheless, Claire Tomalin, one of the original reviewers, flatly declared 'the big centrepiece' of CPS's novel to be 'an account of the Moors Murder trial (so thinly provided with a different cast and location as not to matter)'. It probably mattered more to CPS at the time that her review would not have encouraged the reader to purchase the novel as her judgment overall was that, although CPS's motives had been 'decent', 'the gap between intention and achievement' was too great. Otherwise, *The Sleep of Reason* received a scattering of what CPS's editor at Macmillan called 'Beta +' reviews, but sales, despite the Book Society selection, remained lower than expected, and he continued, as his wife put it, 'in dump'.

The opening scene of the novel, which Pamela had so much admired, and some other key scenes, introduces the reader to a wise child, Eliot's son Charles, identified as a portrait of Philip Snow Junior by his namesake uncle. In November, in real life, the youngest member of the Snow family, to Pamela's relief, unwittingly provided a diversionary tactic in the Eaton Terrace gloom by emulating his parents in his reaction to a new Cold War literary controversy. 'Pops rang up, stifling with rage re Amis attack on Yevtushenko,' Pamela wrote, 'But what to do? If we wade in, we run a risk of harming Zhenya <u>there</u>, whatever finite good we might do him <u>here</u>.' Kingsley Amis, with eleven other writers, all Oxford MAs entitled to vote in the forthcoming election for their university's Chair of Professor of Poetry, had been invited by the *New Statesman* to comment on the candidates (Yevgeny Yevtushenko had been nominated by the Oxford Students' Union). Amis was the only one of the twelve to give an opinion which lived up to the title of the article, namely, 'Parnassian Polemics'. He did not discuss Yevtushenko's merits as a poet, but based his strong objection to him entirely on political grounds. Citing the Russian's (alleged) 'public denunciation of Sinyavski and Daniel as traitors', Amis categorized him as a 'squalid pseudo-liberal', whose election to the chair would be a disgrace. (Edward Lucie-Smith was the only other of the MAs asked to participate in this straw poll to mention Yevtushenko, but he dismissed the whole election as a circus.)

The Snows will not have been surprised that their *bête noire*, Bernard Levin, devoted the whole of one of his *Daily Mail* columns to the subject. In his usual intemperate style, he denounced the Russian poet as:

a party hack pathetically parading as something better. He has come to represent captivity decked out like an ageing whore with the cosmetics of freedom applied with such tastelessness that his true nature is not hidden but proclaimed.

And they might well have anticipated that Robert Conquest would join in against Yevtushenko, as he did in a letter published in *The Times*. The Snows continued to discuss their course of action (or inaction) for a few days. Pamela was despairing: 'What beasts Amis & Conquest are! All they want to do is to make Yevtushenko so disloyal to his country that he ends uselessly in jail or the bin. When I <u>think</u> of the bravery of <u>Babi Yar</u> & <u>Stalin's Heirs</u>!' CPS drafted 'An Apology to Yevtushenko' to send to *The Times*, but Pamela did not record whether he submitted it. It certainly was not printed, so they may well have decided in favour of prudence and waited until they saw whether sufficient others would come forward to defend him. Several indeed did, including a spokesman for the Oxford students, denying that their invitation had been deliberately tendentious. From across the Atlantic, Arthur Miller and Pulitzer Prize-winning novelist William Styron sent messages of support: Miller alleged that 'to the present day Yevgeny Yevtushenko has been a voice of conscience among his colleagues', and Styron called the attacks 'scandalous, cowardly in general and false in its particulars'.[7] Roy Fuller was eventually elected to the Chair, but Yevtushenko came third out of the total of eleven candidates.

Oxford became the focus of Snow family attention again the following month when Philip took the university's entrance examinations, together with vivas at three colleges, Wadham and St. John's as well as his first choice, Balliol. Despite his conviction that he had done badly (a trait he would have inherited from his mother rather than his father), the whole family rejoiced at the news that he had been awarded an Exhibition at Balliol. This was the only good event for Pamela in December. Conchita had not settled down in the new house, and was given to muttering about 'slavery'. Then, worrying as so often about the state of her finances with Christmas looming, Pamela opened her bank statement one morning, expecting a small deficit, to find that she was '£700 in the red. [...] Now seems obvious that Kay (that prize sponge) has called in my £500 – without notifying me.'

Her prayer at the end of her 1968 diary was: 'Lord, send us tranquillity next year.'

It might have been better if she had prayed for better health, as the handwriting in her 1969 diary became progressively spiky and erratic, recording periods of depression and illnesses she believed were minor but which culminated in a hysterectomy from which she took a long time to recover. *The Sleep of Reason* was published in America in January. The early reviews in general were good, but CPS fell back into what Pamela described as 'the horrible gloom [...] despairing (poor chap) of his whole career' after indeed possibly the worst review of his writing career. In the influential *New York Times Book Review*, the playwright and critic Jack Richardson wrote that, in *The Sleep of Reason*:

> Lord Snow obviously wants to present us with a mature, balanced sensibility taking on an ugly caprice of nature, but he manages only to make his detached character seem shallow, if not at times downright silly.

He continued with an overall dismissal of the whole *Strangers and Brothers* series before returning to the novel under review:

> So many men and women drift through Lord Snow's novels without any more substance to them than the bureaucratic awards they have achieved [...]. Stripped of their honors, they vanish altogether, as indeed *The Sleep of Reason* does in the very act of reading it.'

CPS's gloom lasted several days, by which time Pamela became less sympathetic to his 'hellish state of misery & defeat', particularly when he turned on *her*, blaming her for the 'shortcomings of everyone else'.

Earlier that month, CPS had sent a letter, marked 'Confidential', which the recipient, his brother, described as 'curious'. It provides further proof of the secretive, if often irrational, side of his nature, which so frequently distressed Pamela, but this time, the person to be deceived was not his wife, but his long-term mistress. He told his brother that he was withholding from Anne Seagrim, for at least a further two months, the news that their move to Belgravia had taken place, allegedly to avoid her feeling more cut off from him. So, he continued, to their appointed go-between, 'if I should be *incommunicado* up till March and she gets in touch with you I am still to be regarded as in the flat'. His strange logic was that: 'She has been more than good to me, and I want to spare her what little I can manage to spare her from.'[8]

Pamela's first husband arrived in London for a short visit at the end of January, and they arranged a meeting. She wrote:

> Met Neil (first time in 15 years) in Sloane Square & took him to Red Lion for drinks. He looks very grey, is v. gentle. To me, very odd, like meeting just an old acquaintance. Talked politics a lot. What a thing life is!

But she added wistfully: 'Yet, what fun some of it was – especially the hike round the Seine Valley. And the Paris Expo. And Montparnasse.' After this pleasant reunion, there was the expected but nevertheless upsetting ordeal for Pamela when their son Philip departed for his six-month tour of Africa. 'I had', she wrote, 'the extraordinary feeling that it was taking a deep emotional toll <u>which wouldn't consciously register</u>.' It was nearly a month before any relief came in the form of a letter from Philip telling them that he was 'content among the "amiable Zulus", whose hair and fingernails he cuts in the afternoon [...]'.

CPS was beginning to recover from his post-US publication dejection, probably aided by praise from an unexpected source. In the American periodical, *New Republic*, his former adversary, John Wain, opened a long, and more or less favourable, review of *The Sleep of Reason* by saying:

> Lord Snow's sequence of novels, *Strangers and Brothers*, has been going on long enough for most people to have formed their attitude to it. It is liked and enjoyed by many, exceedingly disliked by a few. What the approvers like is clear enough: the books are plain, unpretentious, dealing with credible people, a 'good read'.

Doubtless, to CPS's surprise, Wain continued that 'on the whole I am one of the approvers'.

CPS's emergence from despair was, however, short-lived, triggered by a letter from English Electric setting out the position regarding the termination of his insurance policy. The lump sum payment was approximately one-fifth, and the annual income approximately one-third, of his expectations. The following day was nightmarish for Pamela:

C. so glum that I find myself tiptoeing, as though there's an invalid in the house. [...] Then C. drank wine at dinner & went on & on with it, giving me a tirade about how he wanted to die or to leave all of us & go to Peru, everyone was beastly, etc. He is in an abnormal depressive state and <u>refuses</u> any kind of medical help. It is all v. hard [...].

After a while, they resumed their social and cultural life. They attended the first night of *Hamlet* with Nicol Williamson in the title role at the recently reopened Roundhouse, Camden. Pamela found it difficult to enjoy the performance since the venue was a 'horribly uncomfortable place, with hard seats that make your bottom ache'; the audience had ranged from the Prime Minister and his wife to 'a gaggle of dishevelled Pop stars, the repellent Mick Jagger included, ostentatiously turning up late'.

Pamela then had the first of what would prove to be several serious falls at home. The subsequent hospital examination encompassed a gynaecological examination and an immediate hysterectomy was advised. Pamela wanted to postpone this as they were due to leave again for America, and she felt that CPS would hate her not accompanying him. More heavy bleeding settled the matter (possibly again, earlier diagnosis might have saved her much discomfort and even longer-lasting damage to her general health); she agreed to have the operation as long as it could be carried out before CPS left to fulfil his US engagements. Worried as she was, she managed to get some amusement from her excitable housekeeper's less than sympathetic reaction when she attempted to break the news 'gingerly and obliquely' to her elder son, 'all of which was ruined by Conchita crying out, "I have hystérectomie, Pussie 'as hystérectomie, why not the Lady Snow have hystérectomie?"' Her thoughts, as usual, centred on the effect the emergency was having on CPS. She rang him the night before the operation, and was worried because he sounded 'desolate'. She had no visitors on the day of the operation, but recorded the following day that in the late afternoon, 'darling C. & L.' had come to see her: 'Charles really looked <u>happy</u> that I could greet him so cheerfully. Am sure he will be better off in USA than in brooding in & out of hospital.' And off to America he went the next day, returning twelve days later.

It was now Pamela's turn for 'long, long days of despondency', viewing all work 'with nervous dread', and feeling unable 'to open a pad of paper & write a sentence'. Even her diary entries became less frequent. Nearly two months after the operation, on a day when she felt unable to get out of a mood of 'apprehensive lassitude', she recorded a chance conversation with the psychiatrist Tony Storr who had not cheered her 'by saying recovery from a hysterectomy took about 2 years, after which one felt marvellous!' She forced herself to speak at a day-long symposium organized by the Migraine Trust, and was asked to greet their patron, Princess Margaret. Pamela revealed in *Important to Me* that the princess was herself a sufferer, and speculated on 'how many royal engagements she must gamely have carried out, while migraine had her in its grip' (p.170). Nevertheless, she was not overwhelmed by the Queen's sister at their first meeting:

> She is very tiny – probably below 5 feet. Small hands & feet, huge bust, wears a balloon-like hairpiece which throws her right out of proportion. Fine eyes & skin, but an uncomely profile, nose v. big, chin thickening. Wore a yellow coat & pale yellow dress that looked (apart from bust) like a child's size. During lecture [...] closed eyes several times (well, it was a dull lecture). Brightened later, & seemed to enjoy herself. But she isn't instantly likeable.

Pamela was continuing naturally enough to worry about her younger son, especially as Philip had reached the Sudan just as a left-wing military coup was taking place there. CPS continued to be out most evenings, and when at home during the day and not writing, he would spend the time watching cricket for hours. 'In a mood of self-pity,' she wrote one day, 'I reflected that he had his cricket, his chats at the Lords, his club, etc., & I really get no pleasure. Holidays seem out: never the theatre, never even a cinema.' A turning-point of sorts, however, came a few weeks later with the surprise return of her son. Pamela, as usual at that time, had been lying down, when 'Conchita came bursting mysteriously upstairs to "prepare me", & in walked P. looking very fit, & not the skeleton I had anticipated'. CPS had told her he was going to have a drink with Harry in the nearby pub, the Red Lion, and fortunately on this occasion, this was not an alibi, for Pamela and Philip found them there when they rushed to join them. Her mental health improved after her son's return, but her physical condition continued to be poor.

A further month later, she began 'toying with notes for a book called The Honours Board', although she doubted her ability to complete it. In the first flush of excitement, she found 'writing a sort of sparkling sweat', but soon started losing heart and becoming full of self-doubt. As usual, she asked CPS to read chapters as she went along, and he told her that he considered there were 'fine things' in the draft but also some 'flatness of writing'. She only seems to have registered the latter comment, and she was so downcast that, as she revealed later, this novel was only 'saved from incineration by the efforts [...] of my younger son' (*Important*, p.71). Philip had the distinction of being a character in a novel by each parent consecutively. After his portrayal as the fifteen-year-old Charles Eliot in *The Sleep of Reason*, he became the model for the still younger Peter Quillan in *The Honours Board*.

The novel is set in Downs Park, a boys' preparatory boarding-school. Pamela was worried that the locale would adversely affect its reception in America, but, as Ishrat Lindblad points out, it is 'an unusual school story in that it focuses upon the lives of the staff rather than upon those of the students'.[9] Possibly somewhat unexpectedly to her readers, in view of Pamela's recent campaigns, the opening chapters feature rough marital sex, questionably consensual extra-marital sex, adultery, lesbianism and masturbation, as well as the to-be-expected attachments between adolescent boys. But that year Pamela had been able to define her views on the treatment of sexual themes in the modern novel, when invited, as a practitioner, to participate in an edition of a recently-launched literary quarterly, *Twentieth Century Studies*, dedicated to that topic.[10] 'I cannot see,' she said, 'that the freedoms to depict genital operations in detail, or to employ words hitherto forbidden in print are going to make any revolutionary changes whatsoever in form and style [...]'. She continued:

> I do not feel any compulsion to use the new licence for its own sake, though I have an uneasy feeling that it is being *required* of me; for myself, *Anna Karenina* is the novel most rich in sexual passion, and [...] even if Tolstoy had had the 'permission' to spell out the affair of Anna and Vronsky in detail, I doubt whether he would have taken advantage of it. He did not need to.

'In my own work,' she ended, 'I simply prefer to be oblique. [...] A truly free literature can contain all things, even reticence.'

In line with those precepts, the sexual episodes in *The Honours Board* are rendered without explicit description, and uncensoriously; later in

the novel she deals sensitively with the topics of alcoholism, klepto-
mania and suicide. The mood of the book, however, is not dark; it is
dictated by the benign characterizations of the headmaster, Cyril
Annick, and his wife, Grace, whose protective instincts towards the
boys in their care allow them to overlook anything that will not be
detrimental to the school as a whole. The title of the book is explained
on the opening page: Annick's constant regret is that the academic
record of his school is 'thin', and that the Honours Board, halfway up
the stairs, lists only 'the scholarships of dim boys to dim schools',
although he blames himself for not having had the courage to enter
some of the less dim for 'schools of greater lustre'.[11] Pamela made
teasing use of the new licence in literature at the beginning of the
second chapter, when one of the masters reports to the headmaster
that he had caught some boys 'at their old game of writing rude words
in the sand with a stick'. One boy had ended in tears, having been
'derided by his fellows for writing PHUCK', and, far from being
shocked, Annick feels a leap of hope: 'Surely a boy of eight who could
substitute a "ph" for the most obvious "f" might even be potential
scholarship material?' (p.12).

The dedication on the frontispiece is: 'To Hal and Nancy Milner-
Gulland, whose excellent school is better than this one, with admiring
affection.' Their school was Cumnor House, from which her son Philip,
like Peter Quillan at Downs Park, had gained an Eton Scholarship.
Pamela did take the precaution of sending the Milner-Gullands a draft
copy prior to publication, and was much relieved with their response:
'Thank God, a delighted letter from Hal re THB. [...] Should have
been so distressed if it had in any way distressed them.'

The episodes which had most distressed *her* to write concerned
the alcoholism of the young and pretty wife of one of the masters.
Delia Poole goes to many subterfuges to cover up her addiction, but
to little avail. After a drunken fall which she tries to make light of,
she dreads having to attend school dinner, and the narration becomes
a stream of consciousness:

> She must face it. She was steady now, not bruised. But she would not
> be able to eat, she would be seized by anorexia. The food would stay
> mashed and staling in her mouth, she would be unable to force it down
> her gullet. Well, she must try. (p.90)

In her diaries, Pamela had frequently blamed anorexia for her own inability to eat in public, and worried about her drinking, and now her frequent falls; her fellow-feeling for her character is obvious when she recorded writing 'a depressing chapter on the alcoholism of Delia, which shook me as I wrote'. But another example of her personal identification with her characters adds an instance of the humour which permeates the novel. The Annicks' widowed daughter, Penelope, remarries, and evidently with memories of the Kon-Tiki-expedition-citing clergyman at her own second marriage, Pamela incorporated the comment that, for Penelope, the ceremony had been slightly marred when: 'The vicar gave an idiotic address, implying that the two were to embark on a journey together as perilous as Scott's to the South Pole' (p.231).

Pamela's health continuing to be poor, CPS visited the USA alone that autumn. She was determined to get well by his return, and was rewarded with happy memories, when, as she put it, she 'muscled' her resolution to go out on her own:

> Went walking alone in Royal Hospital Gardens – had forgotten how beautiful they were. There is a marvellous alley of planes, all sparkling with little dots of sunlight & the ground thick with brown leaves. Remembered Dylan there. And wheeling the children there in their prams.

She completed *The Honours Board* a few days later; it had taken her less than two months, at a time when not only was her strength at a low ebb, but she occasionally confided to her diary fears of a complete mental breakdown. She felt 'a slow-growing but immense relief' at the achievement, but, the following month, gave precedence to the delight she felt when recording: 'C. finished "Last Things", & so the whole "Strangers & Brothers" cycle. Feel there [ought] to have been supernatural fireworks.'

Their annual visit to Stratford could not take place until November, so the 'violent gales' and persistent rain were not unexpected. Nevertheless, Pamela was pleased that she had been able to see six plays in six days, even though she worried halfway through their stay whether: 'since my last op., something was lost to me – the capacity for really involved enthusiasm'. She was not over-impressed by the first four productions, but praised 'a charming and subtle production' of

Twelfth Night 'with the proper overlay of melancholy', with Donald Sinden as the best Malvolio she had seen since Olivier. As they left for home, she felt sad: 'Hate leaving Stratford, almost as much as I hate leaving Venice.'

Later that month, she spoke at the PEN Awards Dinner at the Savoy, together with Mark Bonham-Carter, William Douglas-Home, and L.P. Hartley. She was delighted when Rosamond Lehmann, who had then recently been the President of English PEN, told her that she re-read *The Humbler Creation* every year. The year fizzled out uneventfully, and her far sparser diary entries for 1970 are evidence of her reduced professional and social life; they often only record her children's activities and anecdotes about the family's two cats plus a ginger interloper. She continued to be far from well, and worked mostly on short essays and the odd review. Her evenings were spent watching television usually on her own, or with the ever-temperamental Conchita (whose constant threats of retirement added to her worries).

CPS went on his own to Chicago for a week in January, and Pamela comforted herself with her annual re-reading of Proust, 'the only thing', she wrote, 'with power to hold my attention'. She could not bear to let him have another solitary American tour in April, even though the schedule of a fortnight's events in Texas (travelling backwards and forwards between Houston, Austin and Dallas) was taxing for both of them. Pamela had a new experience on this trip, but it was not one which would ever feature in her novels; they were taken by their hosts in Houston to see a baseball match at the Astrodome. She was completely unable to follow the game, 'but dear C. enjoyed it all immensely'. On the flight home, they had an encounter with one of their tormenters of the past, to whom she no longer bore malice:

> Met David Frost on board, who was v. cordial. He really is a pheno-
> menon of the triumph of the 'ordinary' – nothing to look at, acne, quick
> eyes, quick wits, but oddly engaging. C & I remember the old TWTW
> days when we were insulted by Frost! But it all seems so long ago.

The next month, Pamela attended a Cambridge Union Debate in which CPS opposed his friend George Steiner on the motion that: 'This house believes that technological advance threatens the individuality of man and is becoming his master.' Later, Lord Mountbatten and Prince Charles, then in his final year at Trinity College, spoke regarding the motion: the report in the following day's *Times* did not record the outcome of the debate, but concentrated on the contribution from the twenty-one-year-old heir to the throne, who had declared that he had to speak 'from the cross-benches' as he was not permitted to be controversial. Nevertheless, the occasion is still recalled on the official website of the Prince of Wales, because it gave him the opportunity to raise 'in public some of his concerns about the environment and conservation which were to remain central to his thinking over the coming decades'.[12] Pamela's diary yields another perceptive thumbnail portrait:

> Both chatted to Prince, before & after debate, for nearly an hour. He is a very nice young man indeed, rather like a rosy horse, with close-set but v. fine eyes. Humorous & easy: obviously he is a surrogate son to Mountbatten. He spoke modestly & well. The Royal House have been <u>very</u> lucky in that one!

Coincidentally, Pamela had a second meeting with his aunt only a week later when Princess Margaret opened the City Migraine Clinic, and this time found her 'much more cheerful' and 'more chatty'. It might fortunately have been on this occasion when the Royal Patron was in a good mood that an incident occurred which Philip Snow Snr related to me. Pamela had been 'horrified at a function, at which Charles had been indulging in quite a lot of whisky, and he was sitting on a settee with Princess Margaret, and Pam was quite close, and saw him putting his arm around her royal shoulders, while saying: "No, my dear girl, it's not like that."' She had taken CPS to task afterwards for his inappropriate behaviour, because Princess Margaret was known to be prickly if anyone took liberties, but on this occasion, according to his brother, she had taken it well.

One of the few writing commissions that Pamela agreed to undertake at that time had been a review for the *New Statesman* of the recently translated *Story of O*, which at that time was creating a similar stir to *Fifty Shades of Grey* in 2012. She soon regretted her decision, having found the novel 'repulsive <u>and</u> silly, & so repetitious'. Written ostensibly by Pauline Réage, the book, which had appeared in France in 1954, but could not then have been published in England without prosecution, tells the story of a beautiful Parisienne who willingly submits to sexual torture to please her lover. In Pamela's review (19 June 1970), she took issue with the preface written by Jean Paulhan, a member of the French Academy and the director of the literary magazine *Nouvelle Revue Française*, highly praising the book, but anticipating that 'some fool is probably going to raise the hue and cry of masochism'. Pamela, as ever willing to take a stand, responded to this comment with her conviction that: 'This is a sado-masochistic work that would have been on the booklist of Brady and Hindley, had it been published in time for them.' It would not become known until years after Pamela's death that 'Pauline Réage' was the pseudonym used by the French literary critic Anne Desclos, and that Paulhan was both her colleague and her lover. Worried that his interest in her might be waning, and being aware of his penchant for the works of the Marquis de Sade, she told him that she would write something similar from the woman's viewpoint. 'Paulhan', as Geraldine Bedell wrote in an article in 2004, had been 'dismissive', maintaining that 'erotica wasn't a thing women were capable of.'[13] Pamela admitted in her review that 'this stomach-turning little book is [...] fairly well-written', so this had provided an excuse for it to be presented 'as "art" and "literature"'. While she felt the reading public might have preferred to have been spared all the 'sticky descriptions of sodomy and fellatio', she gave examples of its rapturous reception from others (with less personal involvement than Paulhan), as proof that: 'It is amazing what sort of support this degraded stuff can get.' J.G. Ballard, for example, had provided the following endorsement on the jacket:

> Here all kinds of terrors await us, but like a baby taking its mother's milk all pains are assuaged. Touched by the magic of love, everything is transformed. *Story of O* is a deeply moral homily.

'Well,' Pamela observed, 'if this is a moral homily, God help us.' She also took issue with Graham Greene, who had judged the novel to be: 'A rare thing, a pornographic book well-written and without a trace of obscenity.' 'What then,' Pamela asked, 'is obscenity? Silly old four-letter words? The mind boggles.' She concluded: 'We should none of us be frightened not to be 'with it' if we really find this work pretty appalling. Among other human rights is the right to be appalled, and say so.'[14] David Holloway, then the Literary Editor of the *Daily Telegraph*, praised her critique of the novel when they met shortly afterwards, and told her that he thought that, by contrast, most of the other reviewers had been far too cowardly.

Harold Wilson had called a General Election in June, nine months ahead of the statutory end of the term of his government. It is believed that he chose an earlier date because the switch to decimal currency in the United Kingdom was due to take place in February 1971, and was likely to be initially unpopular. But Wilson's political judgment was undone by an unpredictable factor: in Mexico, four days before the election, England lost to West Germany in the football World Cup quarter-finals, and the electorate lost faith in the Labour administration. This was certainly an outcome that Pamela, with her complete lack of interest in sport, would not have taken into account, and as the election results came in, she found them 'a nasty surprise'. While she had disagreed with Labour's education policies, she still supported the party overall. 'Wilson', she wrote, 'is probably the cleverest PM since Lloyd George, & I don't fancy "Grocer" Heath.' She also worried about the 'ugly phenomenon of an increased majority for Enoch Powell, though it was to be expected'.

The Honours Board was published in August; Pamela was now almost as apprehensive about reviews as CPS. 'I am obviously never going to get over publication nerves, which worsen as I grow older', she wrote. To her surprise, for a book about which she had said at the end of the previous year, 'I never wrote anything so much under stress', she was able to record that she had received 'the best press I've had by far since Skipton'. The view of Christopher Wordsworth, in the *Guardian*, was that: 'It is brilliant, chain-reaction entertainment, heightened by the boys'-eye view of adult cantrips, and deepened by the exploration of character, at once relentless and humane.' Julian Symons (*Sunday Times*) more than made up for his luke-warm judgment of *Survival* with a dedicated review, headed 'Top of the Class', accompanied by a large, if unflattering, photograph of the author. *The Honours Board*, he declared,

> is wonderfully readable, a dirty word to apply to a novelist at the moment, although it should be descriptive and not denigratory. [...] If Miss Johnson is so readable, it is partly because of the enviable and apparently effortless skill with which she constructs a narrative.

Derek Mahon (*Listener*) summed the novel as being 'humane, muted and wise', and Norman Shrapnel (*Times Literary Supplement*) called it 'provocative, enjoyable, highly professional'. Pamela was overwhelmed by all the praise, singling out for special mention fellow-novelist William Trevor's lengthy review (*New Statesman*) in which he said that the current novel showed again that 'Miss Hansford Johnson [...] is the most professional, most delicate and cleverest of novelists'.

The Snows went a little earlier than usual, to Stratford-on-Avon for a week to see the plays and also to attend a series of events at the Shakespeare Institute. 1970 was the year of Peter Brook's controversial production of *A Midsummer Night's Dream*. Pamela's reaction to what has come to be remembered as a landmark in twentieth century theatrical history was adverse. She pitied the actors who were 'beautifully spoken', but who had to perform 'in glaring & grotesque production, [...] doing Chinese conjuring tricks' against a background of 'wire hanging from fishing rods for trees, & a hard white snow-blinding glare throughout'. They both thought the production 'visually hideous', and that was the general opinion of others at the Shakespeare Institute: one Polish scholar told them that he thought the set had been 'like Christmas at Harrods'.

Shortly afterward, they left for what Pamela called their 'precious holiday' in Venice. Despite some disruption to their travel plans, and with Pamela suffering initially from a bad cold and digestive problems, she was happy to arrive at the Gritti Palace. On their third night, however, their idyllic dinner on the hotel terrace had been interrupted by a spectacular display of summer lightning and heavy thunder. They had felt just a little inconvenienced when all the hotel lights went out; the following day, Pamela was shocked to hear that the cause of the blackout had been a tornado, which, no more than two miles away, had caused thirty-seven deaths, most of them by drowning, and including twenty-one people on board one of the vaporetti regularly plying in the lagoon. Gradually, Pamela began again to feel 'soothed' in her favourite location, and reflect that this made her 'all too aware how soothed I am <u>not</u> in my own home'. One of the days she most enjoyed was spent with Robert Boothby and his wife Wanda, who had contacted them soon after their arrival to invite them to lunch on the island of Torcello. Their meeting-place was Harry's Bar, where Pamela was delighted to be introduced to 'a very nice old man called Waininger, who had once known Corvo'. CPS's mood was obviously also affected by la Serenissima, when, yielding to his wife's sentimental streak on their final day, they had a 'memorial drink at the old Cavelletto, & remembered all sorts of things together'.

Before they had left for Venice, Pamela's agent had told her that the film director Lewis Gilbert was interested to taking up an option on *The Honours Board*, but on their return, she was disappointed to be told that the film sale had fallen through. She had some consolation in the form of a letter from her American publisher reporting that the US reviews had been 'very fine'. For example, John Knowles, in the *New York Times*, praised the 'mature sympathy' of her 'telling portraits', and provided an answer to her misgivings concerning American unfamiliarity with the novel's setting:

> The essence of prose fiction is particularity, concreteness, the portrayal of a world about which the reader, largely ignorant of it, will say, 'Yes, it must be like this, that's the way it has to be.' At this, Miss Johnson excels.

Judgment day in Britain for CPS's *Last Things* was not far away, and Pamela was reasonably sympathetic about his state of mind: 'C. getting v. wrought up about his publication day [...], poor old boy.' The novel had been published first in America in August, and, while, for once, CPS would have been content with the *New York Times* review in which Stanley Weintraub called the conclusion to the sequence 'a major literary event', he had doubtless brooded over the assessment in *Time* in which Melvin Maddocks declared that, throughout, CPS had written no more than 'the record of middling men and their middling ways in an often middling time. Another Remembrance of Things Past? Never. Another Forsyte Saga? Perhaps.' But the British reviews in October turned out to be in general 'long and impressive'; CPS went happily off 'to club', and Pamela 'drank rather too much out of sheer release & tension', albeit registering her awareness that: 'I mustn't.'

Meanwhile, the new Prime Minister, Edward Heath, was locked in conflict with the trade unions, and a work-to-rule resulted in power cuts throughout December. Pamela recorded 'hideous disruption [...], hospital patients dying [....]. A misery.' She summed up 1970 as having been 'a poor year for this country & the world', albeit with 'literary success for C & me, and success for Andy' (who had successfully completed his doctorate at Imperial College, London). 'But', she ended, 'my spirits have been dark. Pray they grow lighter next year.' Her wish was not to be fulfilled. 1971 began with the necessity to pay £400 to Kay Dick's bank, the balance of the amount she had guaranteed in 1968 (evidently, Pamela had negotiated to have the earlier full withdrawal from her account rescinded). 'Never, never, never again', she vowed. Throughout much of January, she was in a 'miserable state of tremulousness & depression'. Despite what she saw as 'an outburst of anti-smoking propaganda', and acknowledging that she was smoking far too much, she could only reiterate that: 'I can't stop.' She was trying to confine her drinking to evenings when her elder son habitually joined her for his single glass of sherry, but he left that month to take up a Royal Society European post-doctoral fellowship in Genoa, and Pamela lost his moderating influence.

The dramatic alteration in her diary entries throughout February tells its own tale. The shaky and cramped handwriting records what she described as 'a slight stroke', leaving her after three days with 'speech blurred' and 'mouth a bit askew', but 'able to write a little'. Within a week, she was able to write more than single sentences, her speech was clearer, but she still felt 'very down', especially when her bank telephoned to query her signature on a cheque. She was nevertheless able to 'read Trollope for hours'. Two days later, presumably not having had doctor's orders to the contrary, she felt she was again drinking too much and determined yet again to cut down; she would however soon resume 'smoking too heavily for my well-being'. By the beginning of March, she was fulfilling speaking engagements, while still feeling in a 'web of depression'.

She nevertheless was not wholly self-centred at this time. She made time to visit Rayner Heppenstall and his wife, on hearing that the former was in financial difficulties having left the BBC, and she campaigned for him to receive an Arts Council grant. Their reconciliation had been sealed when, the previous year, Heppenstall's first novel for seven years had been dedicated to 'Pamela Snow'. The book, *The Shearers*, dealt with media interest in a notorious American trial in which eight members of an incestuous family were charged with murder, and may well have been influenced by *On Iniquity*. Pamela was then deeply grieved to be told of the death of the 'darling ginger-headed man' of her youth. She remembered Ian Swanson as 'the best of men, graceful in mind & body', and said that she would never forget their meeting in Bruges and subsequent romance, and still felt guilty about having treated him badly when transferring her affections to Frank Saunois.

Pamela continued to be perpetually tired through the spring and early summer, yet was still determined to carry out a planned visit to Hungary and Russia in July with CPS, their son Philip and two of his friends. As an indication of her state of mind and health, the handwriting in her diary can be seen to have improved little by little from the time they left. She seemed to have very much enjoyed the first week; they spent the first two days in Budapest where she took pleasure from sightseeing with no speaking engagements to exhaust her, and then they went on to the holiday resort of Lake Balaton, where they met several literary friends. Their only organised visit there was a morning at the local farmers' Winegrowing Co-operative; after the obligatory wine-tasting in their vaults, 'not surprisingly', she recorded, 'all slept like Breughel's drunkards the entire afternoon'. Their schedule in Moscow was more strenuous with talks, interviews and lectures, but she didn't complain about the full schedule in contrast to her reaction to similar itineraries in the USA when her health had been good. They also visited Progrès, their Russian publishers, to collect royalties: CPS received 900 roubles (the equivalent in 1971 of £600, or nearly £8,000 in 2014) in respect of the Russian editions of his novels, while Pamela, without a gloating comment, recorded receiving twice that amount for hers.

Following their return, however, she reverted to being in a state of lassitude. She despairingly wrote: 'Don't know how to cope. No ideas, either, for a book – not a one. Afraid my stroke spoiled a small piece of brain, too.' Her only work activity for two months consisted of typing up CPS's articles (then regularly appearing in the *Financial Times*). Although she had enjoyed helping him in this way in the past, this chore now increased her depression; she found her eyes full of tears one day, wishing that she was typing her own work. Her love for him nevertheless continued undiminished; on his 66th birthday that October, she wrote that she had thanked him for existing, adding: 'He means so very much to me, more than I can express.'

She convinced herself that she was well enough soon afterward to accompany him on a week's visit to Canada and the United States.

CPS collected another honorary degree (this one from the University of Western Ontario); the exhausting day of the Convocation ended with a reception, a dinner and a library party. Her exasperation was evident as she recorded:

> Met too many people! One damned woman asked me if I was Rebecca West. Tell C. I don't in the least mind walking two steps behind him as a rule, but this was <u>too</u> much! And I hate people who ask me what name I write under, & then give a blank stare.

She did concede: 'Canadians are nice, though.' They flew on to New York where their publishers gave them a party to which all their closest American friends were invited. She enjoyed that occasion, but was relieved to return home.

Pamela again became agitated about her health, and worried about stories about her being spread around by their circle of acquaintances. According, she visited the House of Lords one evening 'in order to show them that I wasn't dotty, senile, or in wretched health', and made a point of talking brightly to their erstwhile host in Venice, Robert Boothby, who, CPS had recently told her to her dismay, was among 'the worst of the gossips'. Nevertheless, her 1971 diary, which, as usual, had carried her Latin motto on its first page, ended with a regretful paraphrase: 'I have neither found out a way nor made one.'

CHAPTER 20

'So End my Fifties...'

T HE MOOD IN the Snow household at the beginning of 1972 was one of familiar gloom, since CPS failed to get the Book of the Month choice for his latest novel, *The Malcontents*. Pamela reported that 'his confidence entirely deserted him', making him 'glum all day', and herself 'both breathless and tremulous'. But, to her surprise, a health check that day found no problems with her heart and lungs, and two days later, she woke 'feeling really better for the first time in a year'. 'Unaccountable. It is really like a miracle', she wrote, and determined to be more active since she had been spending far too long 'glued to my chair in the drawing-room, always in my corner'. She even started planning a new novel, although she had some physical concerns about her previous favoured method of creation, which had been to write the first draft by hand before typing it up. She had to come to terms with the fact that the effects of the stroke were still impeding her handwriting, and that she would have to compose directly on the typewriter. 'It was just like going over the top', she wrote. 'I felt quite unnerved when I sat down to <u>type</u> a novel for the first time!' She was initially 'very excited to be working again, after this last fallow & deadly year', and was able to maintain her usual speed of writing between 1,500 and 2,000 words per day, but gradually became worried that: 'Typing inhibits me, making for a dry, sketchy prose.' CPS attempted to reassure her that this was not the case, but she remained unconvinced.

Despite her working day being affected by the power cuts throughout February which were a by-product of the national miners' strike, she completed her new novel, which had been renamed several times, within two months. One of her provisional titles had been

Captain Keppel's Mast, but she had been swayed by her publishers on both sides of the Atlantic to change this to what they considered a more marketable title, *The Holiday Friend*. The setting, as previously mentioned, was a Belgian seaside resort she named Les Roseaux (or Het Riet in Flemish); the hotel, the beach café, the miniature golf course – and the weather – all had a close resemblance to those of their own family holidays in Le Coq (De Haan). A university lecturer, Gavin Eastwood, his wife Hannah and their now eleven-year-old son Giles, similarly have been frequent visitors to the small town, but this year Melissa Hirst, a student who, without Gavin's knowledge, has become obsessed by him, has followed the family there.

Discussing Pamela's work together with those of John Wain and William Cooper, Rubin Rabinovitz (1967) had declared that none of their novels contained examples of experimental techniques, and that 'their time sequences are chronological, and they make no use of myth, symbolism, or stream-of-consciousness inner narratives'.[1] While he would have had no knowledge of *The Holiday Friend* at the time of writing, one can only assume that he had not read Pamela's early novel, *Blessed Among Women*, which this novel constantly brings to mind, not only because of its focus on fanatical love, but also because of its incorporation of modernist techniques within a realist framework. Flashbacks in this later novel offer explanations of recent events from within the consciousnesses of Melissa and Giles, also, of course, disrupting chronological narration. Most importantly, had the above-quoted original title been adhered to, the symbolism of Captain Keppel's mast and his circus would have been recognized as the underlying theme of the novel.

A similar entertainment was the highlight of the summer season at Le Coq, as Pamela's children remembered. The fictional Captain Keppel's 'Mechanical Circus', and a 'great ship's mast, painted crimson' was the centre-piece of the performing area in the town market-place.[2] By the evening of this event, Melissa had managed to infiltrate the Eastwoods' circle of friends and acquaintances and had been invited to join them to see the spectacle. After dramatic stunt-riding by motor-cyclists ended with their riding through flames, everything became dark, until the mast was lit up, with Captain Keppel standing glittering at its foot:

He saluted the crowd with grandiloquence and began to climb. The audience was hushed. Melissa followed him with her eyes. Up and up he went, a figure tinier and tinier as he climbed the rigging. Her imagination was seized and grew wild. She would climb like that; all things were possible.

At the top, to tumultuous applause, the Captain stood on his head and performed acrobatics (p.90). It is an image which remains with the previous timid Melissa, twice unconsciously in vivid dreams, and consciously later in the holiday when she is self-congratulatory about her strategy to ensnare Gavin despite sensing both his misgivings and those of his wife:

> The shame and fear she had felt had now deserted her. She was filled with a brave and restless energy. She had carried off the morning well, she was climbing almost as steeply as Captain Keppel. [...] There was nothing she could not do, nothing she could not dare. He would come to her in the end, she knew that. (p.191)

But it is not only Melissa who is harbouring a secret, so is Giles, and his dreams turn into Futurist nightmares about mechanical and real animals (p.213). To reveal more would vitiate the cumulative effect of the novel.

CPS was briefly heartened by the news that *The Malcontents* had been selected as the Book Society alternative choice, but before long was again 'as low as he can possibly be' when their son returned home from Oxford after 'Mods', his first-year examinations, convinced, as with his Eton scholarship exams, that he had performed poorly. The results would not be known for almost a month, during which time both parents suffered both mentally and physically. Finally Pamela was able to record that: 'Pops had GOT A FIRST (of course he had)', but the following day, she wrote that she had 'suffered a heavy reaction after these weeks of tension, & trying always to appear in good spirits'.

A few days later, she and CPS left for a fortnight in Miami, ful-filling engagements at the university, and attempting to enjoy some of the tourist attractions, although Pamela felt 'far from well – weak, breathless, nervy'. For this trip she had been supplied by her ever-helpful doctor with the then-fashionable tranquilliser Valium, rather than her usual 'upper', Benzedrine. This medication evidently dulled her senses although she didn't make the connection when regretfully writing about a sail on the yacht of some new friends: 'Water a wonderful emerald, indigo & saffron, & I liked the little mad houses built on stilts over the water, but <u>nothing sang to me</u>. (Oh, for a taste of the madeleine!)'.

The day before her birthday that year, Pamela dolefully wrote: 'So end my Fifties, & I am glad to say good-bye to them. On the whole, they have meant ill-health, & only small oases of happiness. Better luck for me in my sixties.' CPS gave her a 'delightful' pearl and amethyst brooch, and she also received a 'most queer gift' from the manager of the Six Bells in Chelsea. It was a chunk of stone from the fountain in the pub garden to remind her, he said, of when she used to sit beside it with Dylan. She did little on the actual day, which was clouded by the illness of her favourite cat, but Macmillans made a big party for her two days later.

The reviews immediately following the British publication of CPS's *The Malcontents* in June were 'fair', according to Pamela, but there were later sufficient good ones in the more prestigious periodicals to keep CPS's post-publication dejection at bay. The book might be categorized as a political thriller, but it is not worlds away from the first novel in his *Strangers and Brothers* sequence, focusing as it does on a group of young radical students in a provincial university town identifiable as Leicester. Among the reviews which might have been rated as 'mixed', two came from writers of the same generation as CPS's protagonists. The first of these was the 19-year-old Martin Amis, reviewing in the *Observer*. Despite initially mocking CPS's efforts to speak the language of 1970s' students, he went on to praise 'Snow's tolerance and honesty, and his eloquence when writing about the possibilities of doing good and the difficulties of behaving well'. The second review, coincidentally also by the son of an established novelist, came in the *Spectator* from 32-year-old Auberon Waugh. Although he had been critical of CPS's writings in the past, on this occasion Waugh was comparatively benign: the headline was 'C.P. Snow: shows promise', and although much of the content was tongue-in-cheek, he said (obviously with no knowledge of *Death Under Sail*), that: 'The new talent which Lord Snow reveals is that of the mystery suspense writer. [...] I am prepared to bet that he could write a really first-class detective thriller if he set himself to it.'

Kay Dick was now compiling a book of interviews with her writer friends. She had begged Pamela to be the first of her interviewees, on the grounds she wrote, in a lengthy autobiographical afterword incorporating her reflections on the nature of friendship, that, 'Pam, for over thirty years, had seen me through many of the joys and pains of my personal life'.[3] Although most of those events directly related to Kay's twenty-two years with Kathleen Farrell, the latter remains a hidden figure in the book, despite at least two of the other contributors (Olivia Manning and Francis King) being particular friends of both Ks from their joint Hampstead days. King offered an insight into the Hampsteadites' pleasure in gossip which had so plagued the Snows. He discussed with Kay their similar reactions when anecdotes came their way:

> I won't name names, but we have mutual friends, and, if we were ordinary people, you would telephone me, or I would telephone you, and say, 'Isn't it absolutely monstrous what X has done now?' Whereas you ring me up or I ring you up and say, 'I must tell you something absolutely priceless that X has done.' It's a different attitude. [...] We're collectors, and when X has produced some extraordinary example of misbehaviour, we're not scandalised at all; it's as though we'd dug up something in an antique shop. (p.131)

Despite Pamela's annoyance with Kay over the called-in loan, she agreed to her request in July, even though, as both of them had anticipated, she found the process 'extremely tiring'. Kay mentioned Pamela's slow recovery from her stroke the previous year in the introduction to their discussion, saying that her co-operation in these circumstances was 'yet another instance of Pam's instinctual response to friendship' (p.13). The pattern of the interviews was to ask the s ubjects to describe their childhood, the beginnings of their literary career and their political views on a number of issues, and finally to discuss their attitude to death. Kay did not, however, perhaps for once being tactful, ask Pamela about the latter. Pamela spoke at the greatest length very fondly about her childhood and adolescence, and this may have been the seed from which *Important to Me* grew. When invited to comment on the contemporary literary scene, her heartfelt reply was:

> I think I'd loathe to be a young writer today. It's far harder to get going. The costing is so much higher [...]. The sales of novels are

slumping very badly. We've lost so much now the lending libraries are all gone [...]. I think there's a certain polarization between novels that are generally popular, and novels that are not popular at all, but get a lot of admiration. Very miserable.

In September, CPS was invited to attend a Theoretical Physics Symposium in Trieste, and they decided to combine this with a few days in Venice before and after the event. 'Drenching rain', as usual, greeted them, and the following day Pamela had her usual bout of diarrhoea once abroad, but on this occasion it was still more unfortunate, coinciding, as it did, with a rare event, the procession of the Pope up the Canale Grande, which CPS had been able to see from their hotel balcony 'while I', she moaned, 'couldn't move'. But the following day, they had a delightful surprise when their son, who had been travelling again in Africa, nonchalantly strolled onto the terrace where they were having pre-dinner cocktails, 'looking like the historic traveller – shorts & jersey, & miles of bare leg'. Philip accompanied them to Trieste, and attended the symposium with his father while Pamela stayed in the hotel, initially enjoying 'the most idyllic view from the balcony', but then recording her moods 'swinging between a sort of ecstasy & the blackest bouts of depression'. These continued when they returned to Venice, compounded by CPS suffering from what he assumed to be bad bouts of indigestion. Although Pamela still considered that 'Venice remains very much "our place"', she now sadly came to the conclusion that the idea of retiring there which they had occasionally considered was unrealistic, because 'to live there now, with no domestic help & more stairs than we've got already, must be intolerable'. She was also continually searching for a rational explanation of her 'hideous states of depression': 'I couldn't have a more beloved husband, nor be more proud of my children. But the Black Dog (Churchill's) sits all too frequently on my shoulders.'

A short visit to the United States in October also held little enjoyment for Pamela; with CPS's engagements involving travelling between Baltimore, Philadelphia and New York, her feelings were 'that wherever I am, I want to get away'. They returned to England on the day of the publication of *The Holiday Friend*; the initial reviews, she wrote, were 'respectful, but all pretty dim'. She admitted moping about these the next day: 'Have I "had it"? Am I a kind of respected has-been? And can I go on?' She quoted from Macheath's lament in jail in the final act of *The Beggar's Opera*: 'I tremble, I droop. See my courage is out.' But Macheath had a last-minute reprieve, and similarly on the following Sunday morning, her daughter woke her at 10 a.m. to tell her that 'the Sunday press was splendid!' 'And so it was', she rejoiced: 'A great relief. [...] So perhaps I <u>can</u> go on after all!'

In the *Observer*, Anthony Thwaite had written that:

> Pamela Hansford Johnson is marvellously adept at getting the maximum effect out of slyly false trails in the narrative, so that a hint here, a conversation there, make one feel that, though something nasty is looming, it will strike elsewhere. She also manages very well the almost suffocating atmosphere of holiday routine, normality, decency and high-mindedness, and this adds to the tension of a book which slowly poises itself for its final horrific lurch.

An excerpt from Maurice Wiggin's rave review in the *Sunday Times* the same day became the quotation used in Macmillan's subsequent advertisements for the novel. *The Holiday Friend* was, he declared:

> possibly the best novel which Pamela Hansford Johnson has written; certainly right up to her highest standard. It is one of the rather few novels which I have read in recent months which I can recommend with no reservations – with a blithe assurance that any intelligent reader will find it absorbing and rewarding.

Still more satisfying probably for Pamela, Wiggin had addressed the problem of style about which she had been self-critical because she had been unable to write by hand, and he combined this with approval of her reticence in conveying the pleasures of Gavin and Hannah's marital congress:

> No gutter language – Miss Hansford Johnson has the grace to present subtle and illuminating insights in simple language. Lucid and limpid, her admirable novel carries absolute conviction; her people live, every shade and nuance of thought, language and behaviour captured with an art that seems effortless, though of course it is anything but.

Pamela's revival of spirits was sadly short-lived. For the rest of the year, her diary entries are harrowing to read as she felt reluctant to share her despair with family or friends, and also rejected any thought of psychiatric help. 'What a comfort a diary is!', she wrote. 'It is "someone" to tell.' She was plagued with fears of an early death, and sedulously recorded news of the deaths of people she had known from the past as well as those from the present, and public figures. The first category included her wartime friend Ron Payne, and she grieved that she had lost touch with him, remembering 'those lively & apprehensive days at the Wardens' Post'. Hearing, however, about the death of a member of Victor Neuberg's circle left her with an unanswerable question as to whether that woman had been, as both Pamela and CPS suspected, the author of 'those horrible anonymous letters that plagued me for so many years? Or did I do her a grave injustice? I shall never know.' The memory lingered, and would resurface in Pamela's final novel.

1973 was also to be a year of obituary notices and memorial services. The first of the latter in January was for L.P. Hartley whom Pamela remembered as 'a kind old thing', whom she had always enjoyed meeting at parties; the next was in March, for Max Adrian, whose performances in her Proust reconstructions she had delighted in. Elizabeth Bowen died in February, and two further acquaintances died in March. The latter were the theatre impresario Binkie Beaumont and Noël Coward (who, when meeting her some ten years earlier, had been, she had written 'exceedingly nice about my books, which surprised & pleased me'). 'God seems to be swatting people like flies', she commented. In May, she heard of the apparent suicide of 'my old foe, Ken Allsop', and wrote that she felt sorry, and wished she had forgiven him in her heart.[4]

Early in the New Year, Pamela realised that she had forgotten to mention in her diary 'what would have seemed so important once', which was that she had made a tentative beginning on a new book, 'not a novel', but the book which would become *Important to Me*, although her first choice of title had been '*What I Believe*'. Capital letters show that her initial enthusiasm about the book was not so much about its contents as that she felt capable of writing again 'IN HOLOGRAPH'. Once the book was underway, despite her fragile state of health, she felt compelled to write throughout the day: 'I only write well', she said, 'when I am writing quickly.' Her solution to the problem of having to overcome acute tiredness was, as she admitted, to smoke and drink too much. Certain chapters understandably gave her particular difficulties; she was 'dreadfully distressed' when writing about the last years of her mother's life.

Within a month, however, she estimated the wordcount of the first draft at around 60,000 words. 'Don't know', she wrote, 'if it is going to show a bit too much self-love or self-disgust – which are much the same thing.' Her comment might well have been made when she was writing Chapter 29: Depressions. To some extent, she downplayed her own condition, which almost certainly today would be diagnosed as clinical depression; apart from her frequent bouts of acute sadness, her diary attests to other classic symptoms, particularly groundless feelings of guilt. She answered the question she assumed would be in the reader's mind: 'No, I have not consulted a psychiatrist, and I shan't. I am not bad enough for that,' and then attempted to lighten the topic with an anecdote about George Best's attitude when forced to consult a psychiatrist (p.207).[5] Nevertheless, there is pain evident in her desire to understand why she should be so afflicted:

> So, with all the suffering in this tormented world, who am I to have these depressive bouts? But that is an idiotic question, and I dare say I simply put it in to make myself look less callous, and more 'aware'. Those of us who do have to endure these things, know perfectly well that with all our mental strivings and wrenchings, we cannot help them.

'I am writing this,' she continued, 'partly as a form of catharsis, and partly because it may reassure others like me that they are not alone' (p.209). In a postscript added just before publication in 1974, she added in the hope of bringing further comfort to others that her depressions had largely disappeared (p.211); this hiatus was unfortunately to be short-lived. Despite her increasing lack of faith in her doctor, *Important to Me* was dedicated to Sofaer's three children, and despite her husband's almost total antipathy to him, CPS's novel, *In Their Wisdom*, also published in 1974, was dedicated: 'To My Friend David Sofaer'. However, Andrew Stewart told me that CPS did this as a form of revenge in the knowledge that Sofaer never read books and so would be unaware that the character of the odious Dr. Pemberton in that novel had been in part based upon him.

Along with the rest of the country, Pamela had domestic problems caused by the challenges by an increased number of trade unions to Edward Heath's government. Having got used to electrical blackouts, she became particularly worried about the prospect of a threatened gas strike, since she believe this would necessitate turning off the gas supply at the meter: 'This is all a horror to me, as I am not mechanically minded or strong, my chest is weak & I dread the cold abnormally.' Evidently in the belief, despite their past summer experiences, that they might be better off in Belgium in April than in England, she and CPS went to Le Coq with Philip and one of his friends for ten days which would prove atrociously cold, and be combined, for Pamela, with both deep depression and anorexia. However, on one of the last days, she witnessed what was for her a transcendental alteration in the seascape before her as the skies cleared, and shortly afterwards did manage to accompany the others to Ghent to revisit Jan van Eyck's 'Adoration of the Mystic Lamb'. These two events gave her the impetus to add a final chapter to *Important to Me* there and then, which ends:

> From the bitingly cold short holiday on the Belgian coast, I have learned much. The eternal uplifting transformations of the sea, the benediction of Van Eyck. I hope they may stay with me. (p.254)

Sadly in fact, on their return, she reverted to a depressive state, and a resolution to cut down on Scotch and cigarettes seemed to do her little good. She cried out to her diary, her only confidante: 'And the concealment of all this! The concealment! When is God going to help me, or don't I deserve it? I am trying to straighten out my life.' A revelatory entry concerns the brief respite of 'an ecstasy of joy' she experienced one day when CPS had suddenly mused about:

> how it would have been if he had written to me – as he had intended – in 1935, & we had met: "We'd have had four children by now!" As I have so long doubted if he still loved me, this made me marvellously happy.

Her daughter, who had had a number of jobs, including a frantic short spell working for the film director Ken Russell, had decided to accept the offer of a position in a publishing house in Budapest. Her father had worked as a journalist in Hungary after his divorce from Pamela and before his return to Australia; and although the job offer had nothing to do with him, Lindsay told me:

Having for so long been introduced to people as C.P. Snow's daughter (when I was in fact his step-daughter), I was thrilled when people in authority in Hungary said approvingly, 'Oh, you're Neil Stewart's daughter.' It had never previously happened.

She left England in May. Pleased as she was for her daughter, Pamela knew she would miss Lindsay greatly. That month, CPS left for a fairly short visit to Newfoundland – to collect another honorary degree, and she mentioned how lonely she felt each day before his return. She was also very apprehensive about who would be replacing Conchita who was finally determined to leave in October, even though this was some months away. Fortunately, Pamela very much liked one of the applicants for the job of housekeeper; she described Doris Cadney as 'very tall, bony' and 'not lacking in a quiet humour'. Doris was to stay with her for the rest of her life, and become a treasured friend.

During that summer, there was a spate of bombs in department stores; Pamela continued to keep her regular appointments in the hairdressing salon in Harrods, and attempted to make light of the frequent disruptions. 'Must say,' she wrote, 'that sitting under the drier in these circumstances is on the trying side.' She was more concerned, presumably for CPS's sake, when play in the Lord's Test Match against the West Indies was delayed because of a hoax bomb threat, and later the same day, when supporters of the away team invaded the pitch and, she wrote, 'jostled, punched & shoved' Geoffrey Boycott. She despaired at 'the uglification of this world!!'.

Fortunately, her next engagement restored her spirits for a while. Earlier in the year, Pamela had been delighted to be asked to accept an honorary degree from Widener University, Pennsylvania, particularly as she would be the first woman to do so, and, above all, because the ceremony, 'blessedly', would not involve transatlantic travel, but would take place in Oxford in the summer. Although as the time approached, she became fearful about the occasion, she managed successfully to lecture to a large audience of students and members of the university faculty in the morning, before the conferring of the degree in the evening. She exulted: 'Never saw a more beautiful ceremony – and in Queen's College Chapel!'

The seesawing of her moods then took another dip when she learned by chance that CPS had arranged to go to India the following March: 'The habit of secrecy (an old one) is growing on him, & I don't like it. He says I would have tried to stop him – too right I would.' He went on his own to America in the autumn, and she sank into such deep depression that she could not decide whether or not she was longing for his return, writing: 'only hope I am in a fit state to keep him happy'. She was in fact ecstatic to have him home again, because there were to be further major changes in the composition of her household. In addition to Lindsay still working in Hungary, and Philip due to leave for a year in Singapore since he had switched to reading Chinese at Balliol, Andrew left England in September to take up a lectureship in physics at the University of New South Wales in Sydney. Conchita did retire to Catalonia in October (to the accompaniment of many tears from both of them). It would be the first time that all Pamela's children (and Conchita, for the past eleven years) had not been with her at Christmas, but, since she had so often registered her aversion to the festival, she was content to send Doris, her new housekeeper, back to her family in order that she and CPS could be 'perfectly quiet & peaceful' on their own.

On New Year's Eve, Pamela was again glad to bid farewell to a 'horrible year', in which she had felt in 'a state of hebetude'[6] throughout. Her final comment in her 1973 diary was that she resolved to leave 'positive instructions that these diaries are not to be looked at for 40 years after my death. They are so wretched, & make me appear such a wretched creature.' (In fact, a clause in her will reduced the period of embargo to twenty-five years.) It is to be hoped that the readers of the diary entries quoted in this biography will not have that opinion of Pamela, but have sympathy for her, as well as admiration that, despite her failing strength, she was continuing to write to the high standard that she had set herself.

Pamela did begin 1974 more confidently. At the end of the previous October, she had had an idea for a novel, which she intended to call *The Good Listener*, but she did not mention this again until the first day of the new year, when she recorded making extensive notes for this book. She was also re-reading James Pope-Hennessy's 1971 biography of Anthony Trollope, since she had been commissioned to write an article for the *Sunday Times* prior to the television series based on the Palliser novels. She started the new novel at her usual speed, despite her writing, as she put it, being 'execrable' again, and her typewriter breaking down 'hopelessly' for days while she frustratedly awaited a mechanic's visit. She completed the Trollope assignment and was forced to submit it in the form of 'a very bad holograph'. The article, which occupied a prominent position on the first of the *Sunday Times* arts pages (13 January 1974), took the form of an intro-duction for the benefit of viewers who might be unfamiliar with Trollope's novels, and she began:

> I do not know when I have looked forward so eagerly to any television series as I do the BBC'S version of Trollope's Palliser novels. Dickens, the greater novelist, told us about other people, most of them much larger than life: Trollope told us about ourselves, precisely as we are. Among all writers, I know few who are psychologically wiser.

She reiterated again at the end:

> As I have said, I await the series with breath properly bated. Will it come through, all that Trollope has to tell us *about ourselves*? Shall we have that shock of recognition? – "Yes, *I* am like that!" We must wait and see. This will be the final test – but the story will hold us anyway.

However, she was to find the first episode 'unpromising – far too tricky', and although she watched each of the subsequent twenty-five episodes, she was generally very critical of the series.

The same Sunday that Pamela's Pallisers preview appeared, the *Sunday Telegraph* published the first of three full-page essays by her which were published in consecutive weeks under the general title of 'Ruling Passions'. These had been written the previous year at a time of stress, yet they are exemplary, lucid expositions of her beliefs about the issues facing contemporary British society. The newspaper's respect for her was exhibited by the banner announcement of all three at the top of the front page of each issue. The subheadings below testify to the wide range of topics she explored:

> 13 January 1974:
> A woman novelist's critical eye on the forces that make us all tick.
> Silliness about sex – and the realities of power
> Cheapening – an evil of our times
> A message for militants who would like to see society break down:
> Out of rubble came Hitler, and anarchy may bring him again.
>
> 20 January 1974
> Envy and avarice up to date

If you sincerely want to be cured of desire for possessions ...
Privilege – why begrudge it to the academically gifted but not to the
physically bright?
Demands for more – there must be limits
Wanted – a new attitude towards the successful immigrant

27 January 1974
Race, class and sport in the 'seventies
When mass passions ride high

In the first of these essays, she showed herself willing to run the risk
of mockery from the gossipmongers by discussing the role of sex
within a long-term partnership:

> Sex-with-love, whether heterosexual or homosexual, is the most
> wonderful state known to mankind. *And it can last.* [...] the first
> passion may cool to a deep, self-abnegating love – the deepest care on
> both sides being for the other person – which will itself endure, in
> increasing friendship, sympathy and understanding, even after the
> sexual impulse itself has flagged with the growing years or has even
> died away. We must not have the ridiculous hope that our bodily urges
> will be the same at 70 as they are at 17 – though even this has been
> known.

It is clear, though, that Pamela was not as resigned as she might
sound above with regard to the situation in her own marriage which
had remained sexless for many years. While writing about Dylan
Thomas the previous year, a wistful memory had surfaced of her
youthful surprise about the happy sexual relations enjoyed by his
parents 'well into late middle-age'. When she visited Swansea on her
own after breaking up with Dylan, she remembered: 'Florrie would
say sometimes, in the afternoon, "Excuse me, dear, but Jack does like
me to go up on the bed with him"' (*Important*, p.147). Her attitude
might further be surmised from a poignant fiction-within-a-fiction,
recounted in the novel she was now engaged in writing. An admirer
of the writing of a young literary lion reads out to a group of friends
a parable at the end of his latest novel, telling the story of 'a country
where there is no marriage nor giving in marriage', but where, if
a marriage has previously taken place elsewhere, 'a husband and
wife who have loved, may continue to love profoundly and with
infinite tenderness: but without sexuality.' A woman comes to this

country in search of her husband, who has accepted those rules, but she cannot:

> [...] her love had been so overmastering that she wanted him still. It had transcended the gift of eternal bliss. So she continued to ache and to implore, and he to love her and to smile. But, he said, all the rest was over, like a dream forgotten. Surely they existed on the summits of happiness, untroubled, upon the exquisite plateau?'

'So,' the narrator continues, 'for this woman, the country became not a paradise but a torment', and the lord of the country, out of mercy, commits her to a watery grave.[7]

On February 2, she and CPS went to Brighton for the weekend, not on this occasion staying at the Dudley. His declaration of love, sent from the latter hotel, would have been received by her exactly twenty-five years to the day, but she did not say that this had been the reason for their visit. In fact, most of their short stay was taken up with consoling Kathleen Farrell who had been having a brief reconciliation with Kay Dick. As Pamela recorded, the couple had recently 'come to another of the "endings"', adding 'I wonder', despite going on to say that now 'Kay apparently follows Kathleen round the streets yelling abuse'. On their return home, Pamela received a 'most wonderful basket of flowers' from Kathleen; 'Sweet of her', she commented, 'but I think she must be mad: she says C & I gave her such comfort and release. Think we only told her some pragmatic things about Kay and drank her whisky.'

Still at loggerheads with the trade unions, Edward Heath had had to impose a three-day working week with effect from January 1, and after a month during which the National Union of Mineworkers threatened to turn their work-to-rule into an all-out strike, he called a snap General Election. Pamela had little sympathy for the miners' leaders; she had said in her first essay in the *Sunday Telegraph* that 'I have nothing but respect for the long and honourable history of the trade unions. But today's extreme militants [...] seem less concerned about "rights" than about the sheer pushing for power itself.' She predicted that, as it was now all 'a hideous muddle', the likely result was that the Labour Party would get back 'without an overall majority', and she was to be proved right. The Conservative slogan for the election was 'Who governs Britain?' The nation seemed unsure of the answer and a hung Parliament did indeed result, with the Labour Party winning three more seats than the Conservatives, although the latter party polled more votes. After abortive negotiations with the minority parties, Heath agreed to resign, and Harold Wilson became Prime Minister again. The miners' strike was called off, and there was to be a second General Election that autumn, when the Labour Party gained an overall majority of just three seats.

CPS's tour of India was called off on the grounds of 'popular unrest' there. Pamela was sorry about his disappointment, but couldn't help feeling relieved to be spared any further worries. There had been several recent air disasters which had unnerved her (most recently, the crash of a Turkish Airlines plane just outside Orly, in which there had been no survivors). She and CPS were due to fly to New York for a short visit in April and then undertake a strenuous speaking tour in France in May, and she wrote that: 'The American & French trips loom over me like an ordeal.' The American visit did not encompass an honorary degree for CPS this time, but a still more prestigious event at the United Nations in connection with the signing of a declaration on Food & Population. In addition to being one of the signatories, CPS had been chosen to make the formal presentation to Kurt Waldheim, then the UN Secretary-General. Pamela was relieved that she had borne up 'very well on the whole' throughout the long day of receptions, lunch and dinner, having taken care not to drink much. They flew back two days later, but she was not particularly grateful to have been spared a more lengthy tour, reflecting that 'these short Atlantic trips are killers'.

The visit to France should have been far more to her liking, since it only involved one short flight, and there was room in their schedule to spend some time in the area associated with Marcel Proust. Unfortunately Pamela had a new health problem; one of her feet had become extremely painful and cortisone injections had not been effective. Their first day did not augur well; they travelled to Lille via a flight to Brussels and then a train, involving 'awful lugging of heavy bags at station'. Immediately on arrival, they went to a book signing at the largest bookshop in France, then to the University where they jointly lectured on Dickens and Trollope, then to a cocktail party, and finally to a dinner. Her diary entry ended: 'Dead tired, having been in pain almost whole day. Am hoping for the sheer guts to go through this trip.'

Other days followed a similar pattern, with the day in Illiers the only recompense. (The town had been renamed Illiers-Combray three years earlier to mark the centenary of Proust's birth and his depiction of Illiers as 'Combray' in *À la recherche du temps perdu*.) The visit had been all that Pamela could have wished for:

> Were shown privately over the house of Tante Amiot – the little garden & Proust's basket chair, the bell Swann rang. Tante Léonie's & Marcel's bedrooms, the chandelier in the salon. Then took a drive to the Pré Catalan – where there was <u>pink</u> hawthorn as well as white! My main kick of the day. And the 'Vivonnet' looked delightful.
> So did the countryside from the train – gorse blazing, aubépines too, & beautifully planted trees.

She was nevertheless relieved to return home; eventually, after X-ray examinations, a node on the bone of her right foot was found to have been the cause of her pain, but it continued to trouble her.

In a burst of activity, she completed *The Good Listener*; this time, the novel had taken her six months to write. The eponymous description relates to Toby Roberts, a young man initially met in his finals year at Cambridge, with his two friends, Bob and Adrian. Toby is reading History, although he is unsure of his future career path, Bob is expected to gain a First in Physics, and Adrian is reading Theology and hoping to be ordained into a High Anglican order. In the first chapter, the two sides of Toby's nature are established. He has formed a tentative relationship with Maisie, who is reading English at Girton; she is reticent, and Toby knows little about her background, but discovers from Adrian that her mother keeps 'open house for writers and artists and so forth'. Toby listens, as is his wont, but makes no reply while pondering: 'Whom could he expect to meet if he were ever to be invited to the house in Suffolk? He has a somewhat exaggerated faith in the advantages of meeting people.' He also considers whether it might be expedient to ask Maisie first to his modest South London home, and here reveals both his fondness for his parents and the gap he senses opening between himself and them:

> He felt a rush of defensiveness for his parents. They were dear to him, and he was grateful for the sacrifices they had made. But – he could not help it – every time he returned to SE1 he felt like Fanny Price paying a family visit after a long spell at Mansfield Park. (pp.8-9)

He does invite Maisie to meet his parents, and she enthuses about his mother's paintings, which both Toby and his father had always considered to be little more than a hobby. With her mother's contacts in the art world, Maisie arranges a small exhibition in Cambridge, which leads to Mrs Roberts' work gaining recognition, not only in England, but also in America. The omniscient narrator of the novel often interjects a sarcastic comment about the new world which opens up for Toby's mother, as when Maisie's mother brings a group of her friends to the opening night of that first exhibition, who look round 'in the manner of persons at a private view, unspeaking but with looks of infinite arcane knowledge on their faces' (p.62). Ironically, it is due to the success of his self-taught mother that Toby's world also expands, and eventually, the pragmatic side of his nature takes over from the romantic as he transfers his affections from Maisie to Claire, the daughter of a peer who is a merchant banker and intimates that he might be able to offer Toby a job in the City. The destinies of his friends from their undergraduate days form counterpoints to Toby's self-serving progress; Bob gets trapped into a loveless marriage, and Adrian is disillusioned about his calling, yet both of them have a sense of morality that Toby only occasionally exhibits.

After some months of mutually enthusiastic sex, Claire rejects Toby's marriage proposal, but, showing herself to be even more pragmatic then he is, declares nevertheless that 'we've had gorgeous fun together, and [...] we can go on doing so'. Somewhat to his own surprise as well as hers, Toby immediately walks out on her, and knows that he will never return: 'He could not have meant it perhaps, he thought with a flash of insight, if she had really broken his heart, but she had certainly damaged it, and had wrecked his pride (p.224)'. Claire has, however, served her purpose and he prospers in her father's merchant bank. In the serio-comic closing passage of the novel, Pamela reveals that the characterization of Toby had been inspired by a central character in Honoré de Balzac's series of novels, *La Comédie Humaine*. It is New Year's Eve, and he is alone, and, on a whim, Toby drives to the highest point of Hampstead:

> There was all London lying below him, and it seemed to him that it was there for the taking.
>   He did not say, as Rastignac did when surveying Paris from the

heights, "It's between the two of us from now on", since Toby had never read a word of Balzac.

But the challenge was there, and he did think something precious like it.

In the meantime, CPS had completed *his* new novel, *In Their Wisdom*, and had started discussions of a dramatization of the book with Ronald Millar. Alan Maclean, their editor at Macmillan, then, to Pamela's dismay, revealed to her that CPS had 'a certain plan' about which she was supposed to be kept in ignorance. She felt yet again 'immoderately upset, as I hate concealment between C & myself'. About six weeks later, her suspicions were confirmed; CPS's theatrical ambitions were not just confined to writing but also to acting in his own plays. She felt that this would have been 'disastrous for his charisma', but refrained from telling him so. She was extremely relieved when Millar later told her that 'the acting idea is OFF!', due to objections from Equity, the actors' trade union. 'It would <u>not</u>', Pamela told Millar, 'have been in the style of an international sage!', and she further asked him 'if he thought Carlyle would have performed in Ronnie's dramatised version of <u>The French Revolution</u>!'.

Important to Me was published in September. Pamela had anticipated 'a non-event', but the book received notices in the majority of the newspapers and periodicals in which her novels were usually reviewed. She was pleasurably surprised with the first she read, all the more so because it came from Julian Symons. He discussed at some length the concurrencies in their two lives, and continued:

> The personal note seems right, because this collection of jottings and reminiscences which she calls 'Personalia' is basically an autobiography, done with an apparent casualness that conceals a brilliantly skilful shaping and placing of material.

'The portrait that emerges', he continued, 'is of a very intelligent and humane woman whose commonsensibleness conceals a powerful romantic idealism.'

In *The Listener*, the novelist A.L. Barker opened her full-page critique by admitting her long addiction to Pamela's novels, and described why she takes such pleasure from her writing:

She is not in the 'mainstream' of the contemporary novel, and as she
herself says, who wants to be, now that the stream has become a dirty
effluent? She is not a stylist, a turner of phrases. About that, she has
something to say, too: 'It is no use showing off. You will only, when
the chips are down, have produced the effect of having done so.'
Nevertheless, phrases *are* turned, and one remembers them for their
truth as well as their felicity.

Barker's overall judgment on *Important to Me* is similar to that of
Symons: 'These short pieces [...] supply more of the essence of the
writer than any sewn-up autobiography.' Pamela's 'Partial Conclusion'
had considered death, but ended 'Meanwhile, it would be as well if
I started thinking about writing another novel' (*Important*, p.250);
Barker quoted this remark and appended: 'It would, indeed.' A final
review, which also delighted Pamela, came from Sylvia Secker (*Times
Literary Supplement*), and began:

> How often does the reader feel an immediate affinity with a writer?
> The immediacy, in this case, is established in the introduction, in which
> Pamela Hansford Johnson writes: 'It is hard for me to believe in divine
> forgiveness if one has not the forgiveness of the living.'

'So far as I was concerned,' Secker continued, 'Miss Hansford Johnson
had no need to write further for me to be her disciple. This apart, she
writes with the utmost lucidity and with great beauty of phrase.
She is also, praise be, not afraid to voice unfashionable opinions.'
   Unfortunately, CPS's *In Their Wisdom* received a bad press when
published shortly afterward. Worse awaited: his accountant confessed
that, due to his own 'fainéant' (Pamela's description, i.e., slothful)
behaviour, CPS owed £20,000 to the Inland Revenue for income tax.
The timing of this revelation could not have been worse, as they were
due to leave for nearly three weeks in America. Not surprisingly, CPS
remained in a state of depression on both counts throughout, so not
only was the trip the usual nightmare for Pamela as reflected by her
handwriting getting ever more cramped throughout, but, for once,
she criticized her husband to her diary, complaining that: 'Charles's
constant despondency is weighing heavily on me.'
   The year ended with a boost to Pamela's morale. In previous years,
there had been hints that she might be named in the New Year

Honours List, but each time she had been disappointed. Late in November, however, marked with heavy lines in the margin, and in writing noticeably larger and freer than of late, she recorded:

> My CBE at last came up, in letter from PM's office. Felt quite dazed for hours, as I had not been expecting it at all. [...] Am really v. excited – it does seem as though a life's work has at last got some acknowledgment. Keep on even now thinking there may be slips between cup & lips!

But there was to be no slip, and on New Year's Day, 1975, she received many telegrams and letters congratulating her. She was amused to have been honoured in a list that also announced knighthoods for Charles Chaplin, the cricketer Gary Sobers, and controversially, P.G. Wodehouse. Her brother-in-law wrote to say that he considered that she should have been made 'a Dame of the Order', and she replied that she would not have wanted anything more, adding, optimistically: 'When I am 80 I shall accept a pantomime title if they offer it ...'.[8] She did also find Olivia Manning's attempt at felicitations in a telephone call 'rather comic', since it consisted largely of commiserating with her on her bad health. 'Asssured her that I hadn't been better for years,' she wrote, 'but I doubt whether she was so pleased by <u>that</u>!'

An invitation to an evening reception at Buckingham Palace came within a few days, and Pamela took pleasure from feeling that she had been invited to this in her own right, rather than as the consort of CPS. It turned out to be a very mixed gathering, ranging from politicians – 'Lord Home (wearing remarkably well), Macmillan [...] & H. Wilson, most amiable but sloshed' – to John Betjeman and Morecambe and Wise (the latter pair warranted an exclamation mark in her diary). Edward Heath, who had just resigned after having been beaten in the Conservative Party leadership contest by Margaret Thatcher, was also there. Although it was a long evening, Pamela overcame her now usual aversion to big gatherings, and thoroughly enjoyed it. Shortly afterward, she also had an agreeable evening as the dinner companion of Philip Larkin at an event at Sidney Sussex College, Cambridge: he had, she wrote, 'a curious glum humour I find most appealing', adding: 'And he is, I think, a major poet.' The investiture ceremony, a few days later, came, however, as something

of an anti-climax. Pamela had to admit that 'it is dreadfully dull apart
from one's own bit', giving her time to muse about how the Queen
Mother, presiding in the Queen's absence, could stand 'on those dainty
feet for a solid hour'.

Despite her bravado about her health to Olivia Manning, Pamela
now fell back into a state of lassitude. She was unhappy about being
left alone so frequently, but she often chose to stay at home as she was
increasingly exhibiting some symptoms of agoraphobia. After a visit
to Peter Jones, the nearby department store in Sloane Square, she
admitted to her diary: 'I go out so little alone these days that I am
beginning to be afraid of the traffic.' She was not working, and she
seemed to be happiest when watching her old favourites on television
(she had always enjoyed a musical quiz, *Face the Music*, keeping score
and being delighted when she beat the panel). Now she looked forward to some new programmes, particularly *Mastermind* and *Upstairs,
Downstairs*, especially if her housekeeper was able to watch with her.
She was cheered when *Important to Me* received 'most wonderful
notices' when published in America during the spring; she realised
that she had received more letters from admirers for her 'Personalia'
than for any of her previous works. 'What on earth is happening to
that book?' she asked. 'Could it be selling?'

She was forced to come out of her partly self-imposed hibernation
because CPS was keen to attend celebrations being planned in Moscow
to mark the seventieth birthday of Mikhail Sholokhov. Apart from her
now virtually persistent fatigue, she was apprehensive that further
attacks on them would result, and did her best to dissuade him. 'Think
we have done enough for him [Sholokhov], without sticking our necks
out in this way,' she wrote. 'Though I don't believe anyone else wrote
his books.' (There had been, for some time, controversy about the
authorship of *Quiet Flows the Don*.) A month before the event, they
heard that Sholokhov was not well enough to go to Moscow, and
wanted the dinner in his honour to take place at his home. Pamela
was still less enthusiastic as this would involve even more tiring travel
for them, but felt that CPS did intend 'to lug us there'. She persuaded
him to consult James Callaghan, then the Foreign Secretary, but, to
Pamela's dismay, the official advice was to the effect that the Foreign
Office would wish them to go. So they left at the end of May, only to
be told on arrival at Moscow Airport that Sholokhov had had a stroke,

'so nobody will see him, & Veshenskaya trip is off'. A relieved Pamela recorded: 'Must admit the Sholokhov affair has amused C. & me, & will probably save us a lot of embarrassment.' With a certain lack of empathy, she continued: 'Poor chap, I hope he gets better soon. He has been off the drink for a year, because of diabetes. That alone is enough to give him a stroke!'

A lunch in honour of Sholokhov took place at the Writers' Union – 'very much Hamlet without the Prince' – and the remainder of their stay in Moscow was enlivened by Yevgeny Yevtushenko, 'radiating glamour & fun', plus champagne, at their joint press conferences, and inviting them for a day in his dacha (fortunately much nearer than Sholokhov's). He told them a great deal about the present situation regarding Alexandr Solzhenitsyn, who had been expelled as a dissident from the Soviet Union the previous year, and about his efforts to help him 'as best he could'. Pamela remained very enamoured of 'Zhenya': 'He is really one of the most remarkable people I have ever met, & when he speaks seriously, does so with maximum authority. Constantly interesting.' But she had some reservations about his personal life, writing that he was 'an inveterate womaniser & will never change'; he was living at that time with Jan Butler (his English translator, and his current lover), while his then wife and their child were in the Crimea. Arrangements were discussed for Yevtushenko to stay with them in London that autumn.

The Good Listener was published in June. Although this novel, its sequel, and her final novel do not have the descriptive power and emotional depth of her earlier works, the reviews for this book were in general satisfying for her. Pamela mentioned a 'splendid review' in *The Times*, but strangely did not mention in her diary that this had been written by Susan Hill, who had remained in constant touch with the Snow family. Hill began:

> The light shining steadily through each page of Pamela Hansford John-son's new novel is the light of quality – quality of mind, of perception, imagination and prose. She has always been a profoundly wise writer, but has never gone in for showing demonstrations of what she knows, both by instinct and after long reflection, to be the truth.

She admitted that 'there is nothing remarkable or out-of-the-way about the three young men, up at Cambridge in the 1950s' around whom the novel is built, but she believed that the author had never been 'so clever nor so shrewd as in her presentation of Toby' and concluded:

> The Tobys of this world are hard to pin down, but Pamela Hansford Johnson has done it. This ripe, reflective novel is worth a score of those which may make more noise, create more of a fracas. They will explode and vanish. This will endure.

In the *New Statesman*, Julian Barnes, then a reviewer whose first novel would not be published for several years, in general applauded this 'love story with moral connections [which] turns on the failure of feeling and the consequences of faulty emotional decisions', continuing:

> The structure, the leisurely tempo, and the hero's psychology make much of *The Good Listener* read like updated Turgenev. If at times the prose bears an air of *déja lu*, especially in the similes, these are occasional distractions from a wise percipience.

The more critical reviews share a note of regret. Peter Ackroyd, in *The Listener,* said that the novel was not dull, but 'not particularly astonishing either', and ended:

> Of course there are flashes of the old wit and percipience, and some of Miss Hansford Johnson's sentences are turned very nicely; but although there is an acute intelligence at work, it is one that is generally in abeyance.

Anne Duchêne (*Times Literary Supplement*) also harped back to the author's previous achievements:

> Finding the book's centre, its impulse, is the puzzle; the more so, since the writer is one whose attachment to something beyond her stories is usually passionate, and plain. [...] It is a measure of respect for this writer to feel disappointment when she does not impose a stricter, more illuminating pattern.

Both Pamela and CPS at that time were, however, more concerned with awaiting their son's Oxford Finals results. After eight days of tension, he received the news that he had achieved First Class Honours – 'the only one in Chinese in Oxford (or Cambridge, come to that)' – exulted his mother.

A fortnight's holiday in Venice in July proved less than idyllic for both Pamela and CPS. Despite staying in a deluxe room at the Gritti Palace with full air-conditioning, she still suffered from the heat at night, and from her feet by day, and CPS's self-diagnosed lumbago caused him much pain. They therefore were unable to go on the long unplanned walks of discovery they had previously enjoyed. They had also hoped to have left behind them the difficulties caused by union activity in Britain, but, soon after their arrival, a general strike of all hotel staff in Venice was called. 'What a home from home!', she wrote. 'All the Americans seem to take it in good part, & I have to say that to C & me it seems supremely comic!' The next day, the strike was proving fairly ineffective, although Pamela, with a rare metamorphosis into her alter ego, Lady Snow, found it inconvenient that 'we all had to eat inside & there were no tablecloths or cushions on the terrace'.

On their return, CPS's recorded conversation with Roy Plomley on 'Desert Island Discs' was broadcast. He admitted that music played no part in his life, but said that his choices were pieces that meant something to him. His brother was, however, of the opinion that his musical selection could 'go on record as being Pam's choice 100%'.⁹ But it is likely that the record he nominated as the one he would save from the waves was his own choice. It was an excerpt from *Henry IV*, Pt. 2, Act III, sc. ii, in which Falstaff and the local Justice reminisce about their youth, and it contains the immortal line: 'We have heard the chimes at midnight, Master Shallow.' CPS's choice of book was a Russian Grammar, and, predictably, his luxury item was writing materials. Plomley did not probe as deeply into the personal life of his interviewees as those who have followed as presenters of this programme, and Pamela is only mentioned in the context of their discussing their work with each other. She would have agreed with his answer to Plomley's query as to how he would manage on the island; CPS admitted that he would be 'a most incompetent castaway' since he was 'not very good' at looking after himself.

Pamela was now only very occasionally reviewing, and was no longer able to work with the enthusiasm and at the speed to which she had become accustomed; her review in the *New Statesman* (26 September 1975) of Margaret Drabble's *The Realms of Gold* took her two days to write. She had always admired and enjoyed Drabble's novels, but she found writing about this lengthy book a chore: 'My heart is so out for this sort of thing!', she admitted. Nevertheless, there was much in the novel that met Pamela's own criteria. She paid tribute to the way Drabble faced 'the small realities of life squarely; her people have toothache and they go to the lavatory', and thoroughly approved of her ability to be 'one of the frankest of writers now operating, though she sees no need for strings of four-letter words to give the effect'.

That month, Yevtushenko arrived to fulfil various engagements. Despite her fondness for him, Pamela found him a difficult house guest; she could never be sure when or if he would return for meals or for the night. 'He is dreadfully restless, & will pay for this some day,' she wrote. She also thought it 'the height of indiscretion' that Jan Butler was accompanying him (although she didn't stay with them). CPS took the poet to Cambridge, and Jan went with them. She told CPS on that occasion that she would never get married, as Zhenya had spoiled her for any other man. She did in fact marry Yevtushenko three years later, although the marriage was short-lived.

CPS was 70 in October; Pamela reflected that: 'I have known my dear C. for half his life. I wish it had been the whole of it.' He received 'masses of cards & telegrams' plus 'gifts of drink from Bulgarians and Russians'. His biography of Anthony Trollope was published the same day, and received 'a wonderful Sunday press' at the end of the week. His three publishers, then Macmillan, Penguin and Rainbird, gave a 'great party' for him at the Stationers' Hall. Pamela estimated that about 370 people attended the event, and proudly recorded: 'Harold Macmillan presided, made most elegant speech to which C. elegantly replied. [...] All a great triumph for dear C., & of course we sat up late talking it over.' They spent Christmas that year in Belgium, staying in Le Coq, because their son was taking a European Economic Community training course in Brussels. Pamela enjoyed 'the most unChristmassy of Christmas days', although she regretted that she was unable to accompany CPS and Philip on their walks, because she felt so 'tottery', and dreaded falling.

CHAPTER 21

'Why, This is HELL –
Nor am I out of it'

AT A PARTY to celebrate the silver wedding of Joyce and Harry Hoff early in January 1976, Pamela had an eerie experience: as she recounted, she sat next to 'an old lady with a crutch who informed me that she had heard that Snow's wife, Pamela Hansford Johnson, was very ill'. 'She was about to embroider the subject,' she continued, 'when I had to tell her who I was! It was just like reading one's own obituary.' An asterisk on this entry led to the addition dated 24 March 1976: 'How close she turned out to be!'. For nearly three weeks after that party, brief entries in cramped handwriting record her feeling 'rotten' and 'shivery', although she tried to fulfil engagements. Her blood pressure was high, and reverting to shorthand (used now very infrequently), she acknowledged that she had been smoking and drinking too much. They were due to leave for an extended stay in the USA to attend bicentennial events, and Pamela was resisting her doctor's advice not to travel. 'If I stay behind, I shall be abnegating my will,' she wrote, adding: 'And C. would hate it.'

The matter was settled when, at the end of the month, a further stroke resulted in her being taken into the intensive care unit at Brompton Hospital 'very nearly dead', she said when she resumed her diary entries when discharged a month later. She then added, having recovered her powers of descriptive vocabulary: 'Shall not record this time of phantasmagoria & phantasies. I couldn't.' She was only allowed two days at home before being taken for what she hoped would be no more than three weeks' convalescence in Midhurst,

Sussex. During that time, she realised the effect she had had on those around her, and made resolves to change:

> Did <u>not</u> have an urge to smoke, & never must, not again. But at least good to have a drink more or less when I want it, but <u>not</u> so frequently as before. I have misused myself terribly, telling myself that <u>I</u> was the only sufferer, but in fact I have to an extent damaged or worried to death everyone around me.

Her first impression of the convalescent home was that it looked 'pretty pleasant', but she soon became morose. She was strictly forbidden not to smoke, and alcohol was frowned upon; she did have some whisky smuggled in, but her supply kept running out. Family and friends visited frequently, particularly her daughter with whom she played many games of Scrabble, but on other days, she had to fight 'the battle of infinite boredom'. She provided herself with many books, but her first choices were scarcely likely to have improved her state of mind. She mentioned reading Dostoevsky's *The Possessed*, and *The Gates of Hell* by the American author Harrison E. Salisbury; she commented that the latter (which was set in Russia from the 1917 revolution onward) was 'dreadfully depressing reading matter'. Before long, she opted for detective stories which made her 'less lachrymose'.

CPS left for the pre-arranged visit to America; a 'dear' and 'sweet' letter from him led Pamela to believe: 'I am sure he is missing me more than I had expected.' Nearing the end of her anticipated three-week stay, she had a setback, and asked: 'Will my run of personal bad luck ever end?' She had, she realised, still been feeling wretched, and was not totally surprised therefore to hear that jaundice had been diagnosed, but she was not expecting that this would mean a further three weeks in Midhurst. When departure time finally arrived, she was told by her consultant that 'if I so much as have 'flu in future, I must go into Midhurst or Brompton'. As usual, her first thought was how this would affect CPS: 'This terrifies me, since I am afraid to be a wreck on C's hands.' She gathered from his letters that he was having a wonderful time in America, but exhibited no resentment.

One of the first matters she attended to after her eventual return home was to write to Harold Macmillan congratulating him on both their behalfs on his having been awarded the Order of Merit. He promptly replied:

How kind of you to write to me about my O.M.

As you well know, my friendship with you and Charles has been one of the deep pleasures of the last twenty years or more.[1]

This must have delighted her: when writing about her memories of Edith Sitwell, Pamela had observed that 'we are pitifully short these days of people who have "style", that mysterious and immediately recognisable attribute. Edith had it. So has Harold Macmillan (*in excelsis*)' (*Important*, p.75).

Soon afterward, she recorded a 'jour de gloire, after all these desolate months'. Her younger son returned from Peking where he had been continuing his studies, and told her 'wildly interesting travellers' tales', and late that night, CPS returned, jet-lagged as ever, but Pamela was determined to stay up with him until he was sufficiently tired to go to bed. Her high spirits were short-lived; the 'black dog' of depression, which she now blamed on 'the hospital trauma & the deprivation of cigarettes', returned the following day. She forced herself to attempt to write, feeling that this was 'therapeutic, as nothing on earth is', and indeed managed to write a short story within the space of a day. With CPS home, she found the strength to go out to restaurants with him, and to the House of Lords, but her craving for tobacco marred these occasions. She began to consider whether she might secretly allow herself five cigarettes a day, while acknowledging that she might well slip back towards the fifty that she had been smoking prior to her recent stroke. Several shorthand entries in her diary in May seem to refer to surreptitious smoking; by mid-June, she was no longer concealing the fact that: 'I smoked just a little – only a little – too much. Must watch this.' Dr. Sofaer gave her 'a terribly emotional talk' on the subject, which, she said, upset her 'but didn't quite achieve the desired effect'.

Knowing how much 'Hampstead' gossip emanated from Olivia Manning, Pamela seemed charitable in her reaction to that novelist's award of a CBE in the Queen's Birthday Honours List that month, writing: 'I can't like [Olivia], nor forget her backbiting in the past, but I am deeply glad for her now. She is a disappointed woman: so much in her life has gone wrong, & this will help make up for it a little.'

On 21 June, Pamela had a day of hospital health checks. CPS was, she said, 'overjoyed at the rating the Prof. gave me – everything OK'.

She was dubious herself: 'I felt it wasn't, but there we are.' The next day's entry is almost indecipherable; the words are all jumbled together. She had a further number of falls at home, bruising herself badly; a week later, strangely enough with improved handwriting and unimpaired memory for an apt literary quotation, she recorded:

TAKEN BACK INTO BROMPTON HOSPITAL
"Why, this is HELL –
Nor am I out of it." (Dr Faustus)

She decided not to keep her diary until she was discharged from hospital, which would prove to be more than five weeks later. While briefly at home the following day, she summoned up the strength to write a review (to be published in *The Listener*) of a memoir by Katherine Tait, the daughter of the philosopher Bertrand Russell. Pamela's style was as fluent as ever as she praised 'a beautifully balanced portrait of father and of daughter'. While it was clear from the book that the author had adored her father, she ended her critique:

It is extraordinarily rare, in memoirs of parents by their children, to feel that anything approaching the truth has been achieved: but Katherine Tait [...] manages to break the dismal pattern. And for her entire dedication to the truth, I think we have to thank her father.

She might have been contemplating the possibility that, in the now not so distant future, one of her children might consider writing a similar book of reminiscences about her.

She had again been ordered to convalesce, and this time chose a Brighton nursing home, which enabled her friends living locally to visit her. CPS came three times during the three-week stay, but she made no reproaches, indeed, on the final occasion, she wrote about her guilt at seeing 'darling C. [...] so worn, & it is I who have worn him'. But, she added, he was 'so sweet'. It would seem that her doctors had now given up on their attempts to ban her from smoking entirely; she mentioned being on a ration, and being remorseful when occasionally she exceeded it.

Back at home, a highlight of her regular televiewing came about while she was watching 'Mastermind' one evening, and the question was asked: 'To whom did Dylan Thomas write a charming one-paragraph autobiography?' 'I hadn't the slightest idea', she wrote, '– but

it turned out to be me! Can only suppose it is in an early letter.'
(It was indeed an excerpt, headed 'My Life. A Touching Autobiography in One Paragraph', from a long letter to her, written over
several days in November 1933.) Coincidentally, later that year, Pamela
received a long letter from a previously unknown elderly lady called
Evelyn Hamer. She admitted to having removed a photograph of
Pamela when young which she had noticed in an open drawer when
visiting the then near-derelict Boat House, which had been Dylan's
last home in Laugharne. She had meant to return it to Pamela but
had forgotten to do so for several years. 'Don't know how D. came by
it', Pamela commented, 'or how old I was when it was taken. 24 or
so, I suppose.' Mrs Hamer wondered why Dylan had kept the photograph for so many years: 'affection – sentiment or just indifference?
Perhaps you will know.'[2] Pamela declined to speculate.

The only work she undertook throughout September was to write
another review for *The Listener*. Her reading and writing speed being
fully restored, she read Kingsley Amis's novel *The Alteration* in a day,
finding it 'very impressive, funny, tragic & impudent', and wrote the
review the following day. As someone who herself enjoyed switching
genres, she began by commending 'exhilarating Kingsley Amis' for
never doing the same thing twice. She was of the opinion that two of
his other recent experiments – a ghost story, a detective story – had
been less successful, but with this book, she found him 'in full
literary health again'. Amis's genres here encompassed science fiction
and the then newish field of 'alternative history', being set in a contemporary England in which the Reformation had never taken place.
'It would be easy,' Pamela wrote, 'because of its very readability,
to race through it without recognising its depths. For it is basically
serious and scholarly. [...] The whole book is a triumph of tightrope-
walking.'

Pamela was subject to vivid dreams, which she often recorded. At
this time, her description of one of these drew together many strands
of her life:

> I was to be executed, though I didn't know what for. Mother with me.
> Through the window I could see the block & the huge executioner's
> sword. I drank the small whisky & Calvados provided, and as I lit a
> cigarette, said to Mother – 'I always wondered whether I should know
> I was smoking the last one.' Set out among an ordinary crowd, with

Amy & Kalie. A great many businessmen there in Homburgs, & with rolled umbrellas. Of course I was reprieved, & Enoch Powell tipped his hat to me in congratulation. I was bitter. I said to Mother, 'I'm going to take the newspapers for all I can get. This is the last time they have intended to behead a woman. There will be no more.'

Gradually, she found herself able to resume activities, having people in for drinks, and even hosting a dinner party. In her 'first real outing' since January, she and CPS returned to Stratford for a week in November, a highlight of which was a dinner with Ian McKellen (who was playing Romeo, despite being thirty-seven, to Francesca Annis's thirty-one-year-old Juliet, and Macbeth to Judi Dench's Lady Macbeth). Pamela thought McKellen 'very clever & entertaining', and particularly enjoyed his 'superb take-off of Zhenya, hardly distinguishable from the original'.

She started again to take an interest in current affairs, shamefacedly acknowledging her self-centredness since the beginning of the year: 'I feel a bit like Jane Austen not mentioning the battle of Waterloo. But it should be reported that this country is in a very bad way indeed, hideously in debt, & muddled.' (She had not mentioned in her diary Harold Wilson's surprise resignation in April; he had been succeeded by James Callaghan, who had been forced by the end of the year to apply to the International Monetary Fund for a loan of nearly $4 billion.)

Pamela's diary for 1977 is missing, but she evidently did continue keeping one, since she refers to it at the start of her 1978 diary. A review by her of a new biography of Frederick Rolfe (Baron Corvo) was published in the *Times Literary Supplement* in January, but there is no trace of any other published work by her. Her son Andrew remembers that CPS's postponed visit to India did take place that January, and that his mother had been able to accompany CPS to the USA for a tour lasting approximately a fortnight in April. That summer, CPS had his first meeting with John Halperin, who explained how this had come about in the introduction to his 'oral biography':

[C.P. Snow] had written a flattering review in his regular *Financial Times* column of a book of mine, and the publisher we shared arranged a meeting. [...] I was duly summoned to Eaton Terrace. During the course of several hours, the three of us – for Lady Snow, the novelist and critic Pamela Hansford Johnson, was also present – talked books and consumed a great deal more whisky than I, at least, was used to consuming in the middle of the afternoon.[3]

It would seem therefore that both the Snows were continuing to drink excessively. CPS had no work commitments, nor duties in the House of Lords, although he attended debates from time to time, and more often, when not with Anne Seagrim or at the Savile Club with Harry Hoff, spent his evenings in the various bars within the Houses of Parliament. On one occasion, he was indiscreet enough, when extremely intoxicated, to make Francis King his confidant, which was as ill-advised as Pamela confiding personal secrets to Olivia Manning, although the latter insisted that she had done so.[4] King recorded in his autobiography, published in 1993, that one evening in either 1977 or 1978, he had found CPS, 'his usually pallid face blotched and his breath heavy with alcohol, on the door step'. His unexpected visitor apologized, explaining that he was in urgent need of a lavatory, and, having relieved himself, showed no eagerness to leave. Suddenly CPS started talking about Pamela, berating himself for having '"behaved badly to her, very badly"'. He confessed that he had been continuing an affair which had started before their marriage; King only named the woman involved as 'X', but she was clearly Anne Seagrim. 'There followed', King continued, 'a lot of self-laceration.' CPS had insisted that Pamela was '"a wonderful woman, really wonderful, but a man had a variety of needs and sadly one woman could not always satisfy all of them"'.[5] All this would have been grist to the Hampstead/ Brighton gossip mill, but it is to be hoped that King did not broadcast this titbit to that coterie until after the deaths of both CPS and Pamela.

Pamela had started writing a sequel to *The Good Listener*, entitled *The Good Husband*, towards the end of 1977, and was relieved to have completed it early in the New Year, tellingly adding to her diary entry: 'And I can get money on it as soon as it is typed.' The reason for her mercenary attitude was that CPS was still desperately worried about the tax arrears he owed, his accountant having done nothing in the intervening years to rectify the situation brought about by his neglect, and having now suffered a nervous breakdown. In desperation, CPS went to see their editor in the hope of getting some advice, and to the great relief of them both, Alan Maclean arranged a loan from Macmillan of £12,000, which they passed on immediately to the Inland Revenue. But they received further tax demands and Pamela said that she had begun to dread every post. Possibly, in the circumstances, in order to boost their income, CPS arranged for his current secretary, Janet Nalder, to move, with her husband and daughter, into the self-contained flat on the top floor of their house. Their finances stabilized a little further with some moderate fees and royalties for previous works and an advance of $5,000 to CPS for his latest book of non-fiction, *The Realists*, subtitled: 'Portraits of Eight Novelists'.

The strain they were both under, however, came to a head one evening towards the end of March, after they had dined with some friends. Her diary entry was unapologetic, blaming her host for the plight they found themselves in:

> Must have drunk far too much, but was unaware of it till, coming home, I slipped on stairs, and felt I couldn't get up. C., trying to help me, fell likewise. We must have been an hour on the passage floor before I was able finally to rise. Says a lot for the drinks Peter pours.

She was totally unprepared, however, for the next development. CPS told her the next morning that he was leaving the house, and that Anne Seagrim 'would take him in'. She did not express any surprise at the reappearance of Anne into their lives, and believed that his decision had come about because he was deeply depressed as a result of 'many small things for which he blames me'. 'And I love him so much', she still maintained. He stayed away that night, but returned for lunch the following day, and worked upstairs during the afternoon with his secretary. Pamela remained 'shocked and trembling' that day, and throughout the next two. On the fourth day, however, he came in again 'quite cheerful' for lunch, and told her that he would come home the following week, and that they were to go as planned to America together for almost a month in May and June. 'Should have felt huge relief', she wrote, 'and did, but that was cancelled by symptoms of more nervous shock.'

She determined nevertheless to try to do her '<u>very</u> best' throughout their forthcoming US visit, and to that end, forced herself to make 'scarifying' shopping expeditions. Her appearance had always been important to her; her niece Stefanie, the daughter of Philip Snow, Snr., remembered that she had been dazzled by Pamela when they had first met, and that her aunt, in her eyes, had continued for years to look glamorous and well-dressed, with immaculate hair.[6] Pamela was continuing to struggle to the hairdressers each week, although the effort this cost her was evident to the taxi-driver who brought her home on one such occasion at this time, and who refused to take the fare, telling her: '"You need the cab more than I need the money."' However, she was now fretting continually about her 'implacably growing weight', presumably the result of her inactivity and the medication prescribed since her various strokes, and loathed even seeing her reflection in shop windows. She managed to buy two silk jersey dresses but was convinced that both made her look like a balloon.

Not surprisingly, their tour, which involved travelling to Philadelphia, Minneapolis and Louisville, was as harrowing as on previous occasions for Pamela, but this time, it was compounded by CPS's having as many health difficulties as she did. She had breathing problems and vertigo; he was suffering from acute backache, which he still supposed to be caused by lumbago, plus nausea, throughout the four weeks. They both needed wheelchair assistance at all the airports. Returning, both 'absolutely shattered', they called Dr. Sofaer, who told them that there was nothing wrong with them but sheer exhaustion, and prescribed – rest.

The Good Husband was published in October; when correcting the proofs, Pamela had been disappointed in what she then saw as 'a sapless sort of book'. Although she was often pessimistic prior to publication, there was some justification for her verdict this time. The novel continues the story of Toby Roberts on the eve of his thirtieth birthday, and the cast of supporting characters are largely those encountered in *The Good Listener*. The exception is Ann Thorold, a beautiful, rich widow, who becomes Toby's wife. The book is noticeably shorter than its predecessor, but the publishers increased the typeface which gave the illusion of a work of similar length. Whoever the responsible editor at Macmillan might have been, he or she did not seem familiar with *The Good Listener*. There is one particularly jarring error, which had evidently slipped Pamela's memory as well. In the first novel, Toby buys a ring with 'a largish green turquoise in a silver setting' (*Good Listener*, p.218), intending to give it to Claire when he proposes; fortunately, he hadn't produced it before she had turned him down. Shortly afterward, he hears that his first love is to be married and sends Maisie, as a wedding present, 'the green turquoise ring, without any instruction upon which finger she should wear it'. There is no suggestion that *she* returned it; indeed he had a 'very pleasant letter' thanking him for the kind gift (*Good Listener*, p.236). However, in the sequel, Toby still has 'the large silver and green turquoise ring he had bought for Claire' and thinks he might give it to Ann for their first Christmas together; he does not in fact do this until the second year of their marriage when the ring makes another unexplained reappearance.[7]

The main problem with the book lies in sustaining the reader's interest in Toby. Flawed as he may be, he is not as compelling as other of Pamela's anti-heroes, notably William Setter in *An Error of Judgment* and, above all, Daniel Skipton. In an assessment of Pamela's work in 1967, Anthony Burgess had focused on the complexity of the characterization of both. Of the latter he wrote:

> There is nothing good about him, and yet there is this monstrous dedication to art which lifts him to a kind of empyrean: he is as far above ordinary decent plodders through life as the saints and martyrs.[8]

The most remarkable character in *The Good Husband* is Rita, the former wife of Toby's friend, Bob, and now the stalker of the third of the trio, Adrian, now a priest, cursed in his attempts to carry out his duties by being 'spectacularly handsome in an Italianate fashion' and the focus therefore of 'feminine attention' in his 'featureless and rambling parish in Lincolnshire' (pp.26-27). Rita, however, is somewhat arbitrarily disposed of, some distance from the end, without her story seeming to be crucial to the presumable motivation of the novel; Toby's progress toward maturity. Nevertheless, there is much to enjoy in the novel, as Pamela probes the shifting balance of power in the marriage of Ann and Toby.

There were no reviews on the publication day of *The Good Husband* or in the two days afterward. Pamela had been cheered by reading the 'excellent thesis' on her work by Ishrat Lindblad sent to her that week, but she now awaited the verdict of the Sundays on her latest novel. She quoted from Wordsworth's 'The Affliction of Margaret': 'My apprehensions come in crowds', and the *Sunday Times* review was all that she had dreaded. In what Pamela deemed to be 'a shockingly spiteful review from Alan Brien', the critic declared that the novel 'seeks, in vain in my case, to be a Good Read. [...] The dialogue might have been picked up by a bug in Harrods.' He recognized that there was 'a tiny tremor of tragi-comic defeatism towards the end when the once indestructible Ann realises that marriage has delivered her into dependence on the self-centred, once insecure Toby' but continued:

> Since it is difficult to tell quite how consciously Miss Hansford Johnson realises what banal and uselessly ornamental figures they are, the result is simply to lower the temperature of the novel from tepid to chilly.

In total contrast, the critique the same day in the *Observer*, the newspaper in which Pamela usually expected a poor review, could scarcely have been bettered. Hermione Lee, who was unknown to Pamela, but who was to become the Goldsmiths' Professor of English Literature at Oxford and a renowned biographer, began: 'Polished, discreetly malign, and cool as several cucumbers, Pamela Hansford Johnson is a pleasure to read.' She obviously was familiar with Pamela's recent work, as she explained: 'This chill novel about marriage is a sequel to the story of cagey, self-preserving half-nasty Toby in *The Good Listener* [...].' After a brief resumé of the plot, she continued: 'A delicate glee has gone into the treatment of this life-style, and it's hard not to enjoy the book most for its social details [...]', but she warned against underrating the novel 'as a mere comedy of manners'. Lee then reviewed two other novels by women authors less favourably, finally returning to *The Good Husband* to state that: 'Pamela Hansford Johnson would make most other women writers look soft, but the contrast this week happens to be particularly marked.'

The following month, Pamela enjoyed being taken to a private viewing of an Emmy-winning documentary made in 1968, called `*Dylan Thomas: The World I Breathe*, in which John Malcolm Brinnin, Dylan's American agent, presented a portrait of the poet in photographs. She had not previously seen this, although it featured an interview with her. The occasion also provided her with the opportunity to meet Dylan's daughter Aeronwy for the first time, and her small son, Huw. They were, she wrote, 'both so like Dylan that it was almost absurd'.

CPS went to the USA again for a fortnight in December, this time on his own, and returned, Pamela thought, 'in far better form' than from their earlier tour, but over Christmas he was again 'very out of sorts with his lumbago and indigestion'. The following period became known as 'the winter of discontent': James Callaghan, like Edward Heath before him, found the trade unions intransigent regarding the pay restraint which he advocated to deal with the country's economic problems, which paralleled those in the USA. Unusually severe winter weather added to the woes of the populace; Pamela recorded six inches of snow even in central London on New Year's Eve, and she was unable to leave her house for three weeks. Throughout the following January, she listed some of the problems brought about by strikes and secondary picketing, food supplies becoming scarce, no dustbin collections, hospital patients suffering because medical supplies were blockaded, and even dead bodies having to remain in hospital wards: 'An uglier situation I never saw,' she wrote, but, using a cliché she would not have used in her novels, reported one domestic problem solved: 'The greengrocer's roundsman got rid of the rubbish to date. Doris over the moon with relief.'

Pamela had become intrigued by a sensational murder trial which had taken place in 1886, in which French-born Adelaide Bartlett, together with her alleged lover, a Wesleyan minister, had finally been acquitted of poisoning her wealthy grocer husband. Pamela spent two days reading the complete transcript of the trial, after which she could not make up her mind as to whether she did want to write a novel about this 'inconceivably sordid' story. She made a start, but within a week was wishing she could see 'the back of Adelaide' on the grounds that it simply did not suit her style. Handwriting again proving difficult for her, she was forced to type instead, and she found it tedious to be continually having to consult the 'squalid' transcript.

Meanwhile, on the political front, Pamela had totally lost faith in Callaghan, reporting that: 'Things look very bleak for [the] Government, and serve it right.' On 28 March, the Government lost a vote of confidence by one vote, and Callaghan was forced to resign and call a general election. Pamela had never previously imagined supporting the Conservatives, but she was now becoming increasingly pro-Margaret Thatcher. Ronald Millar, CPS's friend and dramatic collaborator, was one of Thatcher's speech-writers,[9] and relayed 'all the latest' about her. As the election drew nearer, she avidly watched current affairs programmes, and was now confirmed in her belief that Thatcher would win, and that it would be good for the country which was in need of a change. They stayed up most of the night as the results came in, and Pamela exulted: 'Obvious that Mrs. Thatcher is going to be our first woman P.M. Hope to God she does well, as this is something for the history books.'

Pamela had now nearly finished her 'beastly book', although she had difficulty in writing the final three pages. She recorded the following day finishing 'ADELAIDE with loathing in my heart'. CPS left for the USA for eight days in June, having spent a similar length of time in Texas in March. She felt, she said, 'as usual [...] at a hopeless loss without him', but nevertheless seemed resigned about the impossibility of being well enough to accompany him. There were again negotiations taking place about a television serialization of CPS's 'Strangers and Brothers' series, leading to despondency when they seemed to be abortive. In the autumn, CPS's latest book, *A Coat of Varnish*, was published; whether or not he had been influenced by Auberon Waugh's jokey advice to him in his review of *The Malcontents*, he had, after more than forty years, written another detective story. Pamela was relieved and delighted that, after some disappointing early reviews, the book turned out to be a 'real success, [...] his best press for years'. Nicholas Shrimpton, reviewing in the *New Statesman*, was among those who remembered *Death Under Sail*, and congratulated CPS on making the return to 'the whodunit [...] with both marvellous assurance and considerable sophistication of intent'.

Their annual visit to Stratford was blighted this year by the pain and nausea that CPS was still enduring. They were only able to see two plays: the first, Eugene O'Neill's *Anna Christie*, was staged in the RSC's studio venue, The Other Place, but they complained that it was inaudible even in the confined space, and left halfway through the performance; the second, a preview of *Julius Caesar*, was, in Pamela's opinion, 'the worst production we have ever seen at that theatre — or perhaps on any professional stage!' Her critical faculties were evidently as sharp as ever; the reviews after the opening night were not quite so damning, but generally unfavourable.

The next disappointment for Pamela was the realisation that she would have to 'jettison Adelaide', as the result of a 'whole heap of

queries from Macmillan', together with the discovery that a book by
Yseult Bridges, *Poison & Adelaide Bartlett*, published in 1962, had far
more information than her own. She did, however, tartly add that
Bridges' conclusion, 'as always with her', was 'screwy'. As it happened,
the following year, she was taken aback to discover that Julian Symons
had also written about the trial in his new book, *Sweet Adelaide*, which
had the bold subtitle: 'A Victorian Puzzle Solved'. Pamela read this,
and deemed it 'so shoddily researched it made me almost wish I'd
published mine!'. She was particularly annoyed about this further
'coincidence' in their lives, if it had indeed been just chance; she
remembered meeting Symons while working on her fictional version
of the story, and talking to him about it, without his having revealed
that he had similar intentions.

On their return from Stratford, CPS had continued to resist the
notion of any further medical examinations, until November when he
decided to see a physiotherapist, who suggested that one or two small
bones might be displaced in his back, and he had 'prodded about',
causing CPS still more pain. Throughout that month, and in the early
weeks of December, Pamela was in despair; on one typical day, she
wrote: 'Poor C. in pain – savage – all day. He is getting so weak &
losing so much weight. I am at my wits' end to know what to do.'
He recovered a little, partly thanks to what had been at last a successful meeting at their house with the television scriptwriter Julian
Bond, the BBC producer Jonathan Powell, and others, at which the
format of the television series to be made from the Lewis Eliot novels
was discussed. 'All rather exciting', Pamela recorded. 'It looks good.
A lot of whisky consumed! C. very chuff. Let's pray that nothing will
prevent the making of it now.'

Pamela, the mother, was to the fore at the beginning of 1980.
Despite her children all now being adults, she continued to be
concerned about them, and still harboured feelings of guilt about her
possible neglect of them when young, due to the hours she had had
to devote to her literary career. She was therefore delighted to record
her contentment about the current happenings in the lives of all
three. Her elder son, Andrew, telephoned from Australia to tell her
that, not only was he to marry, but also that he had been offered, and
accepted, a prestigious academic position as a Senior Fellow in the
Research School of Physics and Engineering at the Australian National

University in Canberra. After her return from Budapest in 1975, her daughter Lindsay had found satisfaction in the permanent job to which she had been appointed in the British Section of Amnesty International; she was now undertaking increasingly responsible tasks there, which would culminate in her later becoming the organization's Refugee Officer and Urgent Action Co-ordinator. And, although Pamela greatly missed her younger son, then working in Peking (Beijing) for the First National Bank of Chicago, she was proud at Philip's progress which would eventually see him evolve into the author of well received books on Far Eastern history including China's relations with Africa and the Japanese occupation of Hong Kong.

Her diary entries otherwise were becoming fewer, and mainly recorded either her own poor health and persistent tiredness, or her anxieties about CPS, who was still intermittently in great pain, although for the first few months of the year, he was occasionally able to go to the House of Lords, or to use the excuse of having tea with Harry almost certainly to visit Anne Seagrim. One of Pamela's longer entries was for the first of April when she had to record the sad news that she had had to agree that the vet should put to sleep their Siamese cat, 'our darling, lovely little Sirikit'. She knew it was inevitable as the cat was nineteen years old, and had been unwell for more than an year, but nevertheless felt bereft when she went to her empty bed (which Sirikit had so often shared), and tried to comfort herself by singing to herself the songs she used to sing to Siri.

At the end of January, Pamela had started work on a new novel, *A Bonfire*, and completed it in May 'or rather', she then wrote, 'it finished itself, juddering to a halt'. Again, it was a book which would have benefited from editing by someone familiar with her previous work, as it revisits episodes from earlier novels, in addition to anecdotes already recounted in *Important to Me*. The characters in *A Bonfire* are clearly based on Pamela's own family. The central character is given, somewhat oddly because it is a sympathetic portrait, the name of Pamela's least favourite aunt, Emma. Emma's mother Agnes Sheldrake and her aunt Issie, both former members of the D'Oyley Carte company, bear strong resemblances to Amy and Kalie (there is a repetition from *Important to Me* of the story about the ever-healthy Yum Yum, who had never missed a performance to the chagrin of her understudy, her mother).[10] Emma's father is still more identifiable with

Pamela's father: his name, Reggie, is unchanged; he has returned from
service in West Africa; and he dies, in the same way as his namesake,
in the lavatory in the middle of the night (pp.27-28). (As mentioned
in Chapter 1, Pamela had already fictionalised the similar circumstances with her description of the death of Christine Jackson's father
in *An Impossible Marriage*.) Emma asks her mother about the facts of
life, and, while Mrs. Sheldrake's explanation is more detailed than
Mrs. Cotton's, Emma's response –'"I would rather be a nun"' (p.25)
– is identical to that of Elsie in *This Bed Thy Centre*. There are also
descriptions of young people's dancing parties at home, chaperoned
by the mother, who provides them with bread pudding, as in previous
novels and her memoir.

More recent autobiographical experiences are also fictionalised by
Pamela in the latter part of the novel. Emma's second husband Alan
becomes an alcoholic, and some of the descriptions of his behaviour
when drunk resemble the return home of CPS when 'popular'. In
this aspect of the novel, the lives of Pamela and Emma do not run
parallel: Emma does not emulate her husband in his consumption of
whisky. Significantly, however, Emma blames herself when Alan's
drinking begins to affect their sex life:

> Emma lay awake, deprived and worrying. He had never failed before.
> She knew he was drinking too much, not steadily, but in bouts. What
> was she to do? She believed it was her own punishment. [...] She
> wished God had not made her so sexually hungry. (p.133)

Alone again, Emma resolves not to remarry, but her strong sexual
urge, like that of Bessie Upjohn, from *Survival of the Fittest*, remains:

> She prayed for it to pass her by, but she was trapped in the poorhouse
> of her flesh. She did not seek sexual self-gratification. She remembered
> her mother's horror when, at the age of nine, she had confessed to the
> habit. "You will either go blind or go mad!" Though she did not believe
> a word of this, it now aroused in her an acute sense of guilt. She wished
> she had been made differently, demanding little, like Agnes, and could
> go to bed each night without the ache and the loneliness. (p.160).

The 'bonfire' of the novel's title is symbolic; at a real bonfire on
a Guy Fawkes night shortly before Emma's confirmation, she feels a
chill, remembering 'the everlasting bonfire'. She had asked her mother

whether she believed in Hell, and 'Agnes had said awkwardly that she believed our punishment for our sins was in our own lives' (p.22). At the end of the novel, Emma wishes that 'she had not been born with so powerful a sense of guilt and knew that Agnes, in all innocence, had encouraged it by her own piety' (p.190). The account of Emma's confused conjunction of sex and religion may explain Pamela's frequent references in her diaries to reverses in her own life being some form of retribution for past sins, however relatively innocuous these may have been. She was aware of the effect this had had on her throughout her life; in the first of many conversations between us, her daughter wanted me to know that:

> She did once say to me, that whatever happens to me, don't you ever feel guilty, and I thought that was a wonderful thing to say to a child. Every time I've thought about it, it quite moves me. So I've done my best not to feel guilty, and I've told the same thing to my son.[11]

Throughout June, Pamela's diary entries centred on her anxiety about CPS, who was experiencing still more acute pain, while resisting any treatment beyond the pain relief pills that Dr. Sofaer kept switching. His brother Philip later found out that he had written to a friend in America, the historian Jacques Barzun, telling him that: 'I have taken such medical advice as might be useful and they say in effect all one can do is endure.'[12] He told others that he was suffering from an 'exceptionally aggravated attack of fibrositis or migratory arthritis', dismissing it as 'what our ancestors would call lumbago', but insisted that it was 'entirely undangerous'.[13] Their son had been sent to Europe by his bank, and so was able to visit him. CPS was also cheered a little by a visit from the Bulgarian ambassador offering him the award of the Order of Georgi Dimitrov for literature and for his work to promote understanding between peoples. He was somewhat bemused to find himself in the company of the three other recipients of the award that year — Andrei Gromyko, the Soviet Foreign Minister, José López Portillo, the President of Mexico, and Fidel Castro, the President of Cuba — and then still more delighted when he found that the award was worth $5000, as they both were still worrying about their financial situation.

For the remainder of the month, CPS was in too much pain to leave the house. In the midst of her distress, Pamela had to cope with 'a tirade' from their doctor, 'about C's treatment of <u>him</u>'. After three days of retching, Sofaer insisted that CPS should go into hospital, and arrangements were made for him to be admitted the following day, the first of July. But it was too late; CPS had a major haemorrhage, and died in Pamela's arms before an ambulance could arrive. 'He was so precious,' Pamela wrote that evening. A post-mortem had to take place, and the cause of death was found to have been a perforated gastric ulcer. It could never be established whether an earlier diagnosis might have prevented his death. There were obituaries in all the major newspapers: the lengthy obituary in *The Times* (2 July 1980) paid tribute to the position CPS had occupied in English life and letters 'such as no other writer has held since H.G. Wells and Arnold Bennett', both in terms of his success as a novelist and his 'extra-literary activities'.

Pamela was supported in her grief by the loving care of her daughter and younger son. Andrew could not arrive in time for the private cremation, so made arrangements to stay with his mother for a month in September, during which time a memorial service was to be held at St. Martin's-in-the-Fields. Pamela had written very few more diary entries in July; there was then a long pause, explained on 29 October:

> I shall not complete the diary of this horrible year.
>   Part of me has died with Charles.
>   The day after his cremation I fell & broke my shoulder in two places.
> When I came out of hospital I felt very ill & shortly after had a stroke.
>   All the children with me, wonderfully kind. Also Andy's wife Donna whom I like immensely. [...]
>   I ache for Charles. It never gets better.

Despite being confined to a wheelchair, Pamela had been able to attend the memorial service, which she described as 'magnificent'. The church was almost full to its capacity. She mentioned in particular their son's Bible reading and the actor Paul Scofield's reading of the final paragraph of *A la recherche du temps perdu*. Her two older children were less impressed by the Address by Harry Hoff, which was, Andrew recalled, read 'very badly in a chatty tone completely inappropriate for the place and occasion', and Lindsay said that Hoff had failed to mention their mother at all.

I am aware that, inevitably, my account of the Snow marriage may be thought to have been one-sided since so much of the evidence comes from Pamela's diaries, and, particularly as her health deteriorated, she recorded many instances of difficulties between them. There is, however, no doubt about the sincerity of a later addition to the final entry in her 1980 diary: Pamela had added: 'It was, & is, a great love.'

By way of further balance, I would also illustrate the high-spirited and inspirational side of CPS's personality by quoting from the obituary by J.H. Plumb in the *Guardian* (2 July 1980). Plumb could have confined his remarks to praising, as he indeed began, CPS's multiple achievements as scientist, civil servant, novelist and politician, but he also provided a portrait of Snow as exhilarating friend to many:

> As a man Snow will long be remembered. He was doggedly loyal to his old friends: he enhanced the days with his vigour, his wit, his courage and his hope. After an evening with Snow all men felt larger, more gifted, happier, and his genial authority was as natural as it was unassuming. He possessed a largeness of heart and capacity of mind beyond the common run of men.

Gorley Putt also wrote movingly about CPS in his memoirs, published in 1990. They had first met at Christ's College in the 1930s, and he touchingly described what he saw as one of his new friend's chief attributes:

> My early impressions of him acknowledged one quality which remained throughout his highly varied career — a great gift of laughter. Laughing with, and at, Snow, both at the same time — this is what his friends miss so much.[14]

CHAPTER 22

The Last Six Months

PAMELA BEGAN her 1981 diary with a brief resumé of the previous six months which she described as 'a nightmare of grief and ill-health'. Although she was then in the London Clinic, her writing was reasonably legible. 'Dear C. could never have imagined my medical expenses or he would not have left me worried to death as I am,' she wrote. She was particularly concerned about her household expenses, being now reliant on three carers, Doris, her housekeeper, Ivy, whom Pamela described as her 'nurse-companion', and Mary, another helper. She itemized their wages, plus the PAYE and National Insurance which she paid for them, none of which was tax-deductible, while meantime she was being taxed at 65% on her royalties. She did, however, manage a touch of black humour as she asked herself: '[Am I] dying beyond my means?' She finally summoned up the strength to dismiss David Sofaer in January, and was then horrified to receive a final bill for the amount of £727.72 for his services in the preceding five months, a considerable proportion of which had been spent by her in hospital. Her new doctor brought in a consultant to examine her, with the result, she wrote, that: 'It is quite obvious now that Sofaer has let me get more & more ill for a long time. Now lungs, heart, etc., all seem dubious.'

The several days of tests in the London Clinic proved inconclusive, but one morning in February, she awoke almost unable to breathe, and was taken to the Westminster Hospital, where the emphysema she had always dreaded since seeing the effects of it on her old friend T.C. Worsley was diagnosed. She was in hospital for five weeks which she translated into 'days & nights of no smoking'. As soon as she was allowed home (with an oxygen machine), she had a cigarette 'out of sheer bravado, but it tasted nasty'.

Two of her oldest friends were regularly in touch with her. She had seen Teddy Lamerton sporadically over the years, and consoled him when he felt that he had not fulfilled his early promise. He was now a widower, living in Dorset, and semi-paralysed; they shared memories over the telephone of 'bread pudding & the Doodah boys!' 'Oh, so long ago', Pamela reflected: 'Nearly half a century.' Eventually, the formerly 'spectacularly good-looking' Teddy managed to visit her, 'looking v. old, with a big white beard'. She wistfully acknowledged that, unlike herself, 'however infirm, he is most courageous & looks after himself most of the time.' Nevertheless, their face-to-face talk proved a disappointment; it was long and dull, Pamela found, and marred by deafness on both sides. The former Babs Freeman, 'the dearest of my friends', also came to see her; she had survived the years better. Pamela was always glad to see her, but was exhausted when she left. She took more comfort from a visit from Father Gerard Irvine, who spoke of John Betjeman's admiration for her writing, and of the poet's opinion that she was 'one of the most attractive women he had ever met'. She did add in her diary, 'among the first 100, I expect', but nevertheless relayed Betjeman's remark in a letter to Babs, saying that 'a little flattery is a quiet consolation'. She was also visited at home by Susan Hill, J.H. Plumb and Harry Hoff.

A Bonfire was published at the beginning of April; reviews were slow in appearing, and Pamela feared that it might be totally ignored. But then her son Philip rang 'with some astounding news':

> Bernard Levin, of all PEOPLE has devoted his space to A BONFIRE! Now that is letting bygones be bygones! One of the best reviews I ever had in my life. It is a good way to go out.

The subheading at the top of Levin's column in the *Sunday Times* read: 'Bernard Levin bids farewell to fiction reviewing', which makes it all the more surprising that he chose *A Bonfire* for his finale. 'This is a cunningly deceptive novel', he began, continuing: 'Short, it crowds a great deal in; all foreground, it implies a much deeper stage; apparently about nothing but its characters' lives, it ends by being about something more important.' He exhibited no knowledge of the repetitions from her previous works, and had therefore been free to enjoy all the positive virtues of the novel. He described the 'great skill in the shaping of the book in the way Miss Hansford Johnson counts off the passing years with the lightest of touches [...]. And all the while, the author's observation is acute.' After this review, others continued to be good. 'How pleased dear Charles would have been! & I think, how surprised!', Pamela wrote, and she wryly observed: 'There is little doubt in my mind that a writer still operating in age becomes either a Sacred Cow or a sheer write-off. Personally, thank Heavens, I seem to be experiencing the former fate.'

Pamela's distrust of her former doctor, as regards his competence towards both herself and CPS, seemed justified when, in May, she gleefully recorded: 'David Sofaer in deep TROUBLE. Has to pay £161,000 for ruining an American's arm, way back in 1976!! He also has to pay costs.'' Sadly though, the increasing deterioration in her health became ever more unbearable for her. Although she had only just passed her sixty-ninth birthday, a typical diary entry in May harrowingly described her experiences of 'the humiliations of the illnesses of old age':

> The hopeless dependency upon others! [...] To watch one's skin slowly wasting! To find people treating one, when off their guard, as a wilful child! It is too much to bear to watch one's mana ending!

Her writing then became illegible, and her entries had ceased by June when she was admitted to the London Clinic for further tests, and developed pneumonia. Her last happiness was being informed that her first grandchild, George Hansford Stewart, had been born in Australia. She died a week later, the pneumonia and the chronic emphysema having led to heart failure. After a private cremation, her ashes were scattered on the river at Stratford-upon-Avon, close to the Royal Shakespeare Theatre.

The obituaries for Pamela praised her work both as a novelist and critic; the longest and most perceptive appeared in the *Daily Telegraph*. David Holloway wrote of her ability to 'happily change her approach, sometimes with a female narrator, sometimes a male, and often in the third person', and to move from novels with serious themes to 'rollicking satire'. He judged her to have been at her best, however, in 'her grave, immensely detailed delineation of middle-class manners', and expressed his view that *The Humbler Creation* had probably been the most important novel of 1959. He concluded: '[...] we have lost a very considerable novelist. The public recognition of her work was never considerable enough, even though she was made a CBE in 1975.'

A memorial service for Pamela took place at St. James's Church, Piccadilly, in August. It was presided over by her friend, Gerard Irvine; Harold Macmillan read the Lesson, and Susan Hill gave the Address. Catherine Lambert read 'The Temper' by the seventeenth century metaphysical poet George Herbert. Ronald Millar read one of her favourite passages from the final book of *A la recherche du temps perdu*, in which memories of the madeleine eaten in his youth, together with his chance recollection of an incident in Venice, lead the narrator to ask: 'But how was it that these visions of Combray and of Venice at one and at another moment had caused me a joyous certainty sufficient without other proofs to make death indifferent to me?'

Finally, her friend Madeleine Bingham read Pamela's description, in the concluding chapter of her memoir, of what had proved to be her final visit to Ghent to see again, and be greatly comforted by, Van Eyck's altar-piece, *The Adoration of the Mystic Lamb*, with its central figure of 'Christ in Glory'. Despite the ill-health and the bout of depression she had then been suffering, Pamela had suddenly felt that: 'I had only to fix my mind on that hand upraised in benediction to become peaceful again at once: peaceful, and still' (*Important*, pp.252-53).

Afterword

A S HAS BEEN SEEN, from the outset, Pamela was governed by
the necessity of having to earn a living not only for herself but
to support her mother, together later with her first husband
and two small children; she was not free of financial worries during
her second marriage, when she had the additional tie of a third child,
born in her forties. Few of her contemporaries had comparable
responsibilities. Cyril Connolly's dictum that 'there is no more
sombre enemy of good art than the pram in the hall' is frequently
quoted, but often misinterpreted as referring to women writers. Many
of the latter have indeed been childless – whether by choice or not –
from Jane Austen and the Brontës to Virginia Woolf and Elizabeth
Bowen. In fact, however, Connolly was only concerned with the
'enemies of promise' that affect male writers, and in particular those
who may, by marrying and having children, 'grow torpid with domesticity'. His solution stipulates 'a wife who is intelligent and unselfish
enough to understand and respect the working of the unfriendly cycle
of the creative imagination', and who 'will know [...] where love,
tidiness, rent, rates, clothes, entertaining, and rings at the doorbell
should stop [...]'.[1] In her second marriage, Pamela, more or less
willingly, not only took on such a role, yet with the equivalent of three
(albeit much-loved and wanted) prams in the hall, had to make time
for her own writing and public appearances, without herself having
the benefit of Connolly's ideal of a wife solely devoted to her needs.
She remained faithful to her motto, in 'finding a way', and the
quality of her writing, as was constantly confirmed by the admiration
of contemporary reviewers, rarely dipped.

There remains the question, however, of how far Pamela's subsequent literary standing has been adversely affected by that second
marriage and her metamorphosis into 'Lady Snow'. Her tendency, in

the early years of their marriage, to adopt CPS's more pedantic vocabulary, did not, as mentioned, go unnoticed, but this was short-lived, and certainly her switch of genres into the satire of the three Dorothy Merlin novels is unimaginable as having been prompted by his influence. Indisputably, however, her admiration for CPS remained unwavering, his literary status being equally, if not more, important to her than her own, and her love for him remained the 'deep, self-abnegating love' about which she had written in her *Sunday Telegraph* article in 1974.

Pamela was, of course, not only a novelist but a poet, a perceptive critic, a social analyst, and, from all accounts, a gifted lecturer. The paradox is that, in seventeenth-century England after the restoration of the monarchy in 1660 and throughout the eighteenth century, a woman with these accomplishments would have been recognized as 'a woman of letters', but, as Norma Clarke has masterfully argued, there was a reaction to the concept in the nineteenth century, when:

> Male paradigms drove literary practice just as they have driven literary history. Men's writings, men's sociable interactions and rivalries, their cultural and political disputes as well as their ventures in publishing led the way. Though there were many women writers, men had social, political, economic and literary power. Literary recognition could only be fully provided by men. Few (perhaps no) women were able to succeed as writers without the support of men.[2]

Some of these factors were lingering on into the twentieth century. Although the relationship of Pamela and CPS certainly began at a time when Pamela was the more influential of the two, this fact became obfuscated after their marriage by CPS's later higher public profile, as well as by the mists of the jealousies, feuds and satirical attacks they attracted through little fault of their own. By the 1970s, Olivia Manning, a writer Pamela had frequently tried to help, had jointly dubbed them 'the Snows of Yesteryear'.[3] Pamela Hansford Johnson needs to be a name still separately recognized for her own achievements as 'a woman of letters'.

The principal cause of opposition directed at the literary partnership of Pamela and CPS relates to the timing of their whole-hearted championship of the novel of realism against the experimental novel. In an article, written in 2003, Kyriaki Hadjiafxendi pinpointed the

1970s as being a key period in which critical positions were taken against the realist novel; she cited, as an example, Colin MacCabe's critique of the presumed ominiscience of novels of this genre, which, she maintained, 'conveniently ignored their use of humour and irony to unsettle the reading public into self-scrutiny'. The opposition to the realist novel continued to be thought valid until challenged by the New Historicism school of thought in the 1990s; Hadjiafxendi tellingly quoted the argument of Catherine Gallagher, a proponent of the latter theoretical approach, who wrote of the capacity of the realist novel 'to interrogate rather than merely reflect the limited middle-class discourses on class and gender by which they were defined'.[4]

My contention is that these defined elements of humour, irony and social exploration run throughout the realism of Pamela's novels, enhancing their many other qualities. Among the latter is another precious ingredient: despite the many changes in her life, there remained within her the attitude of the fourteen-year-old poet who asked the morning to draw back its curtain:

That I may marvel at the world behind!

Notes

LIST OF ABBREVIATIONS

PHJ   Pamela Hansford Johnson

Family and Close Friends

AMS   Andrew Morven Stewart (son of Pamela and Neil Stewart)
CPS   Charles Percy Snow (Pamela's second husband)
DMT   Dylan Marlais Thomas
KD   Kay Dick
KF   Kathleen Farrell
LJS   Lindsay Jane Stewart (later Lady Avebury, daughter of Pamela and Neil Stewart)
NS   (Gordon) Neil Stewart (Pamela's 1st husband)
PAS   Philip Albert Snow (CPS's youngest brother)
PCS   Philip Charles Snow (son of Pamela and Charles Snow)

Archives

CC: CPS   Christ's College, Cambridge: C.P. Snow Archive
CHC: AS   Churchill College, Cambridge: Anne Seagrim Archive
CUL: JHP   Cambridge University Library: J.H. Plumb Collection.
HRHRC: CPS   C.P. Snow Collection, Harry Ransom Humanities Research Center, at the University of Texas, Austin.
LAC   Lindsay Avebury Private Collection, London. (See below.)
SHA   Susan Hill Archive, Eton College Library, Eton College, Windsor, Berks.
SUNY: DMT   Dylan Thomas Collection, The Poetry Collection of the University Libraries, University at Buffalo, State University of New York.

Where quotations throughout the text are unreferenced, they have been taken from the surviving diaries of Pamela Hansford Johnson, which, other than those of 1933-35, are currently in LAC. It is intended that these diaries, together with some existing manuscripts and papers, will be deposited in due course in a British university archive. The diaries for 1933-35 are deposited in SUNY: DMT.

I have in general not given dates for reviews of Pamela's published works, or those of CPS, if these appeared within a few days of publication. If further details are required with regard to the former, I would recommend an excellent article by Mildred Miles Franks: 'Pamela Hansford Johnson: Secondary Sources, 1934-1981', Bulletin of Bibliography (1983), Vol. 40, No. 2, pp. 73-82.

REFERENCES IN THE TEXT

1: A Clapham Childhood
(pp.1-16)

1 Ronald Blythe, 'Ladies of Letters', *Tatler & Bystander*, 6 July 1960.
2 'Sir Charles and Lady Snow', US *Vogue*, 1 March 1961. Snow was awarded his KBE in 1957, seven years after their marriage, and received a life peerage in 1964.
3 Philip Snow, *Stranger and Brother* (London: Macmillan, 1982), p.8.
4 Virginia Woolf, *A Room of One's Own* (London: Hogarth Press, 1929; London: Vintage, 2001), p.98.
5 Roy Newquist, *Counterpoint* (London: Allen & Unwin, 1965), p.367.
6 Pamela Hansford Johnson, *The Listener*, 3 March 1949, pp.367-68.
7 Pamela Hansford Johnson, *Important to Me: Personalia* (1974), p.9. Further references in the text are to this edition, and will be cited elsewhere as *Important*. In general, I refer to it as a 'memoir', although technically it falls into no distinct category, comprising as it does, a mixture of essays and both memoir and memoirs.
8 Mrs Patrick Campbell, *My Life and Some Letters* (New York: Dodd, Mead, 1922).
9 Madeleine Bingham, *Henry Irving and the Victorian Theatre* (London: Allen & Unwin, 1978), p.119.
10 Bram Stoker, *Personal Reminiscences of Henry Irving* (London: Heinemann, 1906), Vol. I, p.305.
11 Bingham, p.259.
12 Original in the possession of Denzil Howson, Australia.
13 Letter from Helen Howson to her sister, Emily, 27 November 1894, *ibid*.
14 The records show the birth-places of the four children of Charles and Helen Howson as four different addresses in South London between 1880 and 1889, so the likelihood is that Pamela was mistaken in her belief that the house was purchased in the mid-1880s.
15 Pamela Hansford Johnson, *An Impossible Marriage* (London: Macmillan, 1954), pp.17-18. Further references in the text are to this edition, and will be cited elsewhere as *Marriage*.
16 Gillian Clegg, *Clapham Past* (London: Historical Publications, 1999), p.78.
17 Noël Coward, *Present Indicative* (London: Heinemann, 1937), p.44.
18 John Raymond, 'A Corvo of our Day', *Times Literary Supplement*, 9 January 1959, p.18.
19 See *Marriage*, pp.80-81, *A Bonfire*, pp.27-28
20 Pamela Hansford Johnson, 'Race, Class and Sport in the 'Seventies', *Sunday Telegraph*, 27 January 1974, p.6.

2: *Aut Inveniam Viam, Aut Faciam*
(pp.17-31)

1 See note above regarding unreferenced quotations throughout the text.
2 *Thomas Wolfe: A Critical Study* (London: Heinemann, 1947), published in the United States as *Hungry Gulliver: An English Critical Appraisal of Thomas Wolfe* (New York: Scribner, 1948).
3 *Ibid.*, p.131.
4 Pamela later annotated this verse in her poetry book, to identify 'the wealthy Mrs. J.' as Mrs. Schuyler B. Jackson, the mother of Schuyler B. Jackson II, who married the poetess Laura Riding in 1941.

3: 'My Darling Dylan'
(pp.32-61)

1 [Horatio Bottomley], 'The Wickedest Man in the World', *John Bull*, 24 March 1923. Ironically, Bottomley himself was a notorious swindler, and if he were indeed the writer of this diatribe, it would have been written from Wormwood Scrubs after his imprisonment for fraud.
2 For further reading on the relationship between Victor Neuburg and Aleister Crowley, see Jean Overton Fuller, *The Magical Dilemma of Victor Neuburg* (London: W.H. Allen, 1965; revised edition, Oxford: Mandrake, 1990); and Arthur Calder-Marshall, *The Magic of My Youth* (London: Rupert Hart-Davis, 1951).
3 Constantine FitzGibbon, *The Life of Dylan Thomas* (London: Dent, 1965), pp.106-07.
4 The reference is to *Hippolytus* by Euripides, ll. 722-3: 'The apple-tree, the singing and the gold'. Gilbert Murray's translation (1902).
5 Calder-Marshall, p.23.
6 Presumably, Pamela had read Evelyn Waugh's *Vile Bodies* (1930), in which he satirized the 1920s generation of 'Bright Young People'.
7 Interview with Eric Hughes, quoted by FitzGibbon (1965), p.70.
8 Dylan Thomas's letters to Pamela Hansford Johnson, as well as her diaries for 1934-36, are in the Poetry and Rare Books Collection at the State University of New York at Buffalo (SUNY: DMT). Selections from these letters were first published in *Selected Letters of Dylan Thomas*, ed. by Constantine FitzGibbon (London: Dent, 1966). FitzGibbon explains that most of the omissions concern Dylan's criticisms of her poems, since he says magisterially that these have 'little interest for most readers'. Occasionally, he also omits passages of 'private jokes' and 'petty gossip about friends'. The full text of all the existing letters is published in *Collected Letters of Dylan Thomas*, ed. by Paul Ferris (London: Dent, 1985).
9 FitzGibbon (1965), *op. cit.*, Paul Ferris, *Dylan Thomas: The Biography,* new edition (London: Dent, 1999), and Jonathan Fryer, *The Nine Lives of Dylan Thomas* (London: Kyle Cathie, 1993).
10 Fuller, p.11.

11 The Welsh League of Youth.

12 Fryer, p.56.

13 FitzGibbon (1966), p.99.

14 Dylan Thomas, *Early Prose Writings*, ed. by Walford Davies (London: Dent, 1971).

15 Pamela Hansford Johnson, in Dylan Thomas Memorial Number, *Adam International Review*, **21**, 1953, pp.24-25.

16 *Sunday Referee*, 25 February 1934.

17 Reviews in the *Times Literary Supplement* were unsigned until January 1975, which led to much speculation as to the authors. Their names can generally now be identified from the *TLS* Historical Archive, and elsewhere, where possible, I have cited them. I could not however identify the reviewer of *Symphony for Full Orchestra*, because the archive at that time only shows multiple names on the 'New Books' pages.

18 Dylan's spelling is often a little wayward.

19 'Nice, round Pamela' rarely weighed more than seven and a half stones at this time.

20 FitzGibbon (1965), pp.144-45.

21 Fragment of letter from Hughes [June 1934] (SUNY: DMT).

22 Ferris (1999), p.100.

23 Fryer, p.61.

24 In *Adam* (1953), *op. cit.*, p.24.

25 FitzGibbon (1965), p.151.

26 See Sandra Gilbert & Susan Gubar, *The Madwoman in the Attic* (New Haven, NY: Yale University Press, 1979), *passim*.

27 Ishrat Lindblad, *Pamela Hansford Johnson* (Boston, MA: Twayne, 1982), p.30.

28 *The Survival of the Fittest* (London: Macmillan, 1968; Harmondsworth: Penguin, 1970), pp.27-28. Further references in the text are to this edition, and will be cited elsewhere as *Survival*.

29 Andrew Sinclair, *Dylan Thomas: Poet of His People* (London: Michael Joseph, 1975), p.61.

30 Interview with Philip Snow, 9 November 2005.

31 Wendy Pollard, *Rosamond Lehmann: The Vagaries of Literary Reception* (Aldershot: Ashgate, 2004), pp.23-30.

32 Frank Swinnerton, *Authors and the Book Trade* (London: Hutchinson, 1932), pp.37-38.

4: 'A Remarkable English First Novel'
(pp.62-84)

1 Ferris, p.399.

2 'Poor Victor', review of Jean Overton Fuller, *The Magical Dilemma of Victor Neuburg*, *The Listener*, 27 May 1965, pp.792-93.

3 Fuller, p.9.

4 Letter to Harold Raymond, 9 May 1927 (University of Reading: Chatto & Windus archive).

5 Letter to Harold Raymond, 26 July 1927 (*ibid.*).

6 Preface to *This Bed Thy Centre* (London: Macmillan, 1961).

7 James A. Davies, 'Glancing Down the Cliff of Time: Pamela Hansford Johnson and Dylan Thomas', *New Welsh Review*, 58, 2002, pp.35-42, p.38.

8 *Ibid.*, p.37.

9 Pamela Hansford Johnson, *This Bed Thy Centre* (London: Chapman & Hall, 1935), p.9. Further references in the text are to this edition.

10 Ferris, pp.209-10.

11 Quotations from Dylan Thomas, *Under Milk Wood* (London: Dent, 1954), pp.1, 14 & 43.

12 Fuller, p.5.

13 *Ibid.*, p.16.

14 Letter to Kathleen Farrell, 11 November 1953 (C.P. Snow Collection, Harry Ransom Humanities Research Center, at the University of Texas, Austin TX, hereafter referred to as HRHRC: CPS).

15 Pamela Hansford Johnson, *Blessed Above Women* (London: Chapman & Hall, 1936), p.2. Further references in the text are to this edition.

16 *Yorkshire Post*, 5 August 1936.

17 *Ibid.*, 9 September 1936.

18 *Ibid.*

19 *Ibid.*, 30 September 1936.

20 *Ibid.*, 7 October 1936.

21 FitzGibbon (1965), p.112.

22 Pamela Hansford Johnson, *Here Today* (London: Chapman & Hall, 1937), foreword on flyleaf 1.

23 *Ibid.*, quotation from the text, spoken by Mrs Bocock, towards the end of the novel, and reproduced on flyleaf 2.

24 Isabel Quigly, *Pamela Hansford Johnson*, Writers and Their Work series (London: Longmans Green, 1968), p.14. In fact, this would not prove to be the only time Pamela repeated herself; as will be seen, there are numerous repetitions in her final novel, *A Bonfire*, but this was not published until 1981.

25 FitzGibbon (1965), p.217-18.

26 *Ibid.*, p.209.

27 Letter, DMT to Caitlin Macnamara, quoted by FitzGibbon (1965), p.218.

5: Married Life amid the Clouds of War
(pp.85-109)

1 Pamela Hansford Johnson, *World's End* (London: Chapman & Hall, 1937), p.2. Further references in the text are to this edition.

2 John Osborne, *Look Back in Anger*, Act III, Sc. 1.

3 I have not been able to trace the English critic who made this comparison.

4 Left-wing support for China following the start of the Second Sino-Japanese War seems not to have entered the general consciousness to the same extent of similar support for the Spanish Government.

5 Pamela Hansford Johnson, *The Monument* (London: Chapman & Hall, 1938), p.7. Further references in the text are to this edition.

6 Pamela Hansford Johnson, 'Scrapbook for 1938', *Spectator*, 16 December 1938, pp.1043-44.

7 Newquist, *p.*368.

8 Pamela Hansford Johnson, *Girdle of Venus* (London: Chapman & Hall, 1939), p.91. Further references in the text are to this edition.

9 Robert Hewison, *Under Siege: Literary Life in London 1939-45* (London: Weidenfeld & Nicolson, 1977; paperback, London: Methuen, 1988), pp.102.

10 Pamela Hansford Johnson, *Too Dear for My Possessing* (London: Collins, 1940; Harmondsworth: Penguin, 1976), p.9. Further references in the text are to this edition, and will be cited elsewhere as *Too Dear*.

11 Hewison, p.103.

12 Author's Note to Penguin edition, *op. cit.*

13 With an early recognition of the racism in the title, *Ten Little Niggers* was retitled *And Then There Were None* the following year.

14 Nap Lombard, *Tidy Death* (London: Cassell, 1940), p.269. Further references in the text are to this edition.

15 FitzGibbon (1965), p.263.

16 Letter to John Davenport, 14 September 1939, quoted by FitzGibbon (1965), p.265.

17 Eventually, however, through the help of friends, Dylan was able to procure a job with a documentary film company, making films for the Ministry of Information, which was deemed to be a reserved occupation, see FitzGibbon (1965), pp.278-79.

18 Fuller, p.291.

19 Letter to Jean Overton Fuller, 19 June 1940, reproduced in Ferris (1985), p.457.

20 Selina Hastings, *Rosamond Lehmann* (London: Chatto & Windus, 2002), p.161.

21 When the series of novels about Lewis Eliot became known as *Strangers and Brothers*, this novel was retitled *George Passant*.

22 John Halperin, *C.P. Snow: An Oral Biography* (Brighton: Harvester, 1983), p.69.

23 There would eventually be eleven books in this series.

24 Review of *Stranger & Brother*, *Liverpool Post*, 4 December 1940.

25 Letter quoted in Philip Snow, *Stranger and Brother* (1982), p.74.

26 Letter, CPS to PHJ, 27 November 1940 (LAC).

6: Surviving on the Home Front
(pp.110-25)

1 Letter, NS to PHJ (LAC).

2 With Snow's active co-operation, Donald Dickson worked for many years on writing his biography, which, due to Dickson's failing health, was never completed. Various versions of his manuscript, together with source material, have been deposited in the C.P. Snow archive, Christ's College, Cambridge, hereafter referred to as CC: CPS.

3 I refer to Charles Percy Snow as 'Snow' while Pamela so names him in her diaries.

To his family, he was always 'Percy', although he always signed letters to them and to close friends as 'CPS'. Eventually Pamela will insist on calling him 'Charles', at which point I call him by his preferred option, 'CPS'.

4 Letter, CPS to PHJ, 4 December 1940 (LAC).

5 Lindblad, p.62.

6 Pamela Hansford Johnson, *The Family Pattern* (London: Collins, 1942), p.149. Further references in the text are to this edition.

7 Pamela Hansford Johnson, *Winter Quarters* (London: Collins, 1944), p.3. Further references in the text are to this edition.

8 Letter, CPS to PHJ, 29 August 1943 (LAC).

9 Halperin, p.125.

10 Philip Snow, (1982), p.16.

11 Letter, CPS to HH, 9 December 1931 (HRHRC: CPS).

12 Halperin, p.142.

13 Lesley Chamberlain, 'Russian Snow: Lost words and a lost woman in the history of The Two Cultures', *Times Literary Supplement*, 20 May 2011, pp.14-15.

14 Letters quoted in Philip Snow (1982), pp.57 & 59.

15 Halperin, p.27.

16 This letter, dated 13 August 1943, is quoted at length in Philip Snow (1982), pp.79-85.

17 Letter, CPS to Sheila Palfreyman, 12 September 1943 (CC: CPS).

18 For an excellent retrospective assessment of this novel, see Jenny Hartley, *Millions Like Us* (London: Virago, 1997), pp.43-45.

19 Letter, CPS to PHJ, 8 December 1943 (LAC).

20 Pamela Hansford Johnson, *The Trojan Brothers* (London: Michael Joseph, 1944), p.5. Further references in the text are to this edition.

21 Aerogramme, NS to PHJ, 13 February 1944 (LAC).

22 Letter, CPS to PHJ, 11 February 1944 (LAC).

23 See note 21.

24 Letter, undated, Morven Stewart to PHJ, c. early 1944 (LAC).

25 Postcard, PHJ to KD, 13 November 1944 (HRHRC: Kay Dick Archive).

26 Postcard, PHJ to KD, 12 December 1944, *ibid*.

7: 'Waving Flags on Top of a Huge Rubble-Heap'
(pp.126-45)

1 Letter, PHJ to KD, 3 May 1945 (HRHRC: KD).

2 Letter, CPS to PHJ, 28 August 1945 (LAC)

3 Letter, Anne Whyte to CPS, 23 July 1945 (HRHRC: CPS)

4 Letter, AW to CPS, 26 September 1945 (HRHRC: CPS).

5 Halperin, p.115.

6 Veglio's was a modest, long-established Italian restaurant at the junction of New Oxford Street and Tottenham Court Road.

7 Letter, CPS to PHJ, 3 December 1945 (LAC).

8 Pamela Hansford Johnson, *An Avenue of Stone* (London: Michael Joseph, 1947;

Harmondsworth: Penguin, 1953), p.73. Further references in the text are to this edition, and will be cited elsewhere as *Avenue*.

9 In Box 54, HRHRC: CPS.

10 Letter, AW to CPS, 30 March 1946 (HRHRC: CPS).

11 Pamela Hansford Johnson, *A Summer to Decide* (London: Michael Joseph, 1948; Harmondsworth: Penguin, 1954), pp.89-90. Further references in the text are to this edition, and will be cited elsewhere as *Summer*.

12 Letter, Robert Lusty to PHJ, 31 July 1946 (HRHRC: CPS).

13 On her return to England, Anne Whyte became the Secretary of the Fabian International Bureau. Her last brief letter to Snow told him that she and her cousin had decided after all not to marry, 31 March 1947 (HRHRC: CPS).

8: Chill Outside and Within
(pp.146-60)

1 Letter, Ivy Compton-Burnett to Robert Liddell, quoted in Hilary Spurling, *Ivy: The Life of I. Compton-Burnett* (London: Cohen, 1995), p.466.

2 Hilary Spurling, *ibid*.

3 Coincidentally, Millar became a friend of the Snows, when adapting Snow's works for the stage and later television.

4 Leslie Halliwell, *Halliwell's Film and Video Guide 2000*, 15th edition, ed. by John Walker (London: Harper Collins), p.550.

5 I am indebted to the website, www.measuringworth.com, for this and other calculations.

6 Pamela's earlier judgment about P.H. Newby's future literary status could be seen to have been justified when he became the inaugural winner of the Booker Prize in 1969.

7 Pamela Hansford Johnson, Preface, *A Summer to Decide* (1948; London: Macmillan, 1975).

8 A.S. Byatt, 'Elegiac Saga', a review of *The Survival of the Fittest*, *New Statesman*, 17 May 1968, pp.654-55, p.655.

9 Introduction, Michael Sissons and Philip French, eds., *The Age of Austerity, 1945-51* (London : Hodder & Stoughton, 1963), 9-12, pp.11-12. See also in this excellent volume, David Hughes, 'The Spivs', 81-100, and John Gross, 'The Lynskey Tribunal', pp.255-76.

10 T.E.B. Howarth, *Prospect and Reality: Great Britain 1945-55* (London: Collins, 1985), p.75.

11 *Ibid.*, p.144.

12 David Shusterman, *C.P. Snow* (Boston, MA: Twayne, 1975), p.22.

13 [Harry Hoff] William Cooper, *Scenes from Married Life* (London: Macmillan, 1961: Harmondsworth: Penguin, 1963), p.179. Further references in the text are to this edition, and will be cited elsewhere as *Married*.

14 Letter, CPS to PHJ, 11 November 1947 (LAC).

15 Letter, CPS to Philip Snow, 24 November 1947, quoted in Snow (1982), pp.95-96.

9: The Dark and the Light
(pp.161-79)

1 C.P. Snow, *The Light and the Dark* (London: Faber & Faber, 1947; Harmondsworth: Penguin, 1962, pp.41 & 42. Further references in the text are to this edition.

2 Patricia K.G. Lewis, *Charles Allberry: A Portrait* (privately published, 1984).

3 Letter, CPS to Harry Hoff (HRHRC: CPS)

4 Robert de Saint-Loup is a character in Marcel Proust's *A la recherche du temps perdu*.

5 Pamela Hansford Johnson, *Corinth House* (London: Macmillan, 1954), p.20. Further references in the text are to this edition.

6 Gordon Crier had previously been principally known as a producer of BBC radio comedy, including the popular and long-running programme, *Bandwagon*, starring Arthur Askey and Richard Murdoch.

7 Bertolt Brecht, *Arbeitsjournal 1938-1955* (Frankfurt: Suhrkamp, 1973), p.122; translated and quoted by Michael Morley, in *Brecht: A Study* (London: Heinemann, 1977), p.98.

8 Father Zossima is a character in Dostoevsky's *The Brothers Karamazov*.

9 Letter, 12 August 1948, quoted in Philip Snow (1982), pp.97-98.

10 William Cooper, *Scenes from Provincial Life* (London: Cape, 1950; London: Methuen, 1983), p.202. Further references in the text are to this edition, and will be cited elsewhere as *Provincial*.

11 *Ibid.*, p.20.

12 William Cooper, *Scenes from Metropolitan Life* (London: Macmillan, 1982; London: Methuen, 1983), pp.32, 45, 163-64, and will be cited elsewhere as *Metropolitan*.

13 Letter, CPS to Maureen Gebbie, 9 August 1948, (HRHRC: CPS).

14 Letter, 3 October 1948, quoted in Philip Snow (1982), p.99.

15 Letter, 12 August 1948, *ibid.*, p.97.

16 Letter, Holly Southwell to CPS, 20 October 1948 (HRHRC: CPS).

17 Letter, Holly Southwell to CPS, *ibid.*

18 Letter, HS to CPS, 14 January 1949 (HRHRC: CPS).

19 Letter, HS to CPS, 16 February 1949, *ibid.*

10: 'I Have Been Infinitely, Infinitely Enriched'
(pp.180-201)

1 The letters from CPS to PHJ are at present in LAC, the letters from PHJ to CPS are in HRHRC: CPS.

2 An echo from a letter from Snow to Sheila Palfreyman on 26 May 1943. Apologizing for a previous letter begging her to see him one more time, he had written: 'I should like to tell you that knowing you has enriched my life with moments of the most extreme intensity. I don't expect to meet again a woman like you, certainly not one with your gifts.' (CC: CPS).

3 Interview with Josephine Pullein-Thompson, London, 7 June 2011.

4 Pamela Hansford Johnson, *The Philistines* (London: Michael Joseph, 1949), p.7. Further references in the text are to this edition.

5 C.P. Snow, *Time of Hope* (London: Faber & Faber, 1949), p.413.

6 Letter, Holly Southwell to CPS, 10 May 1949 (HRHRC: CPS).

7 Letter, Holly Southwell to CPS, 12 June 1949, *ibid*.

8 The text of her broadcast was published under the title, 'The Sick-room Hush over the English Novel', in *The Listener*, 11 August 1949, pp.235-36.

9 Famously, the only copy of the first volume of Thomas Carlyle's *The French Revolution* (1837) was accidentally thrown on the fire by a servant of Carlyle's friend, the philosopher, John Stuart Mill.

10 Philip Snow (1982), p.117.

11 Liz Eliot did find a second husband, who presumably was 'decent and intelligent'; she married the Hon. George Kinnaird the following year, and the couple are frequently favourably mentioned in Pamela's later diaries.

12 A slight paraphrase of the hymn, 'He who would valiant be', from John Bunyan's *Pilgrim's Progress*.

13 Probably a reference to the dry red wine of the Apulia region.

11: 'Divorce-Nausea', 'Wounded Pride', finally 'Wondrous Joy'
(pp.202-20)

1 PHJ, 'A Modern Classic', *Daily Telegraph*, 23 September 1949.

2 Letter, HS to CPS, 4 October 1949 (HRHRC: CPS).

3 Julian Symons, *Times Literary Supplement*, 21 October 1949, p.677.

4 Letter, PHJ to KD, 1 November 1949 (CC: CPS).

5 Pamela had evidently forgotten this incident when she wrote in the Dylan Thomas memorial issue of *Adam* that she and Dylan had lost touch at the beginning of the Second World War.

6 PHJ, *Daily Telegraph* fiction reviews, 20 January 1950.

7 Rubin Rabinovitz, *The Reaction Against Experiment in the English Novel, 1950-1960* (New York: Columbia University Press), p.4 (and pp.97-127, *passim*).

8 Letter, PHJ to KF and KD, 10 April 1950 (CC: CPS).

9 Letter, PHJ to KF, 23 January 1950 (CC: CPS).

10 Letter, CPS to PHJ, 26 January 1950 (LAC).

11 *Corinth House* had a further week's run the following year at the Q Theatre, but never had a prolonged production.

12 Letter, PHJ to KF, 6 March 1950 CC: CPS).

13 Letter, PHJ to KF, 12 June 1950 (CC: CPS).

14 Letter, CPS to PHJ, 15 June 1950 (LAC).

15 Letter, PHJ to CPS, 17 June 1950 (HRHRC: CPS).

16 Letter, HS to CPS, 30 June 1950 (HRHRC: CPS).

17 Transcript of recorded interview of J.H. Plumb with Carl Bode, 3 June 1970 (Cambridge University Library: J.H. Plumb Archive, hereafter referred to as CUL: JHP).

18 W.A. Darlington, 'An Overwritten Play', *Daily Telegraph*, 31 August 1950.
19 PHJ, 'A Great Novelist', *Daily Telegraph*, 26 May 1950.
20 PHJ, 'Latest Hemingway', *Daily Telegraph*, 8 September 1950.
21 Maxwell Geismar, *Saturday Review of Literature* (NY), 9 September 1950.
22 The notebook is among papers in CC: CPS.

12: A Fragile Start to a Second Marriage until the Arrival of 'Borox'
(pp.221-37)

1 Later that year, for example, Pamela was told by Kathleen Farrell that their supposed mutual friend, BBC radio producer Daniel George, had insisted at a party at the Hoffs that '"the Snow marriage was finished"'.

2 Malcolm Elwin, *The Strange Case of Robert Louis Stevenson* (London: Macdonald, 1950), pp.234-35.

3 Lindblad, pp.117 & 123.

4 Despite later audiences turning away from melodrama, Henry Irving nevertheless continued to play the leading role of Mathias in *The Bells* for thirty-four years, giving his final performance in this play the day before he died.

5 Pamela Hansford Johnson, *Catherine Carter* (London: Macmillan, 1952), p.vii. Further references in the text are to this edition.

6 'Willy' was described as 'a high-spirited, Plumbish friend' in Pamela's preliminary sketch.

7 George Eliot, *Middlemarch* (Edinburgh: Blackwood, 1871-72; Harmondsworth: Penguin, 1965), p.225.

8 This remark is quoted without full citation in most biographies of Richard Burton. Paul Ferris, in his *Richard Burton* (London: Weidenfeld & Nicolson, 1981, p.60) admits in a footnote that the origin of Kenneth Tynan's review remains unknown. Tynan would not become a full-time reviewer until the following year.

9 Writing in retrospect about that season at Stratford, however, Pamela wrote: 'Burton now seems lost to the theatre; it is a tragic loss. I cannot but think that despite his fame in the cinema, and the plutocratic glitter with which he has surrounded himself, he has let us down: and by "us", I mean the English stage' (*Important*, pp.88-89).

10 C.P. Snow, *The Masters* (London: Macmillan, 1951: Harmondsworth: Penguin, 1956), pp.86 & 293.

11 Letter, CPS to PHJ, 27 August 1951. Quoted in Dickson MSS (CC: CPS).

12 Letter, CPS to PHJ from Royal Station Hotel, Hull, *ibid*.

13 Interview by the author with Philip Snow, Snr.

14 From her diary entry on the 26th birthday of Philip Snow, Jnr.

15 According to PCS, the nicknames were forms of puns on aurochs, the extinct European wild ox. CPS had been Worox, PAS Jorox (Junior Aurochs) and thus Borox (Baby Aurochs), although the origin of this tradition had never been made clear to the latter. (E-mail to the author, 27 January 2014).

13: Second Exile from the City
(pp.238-63)

1 Letter, HS to CPS, 2 December 1952 (HRHRC: CPS).

2 S. Gorley Putt, *Wings of a Man's Life* (London: Claridge, 1990), p.210.

3 'And I felt, as I say, a sensation of weariness and almost of terror at the thought that all this length of Time had not only, without interruption, been lived, experienced, secreted by me, that it was my life, was in fact me, but also that I was compelled so long as I was alive to keep it attached to me, that it supported me and that, perched on its giddy summit, I could not myself make a movement without displacing it.' Marcel Proust, tr. by Andreas Mayor, *Remembrance of Things Past* (London: Chatto & Windus, 1981), p.1106.

4 'My Books are my Children', in *Winter Tales* 1 (London: Macmillan, 1956), pp.167-89, p.167. Further references in the text are to this edition.

5 C.P. Snow, *Homecomings* (London: Macmillan, 1956; Harmondsworth: Penguin, 1962), p.135. Further references in the text are to this edition.

6 Philip Snow (1982), p.126 & pp.184-87.

7 Philip Snow, *A Time of Renewal: Clusters of Characters, C.P. Snow and Coups* (London: Radcliffe, 1998), pp.200-01.

8 Letter to Marÿke Lanius, December 1961, quoted on flyleaf of Philip Snow (1982), p.xiii. See also *ibid.*, p.128.

9 The information about the date of the resumption of Anne Seagrim's relationship with CPS has been taken from her letter of 8 July 1980 to Professor Joe Maloney of the University of Louisville, Kentucky, in the open section of her archive (CHC: AS).

10 Laker subsequently took all ten wickets in the Australians' second innings for a total of 19 for 90, a record likely to stand for all time.

11 The passage describes an unknown father and daughter playing tennis together, *The Philistines*, p.92.

12 Letter, CPS to PHJ, undated, quoted in Dickson MSS (CC: CPS).

14: '"And Have *You* Ever Written, Lady Snow?"'
(pp.264-94)

1 *The Last Resort* was published in the USA under the possibly less misleading title *The Wedding and the Sea*; it is the only one of Pamela's novels to have been re-titled in the American edition.

2 Quigly, p.44.

3 Pamela Hansford Johnson, *The Last Resort* (London: Macmillan, 1956), p.178. Further references in the text are to this edition.

4 Walter Allen, *Tradition and Dream* (London: Phoenix House, 1964), pp.257-58.

5 Philip Snow (1982), p.113.

6 Moura Budberg received further posthumous journalistic attention when she was revealed to have been the great-great-aunt of Nick Clegg, leader of the Liberal Democrats from 2007 and Deputy Prime Minister from 2010.

7 *Ibid*, p.114.

8 Harvey Breit was then Editor of the *New York Times Book Review*.

9 Quoted in Philip Snow (1998), p.58.

10 Jemmy Twitcher is the betrayer of Macheath in John Gay's *The Beggar's Opera* (1728).

11 Pamela Hansford Johnson, *The Unspeakable Skipton* (London: Macmillan, 1959; London: Prion, 2002), flyleaf. Further references in the text are to this edition.

12 A.J.A. Symons, *The Quest for Corvo* (London: Cassell, 1934, repr. 1955), p.1. Further references in the text are to this edition.

13 Letter, ES to PHJ, Sesame Club, Mayfair, 31 May 1958 (LAC).

14 Letter, ES to PHJ, Renishaw Hall, 26 September 1959, *ibid*.

15 Letter, ES to PHJ, Sesame Club, 8 April 1959, *ibid*.

16 This description was coined by Alfred, Lord Tennyson, in a letter to Edmund Gosse, with regard to a critic called Churton Collins.

17 The full text of John Raymond's *TLS* 'Middle' was reprinted in his collection, *The Doge of Dover and Other Essays* (London: MacGibbon & Kee, 1960), pp.156-63.

18 The other writers portrayed in this series were, in chronological order: John Osborne, Angus Wilson, David Jones, L.P. Hartley, Anthony Powell, John Lehmann, E.M. Forster, Iris Murdoch, V.S. Pritchett, V.S. Naipaul, Evelyn Waugh, William Sansom, John Betjeman, and Graham Greene.

19 Letter, ES to PHJ, 6 May 1959 (LAC).

20 C.P. Snow, *The Two Cultures and the Scientific Revolution* (Cambridge University Press, 1959), p.43. Further references in the text are to this edition.

21 Stefan Collini, Introduction to C.P. Snow, *The Two Cultures* (Cambridge University Press, Canto edition, 1993), p.xxx.

22 PHJ to Susan Hill, 6 June 1957 (SHA).

23 PHJ to SH, 15 April 1959, *ibid*.

24 PHJ to SH, 3 September 1959, *ibid*.

25 Lindblad, p.125.

26 Letter, ES to PHJ, 26 September 1959 (LAC).

15: East and West
(pp.295-314)

1 Bernard Bergonzi, 'The World of Lewis Eliot', *Twentieth Century*, March 1960, pp.214-25, p.215.

2 *Ibid*., p.225.

3 Rayner Heppenstall, 'Divided We Stand: On "the English Tradition"', *Encounter*, September 1960, pp.42-45.

4 Melvin J. Lasky was an American journalist who held strong anti-Communist views in the period following the Second World War. To the embarrassment of Stephen Spender, then editor of *Encounter*, it was later revealed that the journal had received substantial funding from the CIA.

5 C.P. Snow, *Science and Government* (London: Oxford University Press, 1961), p.1. Further references in the text are to this edition.

6 Philip Snow (1982), p.123.

7 Letter dated 7 November 1960, quoted *ibid.*, p.124.

8 Philip Snow (1982), p.25.

9 Pamela Hansford Johnson, *An Error of Judgement* (London: Macmillan, 1962), p.100. Further references in the text are to this edition.

10 Lindblad, p.155.

11 Introduction to *An Error of Judgement* (Oxford: Oxford University Press, 1987), pp.v-ix.

12 Correspondence with Andrew Stewart, 2006.

13 Pamela Hansford Johnson, *Night and Silence Who is Here* (London: Macmillan, 1963; Harmondsworth: Penguin, 1968), p.13. Further references in the text are to this edition.

14 Dog-face is William Setter's word for psychologist, *An Error of Judgement*, p.3 and elsewhere in the novel.

16: Attacks, Scandals and Distresses
(pp.315-44)

1 Robert Conquest, 'Snow on their Boots', *London Magazine*, January 1962, pp.82-84.

2 C.P. Snow and Pamela Hansford Johnson, Introduction to *Winter's Tales 7* (London: Macmillan, 1961), pp.vii-xxi, p.xi.

3 See Robert Conquest, *The Great Terror: Stalin's Purge of the Thirties* (London: Macmillan, 1968), *passim*.

4 Introduction to *Winter's Tales 7*, p.xii.

5 Ian MacKillop, *F.R. Leavis: A Life in Criticism* (London: Allen Lane, 1995), pp.311-14. The essay was by Morris Shapira, a colleague of Leavis's at Downing; he was reviewing *Puzzles and Epiphanies*, a collection of essays by Frank Kermode.

6 Collini, 1993, p.xxiv.

7 *Ibid*, p.xxxii.

8 F.R. Leavis, *Two Cultures: The Significance of C.P. Snow* (London: Chatto & Windus, 1962), p.9. Further references in the text are to this edition.

9 MacKillop, p.321.

10 Nicolas Tredell,, 'Magnanimity', *The Literary Encyclopedia*, 21 February 2013 [http://www.litencyc.com/php/sworks.php?rec=true&UID=34887].

11 Telephone conversation with Richard Ingrams, in the *Oldie* office, London, 13 June 2013.

12 Philip Snow (1998), p.174.

13 Letter, CPS to PAS, sent from English Electric House, 25 July 1962, quoted *ibid*.

14 Court report, *The Times*, 1 August 1963.

15 Tynan as usual could not resist mixing some sarcasm with praise of the play, which he said, more fully in the quoted sentence, 'for all its dear-chapping and

old-sonning and Oxbridge middle-of-the-roading, is something not to be missed'.

16 *Private Eye*, 7 September 1962, p.3. Reproduced by kind permission of PRIVATE EYE MAGAZINE – www.private-eye.co.uk.

17 Pamela Hansford Johnson, 'Literature', in John Raymond, ed., *The Baldwin Age* (London: Eyre & Spottiswoode, 1960), pp.179-88, p.182.

18 Pamela Hansford Johnson, typescript, '1½ Cultures' (LAC). See F.R. Leavis and Denys Thompson, *Culture and Environment* (London: Chatto & Windus, 1933), *passim*.

19 Interview with Philip Snow, Snr., 2005.

20 CPS to J.H. Plumb, Telegram, 28 December 1962 (CUL: JHP).

21 Anthony Storr, who became well-known as a broadcaster and author of books on psychiatry, had gone to Christ's College, Cambridge, in 1939, to study medicine. CPS had been his moral tutor, and as several of Storr's obituaries made clear, it was CPS who had encouraged him to concentrate on psychiatry and who had also given him practical assistance to enable him to complete his degree. They continued to be lifelong friends.

22 CPS to J.H. Plumb, 31 December 1962 (CUL: JHP).

23 Philip Snow (1998), p.132.

24 *Queen*, June 1963.

25 Dickson MSS (CC: CPS).

26 Letter, PHJ to KF, 7 July 1963 (CC: CPS).

27 Letters from Ralph Maud to Oscar Silverman, 19 March 1962, and PHJ, July 1963 (SUNY: DMT).

28 Letter to PHJ from Oscar Silverman, 10 July 1963, *ibid*.

29 The original of the paraphrase is 'your English summer's done' from Rudyard Kipling's poem, 'The Long Trail'.

17: Pamela the Crusader, Part One
(pp.345-68)

1 Quoted in Philip Snow (1982), p.161.

2 *Private Eye*, 30 October 1964, p.3. Reproduced by kind permission of Private Eye Magazine – www.private-eye.co.uk.

3 *Ibid*., pp.13-14.

4 Richard Ingrams, *Muggeridge: The Biography* (London: Harper Collins, 1995), p.202.

5 Peter Cook was one of the first backers of *Private Eye* and the co-owner of the short-lived Establishment nightclub in Soho, which had closed that year. He also denigrated CPS in the course of his performance in that year's Royal Variety Performance, somewhat to the bemusement of the audience (see Philip Snow, 1998, p.100).

6 Neville and June Braybrooke, *Olivia Manning: A Life* (London: Chatto & Windus, 2004), p.132.

7 Pamela Hansford Johnson, *Cork Street, Next to the Hatter's* (London: Macmillan, 1965; Harmondsworth: Penguin, 1968), p.25. Further references in the text are to this edition.

8 As David Eccles, Viscount Eccles had twice been a Minister of Education in Harold Macmillan's Cabinets.

9 PHJ to KF, 11 October 1965 (CC: CPS).

10 PHJ to KF, 26 March 1966, *ibid*.

11 Constantine Fitzgibbon (1965), pp.114 & 116.

12 Letter, Mikhail Sholokhov to CPS, quoted in Philip Snow (1982), pp.170-71.

18: Pamela the Crusader, Part Two
(pp.369-88)

1 Letter, PHJ to PAS, 5 December 1964, quoted in Philip Snow (1998), p.88.

2 Philip Snow (1998), p.88.

3 *Ibid.*, p.101.

4 The full text of the letter was published in *The Times*, 7 April 1966.

5 'Lord Snow: No Regrets and a New Book', *The Times*, 9 April 1966.

6 Elwyn Jones, who was the co-creator and scriptwriter of *Z-Cars*, one of Pamela's favourite television programmes, coincidentally shared his name with Sir Elwyn Jones, Q.C., the Attorney-General, who led for the prosecution.

7 Pamela Hansford Johnson, *On Iniquity* (London: Macmillan, 1967), p.18. Further references in the text are to this edition.

8 Pamela did not mention in *On Iniquity* that Brady had been sufficiently sentient about a connection being made between his book collection and the murders to deposit the books in the Left Luggage office in Manchester Central Station.

9 The BBC has no recording of the programme, nor a copy of the script, which was written by Keith Waterhouse and Willis Hall (both now deceased). Both of the actors very courteously replied to my query as to whether they had any memory of the skit, but regretted that it was too long ago for them to recall.

10 See FitzGibbon (1965), p.83.

11 Philip Snow (1998), pp.113-17.

12 Letter, PHJ to PAS, 13 January 1967, quoted *ibid*.

13 The headquarters of the Communist Party of Great Britain were at 16 King Street, London. W.C.2.

19: 'This World is in a Frightful State'
(pp.389-416)

1 The quotations in this diary entry are from 'The Second Coming' by W.B. Yeats, a poem influenced by William Blake, which also contains the much-quoted lines: 'Things fall apart: the centre cannot hold/Mere anarchy is loosed upon the world.'

2 According to his brother, pernicious anaemia had been diagnosed and, needing constant sunshine, 'only a few months in Sicily [...] saved his life'. Philip Snow (1982), p.30.

3 *Ibid*, (1982), p.177.

4 *Ibid*, pp.73, 108, 177

5 Albert Borowitz, *Innocence and Arsenic: Studies in Crime and Literature* (New York: Harper & Row, 1977), p.1.

6 *Ibid.*, p.25.

7 News Report, *The Times*, 26 November 1968.

8 Philip Snow (1998), pp.134-35.

9 Lindblad, p.163.

10 University of Kent: *Twentieth Century Studies* (November 1969). Other authors who contributed to the presentation of 'the professional viewpoint' included Paul Bowles, Anthony Burgess, L.P. Hartley, B.S. Johnson, Jack Kerouac, David Lodge, P.H. Newby, Kate O'Brien, Georges Simenon, John Updike, and John Wain.

11 Pamela Hansford Johnson, *The Honours Board* (London: Macmillan, 1970; Feltham: Hamlyn, 1981), p.7. Further references in the text are to this edition.

12 See http://www.princeofwales.gov.uk/the-prince-of-wales/biography/education.

13 Geraldine Bedell, '"I wrote *The Story of O*"', *Observer*, 24 July 2004.

14 Pamela Hansford Johnson, *New Statesman*, 19 June 1970.

20: 'So End my Fifties ...'
(pp.417-42)

1 Rabinovitz, p.9.

2 Pamela Hansford Johnson, *The Holiday Friend* (London: Macmillan, 1972), p.88. Further references in the text are to this edition.

3 Kay Dick, *Friends and Friendship: Conversations and Reflections* (London: Sidgwick & Jackson, 1974), p.174. Further references in the text are to this edition.

4 An open verdict was returned at the inquest, the cause of Kenneth Allsop's death being recorded as the result of an overdose of barbiturates.

5 According to Pamela, when forced to consult a psychiatrist, and asked afterwards what the latter had said, George Best had replied: '"I don't know. I wasn't listening."'

6 Hebetude means dullness; it is a word Pamela seems to have acquired from the Snovian vocabulary.

7 Pamela Hansford Johnson, *The Good Listener* (London: Macmillan, 1975), pp.140-41. Further references in the text are to this edition

8 Letter, PHJ to PAS, 2 January 1975, quoted in Philip Snow (1998), p.173.

9 Philip Snow (1998), p.174.

21: 'Why, This is HELL – Nor am I out of it'
(pp.443-61)

1 Letter, Harold Macmillan to PHJ, 12 April 1976 (HRHRC: CPS).
2 Letter from Evelyn Hamer, Stourbridge, 17 December 1976 (LAC).
3 Halperin, p.ix.
4 N. & J. Braybrooke, p.132.
5 Francis King, *Yesterday Came Suddenly* (London: Constable, 1993), p.84.
6 Interview with Stefanie Waine, Welwyn Garden City, 9 November 2005.
7 Pamela Hansford Johnson, *The Good Husband* (London: Macmillan, 1978), pp.117 & 163. Further references in the text are to this edition.
8 Anthony Burgess, *The Novel Now* (London: Faber & Faber, 1967), p.67.
9 Ronald Millar is credited with having written one of Margaret Thatcher's most famous lines: 'The lady's not for turning.'
10 Pamela Hansford Johnson, *A Bonfire* (London: Macmillan, 1981), p.27-28. Further references in the text are to this edition.
11 Interview with Lindsay Avebury, February 2006.
12 Philip Snow (1998), p.181.
13 *Ibid*.
14 Putt, pp.94-95.

22: The Last Six Months
(pp.462-65)

1 Andrew Stewart also informed me that he had been distressed to come across a job lot of correspondence between CPS and Sofaer, including medical records, being offered for sale online, and Jeff Towns of Dylans Bookstore in Swansea similarly was shocked to find Pamela's medical records in the manuscript of *Important to Me*, which she may have given to Sofaer and which had subsequently been sent for auction. Towns returned the records to Pamela's daughter. The manuscript is now in the collection of the National Museum of Wales.

Afterword
(pp.466-68)

1 Cyril Connolly, *Enemies of Promise* (London: Routledge, 1938), pp.152-53.
2 Norma Clarke, *The Rise and Fall of the Woman of Letters* (London: Pimlico, 2004), p.343.
3 N. & J. Braybrooke, p.143.
4 Hadjiafxendi, Kyriaki. "Realism (Literary)", *The Literary Encyclopedia*, (http://www.litencyc.com/php/stopics.php?rec=true&UID=933).

Select Bibliography

WORKS BY PAMELA HANSFORD JOHNSON
(IN CHRONOLOGICAL ORDER)

(a) Fiction

NOTE: My quotations in the text have, as specified in the endnotes, been taken either from the first editions, or from Penguin reprints, referenced below, where the latter are the more easily obtainable. Many of the novels were simultaneously published in the USA, and have also been reprinted subsequently elsewhere.

This Bed Thy Centre (London: Chapman & Hall, 1935)
Blessed Above Women (London: Chapman & Hall, 1936)
Here Today (London: Chapman & Hall, 1937)
World's End (London: Chapman & Hall, 1937)
The Monument (London: Chapman & Hall, 1938)
Girdle of Venus (London: Chapman & Hall, 1939)
Too Dear for My Possessing (London: Collins, 1940; Harmondsworth: Penguin, 1976)
The Family Pattern (London: Collins, 1942)
Winter Quarters (London: Collins, 1943)
The Trojan Brothers (London: Michael Joseph, 1944)
An Avenue of Stone (London: Michael Joseph, 1947; Harmondsworth: Penguin, 1953)
A Summer to Decide (London: Michael Joseph, 1948; Harmondsworth: Penguin, 1954)
The Philistines (London: Michael Joseph, 1949)
Catherine Carter (London: Macmillan, 1952)
An Impossible Marriage (London: Macmillan, 1954)
The Last Resort (London: Macmillan, 1956)
The Humbler Creation (London: Macmillan, 1959)
The Unspeakable Skipton (London: Macmillan, 1959)
An Error of Judgement (London: Macmillan, 1962)
Night and Silence Who is Here (London: Macmillan, 1963; Harmondsworth: Penguin, 1968)
Cork Street, Next to the Hatter's (London: Macmillan, 1965; Harmondsworth: Penguin, 1968)
The Survival of the Fittest (London: Macmillan, 1968; Harmondsworth: Penguin, 1970)

The Honours Board (London: Macmillan, 1970)
The Holiday Friend (London: Macmillan, 1972)
The Good Listener (London: Macmillan, 1975)
The Good Husband (London: Macmillan, 1978)
A Bonfire (London: Macmillan, 1981)

(b) Non-Fiction

Thomas Wolfe: A Critical Study (London: Heinemann, 1947: published in USA as *Hungry Gulliver: An English Critical Appraisal of Thomas Wolfe*, New York: Macmillan, 1948)
I. Compton-Burnett (London: Longmans, Green, 1951)
On Iniquity: Some Personal Reflections Arising out of the Moors Murder Trial (London: Macmillan, 1967)
Important to Me: Personalia (London: Macmillan, 1974)

(c) Poetry

Symphony for Full Orchestra (London: Sunday Referee, Parton Press, 1934)

(d) Stage and Radio Plays

Corinth House, with an essay, 'The Future of Prose-Drama' (London: Macmillan, 1954)
Six Proust Reconstructions (London: Macmillan, 1958)

(d) Detective Fiction, written with Gordon Neil Stewart, under the joint pseudonym of Nap Lombard

Tidy Death (London: Cassell, 1940)
Murder's a Swine (London: Cassell, 1943)

WORKS BY C.P. SNOW CITED IN THE TEXT
(IN ALPHABETICAL ORDER)

Homecomings (London: Macmillan, 1956)
The Light and the Dark (London: Faber & Faber, 1947)
The Masters (London: Macmillan, 1951)
Time of Hope (London: Faber & Faber, 1949)
The Two Cultures and the Scientific Revolution (Cambridge University Press, 1959)
The Two Cultures, with introduction by Stefan Collini (Cambridge University Press, 1993)
Science and Government (London: Oxford University Press, 1961)

NOVELS BY WILLIAM COOPER CITED IN THE TEXT
(IN ALPHABETICAL ORDER)

Scenes from Married Life (London: Macmillan, 1961)
Scenes from Metropolitan Life (London: Macmillan, 1982)
Scenes from Provincial Life (London: Cape, 1950)

SECONDARY SOURCES
(IN ALPHABETICAL ORDER)

Allen, Walter, *Tradition and Dream* (London: Phoenix House, 1964)

Bingham, Madeleine, *Henry Irving and the Victorian Theatre* (London: Allen & Unwin, 1978)

Borowitz, Albert, *Innocence and Arsenic: Studies in Crime and Literature* (New York: Harper & Row, 1977)

Braybrooke, Neville and June, *Olivia Manning: A Life* (London: Chatto & Windus, 2004)

Burgess, Anthony, *The Novel Now* (London: Faber & Faber, 1967)

Clarke, Norma, *The Rise and Fall of the Woman of Letters* (London: Pimlico, 2004)

Clegg,Gillian, *Clapham Past* (London: Historical Publications, 1999)

Connolly, Cyril, *Enemies of Promise* (London: Routledge, 1938)

Dick, Kay, *Friends and Friendship: Conversations and Reflections* (London: Sidgwick & Jackson, 1974)

Ferris, Paul, *Dylan Thomas: The Biography,* new edition (London: Dent, 1999)

FitzGibbon, Constantine, *The Life of Dylan Thomas* (London: Dent, 1965)

Fryer, Jonathan, *The Nine Lives of Dylan Thomas* (London: Kyle Cathie, 1993)

Fuller, Jean Overton, *The Magical Dilemma of Victor Neuburg* (London: W.H. Allen, 1965)

Halperin, John, *C.P. Snow: An Oral Biography* (Brighton: Harvester, 1983)

Hewison, Robert, *Under Siege: Literary Life in London 1939-45* (London: Weidenfeld & Nicolson, 1977)

Howarth, T.E.B., *Prospect and Reality: Great Britain 1945-55* (London: Collins, 1985)

King, Francis, *Yesterday Came Suddenly* (London: Constable, 1993)

Leavis, F.R., *Two Cultures: The Significance of C.P. Snow* (London: Chatto & Windus, 1962)

Lewis, Patricia K.G., *Charles Allberry: A Portrait* (privately published, 1984).

Lindblad, Ishrat, *Pamela Hansford Johnson* (Boston, MA: Twayne, 1982)

MacKillop, Ian, *F.R. Leavis: A Life in Criticism* (London: Allen Lane, 1995)

Newquist, Roy, *Counterpoint* (London: Allen & Unwin, 1965)

Putt, S. Gorley, *Wings of a Man's Life* (London: Claridge, 1990)

Quigly, Isobel, *Pamela Hansford Johnson*, Writers and Their Work (London: Longmans Green, 1968)

Rabinovitz, Rubin, *The Reaction Against Experiment in the English Novel, 1950-1960* (New York: Columbia University Press)

Shusterman, David, *C.P. Snow* (Boston, MA: Twayne, 1975)

Sinclair, Andrew, *Dylan Thomas: Poet of His People* (London: Michael Joseph, 1975)

Sissons, Michael and Philip French, eds., *The Age of Austerity, 1945-51* (London: Hodder & Stoughton, 1963)

Snow, Philip, *Stranger and Brother* (London: Macmillan, 1982)

----, *A Time of Renewal: Clusters of Characters, C.P. Snow and Coups* (London: Radcliffe, 1998)

Symons, A.J.A., *The Quest for Corvo* (London: Cassell, 1934)

Thomas, Dylan, *Early Prose Writings*, ed. by Walford Davies (London: Dent, 1971)

----, *Under Milk Wood* (London: Dent, 1954)

Index